TENNYSON

THE UNQUIET HEART

Tennyson, January 1856, by Richard Doyle.

TENNYSON
THE UNQUIET HEART

❋

ROBERT BERNARD MARTIN

CLARENDON PRESS · OXFORD
OXFORD UNIVERSITY PRESS · NEW YORK
1980

Library of Congress Card Catalog Number 79-41802
ISBN 0-19-812072-9

Printed in the United States of America

For L.N.V.

... for the unquiet heart and brain,
A use in measured language lies;
The sad mechanic exercise,
Like dull narcotics, numbing pain.

In Memoriam, v.

PREFACE

THE chief advantage that a modern critic or biographer of Alfred Tennyson has over his predecessors is that there is no longer any need to justify a study of him; the predictable period of sniping at a writer after his death is long past, and almost no one seriously interested in the subject could fail to recognize that Tennyson is among the great English poets. Perhaps because he, more than anyone else except the Queen herself, seemed an emblem of the Victorian age, there was a lingering critical animosity against him long after the fashion for denigrating Browning and Arnold had died a much-to-be-desired death. If our own age has not learned much else, it has at least come to a belated recognition of the greatness of the age of Victoria. Today the condescension of W. H. Auden and Harold Nicholson to Tennyson seems at least as outmoded as Tennyson seemed to them. A quarter of a century after publishing his study of Tennyson, Nicolson privately admitted to his wife how wrong he had been: 'he truly was a poet, darling, and I wish I had realised that more deeply when I wrote that slight book about him'. It is a statement that might fairly represent the view of modern criticism.

The freedom from having to defend Tennyson's poetry means that one may write far more candidly about him than could the earlier biographers who were afraid that the mention of minor blemishes on his personality and character might result in dismissal of him as a poet. Nor does a modern biographer have to worry that his readers will expect only blind partiality about his poetry, of the sort that Tennyson (it must be admitted) would have preferred himself. To ignore the imperfections of a man is to patronize him, as if the whole truth of his character were not to be faced. Most people who knew Tennyson himself found him difficult and prickly, but those who persevered and were not unduly censorious of his irritability and touchy pride found him capable of inspiring deep affection. The man who hid behind the awkward façade would have made the reservation of conventional judgements worthwhile, even if he had not been a great poet. That has been the vicarious experience of this biographer, and the book itself is an attempt to look at the whole man, not one part only.

One other problem must be acknowledged at once. Literary biography poses the peculiar difficulty of adjustment between 'life' and 'works', however artificial that distinction may be. No one would expect a biography of Wellington to exclude all references to his battles, but many reputable scholars feel that the split between the study of literature and the study of writers' lives should be as sharp as possible. My own belief is that pure criticism and pure biography are like two very different but friendly nations between whom there is an unguarded frontier; it is not difficult to recognize the further reaches of either as very unlike the other, but it is easy to stray across the border without being aware of it. Since the real reason for a biography of Tennyson is that he was a great poet, I need not apologize for including some discussion of his works; it will probably be too little for those whose sole interest is criticism, too much for those who believe that poetry has little to do with real life. Both seem to me to deny the final importance of poetry, and I suspect that both are wrong.

Wootton
Woodstock
Oxford
September 1979

CONTENTS

✻

List of Illustrations   xi

   I The Foundation of a Family   1

   II Childhood and Schooling, 1809–1820   17

   III Dr Tennyson's Breakdown, 1820–1827   32

   IV Early Days at Cambridge, 1827–1829   52

   V Arthur Hallam at Cambridge, 1829   67

   VI The Apostles, 1829   80

   VII Hallam at Somersby and *Poems, Chiefly Lyrical*,
      1829–1830   97

   VIII The Valley of Cauteretz, 1830   114

   IX Death of Dr Tennyson, 1831   128

   X Journey to the Rhine, 1832   145

   XI Crushing Reviews: Bulwer, Croker, Wilson, 1833   161

   XII Death of Arthur Hallam, 1833   174

   XIII Mirehouse, and Death of Tennyson's Grandfather,
      1835   189

   XIV Rosa Baring and Emily Sellwood, 1835–1837   210

   XV Matthew Allen and Thomas Carlyle, 1837–1838   229

   XVI Break with Emily Sellwood, 1838–1842   244

   XVII Financial Disaster, 1842–1843   261

   XVIII Emotional Breakdown, 1844–1845   276

   XIX Civil List Pension and 'The New Timon',
      1845–1846   289

   XX *The Princess*, 1846–1847   301

   XXI Financial Security and Marriage, 1848–1850   317

XXII	The Golden Year: *In Memoriam* and the Laureateship, 1850	337
XXIII	Literary London, 1851–1852	356
XXIV	Farringford and *Maud*, 1852–1855	370
XXV	A Literary Lion, 1855–1856	389
XXVI	The Erosion of Friendships, 1857–1859	410
XXVII	Two and Thirty Years Ago, 1860–1864	429
XXVIII	New Friends, 1864–1868	451
XXIX	Aldworth and London, 1867–1872	472
XXX	*Idylls of the King*, 1872–1874	493
XXXI	Tennyson and the Theatre, 1874–1882	511
XXXII	Death of Old Friends, 1880–1884	532
XXXIII	Declining Years, 1885–1890	554
XXXIV	Silent Voices, 1890–1892	573
	Family Tree of the Tennysons	584
	Acknowledgements	587
	Abbreviations Used in the Notes	589
	Notes	592
	Select Bibliography	616
	Index	625

LIST OF ILLUSTRATIONS

❋

Frontispiece Tennyson, January 1856, by Richard Doyle

facing page

I George Clayton Tennyson, oil painting of the father of the poet — 20

II Alfred Tennyson, aged 15 — 21

III a. Alfred Tennyson, *c.*1830, probably by Anne Sellwood — 52

b. Arthur Henry Hallam, *c.*1830, pencil drawing by Anne Sellwood — 52

IV a. Alfred Tennyson, *c.*1831, attributed to James Spedding — 53

b. Arthur Henry Hallam, *c.*1832, by James Spedding — 53

V a. Alfred Tennyson from the rear, 1835, by Edward FitzGerald — 116

b. Somersby Rectory, by Alfred Tennyson — 116

c. Alfred Tennyson, 1835, by James Spedding — 116

VI Alfred Tennyson, by James Spedding — 117

VII a. Bayons Manor, before 1820 — 148

b. Bayons Manor, *c.*1850 — 148

VIII Tennyson, aged about 30; lithograph by J. H. Lynch of oil portrait by Samuel Laurence — 149

IX a. Tennyson, *c.*1849, by Algernon Langton Massingberd — 212

b. Tennyson, January 1842 — 212

X Emily Tennyson, oil by G. F. Watts, 1862 — 213

XI Emily Tennyson, *c.*1863 — 244

XII Farringford, *c.*1894 — 245

XIII Tennyson reading *Maud*, 27 September 1855, by D. G. Rossetti — 308

XIV Tennyson, *c.*1855, by Richard Doyle — 309

XV Self-portraits by Tennyson — 340

XVI Tennyson, 1856, medallion by Thomas Woolner — 341

XVII Lionel and Hallam Tennyson, 1857, by Lewis Carroll   404
XVIII Tennyson, *c.*1857, by Lewis Carroll (?)   405
  XIX Tennyson, 1859, oil by G. F. Watts   436
   XX Hallam, Alfred, Emily, and Lionel Tennyson, 1863, by
      Rejlander   437
  XXI a. Aldworth   500
      b. Bayons Manor   500
 XXII a. Dickens after death, by Sir John Millais   501
      b. From *Punch*, 22 December 1883   501
XXIII Tennyson, 1888, by Barraud   532
XXIV Tennyson, 1890, chalk sketch by G. F. Watts   533

The author and publishers are grateful to the following for permission
to reproduce pictures and/or for furnishing copies:

Tennyson Research Centre, Usher Gallery, and Lincolnshire Library
  Service: I, II, IVb, VIIa and b, VIII, X, XI, XVII, XXIII, XXIV.
Lt.-Col. J. A. Tennyson, RN: II.
National Portrait Gallery: IVa.
The Master and Fellows of Trinity College: Vb and c, IXb.
Mr J. H. Fryer-Spedding: VI.
Mr John Montgomery-Massingberd: IXa.
Mrs J. D. Wrisdale: IXa.
Mrs I. Dennis: XIII.
Mr R. H. Taylor: XIVa
Department of Rare Books and Manuscripts, Princeton University
  Library: XIVa.
Trustees of the British Museum: XIVb and c.
Beinecke Rare Book and Manuscript Library, Yale University: XV.
Lilly Library, Indiana University: XVIII.
The Hon. Mrs B. A. Hervey-Bathurst: XIX.
Witt Library, Courtauld Institute: XIX.

※

CHAPTER I

THE FOUNDATION OF A FAMILY

NOT long before his death Tennyson was talking with Boyd Carpenter, Bishop of Ripon, about his belief that original sin would not be punished. Carpenter had elaborated with episcopal authority on the necessity of unredeemed man's suffering for what he had not committed. 'Yes,' replied the poet with his habitual gravity, 'but there is heredity; it counts for so much.'[1]

All his life Tennyson was haunted by what he called the 'passion of the past', the regret for a better world irretrievably gone, while at the same time he was aware that the immediate past of his own ancestry was a dark one, throwing its shadow over the present into his own life. What he had actually inherited from his forebears was a crushing weight, but the reality was only a fraction what he believed to be his legacy.

The history of the two generations of Tennysons immediately before his own is fascinating enough for its own sake as a piece of Gothic melodrama, as improbable as the accounts of that other cradle of eccentric northern genius, Haworth, home of the Brontës. For the purposes of Tennyson's biography, however, some knowledge of the Tennyson family is indispensable both to understand the peculiar quality of his personality and to see how often it shaped his poetry, even when he was not totally aware that it was doing so. In particular it is necessary to know about the perplexed, unhappy relationships between Tennyson, his father, his uncle Charles, and his grandfather, for in their miserable misunderstandings of each other lay the direct cause of much of the desperation of the first half of his life. It has been customary to marvel over Tennyson's morbidity and gloom, but it would be more to the point to wonder at the strength of character that kept his mind from total disintegration.

The remote ancestry of the Tennysons was obscure and certainly plebeian. Some of his family (notably his uncle Charles, although Tennyson himself was occasionally guilty) were inclined to fabricate and perhaps believe a romantic nonsense of their aristocratic lineage, but the truth is that they had long been undistinguished. The name is Danish in origin, but their beginnings are otherwise uncertain. In the seventeenth century, while still resident in Yorkshire, they had produced three outstanding clerical cousins, two bishops and an archbishop, but these were collateral kinsmen not direct ancestors of the poet. For the rest of the family there are few records.

It was not until a hundred years later, after a migration to Lincolnshire, that the family began its painstaking climb from obscurity. Tennyson's great-great-grandfather was a solicitor; his son Michael, the poet's great-grandfather, described himself as 'surgeon'. Both those professions, though respectable enough, had considerably less prestige than today. Father and son both prospered, and Michael Tennyson further improved his lot by marriage to the daughter of a well-to-do family, who was certainly descended from the artistocracy and perhaps from royalty as well.[2]

Like many other families making their way upward, the Tennysons often married more for financial gain than headlong romance. Of such hard-headed alliances in the family, the first of which there is record is that of Michael Tennyson, great-grandfather of the poet. To him Elizabeth Clayton brought, as he expected, both her father's money and the blue blood of her mother's family, the Hildeyards.

She also brought another inheritance on which Michael Tennyson had probably not counted: the aberrant mentality that seemed the legacy of the male Claytons. As a family they were quarrelsome, litigious, recriminatory, and distrustful, perhaps even more with each other than with outsiders. There is no longer any absolute proof of an inherited physical characteristic responsible for their difficult personalities, but Alfred Tennyson's grandfather thought there was. More importantly, Tennyson himself probably thought so as well when he was a young man.

George Tennyson, Alfred's grandfather, and his sister Anne were the only children of Michael and Elizabeth. George was born in 1750, and with that event begins the real history of Alfred Tennyson. Five years after his birth, George Tennyson's mother died. If we are searching for psychological explanations of the difficult temper that he manifested in later life, we might find cause in both his lack of a mother while growing up and the unstable mental strain that she had brought from the Claytons. George Tennyson grew up to be overbearing with friends, a bully to his family, susceptible equally to choleric rages and to maudlin self-pity about his treatment by his own children.

We no longer know what kind of woman his mother had been and whether she exhibited any of the Clayton instability; what is certain is that her early death removed him from the normal civilizing influence for which children were then usually dependent upon their mothers. Certainly, he never really liked women in later life except as ministrants to his own comfort or as the bearers of dowries to the family. The wife he chose was more than usually submissive, as were the wives of most of his immediate male descendants.

Nowadays it would be tempting to attribute this example of the Tennyson 'black blood' solely to his lack of feminine training, were it not that his children and grandchildren also suffered from depression, melancholia, and mental breakdowns of all degrees of seriousness, including outright insanity. Presumably, as George Tennyson himself suspected, there was some strain of family predisposition to mental disturbance.

At the age of twenty-three, when he had finished his apprenticeship to a solicitor near Hull, George Tennyson set up practice in Market Rasen, within easy striking distance of Lincoln, Grimsby, and the small market towns of the wolds where so much of the money in northern Lincolnshire was concentrated. His family connections on his mother's side were useful in getting to know the big landholders of the county, for many of whom he was to act as agent or legal adviser. Better still, he was shrewd at buying land at good prices, and before he was thirty he had established himself as one of the cleverest—and most pushing—of the young men making their way in Lincolnshire.

In 1775 he married Mary Turner, daughter of a prosperous landed family of Caistor. Many years later she told her grandson Alfred of the time when she and George Tennyson were courting on the steps of Caistor House, her family home. Just after they had arisen from where they sat, a huge piece of stone fell from the parapet on to the steps. 'It was a special Providence, my dear,' she said to Alfred, 'but for that where would you have been?'[3] Socially, Mary Turner was not apt to help her husband in his climb upward, for her family was countrified of manner, and her parson brother Samuel was notorious for his profligate life, but her connections among the minor squirearchy were useful financially. She was gentle, affectionate, artistic in her interests, and so devoted to her husband (or perhaps so apprehensive of his temper) that her deliciously mis-spelt letters are full of apologies for the inconvenience her own illnesses or those of her children might cause him. Everything she wrote had to avoid a 'sombre cast' for fear

of throwing a gloom over her husband's mind. She was terrified of the
servants in her own house and once confessed that 'she wod. as soon
see a wild beast walk into the House as a Lady's Maid'.[4] As the years
passed her effective role in the lives of her husband and children
dwindled to almost nothing.

The eldest child, Elizabeth, was born in 1776, a year after her
parents' marriage, and then came Mary in 1777 and George Clayton
Tennyson, the poet's father, in 1778. It was not until 1784 that
Charles, the last child, was born; whether there was any significance in
this gap of six years is debatable.

Elizabeth, easily the most charming of the children, was beautiful,
and she bubbled with fun when she was in good health. She had a racy
turn of phrase that must have startled her contemporaries; once she
said that she yearned to be a man not a woman, that her ideal was 'to
be clustered not cloven'.[5] Later in life, when her pregnant daughter
was chased by a bull, Elizabeth reserved her sympathy not for her
daughter or unborn grandson but for the poor animal so sorely
tempted. Her health was never a match for her spirits, and when she
was ill she sometimes suffered from depression. She married Major
Matthew Russell and with him lived in splendour in Brancepeth
Castle, the vast ancestral home of the Nevilles in County Durham,
which the Russells largely rebuilt. Her husband was reputed to be one
of the richest commoners in England as a result of the millions amas-
sed by his self-made father, chiefly from mining in the north. Whether
her marriage came about because Elizabeth and her Matthew fell in
love, or whether it was arranged by George Tennyson, it was an
undoubted success, unlike those of her brothers and sister. She had her
mother's love of poetry and music, and from the time he was eighteen
she regularly gave money to her nephew Alfred, whose early talents
she was the only relative outside his immediate family to recognize.
She loved Alfred and she was truly generous, but her enjoyment of
charity to him was mischievously enhanced by the disapproval that it
engendered in her sister Mary and her brother Charles.

The second child, Mary, was always difficult, a fact that may be
connected with her not marrying until she was well on in her fourth
decade. In her mature correspondence there is no hint that she was
ever fond of her sister, and she was only intermittently so of her
brothers. As an adult she became gloomily and almost spitefully
Calvinistic, sadly rejoicing that she was one of the elect and trying to
regret her own family's certain damnation. Her husband was John

Bourne of Dalby, a few miles from Somersby, one of the few Nonconformist squires of the county; their marriage may not have been
ecstatic, but it was held together by their shared faith. At Dalby,
waited on by servants chosen for their religious rigour, she occasionally entertained her nieces and nephews, reminding them with lugubrious relish of the fate to which they were condemned. Whether
Elizabeth Russell was repelled by the dank religious pall of Dalby or by
the quality of the wine provided by her brother-in-law, about which
she wrote in amused fashion, she seems seldom to have visited there.
Because of her spiritual remoteness from Mrs Russell and her
brothers, Mary Bourne was the member of the family with least
apparent influence on Alfred Tennyson.

At the birth of the poet's father, the first-born son in the family,
George Tennyson gave him his own Christian name and added to it the
talismanic one of Clayton. Obviously, the child's position as eldest son
as well as his names indicated that he was intended to inherit money
and position and to enhance them. As a man George Clayton Tennyson was capable of both his mother's sweetness and his father's rage,
but he had inherited neither the placidity of the one nor the surface
self-confidence of the other, and his life was a turmoil of emotions,
each forgotten as it was succeeded by another. He was several inches
over six feet tall, physically awkward, with long legs and enormous
feet that gave him a lurching gait. His rough, handsome, curiously
unformed face was incapable of hiding the turbulent emotions within,
and his body was a quivering, twitching instrument upon which they
played.

All this physical and psychological maladroitness must have been
manifest when he was a mere boy, for at a very early age he was sent
away from his comfortable home to live for some years with his
grandfather, Michael Tennyson, in Holderness. Unfortunately, when
he returned to his parents, George seemed even more noisy and
ungovernable than before, his voice and speech still more annoying. If
the elder George worked at liking his first son, his efforts were singularly unsuccessful. He tried according to his lights, to be fair, but the
boy would irritatingly show in return the very kind of temper the
father had been trying to suppress in himself. Mrs Tennyson was
probably affectionate to him in her ineffectual way, but young George
grew up an outsider, knowing that he was further from his parents'
hearts than even his sister Mary. Inconstant in mood, vacillating
between frenzy and lethargy, seldom obedient to his parents,

spendthrift and unbusinesslike by nature, driven by lack of affection to accentuate his own worst failings, he led a life that must have been appallingly lonely.

The pride the elder Tennyson wanted to feel in his family was reserved for Charles, last of the children. One cannot help wondering whether his birth six years after his brother's indicates a last attempt by his father to secure an eligible heir to take the place of little George, who was already so unsatisfactory. George was physically uncoordinated, but Charles was graceful. George's craggy great head was smoothed in Charles to a romantic handsomeness when he was grown that was to attract more women than his wife could countenance. Every word George uttered seemed calculated to alienate his father, but Charles knew instinctively how to flatter old George and keep him in temper.

Charles grew up cautious, businesslike, careful to husband his emotion against unproductive waste, efficient and unimaginative as parliamentarian and Privy Councillor, and above all anxious to advance the family socially and financially, to build one of the grandest houses in England, and to procure a romantic sounding title. Unfortunately, he had neither his father's quick-witted shrewdness nor his mother's charm and sense of humour about herself. With all his abilities, the fact seems patent that Charles was a bore. His marriage was the most unsatisfactory of those of the four children; his own offspring frequently turned against him and laughed at his pretensions, and finally his life was no happier than that of either his brother George or his sister Mary.

The elder George Tennyson surely knew in his heart that his favourite son had none of the necessary panache for a rise to power and position, but he was none the less the best material at hand. Besides, his father felt for Charles what has been described as 'an almost morbid affection' and 'a corresponding dislike for his elder brother'.[6] While his sons were still young, he decided to make Charles the major heir, even though it meant going against the position of the elder son and the hopes implied at his christening.

In the future their families were to split hopelessly over the arrangements for the inheritance of old George's fortune, but the amazing thing is that his sons remained good friends all their lives, and young George seldom resented Charles personally for having, as George saw it, usurped his place. Young George was incapable of living in constant peace with someone as close as his brother, but his anger was always short-lived. His sons, however, all detested their uncle Charles. Indeed, it would be fair to say that old Mr Tennyson's decision over the disposition of his fortune was probably the major external fact governing the first half of the life of his grandson, Alfred Tennyson, even though that decision had been taken long before his birth in 1809.

Although he intended to pass over young George, Mr Tennyson had no intention of leaving him with neither profession nor inheritance. The obvious solution to the first of these problems was to make him a parson, since Mr Tennyson's own acquaintance among landed men in Lincolnshire would almost certainly guarantee his son clerical preferment. As early as 1791 he secured the benefice of Benniworth for the future incumbency of George, although the boy was only thirteen at the time, and the same year he was negotiating for the further living at South Willingham, in the gift of Tennyson's friend Mr Heneage. Another clergyman would have to fulfil the parochial duties until George could attend the University and be ordained. Such use of a 'warming pan', as the luckless locum parson was known, was fairly common, to secure a permanent benefice for a boy not yet ready for ordination.

Either young George knew nothing of the activity on his behalf or he was too young to realize that it meant his displacement in the family fortunes, for it was not until he was at Cambridge that he recognized fully what was implied in his ordination, and by then it was too late to gain a proper place in his father's regard.

What he was losing was considerable, and it promised to be a great deal more if the elder George did not succumb to apoplexy in one of his frequent rages. From his father the elder George had inherited properties worth £700 a year, and at the death of his uncle Christopher Clayton in 1794 he became the heir of property bringing in £2,000 annually, but this was only part of his income. During the last quarter of the century he continued buying land with profits from his successful practice in Market Rasen. By 1815 his properties at Grimsby alone were offered for sale at £200,000, and at his death in 1835 he owned lands and manors all over northern Lincolnshire.

In his diary for 1798 Dr John Parkinson described the reprehensible business methods of 'Tennison', a man 'who has always some object in view, which he exerts himself by every trick of a fawning parasite to accomplish; but who tramples underfoot the person whom by this means he has got into his power'. A year later Parkinson called him 'a weak man (only likely to impose on such as he can deceive) who contradicts himself continually'.[7]

Of the properties he acquired, the one with the most sentimental value for George Tennyson was the land he bought in 1784 in Tealby, a pretty little village in the wolds not far from Market Rasen. Sentiment is not a word usually connected with him, but this purchase was certainly dictated by motives beyond mere financial gain. Successive purchases over the next forty years finally made the Tennyson holdings at Tealby into an estate of some 2,000 acres.

In a dominant position across the valley from Tealby were the ruins of an old castle that had once belonged to Lord Lovel and d'Eyncourt, one of the ancestors of George Tennyson's mother, the former Elizabeth Clayton. Below the ruins stood the little seventeenth-century manor house known as Beacons. There is no indication of how clearly defined his intentions were when he bought the property while still in his thirties, but Tennyson must already have had in mind the revival of his family's fortunes and its establishment in what he thought of as the ancestral manor.

Beacons was a thatched house, too small for the Tennyson family, and he did nothing to enlarge it for some time, although he began planting the bleak hillside with trees, against the day when he might either enlarge the house or build a grander one on the foundations of the castle. In the meantime he and his family moved around Lincolnshire, living in some of the various houses he owned. In the early 1790s he bought a fine old house, Deloraine Court, in Minster Yard in Lincoln, but the Tennysons were not taken into the snobbish provincial society of the county town, and in 1797 he sold the house for £1,500 and took the family to Grimsby while Tealby was being made ready for them. Rather than put a new house on the foundations of the castle, he expanded the old house into one of some ten bedrooms, still quite modest by the standard of what it later became. The original thatch was kept, but the name was changed to Tealby Lodge. It took another half-dozen years and the imagination of Charles Tennyson to trace its fanciful derivation from 'Bayeux' to 'Beacons' to 'Bayons Manor', the name by which it finally became known until its destruction a few years ago.

In the thousands of pieces of correspondence of George Tennyson and his four children now in the Lincolnshire Archives Office, there are three recurrent concerns: money, filial ingratitude and disobedience, and health. All very much what one might expect to find in any large group of family letters except that, in this case, they are greatly magnified in the passion with which they are argued.

Probably the correspondence between George Tennyson and his son Charles exaggerates their concern for money, since they were two businessmen trying to consolidate a family competence into a fortune, and naturally their common interests were often financial. All the same, rents, purchases of land, fees, and the peccancy of factors make up an unusual part of the matter of their letters. The carelessness of his children about money was a stabbing worry to old George; his desire to see them rise socially was paralleled by his fear that they were becoming aristocratically extravagant. Money lay, too, behind his preoccupation with the duties of his children and the health of their bodies.

The ingratitude that the elder Tennyson thought was his daily portion from his children frequently provoked him into threats of disinheritance, and in turn they had occasionally to protest their independence of his bullying. At one time or another he was totally alienated from each of his children, for even the normally submissive Charles could be provoked into rebellion against his tyranny. There was deep affection among his children, at any rate between Elizabeth, George, and Charles, but they had inherited some of their father's temper, and they would occasionally flash out at each other. Mary seems to have quarrelled almost constantly with the others, although she tried to remain on good terms with at least one of her brothers at a time, in order to have a confidant about the sins of the others. Elizabeth had by far the most equable temperament of the children, but even she quarrelled seriously with each of the others. It is improbable that there was any considerable period between 1800 and old George's death in 1835 when all four children were on good terms with both their father and each other. Most of the time at least two of the fractious quintet were not on speaking terms, but there is no indication that any of the children ever fell out with their gentle mother.

The intimate correspondence of most families seems to outsiders to be concerned unduly with sickness. When parents must watch over the physical well-being of children, they frequently become obsessively concerned with weakness and illness, and the children in turn find their own health a source of constant interest to their parents. So many families in the nineteenth century had lost at least one child that it was natural for the Tennysons to have scrupulous interest in each other's physical functions. Allowing for all this, however, the correspondence of George and Mary Tennyson and their children and grandchildren sometimes seems to exist primarily for the exchange of news of symptoms. Fevers, tonics, purges, medicines, doctors, and diet were part of their ordinary vocabulary, and few families can have been in more detailed communication about the state of their bowels. But beside this fairly normal preoccupation with health was a dark counterpoint of constant, brooding concern about one disease: epilepsy.

The family letters show that both young George and Charles suffered from time to time with some form of the illness, that one of Charles's sons was a victim, and that perhaps old George himself had attacks of less severity than those of his descendants. One of Alfred Tennyson's brothers was totally insane most of his life, another suffered from some form of mental illness nearly as incapacitating, a third was an opium addict, a fourth was severely alcoholic, and of the rest of the large family each had at least one bad mental breakdown in a long life. If there are any detailed records extant of what precisely ailed them all, I have been unable to find them, and it is impossible to say whether any of young George's children actually suffered from a form of epilepsy. What is most probable is that among Alfred Tennyson's ten brothers and sisters, some had attacks that resembled epilepsy, and that Alfred either had the disease while young and recovered from it in later life, or, more probably, mistakenly feared as a young man that he had inherited a tendency to it that he might transmit to any offspring of his own.*

* Unfortunately, the certificates of death in the family shed little light upon the matter of the Tennysons' epilepsy. When George Tennyson and his son George Clayton Tennyson died, certificates were not required. Victorian doctors, like modern ones, were hesitant to ascribe death to causes that might embarrass the survivors, and we could not expect to find a 'shameful' disease like epilepsy recorded on the death certificates of members of the gentle classes like Septimus Tennyson, Charles Tennyson d'Eyncourt, and his son George Hildeyard Tennyson d'Eyncourt, who, with Edward Tennyson, were the members of later generations most apt to have suffered from the malady. Septimus was certified to have died of 'Chronic Affection of Liver and Brain', from which he had suffered 'Some years, Bronchitis 3 weeks'. His uncle Charles died of 'Disease of brain, paralysis'. George Tennyson d'Eyncourt, whose severe alcoholism was certainly not mentioned, died of 'Chronic Disease of Brain'. Edward Tennyson, who had been confined in a mental asylum for nearly sixty years, was certified as dying of 'Exhaustion (after Mania) 5 months'. The vagueness of the several descriptions may conceal evidence of epilepsy, but in themselves the certificates are neither proof nor disproof of its existence in the family. One frail bit of evidence is that Edward, Septimus, and George Tennyson d'Eyncourt all died unmarried, which in the latter two may indicate that they were afraid to pass on an inherited disease.

There is no clear indication of when epilepsy first manifested itself in the elder Tennyson's sons, but George suffered more severely from it than his brother did, and he probably began having attacks at an earlier age than Charles. If so, this would in part explain their father's decision to pass over the normal expectations of George, since a disposition to fits was no recommendation as head of the great family the elder George Tennyson hoped to found.

Despite his strong preference for Charles, he was even-handed in the education he provided for his sons. George was sent to St. Peter's Grammar School in York before being farmed out to a country parson in Huntingdonshire to prepare for St. John's, Cambridge. In later years he used to lament that he had not been sent to Eton rather than York, so that he would have learned greater polish in classical versifying, and he certainly felt that Eton was the natural privilege of an elder son (when the occasion arose he sent his own eldest son there). It was surely from this sense of deprivation that the tradition arose among the Somersby Tennysons that their uncle Charles had been sent to Eton from York, in express reversal of the normal treatment of elder and younger son.[8] In fact, Charles went to Louth Grammar School from York, and then to St. John's; there is no evidence that Eton was ever suggested. The mistake is important only as it demonstrates how the Somersby Tennysons piled up more and more instances of their grandfather's injustice, even when the instances were untrue.

Some indication of the elder Tennyson's habitual inclination to believe the worst of his sons, particularly George, is contained in a letter to the headmaster of St. Peter's when the boys returned home at the end of June 1793 in good health and spirits: 'George, I am sorry to say, speaks as bad or worse than ever, I fear he will not attend to you in this respect, & not having been favor'd with a line from you, I doubt you have not anything favorable to say of them.'[9]

The stay in Huntingdonshire with Mr Hutchinson suggests that young George was in special need of tuition before going up to Cambridge in October 1796. His subsequent career there was undistinguished, perhaps because he felt no inclination to study in preparation for holy orders, a career to which he was being ineluctably pushed. He did not misbehave badly, but there is a family tradition that he once fired a pistol shot through a window in Trinity chapel; he did no hard work and was more than once called to account by his father for extravagance. 'I assure you upon my honour that I have kept nothing from you and that you know to the last farthing every thing I owe in the world except my next Tutor's bill,' he wrote home on 13 May 1799. To be sure that he was concealing nothing in the total of his debts, his father characteristically added the amounts on the back of the letter.[10] The paternal warning may have been effective, for by July Thomas Catton of St. John's wrote to George's father: 'Notwithstanding a good deal of apparent idleness, it is a proof of real industry that he obtained a good place in the first class, at our late examination.'[11]

George Clayton Tennyson was obviously intelligent, and at Cambridge he acquired a good knowledge of the classics, some Hebrew, and a fair knowledge of French. But after his brief success in 1799 he fell into slack ways again. The following year he wrote to his father, excusing his neglect of mathematics and his unwillingness to work for an honours degree: '. . . though I have by a habitual study of the Mathematics acquired a pleasure in the acquisition of further knowledge in many branches of them, yet were I to aim at the very highest honours it would required such continual application and exertion and a knowledge of such other parts of them which to me are perfectly disinteresting and which I believe are generally acknowledged to be almost useless.' In the remote possibility of taking a good degree, it would be 'an uncertain & at best a transitory honour'.[12]

After this ingenuous plea he studied once more with Mr Hutchinson, finally taking a pass degree. Worse than this disappointment, old George discovered at about the same time that Charles was also beginning to demonstrate spendthrift ways at school at Louth.

After finishing his requirements for his degree young George was ordained deacon at the end of May 1801, as his father wished. Even then he had to continue answering his father's criticism: 'I must say I felt myself rather hurt you should even conjecture that I had not prepared myself sufficiently for orders.'[13] The letter, now among the family papers, is torn lengthwise, as if old George were furious at filial disrespect.

Presumably young George still hoped his father would relent, restore him to the position of elder son, and make it unnecessary to proceed to priest's orders. In the meantime he had one last fling, a trip to Russia in the autumn of 1801, ostensibly to see the coronation of Tsar Alexander, successor to the Emperor Paul, who had been murdered the previous spring. The account of what happened there is wildly improbable, and there are several versions of it, which leads one to distrust them all. None the less, Alfred Tennyson believed his father's story and frequently told it as literal fact, so there may be at least a germ of truth in it.

Although he arrived in Moscow too late for the coronation, George stayed on there as the guest of Lord St. Helens, the British diplomat to whom he had an introduction. At a grand dinner given by St. Helens there were present many Russian notables whose names Tennyson failed to catch. When the death of the previous Tsar was cautiously mentioned, the young Englishman is said to have leaned across a heavily bemedalled man next to him and cried out impetuously, 'Why, St. Helens, what's the use of speaking so gingerly about a matter so notorious? We know well enough in England that the Emperor Paul was murdered in the Mikhailovski Palace, and we know exactly who did it. Count Zoboff knocked him down, and Benningsen and Count Pahlen strangled him.' A deep silence fell over the table.

After dinner, as the guests were going into an adjoining room, Lord St. Helens said to Tennyson in a whisper, 'Don't go into the next room, but fly for your life. . . . The man next you across whose breast you leaned, was Count Pahlen, one of the most powerful nobles in Russia. Zoboff was at the table, too, and you have publicly charged both of them with being assassins.'[14] Tennyson left the palace and took fast horse, without even changing his clothes, while St. Helens kept the company as late as he could. From Moscow Tennyson posted to the home of a Scottish merchant outside Odessa and went into hiding. St. Helens sent a message to listen for the sound of the horn of the English courier who passed through the village once every three months. It came one stormy night, and Tennyson, disguised as a servant, went with the courier who was taking dispatches home. After finding the papers which the courier lost on the journey while he was drunk, Tennyson made his way to an English frigate at Odessa, got safe on board, and so back to England, little changed except for the beard grown in compliment to the new Tsar.

Contemporary letters show that George Tennyson actually was in Russia, but the details sound too wild to be convincing; probably the best suggestion is that made by Sir Charles Tennyson, who said that his great-grandfather may have invented the whole story in a pathetic attempt to give himself a romantic past in compensation for the dullness of his subsequent career. Many years later George Tennyson wrote hair-raising letters from another Continental trip, telling of the narrow escapes he had made from other horrible situations, but by then his mind was already badly deranged. What is common to all his stories is that there was no witness who might have disproved them.

Whatever the reality of the Russian trip, he returned from it in February 1802 to a humdrum clerical existence of which he had never wanted part. In December he was ordained priest and then inducted into the living of the little village of Benniworth, almost equidistant from Wragby, Louth, and — more ominously — Tealby, where his father was by now settled.

For a year or two young George lived at Tealby and from there took care of Benniworth and South Willingham. His sermons were always highly literate but far too difficult for the simple country folk who were his parishioners; he was capable of great kindness, but his innate impatience made it hard for him to spend much time in parish visiting. He was unsatisfactory in most of the ways that were important to a parson in the depths of Lincolnshire.

Robert Burton of Lincoln, a friend of the elder Tennyson, had long been fond of young George, knowing how difficult he was but appreciating how much he had been hurt by his father. While George was still in Cambridge, Burton wrote to Mr Tennyson about the possibility of the living falling vacant for the united parishes of Somersby and Bag Enderby, a benefice of which Burton was patron. The Rector, Mr Chambers, wanted to move, but it was not until 1806 that the vacancy finally occurred; in the meantime George was encouraged to expect to take over the living when Chambers left.

While waiting for Somersby he moved to lodgings in Louth, and neither he nor his father can have regretted the distance put between them. At Louth he met the gentle daughter of a former vicar, Elizabeth Fytche (or ffytche, as it was sometimes spelt). She was beautiful, with merry dark eyes, a rosy complexion, and a simple, lackadaisical manner that appealed strongly to men, perhaps particularly to an uncontrolled and somewhat violent man like George Tennyson. When she was nearly eighty, one of her children, thinking she could not hear, mentioned that she had received twenty-four proposals of marriage before accepting George Tennyson. 'No, my dear, twenty-five,' said the old lady in a simple desire for accuracy.

The elder Tennyson, who is said to have disapproved of his son's choice of a beautiful bride with no money, surprisingly put no effective barriers in the way of the match, and indeed settled 100 acres of land upon his son, but he did not go to the marriage in the summer of 1805. Mary Tennyson drove to the wedding with her brother Charles in the family carriage and sent a detailed account to her sister Elizabeth Russell of the 8 a.m. ceremony at which the bride wore a white beaver hat and 'lilly muslin gown'. George had a new coat and 'a pair of the best silk hose'. The bridal pair drove back to Mrs Fytche's in the Tealby carriage while the rest of the party walked to the 'very plentiful breakfast' of spice cake and coffee. 'After breakfast we danced "come haste to the wedding," cotillions & waltzes followed, fandangos & minuettos closed the revels of the morning,' wrote Mary. When the party was over, the bride and groom went to Tealby to pay their respects to the elder Tennysons, an unpromising but emblematic start to their marriage. They drove to Tealby, as Mary told her sister, with

three outriders all of which together with postillions and every horse had good white satin favors at a shilling a yard, tyed up by the bridesmaids, but trouble was nothing, expense was all!!!!!! . . . Eliza is really a sweet tempered creature and the *very* woman for George. . . . I think you would like her, she is particularly fond of and tender to animals, and quadraped [*sic*] conversation she enters with more interest into than any other, but I have never yet had a quiet half hour with her and therefore cannot with justice detail the varieties of her mind & soul.[15]

After a few days of honeymoon the pair settled down in Louth and began their disastrous life together. Mary Tennyson could not have been more wrong about their suitability for one another. Elizabeth was easy-going, unworried by details, and more than a little feckless about running the household. The life together of two indolent persons created constant mutual friction. George was moved to irritability and occasional brutality by her quiet acquiescence; she protested feebly, unable to understand his alternations of rage and lethargy. It was an unpropitious atmosphere for rearing a family of twelve.

In 1806 the living of Somersby and Bag Enderby at last fell vacant and George Tennyson was inducted by Robert Burton at the end of the year. There was a good deal of tiresome quarrelling between Burton, the new Rector, and the Rector's father about who was to pay for the extensive alterations to the old manor house, now known as Somersby Rectory, to which the young couple intended to move. The elder George agreed first to pay £200, then £500, towards the cost of enlarging the kitchen, adding a nursery, two servants' rooms, stables, and a coal-house. When the money was not immediately forthcoming, young George recklessly wrote to his father demanding interest of more than £50 for the time elapsed since the money had been promised. The irritation this produced in his father was aggravated by the fact that George's sister Mary was also giving trouble to her parents. Old George's first reaction was to turn to Charles for consolation: 'Mary & George's conduct towards myself & your Dear mother have of late made both myself & her low & dispirited,' he wrote. 'You & our dear Eliza have been ever kind & dutiful to us & were they so likewise we could love them equally.'[16]

When all the difficulties over the alterations were settled, young George and his wife moved into Somersby Rectory early in 1808. Technically it was not a rectory but the personal property of Mr Burton, who recognized that the old Rectory, a mere cottage, was totally inadequate for a clergyman with family. All the rest of his life George Tennyson was to tinker with the house, making it more to his liking, expanding its small rooms and narrow passages to house his constantly growing family, and though it was always crowded, it became a comfortable place to live.

Three cramped rooms were thrown together to make a pleasant book-lined drawing-room, with yellow curtains and covers, and on the walls the Rector hung the paintings he had been accumulating with indifferent success; to the locals they were known as ''eathen gods and goddesses wi'out cloäs'.[17] By the windows to the garden stood the harp on which he and his daughters played. In 1820 he built a Gothic dining-hall with the help of his coachman Horlins and himself carved the oak chimney-piece to look like stone. It must have been a charming room with stained glass windows, green brocade on the walls from his mother's wedding dress, and ranks of oil paintings skied to the arched ceiling. The room was, unfortunately, torn down recently.

By the time they moved to Somersby Elizabeth Tennyson had already borne two sons and was once more pregnant. The first child, hopefully named George for his grandfather, had died in infancy in 1806. Frederick was born in Louth in 1807, and Charles was born in Somersby in the summer of 1808. The following year, so near midnight on 5 August that it was difficult to be certain of the date, Alfred Tennyson was born in Somersby Rectory, in the white-canopied bed in the main bedroom. He used to claim that his birthday was the 5th, but his mother held out for the 6th, and in time he agreed that her memory of the event was more apt to be correct than his own.

✻

CHAPTER II

CHILDHOOD AND SCHOOLING,
1809–1820

WHEN he was only two days old Alfred Tennyson was baptized by his father. Tennyson's son says perhaps too insistently that the Rector was merely following the Prayer Book injunction that baptism of infants should not be deferred 'longer than the first or second Sunday next after their birth'. Two days after Alfred's birth, however, was Tuesday, not Sunday, which suggests that there was reason for haste. George Clayton Tennyson, we know, did not follow the Prayer Book slavishly on baptism, for Frederick was more than a year old when he shared a christening with his brother Charles. Hallam Tennyson also records that the Rector said the infant Alfred was like a baby Hercules; 'nevertheless during infancy three times after convulsions he was thought to be dead'.

There are many other possible causes of convulsions in infants, but on rare occasions they may indicate epilepsy. Probably the family set the date forward, privately suspecting the disease that was to become so publicly apparent at Somersby a few years later. To Alfred, looking back, the convulsions must have seemed in retrospect the first onset of what he feared was his own malady.

At scarcely more than yearly intervals Alfred and his two surviving brothers were joined in the Rectory by four more boys and four girls. Such a crowd strained both the sleeping capacity of the house and the temper of the Rector, who was so morbidly sensitive to sound that little Alfred once asked whether he would be permitted to make noise when he got to heaven. The children grew up in awe, even fear, of their father, and they would scatter in every direction when they saw him coming. Away from his family he was popular with many of the county families as an amusing and genial guest who talked brilliantly, but the return to the Rectory brought with it his black depression, and though he did not intend to be hard on them, it was not easy for him to demonstrate his affection to his children.

Mrs Tennyson was probably more genuinely religious than her

melancholy clergyman husband, and she passed on to Alfred her spirit of reverence, although he early deserted her strict Evangelical beliefs. For her he reserved the love he was half afraid to show to his father. She liked to read poetry aloud, and she listened sympathetically to her children's poems, so that they grew up scribbling verse nearly as easily as prose. As her sister-in-law Mary had noticed, she loved animals, of which the house was often inconveniently full; Alfred shared her fondness for them but never conquered his dislike of cats. He once tamed an owl that he had lured to his bedroom window, and it would sit on Mrs Tennyson's head, descending only to give battle to her monkey. The monkey was a difficult pet, but she was not bothered when it scoured the floor with ink or bit the ankles of the housemaids. Soon she was known in Somersby as an easy source of small change for the local boys, who brought dogs to beat beneath her window, knowing that she would pay them to stop.

During their early days in Somersby the Tennysons kept neither horse nor pony; the Rector walked everywhere within fifteen or twenty miles, while his wife took her airings in a donkey chair drawn by a huge 'Newfoundland mastiff'. As the elder boys grew up, they would walk beside her chair, and when the dog insisted on lying down, she read Thomson's *Seasons* to them. She was very small but inordinately proud of the height of her sons, and she treated them with a deeply feminine manner not far removed from flirtatiousness. It was charming but probably not good for their future emotional stability.

The informality and warmth of her affection were necessary to offset her husband's nervous sternness to the children, and without it they might have grown up far more crippled emotionally than they did. But between her easy-going ways and his aloofness, the children were hardly trained in any of the normal modes of social behaviour. Total neglect of the rules of conduct can be as crippling as absolute conventionality, and all during their lives the Tennyson children were at a disadvantage from never having learned the ways of making personal intercourse easy. Only their intelligence, charm, and basic good will carried them through, and even so they were regarded as having extraordinary manners. When he was old and famous, Alfred Tennyson was still to suffer occasionally from the suspicion that other people thought his behaviour curious, which it was.

Even in a rough, unmannerly countryside the Tennysons were noticeably eccentric. They dressed oddly, they were often unkempt and rumpled, they read and talked to themselves as they walked, so absorbed in their own thoughts that they passed others without recognition. The elder boys used to walk about with their eyes stretched wide-open between outspread fingers, so that they might see better. Normal hours meant little to them, and they were as apt to be met in the lanes around Somersby in the middle of the night as in the day. Within the Rectory arrangements were casual to a degree, and Mrs Tennyson was said to forget to order food for her family until they were nearly ready to sit down at a meal, then to send hurriedly to the neighbouring farm for two or three ducks. In church the Rector took snuff in the pulpit, twiddled his fingers nervously as he spoke, and delivered finely balanced sermons in his beautiful deep voice, unaware that his congregation understood almost nothing of his Georgian periods. On weekdays he would sleep until late afternoon, then rise to play the harp. On at least one occasion he could not remember his own name, and he recorded with amusement the exasperation of his brother Charles, who said that the Rector would 'hesitate for half an hour on which peg [he] should hang [his] hat'.[1] No wonder the parish tolerated the family as endearingly odd.

With all its disadvantages, the Rectory was in many ways a splendid place for a poet's growth, since art and learning were accepted there as normal. The Rector himself was a competent amateur poet, with a real love of the classics. For a country parsonage his library was unusually scholarly, a collection of some 2,500 books, many of them bought at the dispersal of the library of Bennet Langton, Dr Johnson's friend. Predictably, there were many volumes of theology, philosophy, and history, and to young Alfred the classical and Oriental sections were important in the development of his poetry. More surprising was the group of scientific books, which influenced Tennyson in his lifelong amateur passion for science. Recently, part of the library has been assembled and housed in the Tennyson Research Centre in Lincoln, where the individual volumes show signs of heavy use.

'Somersby', wrote Tennyson as an old man, 'is secluded under a chalk-hill, called in the dialect of this county, a wold—a village shadowed by tall elmtrees, with here & there a sand-rock jutting out of the soil.'[2] Today it still seems very remote, caught between the wolds to the north and the fens a few miles south. It is green country, heavy and breathless with vegetation in high summer, when moss is thick on the walls and even the churches built of the local greenstone seem to recede into the lush growth. In the winter it is bleak, insufficiently protected from the North Sea winds, and the narrow lanes in those days would turn sullen with mud. Towards Tetford the road rises white with chalk dust between hills sprinkled with sheep, while the road to Harrington snakes eastward through swampy copses. It is a narrow, enclosed world but wonderfully varied, and Tennyson found there the basis of his greatest poetry, in the intimate relation between man and his natural surroundings.

In his time the church at Somersby was still thatched, and its low grey tower with two bells was cobbled up with brick. Beside the door stood a good Norman preaching cross. The interior of the church is intimate but undistinguished save for having been the pastoral responsibility of George Clayton Tennyson.

Across a deep lane the Rectory turns a plain face to the road, as it did in the last century, for its real orientation was to the extensive gardens stretching away from the creeper-covered house towards the cress-filled brook at the bottom of the glebe field. There were 'seven elms, the poplars four' shading the lawns, with sycamores and a Scotch fir full of rooks. Hollyhocks, sunflowers, lilies, and roses grew in charming disorder to match the life of the family. The kitchen garden had gooseberries and an orchard of what Tennyson remembered as 'golden apples—summer apples, we used to call them—I have never seen their like but once long years after at Coniston in the old courts'.

Behind the Rectory was Holywell (Halliwell) Wood, full of snowdrops in the spring, followed by violets; the little village school was in the wood beside a skittle alley and a bath house with steps down to the water, flashing with trout and eels. In the stream Alfred used 'to build cities and castles of sand till the current undermined them and the towers fell'. Down the brook he 'made sail little bits of wood freighted with imaginary wares for China and India till an eddy overwhelmed them'.[3] On its frozen surface he learned to skate in the icy blasts that were said to blow unimpeded from the Ural mountains. How much the brook meant to him is indicated in 'Flow down, cold rivulet, to the sea', his farewell to it when the family left Somersby in 1837.

The picture of the Rectory sounds idyllic, as it undoubtedly was much of the time, but what Tennyson's son records in his biography indicates little of the tensions within the house. It is normal enough to remember chiefly the pleasurable aspects of childhood, but Tennyson deliberately suppressed the less delightful side and told his son little of the perturbation of the family background. Almost the entirety of what we know about it is recorded in the family archives assembled by the elder George Tennyson and his son Charles.

I. George Clayton Tennyson, father of the poet, oil, artist unknown.

II. Alfred Tennyson, aged 15.

Because of the smallness of the house, the three eldest boys shared a combination bedroom-study in a gabled attic under the roof, reached by its own steep stairway, illuminated by a skylight. In the room was a great beam on which they practised acrobatics.

Alfred was close to both his elder brothers, although relations were not always easy with Frederick, who had a hot, almost ungovernable temper which had probably not often been checked by his parents when he was small. Friends would occasionally complain that he was arrogant. He was brilliantly clever, powerfully built, handsome (he was the only one of the family who had fair colouring), and musically gifted, playing both flute and keyboard instruments with great skill; he had the good sense to love Mozart at a time when his music was less well known than it is now. Unfortunately, he was idle and given to insolently flouting any authority he did not totally respect. The Rector had difficulties with all of his children, but between him and his eldest son there was open hostility, and it can hardly have been entirely the fault of the father. It may be significant that of all the family it was Frederick who most resembled his grandfather in both looks and temperament.

Of his ten brothers and sisters, Charles was dearest to Alfred. He was sunny-tempered, whimsically amusing, tender-hearted, and generous to a fault. His sister Mary, who was normally censorious of men, thought Charles the kindest person she had ever known. Although he was but a year older than Alfred, Charles took it upon himself to help and to teach his brother in a way that is unusual in one so little senior. One Sunday when Alfred was only eight, he was too unwell to attend church, so Charles handed him a slate and said, 'See if you can write verse', and assigned 'flowers' as the subject. Before he had returned, Alfred 'had covered both sides of the slate (a large one) with very fair Thomsonian verse and perfectly metrical so that [Charles] said: "you've done it." '[4]

This was presumably Alfred's first written verse, but from the time he was five he had composed individual lines. 'Before I could read,' he remembered in old age, 'I was in the habit on a stormy day of spreading my arms to the wind, and crying out, "I hear a voice that's speaking in the wind," and the words "far, far away" had always a strange charm for me.'[5] When he and Charles went for rambles, they would walk on opposite sides of a hedge, making up lines and shouting them to each other. One that Alfred remembered was 'With slaughterous sons of thunder rolled the flood'. When he was sixty he repeated the line and said, 'Great nonsense of course, but I thought it fine.' What he began so early he continued all his life, for his normal method of composition was to put together individual lines, which then sometimes suggested themselves as the germs of entire poems.

Pope and Scott provided models for many of his poems written before his teens, and he loved Byron's poetry, although he outgrew it in later years. It is indicative of what his mature poetry was to become that what he remembered best of these early efforts, long after they had disappeared, was their metrical perfection. His family, including his father (who tried to be dispassionate), recognized his poetic superiority to his brothers and sisters, but there was probably no real awareness of his genius, however much in later years his brothers and sisters tended to remember predicting his brilliant future. Whatever the others thought, Alfred himself felt early confidence in his own vocation and told his young brother Arthur, 'I mean to be famous.'

One of the earliest surviving examples of a complete stanza of his verse, written when he was about eight, is particularly interesting for showing how quickly the distinctive Tennysonian style developed:

> Whateer I see, whereer I move
> These whispers rise & fall away;
> Something of pain, of loss, of love,
> But what, twere hard to say.[6]

Even in so rudimentary a poem as this, the last two lines give away their creator's identity.

Some fifteen miles east of Somersby lies Mablethorpe, in Tennyson's childhood only beginning to be thought of as a place for seaside holidays. There were few places to stay, and in 1813 the Rector of Somersby had trouble finding lodgings for his brood, since 'Every potbellied grocer and dirty linen draper bespeaks his lodgings from year to year, and they are therefore pre-engaged throughout the season'.[7] But young Alfred loved it as the first place he had ever seen the sea, and all the rest of his long life he could remember the feel of the wind catching him as he stood on the high, tussocked bank that protected the level land behind him from the sea, and he could still see the wet sand flats gleaming at low tide, runnelled by the retreating water, then churned up again when the waves came roaring in with the turning tide. Water, he used to say, was somehow his favourite element, and the surf and sand of Mablethorpe, where he had paddled as a bare-legged boy, remained his prototype for the primeval contest for boundary between sea and land, in its timelessness annihilating the present and releasing his passion of the past:

> Here stood the infant Ilion of my mind,
> And here the Grecian ships did seem to be . . . ('Mablethorpe')

Eight more children were born at the Rectory in the ten years after Alfred's birth: two girls, Mary and Emilia; then three boys, Edward, Arthur, and Septimus; then Matilda and Cecilia; and, finally, Horatio. Such a large family naturally tended to split into groups, but they were happily united in play and amusements. So close were they that for years they hardly ever mixed with other children, since there were enough at home for almost any game they could invent. Knightly feats, jousting, and castles naturally occupied much of their outdoor play, and within doors they loved to write endless stories in letter form, the current instalment each night being slipped under the potato dish to be read aloud at the end of the meal. Alfred's were conceded to be the best, especially 'The Old Horse', which lasted for months. The tightness of the family circle and the relative absence of outside influences only made the social and emotional singularity of the family greater.

To Alfred's grandfather, the elder George Tennyson, everything that was unsatisfactory at Somersby could be traced back to the imprudence of his son's marriage: the chafing of husband and wife, their inadequate income, the extraordinary behaviour of their children, most of all the general lack of respect for the inhabitants of Tealby Lodge. As a bad example, it could at least prove useful for Charles when he looked for a wife.

Two years after his brother's marriage Charles found a suitable young heiress, Frances Hutton of Morton, near Gainsborough, the pretty only daughter of a rich, widowed mother. The prudence in courtship that came naturally to Charles was insufficient for Fanny Hutton, who expected passion in her suitor to match his appearance. She kept urging him on while he was trying to keep the affair from being too headlong, without seeming lukewarm himself. For a month or two in the spring of 1807 he wrote a series of letters that would have delighted Jane Austen and sound as if they had come from the unimpassioned pen of Mr Collins. But Fanny Hutton was as resolute as her milk-and-water lover was indecisive, and she responded to his tentative letters with deep hurt at his wavering, with underlined sentiments and a flinty, mis-spelt obduracy about not letting him go free. By the end of July he had dwindled into an engaged man.

During their engagement Charles wrote frequently to Fanny; his letters were written over and over before being sent, the various drafts crossed out, underlined, and overwritten in a desperate attempt to give them spontaneity. All that he usually managed to achieve in his carefully numbered paragraphs was a prudential, calculated ardour. It is not surprising that Fanny seems not to have kept his letters, although he meticulously filed hers with the various rejected drafts of his own. Their wedding took place in January 1808, and he and Fanny settled down in Caenby Hall, some ten miles west of Tealby, while Charles began the practice of law in Lincolnshire. There they hoped to found the dynasty on which his father had been counting for so long.

Fanny's stubbornness over the engagement might have warned Charles that she would be far less mild than either his mother or his sister-in-law. Perhaps because she knew that her fortune would provide a large part of Charles's income, she was quite aware of what was due to her, and she would not take her father-in-law's arrogance without protest. Her tongue could be as wounding as his, and she gave it free rein. When Charles failed to stand up for her against his father, she would turn her scorn on him. Within a short time after their marriage Charles was suffering from mysterious attacks that kept him debilitated. By 1811 the marriage was already in serious difficulties, and a few years later they began the first in a long series of separations. Charles did not like his mother-in-law any more than Fanny liked old George Tennyson; he liked living in London, she hated it; he seems to have been a physically passionate man in spite of his lukewarm courtship, and Fanny had ailments that made their sexual life difficult. Notwithstanding, she bore him seven children over the years, and the succession to his father's fortunes seemed assured.

The best side of the family temperament is shown in the way that George remained on such good terms with his brother in spite of having been displaced by him. The two men kept up a constant good-natured correspondence, in which George's letters to Charles have the playfulness of a young man: they are lively, humorous, full of Latin and occasionally of coarseness. His letters to the elder George at the same time are leaden, respectful, and timorous, showing how easily the father made the son put his worst foot forward.

By this time the elder George's plans to turn the house at Tealby into a family seat were beginning to crystallize, and about 1811 it was first referred to regularly as Bayons Manor. Unfortunately, Mr Tennyson's temper was becoming thoroughly unpredictable. His wife said that he was 'but too susceptible of Melancholy from every passing cloud'.[8] He was beginning to miss having his sons within easy bullying distance, and as he sat grumpily on his Tealby hillside, fulminating about his family, he became known to his Somersby grandsons as 'The Old Man of the Wolds', a name by which they referred to him until the end of his life.

The younger George Tennyson's emotional difficulties were now accompanied by overt physical symptoms. In 1813 he spent three weeks in London with an eye specialist in the belief that he was going blind. He was told that his eyes were not functionally impaired, but the possibility of blindness continued to prey on his mind. It was the same fear that Alfred Tennyson was to have recurrently all his life, no matter how often he was assured that his sight had not deteriorated. Frequently Alfred complained of spots before his eyes, and at best he was miserably short-sighted. The first reference to his eye troubles comes from his undergraduate days, but before that he was wearing a monocle, so that his sight must have been poor for a long time. It is suggestive that his first extant letter, written when he was twelve, is a long account to his aunt of the 'pathos and sublimity' of 'Sampson Agonistes', with special appreciation of the 'particularly beautiful' complaint by Samson of his blindness. Before he went to Cambridge he had already read so widely about blindness in medical books that he was taken by one doctor for a medical student.

What was as frightening as the prospect of blindness was his continual awareness of how much he had inherited of his father's physical and mental qualities. Of all the sons he most resembled his father, not only in his bad eyesight but in stature, features, walk, and voice, and he was the only one of the sons with a huge head like the Rector's. Like his father, he was subject to recurrent depression, which we are told was usually brought on by the attacks of 'black blood' in his father. When the Rector's moods were at their worst, Alfred would run through the night to the churchyard and throw himself prostrate among the graves, wishing that he were dead. It was a peculiar identification for a young boy; mingled with his sympathy was the dread that one day he would be like his father. At the end of his life Tennyson used to recall how, as a small boy, he believed so deeply in the malignity of fate that when he desperately wanted something to happen, he would loudly assert, 'I know it won't! I know it won't!' to ensure that it would occur.[9]

In some ways the Rector's fortunes were improving. He paid for the degree of Doctor of Civil Law in 1813 and thereafter had the satisfaction of being addressed as 'Doctor Tennyson'. The following year the Old Man of the Wolds decided to give each of his sons an allowance of £250 annually, which greatly helped with the Rectory expenses, as until that time the Tennysons had been living on approximately £450 from the Doctor's combined benefices.

In 1815 the Doctor's financial position was still further improved. His mother's brother, Sam Turner, Vicar of Grasby, heard in the spring that the living of Grimsby was to be vacant, and he wrote to the elder Tennyson to urge him to intercede with his friend Mr Heneage to get it for Dr Tennyson. The manœuvre was successful, and the Grimsby benefice brought in another £545. From this Dr Tennyson had to pay a curate, but since in 1811 he was paying less than £35 for a curate at Benniworth, he still had a good bit in hand. For most clergymen of the time an income of more than £1,000 would have been riches indeed, but it seemed totally inadequate to the Doctor, who regarded himself as the legitimate heir to a wealthy man and consequently adjusted his needs to a good bit more than his expectations. By 1816 he had worried his father into a larger allowance, probably £500 p.a. It was more than Charles was receiving, but Charles claimed that he did not mind, since the money he had through his marriage was due entirely to his father's covenants and financial backing, whereas George's income would stop at his death.

Comparative freedom from financial worry did not improve Dr Tennyson's frame of mind, nor did it lessen his eccentricity. In the spring of 1815 he spent a full day at Tealby, during which he refused to mention his brother or his sisters, and he would not talk to his parents 'on any subject except the most trivial'.[10] What was the matter with him was obvious to his parents, but they refused to mention it until the following year when the Rector, who was ill, came with his wife to spend some days at Tealby.

In 1816 his mother wrote to Charles to tell him that his brother George was having fits about once a week. Charles himself had been suffering from a similar complaint, and she had been afraid of bringing on a recurrence if she were to tell him of George's troubles:

Poor George left us on Friday much better in his spirits and appetite—but his complaint which does not exactly put on the appearance yours did—still returns upon him about once a week—on Thursday Eveng. he sat with his Head on his Hand as though he was musing—when his Wife observed 'he is not well' we spoke—he did not answer—we repeated, he made no Effort to speak & was insensible—when he open'd his Eyes they roll'd without meaning and then he spoke incoherently for a minute, this wandering of the intellect is alarming.

The Doctor's distressed mother sought advice and hopefully reported that the medical man believed it might be 'Catalepsy rather than Epilepsy.' Part of the trouble seemed to be that when he recovered from a fit, Dr Tennyson was careless about taking the prescribed pills, 'for he knows not how much he has been affected—or that any thing has been the matter'. He had been suffering the recurrent attacks for some time, his mother told Charles, and 'when you saw him here he had had one of these fits in the night at this place but said nothing about it & it seems the only one he ever remembers'.

The first day of Dr Tennyson's stay at Tealby his mother had handed him a letter from his sister Mrs Russell, 'when he directly fainted and it ended as the one I have described—but whether to attribute it to bodily weakness or too acute a sensibility I know not'. Until then Mrs Tennyson had told neither Charles nor his sister Elizabeth, 'but I think you should no longer be ignorant of what every one seems to know.' She concluded with the hope that the news would not bring on a fit in Charles himself.[11]

Mrs Tennyson's account of her son's seizure is a perfect description of the 'petit mal' or mild attack of epilepsy. Her worry that others knew of the attacks and her clinging to the hope that they might indicate catalepsy reflect the usual belief that epilepsy was shameful. Medical opinion of the time was divided about a disease with so many manifestations, but on a few facts it was in general agreement. It was usually thought that the disease, or at least a proclivity to it, was hereditary. The original cause of its incidence was obscure, but many doctors believed that it was sexual in origin. Incontinence in males and continence in females were both thought to cause predispositions to the disease, and 'intoxication in one or other parent at the period of conception' was another possible cause.

Heredity, or 'ancestral epilepsy', was the commonest predisposing cause, but the immediate, or 'exciting', cause might vary from too much smoking or drinking to a too-tight prepuce in males. The commonest exciting cause in both sexes, and that which made the patient almost incurable, was thought to be masturbation. The reasoning behind this was simple: nearly all patients in hospitals admitted upon close questioning that they had been guilty at one time or another of 'self abuse', which seemed adequate proof that it was the cause of the malady. Sexual feelings were thought to be strong in epileptics, making them prone to masturbation, which in turn brought on fits. To the horrors of the disease itself was thus added the awareness that its occurrence gave open witness of an addiction to a supposedly guilty practice. Alfred Tennyson's friend Edward Lear was nearly driven mad in the attempt to conceal the debilitating attacks that sometimes occurred as often as twenty times a month, believing that they were caused by the shameful habit he had tried since boyhood to break.

Cure of epilepsy was rare, but there were many forms of attempted alleviation. Hard walking and exercise were thought to ward off attacks. Water taken internally or used externally, as in baths, showers, spinal douches, and swimming, was highly recommended. Both, of course, were traditional Victorian recommendations to adolescents to rid their minds of sexual thoughts. Sedatives derived from opium, such as laudanum and morphia, were prescribed, but their use was chiefly to damp down sexual arousal and hence the attacks. Not until the 1850s was it observed that the drugs acted directly on the disease, rather than merely inhibiting sexual feelings.

When the treatment was uncertain and the cure improbable, the patient usually had little to look forward to but mental deterioration, possible exclusion from the society of others, and the strong probability that his disease might turn him to violence. Parenthood, with the probability of passing one's illness on to children, was a terrible gamble. It is not surprising that the elder Tennysons were anxious to conceal the illness of George and Charles.

Nor can its incidence in Somersby Rectory have made life there any easier. The Doctor and his wife kept the knowledge of it from the children as long as they could (that is presumably why they had gone to Tealby when it was at its worst), but such things cannot be concealed from others, even children, living in the same house.

About this time came the onset of a curious mental phenomenon in Alfred, a trance obviously linked in some way with the times when he threw himself down in the churchyard wishing for death. It was, he wrote, 'a kind of "waking trance" (this for lack of a better word) I have frequently had quite up from boyhood when I have been all alone. This has often come upon me through repeating my own name to myself silently, till all at once as it were out of the intensity of the consciousness of individuality the individuality itself seemed to dissolve & fade away into boundless being—& this not a confused state but the clearest of the clearest, the surest of the surest, utterly beyond words—where Death was an almost laughable impossibility—the loss of personality (if so it were) seeming no extinction but the only true life.'[12] When he wrote this at the age of sixty-five, he thought of it as some kind of beneficent mystic vision, but as a boy it was obviously in part a way of escaping from the reality that lay around him, a more dangerous form of the retreat that he could make creatively in writing poetry, for it represented the near edge of that denial of reality that is insanity. Alfred Tennyson never did lose his sanity, but he was perilously close to it at times, and we can see the direction his mind would have taken had he done so. For Tennyson as a boy it must have seemed horribly like the fits that his father was suffering from.

By the time of Dr Tennyson's attacks at Tealby both Frederick and Charles had been sent away to their uncle's old school at Louth. In December 1816 Alfred joined them there. It may be that his parents thought it would be better for him to be out of the house because of his father's illness. The version of his going to school told by his son is that he was asked whether he would prefer going to sea or to school, and that he chose school in the belief that it was some kind of paradise. This can hardly be literally true, since Charles had been in the school more than a year and Frederick for more than two years, so that he would have known something about it. All the same, he probably had little idea of what lay ahead, and it was certainly not paradise.

Before going to Louth at the age of seven, Alfred had attended classes with Mr Cadney in the village school in Holywell Wood, he had studied music with a master named Smalley from Horncastle, and he had begun the classics with his father. On the flyleaf of the first volume of C. G. Heyne's edition of the *Iliad* Tennyson wrote as a grown man: 'My father who taught us Greek made us—me & my brother Charles—write the substance of Heyne's notes in the margin to show that we had read them, & we followed the same command of his, writing in our Horaces, Virgils & Juvenals &c &c the criticisms of their several commentators.'[13] Dr Tennyson did not consider him ready to go to Louth until he was able to repeat from memory on four successive mornings the Odes of Horace.

Louth Grammar School was an Elizabethan foundation, the best of the local schools, to which most of the county families of Lincolnshire sent their sons. The Reverend J. Waite, who was a relative of Alfred's mother, was headmaster, and from all accounts he was sadistic, even for those unreformed days, in his teaching methods. Tennyson said a half-century after leaving the school that Waite 'thrashed a boy more unmercifully for a false quantity than a modern headmaster to-day would thrash a boy for the worst offence of which schoolboys could be guilty'. One boy was in bed for six weeks from the beating he received for being dilatory with his lessons. The other masters, taking their lead from Waite, were even more brutal in their sarcasm. Alfred, who was a shy and silent boy, was so frightened in his catechism class that he could not remember the words of the Lord's Prayer. 'The masters jeered at me remorselessly,' he said, 'and I have never forgotten their injustice. A little kindness would have saved me.'[14]

On another occasion Alfred 'addressed the boys at Louth school in the person of his Uncle Charles Tennyson', who was then MP for Grimsby. One of the masters heard the impersonation and said, 'You member for [Grimsby]! why you are not fit for the Parish beadle.'[15] Whatever the quality of his imitation, it at least showed how little Alfred thought of his uncle.

The other boys were cruel, and once when Alfred was sitting on the school steps weeping and ill, a larger boy hit him in the wind with the words 'I'll teach you to cry'. It was a shock to find that the boy grew up to be 'the kindest of men', while the only one who had been kind to him at Louth was later hanged for horse-stealing.[16] The result of the bullying was that the Tennysons spent little time with the other boys in games but would either take long walks or sit reading instead of joining the play.

Alfred was a day scholar, and he stayed with his grandmother, Mrs Fytche, and her daughter Mary Anne in their house in Westgate Terrace, near the church. He is said to have sat crying on the edge of his bed each morning, unhappy at having to get up at 6 a.m., and then he would loiter until he had to run to get to the hated school on time. His grandmother was mean (she once refused to light a fire for a drenched cousin of Alfred's because it was an hour before she usually did so), but Alfred's aunt was generous, and he remained fond of her when he was grown.

In 1818 Frederick was withdrawn from Louth to be sent to Eton, leaving Alfred and Charles even more lonely than they had been before. Alfred left at the end of 1820, and for some reason Charles stayed on another year. Alfred so hated the school that in later years when he was in Louth he refused to go down the lane where it stood. He used to say that he had learned absolutely nothing there, but in more charitable mood he said, 'the only good I ever got from it was the memory of the words, "sonus desilientis aquae," and of an old wall covered with wild weeds opposite the school windows'. His memories indicate his sharpened sensory perception at Louth, and since much of his best poetry was concerned with the sound of water and the look of plants, his schooldays may have been less wasted than he thought.*

* It has been pointed out that the words he had in mind were Ovid's *ex alto desilientis aquae* (water leaping down from on high), 'and it is evidence of the auditory quality of his imagination that in his memory he imported the sound (*sonus*) of the water into the phrase' (Culler, p. 6).

✻

CHAPTER III

DR TENNYSON'S BREAKDOWN,
1820–1827

MUCH had happened to the Tennyson family in the four years that Alfred was at Louth. In 1817 Elizabeth Russell's father-in-law died, leaving a huge fortune and several houses, including Brancepeth Castle, which the Russells set about making even more magnificent, reportedly spending more than £80,000 annually in the process for some five years. Their extravagance was to provide the pattern for Charles Tennyson when he began in 1835 to enlarge Bayons Manor. In the meantime all Charles's enthusiasm and considerable artistic flair was put at the disposal of the Russells, and under his aegis the castle became progressively more medieval, with only a few setbacks, such as the difficulty with the bastion, which toppled into the brook.

Possession of such a house inevitably gave Russell hope that he might receive a peerage, but his wife characteristically kept her sense of humour on the subject. 'Our towers look most nobly, but the whole structure is too fine for a commoner,' she wrote to Charles. 'Is Ermine dear, do you think?'[1]

Charles was enraptured with the results: 'The Castle surpasses all my ideas of what it was to be.'[2] Russell's lordly spending on the Castle and his hopes for a title remained an inspiration for Charles, but he unfortunately noticed neither the strain that the building put on the vast Russell resources nor the disappointment that his brother-in-law felt when he was not ennobled.

At Somersby the Brancepeth extravagance naturally embittered Dr Tennyson, who felt he was being left farther and farther behind by his family each year. We no longer know Alfred's reaction at the time, but as an adult the patterns he imposed upon his own life were in part subtle shadows thrown from the past by Brancepeth and Bayons.

To want to take part in the government of the country was a logical extension of the ambitions of the Tennysons, and in the general election of 1818 Russell, old Mr Tennyson, and Charles Tennyson stood for Parliament and in a clean sweep for the family were all returned. While Charles was conducting his campaign, he became ill with serious vomiting, and in one hour he was 'blooded, blistered, clystered, & (attempted to be) purged beside the continued & violent vomiting'. The report of his illness terrified his father, who wrote to inquire 'whether you had any particular fit of the nature of your old ones, I will burn your Letter. . . . If you want money say so, & I will supply you with pleasure, I would at least divide my last penny with you.' Reassuringly, Charles answered: 'I had no fit, except a mere fainting when I was bled.'[3] In spite of his assurances, it showed how near the surface of the family fears was the recurrence of epilepsy.

Fanny Tennyson's dislike of her father-in-law and his children finally prompted her to tell Charles that she and his 'very, very strange' family ought 'in order to keep friends to have as little communication as possible. I have not a word to say against them except that they are not people that at all suit me.'[4] What she could not know was that her deliberate estrangement from her husband and his family provided the opportunity for Charles to have an affair with a friend of Elizabeth Russell, Mary Thornhill, daughter of the squire of Stanton near Bakewell. 'Polly' Thornhill took the initiative in April 1816 in meeting Charles, whose picture she had seen at Mrs Russell's house. For twenty-two years thereafter she wrote constantly to him, addressing him as 'Dearest Beauty' while signing herself 'Your tame and affectionate Beast'. One of the most curious aspects of the affair is that Charles kept her love letters stored indiscriminately with bills, letters from his family, and reports of Parliamentary business, apparently without fear that they would be seen by his family.

There is no indication of whether Alfred Tennyson ever knew about the affair, but he certainly met Miss Thornhill with Elizabeth Russell, with whom she often stayed. If he knew of her connection with Charles, it would have contributed to his dislike of his uncle, for he was unusually censorious of adultery.

Relations between Tealby and Somersby had been bad for a long time, but by 1820 they had reached a place from which there was no real return; the younger George might in the future try to swallow his pride and treat his father with filial respect, and the Old Man of the Wolds might pretend that nothing had happened, but both had now said what they thought, and there was no unsaying it. The letter the Rector wrote on 14 August 1820 has been published before, but it is so remarkable that it deserves to be given in full. 'My dearest Father,' wrote Dr Tennyson,

I find to my great disquietude, that you have thought proper to attribute to my suggestion or instigation certain expressions which may or may not have been used by Miss Fytche reflecting upon your conduct as a parent. I utterly disdain to exculpate myself from this charge. I did intend to have visited Tealby, but an accusation so unjust, so frequently reiterated and so totally unsubstantiated has so far oppress'd my spirits and irritated my feelings that it is impossible that I can do so with any pleasure. With the sentiments you yet entertain and have entertained for more than twenty years, I cannot wonder you told Mr. Bourne you had not a spark of affection for me. The rude and unprecedented manner in which you first address'd me at Hainton, after a long absence, on your return from York (I quote your own words, *"Now you great awkward booby are you here"*) holding me up to utter derision before Mr. Heneage, his sons, and Sir Robt. Ainslie, & your language & conduct in innumerable other instances, many of which have made a deep impression upon my mind, sufficiently prove the truth of your own assertion. You have long injured me by your suspicions. I cannot avoid them for the fault is not mine. God judge between you & me. You make and have always made a false estimate of me in every respect. You look and have always looked upon me with a jaundiced eye & *deeply and experimentally* feeling this, I am sure that my visiting you would not contribute to your satisfaction and at the same time would materially injure my own health and comfort. Conscious also that I am thrown into a situation unworthy my abilities & unbecoming either your fortune or my just pretensions, & resisted in my every wish to promote my own interests or that of my family by removing to a more eligible situation, unaccountably kept in the dark with respect to their future prospects, with broken health and spirits, I find myself little disposed to encounter those unprovoked and sarcastic remarks, which tho' they may be outwardly borne, are inwardly resented, and prey upon the mind—the injustice, the inhumanity & the impropriety of which everyone can see but yourself, and which in your last visit were levelled against the father of a large family in the very presence of his children, and that father between forty and fifty years of age. I should not have proceeded this far had you not by your unjust aspersions set fire to the mass which was already disposed to ignite. You may forget or pass off as a jest what penetrates and rankles in my heart; you may break what is already bent, but there is a tribunal before which you and I may speedily appear, more speedily perhaps than either of us desire or expect—there it will be seen whether you through life have treated me with that consideration and kindness which a son has a right to expect from a father, and whether (as you have been accustomed to represent me to myself & others) I have been deficient in filial affection & obedience.

I am, My dear Father
Your affectionate Son
G. C. Tennyson[5]

The sincerity and anguish of the letter are so obvious that it would seem impossible that Dr Tennyson was exaggerating, or that his father could be anything but a monster. The general tenor of the letter must be a fairly accurate statement of what had passed between father and son, and yet the tone may be in part a phantasm of the Rector's already clouded brain. Six weeks later Dr Tennyson sent his father a second letter, but in it there is absolutely no mention of the subject of the howl of pain in the earlier letter; it is as if he had totally forgotten a bad dream. Old George did not answer either letter until 1 October. His only reference to them was a line at the end of some discussion of other matters: 'We return our love to Eliza, you & yrs. & I remain notwithstanding your unkind, & I can with truth say unjustifiable letter to me of the 14th. Augt last, as I have ever been, Yr. affte far. GT.'[6] He was an unjust man, but his elder son must have provoked him severely.

Although Dr Tennyson felt badly depressed financially, conditions at the Rectory were far from miserable. In 1820 they had begun to keep a horse and carriage, there was a coachman, a governess for the girls, a nursemaid, a cook, the Rector's valet Jonathan, housemaids, and surely several gardeners. In 1822 he hired a housekeeper to supervise the other servants. He complained bitterly in 1824 that there were twenty-three persons sleeping in the house; since there were only thirteen in the family when all were at home there must have been at least ten servants living there and probably others elsewhere. It was a large establishment for a country clergyman, and the Old Man of the Wolds was not completely irrational in thinking that his son must be wasting the money he gave him.

In his first miserable year at home after Louth, Alfred found himself at eleven acting as virtual head of the family. Both elder brothers were away, his mother was loving but ineffectual, and his father was constantly aggravating his epilepsy by drink until his mind seemed to be cracking. It was a heavy responsibility for Alfred, but it was from that time that his brothers and sisters began to turn to him for help and comfort. As an old woman his sister Cecilia told how Alfred would take one child on his knee, put another between his legs in front of the fire, and prop two others against him on either side as he told them stories. When he read aloud, his dramatic ability and the beauty of his deep voice made the family think he would become an actor. After he was Poet Laureate, his brothers and sisters became more detached from him, as if half afraid of his fame, but until that time they naturally looked to him as their chief defence.

In bringing Alfred home, the Rector could at one swoop save

money, improve his son's education, and give himself a regular task, to avoid the introspective brooding that made him drink too much. As preparation for teaching he brushed up his classical versification and his Greek language. His own fiasco with mathematics at Cambridge made him realize that he could not teach that subject to Alfred, so he called in as tutor a Bag Enderby boy, only two years older than his pupil. It was an unsuccessful plan, for Alfred grew up as uninterested in mathematics and as ignorant of it as his father. Had he attempted to sit for a degree at Cambridge, that section of the tripos would surely have been his downfall.

Even at this early age Tennyson was beginning to feel the ambivalent attitude he had about science all his life, fascinated by it but fearful of its results. Many years later he told a young friend: 'When I was a lad, a mere lad, you know, I was given a book called "Conversations on Physical Science," by a good author. The book was simple enough, but somehow, I don't know why, I felt differently after reading it. The oxygen and carbon and all the rest of it unsettled me a little, and made me feel less able to believe, made my faith heavier, duller; I don't know why. I was a mere lad, you know.'[7]

Apparently he had no more music lessons after returning from Louth, although he continued to sing for some years. The time he had devoted to music was now given to drawing, at which he became moderately adept, as did several of his brothers and sisters, particularly Arthur. Many of the manuscripts of his later poems are scrawled over with sketches, occasionally of buildings, more often of profiles or of his own fingers or toes. These little anatomical drawings seem a mirror of his constant self-preoccupation, the detailed introspection that characterized his poetry of the 1830s and 1840s.

When he returned to Somersby he was composing poetry of a more external kind, an epic of some six thousand lines in emulation of Scott, 'full of battles, dealing too with sea and mountain scenery', and said afterwards that he had never felt himself more truly inspired, as he rushed about the fields with a stick for a sword, fancying himself a conqueror advancing upon an enemy's country. At this time he first came across Malory, and almost immediately the conception of King Arthur that he was to use in the *Idylls of the King* came to him.

Dr Tennyson was a demanding tutor, but his recurrent illness allowed his pupil time to compose poetry, and Alfred often startled the housemaids by muttering to himself as if in prayer or by halloaing his poems aloud as he walked up and down the drive.

The most important work of this time was written about 1823, *The Devil and the Lady*, three acts of a comedy in blank verse owing its inception to Alfred's knowledge of Elizabethan and Jacobean drama. In the play the Devil disguises himself as Amoret, the young wife of an elderly magus, who is left behind in the Devil's care when her husband goes on a journey. As Amoret he receives a series of suitors seeking to seduce what they think is an unprotected wife. Much of the comedy arises from the jargon used by the lawyer, apothecary, sailor, astronomer, soldier, and monk in their attempts to seduce the supposed Amoret. The play is full of a clear kind of fun and an uncomplicated acceptance of sex that were sadly not to be repeated in Tennyson's later works.

Bleeding gobbets of erudition are stuck into the text, but that is only the natural swank of a fourteen-year-old displaying what he knows. More interesting is the constant, half-familiar series of echoes from *Hamlet, Lear, The Tempest*, and *Paradise Lost*, showing Tennyson in the process of making Shakespeare and Milton part of his own language, submerging their metaphors in his personal diction. It is a wonderful example of the educative process of a poet, unselfconsciously forging an original style from that of others.

The confidence of the language, the freedom of versification, and the success of the comic sections are startling in so young a writer, but the interest of the play is less intrinsic than in the hints it gives of a mature Tennyson. They are, however, hints of future language rather than of adult attitudes, for the drama is most uncharacteristic of Tennyson in its relative objectivity and lack of personal involvement.

While Alfred was writing, the family was disintegrating even further. At Eton Fred found that the way was not easy for a country boy. He had to ask his father to have new clothes made for him in London because the other boys ridiculed the abominable Lincolnshire cut of his old ones, and having his 'coate Dyed Black' at a cost of four shillings did not serve. His accent was so provincial that even his grandmother feared it might infect his cousins. Instead of entering into the life of the school he spent much of his time playing a flute and being insolent to his masters. On his way between Eton and Somersby he stayed in his uncle Charles's London house in Park Street, but he never knew when to leave. He was a clever boy, and when he went up to Cambridge he was expected to achieve scholarly distinction, but his awkwardness and laziness were by then ingrained. At Eton he had achieved much less than his father hoped for.

By 1822 the physical state of Alfred's elders was as worrying as their mental health. At the beginning of the year his grandfather was so ill that he was not expected to live long. By April the effects of Dr Tennyson's drinking were so serious that he had to go for a cure to Cheltenham, where his brother Charles had been taking the waters. Dr Tennyson reported that the physician 'gives me great hopes that the waters will reestablish my health & says that a schirrus has not as yet formed upon my liver, but that he could not have answered for the consequences if I had not immediately come here. We are advised to stay here a month or five weeks. We found the Russells here. My sister has been complaining of a severe attack of the Rheumatism.' As Frederick enviously told his grandfather, Alfred and Charles were on holiday while their father was absent; 'when he is at home they are almost always at their lessons, and very seldom have any holidays'.[8]

The waters at Cheltenham seemed to help George Tennyson's liver, and his family thereafter had a high regard for their therapeutic qualities. Alfred spent a good deal of time there for his health in the 1830s and 1840s, and his mother made her home there for about ten years. When the family first began descending on it in 1822 for its waters and its mild, provincial social life, Cheltenham had a reputation for being vulgar and full of wife- and husband-hunters, and visitors so bored that their 'whole life is spent in devising one day how they shall spend the next day with as much enjoyment and at as little expense as possible'.[9] There were many foreigners about and Matthew Russell complained that in church the mahogany faces surrounding him made him fancy himself in India.

Russell died in Cheltenham in April 1822, and in all his selfless help to his sister Dr Tennyson forgot his own troubles. But by November of the same year he was back in Cheltenham, this time apparently for treatment of his epilepsy; although it was aggravated by alcohol, his fright of the previous spring had not served to cut down his drinking. 'I trust a happy change of mind may be productive of good effect on his dreadful disease,' his mother wrote. 'O may it please the great dispenser of events to restore this dear afflicted Child to his powers & strength & health—as well also as a calm & quiet mind.'[10]

Although old Mr Tennyson was worried about his son's health, he was almost equally worried about how much the treatment was costing. He agreed to pay £60 p.a. for any of the Rector's sons who attended Louth or a similar school, but he drew the line at Eton, even though Dr Tennyson insisted it cost no more than Louth. Subsequently he raised the Rector's allowance to £700 a year and agreed to pay his heavy outstanding debts and support him in Cheltenham during treatment. Then, to his fury, he found that Dr Tennyson had ordered a new carriage and borrowed its cost from Charles. Mr Tennyson repaid Charles, but it went against the grain: 'He has not, nor has his Wife written even a line of thanks!! . . . I can do nothing even shoud. I beggar myself to satisfy the rapacity of George, however I am sorry to find from you that he is so ill, & shall do my duty & more than my duty to him & his, notwithstg. his bad conduct towards me & yr. mother.'[11]

By now Mr Tennyson's unhappiness was increased intolerably by the news that epilepsy had hit the family once more, this time in the person of his favourite grandson, George Hildeyard Tennyson, Charles's eldest son. Even the boy's apparent recovery did not allay the old man's fears.

Once back at Somersby the Rector again began tuition, but the drudgery brought on bouts of nervousness, followed by drink to steady his nerves, followed inevitably by a recurrence of his fits. Alfred, whose wide but fragmented interests as an adult reflected the undirected quality of this part of his life, was fortunately so infatuated with reading that he continued his own haphazard education in the library even when the Rector absented himself. Only Frederick was absent from the bulging house, and probably Alfred took to books in part to escape the perpetual noise of such a large and exuberant family.

The few letters extant from this period show that Alfred kept his sympathy for his father alive in a way most unusual for a boy of his age put in such an intolerable environment. To escape the schoolroom together they went for occasional visits to Bayons Manor, and when their welcome there wore out, they would visit Alfred's aunt Mary Bourne at Dalby. It was not much fun to stay there, for a curtain of depressing religiosity hung over the house; the Bournes attended a Dissenting chapel and expected their 'Servants to do the same, & also to be in attendance every morning & evening at Family prayers'.[12]

Alfred managed to find some relief in tight-lipped amusement at the rigidity of his aunt's beliefs. Once when she had taken him with her to chapel, she began to weep while listening to a sermon on Hell. He asked her with concern whether it was for pity of the poor creatures in torment, but she said, no, it was because she alone, miserable woman, had been picked out by Providence for salvation. Perhaps it was his amusement that caused her to begin looking hard at the state of

Alfred's soul. On another occasion she saw him across the street and called, 'This reminds me of "A great gulf shall divide the cursed & blessed."' It was perhaps harder to laugh when she said directly to him, 'Alfred, Alfred, whenever I look at you I think of the words, Depart from me, ye cursed, into everlasting fire.' 'Which didn't make a boy of fourteen feel very comfortable,' Tennyson added when telling the story as an adult.[13] Mrs Bourne's excesses may have contributed to his extreme dislike of the doctrine of eternal damnation the rest of his life.

The eccentricity of the Rector was increasing rapidly. Early in 1824, after brooding over the matter for two years, he suddenly decided that his sister Elizabeth had been insufficiently grateful for his help at the time of her husband's death. In a long and vituperative letter, in which he referred to her as 'Mrs. Russell', he complained that she was too taken up with worldly matters even to write to him. 'But money I am well persuaded deadens the feelings. . . .' She had offered to help with the cost of his children's education: 'This of course I refused.' Recently she had asked if she might come to Somersby, but he told her there was no space. 'We are three & twenty in family and sleep five or six in a room. Truly we have great accommodation for Mrs. Russell & her suite. We have not the house at Brighton nor the Castle at Brancepeth.'[14] But within another month his anger at Mrs Russell had dissipated and he had almost forgotten what had so exercised him. It was a pattern of vehement anger and subsequent forgetfulness that imposed itself upon his imaginary hurts and humiliations for the rest of his troubled life.

Much of his confusion came from the increasing frequency of his epileptic attacks. He chafed constantly at having to do the teaching that he had taken on of his own volition and which could easily have been avoided if he were to take money from his sister or father for sending his boys to school. Pride in his children was mixed with a distinct pleasure in his own martyrdom. He refused an invitation from Charles to go with him to Paris, although he acknowledged that 'a removal from the harassing business of instruction would perhaps restore me. But I feel my powers of mind sensibly declining & the attacks to which I am subject must necessarily injure the intellect. I have had two in the last five days. I have known some satisfaction in thinking that my boys will turn out to be clever men. Phoenix-like, I trust (tho' I don't think myself a Phoenix) they will spring from my ashes in consequence of the exertions I have bestowed upon them.'[15]

The next few years were to be a repetitive history of decline in the Doctor's health. In the spring of 1825 his mother reported that George 'thinks he has Water in the Chest, & says he feels it roll about'. Charles wrote to his father, enclosing a letter from the Rector's physician: 'It indeed presents an alarming acct of my poor Bror. I have little doubt that a removal to Cheltenham or any other place where his mind cd. disengage itself from the harassing occupation to which he is daily devoting himself & get it into new channels of thought & his body into more active exercise wd. be very beneficial to him.'[16]

Charles gave generously to the poor Doctor of his time and sympathy, but his generosity was curiously entwined with anxiety about what his brother's attacks implied about his own health. When the Rector's best friend, Mr Rawnsley, wrote to say that the last fit was epileptic, Charles told his father apprehensively, 'Perhaps Rawnsley may merely surmise that the fit was Epileptic.'[17] His own medical history was enough to make him worry that he might end up like his brother George.

The Rector steadfastly refused to go to another doctor, and when his father wrote to him, offering to pay his expenses if he went again to Cheltenham, Dr Tennyson did not even acknowledge his letter. At last old George dispatched one of his friends to engage a physician to send back the truth of matters in Somersby. Mr Vane reported that he had called in Dr Bousfield, but though the Rector had had two fits, the medical man had not witnessed them. The Rector's wife was afraid even to mention to her husband that Dr Bousfield had been engaged. Mr Vane could only say that 'Dr Tennyson had given up the Education of some of his children, which would be a great relief to him in his weak state'.[18]

Dr Tennyson's illness was an agonizing series of temporary recoveries and deep relapses. It is no longer possible to be sure of the exact cause of his deterioration, but it seems to have been primarily epileptic in origin, possibly complicated by heart troubles, and certainly aggravated by alcoholism. By the end of June 1825 he had pulled himself together and gone off to Cambridge with Charles and Alfred to enter Frederick at St. John's, and seemed to bear the journey well. Only three weeks later he was so ill that he was not expected to live, and there was talk of how to dispose of his benefices. After one of his worst attacks he sent for his father in the hope that 'everything would be forgotten that had been disagreeable'[19] between them, but as soon as he was once more strong enough, he resumed the interminable skirmishes with his father and brother.

Of all the children Alfred was probably the most affected by his father's decline. Not only was he fond of the Rector, but he, like his uncle, probably felt that everything happening to his father might be repeated in his own life. For the rest of his father's life Alfred vacillated between tenderness and distress so great that he had to get away from the suffering man. His letter to his uncle Charles on 2 August 1825, telling him that the Rector was having as many as three attacks a night, indicates how deeply he felt his father's state: 'Indeed no one but those who are continually with him can conceive what he suffers, as he is never entirely free from this alarming illness. He is reduced to such a degree of weakness from these repeated attacks, that the slightest shock is sufficient to bring them on again. Perhaps if he could summon resolution enough to get out more, he would be relieved, but the lassitude which the fits leave incapacitates him from undergoing any exertion.'[20]

Released from his father's teaching and the necessity of daily lessons, Alfred tried his best to keep relations with Bayons Manor on an even keel. He would proudly walk the twenty miles of wolds between Somersby and Tealby to take news of his father to his grandfather. Returning from one visit to Tealby, he was buffeted by the wind and rain, which he almost escaped 'by means of a thick plaid & a good umbrella'. He had to stay the night in Louth, for he was so late that he was afraid of being benighted if he set out over the hills for Somersby.[21] Like all his tall brothers and sisters, he loved walking, which was a lucky thing if they did not wish to be confined totally to Somersby.

In spite of all warnings, the Doctor was unable to give up drinking, and by the beginning of 1826 he had added another cause for alarm when he began systematically taking henbane and laudanum for the relief of the 'oppression of the Chest' that made him gasp for life. A few days later he began taking 40 drops of laudanum at night, 'besides other Soporifics', but he still could not sleep and paced the house till dawn.[22] Since laudanum was standard treatment for epilepsy, it is probable that Dr Bousfield had prescribed it for that disease. Although he continued to take the drug, there is no evidence that he became badly addicted. It was, however, probably his example to which his son Charles owed his use of the drug, which nearly ruined his life. Alfred Tennyson thought the use of laudanum was the worst kind of millstone a man could hang around his own neck.

At last the constant vigil broke down Alfred's health. Frederick wrote to their grandfather, asking for money to take Alfred to Skegness, where he wanted 'to try the effect of sea-bathing' to cure his illness. Frederick obviously intended to go along for a free ride, and he had to admit that Alfred needed the trip more than he did, since he was 'younger & of a more relaxed habit'. On the back of the letter their brother Charles added a note, asking if enough money could be sent to allow him to accompany the others, although he confessed that he was not unwell himself but wanted to go from mere love of the surf.[23] Unfortunately their grandfather's reply to this delightful piece of sponging has not survived.

Marooned on his Tealby hillside the Old Man of the Wolds saw his plans for a great dynasty tumbling about his ears: he had written off Mary and George years before, and events seemed to prove his wisdom in doing so. The widowed Elizabeth no longer seemed to worry about his opinion, and she in addition was guilty of the worst act of filial ingratitude: she was now totally independent of him financially, so that he had no weapon with which to threaten her. Only Charles remained, and his marriage was a ruin. Fanny refused offers of reconciliation from both her husband and her father-in-law. She and Charles divided up the house in Park Street, Westminster, so that they could be in London at the same time without having to live together, and Charles put the children in school in Paris to get them away from their mother. Their separation had long since become a matter of common gossip, and it looked as if the elder George might be the only one of the line ever to live in Bayons. When Fanny went off alone to Bletchingley, where she had kept a house for some years, he could stand it no longer and pleaded with Charles: 'for your comfort, the comfort of your Wife, & Children, & for the worlds opinion it is necessary you & yours shd. be more congregated &—particularly that you & Fanny shd. not live so much asunder . . .'[24]

One reason for the coolness between Fanny and Charles was something that old George presumably did not know. Fanny had lost at least one child, and she had difficulties at the birth of others. She seems to have been remarkably uninformed on sexual matters,* and finally her doctor had to write to Charles to say that her pelvis was too small

---

* After more than fifteen years of marriage she wrote to Charles to tell him that a doctor whom she had consulted while away from home had asked whether her usual physician 'ever suspected my disease of the uterus? of the meaning of this word I am ignorant and want you to tell me.'

for childbearing, and that further pregnancies would be dangerous. He advised continued separation, urging Charles to consider 'whether it is worth while for the sake of return to intercourse to encounter a process . . . attended by danger'.[25] The letter throws a different light on Charles's affair with Miss Thornhill, about which his father seems to have been hearing gossip.

It also explains in part the complacency which Charles increasingly showed about his life in London. He was given to boasting with what the Somersby brood thought of as exquisite fatuity on his acquaintance with the great. After attending a levee he wrote that 'His Majesty received me most graciously. He spoke to me by name, smiled & asked me how I did, which is unusual with him to persons going to Court in a common way unless he personally knows them.'[26] No doubt much of this was his own way of coping with his sadness over his family.

To cap all old George's troubles, in the summer of 1825 his wife died. She had been a shadowy figure in his life for years, but her death must have touched him. According to his daughter Elizabeth he reported the death somewhat gnomically: 'I saw her dying, I saw her dead, & *I am alive!*'[27] Whatever emotion, or perhaps lack of it, lay behind the stark words prompted him to erect a beautiful tablet to her memory, the first of the splendid group of monuments lining the walls of Tealby Church. It mentioned her four children and her bereaved husband, for whose own tablet a space was reserved. Ten years later, at his death, this was to split the family even further apart.

With justice Elizabeth Russell told her brother Charles that the entire family was painful when viewed in perspective, 'the branches as well as the stems'.[28]

Bereavement did not soften the Old Man of the Wolds. After his wife's death he asked Alfred to write an elegy on his grandmother and offered him ten shillings, saying, 'There, that is the first money you have ever earned by your poetry, and, take my word for it, it will be the last.'[29] The elegy, if it was ever written, has disappeared, but that is probably less to be regretted than the loss of Alfred's reply.

In April 1827 Jacksons, the booksellers at Louth, quietly published a small volume called *Poems by Two Brothers*, which was the first appearance in print of the future Poet Laureate. He had written more than half of the poems most of the rest were by his brother Charles, and, despite the title, three or four were by Frederick. There has never been a satisfactory explanation of why a provincial bookseller should publish such a book, which could not be expected to cover its costs. It has been suggested that either the Rector of Somersby or one of his relatives secretly paid for part of the publication, but it is unlikely that Dr Tennyson would have done so, since he distrusted the publishers. Jackson, he had warned his brother Charles as long before as 1812, was 'an infernal Rogue'.[30] His wife was so interested in the publication of the book that she would stand in the road outside the Rectory with her sons waiting for the post when proofs were expected, but she had no money of her own to contribute. Most of the other relatives could easily have afforded to subsidize the book, but the only one who had any reason to do so was Mrs Russell, who loved poetry, believed in Alfred and his genius, and was generous with allowances to him in later years. Of her generosity on this occasion, however, there is no proof.

Jacksons offered the two authors £20 in advance in books and cash, which was not bad for unknown young poets who refused to let even so much as their initials appear on the title-page. Alfred's surprising sharpness at bargaining over royalties when he was famous was foreshadowed by his remark that it was 'none too high a price'. At least it disproved his grandfather's glum prognostication that he would never make another shilling from poetry. Only two perfunctory notices of the book appeared, and the sales were practically non-existent, but it established the boys in their own eyes and those of their family as genuine, published poets. Years later Charles told of the glorious day of publication, when the two brothers hired a carriage in which they drove to Mablethorpe to shout their glory to the sea. 'I think that if anyone had met us,' he said, 'they would have thought us out of our minds, and in a way I think that day we were indeed beside ourselves with joy.'[31]

Most of Alfred's poems in the volume were written between the ages of fifteen and seventeen, so it was natural that they were immature. Their most noticeable aspect is that the majority derive directly from his reading, like exercises or improvisations in a variety of styles upon the themes of others. The sheer prodigality of his versification was never to dry up, but in middle age he sometimes found himself without matter. By the time he was famous there was no dearth of suggestions from others: Jowett, Woolner, and his own wife were only too anxious to offer him subjects. His acceptance of them indicates the disjunction in his mind between form and content, producing at worst a loose poetic drapery thrown over a subject with little apparent intrinsic importance for him; in whatever other aspects he was a child of the

Romantics, he was certainly not so in their conception of the organic unity of form and content. In *Poems of Two Brothers* the separation is already apparent. There is a distinct sense that the young Tennyson is turning out mechanically correct versified ideas imitating an approved model: in short, that he is following the dusty path of generations of English schoolboys learning classical languages by writing Latin or Greek verse. These are as competent as one could expect a boy's exercises to be. But they are finally not very good poetry.

Some years ago Professor Paden demonstrated that almost all these poems derive specifically from books in the library of Somersby Rectory.[32] Many of the great poetic masterpieces draw inspiration from literary rather than diurnal experience, but they have become part of the fibre of the poet, rather than mere excuse for language, as the reader is apt to feel in this first volume of Tennyson's. The adoption of other men's ideas as a starting-point in these poems results in a loss of passion and gives the sense of a retreat from reality, as if the poet could not yet afford to treat ideas and emotions of his own because they were too near the heart. Somersby Rectory provided a fifteen-year-old with plenty from which to retreat, but it was a practice ultimately dangerous for both poetry and personality.

As Tennyson's habit of composing discrete lines before thinking of a poem as a whole would suggest, there are fine fragments in these poems, often submerged in pedestrian passages. In six lines from 'Antony to Cleopatra', for instance, the description of Antony's sea-flight in battle has two superbly assured lines sandwiched between other couplets in which the construction seems designed only to piece out the metre:

> Soul of my soul! I saw thee flying;
> I followed thee, to save.
> The thunder of the brazen prows
> O'er Actium's ocean rung;
> Fame's garland faded from my brows,
> Her wreath away I flung.

In the central couplet the delayed verb completes the unity of action with a snap; in the two surrounding couplets it seems mere perverse construction. As the long years of his craft passed, Tennyson increasingly learned to refine out such eccentricities. He used to refer to this first volume as 'early rot', but he admitted with grudging pride when he reread it, 'Some of it is better than I thought it was!'

The wild pleasure Alfred and Charles felt on publication day in Mablethorpe antiphonally shouting their poems above the noise of the spring tide can hardly have survived much longer than it took them to drive home across the marsh in the late evening, for there the stern reality of Dr Tennyson awaited them. To add to his other troubles, he had the previous October contracted 'a violent attack of the Cholera Morbus' during a visit to Cambridge. Like most things that happened to the Doctor, the illness was larger than life. 'The Physician who attended me states that he never almost saw a more serious attack. The worst is that this complaint is now followed by a troublesome and painful dysentery. . . .'[33] The effects of the dysentery were no doubt enhanced by the doses of calomel he was taking with his laudanum. He was still greatly bothered by the chest spasms, which suggest that he had heart trouble as well.

Only a month or two before the publication of his sons' poems he had written to the Old Man of the Wolds for help in paying Frederick's Cambridge bills; tactlessly he used the same letter to reproach his father: 'I have been credibly informed that you make it your business to speak in the most disrespectful terms of me to every one & to one person you represented me as "the greatest lyar that ever spoke" and this you had said immediately prior to writing me a very affectionate invitation. How can you think so ill of me & yet write so kindly is more than I can comprehend.'

In white heat the elder George sat down and drafted a reply on the very sheet of paper on which the Rector had written; it is brief, angry, and unconciliatory. But, as if unwilling to trust himself, he did not send it. Two days later, when he had cooled down, he answered, saying that he would raise the Rector's allowance from £700 to £1,000 if he would not apply for more. 'The concluding paragraph of your letter forbids all comments, your experience & your knowledge of me as a Father & a friend ought to have furnished a ready contradiction to him who cd so slander me. . . .'[34] It was like a repetition of the exchange of letters in 1820; one can only wonder whether the Doctor in his brooding resentment was confusedly remembering what had happened seven years before, or whether the insult had actually been reported to him. Certainly, it does cast doubt on the validity of his accusations of his father on the earlier occasion. Like the first exchange, this one was enigmatically closed by the Rector, with a letter of thanks for the money so bland that he might never have written the furious letter of accusation.

In early June 1827 Alfred and his brother Charles went with their mother to London to visit relatives and have a respite from Somersby. It was probably the first time either of the boys had been out of Lincolnshire, except for a trip to Cambridge, but Alfred could find little in the capital to capture his imagination. His aunt Russell wrote to old George: 'Alfred & Charles have been to see me from Market Street, where Eliza is visiting a relation. Alfred came a second time without his Brother & slept during the time he staid upon the Drawing room sopha. I wish he had something in Life to interest him as well as his beautiful poetry. Westminster Abbey was the only thing which particularly charmed him, it suited the *pensive* habit of his soul.'[35]

A pleasant consequence of the trip was that Mrs Russell offered to help with Alfred's expenses if he went to Cambridge with Charles that autumn. He would need tuition in mathematics, in all probability, and she was willing to pay for that. Mrs Russell realized what was by now very clear to Alfred: that he could not go on for long in the Rectory with his father.

The Fytches, Alfred's mother's family, had never liked old George Tennyson, but their first thought when the Rector behaved badly was to expect his father to handle the matter. But he was by now nearly eighty, and any hope that he could really manage his son was unreasonable. All during the summer of 1827 Dr Tennyson had been drinking heavily and had begun threatening physical violence to his family; it was probably to escape this that Mrs Tennyson had taken the boys to London in June. In October a friend of the Fytche family, William Chaplin, at last wrote to Charles Tennyson, trying to convince him that the only way left to deal with the Rector was to have him certified insane and committed to confinement. Otherwise, said Chaplin, he might murder one of the family, 'which wd. consign him to perpetual confinement for his life. . . . His excessive habits of drinking bring on such repeated fits, that he is as deranged as madness can be described. . . . The children are alarmed at him & the wife is in the greatest fright both in day & night, & I may in truth say in daily danger of her life . . . as long as he is under the uncontroled powers of liquors, daily dangers await him & he may be consigned to imprisonment for murder under the influence of Insanity.'

As dangerous to the children as physical violence was the way they were allowed to run wild: 'he will not allow them to go to school, & he will not clothe them, & what must be the end of all this, for he cannot educate them himself. . . . His duty is sadly neglected, & his fits have come on in the church, so *every one is afraid of him*, & neglect the church. The only person having influence with him is a faithfull servant, a *Coachman*—he can stop some violent paroxysms but that cannot last long—he will not pay any house bills, nor allow necessary food for his family. . . . Nobody knows where George hoards up his money, he pays nobody.'

Mrs Tennyson had unsuccessfully tried to get the children away from the Rectory, Chaplin continued, and she would not leave them alone with her husband. 'She has spent a most dreadfull life for some years—Georges violence is well known in all the adjoining villages & his horrid language is heard everywhere he goes. He has no judgement left or control over his Tongue.'[36]

In his anger at what he considered Chaplin's presumption, Charles showed the letter more widely than he should have done, so that it became a matter of common gossip. He then wrote to the local physician, Dr Bousfield, to ask for another assessment of affairs in Somersby. Dr Tennyson must have been very plausible in his behaviour when he wanted to be, for Bousfield went to dinner and found him, he reported, with 'the same acuteness of mind and playfulness of manner as when I first met with him more than thirteen years ago'. Bousfield realized that Mrs Tennyson really believed that she was in danger from her husband, but he thought she was misled by fear for her children. 'I do not make out that Dr. T's fits have of late been unusually frequent, or that excess of spirit drinking has been more than occasional. He habitually indulges too much in Malt liquor, to which he has been gradually led by its soporific quality. . . .' Dr Bousfield suggested that a Continental tour would probably benefit the Rector, since it would take him away from habitual scenes.[37]

There is no reason to believe that Bousfield was less than ordinarily observant, for others outside the family who spent time with Dr Tennyson during the next few years were convinced he was nothing more than eccentric. However, the combined testimony of his children and his wife, living in the same house with him, is surely to be taken more seriously than that of friends who saw him at his best. The 'playfulness of manner' and 'acuteness of mind' were genuine enough, but they were only a small part of his nature. When he had word from Bousfield, Charles wrote coolly: 'I do not believe that my Brother's health is at all worse in any respect than it was a year ago.'[38] The truth was, however, that he had not actually seen his brother and was merely retailing Bousfield's opinion.

Dr Tennyson's behaviour, and his coarse remarks about his wife when he heard that her family friends were complaining about him, finally reached the ears of his sons Arthur and Horatio, who were staying, as Alfred had done, with their grandmother and their aunt Mary Anne Fytche while they attended Louth Grammar School. Normally Miss Fytche would have turned to her brother for help, but he was away from Louth and her mother was too infirm to write, so, when she heard of Charles Tennyson's noncommittal letter, she determined to write directly to her brother-in-law and to send a copy of her letter to his father. Dr Tennyson's conduct to her dear sister had been unparalleled in its barbarity, and, she said, surely 'it was sufficient misery to be subject to the caprices of so dreadful a temper as yours for twenty two years without having her character vilified when she has no means of justifying herself. You have deprived her of all authority in the family, & encouraged the servants to insult her, she is not allowed to have any Money, & if she asks for some for the necessary expences of the family, she is refused in such language as I should be ashamed to transcribe, these circumstances are so public that your poor Children here are told of them every day by their Schoolfellows, & we should consider ourselves as accessories in your violence did we neglect any means in our power to deliver Eliza from such brutality.' She concluded by telling her brother-in-law that once she had thought highly of his disposition, but that his wilfulness had 'effaced every trace not only of noble feeling but of common humanity'.[39]

Old George's reply to Miss Fytche has disappeared, but he was moved to invite his daughter-in-law to stay at Tealby at the end of October to talk over her husband's condition and to find out how much of what had reached Bayons was true. Mrs Tennyson accepted for herself and her two elder daughters, but then her husband balked at their leaving and would not let her take the horses unless she would promise to remain away for six months, so she was unable to go.

At eighteen Alfred was once more the eldest of the children at home, and surely he was the most responsible person in the Rectory. Frederick had been at Cambridge for a year, and in October, while the furious letters were flying around the family, Charles had gone to join him at Trinity, to which Frederick had migrated after his first year at St. John's. Alfred intended to remain in Lincolnshire and work with a mathematics tutor before going up to Cambridge the following year, but the turmoil at the Rectory was too much for him, and he could not find a tutor whom he liked. It is only fair to add that the man probably did not exist who could have made the subject palatable for him.

He must have suffered particularly over his father's illness, for at the end of October he went to Bayons to stay with his grandfather, a move that in itself suggests his desperation. While he was there his father at last agreed to go to France with his brother Charles. Before they left the country, Charles announced that he was bringing Dr Tennyson to Tealby. This was enough to drive Alfred away. After his departure his grandfather wrote to Mrs Russell: 'The day his father came here, Alfred set out for Cambridge, not wishing to meet him, where he proposes to stay 'till the 100£ you kindly promised him is exhausted. What is to be done with him I dont know.'[40]

Apparently Alfred's flight by coach was so headlong that he did not even stop at Somersby on the way but took the *Umpire* to Stamford, where he transferred to the *Leicester*, which set him down at the Blue Boar in Cambridge.

✳

CHAPTER IV

EARLY DAYS AT CAMBRIDGE, 1827–1829

IN the dusk of the evening of 9 November 1827 Tennyson arrived to take up residence in Cambridge, although he had not yet completed the formalities for admission as pensioner of Trinity College. There were no real difficulties, in spite of his previous worries about mathematics, for he was soon examined by his tutor and the Dean, who said that he 'was fully competent to enter ye. University'.[1]

Since he arrived after the beginning of term, there were probably no available rooms in college, but in any case he would have gone, as he did, to lodgings with Frederick and Charles, who were established in Rose Crescent, a short distance from the college. So far he had only £100 on which he could count, and the meanest garret room in college cost a quarter of that annually, whereas lodgings in the town with most meals were between 18 and 25 shillings a week. A year later he was paying a guinea for new lodgings, which was probably about what he paid initially. He and his brothers took their breakfasts and teas communally, thus reducing their expenditure a little. At the end of the first term he and Charles moved to Trumpington Street, to rooms in 57 Corpus Buildings, where they were comfortable in spite of being what seemed to Alfred an undesirable distance from Trinity. There, to remind him of the troops of animals in Somersby, he kept a snake, and he spent hours watching it wind sinuously over the carpet.

It is difficult to exaggerate the change to Cambridge from the narrow triangle bounded by Tealby, Louth, and Somersby. Trinity was the most self-consciously grand of the Cambridge colleges, and most of the men there had been at a public school, whereas Tennyson had spent four largely wasted years in Louth Grammar School seven years earlier. It was not an entirely unfair story told of the Trinity man who said condescendingly of the smaller colleges in Cambridge, 'They, too, are God's creatures.'[2] On the first night that Tennyson went into hall in Trinity he was so taken aback by the ranks of undergraduates and the splendour of the place that he turned away in shyness; to his

III a. Alfred Tennyson, c. 1830, probably by Anne Sellwood.

b. Arthur Henry Hallam, c. 1830, by Anne Sellwood.

IV a. Alfred Tennyson, c. 1831,
attributed to James Spedding.

b. Arthur Henry Hallam,
    c. 1832, by James Spedding.

myopic eyes that vast room looked limitless, with the candles receding beyond the reaches of his sight. It was probably on that very night that W. H. Thompson, later his friend and still later Master of Trinity, saw him hesitating at the door and said, 'That man must be a poet.'

There was a rough independence about Tennyson that belied his awkwardness and shyness and kept him from feeling inferior over his lack of social experience. Perhaps because of the contempt he felt for his uncle Charles's desire to be the intimate of dukes, he was seldom overawed by mere position, and in the correspondence of his youth there is no indication that rank meant much to him. He could be embarrassed when his own gaucheries were pointed out to him, but they never deeply disturbed his self-confidence.

This curious combination of shyness and self-confidence made him totally unconventional in his conversation, since he would say exactly what was on his mind without regard for its appropriateness. Sometimes his manner could harden into a kind of Tennyson hauteur like that of his grandfather and his brother Frederick. He used to tell of alighting from the coach on his first night in Cambridge and being addressed by a proctor as he walked down Trumpington Street: 'What are you doing without your cap and gown, sir, at this time of night?' Without bothering over who had asked the question, he negligently retorted, 'I should like to know what business it can be of yours, sir.'

He was a conspicuous figure, familiar by sight to men who had never met him. He stood well over six feet, with a singularly broad chest and heavy legs with which he walked long distances very quickly in spite of his appearing to shuffle because he scarcely lifted his feet from the ground. His complexion was swarthy (Spanish was the usual description given by his contemporaries), his long dark hair gleaming with a flash of chestnut, although customarily unkempt, hung gracefully as a frame for his massive head. The slightly remote quality of his gaze from deep-set, hooded eyes gave him a self-contained appearance that set him apart without revealing how near-sighted he really was. To some his withdrawn manner could seem both arrogant and affected. With a beautifully modelled nose and sensuous mouth, he was so startlingly handsome that Edward FitzGerald, who did not know him for some years after, always remembered him walking the tortuous streets of Cambridge looking 'something like the Hyperion shorn of his Beams in Keats' Poem: with a Pipe in his mouth'.[3] His native refinement was made all the more striking by contrast with the ruggedness of his body and the carelessness with which he wore his countrified, often dirty, clothes; it is impossible to imagine his asking his father for a smarter tailor, as Frederick had done at Eton.

Most undergraduates of the time who were not preparing for holy orders went to the University with little purpose. Broadly speaking, they were divided into the 'fast', or 'gay', or sporting set, as opposed to the reading men, many of whom were intent on a clerical career. Most of the former had no intention of ever attempting a degree, and a fair proportion of the reading men expected to take one chiefly as preparation for ordination. Reading men took little exercise except for long walks, and to distinguish themselves from the fast men they went out clad in 'dark coat, black pantaloons, blue stockings, and, in winter, Berlin woollen gloves'.[4] Should there be any doubt of their status, they wore cap and gown all day, even when their walks had taken them miles from the University. Sporting men donned gowns only at night, when they were prescribed by the proctors to distinguish undergraduates from townsmen.

Awkwardly, the Tennysons fell somewhere between the two groups. Certainly, they were not sporting men, and if Frederick had a taste for the 'fast' life he did not share it with his younger brothers. The interests of all three were highly literary, but that did not qualify them as reading men, since the matter of a degree still seemed remote, with the apparently unscalable wall of mathematics lying between them and its possible attainment. Because of the efforts of Christopher Wordsworth, Master of Trinity, it had been possible since 1824 to read the classical tripos, but that privilege was granted only after attainment of honours in mathematics. In any case, the Tennysons felt something of the attitude of Thackeray who said that he knew of some first-class men, 'who are very nice fellows, only they smell a little of the shop'.[5]

All three brothers were to achieve some formal distinction at Cambridge, but in each case it was for poetic rather than strictly academic attainment. Frederick had already won the prize for a Greek ode, Charles was to be awarded a Bell Scholarship in 1829 for his English translations of the classics, and Alfred later won the University prize for English verse. But these were all aside from the more earnest business of winning academic honours and earning degrees. Since they were such distinctive figures and since their poetic reputation had preceded them (there were surely few undergraduates who had already published a volume of their own poetry), and perhaps even more because of the sheer improbability of there being three such gifted brothers, they were soon well known in the University, and for the first time Alfred had close friends who were not of his own family. Frederick already had his own circle, of course, and Alfred and Charles were made part of it. The pithiness and unorthodoxy of his remarks made his new acquaintances pay particular attention to Alfred, and he discovered that the gift for mimicry with which he had amused the family at Somersby entertained his friends. He would do the sun emerging from a cloud by a gradual opening of his eyes and mouth and whole countenance, and then imitate its return into obscurity by slowly closing up once more. Or he would fluff up his untidy hair so that it looked like a wig, hunch up his cravat and collar, and take on the look of George the Fourth. Once he felt at home with other men, he liked to recite poetry aloud, his own as well as the dozens of ballads he knew by heart.

Since he was a poet and not a scholar, most of the traditions about his Cambridge career are naturally unconcerned with what he was meant to be learning. The University was still in part run rather like an advanced school, with a curious atmosphere compounded of rules for the guidance of the adolescent and a freedom that often verged into licence. Chapel rules had been formulated in 1824, made necessary by the general tendency to laxness about the matter. Trinity men were required each week to attend five morning chapels at 7 a.m. and five evening chapels. There were lectures from 8 a.m. until 10 a.m. From then until evening chapel the undergraduates were in theory engaged in study, but in practice they were free to ride, to run to beagles, to fight bargees on the Cam, or to take part in any kind of dissipation. Not infrequently they turned up for evening chapel the worse for drink, but drunkenness was generally held to be a lighter offence than missing chapel. Tennyson had no natural tendency to dissipation, unless one counts his heavy smoking, in which he had indulged ever since his schooldays in Louth. In later life he drank more than his friends thought was good for him, but there is no record of his being addicted to the bottle at Cambridge. For exercise he rowed, fenced, or took the long walks that were habitual since boyhood.

Dinner in hall, which he took occasionally, was a rough-and-ready affair at which only meat was provided, in great joints from which the undergraduates casually and unskilfully hacked their own portions at table. Everything else from soup to cheese had to be paid for additionally, and not many of the undergraduates except the gentlemen commoners, who ate with the Fellows, came regularly to the meal. There was so much profit from uneaten meals that the position of college cook was said to be more lucrative than that of Master.

By modern standards the prevailing atmosphere was highly unintellectual, but Trinity was slowly changing since Christopher Wordsworth had become Master in 1820 and had joined his influence to that of some of the younger Fellows, who wanted to change the college into a place devoted primarily to learning. In their zeal the alternative they provided was often pedantry, but it was probably a necessary step. It was because the college was at this turning point, poised between abuse and reform, that a group like the Apostles, of which Tennyson later became a member, could be so appealing in their combination of fun and moral earnestness. Another man might have fallen into the ways of the Simeonites, then primly flourishing at King's, with 'night services' at Little St. Mary's, but Tennyson, as a parson's son, was already inoculated against religious enthusiasm, and though he was no true intellectual he early cast his lot with those who were.

His tutor at Trinity was William Whewell, who had been a Fellow for ten years when Tennyson arrived, and who was later to be Master. Although he tried to teach Tennyson mathematics and moral philosophy, he was sufficiently aware of his pupil's eccentric genius to turn a blind eye to the fact that Alfred read Virgil under his desk when he was supposed to be working at mathematics. The respect and affection Whewell felt for his pupil was by no means the rule, for though he was a genial man, he was sometimes so impersonal with those he taught that he was said once to have remonstrated with his college servant for not having corrected his mistake when he issued an invitation to one of his pupils who had died the previous term.

With the thought of Somersby constantly in the back of Tennyson's mind, the knowledge of drunkenness, dissolution, and violence as an ever-present threat in the Rectory, Cambridge must have seemed by contrast even more attractive than the University usually does to an intelligent young man away from home for the first time. But his home need not be a totally happy one for the man to be homesick, and Alfred was probably that as well in the brief month of his first term at the University. Above all, he was now eighteen years old, with the affections of an adult, and he had never been in love nor had he ever had the intimacy of one close friendship, as had most of the public school men in Trinity. Cambridge was splendid, but it was not perfection.

The second week in December Alfred and his brothers went back to Somersby for the Christmas vacation. The welcome from his mother and brothers and sisters was to a noisy but peaceful house, unlike that he had left, for the Rector was still in France. At the last moment he had nearly decided to remain in England, refusing to travel unless his brother Charles accompanied him. Charles pleaded that he was too busy but finally went with him to Paris and left him there in charge of the Marthions, the people to whom Charles had sent his own daughters to learn French.

Since his arrival in Paris Dr Tennyson's letters home had been mildly encouraging, for he seemed to be his old self. Just before going back to Somersby for Christmas, Alfred had written to his grandfather to say that he had received a letter from his father, asking to hear in return. 'I have accordingly written to him to day—he seems I think to be in much better spirits than when I last saw him.' Alfred was certain, he said, that the 'constant variation of scene & ideas wh. occur in travelling will operate as an infallible restorative to his unhinged state of mind'.[6]

At Somersby Mrs Tennyson was willing in her simple way to believe that all would be well again. According to her father-in-law, she 'speaks most affectionately of her Husband & she and her children, at home, are looking forwd with delight at the prospect of his return with amended health, his is a fine family, & fervently do I hope they will prove blessings'. Before his return old George hoped to have Dr Tennyson's financial affairs straight once more, and to that end had been gathering in his son's bills and calling at his bankers, to be sure that his account was solvent. With a gloomy pleasure that reminds one of his daughter Mary Bourne's delight in damnation, he would recount to Charles all that had gone wrong, including the fact that he had settled the debts of £400 left unpaid when the Rector left for France.

It seemed to old George and Charles an opportune time to determine the futures of the brood at Somersby while their father was away, since they were sure they could handle Mrs Tennyson's objections if she had any. When Alfred arrived home, Edward was staying at Bayons, where old George proposed to 'let him copy Deeds and Abstracts' and then put him out as clerk to a solicitor. Arthur was to be taken out of Louth Grammar School and go to the Army as a cadet or possibly into the Navy. Septimus, soon to be twelve, was to go to Louth School with Horatio, unless he could be got into the Army or Navy; in the meantime he was sent to Bayons to join Edward under the appraising eye of his grandfather. Before going back to Cambridge Frederick and Charles were expected to go to Bayons in the carriage that was to take Edward and Septimus home. Matilda and Cecilia

were to be taken for their grandfather's inspection by their new gover-
ness. There is no mention of Alfred's seeing his grandfather; old
George did not think he need withdraw from Cambridge for the
present. When the Old Man of the Wolds announced his plans for the
Somersby children, his son Charles loyally assured him, 'I think my
Bror. will not disapprove of your arrangement for his boys.'[7]

Old Mr Tennyson was particularly interested in having his grand-
daughters' governess accompany them because their brother Charles
had been in love with her predecessor. It had been an opportunity for
Mr Tennyson to indulge in what Samuel Butler called will-shaking. 'I
must confess this distresses me & your family most seriously,' he
wrote to Charles, 'and may if persisted in prove the utter ruin of you
and her. It wd. interrupt your studies, and prevent your ever providing
for yourself & a family of your own besides your persisting at present
to a conclusion would certainly leave you pennyless, for you could not
expect any fortune from your *uncle Turner*, your father or myself.'[8]
Within a few days he discovered to his delight, if not that of Charles,
that Miss Watson had been taking goods on credit and then selling
them. With some relish he reported that she 'was arrested at Somersby
for a Debt of £24 but escaped in the Night'.[9] Charles appears not to
have suffered much damage to his heart at the end of the affair.

Some evidence of how disturbed the children at Somersby were by
their grandfather's interference with their lives, by what they had been
going through while their father was at home, and by the prospect of
his return, is shown by the attempt of one of the daughters to run away
early in January 1828, leaving without knowing where she was going
and without even time to have her trunks strapped. It was probably
Mary, eldest of the girls, who tried unsuccessfully to escape from the
Rectory. She was only a year younger than Alfred, to whom she was
closer than were any of her sisters. Although an accident while she was
small had left her with a pronounced limp, she was extraordinarily
beautiful by the time she was in her teens. She was devoted to Alfred
and Charles, and it may have been their impending departure for a
second term at Cambridge, to leave her in the Rectory when her father
returned, that led to her attempt to run away.

In the middle of January Alfred was staying with his grandmother
Fytche in Louth before going back to Cambridge. The Rector landed
in England on 20 January and spent some days in London to find a
new replacement for Miss Watson. From London his brother Charles
reported that 'He looks tolerably well & talks of proceeding into

Lincolnshire in the course of a few days'. Whether by design or accident he got home too late to see his three elder sons, who had returned to Cambridge. At first all seemed to go well, and he was reconciled with his old father, but that was too good to last. By the end of February Charles had to reassure his father, who thought that Dr Tennyson had been rude to him: 'My brother George, I am quite sure feels for you & will act towards you as a son ought. He may be carried away for a moment, *but his Heart is right.*'[10]

Things went rapidly downhill at the Rectory again. During his spring holiday from Cambridge Alfred was at Somersby when the young woman who was the family cook had her dress set alight in a kitchen accident. According to the story afterwards, she was afraid of the Rector's temper and ran up and down in the yard, screaming for help rather than going to his study; her burns were so bad that she died soon after. It is indicative of the malicious stories told of Dr Tennyson that it was soon believed that he had thereafter put a large butt of water outside the kitchen door, with instructions for future cooks not to bother him should they be set afire. Perhaps in part from the cook's accident, the Rector was soon in a condition as bad as that before he went to France, and by autumn he was writing letters to his father so abusive that at first they seemed a joke.

As before, the confusion and pain of his mind was closely linked to his physical condition, and the fits that the family dreaded were returning, as well as the spasms of the chest. Alfred's brother Charles wrote to his grandfater about the Rector's condition: 'Last night he suffered very much from the same cause. To night it has recurred with great violence. My Father is lying for ease on the floor & it is now midnight.'[11]

When he returned to Cambridge in January 1828, Alfred was probably much less bored and world-weary than he pretended to be when writing to his aunt Russell. Sure of her affection and tolerance, he would try out roles in his letters to her. 'I am sitting Owl-like & solitary in my rooms,' he wrote, '(nothing between me & ye stars but a stratum of tiles) ye hoof of ye steed—ye roll of ye wheel ye shouts of drunken Gown & drunken Town come up from below with a sealike murmur—I wish to Heaven I had Prince Houssain's fairy carpet to transport me along ye deeps of air to your Coterie . . . What a misery not to be able to consolidate our gossamer dreams into reality! Be it so. I must take my cigar philosophically & evaporate them in smoke, twirl my thumbs, rotatorily cross one leg over ye other & sink back in my chair. . . . ye eternal riot of this place ye wear & tear of mind & body are a very insufficient balm to ye wound of recollection. . . . I know not how it is but I feel isolated here in ye midst of society, ye country is disgustingly level, ye revelry of ye place so monotonous, ye studies of ye University so uninteresting, so much matter of fact—none but dry headed calculating angular little gentlemen can take much delight in . . . Logarithms, Involution & Evolution, properties of curve lines, resuming Series, indeterminate Analysis, Method of Increments! Do not they look annihilatingly barbarous? "There is no pleasure like proof" cries ye Mathematician. I reverse it "there is no proof like pleasure".[12]

Mrs Russell unprotestingly put up with his affectations, sent him reassurances and regular cheques (she gave him £100 p.a. until long after his marriage), and forgave him the numerous times he forgot to thank her or to let her know what he was doing. With her more than any other adult in his family he found intelligent, trusting, and uncomplicated love, and for her he had his own affectionate name, Asile, a reversal of the letters of the name by which she was known to the rest of the family.

Few other letters have survived to indicate his state of mind during the spring and summer terms of 1828, but behind the assumed languor and fashionable drawl of his letter to her it is easy to see a poignant loneliness. Although he still lacked real intimates, he was already well known in Cambridge. The same month that he wrote to his aunt, one of his new friends, Charles Merivale, wrote to his father: 'I have got the third of the Tennysons in my room, who is an immense poet, as indeed are all the tribe—was the father so? I am very glad to find that the eldest has received great praise in the Trinity Scholarship Examination, though they would not give him one from lack of mathematics.' A few months later he wrote that when in need of conversation, 'I fly to Birkbeck or Tennyson at Trinity, with the latter of whom especially I exercise dialectics by constant argument.'[13]

By the autumn of 1828 Alfred was so well entrenched in Cambridge as to startle his cousin George Hildeyard Tennyson, who came up in October. Alfred and his brothers helped their cousin find lodgings, and he fell into the habit of dining with them, 'each man subscribing a dish, which encourages society at a cheap rate'.[14]

Uncle Charles Tennyson had been so apprehensive about the behaviour of his Somersby nephews that he did not want his eldest son even to be in the same university with them. Unfortunately, he was unable to place him in Christ Church, Oxford, so he had to settle for Trinity. The propinquity of his nephews, he explained, was dangerous: 'I am *far* from wishing you not to be on kind & affectionate terms with your Cousins, on the Contrary, it is desirable that you shd. be & remain so—but one object of going to Cambridge is to cultivate a variety of acquaintance & therefore I wd. not have you confine yourself entirely to them or to the circle to which they may introduce you. . . . Your Cousins are I doubt not very respectable young men & very clever—but their *habits* may be confined & their Society limited. It is not that I am fearful of any improper conduct on their parts but do not, I repeat, suffer yourself blindly to be drawn into *confined muddling* habits. . . . Cambridge shd be a preparation for the World & if you live exclusively with a certain set, you may as well be in the Country except for the advantages which the studies of the University afford. Your Cousins are very well informed on many literary matters & may be of use to you. Avoid all conversation (without seeming to do so) on family matters—otherwise *it will & must* end ill, particularly with Frederick.'[15] Possibly most fathers giving advice to undergraduate sons sound remarkably like Polonius.

For a time Uncle Charles addressed his son as 'Hildeyard', but warned him not to abandon his first name, since it might not please his grandfather. The change of name was intended to keep people from confusing him with his cousins: 'to adopt *Hildeyard* as a sort of *addition to your Surname*, in order to secure a permanent distinction from others of your family'.[16] The new name was soon dropped, but it had been a rehearsal for Uncle Charles's later change of name to Tennyson d'Eyncourt to keep his family from being associated with the crowd at Somersby.

To young George's surprise his cousins were far from being the disgrace his father had prepared him for. 'Frederick is I think much improved,' he wrote home. 'I think the society they keep is by no means *middling*. They have introduced me to 2 men who are both gentlemanly & clever. . . . De Vere the son of Sr. de Vere Hunt, Bart, an Irishman is one & is accomplished. He plays beautifully on the Piano. Frere is the name of the other, the son of the Master of Downing College. Wordsworth the Master of Trinity is I hear a complete *humbug* & *not* a very clever man. He is brother to the poet, who I think is by no means, a first rate one. . . . My cousins scarcely ever go to chapel & I expect they will have a thundering imposition one of these days.'[17]

George Hildeyard Tennyson had good instincts and was grateful to his cousins, but he was too much the son of his father not to worry about their unconventionality. 'I scarcely see anything of Charles or Alfred,' he wrote to his father a few months after they had introduced him in Cambridge. 'They only move in one sphere; their society so far is good, being literary: but I think to be a man of the world, one ought to live in different societies.'[18]

Uncle Charles had met the Rector and his wife in Lincoln at the Stuff Ball and told them that his son was now living in lodgings, to which Mrs Tennyson replied, 'Fredk & Chas & Alfred will be very sorry for that as they wanted *a room* in College.'[19] The Somersby Tennysons were so unthinkingly hospitable to their acquaintances that it never occurred to them that others might not like sharing their rooms or houses for an unannounced visit. To Charles Tennyson it proved that his nephews intended to use his son for their own advantage.

However much he might avoid his cousins and change his name, George Hildeyard Tennyson had one kinship with the family that he could not renounce. At Trinity he had a recurrence of a 'serious indisposition', of which the name was never mentioned, although the symptoms were obviously those of epilepsy. His father suggested that he give up drinking totally for some years lest it 'bring back what we had hoped was already eliminated. . . . if once those frightful attacks recurred, they might at your present age, *fix*, & produce an effect not only on your health but on your mind, which it wd be horrible to contemplate. Above all things take care of your bowels.'[20]

At the end of 1828 came the apparent proof of everything his uncle Charles had suspected of Frederick. As his cousin had noticed, Frederick was more than usually lax in his chapel attendance, and when an imposition was laid on him, he neglected to 'get' it. He was called to the Dean of the college for an explanation, and instead of telling the Dean of the illness from which he had been suffering, he sarcastically asked why it was that the Master's son, who was guilty of approximately the same offence, had been given a lesser imposition. The Dean then referred him to the Master, and he was called before governing body, where he was 'smilingly & satirically impertinent'. The upshot was that he was rusticated for three terms. The Dean wrote to Charles Tennyson: 'I must say that considering his conduct his sentence is mild; in most instances expulsion would have been the punishment.'[21]

Dr Tennyson went for help to Edward Maltby, who had married his wife's cousin and who was already embarked upon a worthy clerical career that was capped by his becoming successively Bishop of Chichester and of Durham. Maltby heard Frederick's explanations, which seemed to both him and Dr Tennyson so reasonable that they decided the sentence 'was most harsh and unjust'. After all, Maltby concluded, Frederick had inherited both talent and eccentricity from his father, and it was not surprising that he was 'always *distrait*, and more like an inhabitant of Laputa than of England'.[22]

Predictably, Frederick's failure threw his grandfather, uncle, and father into wild recriminations and plans. Old George called Alfred and Charles to Bayons to see if they had been infected by Frederick. 'They did not act *dis*respectably to me,' he informed his son Charles, 'but they are so untoward & disorderly & so unlike other people I dont know what will become of them, or what can be done with, or about them. I tried to impress them with the feeling that they and Fredk. were spending or wasting half their Father's income & he had only half to maintain himself his wife & to educate 4 other Boys & 4 Girls, and that unless the money expended for their education was to fit them for professions to get their livings, so that they might be out of the way for an expenditure on the Education of their Bros and Sisters & for putting their Bros in a way of getting their livings, they, Fredk, Chas & Alfred would be the ruin of them & act most unkindly & dishonorably. Those 3 boys so far from having improved in Manner or Manners are worse since they went to Cambridge.'[23]

At Somersby the friction became unbearable as the Rector and his wayward eldest son were thrown upon each other. The father claimed that Frederick tried to 'prescribe laws for the management' of the rest of the family, and that he would ruin them, as he had Alfred and Charles: 'I regret the day I ever sent Frederick to Eton.'[24]

It is difficult to be sure of what happened at Somersby in the winter of 1828 and spring of 1829, not because there is little evidence but because there is too much. In general, however, it seems safe to believe that Mrs Tennyson and her children were telling the truth, even if it was somewhat coloured by their emotions. Poor Dr Tennyson was by now so confused that his own accounts, conflicting as they were, can scarcely be trusted. As always, he had a very plausible manner when he was not in the actual grip of his illness, and he was such a kind and reasonable man at times that he could convince his friends that everything that had been said of him was false. The result is that much of the evidence is contradictory.

At last in February 1829 Mrs Tennyson wrote to her father-in-law to announce her intention of living separately from her husband and to explain why, although she knew the old man would not believe most of her account. Her husband had been getting more and more abusive and using 'such degrading epithets to myself & children as a husband and a Father & above all a person of his sacred profession ought particularly to avoid'. He kept a large knife and a loaded gun in his room, and he was with difficulty persuaded not to fire the gun through the kitchen window. In his mania he often had his time confused and probably thought he was back in Cambridge as an undergraduate, firing through the chapel window of the college that had fostered his sons' ingratitude. When he was persuaded to give up the gun, he said he would take the knife and kill Frederick by stabbing him in the jugular vein and the heart. 'We may thank God that we do not live in a barbarous Country,' said Frederick, 'or we should have murdered each other before this.'[25] Thereupon Dr Tennyson called the constable and turned Frederick out of the house. The sensible constable took Frederick home for three days, where he behaved well, then sent him off to Louth to stay with his aunt Fytche.

Mrs Tennyson had to beg her father-in-law for the return of her own grey pony and pony chaise that her husband had sent to Tealby as a present for his father. She wrote that Mrs Russell had given her the chaise and that she had bought the pony herself, so that they were not Dr Tennyson's to give, but old George refused to return them to her, leaving her with no means of getting away from the Rectory.

The confused accounts that reached Tealby were hard to evaluate, and old George sometimes turned to other sources of information. 'I understand Fredks. abuse to his Father was *shocking*, so bad I cannot repeat it,' he wrote to his son Charles. 'I had the acct from Ingham the servt.'[26] Apparently he was totally unabashed at seeking gossip about his son and grandson from their servants.

In one of the lightning changes of mind that made him so hard to deal with, Dr Tennyson then informed Frederick that he would allow him £100 a year, stipulating that he must not come back to Somersby. Mrs Tennyson reluctantly decided to take lodgings in Louth, 'the only step that can effectually secure myself & family from the consequences of his ungovernable violence'. Her brother, John Fytche, whom Dr Tennyson called a 'perfect Demon', was determined to 'sue for a separate maintenance in Doctors commons' on her behalf.[27]

When George Hildeyard Tennyson at Cambridge heard of the quarrel between Frederick and the Rector, he found it particularly painful, he told his father, 'when we consider that we are allied to them by blood. To read this even in a newspaper, would excite some sympathy.' Correspondence with his father always brought out young George's priggish side, and he added that 'the Tennysons are naturally rather hot, and it only shows us how we ought to value that Reason which I trust is imparted to us in a degree equivalent to our temperament. . . . I heard from Alfred & Charles the other day that they had heard from home, but they did not mention anything about this matter.'[28]

All through his years of illness Dr Tennyson's best friend had been T. H. Rawnsley, the incumbent of Halton Holgate, a village some ten miles from Somersby. On 12 March 1829 Rawnsley wrote to Charles Tennyson to say that he had taken Dr Tennyson into his own house, since the rest of the family had quitted Somersby, leaving the Rector 'alone, & so ill, that his neighbour sent an express for me, fearing he would sink under his depression, & Epileptic tendencies—when I arrived on Monday, I found your brother *feeding upon himself*, & most miserable'. Mr Rawnsley's advice was that he take another Continental trip as soon as possible. 'I need not add how deeply I . . . sorrow over the decay of such a powerful Intellect. . . . the Dr. is better this morning & better he will be if he gets into Society, but *alone* he must not be.'[29] Subsequently Dr Tennyson took to his bed and did not leave it for more than forty-eight hours. Once he was away from his family he was so persuasive in his account of what had happened that Rawnsley's letters during that spring all indicate that Dr Tennyson had been shamefully abused by his family.

In a kind of waking delirium Dr Tennyson began even wilder imaginings than before; at one point he was convinced that he was about to have a duel with Mr Vane, a friend of his father's. It was clear that he must be got out of Lincolnshire, both in the hope that he might make some recovery, and that his wife and children might come home again. Although old Mr Tennyson had long given up the Rector as a lost cause, through everything that had happened he had insisted that his son was innocent and that all the trouble at Somersby had been the fault of his daughter-in-law. At last even he had to agree that, though it was possible for the Rector to return home, 'unless *he will determine* to give up drinking, in a week all will be as bad as ever'. Even so, Mr Tennyson was unwilling to admit that there was anything wrong with his son that abstinence would not put right. 'I am sure that wd he give up drinking, all might yet end more to all our credits.'[30]

On 14 May Dr Tennyson left for a second trip to Paris in search of health, but not without giving a power of attorney to his father and brother to act for him in his absence, showing how little he trusted his sons, who must have sided with their mother. Surely none of the family really believed that he would be better for the trip, but for their own sanity he had to be removed from their lives.

There is no mention of the presence of Alfred during the violence at the Rectory and the subsequent events, but none of the letters of the period mentions that he was not at home with the other children, so we must assume that he had come back to Somersby for his spring holidays. It was presumably while he was at home that the Rector in one of his intermittent periods of lucidity had insisted that Alfred enter for the University Prize for English Verse, for which the subject that years was announced as 'Timbuctoo'. Alfred reluctantly agreed to do so, and tinkered up an old poem about the battle of Armageddon for submission when he returned to Cambridge. The poem won the prize, but, far more importantly, its submission brought about the deepest friendship of Tennyson's life.

CHAPTER V

ARTHUR HALLAM AT CAMBRIDGE, 1829

LIKE most artists with a conscience, Tennyson was plagued all his life with the conflicting claims of his duty to society, to the world at large, and his duty to his own sensibilities. Was the cultivation of his poetic talents mere selfishness, or did their existence oblige him to forgo some of the more normal domestic virtues? For a poet whose self-confidence was as poorly insulated as Tennyson's the problem was particularly intense, so that public conscience and private were at constant war, and he had to face the possibility that his poetry might be only an escape from external difficulties.

Even in so apparently simple a matter as his return to Cambridge at the end of the spring holidays in April 1829 the question was important. The coach in which he went to Cambridge took him to a world where fathers and sons were not in frequent danger of murdering one another, where voices were raised in laughter more often than in menace, where even the winds that filled the winter streets were abating into the promise of something softer, where the very regulations that seemed mindlessly confining also gave a shape to life. But the wrangling at home was unresolved, and for all he knew there might not even be a home to which he could return in the summer. Leaving Somersby behind might be nothing but a form of escape, from social responsibility to a world of enthralling artifice, precisely as he knew that the composition of poetry was sometimes a flight from the grim reality of the Rectory.

It is probably significant that during this period he 'took a lively interest in politics', as his son said. Under the influence of his politically minded friends he talked a great deal about Reform, tyranny, and revolution, but his interest was never profound, for he lacked the theoretical mind that makes politics more than personal emotions writ large. Independence, the struggle against oppression, heroism: all naturally moved him, but they touched his heart not his mind. During his undergraduate years he wrote poems on Napoleon, the Reform

Bill, and the Polish insurrection, but they would not detain a modern reader were they written by someone less famous. Probably more important in his development was a little poem, 'Written During the Convulsions in Spain', that had appeared in *Poems by Two Brothers*, composed in response to the liberal revolution against King Ferdinand, for it shows that he was predisposed to the revolutionary cause that he was to attempt to help in 1830.

As an older man Tennyson had the usual prejudices that pass with most of us for political theory; although certainly curious, he never gave much of his mind to the subject. His instincts were deeply conservative, but otherwise he tended to confuse political thought with a xenophobic patriotism. When asked what his beliefs were, he would say, 'I am of the same politics as Plato, Shakespeare, & Bacon, & any sane author.'[1] At the University he thought himself constrained to political talk with his friends in the Apostles, but he felt little more than an uneasy sense that the artificiality of the small world of Cambridge made it imperative to connect himself with larger issues.

The fragility of his ties to all that Cambridge represented had already been demonstrated by the departure of Frederick, who had been one of his major links to the rest of the University. Alfred still had plenty of friends but no intimates. What he was studying had no vital relation to his own personality. Where he located the centre of life is made explicit in the bitter 'Lines on Cambridge of 1830', in which he rails against the senior members of the University, whose 'manner sorts/Not with this age wherefrom ye stand apart', since they 'profess to teach/And teach us nothing, feeding not the heart'. Though he might look to the external world of politics for consolation, it was the unfed heart that disturbed him, a world without internal coherence because as yet he had none himself.

He seems, too, to have felt contempt for the University's attitude towards poetry, the traditional nurse of the heart and emotions. His entry for the Chancellor's Gold Medal for English Verse was written in blank verse, rather than the usual heroic couplets in which previous winning poems had been written, but that does not indicate that he was conscientiously attempting something novel. He had not wanted to enter the competition, and did so only after a wrangle with his father, yielding at last in deference to Dr Tennyson's illness. In grudgingly retailoring his old poem on Armageddon he was taking the easiest way, and probably, by deliberately submitting a poem in blank verse, flaunting how little he cared for either competition or prize.

Whatever Tennyson's attitude to it, the prize was a respectable one. It had been inaugurated by the Duke of Gloucester in 1813, and Macaulay, Praed, Christopher Wordsworth, and Edward Bulwer had all been past winners.

A rather more conventional entry than Tennyson's, although it was written in *terza rima*, was that by Arthur Henry Hallam, also of Trinity. It was over the submission of their poems in April that Tennyson and Hallam first became friends, but they may have met casually before that, since Hallam used to claim that Tennyson had borrowed from him the pervading idea of his poem, so that he deserved at least the 'honours of a Sancho Panza'.[2] That may merely mean, however, that they had discussed Tennyson's cobbling up of the old poem immediately before Tennyson submitted his entry, which was put together hurriedly.

At first it seems surprising that they should not have known each other before, but Trinity, where Hallam lived in first-floor rooms in New Court, is a huge college; Tennyson was in lodgings and took few of his meals in hall; Hallam was two years his junior and a year behind him in the University. Most of Tennyson's friends were concerned with poetry and literature, and in spite of his spurt of interest in politics, he was essentially non-political. Hallam had a deep feeling for poetry, but he gave his heart to metaphysics and politics, and these, combined with his outstanding ability at debate, naturally led him to the Union, where Tennyson had probably not set foot before meeting him. Most of Hallam's wealthy friends at this time were from Eton (where he had known Frederick casually). Tennyson was rapidly running into debt, for his aunt's initial gift of £100 had not gone far, and he had to ask for money from his father and grandfather, two totally undependable sources. Hallam, on the other hand, had an allowance of £300 a year, equivalent to the living of a clergyman in a fairly good benefice. The external circumstances of their lives were so different that it is surprising the most celebrated friendship of the century should ever have begun at all.

Hallam's father was the great Whig historian Henry Hallam, and his mother was the former Julia Elton of Clevedon Court, near Bristol. The elder Hallam had inherited a good deal of money, property near West Bromwich and Boston, and several houses. He moved in the magnificence of the Whig aristocracy and its strongholds around the country, although he was not loved everywhere, particularly by the young Whigs, whom he was reputed to snub. Henry Fox, for example, said that he was 'one of the most disagreeable members of society I ever have [had] the misfortune to meet'.[3] In Hallam's own home, history, politics, and philosophy were matters of constant and every-day interest. But all their wealth, connections, and cultivation could not protect the Hallams from fatality. Like Tennyson, Arthur Hallam came of an enormous family, but by 1829, when they met, he was one of only four left of the original eleven children, and of the whole family only one daughter survived the elder Hallam at his death in 1859. The hopes that Henry Hallam had for his talented children had become concentrated on the cleverest of the lot, Arthur, with all the well-meant oppression that such a loving burden implies.

Arthur was precocious enough naturally, but his father's ambitions for him undoubtedly pushed him at great speed, as John Stuart Mill's father had nudged him along in his precocity. By the time he was seven Arthur could read French, and two years later he was proficient in Latin. He was also writing tragedies which so dazzled his parents that 'the circumstances of these compositions was hardly ever mentioned out of their own family',[4] lest it seem boastful and spoil him for a brilliant future. Another probable reason they were not spoken of was that Henry Hallam, for his interest in literature, finally did not regard it as a reasonable full-time pursuit, and he was afraid Arthur might become too devoted to it to the exclusion of more practical matters.

At Eton Arthur's closest companion had been the young Gladstone, who, like Tennyson after him, used to envy Arthur his family back-ground of easy acquaintance with intellectual matters and the fluency it developed in talking about them. Arthur was periodically ill at Eton and suffered so severely from headaches that he was unable to take part in games. Gladstone would scull him upstream to the Shallows when he was unwell, saying that this proved how much he valued Arthur's company and talk, and as often as possible they took meals together, although they were in different houses. Their friendship was not always untroubled, and Gladstone's diary shows that he seldom knew how long he would remain in favour with Hallam, who might unaccountably transfer his interest and affections to another boy, leaving Gladstone puzzled and deeply hurt. All the same, at the end of his life Gladstone remembered him as the most richly endowed with natural gifts of anyone whom he had ever met.

Nor was Gladstone alone in his estimate of Hallam's abilities. When he left Eton in 1827, at the age of sixteen, he was generally regarded as the outstanding boy of his time, although a certain prim didacticism in his manner had earned him the school name of 'Mother Hallam'. Most of the next year, before going up to Cambridge, he spent in Italy, learning the language so well that he wrote respectable verse in it, and working hard at Dante's poetry, which remained for the rest of his short life the test of all literature.

As he was considerably more experienced than Tennyson in male friendship, so he was in his relations with the opposite sex. While in Italy he knew a beautiful young English woman, Anna Wintour, some ten years his senior, the daughter of one of his father's Christ Church friends; he is said to have fallen deeply in love with her. Certainly, he and his friend James Milnes Gaskell were in amicable rivalry over their affections for her, so generously indeed that they only became closer friends, which scarcely points to desperate love on the part of either. They both wrote poetry to her, or at least about her, and indulged in all the antics of well-read boys who know perfectly well how lovers should behave. Arthur's feelings for Anna Wintour have been described as precocious love, but they were more like adolescent infatuation, and a very conventional one at that. His own wry awareness that it was all a bit forced is suggested in a letter to Gaskell, who had written a particularly rhapsodic piece of praise of Anna; Hallam urged him 'to moderate a little the vehemence of that adoration'.[5] Miss Wintour probably never even knew of the broken hearts they boasted, and by 1829, when Hallam met Tennyson, she was already engaged to be married; Hallam muttered darkly about the unworthiness of her fiancé, but there is little to indicate that her loss deeply affected him. Gladstone once said wisely of the affair that 'people fell in love very easily in those days'.[6] And, one might add, out of love.

This is not to deny Hallam's pain over Anna Wintour, only to suggest that the hurt was neither deep-seated nor long of duration. No one who has ever felt it needs reminding of the poignancy of adolescent love or, for that matter, of its brevity. In Hallam's case it was almost certainly the normal step towards mature feelings taken by a young man with strong sexual impulses that seem to have manifested themselves with remarkable alacrity.

Arthur's father could see nothing that was not deplorable in his gusty passion for Miss Wintour, and it clearly did not help in the straight march forward intellectually that Mr Hallam wished. His acquaintance with the classical languages, thought his father, was 'not improved, to say the least, by the intermission of a year, during which his mind had been so occupied with other pursuits, that he had thought little of antiquity even in Rome itself'.[7] At best Henry Hallam was lukewarm about the utility of the emotions, and the whole affair of Anna Wintour only added to his distrust of the ardour of Arthur's affections. It was surely a wrench to him not to send Arthur to Christ Church, his own college, but he thought it wiser to separate his son from Gaskell and Gladstone, who were already at Oxford, so Trinity it was for Arthur. At this distance it is hard to understand that such genteel sadism was the result of a genuine wish for Arthur's welfare, but it undoubtedly was.

At Cambridge Hallam missed his closest Eton friends as much as Tennyson missed his brothers and sisters, and as a consequence he initially despised the University as inferior to the one where he would have preferred to be. 'There is nothing in this college-studded marsh, which it could give you pleasure to know,' he wrote to his sister. His letters to Gladstone constantly indicate the inadequacy of the new acquaintances he was meeting. 'I am sick at heart and chill in feeling, and perish without something to invigorate, something to refresh,' he told Gaskell at the beginning of his first winter term. When Gaskell went to visit Hallam, he reported back to Gladstone that he was not surprised that their friend did not like Cambridge, and Gaskell himself 'was anything but pleased with the tone of society at Cambridge and was a good deal disgusted' at much of what he heard there.[8]

Like Tennyson, Hallam lacked intimates, although his unusual gifts of intellect and articulateness had already made him a marked man among the 'metaphysical set', of which he had become part. There is plenty of testimony to his kindness and sympathy to those in trouble, but in his early Cambridge life there is little record of that spontaneous opening of his own heart that is the sign of the man made generous by happiness.

It is difficult to write of the meeting of Tennyson and Hallam because of the inadequacy of our language to deal with deep friendship. There should be a phrase analogous to 'falling in love' to describe the celerity of emotion that brings two persons together almost at first meeting; 'falling in friendship' is what happened to Tennyson and Hallam. In February Hallam had been writing to Gladstone that it was difficult to find a true friend: 'There are many, very many, whom I like, and esteem: but in the higher point I am difficult to please.'[9] When he had known Tennyson less than a month he had already transferred his allegiance from Gladstone and written a sonnet 'To A.T.', in which he says that it was only priority in time that had made Gladstone his best friend:

> Oh, last in time but worthy to be first
> Of friends in rank, had not the father of good
> On my early spring one perfect gem bestowed,
> A friend, with whom to share the best and worst.

'Perfect gem' was praise indeed for Gladstone, but it could hardly mask the fact that he had owed his initial position in Hallam's affections to the absence of the new friend, who is addressed at the conclusion of the sonnet in words that must have been a conscious echo of Shakespeare's protestations of timeless allegiance:

> And well I ween not time with ill or good
> Shall thine affection e'er from mine remove,
> Thou yearner for all fair things, and all true.

Tennyson's reaction to Hallam was simple: 'He was as near perfection as a mortal man can be,' he said long after Hallam's death, when his memory was as green as if all the intervening years had dropped away.[10] It would be hard to exaggerate the impact Hallam made on Tennyson; their friendship was to be the most emotionally intense period he ever knew, four years probably equal in psychic importance to the other seventy-nine of his life.

It is always difficult, when simple adulation is unsupported by much other evidence, to make an assessment of the character of a man whose impression on others was dependent upon the immediate impact of his personality. The brevity of Hallam's life and its brilliance make the accounts of his friends seem as inadequate as the description of a rocket shot into the night. The fact that he was only twenty-two at his death naturally exaggerated for those who were left the importance of what had been lost, since it is far easier to be certain of the genius of a man who has not lived to demonstrate human failure. The briefer the life the more extravagant the hagiography. One natural instinct is to doubt the validity of undiluted praise, a reaction which may be misleading in trying to arrive at the truth of the matter. Certainly, a significant few of those who knew Hallam reacted against the adoration offered to him by most of his friends, but that does not automatically make their opinion trustworthy. Since few of his contemporaries saw him as a normal blend of many qualities, admirable and otherwise, there is something faintly inhuman about his image as it has come down to us.

Hallam's surviving writings do not quite bear out the accounts of the splendour of his intellect and charm. His letters are full of both serious consideration of serious ideas and an engagingly boyish play-fulness, but they usually lack the personal immediacy to set them apart as essentially more interesting than those of his friends and contemporaries. His poetry is fluent and well-tailored, but most of it suffers from wordiness, so that it is easy to see why R. J. Tennant said he had more of the philosopher than the poet in his make-up. The surviving essays are intelligent, well-informed, and maturely constructed, but there is not much hint of genius in them.

All this makes it difficult to understand the usual opinion of Hallam, but whatever other evidence is adduced there is one central fact to be remembered: the two men usually regarded as the foremost of all Victorians both loved him deeply, thought his death had deprived the world of great gifts, and felt the continuation of his presence so strongly that sixty years after his death the Prime Minister and the Poet Laureate were still jealous of each other's place in his affections. It was certainly no ordinary man who inspired that kind of devotion.

Even during his lifetime there were plenty of tributes to the quality of Hallam's intelligence. 'What a rare thing is a grown-up mind!' Richard Monckton Milnes said of him once, and on another occasion, 'He really seems to know everything from metaphysics to cookery.' James Spedding shrewdly saw the dangers of Hallam's intellect, even though he admired it greatly. 'Thompson will be the greatest man among us yet,' he told his brother Edward. 'His mind, if it wants something of the energy and Glory of Hallam's, has a much steadier and more sober power of self review: and besides the said Hallam's natural skill in the dazzling fence of rhetoric is in great danger of misleading and bewildering him in his higher vocation of philosopher.'[11]

Henry Alford, a Cambridge contemporary, was one of those who saw only the lovable, tender side of Hallam: 'I long ago set him down for the most wonderful person altogether I ever knew.' Once he described him as 'full of blessings, full of happiness, drawing active enjoyment from every thing, wondering, loving, and being loved. . . . At night [he] came full of love and happiness, sat up with him till four a.m.'[12]

The tenderness that Alford knew in Hallam was sometimes hidden behind a mask that made less intimate friends think him heartless. Beside Alford's picture of him we should set the diary entry of the Revd John Rashdall at Hallam's death: 'the accomplished-vain philosophic Hallam, dead, suddenly—at 23'. But then Rashdall was not an intimate of his. How differently even members of the same family could feel about Hallam is shown in a letter to Edward Spedding from his elder brother James, who was to succeed (but not replace) Hallam as the man nearest Tennyson's heart: 'I do not agree with you as to A.H.H.'s flippancy. It seems to me to be all very graceful & courteous—and the medium nicely hit. But we always differ on this subject, as on most others. And no wonder; seeing that we regard his multitudinous majesty with such different eyes. I like to be amused with him & his pursuits & his amusements—you, if I mistake not, despise him so cordially that even where his taste coincides with your own natural taste you will not laugh or weep with him—if you fancy that a thing would please him it is enough to make it displease you.'[13]

The truth is that Hallam was neither perfect nor despicable, but that the separate aspects of his character were often kept discrete, rather than being mingled as in most men. He was at his best with those who elicited his sympathy, for to them he could show his own weaknesses without fear. He may have begun by sympathizing with Tennyson, but he finished by receiving at least as much as he gave.

They had a lot in common, for all their surface differences. Dr Tennyson was extraordinarily trying for his sons, but Alfred shared this burden with Arthur, for in spite of all Henry Hallam's love of his son he may have been as difficult a father as Dr Tennyson, since he was so exigent in his demands. Even after Arthur's death his father kept thinking of ways he might have improved his son's mind: 'A little more practice in the strict logic of geometry, a little more familiarity with the physical laws of the universe, and the phenomena to which they relate, would possibly have repressed the tendency to vague and mystical speculations which he was too fond of indulging.'[14]

Henry Hallam was seldom in doubt about the correctness of his own decisions and never hesitated in giving others the benefit of his wisdom. Sydney Smith, who was particularly tried by him, was once talking to Lord Melbourne, who began, 'I think I may assert without fear of contradiction. . .'. Smith interrupted, 'Are you acquainted, sir, with Mr. Hallam?' Even Tennyson, who had much reason in later years to love the elder Hallam, remembered near the end of his life how contentious he had been and used to tell how on another occasion Smith had said, 'There is Hallam, with his mouth full of cabbage and contradiction.'[15] Henry Hallam was also reputedly a domestic autocrat, and this probably went a long way towards neutralizing the benefits of the intellectual atmosphere he fostered in his house. The delight Arthur took in the eccentric household at Somersby shows how much he missed that erratic warmth and companionship at home. He was as alienated from his parents, because of his father's constant demands, as Tennyson was alienated by the violence of Somersby.

The ebullience that Alford and James Spedding saw in Hallam, and his willingness to help others, have given the mistaken impression that his unshakable emotional stability was a rock to which Tennyson could cling, but he was probably much nearer neuroticism in many ways than Alfred. 'I really am afraid of insanity,' he wrote to Richard Monckton Milnes in the summer of 1829,[16] and it was a fear that continued to haunt him. He told at least two correspondents during the same period that he was seriously considering suicide. It was a threat surely more real than Tennyson's throwing himself on the ground of the churchyard, wishing he were dead; poems like 'The Two Voices' indicate that Tennyson had probably known the urge to suicide himself, but that poem may have derived in part from what Hallam had told him of the feeling.

Like Tennyson, but with better reason, Hallam was despondent about his own health; all during the first year at Cambridge he suffered from a terrible mental fatigue caused by 'a too rapid determination of blood towards the brain',[17] as he had done during his year in Italy. The headaches continued, and during the summer of 1829 he was constantly ill and deeply depressed. Curiously, it seems to have been only after his death that his family and most of his friends recognized the seriousness of his complaints. Practically all of the correspondence between Arthur and Alfred was destroyed, so how much they told each other of their problems can be only conjectural, but since each was the other's closest friend they would have exchanged their worries about insanity, suicide, Arthur's disordered health, and the epilepsy and alcoholism that were ruining Somersby Rectory.

Both men were lonely when they met, Hallam particularly so because of the imminent marriage of Anna Wintour, both felt they were alien spirits moving through Cambridge, both were bored and dissatisfied with their studies, and both had to struggle to maintain their religious faith against the anguish of disbelief. Many of the feelings they shared might have been claimed by a large number of the young men at the University, but the moment was propitious, and at the right time it seems a miracle to find another person sharing one's views. By June 1829 their friendship was already so close as to become a matter of course, and Gaskell could refer casually to Tennyson as 'a great friend of Hallam's', as if the two-month-old intimacy were already one of long standing.[18]

On 6 June it was announced that Tennyson's poem had won the Chancellor's medal. Hallam felt no jealousy of his triumph, and the two men vied in praising each other's poem, each saying that the other's was better than his own. Disappointingly, the formal reading of the winning poem took place after Hallam had gone abroad to convalesce from the illness that so depressed him that summer.

One result of Alfred's success was grudging praise from his grandfather, which may have been the result for which Dr Tennyson had hoped when he insisted on Alfred's entering for the medal. Alfred's cousin George wrote to his grandfather the day after the winner was announced: 'You will be glad to hear that Alfred has gained the prize for the English poem (Timbuctoo)—a gold medal worth 15 guineas. I understand he is also very likely to gain the prize for the Greek ode.' Alfred did not get the Greek prize, but perhaps the value of the medal influenced his grandfather, who told Frederick: 'It gives me satisfaction that Alfred has succeeded so well.' If he wrote to congratulate Alfred personally the letter has disappeared, but probably he did not, for he was much occupied with how put upon he was by the family of his elder son: 'I am & have been much exhausted in mind & body on your Family affrs in consequence of the unhappy differences in it, & am now in my 80th year Gouty and infirm, & shd be spared.'[19]

The poem was recited on 5 July in the Senate House, not by Tennyson but by his friend Charles Merivale, who had won the prize the previous year. As an old man Tennyson blamed his own shyness: 'I couldn't face the public recitation in the Senate House', but at the time he wrote to his grandfather to explain Merivale's standing in for him: 'he has read it for me which is a customary thing if the Author be in any manner detained; as I have been by indisposition; indeed for the last quarter of a year I have been much distressed by a determination of blood to the Head, for which, as it affected my eyes with "muscae volitantes" (I speak medically: they are what are called in Scripture "the mote in the eye") I was ordered to be cupped by Alexander the great oculist No. 6 Cork Street.'[20] It is a delightful combination of youthful pomposity in the medical jargon and the factual circumstance of the physician's address, probably all calculated to appeal to old George, who could understand physical affliction but not shyness.

As the circumstances of its composition suggest, 'Timbuctoo' is a strange mixture. Tennyson was accustomed to converting single words or individual lines into whole poems, and here he transforms an entire early poem into something quite new. 'Armageddon', from which it comes, supplied about half its length, a splendid vision now framed in a new beginning and conclusion. The theme of 'Timbuctoo' is the relativity of truth in myth and religion, which may both spring from man's mind and then in turn become the object of his devotion:

> And much I mused on legends quaint and old
> Which whilome won the hearts of all on Earth
> Toward their brightness, even as flame draws air;
> But had their being in the heart of Man
> As air is the life of flame.

The suitability of the theme is apparent when we consider how casually Tennyson mined one poem for another of totally different purposes, since poetry, dependent upon myth, then seems to have the meaning that man postulates for it, rather than containing an inherent truth. This poses disturbing questions about the final validity of poetry, and it is hard to believe that Tennyson would have started such a hare as a mature poet. In 'Timbuctoo' the mutability of beauty is demonstrated by the way in which science and discovery can change one's perception of it, and finally rob it of all life. It is a Keatsian concept, and there is more than a hint of 'Ode to a Nightingale' or 'La Belle Dame sans Merci' or 'Lamia' in the ending of 'Timbuctoo', when the radiant seraph departs 'Heaven-ward on the wing', and, the poet says,

> I
> Was left alone on Calpe, and the Moon
> Had fallen from the night, and all was dark!

An unfortunate consequence of the method of composition is that the poem is needlessly difficult to follow because of the looseness of organization, so that the impression it leaves is one of splendid, disordered images. The Keatsian luxuriance of colour and the Miltonian mellifluousness of the blank verse is that of the best of Tennyson's early works, as in the poet's vision of the earth when he is supernaturally excited:

> I saw
> The smallest grain that dappled the dark Earth,
> The indistinctest atom in deep air,
> The Moon's white cities, and the opal width
> Of her small glowing lakes, her silver heights

Unvisited with dew of vagrant cloud,
And the unsounded, undescended depth
Of her black hollows.

If, as seems probable, the poem was in part a gesture of contempt for the whole competition, it is easy to see why he included a prose argument for the judges and prefaced the poem with an epigraph:

Deep in that lion-haunted inland lies
A mystick city, goal of high emprise.

Chapman.

As critics have noticed, the lines are unknown to Chapman scholars, and they have a suspiciously Tennysonian ring. Tennyson was thus providing himself with a built-in insurance against any adverse judgement of the poem: if the judges failed to notice the imposture of the epigraph, then they were unfit to assess what followed.

Hallam told Gladstone that the work gave promise of Tennyson's becoming the greatest poet of the century, but a possibly better balanced judgement was that of Charles Wordsworth: 'If such an exercise had been set up at Oxford, the author would have had a better chance of being rusticated, with the view of his passing a few months at a Lunatic Asylum, than of obtaining the prize. It is certainly a wonderful production; and if it had come out with Lord Byron's name, it would have been thought as fine as anything he ever wrote.'

Poems by Two Brothers had been, if anything, a regression after *The Devil and the Lady*, but in 'Timbuctoo' Tennyson moved forward immeasurably, showing for the first time, despite its defects, the opulence of the great poet that he became.

Another Trinity undergraduate, not yet acquainted with Tennyson, was moved to verse by the competition, and though he did not submit his poem to the judges, it does foreshadow the future accomplishments of William Makepeace Thackeray, of a rather different kind from those of Tennyson:

If I were a cassowary,
I would go to Timbuctoo,
And eat up a missionary,
Him and his hymn book too.[21]

It is fortunate that Tennyson presumably never saw the squib, for he and Thackeray later became close friends; burlesques of subjects he treated seriously were always offensive to him.

CHAPTER VI

THE APOSTLES, 1829

WHEN Alfred returned home from Cambridge in July 1829 the Rectory was more peaceful than it had been for a long time. In Dr Tennyson's absence relations with Tealby were easier, so that the post did not bear constant recriminations from one house to the other. Mrs Tennyson was once more moved to ask for either the pony or the carriage horses that her husband had given to his father, and again old Mr Tennyson refused, saying that 'it would be improper to keep Horses for the close carriage particularly as your husband ordered they shd be sold & the land let'.[1] This seems, however, to have been the only time that summer when the two households were openly at cross purposes, which was a welcome improvement over the spring.

There were no letters at Somersby from Paris, where Dr Tennyson was spending more time nursing grievances than his own health. 'I shall not write to my Wife at present, nor to any part of my family,' he told his brother Charles. 'They have (the more I consider the subject) treated me in too infamous a manner.' Mrs Russell was in Paris as well, living with her daughter and son-in-law in the Champs Elysées, but he refused to see them. In the endlessly recurring confusion of his illness, he began cutting himself off once more from the other members of his family to whom he had been reconciled. By the end of June he was convinced that his brother had neglected him, and when he refused to write, Mme Marthion had to notify Charles that the Rector had seemed to improve physically for a time, but now he 'had a spitting of blood, & his spirits at times much depressed'. When Charles did not come to join him, he left for Geneva in a rage: 'I have *positively waited for you three weeks in Paris*.'[2]

All during July he made his companionless way from Geneva to Lausanne, to Villeneuve, to Neuville, to Berne, where he had to stop because he was suffering from vomiting and diarrhoea. Like many lonely travellers, he began to blame his solitary state on the foreigners among whom he found himself and their stubborn insistence on using an alien tongue. Left with no one to talk to, 'for almost everybody speaks German', he brooded on his wrongs at home. 'Mr. Fytche & Mary Anne Fytche have encouraged my family to act in open rebellion against me. . . . Mr. Fytche may perhaps have some time or other rebellious children himself, & he will then be able justly to appreciate his own infamous conduct towards me.'[3]

The trouble and expense of the tour seemed to be doing him little good, and the only apparent benefit was such an improvement in the steadiness of his hand when writing that his brother was encouraged to believe that it 'proves that he abstains from a habit which we have lamented'.[4] Clearly, old Mr Tennyson had been too sanguine in thinking that if he stopped drinking all would be well. After the end of July Dr Tennyson apparently did not write to Somersby or Tealby for nearly five months, hoping his relatives would spend their time in worry and repentance over their ill-treatment of him.

When his father was not around to quarrel with, Frederick's disposition improved so immeasurably that he began considering supporting himself. While in London for medical treatment he talked about his prospects to his uncle Charles, who reported dutifully to Bayons: 'He seems to prefer the idea of being a Tutor to some Young Nobleman at Eton to going to the Bar & laments that his name was taken off the Boards as he thinks he could by those means have succeeded *in the Church*, whereas he says he has not the sort of talent necessary for the Law. He seems to think you wd not like his taking the situation of a Tutor. I said I was sure you would be far from disapproving *any* indication on his part of a desire to make himself useful in life.'[5]

At great length Frederick wrote to his grandfather, giving his own version of what had happened at Somersby ('I never expressed any desire to murder my father'),[6] protesting his innocence in his Cambridge difficulties, and stating his wish to be reconciled with both father and grandfather. When old Mr Tennyson had relented, sent him money, and invited him to feel free to come to Bayons, Frederick set off for Paris to repeat the process with his father, but when he arrived Dr Tennyson had already started for Switzerland.

With the chief troublemakers of the family away, the Rectory was a pleasant place to entertain, and the Tennysons embarked on a modest social life, welcoming their neighbours, since without horses they were confined to Somersby and the vicinity unless they were driven by friends to make overnight visits. Charles was twenty-one, Alfred twenty, and Mary and Emily were nearly nineteen and eighteen respectively. Much as they loved their family, Charles and Alfred could hardly have been satisfied without branching out further for company, for the Rectory must have seemed limited after Cambridge, apart from its sad associations with their father's troubles.

The young Tennysons were an attractive lot, all of them except Matilda exceptionally handsome, furnished with intelligence and charm, and in the country their manners were acceptable if a bit rough. Alfred in particular was much in demand, not only because he danced so well at the frequent balls around the countryside but because of his romantic appearance and his reputation in Cambridge as a promising poet.

The Rawnsleys at Halton Holgate were their particular friends, but there were also other families in that part of the county who visited Somersby and invited the young Tennysons to stay. Most of their friends were naturally of the degree of squire or parson, rather than the great titled families. There were the Heneages, the Massingberds, the Brakenburys, and the Cracrofts, scattered around the county in their pleasant big houses, and there were local gentlemen, not quite reaching the level of county gentry but highly respectable, most of them of the professional classes. Among them was a Horncastle solicitor, Henry Sellwood, son of a landed Berkshire family who had lost their money in the previous generation. Mr Sellwood had three attractive daughters, Anne, Louisa, and Emily. They were cousins of the Cracrofts of Harrington Hall, a mile or two from Somersby, where they often stayed, and their dead mother had been one of the seven sisters of Sir John Franklin, the Arctic explorer. In 1829, when the two families probably first became acquainted, Emily was a slight, pale girl of sixteen, of an age to be friendly with Mary and Emily Tennyson but probably a little too young to be of particular interest to twenty-year-old Alfred.

He had a playful, elder-brother kind of relationship with some of the younger daughters of the families he knew. Sophy Rawnsley, a lively twelve-year-old at the time, loved to dance with him, aware of the contrast between her dainty figure and that of the great dark undergraduate. He teased her and wrote poems to her, but there was not much more than that to their friendship, although some of the Rawnsleys of the next generation liked to think his affections had been deeply involved.

Indeed there is no indication that Tennyson had romantic inclinations towards any of the girls he knew at this time, but many of them were quite aware of his swarthy good looks and his interesting mind. His unconventional manners could be daunting, and one girl remembered years later that with his eye-glass he 'looked you thro' and thro' and made you feel that he was taking stock of you from head to toe'.[7] His short sight made him scrutinize faces carefully when he was interested, and he seldom bothered to explain the reason for his behaviour, which could strike fear into a shy girl. All his life Tennyson liked women and girls who would respond with spirit and humour to his brusqueness and unintentional rudeness, and he regarded as negligible those who were frightened away.

One of the great attractions of parties at Somersby was their informality. Since the house was already so crowded, guests had to share rooms in threes and fours, and the meals and the hours at which they were served were sufficiently flexible to allow for expeditions whose duration could not be accurately predicted. Long walks were the opportunity for lively discussions, and everyone used to pace endlessly around the paths of Holywell Wood, deep in talk and mild flirtation. Like many big families, the Tennysons had the gift of forgetting age, and they all took part in entertaining the guests, from the ten-year-old Horatio and the family pets to their gentle, complaisant mother, mildest of hostesses. All the children were known by nicknames, all of them admired each other inordinately and unselfconsciously.

They loved group games and there was music most evenings, with Ally singing to the harp, followed by impromptu dancing. If the night was fine, they would carry the harp out under the trees for Mary to play as the others danced, and later the tea urn was brought out as one of them recited poetry. If some of them were too excited to sleep because of the poetry or the flirtations or merely by the exhilaration of youth, Mrs Tennyson was not disapproving if they decided to walk through the night. It was a way of life, however, that did not commend itself to Charles Tennyson's family, who found the manners of Somersby lax. Once in the summer of 1829 George Hildeyard Tennyson came to stay, but there are few other records of his brothers and sisters ever visiting Somersby.

Yet the black mood that underlay so much of Alfred's personality had the power of striking at the moments when he had most reason to be content. Of these years he said, 'I remember that sometimes in the midst of the dance, a great and sudden sadness would come over me, and I would leave the dance and wander away beneath the stars, or sit on gloomily and abstractedly below stairs. I used to wonder then, what strange demon it was, that drove me forth and took all the pleasure from my blood, and made me such a churlish curmudgeon.' Many years later he claimed to know the reason: 'It was gout.'[8]

Gout? The effect would seem one that medical science has not recorded. The truth is that 'gout' was a word used loosely in the family, and now we no longer know precisely what they meant by it. In 1885 Edmund Lushington, who married Alfred's sister Cecilia, wrote of the mental disturbance and depression of his wife: 'Many complaints that formerly had different names, are now often classed under the head of gout, supprest or otherwise; Cissy is apt to consider that her ailments mainly come from gout.' In his own old age Tennyson suffered from what he called gout, which was probably much closer to the modern meaning of the term, for he had great pain and was forbidden by his physician to drink port. During his illness in 1888 he remembered his grandfather Tennyson as an old man suffering from gout, 'tho' he had never touched anything but water to drink.'[9]

What drove him forth as a young man from the dancing was probably related to the mysterious trances into which he had fallen ever since he was a boy, and which he was able to enter until the latter part of his life. Gout was a respectable name by which to recall them, but when he was a young man he had every reason to think they were connected with the epileptic fits into which he had seen his own father fall, and which had afflicted his uncle and cousin, and perhaps his brothers. They must totally have obscured the light of heaven for him when they came, until late in the 1840s when he realized that what had ruined his father's life need not be his own inheritance.

Another description of his of the same phenomenon was recorded in his old age by his daughter-in-law: 'In my youth I knew much greater unhappiness than I have known in later life. When I was about twenty, I used to feel moods of misery unutterable! I remember once in London the realization coming over me, of the *whole* of its inhabitants lying horizontal a hundred years hence. The smallness & emptiness of life sometimes overwhelmed me—. I used to experience sensations of a state almost impossible to describe in words; it was not exactly a trance but the world seemed dead around and myself only alive. It might have been the state described by St. Paul "Whether in the body I cannot tell; or whether out of the body I cannot tell." It sometimes came upon me after repeating my name to myself; through excess of realizing my own personality I seemed to get outside of myself.'[10]

Following Tennyson's own lead in old age, when he no longer had reason to be afraid of talking of his trances, one recent critic has described them as a form of transcendental meditation upon the mantra of his own name.[11] That is certainly the impression Tennyson tried to convey, and it is the burden of the famous passage in 'The Ancient Sage', in which he speaks of the experience as giving glimpses into the Nameless. What this neglects is the fact that in his youth the trances were connected not only with illumination but with misery and fear. The form of the trances was so like the epileptic seizures of his family that it is not surprising he should be terrified.

Aside from this nameless sadness that swept over him with little warning, the summer of 1829 was moderately happy, the beginning of what was to be embedded in his memory as the golden period of his youth. He never knew deep, untroubled contentment in all his years; the facility for happiness, like a good French accent, is usually learned either early in life or never at all. By the time life had done well by Tennyson it was too late for him to develop the art of serenity, but these few years from 1829 to 1833 had more moments of unrelieved happiness than any other comparable period.

During the summer of 1829 he apparently did not see Arthur Hallam, who was travelling with his father in Scotland and on the Continent. Hallam returned from Scotland miserable and ill, saying he was afraid he was going insane. He was frequently reminded of his love for Anna Wintour, but the core of his desperation was deeper than frustrated adolescent infatuation and was probably connected with the physical condition from which he died four years later.

Characteristically, Tennyson still had not written to Arthur two months after leaving Cambridge. It was hard for his friends to accept that the dearth of letters did not mean lack of affection. The rest of his life was littered with the misunderstanding of those to whose letters he sent no response, for he would claim that he needed his energy for writing poetry and that he would as soon kill a pig as write a letter. Like most of his brothers and sisters, he had an egoistic lethargy beneath the surface of his magnetism, which often manifested itself in the neglect of the feelings of his friends. The closest of them, like Hallam, understood his apparent lack of regard and were not wounded.

On his return to Cambridge Tennyson became a member of the secret club which has been associated ever since with his name. On 31 October he was elected to the group officially known as the Cambridge Conversazione Society, although it was called 'The Apostles' by both its members and outsiders. Hallam was already an Apostle, having been elected the previous May. Tennyson was proposed for membership by R. J. Tennant, but there can be little doubt that Hallam had been active in recommending Tennyson to the society. Tennyson's formal membership was not destined to last long, but the brevity of the time is no indication of the importance of the Apostles to him, since the group remained all his life the model of what such an organization should be. Many of the clubs to which he subsequently belonged owed part of their character to the example of the Apostles. The Sterling Club, the Cosmopolitan Club, the Metaphysical Society, and even the London Library, of which he was President at his death, have all been claimed as offspring of the Apostles.

The society was founded in 1820 but did not flourish until about 1824, when it was given great impetus by two young members, Frederick Denison Maurice and John Sterling. It began as a group devoted to the discussion of serious philosophical subjects that did not fit easily into the prescribed studies of the University. Politics, science, poetry, aesthetics, metaphysics, and religion all came within the scope of their talk. Under the leadership of Maurice, who left Cambridge the year Tennyson arrived, it had established an elevated, rather solemn level of discourse, one at variance on occasion with the natural high spirits of undergraduates. Because of its secrecy the society attracted some hostility, and its apparent snobbishness in restricting its usual membership to about a dozen prompted its nickname, a word with double significance, since in Cambridge slang 'Apostles' referred also to the twelve men with lowest standing on the list of bachelors of arts.

Like most undergraduates the Apostles delighted in the envy of their fellows and happily accepted the nickname, choosing to recognize only the sense in which it referred to their superior and exclusive status. The group had originally had its centre in St. John's, but it had gradually shifted to Trinity, until by Tennyson's time there were few members outside his college. Theoretically, the Apostles were chosen for their outstanding minds and personalities, and it was not surprising that they should regard themselves as the top of the heap in Cambridge, belonging, as they did, to the most exclusive set in the most exclusive college in what they thought of as the only existing university (to indicate their opinion of any rival institution, they habitually spelt its elder sister 'oxford'). Most of the assumed superiority was simply high spirits, but there was also a residue of real feeling that they were Tritons among the minnows. It was heady, perhaps too much so, for a man who had hardly been out of the centre of Lincolnshire before coming to Cambridge. Such was the prestige of being an Apostle that Thackeray said it was considered, when he first came up to Trinity, to set a man apart to be seen in the company of William Brookfield, who was not an Apostle himself but was on intimate terms with several.

To be elected to the Apostles a man had to be known personally to each of them and approved by all. In practice this meant that those who knew him least might satisfy themselves as to his clubbability by a call on him in his rooms. There were men in Trinity who were never invited to become Apostles who were far more distinguished in later life than some of the members. Thackeray, for example, and Edward FitzGerald were both in the college in Tennyson's time but were not asked to join. This period was the high-water mark of the society, for practically all the members of the time became at least sufficiently distinguished to be included in the *Dictionary of National Biography*. There have been several tight-lipped assertions that it was not really such a splendid company, since it included only one authentic genius while the rest became no more than well-known writers, editors, scholars, archbishops, deans, and even simple parish clergymen. True, but it would be difficult to find another undergraduate club of so few members, during the whole nineteenth century, which rose to such a level of achievement. Were it not for Tennyson the group of 1829–31 would not be famous, but it was a circle of considerable distinction even so. The individual Apostles took the honour of membership so seriously that James Spedding suggested that Wordsworth and Hartley Coleridge were both such impressive men that they deserved to have been members.

John Kemble wrote reminiscently of his own years with the Apostles: 'To my *education* given in that society I feel that I owe every power I possess, and the rescuing myself from a ridiculous state of prejudice and prepossessions with which I came armed to Cambridge. From "the Apostles" I, at least, learned to think as a *free man*.'[12] With some justice the members referred to themselves as 'the wise society'.

There was a new spirit moving among them, which did not neglect the seriousness of which Kemble wrote but took cognizance of other parts of man's nature. Tennyson's election was an apt symbol of the change. The subjects they discussed in his day were much the same as those that Maurice and Sterling had considered, but there was now an insistence on pleasure as well as edification in the essays that were read. No one who knew him could have mistaken Tennyson for a man of profoundly philosophical mind, and it is certain that he was elected because of his quirky humour, quiet companionability, and great poetic promise, rather than for the intellectual distinction that Maurice thought the Society should foster. Probably without such a change the Apostles were in danger of priggishness.

Even better proof of the alterations in the society was the election on the same day as Tennyson of Richard Monckton Milnes, afterwards Lord Houghton. He had a passion for poetry, at which he was mediocre, and for intellectual discussion, in which he was not out-standing, but he also had great talent for talking so wittily that he was known as the Bird of Paradox, and a positive genius for acquaintance. Intimacy with him was apt to produce disappointment, but there were few who could initially resist his good-natured Italianate face, sadly lacking in chin but shining with enthusiasm, or the affection with which he would throw his arms around the embarrassed neck of any of his 500 most intimate friends. When Tennyson first saw him, he thought Milnes looked the best-tempered creature he had ever seen and asked to meet him. At the beginning of 1830 J. W. Blakesley sent Richard Chenevix Trench news of Cambridge: 'Milnes is now an Apostle. The Society doth not, I think, gain much from him, but he will leave Cambridge in a few weeks. . . . The Society has received a great addition in Hallam and in Alfred Tennyson . . . truly one of the mighty of the earth. You will be delighted with him when you see him.'[13] Although they remained friendly all their lives, Tennyson and Milnes were poles apart temperamentally. On any subject they discussed, Milnes skated blithely and gracefully over the ice through which Tennyson was always breaking into ankle-deep waters.

The Apostles met formally on Saturday evenings after hall, nor-mally in the rooms of the man whose turn it was to give a paper on a subject of his own proposal. In theory no outsider knew about the meetings, but it was easy to guess what was happening when the same group of a dozen men disappeared each Saturday night into the rooms of one of them, slamming the outer door behind them. Once they were assembled, even the inner door was locked to preserve the privacy in which they could talk in unbuttoned freedom with no fear of being reported abroad. To the same end, only the sketchiest of minutes were kept of the meetings, chiefly the topic discussed, the speaker, and the division on the vote afterwards.

No wine was allowed, for fear of muddying the crystalline tenor of the talk, but the members consumed prodigious amounts of food, of which two unvarying items were coffee and anchovy sandwiches, perhaps inevitably known as 'whales'. The host (or moderator) delivered his paper with his back to the fire and the rest of the company spread out before him in a semicircle, a lucky few on chairs and sofas, the others lounging on the floor. No wine, but the air would be thick from their pipes, the dreadful shag that Tennyson used cutting an acrid way through the rest of the smoke.

Tennyson loved the society of other men, but community discussion never came easily for him. The accounts of his talk in company in later years fall almost entirely into two rigid categories: either he would take the lead and keep the conversation on poetry and his own attitudes about religion, topics where he felt safe from contradiction, or he would lapse into silence as others tossed the conversational ball, interjecting little but the curtest of grunted remarks. With the Apostles he took the latter course, for he did not have the logical kind of mind to develop an argument in the give-and-take of discussion. From behind the clouds of shag he would listen to papers with such titles as the one given by Hallam on 5 December 1829, 'Whether the existence of an intelligent first cause is deducible from the phenomena of the Universe', or another, 'Whether the poems of Shelley have an immoral tendency'. (Hallam and Tennyson voted no to both questions.) In the ensuing discussion Tennyson listened intently but said little.

Even in this friendliest of environments Tennyson could not overcome his innate shyness nor could he put enough of himself at risk to say directly what he thought on a question of which he was not master. He belonged to several clubs in later life, but he never learned the easy exchange that was their excuse, and he eventually drifted out of them. Rather ominously, he was fined five shillings for non-attendance the week after he had been elected to the Apostles. In all he attended but five meetings of the society.

On 13 February 1830 it was Tennyson's turn to act as moderator, and he had proposed to speak on 'Ghosts', but he was so nervous that he tore up most of what he had written and threw it on the fire. When the other members arrived in his rooms he resigned his place in the society.

Tennyson believed that he had given up very little by formally leaving the Apostles, but he might have learned a great deal if he had persevered. The discussion had never been the most important part of the society to him, for what had mattered was the intimacy and love to which he had been admitted, and that continued without diminution. After his resignation he still spent practically all his time with the Apostles, over wine, at meals, in and out of their rooms, all shouting at each other as they walked beside the windy Cam. He was still consulted about new members, and he remained so close to the Apostles that many of them thought they vaguely remembered his having been made an honorary member, allowed to attend meetings without the necessity of reading a paper. In fact it was not until 1855 that Fenton Hort wrote on behalf of the society to say that Tennyson had been elected an honorary member. Normally he would have been elected immediately upon leaving the University, but there was a mythical understanding that no one could be re-elected who had not written at least three essays. When it was found that this was not true, F. D. Maurice proposed his name and he was duly taken back into the society. By then, of course, it mattered little to him, and he seems never to have attended the annual dinners for past and present members.

What might have been the most valuable contribution the Apostles could make to Tennyson's education was their new-found insistence on wit and on trying to take one's self, but not others, lightly. Aubrey de Vere, who went up to Cambridge ten years after Tennyson, found the Apostles more concerned with word-fencing and love of paradox than he liked. They were, he said, 'the opposite of the grave and courteous Doctors of Oxford. They are full of "Irony" and have a manner of playing with Theories and putting Thoughts into a fanciful combination and making them go through evolutions like troops at a review. It is very amusing, though Newman would say that the amusement was sometimes "not less than profane." ' It would be idle to pretend that their profane amusement turned Tennyson into a wit, but it probably helped to leaven a certain native solemnity in his nature. One of the more earnest members of the society, Thomas Sunderland, lamented the frivolity of the others and complained to Milnes, most sociable of that sociable company, 'We really must introduce someone among them who is not so vulgarly gregarious as the larger portion of our worthy brother Apostles.'[14] Even Milnes could not find a suitable reply to that remark.

It would not be worth insisting on the exuberance of the young were it not that some critics like Harold Nicolson, writing out of 'inevitable dislike of the Apostles', have tried to make them into a prim band of Nonconformist divines contemplating the rest of the world in narrow-eyed disapproval. They were undoubtedly more accurately described in a letter from Tennant to Tennyson, after he had left the society, telling him about a dinner at which Tennyson's health was drunk: 'Edmund Lushington & I went away tolerably early but most of them stayed till past two: John Heath volunteered a song, Kemble got into a passion about nothing but quickly jumped out again, Blakesley was afraid the Proctors might come in, & Thompson poured huge quantities of salt upon Douglas Heath's head, because he talked nonsense.'[15] In short, undergraduates behaved like undergraduates, mixing their solemnity and frivolity without worrying unduly about the categories.

Comradeship was the cornerstone of the society, which took as its guide the definition of friendship by St. Augustine: 'To talk and laugh with mutual concessions, to read pleasant books; to jest and to be solemn, to dissent from each other without offence, to teach one another somewhat, or somewhat to learn—to expect those absent with impatience and embrace their return with joy.'[16] Above all they had the grace to assume the best of each other. Like all closely-knit groups they developed their own 'little language', with such terms as 'Stumpfs' for the Philistines of their acquaintance and 'pill' for humbug. They were generous in lending each other money in their inevitable financial scrapes, and even after leaving the University they were expected to continue an active interest in the society as honorary members, supporting each other in their claims for public attention as they had helped one another as undergraduates.

Inevitably, in such an intimate society, individuals began taking on specific roles. The acknowledged father of them all was James Spedding, whom Tennyson called the 'Pope'. Calm, judicious, and loving, he listened to the others without intruding his own personality. He was a born scholar, hesitant between an academic and a clerical career, to the dismay of his father, a wealthy landowner in Cumberland who thought he should be interested in public life. The delicate modelling of his mouth and chin made him a handsome man, but since his schooldays in King's Lynn he had been nearly bald, with a great domed forehead that the other Apostles insisted had often been mistaken by the Navy for Beachy Head and given a full salute. It was a forehead that inevitably attracted the wonder of phrenologists, and one amateur said 'that all his bumps were so tempered that there was no merit in his sobriety. . .'.[17] Spedding's loves were the works of Bacon and the florid operas in which Jenny Lind was later to make her name. It was his enviable ability to give himself totally to his friends, then to enter single-mindedly into the studies that made him a great editor of Bacon after he left the University. Next to Hallam he was Tennyson's closest friend.

Hallam rapidly took upon himself the role of intellectual centre of the society, since his curiosity ranged so widely. He had developed the ability to read so quickly that he seemed to get through more books than all the others and still have time to stimulate the questionings of his friends. To them he seemed the natural successor to Maurice.

Tennyson's role is shown by the way that he was immediately adopted informally by the society after he had resigned from it. Improbable as his size and presence might make it seem, he was essentially the pet of the others, to be indulgently and affectionately pampered in his disregard of the conventions and prescribed studies of the University. To their credit, it should be noted that the Apostles decided early that he was a poetic genius and that it was their duty to foster him. Part of their feeling may have stemmed from pride in one of their own, but certainly part was real recognition of his promise, and they spread his fame in every way they could.

One quirk of his character they were careful to indulge. Then, as for the remainder of his life, he was inordinately sensitive to adverse criticism, either of himself or of his poetry, which he thought of as inseparable. They listened closely as he read, or more often recited, his new poems, usually praising him but remaining silent when they could not do so. They also took upon themselves the burden of getting Tennyson to write down his poems, since he hated to record them after composing them in his head. He said he preferred to roll them around to himself before committing them to a more final form, but much of his reluctance was simple indolence; he used to say that thousands of lines had blown away with the fumes of his pipe. Once he was sitting smoking with his feet on the chimney-piece as he spouted 'The Lotos-Eaters' in its first form; unknown to him, Hallam darted around to a table behind him and took it all down as fast as he could to rescue it from oblivion.

The effect of the Apostles upon Tennyson was double-edged. There is no doubt that he desperately needed the calm confidence and affection they gave him, so unlike the turbulence of Somersby when Dr Tennyson was at his most disturbed. But it is also true that their spoiling of him confirmed his natural inclination to feel that others owed him more than he owed them. It is not only a puritanical feeling about his responsibility that makes one wish he had been forced to pay more attention to the sensitivities of others, for it is essentially his lack of understanding of the motivation of men unlike himself that is at the heart of the failure of almost all his poems in which he tried to create the consciousness of a mind that was not a carbon copy of his own.

In assessing his relations with others, one must add the physical limitations of Tennyson's sight to the pampering of the Apostles. By the time he was in the University he customarily read only with a monocle or reading-glasses, with the book held close to the end of his nose. He used the monocle habitually at meals and was unable to see to eat without it. For looking at things in the distance he had another pair of spectacles, but it was impossible to compensate totally for his myopia, and to the end of his days he was never able to see clearly the stars at which he stared for hours at a time, trying to pierce beyond the concentric rings he saw to an accurate perception of their appearance. It is obvious in his poetry that what he knew best was the minute examination of forms, such as the flowers or leaves that he peered at by throwing himself on the ground and thrusting his face into them. Against that must be set the evocation of enormous misty distances, of the blank loneliness of sea and sky that fascinated him and that so often furnished him with the similes for dimly perceived abstractions, for the capitalized words like Immutability or Immensity or Unknowable. In his poetry there is little middle distance, and that includes the accurate perception of persons. Tennyson never really saw the play of emotion on the face of other men, nor could he perceive minute changes of expression, so that it is no wonder his characterization in the narrative and dramatic poems is often unsubtle.

It has been commonly noted that both the deaf and the blind are apt to become defensive, even withdrawn, and that they may believe that others are secretly communicating without their knowledge. Tennyson's insistence on taking the lead in conversation or, conversely, his retreat from participation in it, can be partly blamed on his inability to see clearly those with whom he was talking, for he was cut off from half of normal communication. His vocation as poet and his attention to verbal detail are natural concomitants of the partial loss of communication through sight, and his insistence that friendships exist on his own terms was the inevitable result of being unable to participate in the normal intercourse of others. In his case his basic personality was combined with his physical disability to produce a particularly painful form of self-awareness and introspection that dogged him all his life. By their kindness to him and indulgence of his temperament, the other Apostles succeeded only in confirming a habit of mind that would better have been eradicated.

Of all the Apostles it was Hallam who was closest to him and who was generally regarded by the others as his especial friend. The intimacy of their connection has given rise to a good deal of speculation about its exact nature and considerable unexamined assumption that it was sexually abnormal, so that it is perhaps necessary to turn briefly to the subject.

It has been the tendency in post-Freudian times to look at such matters in an increasingly unsubtle fashion and to fasten categorical labels that are inexact at best. Love is described as either homosexual or heterosexual with little awareness that it may consist of a good deal that defies those categories. Sexual feelings may be the most common stimulus to love, but even in relationships that are deeply sexual there are many other factors that have little to do with sex. Sympathy, companionship, likeness of interests, and even habitual proximity often form a great part of love, although they are not obviously sexual in prompting. It was surely these feelings that were at the heart of Tennyson's friendship with Hallam.

Love would be the more exact word to describe their relationship, since such deep affection has no other proper name, were it not that for the prurient it sometimes carries the wrong connotation. Perhaps all relations have at least a slight element of sexual awareness, and it is probable that Tennyson's regard for Hallam had more of that than he would have wanted to admit, even to himself. For his part, Hallam was deeply heterosexual, and there is little evidence that he ever felt anything more than a brotherly affection for Tennyson (if even fraternal love can be described as harmless today).

In the pre-lapsarian innocence of the Apostles such affection could be more openly expressed because there was little fear that it was only the skin over an unperceived gulf. Tennyson's brother-in-law, Edmund Lushington, wrote to Hallam Tennyson at the time of Tennyson's death to say that in a dream he had kissed Tennyson when they were walking. There is no suggestion that such displays of affection ever took place in the waking state, but Lushington's frankness surely indicates how little sexual store he set by the dream. It is in this context that one must put Tennyson's remark to James Knowles when they were discussing *In Memoriam*, CXXII, which begins, 'Oh, wast thou with me, dearest, then'. In denying the literal parallel to his relations with Hallam, Tennyson said, 'If anybody thinks I ever called him "dearest" in his life they are much mistaken, for I never even called him "dear".'[18] The bluff openness is surely evidence of his lack of self-consciousness about the matter, which would not have been true had he been aware of having sexual feelings for Hallam.

But, some critics would say, wanting to have it both ways, his lack of awareness is the final proof of how deeply sexual his feelings were, since he had to deny them to himself. Possibly, but there can be no discussion in the face of such a claim. What seems nearest the truth when all the evidence is examined is that Tennyson was not a deeply sexual man, and that his emotional needs at Cambridge were largely fulfilled by his friendship with Hallam, probably making the love of a woman less necessary for him than it would otherwise have been. A qualified answer, but more accurate than a label of either total heterosexuality or complete homosexuality. James Spedding once told W. B. Donne that his circle knew more of the 'darker passions' from Shakespeare, Scott, and Byron than from life: 'as for anything more, we are as innocent as lambs unborn'.[19] The reference was presumably to heterosexual matters, but it might stand as a description of Tennyson's total sexual experience at the time.

The pairing of friends such as Hallam and Tennyson was both common in the Apostles and perfectly open. Mrs Brookfield wrote of the group: 'most of them chose out of their number one to be his bosom friend, and kept him through all times and changes, troubles and vicissitudes—always generously submitting his will, always unselfishly helping his needs'.[20] As Maurice and Sterling had been each other's closest friends at an earlier date, so Kemble and Donne, Robert Monteith and Francis Garden, G. S. Venables and Henry Lushington, all found a special friendship within the larger group, one to give a centre to their affections.

Such deep but frank feelings were by no means confined to the Apostles. Edward FitzGerald's affection for John Allen was so intense that one of Allen's family wrote that 'since Jonathan no man ever loved another with a purer or more loyal devotion than that with which his dearest friend loved him'. Allen himself felt a jealous affection for Henry Alford, FitzGerald described his college friendships as more like loves, and Thackeray remembered Cambridge with a sigh: 'What *passions* our friendships were.'[21]

At this distance all the insistence upon passion seems a little hectic, and no doubt at times it became dangerously intense. The historian of the Apostles has said that George Venables was deeply in love with Henry Lushington and was even jealous of Tennyson's friendship with him. It is certainly probable that Milnes had some homosexual experience at Cambridge, and in later life he had an interest in pederasty so intense that it is difficult to believe it was only speculative. Some sense of this lay behind Hallam's apparently ungracious rejection of special friendship with Milnes in July 1831: 'I am not aware . . . that, in that lofty sense which you are accustomed to attach to the name of Friendship, we ever were or ever could be friends. . . . That exalted sentiment I do not ridicule—God forbid—nor consider it as merely ideal: I have experienced it, and it thrills within me now—but not—pardon me, my dear Milnes, for speaking frankly—not for you.'[22] It is the admonitory tone of Mother Hallam of Eton, but perhaps forgivable in its priggishness if Hallam was worried about the exact nature of Milnes's proffered affection. Hallam's friendship with Tennyson was sufficient to engage one part of his nature, and by the time of the letter to Milnes Hallam had already formed another attachment that was proof of how little apt he was to enter into a homosexual relationship.

CHAPTER VII

HALLAM AT SOMERSBY AND *POEMS, CHIEFLY LYRICAL*, 1829–1830

AT the end of November 1829, in the last weeks of the Michaelmas term, Hallam, accompanied by Milnes and Sunderland (who had complained to Milnes of the deplorable gregariousness of the Apostles), set out through the snow for Oxford as representatives of the Cambridge Union, to debate with their Oxford counterparts on whether Byron or Shelley was the greater poet. Gladstone and Francis Doyle, another of Hallam's Eton friends, had issued the invitation. The plan had presumably been cooked up by Gladstone and Hallam in October, when they spent some time together in Malvern and Oxford before the beginning of term.

Indirectly it was probably Tennyson's influence that had brought up the name of Shelley, whose reputation was still slight. Before going to Cambridge he and Frederick and Charles had learned to love Shelley's poems, and he had talked a great deal to Hallam of his enthusiasm, which may finally have accounted for the proposed subject of debate. Curiously, the Cantabrigians were to uphold the Oxford Shelley, and the Oxonians to defend Byron of Trinity.

Another reason lay behind the trip. Gladstone was aware of how quickly Hallam had transferred to Tennyson the affection that had once been his. Three months before the debate he had sadly put down in his diary the disappointing progress of his friendship with Hallam, from the time that Arthur sought him out at Eton in 1827 until the present, when it seemed to be crumbling away under the joint stress of their absence from each other and Hallam's new friendship with Tennyson. It had always been an up-and-down business, and by September 1829 Gladstone felt painfully uncertain whether he could even call Hallam a friend. In an effort to repair the breach he went to Malvern to see Hallam, and then invited him to Oxford before he returned to Cambridge. Hallam had spent four days with Gladstone, but he talked much of the time of Tennyson and read 'Timbuctoo' over and over to Gladstone, who had trouble understanding it. At last Gladstone agreed that he liked the poem immensely, but the visit had not been a total success. The Shelley–Byron debate was another opportunity to restore the old intimacy with Hallam.

Milnes had applied to the Master of Trinity, Christopher Wordsworth, for an exeat for the three men, since term was not yet over. Later he admitted drolly that he thought it was possible that he had substituted William Wordsworth's name for Shelley's in order to get the Master's permission. The conversation in the chaise to Oxford must have been amusing, with Sunderland talking of the necessity for less Apostolic levity and gregariousness to Hallam and the ebullient Milnes, possibly even referring to Tennyson, with whom he shared a mutual antipathy. One of Tennyson's few satirical poems was 'A Character', in which he described Sunderland anonymously, touching on his speaking style and arrogant manner:

> . . . with a sweeping of the arm,
> And a lack-lustre dead-blue eye,
> Devolved his rounded periods.
>   . . .
> With lips depressed as he were meek,
> Himself to himself he sold:
> Upon himself himself did feed:
> Quiet, dispassionate, and cold.

When Sunderland learned of Tennyson's unflattering portrait, he said in his most supercilious manner, 'I hear that one of the Tennysons has been writing a Poem about me. Which was it? The one in the dirtiest shirt?' Edward FitzGerald called him 'a very plausible, Parliament-like, & self-satisfied Speaker at the Union Debating Society',[1] but Sunderland was generally accounted the most brilliant of the debaters then at Cambridge. Hallam thought little of the style of the Oxford speakers, but one of them, Henry Manning, reacted vividly to Sunderland: 'Both . . . Milnes and . . . Hallam took us aback by the boldness and freedom of their manner. But I remember the effect of Sunderland's declaration and action to this day. It had never been seen or heard before among us; we cowered like birds, and ran like sheep. . . . I acknowledge that we were utterly routed.'[2]

Afterwards Milnes liked to pretend that there was an unfortunate misunderstanding on the part of the Oxford speakers, who had never heard of their own Shelley and hence had debated under the delusion that Shenstone's was the name in question. Even sweeter was Hallam's knowledge that among the Shelley poems they had quoted were a few by Tennyson that had been slipped in by William Brookfield before they left Cambridge, and that none of their opponents had noticed. Good reason to deny oxford its capital letter. Despite Manning's tribute to their speaking the Cambridge men were outvoted in the division, but they felt that theirs had been a victory since they had at least brought some culture to the wilds of oxfordshire. To some of their friends they seemed less successful. John Spedding wrote to his brother James to ask, 'How goes on the Union. I heard their orators made a shitten piece of business of it at Oxford.'[3]

Hallam spent a good deal of the day and a half in Oxford with Gladstone, and their breach was patched over at least temporarily. None the less it was Tennyson to whom he was returning in Cambridge, and it was Tennyson whom he invited to his home immediately after the end of term.

Alfred and Charles Tennyson went to London with Hallam, where he introduced them to his Eton friends down from Oxford. Francis Doyle wrote of the two young men from Lincolnshire: 'Alfred Tennyson I like but to use their own cant . . . he is a strange form of Being. Charles is a nice fellow too and by no means one of the set.'[4]

The short visit to his aunt Russell in the summer of 1827 had been Tennyson's first trip to London, but then he had not seen much of its glitter. In this stay with Hallam he was seeing for the first time the world in which his new friend normally lived, and he found it exhilarating. He discovered the great city and the fascination of its 'central roar'. One of the most exciting of their doings was a theatre party to see Fanny Kemble, the young sister of their Apostolic friend, Jack Kemble, who was making a sensation at the beginning of her acting career. They fell collectively under her spell. Tennyson can hardly have attended the theatre before this, except in Cambridge and Lincoln, but he loved it thereafter with some disadvantageous results.

The Tennysons and Hallam went back to Cambridge for a short time to hear a debate on Milton at the Union, then set out for Lincolnshire. On 20 December they arrived at Somersby for what was to be Hallam's first visit to the Rectory. He stayed for only a few days before returning to London for Christmas, but the visit was a momentous one, for there he met, among the other members of the family, Alfred's eighteen-year-old sister Emily, who was just seven months younger than Hallam.[5]

Although her family and friends called her Emily, the second daughter of the family had been christened Emilia, a name suitable to her dark Latin beauty which was just maturing into rivalry with that of her startlingly beautiful sister Mary. 'Testa Romana', one admiring Italian said of her chiselled profile and big dark eyes, luminous with 'depths on depths'.

Hallam was not a conventionally handsome young man, in spite of a noble forehead with a broad bar of frontal bone, of which he had once said as he came into Tennyson's Cambridge rooms, passing his fingers across his brow, 'Alfred, I've got the real "bar" of Michael Angelo.' His circulatory problems, which included high blood pressure, made his colour so pronounced that it was described by one disbeliever in the Hallam legend as 'beery', but the intensity of his brilliant blue eyes and the splendid carriage of his well-shaped head gave him great presence beyond conventional good looks. With beatification apparently in mind, Fanny Kemble wrote of him after his death: 'There was a gentleness and purity almost virginal in his voice, manner, and countenance; and the upper part of his face, his forehead and eyes (perhaps in readiness for his early translation) wore the angelic radiance they still must wear in heaven.'[6] What she tactfully did not mention was one of the most striking features of his portraits, a narrow, ungenerous mouth beneath a sharp nose, which almost succeeds in cancelling the radiance of the upper part of his face. If physiognomy is a clue to character, one might feel that his mouth pointed to the teasing, not altogether pleasant quality of his later relations with Emily.

Hallam was to keep 20 December, when he first met Emily, as 'a saint's day'. Family tradition had it that the first day of his stay at Somersby was sufficiently mild for him and Alfred to play in the garden with Billy, Mrs Tennyson's monkey. He was so delighted with the younger Tennysons that Matilda said forty years later they 'were all in love with him from the first'.[7] Dr Tennyson was still in France, and the Rectory was breathing easily in the absence of family quarrels. Hallam seems to have fallen in love at once, but with the whole family rather than with a particular member. Certainly he had never known at home any of the informal atmosphere that Mrs Tennyson's casual warmth created so easily, nor had his own family been so loving, impetuous, and endearingly odd as the Tennysons *en masse*.

Like most lovers he later thought, or claimed to think, that he had fallen in love with Emily almost at once, but there was no overt recognition between them. On writing for her twenty-first birthday in October 1832 he remembered fondly: 'It is now near three years since you arose upon my life, like a star. At first the beams were clear, but distant . . .'[8] They had little time to be anything but distant, since Arthur spent only three or four days in Somersby before returning to London for Christmas; it was not until the next year that they were to make declarations to each other on the yellow sofa in the Rectory drawing-room. In the meantime Arthur went about the pursuits of a sociable young man in London, apparently having forgotten Anna Wintour in the pleasures of the season and the acquaintance of a number of young ladies. Among these was Fanny Kemble, to whom he wrote some ecstatic sonnets in the initial flush of his enthusiasm, but it is unlikely that there was more than that to the affair, for Fanny Kemble's later correspondence shows that she was infinitely more interested in Alfred Tennyson than in his apparently conventional friend Hallam. (Tennyson admired her in return, and they were friends all his life, but he paid little more serious attention to her than she did to Hallam.) Since Hallam's love for Anna was dead, and since not being in love was a state that he found highly uncongenial, he continued in his poetic devotions to Fanny Kemble until his next visit to Somersby. From his poems to Fanny and his letters to Emily it would be easy to conclude that they were twin stars, but it is doubtful that he felt seriously about either until April 1830. All his social activity in London made him ill once more, and he had to return to Cambridge. His friend Blakesley wrote to Tennyson that Hallam had been 'submitting himself to the influences of the outer world more than (I think) a man of his genius ought to do'.

Blakesley had difficulty in getting Tennyson's address because the Apostles professed to disbelieve in the existence of Lincolnshire. 'To be sure,' he wrote, 'Spedding informed me that a letter directed to Mount Caucasus would be sure to reach you, but altho' I had full faith in the fact, the extraordinary postage which Sir Francis Freeling demands on letters sent thither somewhat staggered me.' It was by now openly known that Tennyson was considering publishing another volume of poetry, and that when he had sufficiently overcome his lethargy he would begin assembling it. Like the other Apostles, Blakesley was worried that he might never get around to the matter at hand. 'I trust that you have taken advantage of the inspiration derived from seeing Miss Kemble and the leisure afforded by the vacation to ingratiate yourself yet more with the Muses, and it is the earnest wish of me and all the rest of your friends, that you will desist from flirting with each of them alternately, and declare at once what your intentions are to some one of them.'[9]

This time Tennyson intended to publish under his own name, and the other Apostles assumed that he would be the sole author of the volume. He was, however, preparing another joint publication like *Poems by Two Brothers*, but the co-author was to be one who was already closer than a brother: Arthur Hallam. In later life Tennyson admitted that Hallam's genius was not essentially poetic, but he had such admiration for him that he seems at the time to have thought that he was his own equal in poetic talent. We must believe that he genuinely thought so, for one thing on which he would not budge an inch in all his long life was his poetic integrity. He was ruthless on some of his own poems, refusing to publish them until they seemed to him worthy of public notice, and it is a certainty that he would not have considered publishing with Hallam out of mere friendship without believing that Arthur's poems were first-rate. Blinded by affection he may have been, but he was sincere. Nowadays, few readers would agree with him about the quality of Hallam's poetry.

Charles Tennyson was also preparing poems for publication, assuming that once more they would appear with his brother's, but Alfred told him that he did not want a third. Milnes, too, asked to publish jointly with Tennyson and Hallam, but Arthur frightened him off by telling him of Alfred's refusal to Charles.

At last the arrangements were complete for the publication of the new volume by Effingham Wilson. 'In Alfred's mind,' wrote Kemble to Trench, 'the materials of the very greatest works are heaped in an abundance which is almost confusion. . . . [He] and Hallam are about to edit their poems conjointly. One day these men will be great indeed.'[10]

It is no longer clear why Effingham Wilson undertook the book. Tennyson was co-author of *Poems by Two Brothers*, and he had won a modest local fame at Cambridge for 'Timbuctoo', which was published with earlier prize-winning poems, but these facts do not explain why a publisher should wish to undertake the poems of an almost unknown young man. A copy of a letter from Hallam to Tennyson, now in the Tennyson Research Centre, indicates that Wilson sent Tennyson a bill for £11, which Hallam said was a mistake and told

Tennyson not to pay. 'Take no step yourself. Leave it to Moxon, Tennant, Heath & myself.'[11] This suggests that Hallam and perhaps others had guaranteed the publication costs. Mrs Brookfield wrote that Arthur Hallam was responsible for finding the publisher in the first place.[12] He had unquestioning admiration for Alfred's poetry and probably first suggested that he publish his poems; he may then have been invited by Tennyson to publish jointly with him.

The plans behind publication remain obscure, but by the winter term they were so advanced that Tennyson was writing out his poems, as Blakesley had urged him to do. Some of them came from his own copies, some from those taken down and surreptitiously circulated by the Apostles, and some of them certainly out of his own head, where they had been rolling around since first he thought of them.

In April 1830 Tennyson once more took Arthur Hallam with him to Somersby, for the Easter vacation. By now letters from Dr Tennyson were arriving at the Rectory, but he had not yet mentioned coming back to England and the atmosphere was as pleasant as it had been during Hallam's visit in December. This time he had come for a much longer stay, with the idea that he and Alfred would be working on their joint volume of poetry. So far as Arthur was concerned, something of far greater moment happened: the beams of affection that had seemed 'clear, but distant' at Christmas suddenly came from heaven to earth. A year and a half later he wrote to Emily of the moment when their love was first brought home to him with full force, as he walked in Holywell Wood and suddenly came upon her. His letter concerned *Undine*, of which he had given her a copy: 'Cannot you indeed find any one like her in the world? So I thought for a good many years; but one fine spring I came to a wooded glen among wolds, where I saw a being more like Undine than I had ever thought to see. She was not indeed so frolicsome; she had neither blue eyes, nor was she a "wonder-fair blonde" as the German original calls Undine: but the soul of the creature I speak of had something Undinish, to my fancy.'[13]

Hallam's infatuation with Anna Wintour and his admiration for Fanny Kemble had further sensitized his already quick emotions, so that he was ready to fall in love, and his deep affection for Alfred had predisposed him to choose one of the daughter of the Rectory. It is not certain whether he declared his love on the spot to the Undine of Holywell Wood, but his natural impulse would have been to tell Alfred at once what had happened, thus knitting still more tightly the bond of their friendship.

During the nearly three weeks that Hallam spent at Somersby the Tennysons gave parties to introduce him to the neighbourhood. On one occasion the guests included Emily Sellwood, who was making her first overnight visit to Somersby. In the evening after dinner they all played at capping verses. Sixty-five years later Emily remembered that they had played at 'The Emperor of Morocco is Dead', and that 'Arthur Hallam was pleased with me because I went through the trying story between my two big candles with so much gravity'. Tennyson must have noticed Hallam's pleasure at the Horncastle visitor, although any reactions of his own have not been preserved.

The next morning some of the party were walking in Holywell Wood, and Hallam was accompanying Emily Sellwood. Suddenly Tennyson made his appearance wrapped in a long blue cloak. As he looked at Emily, who was wearing a light blue dress, he asked, 'Are you a dryad or a Naiad or what are you?' It was a greeting that Emily never forgot, and she fell in love on the spot.

Tennyson's feelings are harder to assess. What is striking about their meeting is that it was so precisely like that of Arthur Hallam and Emily Tennyson a few days before: the same setting in the little wood like a classical grove on its stream behind the Rectory; the comparisons of the two girls to spirits of the wood and water; not least the identity of their names. Love, or the thought of love, is notoriously contagious, and it seems evident that Alfred was unconsciously imitating what had happened to his friend. Emily Sellwood was undoubtedly attractive to him, but Arthur still fulfilled many of his emotional needs, and there is no evidence that Alfred even flirted with Emily Sellwood beyond the words that she remembered so clearly.

Emily ever afterwards recalled each detail of his appearance, which was 'magnificent, kingly with his masses of fine wavy hair, almost black with gold streaks, as was then worn'. His face she thought 'Elizabethan', 'his eyes long and dark, having a languid light . . . His nose aquiline . . . his skin soft as a woman's. His foot under which a stream could pass. . . . His smile, most beautiful.' In short, he seemed to her 'a mysterious being lifted high above other mortals'.[14] The only drawback was that he apparently paid little more attention to her than he did to the young sisters of his Lincolnshire friends.

It was perhaps at the same party that Emily Sellwood's younger sister Anne sketched Tennyson and Hallam, taking a much less flattering look at them both than did Emily. Even allowing for her inadequacies with the pencil, one can see that Anne viewed them as mortals not gods. The sketch of Hallam must have been a good likeness, for it hung over Tennyson's fireplace the rest of his life; the original was unfortunately spoiled by the heavy outlines drawn on it at a later date, probably when Hallam Tennyson was using it as an illustration for *Tennyson and His Friends*. (See Plate III).

Tennyson's poems for the new volume were all copied out before the end of the vacation, but one night returning home by foot from Spilsby he dropped the entire manuscript out of the pocket of his greatcoat, and it was never recovered. Most poets would have been in despair, but Tennyson was able to reconstruct the whole book from his memory. His practice of working the poems over in his head paid off, for they were so engrained that 'the invisible ink was made to reappear, all the thoughts and fancies in their orderly series'. Years later he told Carlyle of the experience and asked how he had felt when the manuscript of the *French Revolution* had been burned. 'Well,' replied Carlyle, 'I just felt like a man swimming without water.'

In the early spring of 1830 Charles's little volume of *Sonnets and Fugitive Pieces* was published. Many of the poems in it are charming if slightly pastel in effect; the response to them seemed encouraging after the reception of *Poems by Two Brothers*, which had received only two reviews. Coleridge compared Charles to Wordsworth and Southey, and Spedding reported a droll letter in which Charles said he was 'inspired with profound respect for the Lake Poets by hearing the judgment of Wordsworth & Southey on his poems'. It was typical of Charles to take his praise so lightly. From Trinity Spedding wrote to his brother to 'proclaim C. Tennyson's praises boldly, for he has been praised by a Doctor of Divinity. The Master sent for him the other day and complimented him till he could hardly stand, and did actually drop his glove—upon which the Master stooped and picked it up for him—an honour which affected the poet beyond all the compliments wh. went before.'[15] It is easy to see why Charles was better known at Cambridge for his humour than his poetry. All the praise he received seemed a good augury for the joint volume Alfred was publishing with Hallam.

When he got back to Cambridge there was a great disappointment for Alfred. The poems were already in print and the preface written when Hallam's father decided not to let him publish his poetry. His reluctance to let Arthur devote himself to literature was undoubtedly at the base of his objections, but he may also have taken exception to the love poems to Anna Wintour, for he said that some of the short poems were 'unfit even for the limited circulation they might obtain, on account of their unveiling more of emotion than, consistently with what is due to him and to others, could be exposed to view'. Hallam put a brave face on his disappointment and claimed that withdrawing the poems had been his own idea, since he had been conscious of a 'growing conviction of the exceeding crudeness of style' in his poems, 'and in parts morbidness of feeling, which characterised all my earlier attempts'.[16]

Hallam's generosity to Tennyson is shown in a letter he wrote to Donne after hearing that they would not be allowed to publish jointly. 'Friendship certainly plays sad pranks with one's judgment in these matters; yet I think if I hated Alfred Tennyson as much as I love him, I could hardly help revering his imagination with just the same reverence. The book will be small; but did not Samson slay some thousand Philistines with a jawbone? and what hinders but a little 12 mo. of a hundred & fifty pages may in the hand of a right and true spirit do the Lord's work against the Philistines of this viperous generation? His brother's Sonnets you have seen, I am told, and I rejoice much that you like them: but Charles, though he burns and shines, is a lesser light than Alfred.'[17]

The cancellation of their joint publication was particularly frustrating to Tennyson and Hallam because the volume had been intended 'as a sort of seal' of their friendship, which was now knit closer than ever by Hallam's love of Emily. Nevertheless, Hallam circulated his own poems privately while publication went ahead on Tennyson's *Poems, Chiefly Lyrical*. It is an indication of changing publishing practice that apparently only a month intervened between the confusion attendant upon Mr Hallam's decision and the actual publication of Tennyson's volume.

Poems, Chiefly Lyrical appeared in June 1830. The only indications that it was originally intended to include Hallam's poems as well are a reference in the preface and perhaps the excessive slenderness of the volume. The contents are uneven in quality, and some of the poems are bad by any standard, but there are none the less a handful of poems that show for the first time that Tennyson was a great poet in the bud. 'The Kraken', 'Ode to Memory', 'Supposed Confessions of a Second-Rate Sensitive Mind Not in Unity with Itself', and 'Mariana' are the poems that matter most, although only 'Mariana' is one of the staples of English poetry.

The impression of the volume is of intense introspection, largely reflecting a state of mind or being unable to move beyond dead centre. In most of the poems the range is from totally static description to a state in which the action might be possible were the energy and certainty there to lead on to some kind of movement. Curiously enough, since the poets are so unlike in most respects, the reader is frequently reminded of the same state of mind in the poetry of Matthew Arnold, that paralysis of soul that he described as 'Wandering between two worlds, one dead, / The other powerless to be born'. It may be thought of as the typical dilemma of the Victorian poet, but it is put forward with unusual pathos in these poems, argued with what might be called a passionate lethargy.

One of the difficulties with confessional poetry, particularly that by young men, is that it too often degenerates into mere description of a mental state. 'Supposed Confessions', 'The Kraken', and 'Mariana' seem particularly successful because in each the stasis of being is used dramatically as well as being simply described. The binocular effect of looking at the emotions from more than one point of view in these poems foreshadows Tennyson's success in later works that were in all but name dramatic monologues.

'Supposed Confessions', perhaps the least skilful of these three poems, shows how Tennyson managed to objectify and make tolerable his own feelings of frustration by stepping back to examine them and taking an attitude towards them, thus turning them into more than flat autobiographical writing. He subtly exaggerates their poignancy, almost to the point of caricature, so that we cannot help looking at them from two points of view, sympathizing warmly with them at the very moment of recognizing their exaggerated nature. It is a method that he was to use later with great skill in *Maud*, and it is probably not accidental that both poems ring with echoes of *Hamlet*, the *locus classicus* in Western literature of character rendered inactive by uncertainty of belief and made almost grotesque by introspection. Nor, to turn the matter around, is it surprising to find in the poem anticipations of T. S. Eliot's poetry of uncertainty, such as 'Gerontion'. For the problem is, of course, the loss of faith, with the poet looking backward to a time when a simple formulation was adequate to his needs, aware that it will no longer serve him. In the poem Tennyson even manages to turn to his own advantage one of the persistent failures of his verse, the mawkish sentimentality about such matters as motherhood and children's prayers. The following lines, for example, would be intolerable did he not show that what was once honest emotion would now be sentimentality if it were persisted in without change:

> Would that my gloomèd fancy were
> As thine, my mother, when with brows
> Propt on thy knees, my hands upheld
> In thine, I listened to thy vows,
> For me outpoured in holiest prayer—
> For me unworthy!—and beheld
> Thy mild deep eyes upraised, that knew
> The beauty and repose of faith,
> And the clear spirit shining through.

What cuts through the treacle is the poet's acute awareness that the childish attitude he fondly remembers is a sickly one for an adult.

The end of the poem is a plea for light and an iteration of the pain of the present:

> Oh teach me yet
> Somewhat before the heavy clod
> Weighs on me, and the busy fret
> Of that sharp-headed worm begins
> In the gross blackness underneath.
>
> O weary life! O weary death!
> O spirit and heart made desolate!
> O damnèd vacillating state!

The deadly energy of the worm is pitted against the inertia of the paralysed heart in a most effective conclusion, vibrant with tension between the two states.

More typical of the young Tennyson in their ornate language and encrusted images are 'The Kraken' and 'Mariana'. The first of these tells of the sleeping trance of the sea monster, couched in 'the sickly light', among 'Unnumbered and enormous polypi' that 'Winnow with giant arms the slumbering green'. But though the picture is one of luxuriant languor, the beast becomes the symbol of bottled-up, potential power (the power of poetry? of death?):

> There hath he lain for ages and will lie
> Battening upon huge seaworms in his sleep,
> Until the latter fire shall heat the deep;
> Then once by man and angels to be seen,
> In roaring he shall rise and on the surface die.

Even in his death there is cataclysmic energy, and into the foreordained eruption Tennyson packs much of the explosive force that Hardy was later to see in the collision of the *Titanic* and the iceberg in 'The Convergence of the Twain'. The exotic submarine growth becomes emblematic of the unknowable, slowly stirred poetry of the natural world. In this poem, as in 'Mariana', Tennyson succeeds in giving vitality to listlessness as a poetic subject.

The central figure of 'Mariana' seems to have wandered a long way from Shakespeare's Vienna in *Measure for Measure*, where Tennyson first found her. She has taken up residence in a moated grange more English than Austrian, and both the flora and fauna take their being from the air of Lincolnshire. Rather than making the situation ridiculous, it is this very domestication of Angelo's deserted fiancée that is responsible for the success of the poem. So lovingly detailed is the description of the lonely farmhouse that many of Tennyson's readers understandably assumed he must have in mind a particular building, but he wrathfully insisted that he had conjured it up like Orpheus 'to the music of Shakespeare's words'.

The scene is not of decay alone, but also of motion and life frustrated of their normal function while still retaining their potential vitality, precisely as Mariana herself is, in her deserted, unloved state. The house is not used for its proper function, and even the doors creak without being opened:

> The blue fly sung in the pane; the mouse
> Behind the mouldering wainscot shrieked.

It is nature unnaturally constrained and distorted by man. The horror of life unlived is indicated by the slowly changing hours of the day that bring no change to Mariana and little to the refrain, 'I am aweary, aweary, / I would that I were dead.'

Much of the effect of the poem is dependent upon the contrast between the carefully detailed, sensuous description of the physical world and the utter sterility of Mariana's emotional state. It is a picture as static as anything else in the entire volume, but the poem is given life by the ability of the poet to stand back and contemplate the implicit meaning of the moralized landscape. When it is done as effectively as this, Tennyson need make no overt comment upon its significance.

These poems stand in stark contrast to many of the others in the volume, such as the passionless verses to anaemic young ladies like

'Claribel' and 'Adeline' and 'Madeline'; one constantly wishes that Tennyson had exercised on them the threat made in grotesque humour to 'Lilian', who laughs too constantly:

> If prayers will not hush thee,
>   Airy Lilian,
> Like a rose-leaf I will crush thee,
>   Fairy Lilian.

It is only because the best of the poems are so good that the rest cause impatience, since they are after all the work of a man less than twenty-one years old. His youth constantly shows in the repetition of words like 'sheeny', 'reflex', or 'marish', in the frequent self-rhymes, in the repetition of lines without the dramatic function they have in 'Mariana', and in the self-indulgence of unhyphenated combinations of words and accents marked in direct opposition to their normal pronunciation. It was these last in particular that understandably annoyed some of the reviewers:

> Both in blosmwhite silk are frockèd;
> Both, unlike, they roam together
> Under a summervault of golden weather;
> Like, unlike, they sing together
>   Side by side,
> MidMay's darling goldenlockèd,
> Summer's tanling diamondeyed.   ('Dualisms')

The uncertainty and doubt that pervade this volume are undoubtedly indicative of Tennyson's morbid despondency during the years in which it was written. Some, although not all of the depression was to lift under the influence of Hallam's affection, and certainly the poems he published two years later were to exhibit an energy and vitality that were often lacking in 1830.

The reviews of *Poems, Chiefly Lyrical* were generally good, although they must have seemed to appear with wearying slowness. In August the *Spectator* noticed the poems favourably, and early in 1831 both the *Westminster* and the *New Monthly* were flattering in their reviews. Hallam, who was not particularly patient, felt that not enough attention had been paid to the volume, and he arranged to write anonymously for the *Englishman's Magazine* in 1831. Although critics as diverse as Yeats and H. M. McLuhan have praised his review as anticipating the Symbolist poetic credo in a startling way, it reads rather tamely today. Not unexpectedly, it is full of high praise for Tennyson, quite properly identifying him as a poet 'of Sensation' rather than of reflection. Hallam singled out five characteristics of Tennyson's poetry for commendation, of which only two now seem to mark out what is specifically Tennysonian: '. . . his vivid, picturesque delineation of objects, and the peculiar skill with which he holds all of them *fused*, to borrow a metaphor from science, in a medium of strong emotion' and 'the variety of his lyrical measures, and exquisite modulation of harmonious words and cadences to the swell and fall of the feelings expressed'. Hallam also fairly recognized the shortcomings of the verse, such as the occasional misuse of language when Tennyson simply mistook the meaning of a word. What was probably most helpful to Tennyson's fame was that Hallam reprinted in full the text of 'Recollections of the Arabian Nights', 'Oriana', and 'Adeline'.

James Spedding's brother Edward thought the review would 'serve the holy cause but little after all', and said that Hallam's language was more obscure than Tennyson's. 'At least it is all I can do favoured as I have been with the conversation of the wise and good to make out what it means in most parts', and 'how those who like most of our benighted countrymen . . . think Alfred the Great a dreamer . . . should make out the distinction between the "logical relation of ideas" and "the congruity of the sentiments to which they refer"' he was puzzled to understand.[18]

By modern standards the review seems neither fulsome nor obscure, but in 1831, when reviewers were accustomed to using the cutlass, it offended at least one reader, Professor John Wilson, better known as 'Christopher North', who was one of the most influential critics of the day. In February 1832, in *Blackwood's Magazine*, Wilson mentioned Tennyson's poems in passing and praised them, but by May, when he came to write a full-scale review, he was clearly irritated by Hallam's article. He took Hallam and the *Westminster* reviewer to task for what they had written, calling the latter an 'idiot lunatic, slavering in the palsied dotage of the extremest superannuation ever inflicted on a being . . . now sensibly and audibly reduced below the level of the Pongos'. Having thus worked himself up, he proceeded to tear some of the poorer poems to pieces (not unjustly), and so fell into such good humour that he finished by praising Tennyson and quoting several of the best poems.

Hallam took the review in good part, professing to feel amused at the attack and saying wisely that the length of what Wilson had quoted, as well as his praise, would enhance Tennyson's reputation. Tennyson, however, demonstrated the habitual thinness of his skin by the fury of his response to a reviewer who not only poked fun at some of the poetry but dared to be insulting to Hallam. As we shall see, it had unfortunate results for Tennyson.

The Apostles were in ecstasy over the volume and tried to think of ways to bring it to wider public attention. Only Trench was not enthusiastic, but his jaundiced view of Tennyson may well have sprung from a feeling that his own poems received less attention from the other Apostles than they deserved. After *Poems, Chiefly Lyrical* appeared, Trench told W. B. Donne that Tennyson's 'friends at Cambridge will materially injure him if he does not beware—no young man under any circumstances should believe that he *has* done anything, but still be forward looking'. Sound advice but less than generous in the circumstances. A year later Trench told Donne that Tennyson was 'certainly the best of the young Poets and the perversest, but this must chiefly be laid to the charge of his Cambridge advisers (Hallam, Blakesley, Kemble and Co) who in a short time did much to spoil and pervert him, flattering in every way his Antinomian Spirit, which needed rather a check and no such encouragement'.[19] Trench's judgement would be sensible if Tennyson had been an average man, but with his morbid fear of criticism he would probably have dropped his friends if they had tried to reform him, and in so doing he would have lost what he needed most, their affection.

Hallam was the natural mediator between his friends, and he tried to make Trench see that he was making a superficial judgement on Tennyson: 'His nervous temperament and habits of solitude give an appearance of affectation to his manner, which is no true interpreter of the man, and wears off on further knowledge. Perhaps you could never become very intimate, for certainly your bents of mind are not the same...'.[20] In spite of his efforts relations between the two men always remained cool.

The other Apostles took heart at every favourable notice of Tennyson. Robert Monteith asked Milnes, 'Have you seen... the review of Tennyson's poems in the Westminster? It is really *enthusiastic* about him, and is very well written on the whole. If we can get him well reviewed in the Edinburgh he will do.'[21] Blakesley was worried that Milnes had no authority for saying that Tennyson's poems were selling well: 'I fear that your wish has been father to yr. thought. They however have been highly admired by some men of considerable influence in the literary world & will very probably soon be reviewed in some periodical of note.'[22]

Trinity was not Tealby, however, and when Tennyson's uncle Charles heard that Alfred had published a book of poems, he said with disgust that he would have preferred hearing that he had made a wheelbarrow.

✻

CHAPTER VIII

THE VALLEY OF CAUTERETZ, 1830

In his surviving correspondence there is no indication of what Dr Tennyson thought about the publications of his sons in 1830, or whether he even knew of them before his return to England that summer. In March he had written from Rome to complain that he had not heard from his family for four months, and the terms of his complaint suggest that the death by fire of the unlucky cook still weighed heavily on him: 'My family may all have been burnt for what I know.'[1] By now, however, the balance of his reason was so precarious that he might not have remembered even if he had heard of Charles's and Alfred's poetry.

In his loneliness he sent long letters to his father and brother describing the scenery in great detail, to make up for having little to tell of persons. Old Mr Tennyson wished testily that 'instead of his elaborate descriptions of Mount Vesuvius &c, he had given some of his state of health, the society he is in, and an intimation as to his return'.[2] Pathetically, Dr Tennyson would abuse his family, then wonder why they were not warmer to him. At last in April he decided that the letters from Somersby were affectionate enough to warrant his return.

He landed in England at the end of June, then went to stay with his brother in London. The poor man seems not only to have been ill himself but to have been the cause that there was illness in others. He had been staying with Charles only a week when his brother began having 'Spasmodic seizures' once more. 'No one knows any thing about that disorder,' Charles wrote to his father, 'it is brot. on by any thing affecting the Nerves—whet. the cause be bodily or mental.'[3] Perhaps to help restore his brother's health, Dr Tennyson then left for Bayons Manor to stay with his father, but so far he had not bothered to notify his wife directly that he was in England.

At last, at the end of July, he returned to Somersby, full of wild stories about what had happened to him on the Continent while his family had been neglecting him so scandalously. Once he had nearly been buried alive in an avalanche, and once he was saved by the timely intervention of another man from falling over a cliff when he was giddy. His son Charles wrote to a friend about more of his father's adventures: 'On one occasion proceeding along in a small carriage over the mountains he was hurled down in a precipice & stunned but saved himself from certain death by convulsively grasping a pine that grew out of a ledge: while the driver carriage & horse were dashed to atoms thousands of feet below him. Again, at the Carnival in Rome, a man was stilettoed in his arms, drawing first, suspicion and then violence on his person: the excess of wh. he prevented by exclaiming that he was an Englishman & had not done the deed.' After the 'neck-break adventures' his father had encountered, Charles wrote drily, he was 'much surprised to see him so well'.[4] Like the accounts of his escapades in Russia when he was a young man, Dr Tennyson's stories now were clearly pathetic attempts to bolster his own waning self-confidence. From this time until his death a few months later he declined quickly, and he seems to have had only intermittent periods of total clarity.

By the time Dr Tennyson arrived in Lincolnshire, Alfred had gone to London. His father had written an abusive letter to Frederick, apparently while drunk, and Alfred probably wanted to avoid meeting him for as long as possible. 'Alfred is very ill & went to London to consult an eminent physician, as he supposed, on a case of life or death,' his mother wrote to her brother-in-law. 'He writes to me now that the Physician hopes he is mistaken, but desires him to remain in London for a fortnight & then come to him again & has given him some medicine to take.'[5] The casual air of her letter suggests that even she believed his illness had never been so bad as Alfred thought. Half a century later Tennyson said that a country doctor had once told him he had 'a travelling clot' in his veins and that he might die at any moment without warning. With due allowance for his habitual hypochondria and exaggeration of his symptoms, Tennyson did have some reason to worry about his health, and it was probably the threat of unexpected death from the clot that was the excuse for his trip to London.

In town he had been staying with the Hallams at 67 Wimpole Street (Arthur used to say that they were all at sixes and sevens), filling Arthur's den at the top of the house with smoke as they hatched schemes for a Continental trip. Before this Arthur had planned on spending the summer in Germany, but now he and Alfred decided on going to France with Frederick before going south to the Spanish border. On their return they intended to join forces with another Trinity undergraduate, Robert Robertson, who had been with Arthur in Italy. Arthur's reasons for the trip were political, and though Tennyson was less interested in revolution than in scenery he was pleased to accompany his friend. It was to be the trip that meant most to Tennyson in all his life, one that he tried again and again to repeat as he remembered the pleasure of travelling with Hallam.

What lay behind their plans was the interest a few of the Apostles had taken in the cause of the Spanish exiles in London who had fled their native country in 1823 when Ferdinand had been restored to the throne, revoked the constitution, and set about harsh reprisals. Tennyson's imagination had been captured by the failure of the liberal revolution, as we have seen, and he had written about it in *Poems by Two Brothers*.

The leader of the exiles was a young general, José Maria Torrijos, still in his early thirties, handsome and as dashingly impetuous as a Spanish revolutionary should be. He met John Sterling and through him was introduced to other Apostles in 1828. Carlyle wrote in his biography of Sterling of seeing the sad, proud Spaniards who lived in squalid lodgings in Camden Town. Most of them were unable to speak English, and in any case had no real wish to domesticate themselves in London and find employment. Their meeting place was the area around Euston Square, where they would walk silently and tragically, muffled in threadbare long cloaks against the cold of the Northern capital, dark Iberians among the London traders.

Through Sterling Torrijos met John Kemble in Cambridge. In his own way Kemble was every bit as romantic and flamboyant as the Spaniard. He was as darkly handsome as Torrijos, with all the flair of his theatrical family; he was brilliant, arrogant, hot-tempered, and thoroughly beloved by the other Apostles, who were amused by his histrionics. He was seldom guilty of not taking himself seriously enough and once announced to his delighted friends, 'The world is one great thought, and I am thinking it.' Kemble threw himself into the Constitutionalist cause with his usual fervour, introducing Torrijos to his friends, including Hallam and Tennyson.

By the time his mother was reporting his trip to London to his uncle Charles, Tennyson must have been reassured about the seriousness of his illness, for he had already been gone from England for three days, in the company of Hallam and presumably Frederick. Mrs Tennyson

V a. Alfred Tennyson from the rear, 1835, by Edward FitzGerald.

b. Somersby Rectory, 1835, by Alfred Tennyson.

c. Alfred Tennyson, 1835, by James Spedding.

VI Alfred Tennyson, 1835, by James Spedding.

certainly knew of the journey they had planned, although she may not have known their destination or the exact date on which they expected to leave. In June she had received a letter from Hallam with an advance copy of Alfred's new book and a copy of his own poetry: 'I am afraid it is quite impossible for me to accept your very kind invitation before my leaving England early in next month. I earnestly hope Alfred & Frederic will be able to join me then; I think nothing will do the former especially so much good as travelling awhile.'[6] In not mentioning the Spanish trip to her brother-in-law she was shielding Alfred, for Charles and his father would certainly have disapproved of the trip, and she was inclined to take the side of her children against their elders at Bayons.

Behind the secrecy lay the reality of a plot for the Constitutionalists to retake power in Spain, and Alfred and Hallam were committed to taking money and coded dispatches in invisible ink to the revolutionaries, who were gathering in the Pyrenees. It is tempting to say that it was literally a cloak-and-dagger affair, for it seems to have been at this time that Tennyson began wearing a Spanish-style cloak and the 'sombrero' that were to distinguish his appearance for the rest of his life; probably he first wore them in emulation of the exiles and then continued with them in memory of the summer's trip.

Sterling's cousin, Robert Boyd, had inherited £5,000 which he invested in buying a ship to take the rebels to Spain and in outfitting it with arms and provisions. In return for his help he was to be made a colonel in the Spanish cavalry if the revolution succeeded. Hallam and Tennyson left on 2 July, Kemble sailed for Gibraltar five days later without telling his family where he was going, and later in July Boyd's ship was to take the Spaniards home. Unfortunately, the Thames police came aboard shortly before it was due to sail, acting on the orders of the Home Secretary, to whom the Spanish consul had complained. Boyd and Torrijos jumped overboard to escape arrest, and Sterling leapt into a passing rowing-boat. Without the gunboat Boyd and the Spaniards had to find their way to Gibraltar as best they could. There they met Kemble and Trench, who had gone to act as spies working with the forces in the south of Spain. As a gesture of undergraduate resolution, both of them were growing beards, which they swore they would not shave until Spain was once more free. In the meantime they gave themselves up to the considerable pleasures of Gibraltar, where handsome and charming Cambridge undergraduates were at a premium. It was to be more than a year until the actual attack took place, and before then Palmerston had asked the Constitutional-ists to leave Gibraltar because they were endangering relations with the Spanish government.

After all the secrecy surrounding their departure from England, once they got to France there seemed to be little urgency about the enterprise in which Hallam and Tennyson were engaged. The evidence is scanty for what they did on their way south, but they stopped in Paris, where they had introductions to Guizot, who was a friend of Hallam's father. Tennyson and Hallam had composed a joint poem in French, beginning, 'O Fontainebleau! O Fontainebleau', which Ten-nyson began to recite. Guizot stopped him and said it would not do because Fontainebleau has four syllables in poetry, so that the first e is pronounced. Tennyson remembered that it made them both 'feel very small'.[7] It was presumably on this trip, his first to France, that Tenny-son went each day for a fortnight to the Louvre, where he claimed that he had looked each time in single-minded concentration at only one picture, 'La Maîtresse de Titien'.

Frederick accompanied Hallam and Alfred on their way south by diligence, their circuitous route taking them to Poitiers, then eastward to the Mediterranean coast. Alfred was desperately tired from the long and dusty journey, on one occasion falling sound asleep on the lap of the lady sitting next to him, a French countess who reacted angrily by shaking Frederick and pointing to his sleeping brother. At Montpellier they had to break the journey for some days when Alfred's fatigue gave way to a fever. When he was convalescent, he and Hallam continued west to the Pyrenees. Much as he loved the gentler countryside of England, Tennyson always had a deep craving for more exotic scen-ery, and on this, his first trip abroad, he could scarcely keep his mind on the mission to the revolutionaries because he was so busy absorbing the novelty of the Mediterranean landscape. As they passed through a particularly desolate area between Narbonne and Perpignan, he recognized the barrenness as precisely the background he needed for 'Mariana in the South', which he intended as a pendant to 'Mariana', and he copied faithfully what he saw. Hallam was bothered by the heat, but he wrote to Charles Tennyson that 'Alfd. is delighted with his journey, tho' regretting the impermanence of his impressions in the hurry of travel.'[8]

At the southern extremity of their trip lay disillusionment. They finally made contact with the leader of the Pyrenean party of the insurrectionists, one Ojeda, at Pont d'Espagne, a remote border village at the confluence of the torrents of Gaube and Marcadou, where they turned over their concealed money and secret messages. It was only then they learned that the revolution was aimed as much at the Church as the King; Ojeda casually mentioned his own desire to cut the throats of all the priests ('couper la gorge à tous les curés'). Aware that he had shocked the Englishmen, he clapped his hand over his heart and said, 'Mais vous connaissez mon coeur.' Tennyson muttered, 'And a pretty black one it is.'

The episode was discouraging to young men as idealistic as Hallam and Tennyson, but there was better to come. Frederick had promised to join them at Bagnères, but when they got there they found only a letter asking them to follow him to Paris. Instead they stayed on in Cauteretz, for Tennyson was still unwell and Hallam was tired. With them was Hallam's friend Robertson, with whom they planned on returning to England, as well as a cousin of his. At last Tennyson had the leisure to look at the surrounding country as long as he liked. In spite of his bad health they all climbed mountains, swam in the high lakes, and walked endlessly. The black rocks in the mountain torrent running through the little town threw up flashing white spray as the stream frayed its way through the defile; out of the implacable sun there was deep mysterious shade; pine trees hung on the sides of the ravine where 'the swimming vapour slopes athwart the glen'.

Tennyson had stumbled upon a totally new dimension of natural beauty on which to draw for the kinetic, metaphorical landscape that he was beginning to mark out as his own particular poetic domain, and with this accession of territory began an amazing creative spurt. While he was still in Cauteretz he began writing 'Œnone', in which the vale of Ida is drawn from the magical landscape then surrounding him. When they went to the Cirque de Gavarnie, the spray, 'like a downward smoke', brought to his mind the line 'slow-dropping veils of thinnest lawn', and from these two phrases was generated much of 'The Lotos-Eaters'. At the Lac de Gaube he observed a little picture that finally found a poetic home in *The Princess* years later, when the Princess Ida is described as

> standing like a stately Pine
> Set in a cataract on an island-crag.

Wheeling overhead at the Pic du Midi were great bald-necked predatory birds, stooping threateningly at the sight of the climbers, to be recreated in those marvellous six lines of dizzying height, 'The Eagle'.

The poems of the 1833 and 1842 volumes are haunted by the sight, sound, and rough feel of that small section of the Pyrenees; 'an artist', Tennyson told Hallam, 'ought to be lord of the five senses'. For the rest of his life the echoes of the trip and his stay in Cauteretz were to reverberate through his work. He came again and again to walk beside the stream bisecting the deep gorge, until his final visit forty-four years after he had first seen it. And of course it inspired one of his finest lyrics, 'In the Valley of Cauteretz'.

The Pyrenees provided him with a local habitation for the classical myth and poetry which he had loved since childhood, and which were to suggest much of his best work. The miles of uninhabited mountains, little changed in the generations that they had been known, stood in for those of Italy and ancient Greece, and even the peasants in their alien, traditional costumes held no suggestion of modernity. He always needed an exact picture in his memory or his imagination to reproduce in his poetry, and the new-found grandeur gave him what no English landscape could have done in quite the same way, the vision of an uninterrupted timelessness, the emblem of classical antiquity. It was years before he saw Italy, and he never did get to Greece, but they were not necessary to the man who had already domesticated Greek and Roman literature in the Pyrenees.

Something even more profound than his perception of the metaphorical meaning of the evocative landscape must have happened to Tennyson in Cauteretz, although it is impossible to know exactly what it was. Recurrently sounding through the poetry written after the Pyrenean trip is the word 'valley', always connected with love, usually with youth, and frequently with Arthur Hallam. Any supposition that one totally understands why the word had such subterranean power for Tennyson after his visit to Cauteretz is almost certain to be wrong. Was it there that Tennyson recognized fully for the first time how much another person meant to him? There is really no telling. What seems certain is that the unexpected romantic beauty of that ravine, 'lovelier / Than all the valleys of Ionian hills', fused with some deep personal perception to make it the most potent spot poetically that Tennyson ever knew. As he was to write in *The Princess*, nearly two decades later, 'Love is of the valley'. In the year of his own death he published 'The Death of Œnone', in which the imagery proves that the memory of the valley of Cauteretz was as green as it had been sixty years before.*

---

* One possible clue, admittedly faint, to what happened to Tennyson at Cauteretz may be found in the poem he started there, 'Œnone'. It is spoken by the nymph and

On 8 September the friends boarded the *Leeds*, bound from Bordeaux to Dublin. To their delight they found on board Mr and Mrs John Harden and their three daughters, who were neighbours of the Speddings in Cumberland and whose relatives were friends of Robertson's family. The three young ladies wore magnificent coal-scuttle bonnets on which they were pleased to be complimented by the undergraduates. The first day Hallam, whom they noticed as 'a very interesting, delicate-looking young man', was too seasick to appear, but the next day he joined the others on deck in the sun, where he lay on his back reading Scott aloud while Tennyson and the others watched the girls sitting in a prim row with their mother. Mr Harden made two pencil sketches of the group that are now in the library at Trinity; one of them is probably the only extant picture of Hallam and Tennyson together. One of the Misses Harden remembered Tennyson as 'all large cape, tall hat and decided nose', so she was not surprised when he was sometimes taken for a foreigner: 'I never saw a more Spanish looking man in my life'.[9] Under the relaxing atmosphere of shipboard the girls were allowed on deck under the stars with the young men, to sing and play games, much to Hallam's pleasure. Four days after boarding the *Leeds* they landed in Dublin and Hallam and Tennyson set out for England.

Years later Tennyson used to tell how they had arrived in Liverpool in time to take the first train that ever ran between that city and Manchester, on 20 September, the date that sealed the fate of the unfortunate Mr Huskisson. In their hurry to get aboard the crowded train they were unable to see the wheels because of the press of spectators on the platform, and the near-sighted Tennyson could not see them later in the dark, so that he assumed they were running in grooves. The result of his myopia was a line composed that night which became one of his most famous when it was ultimately embedded in 'Locksley Hall': 'Let the great world spin for ever down the ringing grooves of change.' From Manchester he returned to Somersby, and the holiday was over.

For the Spanish patriots still in Gibraltar, however, it had never been a holiday, and they clung on miserably for another year. Sterling

---

tells of her grief at being deserted by Paris for the promise of Helen. Perhaps this is the unconscious reflection of Tennyson's own awareness, first recognized at Cauteretz, that Hallam's love for Emily inevitably meant the end of part of their intimacy. Such an awareness need not have erotic significance; its occurrence is, in any case, highly speculative.

got married in the autumn of 1830, then fell ill and went off to the West Indies, leaving the cause behind. Ultimately Trench and Kemble lost their enthusiasm, shaved their beards, and returned to England. Kemble continued to sing revolutionary songs when he had had too much to drink, and to tell increasingly tall stories of having single-handedly slaughtered large numbers of Spanish government troops, but his heart was no longer in it. Trench quite simply became apathetic about politics. Of the Apostles and their friends, only Boyd remained in Spain.

In November 1831 the Constitutionalists were asked to leave Gibraltar. With a force of little more than fifty men they landed at Fuengirola, but they were betrayed by the governor of Malaga, who had promised to join them when they landed. He led the party that captured Torrijos's men and sentenced them to death by firing squad. In the Bodleian library is a letter to a friend written by Robert Boyd at midnight on 10 December 1831. It is calm and affectionate, moving in the dignity with which Boyd contemplated the hours that remained before he had to face the rifles of the government troops on the beach near Malaga. When he learned of Boyd's death Sterling said, 'I can hear the sound of that musketry; it is as if the bullets were tearing my own brain.'[10]

It was the end of a romantic dream, in which a number of well-intentioned young Englishmen learned that what began as little more than an undergraduate lark for them ended in death and in even greater repression for the Spanish people; revolution, once begun, had consequences more serious than any of them had foreseen. It is no wonder that Tennyson became increasingly chary of anything that undermined the stability of the world as he had inherited it.

When Tennyson came home from Spain the execution of the Constitutionalists was still more than a year in the future, but he was in a sombre mood. It was the first time he had seen his father since the spring of the preceding year, and by now it was obvious that he could not continue as Rector in his present state of health, particularly as he seems to have begun using increasing amounts of opium. The family began making plans to move some time during the following year, but they had no idea where they might go.

Alfred had come back in better physical shape than he had been for some time, but his health began to decline as soon as he returned to Somersby. The fact that he fell ill so often when around his father hints that much of his bad health was psychosomatic. Now he did not even have the company of Hallam, who was in Leyton, Essex, with his family, and they would not meet until the beginning of term, if Alfred had recovered sufficiently to return to Cambridge.

Hallam was bored after the excitement of the Spanish venture; 'a wild bustling time we had of it,' he remembered.[11] Besides, he greatly missed Emily and Alfred. From the country house where he was living with his family he wrote that he passed his free time by knocking balls around the table in the billiard room. The essentially serious side of his nature comes clearly through the description of his academic work under his father's direction:

I read six books of Herodotus with him, and I take occasional plunges into David Hartley, and Buhle's *Philosophie Moderne* for my own gratification. I cannot find that my adventures have produced quite the favourable impression on my father's mind that his letter gave me to expect. I don't mean that he blames me at all; but his old notions about the University begin to revive, and he does not seem quite to comprehend, that after helping revolutionize kingdoms, one is still less inclined than before to trouble one's head about scholarships, degrees and such gear.

To the chagrin of his father he had already decided not to try for first-class honours, and the constant grinding hardly seemed worthwhile.

Even reunion with his brother Charles was less pleasant for Tennyson than it should have been, for Charles had been bored studying at Somersby all summer. 'I walk much and am in training for my next term's studies,' Charles wrote to Spedding. 'I am sure to be plucked but do not intend to shoot myself on the occasion . . .'[12]

By the beginning of the Michaelmas term of 1830 Alfred was too unwell to return to Cambridge, even though it meant staying at home in Somersby, with little to look forward to but visits to Dalby or Tealby. Frederick had succumbed to the ill health the Tennysons suffered when their father was at home, and he had gone to London and was 'under Stanley's care for a stricture'. After the summer's study Charles had decided not to return to the University after all. Although his letter to Spedding tried to conceal his fear of failing in his examinations, that may not have been the whole reason for his not returning. One clue is in a letter that Alfred wrote to Brookfield when he heard that Brooks had fallen into the habit of taking opium:

Hollo! Brooks, Brooks! for shame! what are you about—musing, and brooding and dreaming and opiumeating yourself out of this life into the next?

Awake, arise or be for ever fallen. Shake yourself you Owl o' the turret you! come forth you cat-a-mountain—you shall chew no more cud. . . . Is there not cakes and ale? is there not toddies? is there not bacchies? is there not pipes? smoke negrofoot an thou wilt but in the name of all that is near and dear unto thee I prythee take no opium—it were better that a millstone were hung about thy neck and that thou wert thrown into the Cam. . . . I think you mentioned a renewal of your acquaintance with the fishermen, which may possibly occur if you will leave off the aforesaid drug, if you do not I can foresee nothing for you but stupefaction, aneurism, confusion, horror and death.[13]

In spite of his joking language there is no mistaking the horror Tennyson felt at opium addiction, and it did not come only from experience with his father. By 1834 Charles had become a hopeless victim of the drug, and it is probable that in 1830 he was already in the first stages of his addiction, so that it would have been difficult for him to go back to Cambridge for term. As a boy he suffered from asthma, for which opium may have been taken, and there is a family tradition that he had bad neuralgia, for which it was prescribed, but the example of his father's opium-taking seems as probable a source of his habit as an unwise doctor's prescription.

Charles and Alfred remained at home when term began, chafing for a fortnight before deciding they could stand the atmosphere at Somersby no longer. Charles was presumably in control of himself, and he decided to accompany Alfred back to Somersby. 'Alfred Tennyson has been very unwell, and it was supposed would not keep this term,' Hallam wrote to Donne on 3 November, 'However he returned last night.'[14] Once he was away from Somersby his health returned as if by magic, and within two more weeks Blakesley wrote to Milnes: 'Alfred Tennyson is in Cambridge, reading & writing, & (much to his own annoyance) looking better than I ever recollect seeing him.'[15]

One of the poems he wrote in the autumn of 1830 was 'Anacaona', which owed its inception to the Spanish trip. There is a new sensuality in the account of the native queen of Haiti, 'Naked, and dark-limbed, and gay', and in the loving, too carefully researched description of lush Caribbean flora and fauna. At the end of the poem Anacaona welcomes the Spaniards to her island. Unstated but hanging over the conclusion is the knowledge that she was subsequently put to death by the Spaniards. The fate of Boyd and the other conspirators was still a year away, but the bitter aftertaste of the meeting with Ojeda was strong for Tennyson, and it seems to have contaminated the otherwise luminous quality of the poem. It rapidly became a favourite of the Apostles, who were perhaps unduly influenced by the allure of the sun on the golden bodies of the maidens. They copied it out for each other and urged Tennyson to publish it, but the passion for literal accuracy that later seemed to obsess him now asserted itself, and he refused, saying that it 'would be confuted by some Midshipman who had been in Hayti latitudes & knew better about Tropical Vegetable and animal'.[16]

During the Michaelmas term Cambridge was full of talk of the demonstrations and troubles in connection with the Reform Bill. There were riots in Huntingdon, which was uncomfortably near Cambridge, and a threat was made to burn the University library and to attack the town itself on 4 December. Hundreds of special constables were sworn in, and the undergraduates formed themselves into companies of ten or twelve men armed with stout sticks. In a letter home Spedding described the preparations of the Apostles: 'Blakesley is Captain of the Corps of Poets & Metaphysicians,—& visions of broken heads & arms, scythes & pitchforks disturbed the purity of our unselfish contemplations, & the idealisms of our poetical imaginings. But the threatened army did not make the threatened attack: & our heads are still sound to talk nonsense & metaphysics; very much to my satisfaction & the disappointment of the more adventurous spirits among us.'

A mile or two away at Coton a farmhouse was set on fire: 'a very magnificent sight it was,' Spedding said. 'The gownsmen worked most meritoriously: and were the sole cause of saving the stables & the dwelling house.' So zealous were some of the undergraduates that they began to tear down the house to preserve it from being burned and were restrained only by the pleas of the distressed farmer.

Tennyson went with the undergraduates to operate a fire engine. 'Poets are not always living out of the world: for Alfred Tennyson, when we came within sight of the flames, was struck with the truth of the case: and declared that it was really time that these things sd. be put a stop to.'[17] According to his son, Tennyson felt sympathy for the demonstrating labourers, but there was never any real question of his siding with them.

At the height of the troubles over the Reform Bill, William Wordsworth came to stay with his brother at the Lodge in Trinity. He found 'a great deal of intellectual activity within the walls of this College,' he wrote, 'and in the University at large. . . . We have also a respectable show of blossom in poetry. Two brothers of the name of Tennyson, in particular, are not a little promising.' Wordsworth stayed in Trinity for several weeks, and with Southey on Commemoration Day, 16 December, he attended the chapel, where among 'the assembled worthies of Trinity, and the ghosts of the Benefactors of Trinity, & fellows that are, and Senior wranglers, & senior Medallists', he heard Spedding deliver his prize declamation. Hallam also spoke, and Robert Monteith wrote to Milnes of the declamation: 'it was verily splendid to see the poet Wordsworth's face, for he was there, kindle as H proceeded with it'.[18]

This was the first of several occasions on which Tennyson might have been expected to meet the man who dominated English poetry in the first half of the century as Tennyson was to dominate it in the second, but the meeting did not take place. Spedding, after his success, was introduced to the Master of Trinity, to Southey, and to William Wordsworth, 'the Great Poet—& heard him dilate largely on matters moral, poetical, and philosophical—also received a free offer to walk with him and talk with him, which if the Gods permit I mean to avail myself of'.[19] Spedding's father was a former schoolfellow of Wordsworth, and James soon became close to the poet. On 19 December he entertained him at coffee in his rooms in Trinity, with a company consisting of Alford, Blakesley, Brookfield, Tennant, and Thompson. The names conspicuously absent from the list are those of Spedding's best friends, Hallam and Tennyson. There is little doubt that he would have invited them, for Tennyson was probably the single undergraduate whom Wordsworth would most have liked meeting, but he and Hallam had departed for Somersby the previous day.

Wordsworth, according to Tennant, 'was in good talking but furiously alarmist—nothing but revolutions and reigns of terror and all that. . . . But upon the whole, although he said nothing very profound or original, yet I enjoyed his talk till 1 o'clock in the morning.' Years later, with the experience of public life heavy upon him, Tennyson commented on Tennant's letter: 'How can you expect a great man to say anything "very profound" when he *knows* it is expected of him?'[20]

For some deeply felt reason Tennyson was reluctant to meet Wordsworth. He was modest about inflicting himself upon the greatest of living English poets, but there may have been some more complicated reason for his diffidence, since Spedding was to find him equally difficult to bring to Wordsworth five years later. Hallam's Somersby visit was to be a matter of only a few days, and Tennyson presumably felt he should be there when Arthur met Dr Tennyson for the first time, particularly as he no doubt knew that Hallam intended to propose to Emily during his stay. All the same, Hallam would probably not have put any barrier in the way of staying an extra day in Cambridge, especially as the coach for Louth did not leave until 2.30 a.m., well after the hour when Wordsworth was safely abed in the Master's Lodge. The relations between the two great poets were never to be totally comfortable, and this was the first overt manifestation of that lack of ease.

We know little of the details of Hallam's visit to Somersby except that by the end of his stay he and Emily had made their protestations to each other in the yellow drawing-room of the Rectory, although there must have been some kind of avowal the previous spring. Hallam returned to London for Christmas, and it is probable that his father did not know until then that he had gone to Somersby for any reason other than to accept a polite invitation from the elder Tennysons and to see them all in the Rectory once more before they moved elsewhere. Very probably the elder Hallam did not even know of the existence of Emily Tennyson until his son's return from Somersby.

Mr Hallam had met Alfred, but there was not much in the untidy young poet to appeal greatly to the austere older man. He came from an obscure country family, and when Mr Hallam had enquiries made about the Tennysons he could only have found out their grandfather was a hard, pushing tyrant; that the elder Charles Tennyson was a Radical MP separated from his wife and with a reputation for social climbing; that Emily's father was an embittered, crazed rural parson, addicted to drugs and alcohol, subject to epileptic fits, and intermittently cut off from his family by mutual threats of murder. Mr Hallam therefore naturally took a jaundiced view of Arthur's new love affair, particularly when it followed so hard upon the heels of his infatuation with Anna Wintour.

CHAPTER IX

DEATH OF DR TENNYSON, 1831

At Cambridge Tennyson had become increasingly involved with the Apostles and their friends. The warmth, love, and security that he felt with them made it all the more difficult when he had to leave unexpectedly.

Besides intellectual discussion and talk of poetry there was plenty of the usual undergraduate horseplay, a few nights when the wine was red, and some mild dissipation. Once when they were gathered in Hallam's rooms in New Court, the Dean came furiously into their wine party. 'What is the meaning, Mr Hallam, of all this noise?' As Tennyson used to tell it, Hallam said, 'I am very sorry, sir, we had no idea we were making a noise.' 'Well, gentlemen,' replied the Dean, 'if you'll all come down into the Court, you'll *hear* what a noise you're making.' In later years Tennyson admitted slyly, 'Perhaps I may have put in the *all*.'[1] Another time Brookfield created a row in the quadrangle before another man's rooms, and when he came hurrying out stark naked to find out what the noise was about Brookfield slammed the door, locking him out in the cold quadrangle, where he stood shouting that he would shoot his tormentor as soon as he could regain his pistols.

There were intimate productions and readings of Shakespeare, in which Tennyson was especially good as Malvolio. In *Much Ado about Nothing* Hallam played Verges, Kemble was Dogberry, and Milnes was an overweight Beatrice, whom Kemble said he played 'like a languishing trull'. At one point the sofa on which Milnes sat collapsed, and he fell with his petticoats over his head, saying aloud a short vulgarity that Shakespeare had not provided for the 'elegant and high-minded Beatrice'.[2]

In such company Tennyson lost much of his touchiness. When Douglas Heath complained that his shirt was less than immaculate, Tennyson only muttered good-naturedly, 'H'm, yours would not be as clean as mine if *you* had worn it a fortnight.'[3]

It was the sort of companionship that Tennyson needed for the peace of his soul, and all during the beginning of the Lent term in 1831 he was still in the marvellous poetic spate that had begun in the Pyrenees. This did not, however, help him with his studies, which were falling so far behind that a degree became an increasingly remote possibility. At the end of February 1831 Merivale wrote that 'Alfred is trying to make his eyes bad enough for an aegrotat degree'.[4]

Even Hallam was not reading with his usual fire. He had come back from the Christmas holiday so full of confidence from his love of Emily that Robert Monteith said he 'has recovered his amiability of late. He is not so dissatisfied with *himself*, not so morbid as he used to be and therefore more in possession of his naturally exuberant loving kindness towards others.'[5] Now, however, Mr Hallam had been rethinking the whole business of the engagement, and he had written to Dr Tennyson, saying that it would be impossible to countenance the marriage of a son so young, particularly as he would be unable to provide him with 'such an allowance as could suffice by any means to maintain a family as respectably as the situation of the parties required'. Mr Hallam apparently suspected that Emily had entrapped his son, and as delicately as he knew how he intimated that right feelings ought to make her release 'a promise made by a boy of 19'.[6] By luck his letter caught Dr Tennyson in one of his more lucid moments, and he answered in what Mr Hallam thought a highly sensible manner. Although he ignored the aspersion on Emily, he did agree with Mr Hallam that Arthur ought not to visit Somersby again during the ensuing year before he achieved his majority. Whether or not he said so specifically, Mr Hallam assumed that Arthur and Emily would not correspond during the year of their separation, but he must have forgotten to make it an explicit condition, for neither the young couple nor Mrs Tennyson thought there was any reason they should not be in touch with each other.

Soon Arthur was denied even the comfort of Alfred's company. After a particularly prolonged bout of drinking Dr Tennyson suffered another relapse in February, and it was clear by now that he was dying. At the end of the month or the beginning of March Alfred and Charles were summoned home to their father's bedside. The knowledge that he would soon be totally dependent upon the charity of his grandfather, and the awareness that his academic record was so poor combined to convince Alfred that he would not return to Cambridge as an undergraduate. 'Both the Tennyson's have gone home suddenly,'

Spedding wrote from Trinity to his brother; 'their Father is dead or dying. Alfred will probably not return to Cambridge; Chas: will take his degree next term; when he will make out his terms reading with me.'[7]

On their last night in Cambridge Charles and Alfred spent the evening with Spedding and Thompson. After hall in Trinity they all went to Tennyson's rooms in Trumpington Street to wait for the coach, which left from the Bull Inn at 2.30 a.m. Conversation at last flagged after hours of talking in the stripped room, and the four men solemnly danced a set of farewell quadrilles to while away the time. As the coach pulled out from the Bull in the wintry night, Tennyson turned and caught a last glimpse of Thompson's handsome face gleaming in the light of a street lamp. Although he was to return often to Cambridge in the succeeding years, he always felt thereafter that odd sense of age and alienation that overtakes a man coming back to the scenes of his undergraduate years.

Hallam was not there to say good-bye to the Tennysons because he had gone to London in the hope of persuading his father to change his mind about the engagement and year-long separation. He told Tennyson that he was going 'girded up for warfare. I hope to fight, like a true knight, although Emily's eyes will not be there to "rain influence." Oret pro nobis.'[8] Neither prayer nor warfare succeeded, however, in moving the elder Hallam's stony disapproval of the match. When Arthur got back to Cambridge, he no longer had the minimal consolation of talking about Emily to Alfred.

Since his return to Somersby the previous summer, the Rector had been drinking heavily and taking increasingly large doses of laudanum, so that his collapse in February was not unprepared for. Frederick wrote to his uncle to say that Dr Tennyson had been attacked 'with a disorder of the stomach, which has been succeeded by a pressure on the brain & for the last two days he has been nearly in a state of insensibility'. As always, he could be perfectly lucid at times, but his nephew George wrote that he 'at others, talks wildly & is evidently deranged for the time being. Dr. B[ousfield] says his disorder is depression of the Brain.'[9]

To his family, knocking upon each other in the crowded Rectory, it was incredible that neither Dr Tennyson's father nor his brother nor his sister Elizabeth bothered to come to see him on his deathbed. Old George Tennyson pleaded that he was laid up by gout and hence too miserable to go to Somersby by carriage, but his infirmities did not prevent him from riding around his Tealby properties in the rain, which in turn aggravated his gout and made it settle painfully in his knee, giving him still further excuse for not going to Somersby.

Charles Tennyson said that he was too taken up with parliamentary affairs in London to make the journey to see his brother. Besides, his daughters were just then being presented at Court and making their début in society, with such grand occasions as a ball given by the Londonderrys. Charles did send his elder son George to spend an unwilling night in the Rectory and then to write the news to his father.

There is no indication of why Mrs Russell was unable to come. Only the difficult Mary Bourne came to see her brother in his extremity, swallowing her righteous Calvinist anger at the man with whom she had so often quarrelled. To the Rector's family such neglect by their relatives seemed grossly unnatural, as it must still seem today. Hoping to ease his father's conscience on the matter, Charles wrote to suggest that the crisis was exaggerated: 'Our family have weak health, but we have strong constitutions & great tenacity of life.'[10] But it was flying in the face of clear evidence to suggest that his brother was going to live.

At the end of the first week of March Dr Bousfield made a diagnosis of typhus, and thereafter only the servants who were nursing him saw Dr Tennyson regularly. There is no longer any accurate evidence about the cause of his death, but the symptoms sound like those of cerebral haemorrhage and very unlike those of typhus. Bousfield's correspondence with the Tennyson family indicates that he was a benevolent man without any particular qualities of observation. He may have believed that Dr Tennyson actually had typhus, or he may have made his diagnosis in a well-meant attempt to conceal the under-lying causes of the Rector's ill health: alcoholism, epilepsy, and drugs, since any further emphasis on them could cause nothing but pain for the family.

The Somersby family kept their relatives informed by daily letter of Dr Tennyson's condition, and on 15 March Alfred wrote to his uncle to say that death was imminent. 'Yesterday he lost the use of one side. It is evident that he cannot last many hours longer. It is a great consolation to us, however, that he is free from all suffering & per-fectly mild & tranquil, seeming not to interest himself in anything that passes.'[11] The next day Dr Tennyson was found leaning back in the armchair in his room, where he had died an uncharacteristically peaceful death. Either to protect the rest of the family from infection or to preserve the fiction that Dr Tennyson had been suffering from typhus, Dr Bousfield ordered the body to be removed hurriedly from the house, to await the funeral a week later.

Frederick, who had gone to London, was summoned home. He wrote of his father's death to John Frere: '. . . a melancholy change has taken place in our House since I saw you last. My Poor Father, all his life *a man of sorrow & acquainted with grief*, has gone to that Bourne from whence no traveller returns. After an illness of about a month's continuance he died last Wednesday at Eleven o'clock in the Day. He suffered little, & after Death, his countenance which was strikingly lofty & peaceful, I trust was an image of the condition of his soul, which on earth was daily racked by bitter fancies, & tossed about by strong troubles.' Mrs Tennyson gladly forgave her husband all the trouble he had caused her in life; to her brother-in-law she wrote a fitting epitaph: 'His errors were owing to the state of his nerves, which made him view everything in a gloomy light & deprived him of almost every enjoyment of life.'[12]

There are no letters to tell us what Alfred Tennyson had to say of his father at the time of his death, although he was probably the one of the family who suffered most. One clue to what he went through occurs in a letter from Arthur Hallam at this time: 'I hope you do fare well, and make head against "despondency and madness."' All the sympathetic illnesses that Alfred suffered with his father should have been over now, as well as all the bitterness, but Dr Tennyson's death provided no easy solutions for his son. In a strikingly Hamlet-like gesture, Alfred slept the night in his father's own bed soon after his death, hoping that his ghost would appear and confirm the continuity of life after death. A half century later he said, 'A poet never sees a Ghost.'[13] His use of the bed seems, incidentally, to confirm the impression that the family did not believe that Dr Tennyson had died of typhus.

What had been a resentful feeling on the part of the Somersby Tennysons that their relatives were behaving shamefully was fanned by the funeral arrangements into real dislike of their uncle and grand-father, causing ill-will far deeper than even the disinheritance of their father had done.

Charles Tennyson was covertly ashamed of not having gone to see his brother, and he wrote apologetically to Mr Rawnsley: 'I was unable to get down to Somersby, my official business requiring my presence in town. I would however have broken through all, if I could have been of use or comfort to my poor brother.' Hallam Tennyson, aware of the hypocrisy in the last sentence, charitably changed the final words, in his *Memoir* of his father, to 'my poor brother's widow'. The real feelings of most of the family were probably better indicated by a son of Emily Tennyson, who many years later clipped out the letter from the *Memoir* and added: 'Humbug. Charles so influenced his father, that he got all the unentailed property. In the family he was sometimes called "The Rt. dishonourable."'[14] The reaction was unjust, but it reflected Somersby opinion.

At his brother's death Charles developed a bad cold and a convenient attack of sciatica that kept him from going to the funeral, although it did not prevent his attendance in the House. His son George represented the family at the church, and he assured his father that in dealing with the Somersby relatives he had 'urged strongly the point of your illness, in preference to that of the entreaties of the Govt. in order to secure your vote', since it would be more convincing to the relatives. There followed a series of letters in which Charles worried about what outsiders would think of him for not going, and his son constantly reassured him: '. . . your future conduct to the Somersby family will convince the world of the substantial goodness of your heart, & will far more than compensate for deficiency in a matter of form.'[15]

Old George's gout was too severe for him to attend the maimed rites. Mrs Russell was not at the funeral, and her daughter Emma refused to go into mourning or even to stay at home from balls in London. The realization that she was carrying on her usual social life horrified her uncle Charles: 'Is it not disgraceful to be allied to such a creature!'[16] Only Mrs Bourne came to see her brother interred.

Mrs Tennyson had naturally expected that her husband would be buried at Tealby, now the seat of his family, where his mother lay, and she had so informed her father-in-law. Old George thought over the matter a few days, then asked his grandson to reply for him. Young George began placatingly by saying that 'He begs me to say that you & the family will find both a parent & a friend in him, being desirous of establishing your Welfare, & furthering your Interests, as far as lays in his power'. After the last ungrammatical, hedging condition he continued into the real meat of the letter: 'My Grandfather . . . thinks it is better that the last rites shod. be performed at Somersby,—he says independantly of the great expense which wod. be entailed, in his present weak state of health, he cod. not undergo the bustle which wod. be occasioned by having the funeral here.'[17] To Dr Tennyson's family all this seemed both cruel and a bad omen for their future relations with the Old Man of the Wolds, and they were right. He admitted in other letters that he was afraid that if the funeral arrangements were not what the Somersby Tennysons wanted, they might attack either him or Charles, so that it was better to avoid the whole possibility of such trouble. Besides, a tablet to his son's memory would hardly have fitted into the series of grand monuments in Tealby Church that he envisaged to commemorate the splendour of the family from Bayons Manor. Also, it might have been a wedge to open the church to unkempt grandchildren and a troublesome daughter-in-law.

Dr Tennyson was buried outside the door of Somersby Church, carried by six neighbouring clergymen to the grave in which he was to rest alone, separated in death from the family from which he had been alienated in life.

The day following the funeral Mr Rawnsley duly reported to Charles that it had 'passed off calmly & with the greatest *propriety*'. After it was over he had read Dr Tennyson's will to the three eldest sons, who all behaved well, including even Frederick, who spoke with 'as much propriety as could be expected under the feelings naturally excited by the remembrance of his former conduct'. When Rawnsley inquired how he intended to keep himself, Frederick assured him that he would now go to the Bar. Rawnsley took the occasion to urge 'the others to every proper exertion, & set before them *their entire dependence* upon the good opinion they induce their *grandfather* to entertain towards them'.[18]

Mrs Tennyson was actually in excellent financial circumstances so long as her father-in-law lived, for he allowed her £800 p.a., which included £70 for each child at home, to be increased if necessary. In practice he usually allowed his grandsons to have the £70 even after they had left home. In addition Mrs Tennyson had her jointure of £200 and an annuity of £300 charged to land in which her husband had a reversionary interest. The total was a handsome sum, but it would have taken a better manager than she to support three sons in the University while maintaining a houseful of children at home and in school.

At first it appeared that one of the greatest privations would be the necessity of moving the household. Arthur Hallam wrote to Emily in an attempt to comfort her, musing about what would happen if the name of Tennyson passed away from Somersby: '. . . many ages, after we all have been laid in dust, young lovers of the beautiful and the true may seek in faithful pilgrimage the spot where Alfred's mind was

moulded in silent sympathy with the everlasting forms of nature.'
With real prescience he added that 'Critic after critic will track the
wanderings of the brook, or mark the groupings of elm and poplar, in
order to verify the "Ode to Memory" in its minutest particulars'.

Fortunately, the family was able to remain in Somersby because the
new incumbent was a young bachelor, George Robinson, who was
merely keeping the living warm until the patron, Mr Burton, could
install his own son as Rector in two years' time. The Rectory was far
too large for Robinson, and the Tennysons rented it from him, and
then were able to extend their tenancy a further four years when the
new Rector was installed.

Dr Tennyson had left little money, less than the debts outstanding,
and at his death the Cambridge tradesmen who had given his sons
credit began asking for their money; it was found that Frederick and
Charles had unpaid bills totalling about £235 each and that Alfred
was £180 in debt. With his usual bad grace old George Tennyson paid
off all the bills, feeling with some justice that he had already given Dr
Tennyson so much money that there should have been no debts. Had
he insisted upon the sale of the furniture and plate, the bills could have
been met from the estate, leaving the family without even furnishings
for the Rectory. Instead of either forgiving the debt or insisting upon
the sale of household effects, he took two bonds signed by the three
eldest brothers and their mother, the principal to be paid to his estate
after his death for the benefit of the Rector's younger children. Meanwhile Mrs Tennyson had to pay interest at the rate of $4\frac{1}{2}$ per cent. The
combination of generosity over large matters and meanness about
small was only too typical of old Mr Tennyson. At another time it
might have passed without resentment, but now the Tennysons knew
that his sharpness with them constrasted bleakly with the open-
handedness he constantly displayed to his son Charles. All this, they
felt, from a man who had not thought it necessary to attend the funeral
of his own eldest son.

For years the habits of the young Tennysons had irritated their uncle
and grandfather, who now set briskly to work to straighten out the
deplorable lack of planning in the Rectory. A great deal of money had
gone down the drain in the education of the three eldest sons, none of
whom had taken a degree. Their example could only be deleterious for
the four younger sons, and might make it impossible to marry the
daughters to anyone suitable. Old Mr Tennyson began inviting the
sons to Tealby, to see for himself what they were fit for, while Charles

came from London to join Mr Rawnsley in urging the elder sons to 'put their great Talents into exercise, & to exert them for their own Maintenance & Respectability'.[19]

As usual, Frederick provided the worst problems. Having initially said he wanted to go to the Bar, he now became as abusive as possible about the law, presumably to irritate his uncle and grandfather. When he had established that the Bar would not do for him, he reverted to saying that he thought being ordained would suit him, perhaps in preparation for teaching at Eton, and that he would therefore have to return to Cambridge for his degree. A month or two later another way of supporting himself suggested itself, better than ordination. In July he proposed to Charlotte Bellingham, one of the three handsome daughters of a wealthy landowner near Louth, but she turned him down. When that possibility fell through, he developed qualms about the Church that he communicated to his grandfather: '. . . it is the consciousness of being no better than other men, that awakens me to the danger of taking [holy orders] unguardedly. . . . I should require nothing more to determine me never to see [Cambridge] again, so great is my aversion for it, than to know for certain that I did not intend to enter into the Church.'[20]

Old Mr Tennyson was not interested in such vapourings as the religious conscience when a living was at stake. Tersely he answered with the implied threat of cutting Frederick off without a penny and signed himself as 'trusting that you will fully consider, as well your own, as the circumstances of your Mother, Brothers and Sisters and ultimately act properly'.[21] Thereafter Frederick kept his conscience quiet for some time.

His brother Charles was an easier matter, for he had been promised by his great-uncle Samuel Turner that he would inherit from him the incumbency of Grasby and enough properties at Grasby and Caistor to live well. In the meantime all that was required was for him to return to Cambridge in mid-April and keep enough terms for a degree and then be ordained. It is possible that he felt no more sense of vocation than Frederick, but he was more amenable. Even so, he lost his nerve about taking an examination after he had returned to Cambridge. James Spedding told his brother Edward that 'Charles Tennyson has craned—and will try again (he says) in October'.[22] It may say something about his attitude towards ordination that his addiction to opium first came to an open crisis once he had taken holy orders.

The elder Charles Tennyson had a limited imagination about what to do with his nephews, for at first all he could think of to suggest to Alfred was ordination. 'Alfred is at home—but wishes to return to Cambridge to take a degree,' he told his father. 'I told him it was a useless expense unless he meant to go into the Church. He said he would. I did not think he seemed much to like it. I then suggested Physic or some other Profession. He seemed to think the Church the best & has I think finally made up his mind to it. The Tealby living was mentioned & understood to be intended for him.' Of the three sons Alfred was the only one who got on well enough with his relatives to be considered for the parish in which Bayons stood. A few days after his interview with Alfred at Somersby, his uncle Charles met him again at Dalby, and already his resolve seemed to have come unstuck. 'Alfred seems quite ready to go into the Church, altho' I think his mind is fixed on the idea of deriving his great distinction & greatest means from the exercise of his poetic talents.' In letters of the period there are a few more casual mentions of the possibility of his being ordained, but they were probably never entertained seriously, for poetry was the only calling he really thought of following. As it turned out, only he and Charles of all the brothers ever earned a living, he from poetry, Charles from the Church. It must have been galling to his uncle Charles to know before his death that Alfred was already on the way to a modest fortune from the proceeds of his writing.

Edward, the next son, was eighteen when his father died. For some years Dr Tennyson had found him a thorn in the flesh, by his impudence and ignorance seeming to be set upon the very path of ruined promise that the Rector himself knew so well. Old Mr Tennyson, who liked to prove how mistaken about his grandsons their father was, for some time regarded Edward as his favourite and planned a thoroughly unsuitable University career for him. By the time of Dr Tennyson's death his future had contracted to the possibility of his becoming a farmer, but when his uncle Charles talked to him about his plans he found him 'unfit for *any thrift*'. Alfred, who was peculiarly sensitive to mental instability in his family, feared that Edward's mind would 'so prey upon itself' that he could not answer for the consequences. Edward would sit for days weeping, saying that he could not endure his wretched existence. By the end of 1832 it had become apparent that he was a present danger to himself and others, and he later had to be sent off to a home for the insane in York, where he stayed until his death in 1890, provided for by money from his grandfather. I have found no record that the other members of the family ever saw him after he went to York.

The sixteen-year-old Arthur was good-looking and quick, but his family thought he was not 'qualified for any profession requiring considerable talent'.[23] Since he was deft at drawing, his uncle thought vaguely that he would be apt at figures and bookkeeping, and so suggested that he might be suited for a job with a land surveyor. When his grandfather summoned him to Bayons, Arthur behaved so oddly that the old man wrote in desperation, 'I dont know what Arthur is fit for. He still does not know the Multiplication Tables or indeed anything useful. He cd learn if he wd but is as idle as a Foal. He must be instructed before he can be fit for anything and his gestures & twitchings &c. are ridiculous & he would be a subject of ridicule anywhere. They are all strangely brot. up.'[24] None of the plans for Arthur came to fruition, and within a few years he had become so hopelessly addicted to alcohol that in 1842 he had to go into a mental hospital in Scotland, unsuccessfully taking the cure.

Septimus at fifteen appeared to be 'a clever sharp fellow', who was well suited to being articled to a solicitor. Nothing that was suggested for him worked out, his considerable poetic talent came to nothing, and until his death he spent his time wandering vaguely in and out of the lives of his brothers and sisters, who all loved him and were unable to do anything to make his life happy. He suffered from nervous depression, and he was speaking the unvarnished truth when he once introduced himself to a stranger by rising from the hearth-rug where he had been lying, extending a languid hand, and saying, 'I am Septimus, the most morbid of the Tennysons.' He died in 1866, just short of his fifty-first birthday, which in the Tennyson family was being nipped off in the prime of his youth.

Horatio, youngest of the children, was eleven and still at Louth School when his uncle and grandfather took stock of him. Ignoring the horrified protests of the boy's mother, his uncle Charles decided that he might as well go into the Navy. It was only the fact that he was two years too young to be accepted that kept him from being shipped off.

The four daughters of the house were, naturally, to stay at home, and it was hoped that their strange manners would not prevent their marrying. Emily, to be sure, thought she was engaged to Arthur Hallam, but it seemed improbable to her uncle that anything would come of that.

It is worth noticing that of all the careful plans the elder Charles

Tennyson and his father cooked up for turning the young men of Somersby into useful members of society, none eventuated as hoped. Charles, of course, did become a clergyman, but that was the result of the wishes of his great-uncle, Sam Turner. Through the summer it was expected that all three of the elder boys would return to the University, but when term began only Charles left for Cambridge. We no longer know what reasons Frederick and Alfred gave for remaining at home, but it must have been evident by now that both of them were reluctant to take holy orders. By October their grandfather was shaking his head over the children again, and angry at the thought that only Charles would take his degree: 'They are, at least Fred. & Alfred are, impracticable.'[25] Apparently at the last possible moment Frederick changed his mind once more and set out for Cambridge, where he sullenly waited out his term for a degree, cutting himself off from college, studying little, and putting himself resolutely against attendance at chapel.

The Old Man of the Wolds was undoubtedly correct in saying that Alfred was 'impracticable', but there was more bothering his grandson than the matter of how he was to earn a living. During his father's illness he had become seriously ill himself. Some time after Dr Tennyson's death Alfred made Brookfield a half-joking apology for not having written: 'I have been and still continue to be very unwell, Brooks, and my eyes grow daily worse; otherwise you should hear oftener from me, but you must not be sullen and fall out with me and abuse me in public and private because I am sometimes selfish enough to prefer a state of purblindness to one of utter amaurosis which would speedily succeed any continuous exertion of that sight which I am only anxious to preserve . . .'[26]

Merivale's statement that Tennyson was deliberately ruining his eyes in order to take an *aegrotat* suggests that his friends thought his illnesses imaginary. No doubt much of his ill health was psychosomatic, but it was real for all that, and after Dr Tennyson's death he failed to make the recovery that had been customary when he was away from his father's presence. By summer he was in bad shape, so certain he was going to lose his eyesight that he went to London to consult the great surgeon Benjamin Brodie. It was apparently he who prescribed the milk diet that Tennyson took to for months and which he claimed was so beneficial that he was enabled by it to see the reflection of moonlight in the eye of a nightingale in a hedgerow.

Even Hallam, sympathetic as always to Tennyson's misery, was not certain that the cause was physical. 'Poor Alfred has written to me a very melancholy letter,' he told Frederick. 'What can be done for him? Do you think he is really very ill *in body*? His mind certainly is in a distressing state.'[27]

All his life there was a too-close connection between Tennyson's emotional state and his physical health. At this time he was reading everything he could lay his hands on that would tell him about blindness and the inheritance of mental illness. Edward's mental confusion was beginning to be even worse than his father's before him, and Septimus was showing symptoms of mental breakdown. Charles seemed to have inherited a tendency to take drugs, and Frederick and Arthur drank too much, as the Rector had done. There was no reason that Alfred could see why he might not inherit any or all of the taints that seemed visited on his brothers, and there was even the possibility that he had inherited the epilepsy that made his father's life such hell. For all this the only available anodyne was poetry.

It is difficult to determine exactly what role the writing of poetry had for Tennyson in numbing the pain that his hypochondria brought on him. It was not a cure, but it was certainly an alleviation. In creating the harmonies and the symbolic order of the poems, he was able to perceive momentarily some kind of unity and wholeness that was applicable to his own life, and so it remained for him until his death.

One of the difficulties with poetry that serves so private a purpose is that it is not essentially directed to a reading public, and for this reason Tennyson was often reluctant to publish, particularly while a young man. Not that he feared the revelation of private emotions; rather, the act of creation had already accomplished that which was most immediately valuable to him in writing poetry, so that publication was supererogatory.

For all his empathy with Alfred, Arthur Hallam was too much his father's son to think that writing had any function save that of communication. If Alfred did not publish, there was no chance of his winning fame and supporting himself by poetry, as he had told his uncle he hoped to do. With Tennyson's permission Hallam constituted himself his publicist and business manager. He had already written in January 1831 to Leigh Hunt, as 'a perfect stranger', to send him for review the volumes of poetry by both Alfred and Charles Tennyson, saying, 'I do not suppose that either of these poets is at all likely to become extensively or immediately popular', although he did claim that Alfred was the legitimate heir to Keats, the 'last lineal descendant of Apollo'.[28] In four issues of the *Tatler* in February and March,

Hunt's leisurely review was highly commendatory to both brothers, although the scales tipped in the favour of Charles.

In the summer of 1831 Hallam found out that the *Englishman's Magazine*, a new periodical, had been taken over by a young publisher, Edward Moxon, who was anxious to make his first issue a 'flash number'. Moxon had given up his struggle to make a name by his own poetry, but he was greatly interested in promoting other new poets. Hallam determined on a frontal assault on Moxon to persuade him to publish Tennyson. Moxon agreed to take one of Tennyson's poems, and Hallam told Alfred that he would be in the company of Wordsworth, Southey, and Charles Lamb. Hallam realized that the major drawback to his plans was Tennyson's dislike of serial publications ('Have I not forsworn all annuals provincial or metropolitan,' he asked). For Hallam almost any publication was better than silence: 'and why should you disdain a mode of publication which Schiller and Goethe chose?' he demanded.[29]

Typically, Tennyson did not answer the letter from Hallam, who a few days later, without waiting further, sent to Moxon a copy of a sonnet that Tennyson had shown him. Moxon was pleased with it, and so began the long and friendly connection between Tennyson and his first regular publisher. The poem stemmed directly from the wonderful days with Hallam beside the stream in Cauteretz the previous year; to those memories Tennyson had added the homely details of a Lincolnshire summer:

> Check every outflash, every ruder sally
> Of thought and speech; speak low, and give up wholly
> Thy spirit to mild-minded Melancholy;
> This is the place. Through yonder poplar alley,
> Below, the blue-green river windeth slowly,
> But in the middle of the sombre valley,
> The crispèd waters whisper musically,
> And all the haunted place is dark and holy.
> The nightingale, with long and low preamble,
> Warbled from yonder knoll of solemn larches,
> And in and out the woodbine's flowery arches
> The summer midges wove their wanton gambol,
> And all the white stemmed pinewood slept above—
> When in this valley first I told my love.

It is easy enough to see why Hallam had enlisted Tennyson among the sons of Keats.

In the same issue of the *Englishman's Magazine* in August 1831 Hallam published his review of *Poems, Chiefly Lyrical*, which has already been referred to. Immediately upon publication Hallam wrote to Merivale to ask him to call on Moxon and 'to pop the question to him, "What do you pay your regular contributors? What will you pay Alfred Tennyson for monthly contributions?" ' By now Tennyson, Hallam said, was 'not intending to go into the Church, as the grand-father who has "patria potestas" over him wishes and not having yet brought himself to cobble shoes for his livelihood', had begun to realize that he must write for profit. Hallam also wanted to know how much Moxon would offer for the copyright of a new volume of Tennyson's poems, since it was time that a publisher should take on the burden of subsidizing his works, rather than his friends. Hallam promised that he would puff such a volume in either the *Edinburgh* or the *Quarterly*.[30] Moxon, who was anxious for more poetry for the magazine, agreed to take on the risk of a new volume, and plans went ahead for its publication the following year. However, the project of monthly contributions came to nothing, since the magazine failed shortly thereafter. All the same Tennyson now had some small basis for his belief that he could support himself by poetry, at least if he could continue to count on the energies of Hallam in promoting it.

Much of the abandon with which Hallam threw himself into help-ing Tennyson may have been the result of trying to forget his own troubles. Although he wrote frequently to Emily, she occasionally appeared to be negligent about answering, and when she did write it was often to complain of her health. It was far from clear to him whether there was anything wrong physically or whether she simply shared her family's tendency to hypochondria. She wandered unhap-pily between Somersby and her aunt Bourne in Dalby and her aunt Fytche in Louth, yielding more and more to a lethargy that kept her from any serious reading of the kind that Hallam thought she ought to be doing. She had begun studying Italian, in order to share Arthur's pleasure in Dante, but that slowly tailed off, even though Alfred studied with her. His own Italian vocabulary he wrote on the white surround of the fireplace in his attic bedroom until it was wiped off by an over-zealous housemaid.

In August Emily went off to Cheltenham, hoping as her family always did to find renewed health there. Grudgingly, her grandfather sent money for the journey, then deducted it from her mother's income. Alfred accompanied Emily, and the possibility of seeing them together was too much for Arthur Hallam, who secretly spent a week there, 'in the constant glory of seeing Emily, talking to her and sitting beside her'.[31] To be sure, he was not directly violating his father's restrictions, for Mr Hallam had thought that all contingencies were covered if he specified that Arthur should not visit Somersby, but he could hardly claim his father's implicit approval, as he did over the matter of correspondence. The fact that Emily, Alfred, Frederick, and Mrs Tennyson all knew that he was flagrantly disobeying the spirit of his father's conditions seems clear proof that they were willing to conspire against what they thought was an unjust provision.

All this scarcely pointed to the peace that Hallam envisioned. 'The life I have always desired is the very one you seem to be leading,' he wrote to the newly-married W. B. Donne. 'A wife and a library—what more can man, being rational, require, unless it be a cigar?'[32] He was in constant alternation between fear for Emily and a scarcely masked irritation that she might be imagining her illnesses.

The only comic relief to leaven the gloom of the summer was unwittingly provided by the Tennysons' uncle Charles, who had now risen to the position of Clerk of the Ordnance, although the current joke was that he had hesitated over taking the post because he disliked being described as a clerk. In a hotly contested election in May 1831 he was returned as MP for Stamford as a Reform candidate. Lord Thomas Cecil publicly made a number of unhandsome remarks about his methods of canvassing and claimed that he had employed troops of supporters with bludgeons to secure votes. Charles Tennyson swallowed his pride as long as he could, until he received an anonymous letter, addressing him as 'a low foul mouthed blackguard', who was apparently no gentleman and certainly a coward.[33]

Goaded into action at last, Tennyson challenged Lord Thomas, no doubt in part bemused by the romance of taking part in a duel and by the possibility of winging a member of the Cecil family. At 6 p.m. on 18 June the two men met unromantically enough at Wormwood Scrubs, Lord Thomas attended by Lord James Fitzroy, Tennyson by Sir William Ingilby. They exchanged harmless shots, both then said they were satisfied, and Lord Thomas made one or two further nasty remarks to Tennyson before they departed. Anticlimactically, as they left they were taken into custody by the police, who drove them to Paddington Station. Since the affair was finished, they were not bound over to keep the peace, and the matter was dismissed. Lord Thomas Cecil had behaved in a brutish fashion, and Charles Tennyson had made himself ridiculous. For several days the London newspapers made fun of both men, to the pleasure of the Tennysons at Somersby. In one of the few jokes that Charles Tennyson is remembered as making, he told his father that 'this is only No. 1 of a series of Reform Duels, & it is thought a very proper thing that the Clerk of the *Ordnance* should commence the Shooting Season'.[34]

⁕

CHAPTER X

JOURNEY TO THE RHINE, 1832

ARTHUR Hallam finished his last term in Cambridge with a flourish by winning both the college English essay prize and the prize for declamation, the latter delivered on 16 December 1831, in the chapel. Tennyson, who had come from Somersby, sat on a bench immediately below Hallam, who spoke from a platform above the aisle. The intentness with which Tennyson listened attracted the attention of another undergraduate, who had never seen him before and who was to remember his look for sixty years. Ten years after seeing Tennyson for the first time, Edmund Lushington married Cecilia Tennyson in the ceremony that was to stand surrogate at the end of *In Memoriam* for the wedding that never took place between Hallam and Emily.

A month later Hallam took his degree, two days before Frederick and Charles Tennyson, the former of whom was two years late in doing so. Frederick wrote to John Frere that he had determined to comply with what he called 'a crotchet of my Grandfather's, that we are all to take orders, myself especially, which puts me into a demi semiquaver. . . . I expect to be ordained in June, without much reason, for hitherto I have made no kind of preparation, & a pretty parson I shall make, Im thinking . . .' Alfred and Frederick were saved from ordination when their grandfather decided that the passage of the Reform Bill meant that the Church of England was soon to be disestablished and that it would not be a good financial risk for them. By the end of the year Hallam informed Leigh Hunt: 'Alfred has resisted all attempts to force him into a profession, preferring poetry, & an honourable poverty.'[1]

For a fortnight after taking his degree Hallam bided his time, knowing that on the first day of February he would be twenty-one and the agreed period of banishment from Somersby would be over. Meanwhile he stayed quietly at home, feeling that he had too often neglected his parents in the past and wanting to secure their good regard before he returned to the subject closest to his heart. As he told

Brookfield, the waiting worried him: 'I am oppressed with the weight of the future—sometimes I feel as if it would be gain to lie down & die. Don't be a fool, you will say; much better get up, & be married. Why so I think too on the whole. Not a syllable have I spoken yet about my intentions to Pa or Ma; but in a day or two that debate must come on. May it produce no division!'[2] When he did speak, he found that his parents had only interpreted his silence as evidence that he had forgotten about the whole matter, so that his tact had produced no results. All the same, in agreeing to his going to Somersby they kept their part of the bargain rather better than he had kept his.

At the end of February he went through Cambridge to see his old friends before going to visit 'the lady of the Mere'. This time he openly came to Somersby 'not only as the friend of Alfred Tennyson, but as the lover of his sister'. It was, he said, 'only the commencement of an union which circumstances may not impair and the grave itself not conclude. My father imposed a very unpleasant, but very natural, prohibition not to come here till of age, so that it is but just now that I have been able to reap in actual enjoyment of her society any fruits of that assurance which a year since poured a flood of hope on a mind much depressed and benighted.' Everything that he remembered was true, and more. 'I love her madly,' he wrote: 'I feel as though I had never known love till now.'[3]

Emily was in better health and spirits than he had expected. Charles and Frederick were well and, with Alfred, had 'taken to digging—one more resemblance of Somersby to Paradise. . . . Emily & Mary have shamefully neglected their singing. . . . There are no horses ridable, wch is a bore: on the other hand, there are curtains in the dining room, wch is a lounge. Charles sleeps much less than he did, but never reads.' Mary, he thought, had diminished in beauty, but he admitted that previously he had not looked much at her, in the presence of Emily. Alfred had nothing serious wrong with him, his spirits were better, 'his habits more regular; his condition altogether healthier'. He was now 'fully wound up to publication', and talked of going abroad with the £100 that his aunt Russell had sent to him.[4]

There was one cloud on the horizon, no bigger than a man's hand. He felt that Alfred had constantly exaggerated Emily's illnesses in reporting them, and hence had cast him down unnecessarily; for the first time in their friendship he had to apologize to Alfred for 'the many little hasty things' he had done and said. No doubt he was occasionally irritated by the way that Alfred complained 'constantly & eloquently of total decay', but his genius was growing 'brighter & more vigorous every day'. Charles and Frederick he found taking 'positive steps towards entering the Church; they toil not however, neither do they spin (sonnets); very fat prelatical lilies they are likely to make!'[5]

Full of new confidence, Hallam asked to meet old George Tennyson, who replied irritably that he was too ridden by fevers and gout to see visitors. Once Hallam had left Somersby, Mr Tennyson complained that he had been taken at his word and that Hallam had not come to see him. Not surprisingly, his chief objection to the proposed marriage was that young Hallam had little money of his own. In spite of the difficulties that he foresaw with the Old Man of the Wolds, Hallam left Somersby after five weeks there, in his most ebullient mood. As Spedding remarked, his difficulties had 'not done much in the way of making his heart old or hair grey or quenching the red upon his cheek'.[6]

When he stopped at Cambridge on his way back to London, Hallam found everyone wanting to know more about Tennyson's poems, and particularly anxious to hear more of 'The Palace of Art', in which they felt a personal interest since it was Alfred's considered response to Trench, who had said reprovingly to him, 'Tennyson, we cannot live in art.' Those Apostles still in Cambridge had formed a 'daily Divan' to read the poem aloud to each of their friends as he came back from holidays. Otherwise, Hallam, at twenty-one, found himself already too old for Cambridge, which he had left but three months before. 'New customs, new topics, new slang phrases have come into vogue since *my* day which was but yesterday. I don't think I could reside again at Cambridge with any pleasure. I should feel like a melancholy Ptero-dactyl winging his lonely flight among the fowls and flying fishes of the post-adamic world.'[7] Later in April he was to keep term in the Temple, in preparation for a career at the law, and then in the autumn he expected to begin working with a conveyancer.

After Hallam had gone, Tennyson's health deteriorated again, and he became too nervous to settle down in Somersby, even for writing poetry and preparing the new volume. He went for a few days to stare at the waves at Mablethorpe, and thence to Sutton for more communion with the sea. He thought of going to Jersey with his aunt's money and considered a trip to Italy with Monteith and Garden, but neither plan came to anything. Without guests he was unable to face the Rectory, but after his return from Sutton, when he entertained Brookfield and Tennant at Somersby, he seemed much calmer.

As a host Tennyson could be delightful, helping his mother with the entertaining, telling stories, organizing games after dinner, singing ballads, and generally keeping the social wheels well greased. While Brookfield and Tennant were guests, there were parties most days. Once the other guests included the young nieces of his aunt Bourne's husband, and to entertain them by showing off his strength Tennyson picked up a small pony Charles had bought for his sisters, carrying it around the lawn in his arms. Brookfield looked in amused envy at the breadth of his chest, then felt his sinews. 'Come now,' he said, 'you mustn't be wanting me to believe that you are both Hercules and Apollo in one.' Tennyson would read his own poems, and in the right mood he could even be amusing at their expense. On one occasion he read his new poem, 'The Sisters', with great dramatic gusto, pronouncing the climactic line, 'Three times I stabbed him thruff and thruff'.[8] Although Hallam had complained that they neglected their music, Emily and Mary would sing at the parties too.

A few days after the departure of Brookfield and Tennant, Monteith and Garden, 'the Scotch duo', arrived for a short stay before returning to Cambridge. Alfred enjoyed their visit, but Frederick found them 'rather too magnificent for a little Parsonage in a remote corner of Lincolnshire', although he admitted they were 'excellent fellows particularly at the head of their own tables asking you to drink Champagne'.[9]

Only a few days after the Scotsmen had gone back to Cambridge the May issue of *Blackwood's* appeared with the previously mentioned review of *Poems*, *Chiefly Lyrical*, in which 'Christopher North' damned some of Tennyson's poems, as well as thoroughly denouncing Hallam's review in the *Englishman's Magazine*. As soon as he had seen it Hallam sent a copy to Tennyson at Somersby, hoping to forestall the pain Alfred would feel if he came on it unawares. The Apostles remained loyal to their own, and a few days later Hallam reported to Emily that at their annual dinner they had drunk Alfred's health to tumultuous applause and then given three groans for *Blackwood's*. Tactfully he told Alfred that he felt more amused than savage at the unkind things Professor Wilson had said of his own review of Tennyson: 'as he has extracted nearly your whole book, and has in his soberer mood spoken in terms as high as I could have used myself of some of your best poems, I think the review will assist rather than hinder the march of your reputation'.

Tennyson was unable to take the same Olympian attitude; typically, he could see only the abuse and not the praise. It was particularly

VII a. Bayons Manor, before 1820.

b. Bayons Manor, c. 1850.

VIII. Tennyson, aged about 30; lithograph by J. H. Lynch
of oil portrait by Samuel Laurence.

unfortunate that the review, coming nearly two years after the publication of the book, should have been published just when his own
emotions were at such a low ebb. He never did recover from the hurt
he received from Wilson, and two years later he was still pretending
that he had not even seen the review until some five months after its
publication. To deny his knowledge of it was one way of dealing with
the pain. The real measure of what he felt was the blind fury with
which he dashed off an epigram to Wilson in his character as
'Christopher North':

> You did late review my lays,
>> Crusty Christopher;
> You did mingle blame and praise,
>> Rusty Christopher.
> When I learnt from whom it came,
> I forgave you all the blame,
>> Musty Christopher;
> I could *not* forgive the praise,
>> Fusty Christopher.

Originally the refrain had been 'Tipsy Kit', but Tennyson wisely
accepted the emendation of one of his sisters. Less prudently, he failed
to take Hallam's advice not to publish the lines, and they were
included with the other poems he was preparing for Moxon. They no
doubt relieved some of Tennyson's anger, but they were not good
enough to risk the offence their publication occasioned.

Smarting from the review and lacking the urgency of Hallam's
presence, Tennyson flagged in the preparation for the press of the new
poems. In June, chafed by his isolation in Lincolnshire, he left for
London, hoping to convince Hallam that he should accompany him
on another trip to the Continent, one that might prove as sanative as
the stay in Cauteretz two years before.

Although Tennyson still knew many happy moments, this was the
onset of a desperately long period of discontent and restlessness. For
the next eighteen years, particularly after Hallam's death, he was to be
almost homeless, wandering from friend to friend, settling briefly with
his family, then pulling up stakes and going off unexpectedly. The
causes of his instability were many, although none of them was in itself
sufficient to explain it. He felt short of money all during the next two
decades; he was emotionally torn by the death of his father and that of
Hallam in 1833; his family was never permanently settled in that time;
nothing of his family background disposed him to think of marriage as

a source of stability; he was worried about the ills of mind and body that he thought were his heritage. A dozen more possible reasons suggest themselves, but the final amalgam is probably as hard for us to understand as it was for Tennyson himself. He usually turned in his loneliness to those who had shared his life in Cambridge. It is only too easy to see that in his constant turning to the past and in his refusal or inability to take on the normal responsibilities of a man there was something fairly immature. As he had been the cosseted pet of the Apostles, so he sought afterwards for someone to take care of him, to give an organization to his life that he was incapable of providing himself. Even in his marriage in 1850, at the age of forty-one, he chose a woman who had many of the qualities that he had found in his own mother. During the long period before 1850 he was almost a nomad; what William Howitt wrote of him might apply to almost any portion of those years: 'it is very possible you may come across him in a country inn, with a foot on each hob of the fireplace, a volume of Greek in one hand, his meerschaum in the other, so far advanced towards the seventh heaven that he would not thank you to call him back into this nether world'.[10] Neither the meerschaum (his pipes were made of clay) nor the seventh heaven is accurate, but the loneliness and the forgetfulness of the world are. Like the scholar-gipsy, he was waiting for a spark to fall from heaven.

When, in the middle of June, unable to stand the loneliness of Somersby any longer, Tennyson went to London, it was as if two years had dropped away and he was once more in the society of the Apostles. He stayed for a time with Jack Kemble, whom Blakesley described as 'reading law five hours a day (or at least was doing so before Alfred Tennyson came up to town, for now these five hours are consumed [together with much shag tobacco] in sweet discourse on Poesy)'. When James Spedding heard that 'the great Alfred' was in town, he set out from Westminster to see him, accompanied by his brother Edward and by the Heath brothers, Douglas and John. As they walked along in the twilight they met John Allen, who dropped his own plans in order to go with them. Soon they were joined by Charles Merivale, and when they got to Southampton Row they found Hallam with Kemble and Tennyson. During the long evening the other men naturally grouped themselves around Tennyson; it was, Kemble said, 'a happy time and a holy time, for it is the mighty privilege of such men to spread their own glory around them'.[11] Kemble held forth flamboyantly among the clouds of tobacco smoke about his stay in Germany, and by the end of the evening Tennyson knew where he wanted to go for the summer, and Hallam, though still hesitant, knew too.

At gatherings like this Tennyson's sense of humour rose to the surface, and as the evening wore on he entertained his friends with his mimicry. First he took the part of a Teutonic deity, then he transformed himself into the sun coming out from behind a cloud, next he was a man on a close stool, and finally he put a pipestopper in his mouth by way of beak and appeared as a great bird sitting on a bough.

In the midst of his pleasure in London, Tennyson was suddenly struck by the need of quiet for writing, and rushed off to the Star and Garter at Richmond, intending to write a poem, 'The Innkeeper's Daughter', as companion to 'The Miller's Daughter', which he planned to publish in the new volume. To Monteith, who was coming to London to see him, Hallam sent warning of the need for haste, 'as by the time the Innkeeper's Daughter is written the poet may be off to some other *star*, & be occupied on some remoter *garter* than that which encircles the fair leg of the Richmond barmaid who doubtless will serve as the prototype of his ideal creations'.[12] The poem has not survived, if ever it was written, which is improbable, for on the evening of the day he went to Richmond Tennyson came pounding back to London to dine with the Hallams in Wimpole Street.

He and Hallam went to see Jackie Kemble's sister Fanny in *The Hunchback* at Covent Garden, and she 'acted better than ever . . . *because she knew Alfred was there*'. Fanny Kemble had more than a passing admiration for Tennyson, of whose appearance she wrote, 'I am always a little disappointed with the exterior of our poet when I look at him, in spite of his eyes, which are very fine; but his head and face, striking and dignified as they are, are almost too ponderous and massive for beauty in so young a man; and every now and then there is a slightly sarcastic expression about his mouth that almost frightens me, in spite of his shy manner and habitual silence. But, after all, it is delightful to see and be with any one that one admires and loves for what he has done, as I do him.'[13]

Fanny's sister Adelaide copied out 'The Sisters', 'raving about it at intervals in the most Siddonian tone', and Fanny set it to music. A few days later the Speddings met Tennyson and Hallam at the Kembles' house, where Fanny sang her setting and Alfred read 'A Dream of Fair Women'.

Fanny Kemble was usually described as a bit too short, a bit too stout for beauty, but she had great magnetism all the same. Tennyson admired her in return, more for her generous heart, her mind, and her untutored dramatic ability than for her looks. Fanny made no secret of her admiration for him, and one night at a crowded party given by the Sothebys she shouted aloud, 'I am glad! I am glad!' 'Of what, Miss Kemble?' asked her startled host. 'Glad that there is yet a man in England capable of performing such glorious things', adding, 'he is the greatest painter in poetry that I know.'[14] Any feelings of his own that Hallam had entertained for her were now gone, and he was only amused, not jealous, at her theatrical enthusiasm.

With so much affection and admiration wherever he went, it is no wonder that Tennyson made this trip to London, the first he ever undertook alone, the prototype for the hundreds of times that he was to fly to the city in succeeding years. The warmth and welcome were to continue, but repetition dulls the edge of delight, and in time some of his friends came to feel that his descent upon them, usually without warning, could be disruptive to their own lives, however necessary it might be to Tennyson.

But on this visit there was no flaw. He would sit contentedly smoking with Hallam and Kemble, rarely speaking or even thinking about his ailments, real or imagined. He wanted to stay in companionable London, but he also longed for more exotic sights, countries 'of colour'. At last he complained so much of his hard lot in having to travel alone that Hallam agreed to accompany him 'in spite of law & relatives'. Hallam also needed relaxation, for he had been in bad health since leaving Somersby.

On the first day of July they sailed for Holland in the *Batavier*, an uncomfortable twenty-four-hour crossing. Immediately on docking they were clapped into quarantine for six days because of the cholera then raging through Europe. They had a choice of living under Dutch guard on an island in the river Maas near Hellevoetsluis, or remaining on a converted steamboat in the river. They chose the vessel, but it was as unpleasant as the island would have been. There were six or seven dirty cabins with broken floorboards, sullen attendants, bugs and fleas in the beds, gnats on deck, and the worst dinners that either Hallam or Tennyson could remember. For this, they complained, they were paying nearly ten shillings a day. For exercise they were allowed off the vessel to walk under guard a few paces from one side of the tiny island to the other, with the constant threat of being shot if they stepped off the path, and under what seemed even greater menace of having their imprisonment extended another fifteen days if they so much as touched members of other parties in quarantine. Since the *Batavier* would not allow them back on board, they said they would return to England on their own if the quarantine was lengthened. Hallam said he would swim, while, typically, Tennyson's lazier idea of revolt was to return by open boat.

At night they could see the boats from the cholera vessels stationed in the river taking corpses to the island, to be dissected and put into coffins kept stacked there, before burial by lantern-light. Even the path on which they paced under guard was said to lead over the grave of the mate of the *Batavier*. The other passengers eyed each other suspiciously, fearing cholera. Hallam could not read, and Alfred was totally unable to write. He was, said Hallam, 'as sulky as possible; he howls & growls sans intermission'. Tennyson told his aunt Russell: 'We at last got so enraged that we pulled down the Dutch colours & reversed them, which put the ancient skipper into such indignation that he swore he would hang us at the yard-arm.'[15] When they were finally released Hallam discovered that he had left on board the quarantine ship the copy of Blackstone he had been ineffectually trying to read.

Money was scarce on the trip; even before leaving London most of Tennyson's £100 was gone, and we know from his letters that Hallam was constantly short of money at the time, frequently borrowing from his friends. As they had so little between them, Hallam wrote to Brookfield, they 'talked much of economy, but the only part of our principles we reduced to practice was the reduction of such expenses as letter-writing &c. Really I often vowed to Alfred I would write to you, & as often he got into a pet, & jingled the bag of Naps, whose glad ringing sound began to come daily fainter on the ear, and their fair golden forms daily to occupy less space in the wellstuffed portmanteau.'[16]

From quarantine they went to Rotterdam, Delft, and the Hague, and Alfred was put out to discover that the dull Dutch plains resembled nothing so much as the flat fenland of Lincolnshire. They were both bored by the landscape of the Rhine until they reached Cologne, where they fell in love with the cathedral and what seemed its acres of painted glass, which Alfred complained he had insufficient time to study. Bonn made them agree that it had a strong family resemblance to Cambridge, beautiful but not very exotic. Then followed a splendid climb up the Drachenfels, winding through vineyards to the ruined tower at the top, where they sat eating cherries and watching the traffic on the Rhine, all the way from Bingen, glooming in the distance, to the unfinished spire of Cologne cathedral hazy in the north.

When they had scrambled back down the mountain they found a small boat, rowed by a strong-backed peasant woman, to take them across to Nonnenwerth, and were nearly run down by a steamer in their crossing. Hallam expostulated mildly with the woman, but she took no notice of him since his advice, as Tennyson claimed, would have taken them directly under the steamer. In Nonnenwerth they put up at a comfortable hotel in a former Benedictine convent on an island in the Rhine, with a superb view of the Siebengebirge. At last it should have been the sort of scenery which Tennyson had been seeking, but now he complained irritably that the weather was not hot enough. Even the trip through the deep valley near Bingen failed to convince him of the majesty of the Rhine and he swore he could make a better river himself. The truth was that it was not a landscape into which he could imagine himself so deeply that the physical reality melted into metaphor. The continuity with the past that was so important to him was less easy to imagine on the reaches of the Rhine than in the near-classical mountains of the Mediterranean. It is also possible that the slight irritation Hallam had felt with Tennyson at Somersby now loomed larger. In any case, Hallam was aware that Tennyson had not found the inspiration he sought from the excursion. 'We have drunk infinite Rhenish, smoked illimitable Porto Rico,' he wrote to Kemble, '& eaten of German dinners enough to kill twenty men of robust constitution, much more one who suffers paralysis of the brain like Alfred. He has written no jot of poetry.'[17]

On their return journey they went to Aix-la-Chapelle and Brussels. At the former place, Tennyson wrote, 'I was so happy as to get a sight of the Virgin Mary's—I suppose I mustn't mention the word—it was that part of her dress which corresponds with the shirt in the male. I saw it streaming from the top of the Cathedral over the heads of adoring thousands & truly I must say that the Virgin wore marvellously foul linen.'[18] Until his death Tennyson remained condescending to foreigners and their religion, insular to a degree in real life however much he might seek universal kinship in his poetry.

Before reaching the port the two young men had another escape when their carriage turned over into a ditch, and was put back on the road only when Hallam had commandeered what he described as fifty Belgians, to push it backwards through a hedge into an orchard.

They arrived back in England the first week in August and set out for Somersby without informing the elder Hallams of their arrival, for fear they would try to prevent Arthur's going to Lincolnshire. On the way they stopped to see Spedding, who was back in Cambridge for the remainder of the long vocation. He invited them to breakfast with Tennant and the young undergraduate, Edmund Lushington, who had been so struck with Tennyson in the college chapel. There was talk of Shelley and Keats, and Tennyson recited some Virgil and an unpublished sonnet of his own, 'Mine be the strength of spirit'. Spedding was amused at their conflicting accounts of the journey. 'Hallam is brimful of adventures and anecdotes of a satirical description, all of wh. Alfred denies in their material facts. But they are very good for all that, and, as Hallam himself justly distinguishes, though they may not be *facts* they are nevertheless *true*.'[19]

There were a number of changes in the Tennyson family since Hallam had last been with them. First of all was the fact that old George Tennyson had given up his pretence that all his descendants were to be treated equally. Although he greatly disliked his son Charles's wife, Fanny, he had invited them both to come to live in Bayons with him, with the idea that Charles would retire from politics and prepare for the time when he would inherit the estate. He was even willing to move out of his own house if it proved impossible for Fanny to live under the same roof with him. When Charles agreed to live half the year in Bayons and half in his town house, he began dreaming of his succession. First he ordered the rising architect, Anthony Salvin, to begin plans for the eventual enlargement of Bayons; Salvin had designed other houses for rich Lincolnshire landowners and Charles now had in mind a seat to eclipse even Harlaxton Manor, the vast place Salvin had recently planned for the Gregorys near Grantham. To have one of the grandest houses in the county was scarcely more than was due to the position of the Tennysons. It would, however, be necessary to distinguish themselves from the scruffy crowd at Somersby, and Charles was again thinking of possibilities of varying his name, although old George was reluctant to change his. Charles expected to get a title in time, and that would solve the problem of what he was to be called.

Sitting uncomfortably in the midst of all the ferment at Bayons was Alfred's brother Charles, who had just been ordained and now was curate at Tealby, acting for the absentee incumbent, his great-uncle Samuel Turner, who held the living in conjunction with four others. It was probably fortunate for family peace that Turner seldom came near Tealby, for his wife was a former barmaid, a connection the Bayons family would not have welcomed. Young Charles wrote unhappily that he was 'under my grandfather's nose, wh. I call being too near . . .'.[20] He expected to inherit the living of Grasby and the estates at Caistor at the death of his great-uncle Turner, but there was no telling when that would be.

Before this time Frederick had been hoping that his grandfather would relent and leave his money properly, to the eldest son of his own eldest son. As a result Frederick had been on good behaviour for what was, for him, an extraordinarily long time. Then, while Alfred was abroad, after old George's invitation to his son to live with him, Frederick had gone to Tealby and quarrelled with the old man over what seemed to him his own disinheritance. Old Mr Tennyson wrote to his son Charles that Frederick had 'treated & left me in the most brutal manner. He is a savage. . . . on his leaving me I said he would kill me by his conduct, his answer was, you will live *long enough*!' The old man's reaction was predictable: 'I have been at Rasen today & given instructions for an alteration in my will.' He also directed that his grandson Charles was to have only one bedroom in Grove House, where he was living in Tealby, so that he could not entertain 'this Brute' Frederick. Truly it seemed to Hallam that in the Tennyson 'family there is an unfortunate spell against concord'.[21]

Hallam saw that he and Emily must soon marry; apart from his own naturally strong sexual impulses it was apparent that they grew little closer through correspondence and that enforced separation for long might build up tensions that would ultimately ruin their marriage. So far there had been little discussion of the financial arrangements for their marriage. In mid-August Mr Rawnsley heard that Arthur was at Somersby 'paying his addresses to & engaging himself with Emily'.[22] As one of Emily's guardians, he informed old George Tennyson of what was going on, and he was enjoined to write to Mr Hallam about the matter. There followed several exchanges of icy letters between the elder Hallam and Rawnsley, old Mr Tennyson, and Charles Tennyson. The only matter on which they agreed was that the marriage was inadvisable; for the rest, each side took a condescending attitude to the other.

In answering Rawnsley, Mr Hallam blamed Emily's mother for approving the correspondence that had been carried on, accusing her of having 'done all in her power to frustrate not only my intentions, but those of her husband as signified to me'. Because of this, Mr Hallam said, Arthur 'considered himself too far engaged in honour' to marry anyone else. (It should be stated, however, that there is little in Arthur's correspondence to support such an ungenerous assumption.) Mr Hallam, pleading straitened circumstances, offered to increase Arthur's allowance to £600 in the event of his marriage, but said that was all he could afford. In the last paragraph of his letter he admitted his true motive for allowing Arthur no more: 'I shall be perfectly willing to make an adequate settlement on any lady whom my son may marry with my consent.'[23] Some time after, he agreed to supply a jointure of £500 for Emily in the event of Arthur's death.

In the meantime young George Hildeyard Tennyson had been making enquiries about the Hallams for his grandfather: 'I understand Mr. Hallam to be a man of some property—whether funded or landed I cannot make out.' Old George's counter-proposal was to continue giving £70 a year to Emily on her marriage and, at his death, for her to have her share of the property set aside for the younger children at Somersby, which would be about £3,000 each. This seemed inadequate to Mr Hallam, as his own proposal seemed inadequate to the Tennysons, and in spite of attempts to budge each other there the matter remained, with Arthur and Emily caught between their families. Desperately, Arthur tried to get help from Mrs Russell or Mrs Bourne, and even suggested that Frederick should heal the breach with his grandfather, so that he could advance money to Arthur from his expectations. Somewhat pompously he assured Frederick that the 'hearthstone which you would thus contribute to raise would be sure & lasting asylum, not perhaps useless or [devoid] of comfort to you all, when the foot of an alien shall be on the soil of Somersby'.[24] Mr Tennyson stipulated, however, that no negotiations could be conducted if Frederick were a party to the business, and frostily requested that all Hallam's correspondence should be through Rawnsley, and that Hallam should not bother either himself or his son Charles on a matter that seemed to him concluded.

At the end of August Arthur Hallam went unhappily to stay with his family in Croydon until the middle of October, when he was to enter a London conveyancer's office. He told Gaskell that he was 'a moping, peevish creature—a sort of dog who wanders about sulkily in the darkness, and bays at the unsteady moonlight which here and there breaks through it. . . . A negotiation has been going on between my father and the old man whose only good quality is his relationship to the person I love best in the world. The wretch makes most shabby, beggarly offers which my father considers inadequate; and unless I can by hook or crook induce him to bid higher, I am not likely to be married before the Millennium.'[25]

At Croydon his chief comfort was to talk of Emily to his sister Ellen. When he went to London he was denied that solace, and since he hated the law passionately he threw himself into an active social life. Emily's letters no longer exist, but she must have felt that he was forgetting that she suffered her own physical and mental woes in Somersby. Certainly, she complained increasingly about them. Arthur, hoping by provoking her jealousy to move her mind from her misery, wrote constantly of the young women he was seeing, how beautiful they were, and how they flirted with him. Apparently the same strategy had worked the previous year when he had written in unnecessary detail of his previous love for Anna Wintour, although he had assured Emily that he could see that beautiful face again without a single disloyal thought. Now he wrote of Fanny Kemble; of the almost identically beautiful sisters, Charlotte and Kitty Sotheby; of another pair of sisters in Blackheath named Marianne and Emily; and of how all those young women would be furious if they knew that he was discussing them with the only girl he really loved. It was pathetically immature and unintentionally cruel behaviour, deriving from Arthur's deep frustration at their inability to marry.

To his surprise none of this seemed to make Emily forget her troubles, and he then had to reassure her, but before long he could not resist telling her of a Miss Morris, who had made 'a dead set' at him. At the time when they most needed all the reassurance that mutual affection could give, they were incapable of the emotional maturity to help each other. They could only hope that Arthur's visit to Somersby at Christmas, the first he would have spent with the Tennysons, would be productive of a deeper tranquillity. Arthur made Emily promise to resume studying Italian, to give up staying in bed until noon, and to stop the weeping that she had reported as habitual. All in all, the auguries were not good for their happiness, particularly as the best hope that Arthur could offer was that their marriage would not be delayed more than two or three years further.

Rather more constructively, Hallam threw some of his excess energy into promoting Alfred's poems. For a year he had been urging him to publish, and during his spring visit to Somersby he had thought he had him screwed up to the point, but once he had returned to

London Alfred had lost his impetus again. Just before Alfred arrived in London before going to the Rhine Hallam had spoken to Moxon, who was justifiably beginning to wonder whether Alfred still intended to publish. It was Hallam's impression that Moxon would publish without subsidy, which would perhaps make Alfred a little money in addition to giving him further renown. Hallam could see no reason Tennyson should not publish at once.

During the Rhine journey Alfred had written almost nothing, but to assuage his worries over Emily and Arthur he set about work at last in assembling the new volume. Near the end of September he sent a packet of poems to Hallam to be turned over to Moxon. Hallam 'felt a thrill of pleasure' on receiving them, since he had, he told Tennyson, 'begun to despair of your volume getting on, as you seemed so indignant at our endeavours to hasten it'. In particular Hallam liked the stanzas 'All good things' (later called 'My life is full of weary days'), since he recognized that they were addressed to him, even though he knew Tennyson would take refuge in his 'convenient station in the Ideal' if they were said to refer to actual events or persons. Arthur had read part of 'Œnone' to his father, and 'he seemed to like Juno's speech and the next but was called away in the middle of Venus'. Arthur was going to London to turn the manuscript over to Moxon, but, knowing Tennyson as he did, he specified that it should not be printed until the first of October, in case Tennyson should decide to alter the proposed order of the poems.[26]

In spite of delay because of a shortage of type, Moxon was able to give Hallam the initial proofs in less than a week, and Hallam set about reading them even though Tennyson still had not sent in the last of the poems. For another month and a half he was to shilly-shally in making his decision about the contents of the volume. Hallam, to whom publication was more important than niggling over a word or two, wrote in desperation, wanting to hurry Tennyson but afraid to antagonize him so that he would refuse altogether to publish. Perhaps because he had the normal publisher's reaction to a dilatory author, Moxon finally decided to publish only if Tennyson were to take half the risk.

The Apostles whom Hallam consulted were disappointed when Tennyson decided not to include 'Anacaona', and when he withdrew 'The Lover's Tale' after it had been set up in print Hallam wrote to 'Dear Nal': 'By all that is dear to thee—by our friendship—by sun moon & stars—by narwhales & seahorses—don't give up the Lover's

Tale. Heath is mad to hear of your intention. I am madder.'[27] But Tennyson was adamant. By the time he agreed to the final form of the book, Moxon had been forced to provide at least three sets of proof. One result of Hallam's reading the proofs was that he took a set with him to Kitlands, the Heaths' house, and there he talked about it with the old poet Samuel Rogers, who expressed his admiration for Tennyson.

After all Tennyson's vacillations the book appeared in the first week of December 1832, with a title-page dated 1833. On 6 December a parcel of copies was sent to Tennyson. Hallam reported to Emily that it 'shines in Moxon's window, resplendent with lilac covers, & tempting [passers-by], I hope irresistibly'. Nearly a hundred copies were sold in the first two days. Hallam was not satisfied with Tennyson's deletions but still concluded that 'the faults are human; the genius divine'.[28]

✻

CHAPTER XI

CRUSHING REVIEWS:
BULWER, CROKER, WILSON,
1833

TENNYSON was not specific, perhaps not even analytical, about why he thought 'The Lover's Tale' unworthy of publication, but his instincts were right. As he tells it, the story is pallid, full of unrequited love and renunciation, the characters are remote and passionless, their feelings described in tired language even more second-hand than the plot. It has been plausibly suggested that the real subject of the poem is 'a Romantic exploration of the psychology of the teller',[1] but the action and the characterization on which the theme is hung are so meagre that few readers feel inclined to go behind them to deeper concerns. Not until nearly forty years later did Tennyson finish the poem by adding a rather incongruous conclusion from Boccaccio, and this he did only because the first three parts of the poem had been published piratically.

Yet 'The Lover's Tale' is certainly not a worthless poem, because of the springiness and vitality of the blank verse whenever Tennyson turns to setting and scene as a way of investigating character. Blank verse came to him with the greatest of facility, and he handled it with increasing subtlety throughout his career. It was unfortunate that there was such a long tradition connecting the verse form with the dramatic and narrative modes of poetry, for they are precisely those least congenial to his talent, so that in his plays and long narrative poems there is often a total disjunction between the suppleness of his verse and the wooden speech and action of his characters. No extended poem in blank verse that Tennyson ever wrote is negligible, but too often he makes it tolerable more by the vehicle than by the passengers.

Without 'The Lover's Tale' the 1833 *Poems* were slimmer by some 1,500 lines, but in the little volume are a number of poems that must be taken into account in any serious consideration of English poetry: 'The Lady of Shalott', 'Mariana in the South', 'Œnone', 'The Palace of Art', 'The Lotos-Eaters', 'To J. S.', and possibly 'A Dream of Fair Women' and that teasing enigma about the poetic gift, 'The Hesperides'. Of these 'The Lotos-Eaters', 'Mariana in the South', and 'Œnone' are redolent of the Pyrenees trip in 1830.

Trench's remark, 'Tennyson, we cannot live in art', which inspired 'The Palace of Art', might not have taken root had it not encapsulated the attitude of many of the Apostles who thought that a great poet such as Tennyson promised to become, ought to consider contemporary problems rather than being content with a rapt, self-searching lyricism. Not even the combined efforts of all his friends would have prevailed upon him had their attitude not been one that he recognized as an aspect of his own aspiration. In part he believed with Shelley that poets should be legislators of the world, and he would have been less than human if he had wanted to be forever unacknowledged. Although he would not have liked to admit it, the arguments of his uncle and grandfather were not totally unlike those of his friends, for at the heart of the attitudes of them all was the assumption that Tennyson was in danger of remaining the unknown celebrant of a private rite of communion with Beauty, impotent in worldly matters and ultimately wasteful of his powers.

The 1833 *Poems* are remarkable for the pervasiveness of the tension between isolated creativity and the social allegiance of man or the poet. At least six of the poems just mentioned have at their core the conflict between privacy and social involvement. The most celebrated of these is 'The Lady of Shalott', in which the Lady, standing for the poet, weaves away in seclusion at a web or tapestry, looking into a mirror to see the life that surrounds her tower, then translating what she sees into the fabric before her, a reflection of a reflection. At the intrusion into the glass of the vision of Lancelot on his horse she recognizes the emptiness of her existence, cries aloud, and the mirror cracks as the web floats away. But she is unable to live in the world that she now attempts to enter. As her body floats down the stream to Camelot, Lancelot and his brother knights stare benignly but uncomprehendingly at her dead beauty.

What is disturbing about the quality of the conscientiously medieval life outside the Lady's tower, which Tennyson puts in contrast to her withdrawn art, is that it seems so like the art of the tapestry itself:

> Sometimes a troop of damsels glad,
> An abbot on an ambling pad,
> Sometimes a curly shepherd-lad,
> Or long-haired page in crimson clad,
>   Goes by to towered Camelot . . .

There is a curiously unreal quality to Tennyson's description of daily life, almost as if he knew too little about it.

In 'The Palace of Art' the narrator builds the soul a withdrawn but 'lordly pleasure-house', a retreat for her to live in forever. Most of the poem is detailed description of the art adorning the building, which sounds rather like Xanadu as constructed by the architect of the Crystal Palace. At the conclusion of the poem the soul, like the Lady of Shalott, shrinks from her solitude:

> 'No voice,' she shrieked in that lone hall,
> 'No voice breaks through the stillness of this world:
>   One deep, deep silence all!'

Her shriek, like the anguished cry of the Lady of Shalott, is the signal to leave the place of lonely art.

In both these poems Tennyson depicts the failure of an isolated creativity, almost as if he were trying to comply with the feelings of his friends about poetry, but his own sensitivity constantly betrays him, so that the vitality of both poems lies not in the descriptions of the socially engaged life but in the account of the withdrawn existence. The shriek and the cry both seem desperate lunges at another form of life, not conversion of any depth. The formal allegiance of the poems is to the external world, but it is subverted by the poetic energy of the world of the imagination, and it is that energy which is responsible for the success of the poems. It is as if Tennyson's subconscious beliefs and loyalties make their own assertion in opposition to what he is protesting. The divided nature of his attitude to the problem is reflected by the fact that he was to work over the poems in this volume and change them in subsequent editions almost more than any others he ever wrote.

The debate is continued more formally and more successfully in 'The Lotos-Eaters', with the tussle in the minds of the mariners between the claims of their duty and the vague but sensual pleasures of the enchanted island. In the Choric Song the reminders of the strenuous life in the even-numbered stanzas are almost irritable, in contrast to the serenity of the odd-numbered stanzas, which gently urge the beauty of the life of magic, symbolized by the herb moly. It is no accident that the most famous lines of this poem nearly all come either from the stanzas pressing the claims of the magical isle or from the conclusion, in which the mariners decide to remain there. Tennyson is subtly loading the dice by the sheer mellifluousness with which he presents one side of the case, so that stern devotion comes out a poor second. This may not have been totally intentional, but whether or not it was is irrelevant; what matters is that Tennyson's best method of argument was not rational but sensual.

The converse of the method is shown in the continuation of the series of poems about young girls, following those of the earlier volume. 'Marion', 'Lisette', 'My Rosalind', 'Margaret' all trail listlessly by, displaying by the tinkle of the rhyming short lines the real inertness of Tennyson's unengaged imagination and probably indicating that his knowledge of women at this time was neither deep nor sensual. His lack of comprehension of them as individuals makes them seem little more than bundles of conventional attitudes given the name of a girl or woman. The lack of individuality permitted some of Tennyson's feminine friends to think they had found in the lines a covert description of themselves, although Tennyson insisted that 'All these ladies were evolved, like the camel, from my own consciousness'.[2] Fanny Kemble thought that she had inspired 'Eleanore', which she therefore admired boundlessly. As Edward FitzGerald wrote rather acridly, 'She has sat for it ever since, I believe. Every woman thinks herself the original of one of that stupid Gallery of Beauties.'

What seems a too shrill note of praise in the poems about young women is powerfully altered to bass organ tones in a little-known sonnet like 'Poland'. Tennyson was not a political animal, but his imagination was stirred by heroism, and it shows:

> How long, O God, shall men be ridden down,
> And trampled under by the last and least
> Of men? The heart of Poland hath not ceased
> To quiver, though her sacred blood doth drown
> The fields, and out of every smouldering town
> Cries to Thee, lest brute Power be increased,
> Till that o'ergrown Barbarian in the East
> Transgress his ample bound to some new crown:—
> Cries to Thee, 'Lord, how long shall these things be?
> How long this icy-hearted Muscovite
> Oppress the region?' Us, O Just and Good,

> Forgive, who smiled when she was torn in three;
> Us, who stand now, when we should aid the right—
> A matter to be wept with tears of blood!

The conviction that breathes through the poem comes not from intellectual persuasion but from the sustained nobility of the sound, as solemn and exalted as Mozart's music for Sarastro. From Milton's sonnet 'On the late massacre in Piedmont' Tennyson had learned to contain his indignation in the monumental calm at the heart of the poem rather than to express it shrilly.

There is something of the same certainty of tone in 'To J.S.', the elegy on Edward Spedding, who died in the summer of 1832, shortly after Tennyson had seen his brother James in Cambridge. The poem opens with a touching address to James Spedding and his quiet courtesy that Tennyson so loved:

> The wind, that beats the mountain, blows
>   More softly round the open wold,
> And gently comes the world to those
>   That are cast in gentle mould.

Tennyson asserts his brotherhood in sorrow to James Spedding because of his own loss of a father, then restates it by speaking of his affection for Edward and his desire to ease James's pain. The closing lines, addressed to the dead man, are as gentle and tender as the opening:

> Sleep sweetly, tender heart, in peace:
>   Sleep, holy spirit, blessèd soul,
> While the stars burn, the moons increase,
>   And the great ages onward roll.
>
> Sleep till the end, true soul and sweet.
>   Nothing comes to thee new or strange.
> Sleep full of rest from head to feet;
>   Lie still, dry dust, secure of change.

For one so unsure as Tennyson of his relations with his own day it was natural to fall into the elegiac mood, with its contrast between the implied character of the past, free from change at last in death, and the uncertainties of the present and future. The elegy fitted him comfortably because it allowed his own innate sadness legitimate scope for expression and because it permitted him to use the beautiful melancholy that sprang so spontaneously to him. 'To J.S.' was the first of the great elegies that he was to write.

Tennyson could not have complained that the reviews of the new book were slow in coming, but their appearance was hardly a satisfaction. On 8 December, only three days after Hallam had reported seeing the volumes in Moxon's window, the *Literary Gazette* turned its guns on Tennyson, in part damning him by association with Lamb, whose newest volume it had pilloried. Moxon's wife was a family connection of Lamb's, but aside from that exceedingly tenuous link there was no actual connection between Tennyson and Lamb, and the reviewer doubtless knew it, but he asserted that Tennyson was of what he called the 'Baa-Lamb School', which he seemed surprised to discover did not like harsh criticism. With some justice he complained that Tennyson was too addicted to archaism, and finished with a blow of staggering unsubtlety: 'Low diet and sound advice may restore the patient: in the meantime we must commit him to what his publication does not deserve to have—a cell.'

Even in a day when reviewing more often smelled of the abattoir than of criticism, this was rough stuff, hurtful to Tennyson, but there was worse on the way. Fortunately, it did not hit until after the holidays, when Arthur Hallam came to Somersby two days before Christmas 1832 to spend that feast with the Tennysons for the first time. Negotiations about Emily's dowry and his father's allowance to him were still precisely where they had been, but at least it was acknowledged on both sides that he and Emily were betrothed. Old George Tennyson would not even listen to any further proposals, but Hallam tried to find some consolation in the fact that therefore he and Emily no longer had to worry about what the old man thought, and could now turn their opposition into pity for his obduracy.

The Tennysons had not yet secured tenure of the Rectory beyond what was first arranged, and they were afraid they might have to move after all. At the time one of the periodic reconciliations with Mrs Bourne took place, and she hinted that she might leave her money to the Somersby family. She also proposed that they all move to Dalby, although it is not clear whether she invited them to live in the same house. Fortunately for family peace the suggestion came to nothing, and the Tennysons were soon able to arrange an extension of their stay in Somersby.

While Hallam was in Somersby for the Christmas of 1832 there were parties with round games and reels in the drawing-room, but little other concrete information about his stay has survived. Disappointingly, Emily's illness showed no improvement with his arrival, and during most of the holiday she was confined to her room, communicating with Arthur only by the notes they wrote to each other in Italian. To Hallam, who was disinclined to pay much attention to his own troubles, her illness sometimes seemed to owe as much to her imagination as to physical weakness. His love for her was as bright as ever, but it was by now apparent that there were real differences of temperament between them, which may have been part of the reason that he left for Cambridge after only a fortnight rather than staying in Somersby until he had to return to London. Alfred went with him as far as Spilsby to say good-bye as he caught the Cambridge coach.

It would be interesting to know whether the Tennysons included Emily Sellwood among their guests while Hallam was there. As we have seen, Hallam liked her on first meeting in April 1830, and she was becoming a close friend of the Tennyson daughters, so it is not improbable that she took part in the reels. By now the sixteen-year-old 'Dryad' whom Tennyson had seen in Holywell Wood was nineteen, but she was still slender and so frail that her lack of health became almost a measure of illness in the Tennyson family.

We know little about his attitude to Emily Sellwood at this time, but Tennyson was beginning to be more involved with women than ever before, although none of his interests was overwhelming. He was certainly aware of Fanny Kemble's interest in him, and the sister of Douglas and John Heath once went all the way to London from Kitlands when she heard that there was a chance of catching a glimpse of him in the National Gallery. Unfortunately, when she did see him there, he had a glass in his eye to look at the pictures and seemed disappointingly out of sorts.

Another friendship with a young girl was with Rosa Baring, the granddaughter of Sir Francis Baring, founder of the family fortunes. When she was about eighteen years old her stepfather, Arthur Eden, had taken the lease of Harrington Hall, two miles from Somersby.[3] It has been suggested that by November 1832 Tennyson was greatly attracted to Rosa,[4] although it seems more probable that he did not become so until after Hallam's death. Sophy Rawnsley, too, was much interested in Tennyson, but hers remained only the affection of a young girl for an older brother. None of the relations was very serious, but Tennyson was for the first time becoming involved with girls in the way that one would expect of a twenty-three-year-old man, a way not yet apparent in his poetry.

In January 1833 there was an unsigned review of Tennyson in the *New Monthly Magazine*, under the revealing title of 'The Faults of Recent Poets'. It was an open secret that it had been written by the editor of the magazine, Edward Bulwer (he did not become Bulwer-Lytton until 1843), who liked to attack other writers under the shelter of anonymity. Although he was scarcely half-a-dozen years older than Tennyson, Bulwer was already MP for Lincoln; during the course of his election there he had become friendly with his most ardent supporter, Tennyson's uncle Charles, with whom Bulwer shared a passion for a romantic past that had never existed. Some measure of the general dislike Bulwer inspired is indicated in a contemporary description: 'He is artificial throughout. . . . You see art and affectation in his very personal appearance—in his mode of dressing, and in his every movement. . . . He is a great patron of the tailor and perruquier. . . . He sometimes affects a modesty of demeanour; but it is too transparent to deceive anyone who has the least discernment. You see at once that he is on stilts; that it costs him an effort even to assume the virtue which he has not.'[5] The description is obviously highly prejudiced, but it shows the feeling he engendered in others.

Bulwer was the author of several successful novels and was on his way up in the world of the reviews, where a knock-out style was more prized than fairness. Like Tennyson, he had won the Chancellor's Prize for poetry at Cambridge, but he did not let that bit of linkage between them soften the attack.

In common with most other reviewers of the time Bulwer enrolled Tennyson in the Cockney school with Keats and Shelley, whom he rapped for being affected, and said of Tennyson that 'his muse will be wasted in affectation'. It was hard, since Tennyson had so conscientiously pruned many of the over-exuberant mannerisms that had been pointed out in his earlier volume. It may be said that few men knew more of affectation than Bulwer himself, who strutted through literary and political London with an intolerable, out-dated dandyism. The first two poems he printed, in order to make fun of them, were 'O Darling Room' and 'To Christopher North', both certainly poor efforts. 'The severity of the last poem is really scalding,' he wrote; 'an infant of two years old could not be more biting.' The sarcasm may have been an attempt to curry favour for his own works with 'Christopher North', who was certainly one of the most influential reviewers of the day. Bulwer did single out 'The May Queen' and two other poems for approval, but since they were among the least successful in the volume his commendation seemed almost an attempt to damn by loud praise. Repeatedly he accused Tennyson of the 'effeminacies' of the Cockney school and of 'a want of all manliness in love . . . an eunuch strain . . .'.

Tennyson's subsequent hatred of Bulwer makes it almost certain that he knew the identity of the anonymous reviewer. It was painful in any case, but what made the review even more wounding was that Bulwer was a frequent visitor to Bayons and the Charles Tennysons' London house. It must have seemed obvious that Bulwer would not have written as he did if Tennyson's uncle Charles had not agreed with the tenor of the review.

In the April issue of the *Quarterly Review* John Wilson Croker had his turn at Tennyson, in what has generally been regarded as the most damaging review of Tennyson's career. The level of invective in the periodical is indicated by its nickname, 'Hang, draw, and quarterly', and its authority by the remark made to Tennyson by a venerable Lincolnshire squire that it was next in influence to the Bible. Croker was already infamous as a self-seeking politician, who prided himself on his scathing review of 'Endymion' in 1818, which was said by Shelley to be the direct cause of the death of Keats. It has been suggested that Croker wrote the review as revenge upon Tennyson for his epigram 'To Christopher North', since *Blackwood's* did not deign to review the book. Croker, however, had no need of prodding from 'Christopher North', since he had sufficient malice of his own. On 7 January he had written to young John Murray, 'Tell your father and Mr. Lockhart that I undertake Tennyson and hope to make another Keats of him.'[6]

In case anyone missed his intentions, Croker began by describing Tennyson as 'another and a brighter star of the galaxy or *milky way* of poetry of which the lamented Keats was the harbinger'. The rest of the review is written in heavy sarcasm, with much ironic praise of bad poems, heavily italicized quotations, exclamation marks, and misquotations deliberate or not. Like Bulwer he reserved most of his vitriol for 'To Christopher North' and 'O Darling Room'.

The latter is perhaps the worst poem Tennyson ever published, eighteen lines of a joke gone wrong; it would be neither fair to Tennyson nor worthwhile for the reader to consider them were it not that they were made to bear the brunt of much of the criticism of the entire volume and, less directly, of the character of the poet himself.

I

O darling room, my heart's delight,
Dear room, the apple of my sight,
With thy two couches soft and white,
There is no room so exquisite,
No little room so warm and bright,
Wherein to read, wherein to write.

II

For I the Nonnenwerth have seen,
And Oberwinter's vineyards green,
Musical Lurlei; and between
The hills to Bingen have I been,
Bingen in Darmstadt, where the Rhene
Curves toward Mentz, a woody scene.

III

Yet never did there meet my sight,
In any town, to left or right,
A little room so exquisite,
With two such couches, soft and white;
Not any room so warm and bright,
Wherein to read, wherein to write

From the embarrassing first line (the vocative 'O' is often a red flag to indicate the imminence of sentimentality in Tennyson's poetry), through the tortured rhymes, to the last repetition, the poem is so unsubtle that there should be no problem with it. Croker recognized that Tennyson meant simply that his room in Somersby ('the author's study') was so snug that even his Continental travels had failed to find anything to match it. There was no such room, Croker wrote, 'in the ruins of the Drachenfels, in the vineyard of Oberwinter, or even in the rapids of the *Rhene*, under the Lurleyberg. We have ourselves visited all those celebrated spots, and can testify, in corroboration of Mr. Tennyson, that we did not see in any of them anything like *this little room so exqui*SITE.'

Heavily, Croker underlined the unfortunate likeness of the effusiveness to that of a romantic young lady's rhapsodies: 'In such a dear *little* room a narrow-minded scribbler would have been content with *one* sofa, and that one he would probably have covered with black mohair, or red cloth, or a good striped chintz; how infinitely more characteristic is white dimity!—'tis as it were a type of the purity of the poet's mind.' It is brutal stuff but not entirely unfair in indicating an essential lack of masculinity in the poem. But even Croker did not go so far as Bulwer, in speaking of 'an eunuch strain'.

Why, one might ask, does Tennyson specify two beds, and specify the number twice at that? Surely, the simple answer is that there were two in the attic room in Somersby Rectory. Charles was gone from home, and Frederick was seldom there. With the reduction in household consequent upon the Rector's death, the twenty-three-year-old Alfred no longer had to share a room, but the bed that one of his brothers had slept in still stood there for use on the frequent occasions when there were guests in the house. But that would not have been apparent to casual readers unacquainted with Tennyson, and even the least prurient of them might have thought there was something vaguely sexual about the poem and those otherwise-unexplained beds. Croker was not a casual reader, although he was certainly prurient, and he had seized upon the ambiguities of the poem to stick a pin into Tennyson.

It is unclear why Tennyson published the poem in the first place, since he was usually so fastidious about what he printed. It presumably began as a light-hearted exercise from John Walker's *Rhyming Dictionary*, but somewhere the joke misfired. In spite of 'Rhene' the second stanza seems to leave the jest behind. One can only guess that the references to the river excursion inadvertently brought together the pleasure of being with Hallam and the comfort of being in a decent hotel in Nonnenwerth after the rigours of the quarantine and the boring trip up the Rhine, and that retrospection left the flippancy behind. In the enclosing stanzas Tennyson added his love for some aspects of life in Somersby. His personal feelings outside the poem clouded his judgement of his own work, so that he was unable to recognize the mawkishness of the finished poem.

Beyond this one has to tread carefully, but there is a little more to be said. From a letter written in February 1833 it seems probable that Hallam shared his room when visiting Somersby, and this leads to speculation whether Croker's offhand nastiness may have brought sudden doubts to Tennyson about the subterranean nature of his own feelings for the man who was engaged to his sister. The poem had unwittingly brought into juxtaposition two different rooms, both connected with Hallam, and brought them so close that it was easy to confuse them. Had Tennyson's own deep feelings led him to say more than he intended, or even knew, about the nature of his affection for

Hallam, and had Croker noticed this when Tennyson had not? It is not necessary to believe that Tennyson thought the matter out carefully, but the nature of his reaction to later reviews suggests that it had occurred to him.

Years later Tennyson professed to read the review with amusement, but even then he had to admit that at the time he had been crushed by it. With their usual loyalty Spedding and Hallam assured him that the Croker onslaught only proved how important a poet he had become for such an attack to be mounted, and that it would bring further attention to his poetry. Moxon was unperturbed by the review and said that he hoped to continue publishing Tennyson's poetry. None the less, the adverse reviews meant that in two years only 300 volumes of the 800 originally printed were sold.

The Croker review provoked considerable gossip in literary circles. At an evening party the wife of H. H. Milman, who contributed to the *Quarterly*, asked Fanny Kemble whether she had read the review: 'It is so amusing! Shall I send it to you?' Fanny Kemble answered levelly: 'No, thank you, have you read the poems, may I ask?' Mrs Milman laughingly admitted that she had not, to which Miss Kemble replied with no trace of laughter: 'Oh, then, perhaps it would be better that I should send you those?'[7]

As characteristic as Fanny Kemble's defence of Tennyson was his uncle Charles's reaction: 'As to Alfred's poems—some of them were good & some rubbish but I had not patience to read scarcely any of them. I do not & never did like his affected & lame style. It is perhaps want of taste—but I felt that the Quarterly Review was scarcely too severe.'[8]

Another reader who had closely followed Croker's review was Professor Wilson, 'Christopher North' himself. Although there was no review of Tennyson's poems in *Blackwood's*, Wilson took an offhand fling at Tennyson in April 1833 for the epigram directed at him, while criticizing him for the adulation of a 'set', and called him 'the new star, no less of Little Britain'. It is evident that he had smarted over the squib more than he wanted to admit.

He returned to the attack in September with a passing sneer at Tennyson, and in December, in the course of reviewing another book, he said that in order to read it, 'We laid ourselves on a sofa (not a little white one like the two dimities that simpleton Alfred Tennyson coquetted with in a German Village-Inn—but a strapping sofa in buff)'. The assumption that the two beds were in a German inn was probably a deliberate misreading. The insulting remark he made so casually was an expansion of the implications of effeminacy by Bulwer and Croker, and he made it by a contrast between his own buff (bluff?) sofa and the two 'little white . . . dimities' that Tennyson had 'coquetted' with. In case his implication needed reinforcement he added 'strapping' with an unstated contrast between its masculinity and the dimities normally used in girls' rooms.

By the time 'Christopher North's' last reference had appeared, Tennyson was already mourning the death of Hallam, the only one of the 'set' whom he had any reason to believe the reviewer had ever heard of, since it had been Hallam whom he had attacked in his first review of Tennyson. All in all, it was understandable that Tennyson believed 'Christopher North' was taking revenge for the offensive epigram, and taking it in the most virulent fashion by sexual innuendo about the poet and perhaps about his dead friend. The silly little poem, so unimportant in itself, had been used as a reviewer's bludgeon. Needless to say, Tennyson never reprinted it.

If these had been isolated examples of the attitude of the reviewers they would have bothered Tennyson less, but much that was written about him at the time was hostile. Even Coleridge said, while admitting the beauty of some of the poems, 'The misfortune is, that he has begun to write verses without very well understanding what metre is. . . . What I would, with many wishes for success, prescribe to Tennyson . . . is to write for the next two or three years in none but one or two well-known and strictly defined metres . . . as Eton boys get to write such good Latin verses by conning Ovid and Tibullus. As it is I can scarcely scan his verses.'[9]

Hallam wrote in the spring of 1833 to say that the Cambridge Union was debating the question: 'Tennyson or Milton: which the greater poet', but since the Union's minutes apparently record no such debate Hallam's account may have been a kindly fiction dreamed up to console Tennyson for the reviews.[10]

He had to wait more than two years for the first favourable review of real consequence, that by John Stuart Mill in the *London Review* in 1835, and by then he was so tender that he wished only to remain unnoticed, even by an approving critic.

CHAPTER XII

DEATH OF ARTHUR HALLAM,
1833

IN his biography of his father Hallam Tennyson gives a pathetic impression of old George Tennyson in 1833, forced to move out of Bayons Manor 'because his son Charles Tennyson d'Eyncourt pressed to be installed in the squiredom'. The truth, however, is that old Mr Tennyson had constantly begged Charles to come to live permanently at Tealby in preparation for owning Bayons. In part he was moved by worry about the way that he thought Charles squandered his money; if he could not get a lucrative government post to pay for the expenses of the London house, it would be far better to give up politics altogether: '. . . ruined we should be laughed at deserted & ridiculed.'[1]

As always, the real difficulty in the way of joint residence was that Charles's wife and his father fought furiously whenever they were together. Old Mr Tennyson, his granddaughter said, could not 'correct that innate propensity & pleasure of his life of finding fault with everything',[2] and Fanny Tennyson had an unattractive love of scenes and confrontations, which she saw no reason to deny herself with the old man. Afterwards she would triumphantly proclaim her victory over him, while he was left spluttering with rage.

Charles's move to Tealby became possible in December 1832, after he had resigned his post as Clerk of the Ordnance and found a safe seat at Lambeth, one which he held for twenty years. By the summer of 1833 Charles and Fanny agreed to move more or less permanently to Bayons, but by that time old George had realized that living with them would be impossible. At first it was suggested that he move into another house in Tealby, but Julia Tennyson told her father that 'He declares that he will not live either with or *near* Mama . . .'. Fanny was equally determined not to be near her father-in-law, since he had been 'insulting and scornful' to her.[3] At last the matter was settled by Mr Tennyson's removal to another of his properties, the manor house at Usselby, some five miles away. By the end of 1833 he was settled there for the last year and a half of his life, with Charles's daughter Julia acting as his companion.

Although reluctant to move to Bayons during his father's lifetime, Charles was not backward about planning his future as squire there, and all during the early part of 1833 he pressed his father hard on the subject of changing the family name. What he had in mind was the revival of that of his grandmother's remote ancestors, the d'Eyncourts, who had once lived at Bayons. Since the old title descended only through the male line, it seemed lost to their part of the family, but he assured his father that he could at least claim the name 'as descended from the antient family of D'Eyncourt' (his spelling became more archaic when he considered the antiquity of his line). As the editors of *The Complete Peerage* have pointed out, Charles Tennyson's 'absurd pretentions' to the name were no more valid than those of several thousand other descendants of the female line, none of whom had the slightest claim to it. All that did not deter him. What he admitted was worrying him was that his father might die without having made the change of name, and if this happened Frederick Tennyson would have a greater claim to the old name than he had. Poor Charles wanted to maintain the appearance of keeping up the traditions of an ancient family at the same time that, as a younger son, his own succession to the family fortunes was a violation of the very traditions with which he yearned to be allied.

Old George hated to give up an honourable patronymic: '. . . it wd hurt my feelings to lay aside the name of Tennyson for this Frenchyfied name and shd not I and we be laught at and held in derision for so doing?' In one letter he signed himself 'Geo Tennyson, no D'eancourt'. At last, however, after repeated urging, he agreed to sign a petition for the exchange of Tennyson for Deincourt, although he was still concerned 'that in grasping at the shadow we shd not endanger nor lose sight of the substance'.

A few weeks later they heard from Lord Melbourne, the Home Secretary, that the petition had been denied. Old Mr Tennyson was relieved, but Charles then set about getting his father to change his will, so that the inheritance of the manor of Usselby would be contingent upon his son's changing his name to Tennyson d'Eyncourt, and to this Mr Tennyson reluctantly agreed since it would almost certainly guarantee permission for the change of name. It had the additional advantages that he would never have to assume the new name himself and that Charles would be relieved of the onus of seeming a climber, since he would only be following his father's wishes. There was still some debate about how the second name should be capitalized and spelt, and whether there should be a hyphen, but the matter had been close to the partial satisfaction of Charles. Within a few months he was dreaming again of the revival of the peerage itself, and in the Lincolnshire Archives is a scrap of paper on which he practised signing the title for which he hoped, boldly underlining the 'D'Eyncourt' with a heavy stroke.[4]

Alfred tried to view the division of the family with ironic amusement. In the spring of 1833 he wrote to his aunt Russell, who was currently estranged from her father, to tell her the news his brother Charles had brought from Tealby, that the Old Man of the Wolds was suffering from severe bouts of gout. 'Of my Grandfather I have seen little for the last three years: he has so rooted an antipathy to me, from some cause or other, that it is not pleasant to visit him without a special invitation. . . . I fear he has little sympathy with any of his numerous descendants, except my uncle's family, who live with him half the year & never pay us a single visit & yet are so amusing as to wonder that one does not call at 4 Park Street, when in town.' Wryly he congratulated his aunt on her first grandson: 'I hope, for his own peace of mind, that he will have as little of the Tennyson about him as possible.'[5]

In spite of family troubles and the early, adverse reviews of his book, Tennyson was not totally unhappy, although he was unsettled and found it difficult to write. In the early spring he went on one of his flying trips to Mablethorpe, 'a miserable bathing place on our bleak, flat Lincolnshire coast', then at the end of March he went to town with his sister Mary to visit the Hallams (there is no indication that he called at his uncle's house at 4 Park Street). 'Alfred Tennyson is in town with the professed purpose of studying the Elgin Marbles,' Blakesley told Trench. 'He has a sister with him—the besonneted, not the betrothed one—of a noble countenance and magnificent eyes, as far as I could judge from a very short visit by candlelight.' Elsewhere Blakesley described Mary as 'really a very fine looking person, although of a wild sort of countenance, something like what Alfred would be if he were a woman, and washed'.[6]

It was the first time the Hallam family had met any of the Tennyson daughters, but it was Emily not Mary whom they were most anxious to see. She, however, had pleaded her liver complaint and stayed in Somersby. No doubt she was really ill, but her knowledge that the

Hallams had not approved of the engagement, as well as her own self-consciousness about her Lincolnshire accent and her country manners, made her fight shy of meeting Arthur's family. The Hallams found that their uneasiness about Emily was in part allayed by their immediate liking of Mary. Ellen Hallam felt she had acquired another sister, and Mrs Hallam said that no one could see Mary enter a room without being struck by her beauty.

Arthur Hallam had been unwell frequently during the spring, suffering from headaches so painful that on at least one occasion his distress made him break off a letter he was writing in order to lie down. Alfred and Mary found him looking fatter and much healthier than had been reported, although he hated the routine of the law and thought most of his fellows in the Temple were red-whiskered snobs. In reaction he was throwing himself into the social round with a hectic brightness. Garden thought him 'most absurdly gay . . . a mood & habit so unsuited to his character, that I can't believe the tendency will last long'.[7] One pleasant result of his undue sociability was that he had begun seeing Gladstone again at frequent intervals after a long period of neglect.

During their visit he put himself out to make the stay happy for Alfred and Mary, who had probably not been in London since she was a little girl. They made the obligatory visit to the Tower and went boating on the Thames with the Heaths. The senior Hallams gave dinner parties to which they invited Alfred's Cambridge friends, including John Heath, who now seemed to be falling in love with Mary, as Arthur had done with Emily. They all went to the Abbey for Sunday service, and Mrs Hallam and Ellen took Mary driving in the park. Alfred went to a supper party at Moxon's and met Leigh Hunt, with whom he was charmed, and stayed until 3 a.m., while Mary entertained Hallam, Tennant, and the Heaths at tea. There were visits to the Gallery of Practical Science and to the Zoological Gardens; they looked through a microscope at a drop of spring water, in which they seemed to see floating moths' wings and gnats' heads, even miniature lions and tigers. With his usual ambivalent feelings about science, Alfred said at the sight, 'Strange that these wonders shd draw some men to God and repel others—no more reason in one than the other.' It shows something of the essential seriousness—and innocence—of Tennyson and Hallam that they did not join a party composed of Brookfield, Thackeray, Garden, and Arthur Buller, who went to a 'divan where a female—of course naked—danced for the edification of the company'.[8]

On 10 April the Tennysons set out for Cambridge, on their way back to Somersby. It had been a totally successful visit, and the Hallams were now reconciled to the idea of Arthur's marrying into the Tennysons. Mr Hallam had taken to Alfred and all of them thought Mary charming. After three years of waiting Arthur now saw his way clear to marriage to Emily. When all seemed to be going so well, it was particularly disheartening for him to fall seriously ill once more. After the departure of the Tennysons he caught influenza, then epidemic in London, and that was followed by an ague or intermittent fever, from which it took him more than a month to recover. He made light of his illness, but it had obviously weakened him. Once one obstacle to his marriage was overcome, another seemed to rise in view, but each time the natural ebullience that was so strangely mixed with the gloomier aspects of his character would reassert itself.

As always, the companionship of Hallam only made Tennyson feel more keenly the loneliness of the succeeding period. When he returned to Somersby it was to receive the Croker review, which stopped him in his tracks. He had been meditating a long poem on the Arthurian legend, a task that he estimated would take him twenty years to complete, but the hostility of the reviewers froze the project to death. All the happiness generated in London was evaporated.

To add to his troubles, it now became clear how badly addicted to drugs his brother Charles had become. Living by himself in Tealby, hating his clerical career, ignored by his relatives in Bayons, Charles could only wait dismally for the death of his uncle Samuel Turner and try to mitigate his boredom with opium. To Alfred it must have looked like a repetition of the end of his father's life.

Hallam Tennyson, who inherited the papers of his father, tried to eradicate every reference in the family letters to his uncle's opium-taking, scraping off some words, inking out others, and often cutting letters to bits. In a letter from Alfred Tennyson to Spedding written on 7 February 1833, now in the Tennyson Research Centre, the original has been scraped and the copy inked, but it once read: 'You inquire after Charles—we see little of him. I believe his spirits are pretty good, tho' he sometimes takes some drops of laudanum by way of stimulus.' A month later Spedding saw Charles at an evening party and reported that he 'looks well—and denies laudanum, except in asthmatical intervals'.[9] In spite of his denial, Charles was seriously addicted by the spring of 1833.

He had fallen in love with Catherine Burton, a relative of the patron of Somersby, but by the middle of the summer she had broken off their attachment. 'Charles is very nervous in the church & does not make a very active country Parson,' Julia Tennyson told her brother George.[10] In a desperate attempt to cure his loneliness, Charles wanted to share Grove House in Tealby with his sister Mary, but the Tealby Tennysons felt that there would be too many unruly cousins on their doorstep. 'G.[rand] P.[apa] will not consent,' Clara Tennyson wrote to George. 'I pity poor Charles who is almost killing himself with laudanum & suffering so much from lowness of spirits—but it would be very disagreeable in many respects to have a tribe of Somersby people near us, as of course Mary wd. expect to go every where we did.'[11]

Charles found that loneliness killed his poetic instincts, which had already suffered a severe blow from his addiction. It was, Frederick said, 'a mournful thing, that a man whose works (the Sonnets) Wordsworth "The Prince of the Bards of the Time" confessed he never recurred to without increasing admiration, should be a slave to the "Tyranny of Dreams" & make no use either of Body or Soul'.[12]

Restlessly Tennyson kept on the move during the spring of 1833. In June he went to Cambridge to see Kemble and Hallam, then he set out again for Mablethorpe to take advantage of the unusually hot weather, to swim, to laze in the burning sun, and to find consolation in watching the great rolling waves pounding in on the flat shore, above which he stood on the tussocked dunes as if on the spine-bone of the world. Oddly enough, Mablethorpe was always linked in his mind with the Mediterranean and the Aegean, particularly when the surf was shot through with brilliant sunshine. After such exotic associations he was disappointed when he went to Scotland in the second half of July. The weather was bad, the countryside seemed bleached of colour, Francis Garden was gone from home, and the senior Monteiths were away when he went to stay with Robert Monteith in their big house near Carstairs.

After Hallam left Cambridge he went to Somersby for the first time without Alfred, a quietly happy visit although he missed his friend. Hallam had to cut short his stay to accompany his father on an extended trip to the Continent, to visit Vienna and Pesth. Since his engagement to Emily had now been accepted by the senior Hallams he liked to fall in with his father's plans whenever possible, although he was reluctant to make the trip, saying that 'too much contact between the govr. & the governed is the worst possible thing'.[13]

Before leaving, Arthur wrote to Tennyson, probably on 28 or 29

July, to ask about his Scottish stay. 'I feel to-night what I own has been too uncommon with me of late, a strong desire to write to you. I do own I feel the want of you at some times more than at others; a sort of yearning for dear old Alfred comes upon me, and that without any particularly apparent reason.' He added that he was leaving on the following Saturday.[14]

The affectionate letter was all that Tennyson needed to detach him from his Scottish boredom and bring him posting to London. Tennant joined Hallam, Moxon, and Tennyson's new acquaintance, Leigh Hunt, at a supper in the rooms Tennyson had taken, and the talk continued until half-past four in the morning. Tennyson repeated part of 'The Gardener's Daughter', on which he had been working in Scotland. The poem had private meaning for Arthur and Alfred, since it told the story of two dear friends brought even closer by their love for two young women; Eustace and Juliet are obviously drawn from Hallam and Emily Tennyson, while Alfred's feelings for Rosa Baring and Emily Sellwood probably contributed to the picture of the love of the narrator for Rose, the gardener's daughter. In a prologue that later became a separate poem, 'The Ante-Chamber', Tennyson referred to himself and Hallam:

> My fancy was the more luxurious,
> But his was minted in a deeper mould,
> And took in more of Nature than mine own . . .

Even without recognizing that special association, Leigh Hunt was as impressed as he had been with Tennyson's earlier poems.

The friends went in a flock to the house of the old poet Samuel Rogers in St. James's Place, to see his gallery of pictures. After the publication of Croker's review of Tennyson in the *Quarterly*, Rogers had gone around London defending Tennyson as the most promising genius of the day. Several of Tennyson's friends, including Hallam, knew Rogers, but this was Tennyson's introduction to him.

At seventy Rogers was the most assiduous literary tuft-hunter in London, and he liked nothing more than to invite promising young men to eleven o'clock breakfast in his palatial house. All during the meal Rogers, looking like a withdrawn death's head, would sit in his place at the head of the table, eating nothing and taking no part in the conversation but saving his energies for sallies of wit once the meal was over. Skied above his head around the walls, so that the light was directed on to them rather than into his weak eyes, hung his collection of paintings: a Raphael, a Titian, a dubious Giotto, and other spoils of his Italian journeys.

What Rogers asked in return for generous hospitality was recognition of his poetic genius, of which he was inordinately and wrongheadedly proud. At the beginning of their friendship Tennyson was willing to make the longed-for acknowledgement, but in time the words began to stick in his throat. For all that, there was a real streak of generosity in Rogers, who liked launching promising literary men as much for their own good as for the pleasure of saying he had discovered them. There is no indication that he ever gave Tennyson any money, as he did to other young poets who were in financial straits, but he certainly helped a few years later in getting him a pension.

Rogers, who had a waspish tongue, rather surprisingly defended his lack of charity: 'I have a very weak voice, and if I did not say ill-natured things no one would hear what I said.' Fanny Kemble claimed that he had the kindest heart and the unkindest tongue in London, and Thomas Campbell indicated the good will behind his malice: 'Borrow five hundred pounds of him and he will never say a word against you until you want to repay him.'[15]

On this, their first meeting, Rogers and Tennyson got on well as the young men walked through the big rooms, admiring the statuary and looking up at the pictures. The Titian was singled out for special attention, since Hallam claimed that Tennyson thought his own talents were most analogous to those of the painter. The only blot on the visit was that when they went into the library they found a copy of Charles Tennyson's poems but none of Alfred's.

The London trip was an affirmation of the affection between Alfred and Arthur, the best of farewells, more than worth the trouble of the hurried journey from Scotland. After his death several of Arthur's friends said that, because of his health, they were shocked but not surprised. It is natural to wonder whether Tennyson, in his wild scramble to London, had some vague premonition that he might not see Arthur Hallam again.

Through the late summer the tedium of Somersby was relieved by Hallam's letters to Emily and Alfred from Austria and Hungary, as full of enthusiasm as if the trip had been his idea, not his father's. The languour of the spring was gone. Never had mountains seemed so sublime to him as those of the Tyrol, nor could the inhabitants be more independent and self-respecting. 'Perhaps coming to them fresh from Somersby, I was better fitted to enjoy them than if I had come from the

vulgar occupations of the world. All noble sentiments are congenial &
accustom the mind one to another.' Salzburg was so pleasant that he
suggested Alfred should take his annual gift of £100 from Mrs Russell
and settle down there. At the beginning of September the Hallams
were in Pesth, then turned home by way of Vienna, which they had
passed through on their way to Pesth and now planned to inspect at
their leisure. For all the beauty of the city, Arthur found the Prater
commonplace, but the Venetian collection in the Imperial Gallery
brought out his exuberance again: 'such Giorgiones, Palmas, Bor-
dones, Paul Veroneses! and oh Alfred such Titians! by Heaven, that
man could paint!'[16]

The glittering city, handsomer than even Paris, was dimmed by the
rain through which he went on his sightseeing, and when he began to
feel ill on Friday, 13 September, he put it down to a recurrence of the
ague, brought on by the damp. He took quinine and stayed in the
warmth of the hotel. The next day the chills were worse, but neither he
nor his father saw any reason to be alarmed. On Sunday he felt
sufficiently better to take a short walk with his father in the evening,
and when he returned to the hotel he felt tired and lay down on the
sofa, talking cheerfully all the time. His father went out for a further
stroll, leaving Arthur to rest in front of the fire he had ordered to be lit.
When Mr Hallam returned he found him apparently sleeping quietly.
Only gradually did his father, looking up occasionally from where he
sat, realize that Arthur had not moved. He called a surgeon, who
opened a vein in Arthur's arm and one in his hand, but no blood
flowed, and he was either dead already or died shortly thereafter,
peacefully and painlessly.[17]

Mr Hallam remained in Vienna for the post-mortem examination,
which revealed that his son had died of apoplexy and that there was a
congenital malformation of the brain that would have caused an early
death even if he had survived the first attack. Totally overcome, Mr
Hallam arranged for the body to be shipped back from Trieste for
burial, then left for home.

The news of Arthur's death apparently did not precede his father to
England, and there is no indication that anyone outside the family
knew it before it reached Somersby. It was during the period between
his death and the arrival of the letter telling of it that Mary and
Matilda Tennyson thought they saw his ghost. Many years later,
reminded by the mists and rain of that long-gone September, Matilda
told how she and Mary had been walking in the deep lane in Somersby

when they saw a tall figure clothed from head to foot in white, followed it down the lane, and watched it go through the hedge where there was no gap. Matilda was so perplexed that she went home and burst into troubled tears.[18]

Mr Hallam arrived in England on 1 October, but he and his immediate family were too prostrated by grief to write. That evening Arthur's uncle, Henry Elton, sent a letter to Alfred, to break the news to him. John Heath was staying at Somersby at the beginning of October, primarily to see Mary. They were all sitting at an early dinner when Matilda came in from her dancing lesson in Spilsby, bringing with her the post for the day, among the letters one from Clevedon addressed to Alfred. She went upstairs to take off her bonnet after she had handed his letter to her brother. There was a long pause as he read it, then he too went out of the dining-room and sent a summons to Emily, to whom he told the contents of Mr Elton's communication. He caught her as she fainted.

Because Emily had been engaged to Arthur and Alfred was his closest friend, the Tennysons were the first to be notified of his death. On 3 October Francis Doyle called at 67 Wimpole Street to ask when Arthur would be coming home, only to be told by a maid that he had been dead more than a fortnight. Gladstone received the news on 6 October: 'When shall I see his like?' he wrote. 'I walked upon the hills to muse upon this very mournful event, which cuts me to the heart. Alas for his family and his intended bride!'

For Gladstone, as for Hallam's other friends, the world at his death 'lay clad in the softness and solemnity of autumnal decay'.[19] After the initial period of disbelief the friends began looking to the others who remained, huddling together like survivors of a surprise raid clustering against the enemy. Robert Monteith spoke for them all when he wrote to Tennyson of his 'longing to preserve all those friends whom I know Hallam loved and whom I learnt to love through him'. The letters of the circle at the time are full of affectionate condolences to each other, sympathy for the Tennysons and reassurances of Hallam's greatness, as if their own being were dependent upon his having been a man of transcendent promise. The Hallam mythology had begun. It was half a century before W. H. Thompson could casually answer Montagu Butler's question '*At the time* did you consider him or Tennyson the greater man?' with the off-hand assertion, 'Oh, Tennyson, beyond a doubt'.[20] Fanny Kemble as an old woman was slightly sceptical about Hallam's genius, for she thought that his early death and his canonization in *In Memoriam* had 'tended to give him a pre-eminence among the companions of his youth which I do not think his abilities would have won for him had he lived; though they were undoubtedly of a high order'.[21]

At Somersby the news of his death undermined what fragile happiness Emily and Alfred had felt. Emily's already bad health broke down completely for more than a year. The rest of the family were nearly as shattered, for the approaching marriage of Arthur and Emily had represented for all of them the re-establishment of an order that had been violated by the illness and death of their father and the estrangement of the family from the other Tennysons. To this was added the love each of them felt for Hallam and the awareness that he could see beyond their eccentricity to what was admirable in their characters. 'We all looked forward to his society, & support through life in sorrow & in joy, with the fondest hopes,' Frederick told his cousin George, 'for never was there a human being better calculated to sympathize with & make allowance for those peculiarities of temperament & those failings to which we are liable. His loss therefore, is a blow from which you may well suppose, we shall not easily recover.'[22]

Unlike Emily, Alfred did not visibly sink under the weight of Hallam's death, although he probably felt it as deeply and it certainly affected him long after she had recovered from it. He kept up the motions of normal daily life, but he had lost his most important anchor to reality. His one remaining resort was to poetry, used as a narcotic for an existence made temporarily meaningless. On the very day that Gladstone heard that Hallam was dead, Tennyson began the first of the lyrics that he was ultimately to collect as *In Memoriam*. Like many who have been recently bereaved, he clung obstinately to the memory of his friend's body, unable to think of Hallam in any form other than the physical one he had known, imagining himself with it on the long journey back to England in the ship that Henry Elton had said would bring the remains:

> Fair ship, that from the Italian shore
>   Sailest the placid ocean-plains
>   With my lost Arthur's loved remains,
> Spread thy full wings, and waft him o'er.
>
> So draw him home to those that mourn
>   In vain; a favourable speed

Ruffle thy mirrored mast, and lead
Through prosperous floods his holy urn.

All night no ruder air perplex
   Thy sliding keel, till Phosphor, bright
   As our pure love, through early light
Shall glimmer on the dewy decks.

Sphere all your lights around, above;
   Sleep, gentle heavens, before the prow;
   Sleep, gentle winds, as he sleeps now,
My friend, the brother of my love;

My Arthur, whom I shall not see
   Till all my widowed race be run;
   Dear as the mother to the son,
More than my brothers are to me.

Henry Hallam was suffering not only from the loss of his son but also from the knowledge that he might have made the last year or two of his life much happier had he given support to Arthur's engagement to Emily. Ten days after arriving in England he was at last able to write to Somersby, assuring Alfred of his 'heart-felt & lasting affection' for Emily, who was 'ever a sacred object' of his thoughts. Behind his grief his deep feelings of self-reproach are easily visible. He asked Alfred to come to London to meet him in Wimpole Street: 'We cannot express in letters what we would say to each other.'[23] It shows the innate generosity of the Tennysons that there is not the slightest scrap of evidence that they ever held a grudge against Mr Hallam. Until his death in 1859 they only grew closer to him, the affection on both sides deepening as Hallam's sternness melted in his grief and their own sorrow was transmuted into sympathy for Arthur's father. During his lifetime he gave Emily £300 annually, as he had planned to do when she married, and in his will he left her £1,000 and Alfred £500.

At the end of October Tennyson had been in London for some time, seeing Mr Hallam and continuing his writing. Edward FitzGerald told Donne that 'he has been making fresh poems, which are finer, they say, than any he has done. But I believe he is chiefly meditating on the purging and subliming of what he has already done: and repents that he has published at all yet. It is fine to see how in each succeeding poem the smaller ornaments and fancies drop away, and leave the grand ideas single.'[24] To stay on in London talking poetry to his friends may seem an unusual way of dealing with his grief, but it was the only mode of handling his problems that Tennyson had. One concrete result was 'Ulysses', written in London and dated 20 October, which Tennyson used to say gives the 'feeling about the need of going forward, and braving the struggle of life perhaps more simply than anything in *In Memoriam*'. But it is worth noticing that the poem is full of the *need* of going forward not progress itself; there is much exhortation, little action. If one were in doubt about the connection of the poem with Hallam, it would be obvious from the linking of the pervading images of death with the vessel and the dark broad seas. The Italian ship and its 'dark freight', which were not even to set out for England until two more months had passed, clearly obsessed Tennyson during the long wait for the arrival of the body.

In October and November Tennyson was writing hard and producing some of his best poems. Besides the lyrics that went into *In Memoriam* and 'Ulysses', he wrote 'Tiresias', an early version of 'Tithonus', the 'Morte d'Arthur', 'The Two Voices' (begun earlier but not completed), 'On a Mourner', 'St. Simeon Stylites', and 'Oh! that 'twere possible', besides other, less important lyrics. Not all of them were finished at the time, and few were in their final form, but the great burst of energy and the growing technical mastery fully justified FitzGerald's enthusiasm. It was to be expected that so many of them should deal with bereavement, suicide, and other aspects of death, since most of them were inspired by his grief over Hallam. Some measure of their therapeutic effect is the statement by Frederick Tennyson in December that Alfred would 'most probably publish again in the Spring',[25] a prediction which he was to repeat a few months later. Frederick's prognostications were wrong, but they show that Alfred's state of mind had become less worrying to others if not to himself.

By November he seemed to his friends to be back in almost normal spirits. He carried on a lively correspondence with Milnes, Kemble, and Stephen Spring-Rice, in which the subject of Hallam was tacitly avoided. We catch glimpses of him at home in Lincolnshire through the diary of a young clergyman, John Rashdall, curate of Orby, a few miles from Somersby. On 26 December the Tennysons came to see Rashdall and nearly emptied a barrel of oysters. Four days later Alfred and Mary were among the guests at the Rawnsleys' house for dinner followed by dancing. Rashdall and the Tennysons paid constant visits to each other, which might suggest that Alfred was nearly recovered, but the truth is that he was carefully keeping his feelings to himself. The only real glimpse Rashdall got of his condition in all their talks was recorded on 16 January 1834, after Tennyson had spent three days with him: 'A.T. improves greatly: has evidently a mind yearning for fellowship; for the Joys of friendship and love. Hallam seems to have left his heart a widowed one.'[26]

While Tennyson was dancing and eating oysters and smoking with Rashdall, his mind was still on the ship bearing Hallam's body back to England. On 9 December Henry Hallam had written to say that he understood Tennyson wanted to attend the funeral in Clevedon, Somerset, although he did not know when that would be since he had had no word that the ship had sailed: 'If that is the case, I have a place for you in my carriage.'[27] Tennyson apparently changed his mind about going to Clevedon, for on 30 December Hallam wrote to say that the ship had arrived and that the funeral would be held on 3 January. 'My first thought was not to write to you till all was over: but you may have been apprehensive for the safety of the vessel. I did not expect her arrival so soon. Use your own discretion about telling your sister. . . . I fear the solitary life you both lead in the country is sadly unpropitious.'

An unwillingness to go through the grim ceremony, the cost of the journey, or even Tennyson's habitual indolence: any of these may explain why he did not go to Clevedon for the funeral. Instead he was helping to entertain Tennant, who had come for three days to Somersby, as he was apt to do whenever he was suffering from depression, whether from love, poverty, or religious doubts, all of which afflicted him painfully and often. A letter Tennant wrote some time later suggests that there had been 'merry Christmas sports, and . . . New Year Revels'[28] at Somersby that first holiday season after Hallam's death, a picture of the Rectory greatly at odds with the grim description of it in *In Memoriam*, and certainly not the solitary life about which Henry Hallam worried.

While Tennyson was comforting Tennant by taking him around the county society, Hallam's embalmed body was moved to Clevedon from Dover, where it had been landed. The heavy sealed coffin was drawn on a hearse by sixteen black Hanoverians across the breadth of England and then taken to Clevedon Court, the home of Mrs Hallam's family. The next day it was borne on the shoulders of the Eltons' tenants through the streets of Clevedon to the lonely church of St. Andrew, where it was lowered into the family vault in the manor aisle.

The church is squat and solid, hunched as if to resist the winds from the Bristol Channel, above which it stands, protected by two green headlands, so that the roar of the broad, unseen tidal estuary of the Severn is softened when heard from the churchyard. From the front door of the church the vista, now obscured by a skirt of bungalows and villas, was of reeds in the long salt marshes. Almost as if to emphasize the bleakness of the occasion, there were no flowers, and the service was the simplest possible, as the Hallams watched the burial of the eighth of their eleven children. Whatever the reason Tennyson gave for not going to the funeral, he must have been at least obscurely motivated by self-preservation, for it is improbable that he could have retained the composure he had been so carefully cultivating if he had been present that day.

※

CHAPTER XIII

MIREHOUSE, AND DEATH OF TENNYSON'S GRANDFATHER, 1835

TENNYSON found one of the most apt metaphors for the ebb and flow of his sorrow in the tidal movement of the Severn as twice daily it filled the Wye at their confluence:

> The tide flows down, the wave again
> Is vocal in its wooded walls;
> My deeper anguish also falls,
> And I can speak a little then. (*In Memoriam*, XIX)

It is not surprising that he was enjoying himself moderately with Rashdall and Tennant on the day of Hallam's funeral, for even deep grief is seldom unrelieved. There was no real contradiction when he remembered years later that at Hallam's death, 'I suffered what seemed to me to shatter all my life so that I desired to die rather than to live'.[1] The little pencil drawing of Arthur that Anne Weld had made at Somersby hung over his fire for the rest of his life, wherever he moved.

The hostility of the reviewers, he said, convinced him that the world had no place for his poetry, and after Hallam's death he half-resolved to go abroad, to Italy, southern France, or Jersey, to live on his tiny income, writing but never publishing again. Even on the £100 that Mrs Russell gave him annually, life would have been possible abroad. John Frere, who went to Hadleigh, Suffolk, as an underpaid curate, counted himself rich, estimating that he spent about £60 annually for four rooms, mutton, beer, cooking, milk, coal, candles, soap, and washing. Since it was even cheaper to live abroad then than in the depths of the English countryside, Tennyson could have managed the life of an exile with some care.

In his announced intention not to publish he was of course inconstant, and in February 1834 Frederick worriedly repeated his belief that 'Alfred will probably publish again in the Spring but his health is very indifferent, & his spirits very variable. He too if he does not mind will be obliged when he has lost the plumage of his Imagination, to fledge it with Tobacco leaves, if he does not take to some stronger & more fatal stimulant.'[2] The last grim clause obviously refers to Charles's opium addiction.

Alfred Tennyson did not go abroad, stop writing, or even take to opium. Instead he settled down to work at the Rectory, glumly drawing up a daily schedule of reading to give regularity to his life.

Monday, History, German
Tuesday, Chemistry, German
Wednesday, Botany, German
Thursday, Electricity, German
Friday, Animal Psychology, German
Saturday, Mechanics
Sunday, Theology
Next week, Italian in the afternoon
Third week, Greek
Evenings, Poetry and Racine, Moliere etc.[3]

Probably Tennyson did not observe such a schedule for long, but he continued composing poetry, with every intention of publishing it eventually. Chief among his works at the time was the 'Morte d'Arthur', which he polished for at least two years, showing successive versions to his friends. Kemble, Spedding, Spring-Rice, and FitzGerald all read it or heard him recite it. His sisters copied it and read it to their friends with particular emotion because of its obvious connection with Arthur Hallam. 'Ulysses' was another poem which he repeated whenever he had a chance. One line in particular he liked, 'And see the great Achilles, whom we knew'. Rather uncharitably Thackeray said that 'he went through the streets, screaming about his great Achilles, whom we knew, as if we had all made the acquaintance of that gentleman, and were very proud of it'.[4]

Although Tennant wrote to congratulate him on his 'East Indian reputation ... Fancy your poems being reviewed at Calcutta!', the truth was that in England he no longer seemed the first of the young poets after the adverse reviews. The *Oxford Magazine* spoke of him as 'still more laughed at than wept over'.[5] When Spedding talked to Wordsworth about Tennyson's poetry, the old man admitted he had not read much of it, but he said that perhaps his lack of admiration came from his own inability to accommodate himself 'to a new style of beauty. . . . But he doubts not that Alfred's style has its own beauty.' As a parallel case of his inability to appreciate splendid poetry, Wordsworth generously cited the choruses of *Samson Agonistes*, 'the measure of which he has never been able to enjoy, which comes to perhaps as high a compliment as a negative compliment can'. For all his attempted charity, it was clear that he did not much care for what he had read, and Spedding wisely gave up attempting a conversion. It must have seemed thin consolation to Tennyson to hear from Milnes that at least the Apostles were still faithful to him: 'if you had heard the cheer that followed the health of A.T., the Poet of the Apostles, at our dinner, if you had!'

Tennyson was normally a man of intense pride, and it is an indication of how low his self-esteem had fallen that in April 1834 he wrote to Professor Wilson ('Christopher North'), bravely claiming that he had not been hurt by the review in *Blackwood's* three years before, which he said was redeemed by 'a tone of boisterous and picturesque humour such as I love'. Then he said that the weakness of his own squib, 'To Christopher North', only proved how little he had minded the review, 'for I trust that you will give me credit for being able to write a better'. With an apology for the worst of his poems, written 'before I had attained my nineteenth year', he offered to shake hands with the reviewer. Wilson apparently took no notice of the letter, which hurt Tennyson after he had so ignominiously swallowed his pride. The episode of 'Christopher North' was closed. He would surely never have written the letter had he not intended to publish again and been afraid of how he might be handled by Wilson. Never before or after was he to come so close to cringing to a reviewer, and the bitter taste of having once done so with no success partially explains why he so distrusted and hated critics in his later years.

In early 1833 Edward Tennyson, 'in a hopeless state of fatuity', had been sent off to the asylum in York where he spent the rest of his life, and for a time it looked as if Septimus would have the same fate, for his symptoms were like those with which Edward's derangement had begun. He would sit for whole days weeping, complaining that all his relatives were neglecting him, and at last Alfred had to write to his uncle Charles, begging that he be taken away from the 'morbid influence' of the Rectory. After being apprenticed to a Lincolnshire physician, Septimus's condition got better, but the improvement did not last long.

The other children went frequently to stay with Charles in Tealby and take care of him in his opium addiction; Eustace Tennyson

commiserated with his father for having 'the swarms of Goths &
Vandals' descending upon Tealby every week.[6]

Relations with Usselby became easier after Frederick had made yet
another peace with his grandfather. In February he called on him and
found him sitting by a roaring fire, surprisingly calm after having 'left
his house, his old haunts . . . & gone to live on a sandy moor. . . . My
uncle's family are already installed in the Squiredom, but such things
do not make him like Lear to double his fist at heaven, or think the
wintry winds nothing to it.'[7] In 'approaching dissolution' old George
became progressively more amenable, entertaining his grandchildren
from Somersby and making his peace at last with both his daughters. It
was too late to establish the ties of love he had neglected so long, but he
had found tranquillity of a sort he had never known before. The old
Adam died hard, however. His grandson Charles had just taken on a
second curacy at Rothwell, for the sake of the £50 income; when he
heard of it old George withdrew an equal amount from the £70 he had
given his grandson annually before that. After all, his charity was
intended to keep his family from want, not to let them live in unearned
luxury. Naturally, even the mild-mannered Charles was furious. After
this last triumphant economy, old George settled down contentedly to
wait for death.

At the end of the summer Frederick went to Italy, then on to Corfu
to stay with his cousin George, who was on the staff of Lord Nugent.
Frederick was uninvited and unwelcome, but he never noticed that
George only wanted him to leave. The elder Charles Tennyson was
appalled at what might happen to the career of his son if he were
saddled with this least favourite of all relatives.

The daughters of the Rectory were in somewhat happier situation.
John Heath and Mary were by now in love, and in June he and his
brother Douglas came to stay at Somersby. By then Emily had begun
to recover her spirits, and on the first day after Arthur's death that she
felt like seeing anyone outside the family she came into the drawing-
room, pale, dressed in black, 'but with one white rose in her hair as her
Arthur loved to see her'.

Love at the Rectory was contagious, and Tennant became the third
Apostle to fall in love with one of Alfred's sisters. The sixteen-year-old
Cecilia did not return his regard, so Tennant had to assure Mrs
Tennyson that he would not renew his attentions if only he were
allowed to continue coming to Somersby. After his summer visit he
wrote in gratitude to Alfred: 'The sight of Somersby and your kindness

have overcome the hard hearted stubbornness that shut up all my feelings. Forgotten friendships have been revived and correspondences been renewed that had long since dropped and home feelings aroused that had slept a long sleep.'[8]

In July Alfred, Emily, and Mary were invited to go south for a month; Emily was to go to Molesey Park to stay with the Hallams for her first introduction to them while Alfred and Mary went to Kitlands, near Dorking, to visit the Heaths. At the last minute Emily once more backed out of the trip, and her mother had to apologize for her: 'The great lassitude she feels makes her fear she is unequal for such an exertion.' Without Emily, Mary felt she could not make the trip, and Alfred went alone. He was depressed, and the Heaths did all they could to cheer him, taking him to see Worthing and suggesting a trip to Brighton. But he preferred to walk alone by the streams running through the wooded valleys near Leith Hill. The Heaths were fortunately not put out by the curious manners of their morose guest, recognizing his sadness as evidence of real distress.

One evening early in July he went to Molesey Park to the Hallams, presumably the first time he had seen any of them except Mr Hallam since Arthur's death. The family was downcast that Emily had been unable to come, over the whole group hung the memory of Arthur, and the visit was unsuccessful. Arthur's young sister Ellen sat for a time on the sofa beside the silent Alfred, unable to think of anything but her dead brother. 'Oh! what a wretched evening for all of us,' she wrote in her diary.[9]

Mr Hallam gave Alfred copies of the *Remains in Verse and Prose* of his son, which had been recently printed. When first he had suggested the volume in February 1834 he wrote to Alfred to ask him to contribute a memoir of Arthur; he made it clear that the work, although intended for private distribution only, would have almost nothing personal in it, and that he intended to print nothing that would 'too much reveal the secrets of his mind'. Alfred replied that his heart was 'too crushed and all [his] energies too paralysed' to help,[10] so Mr Hallam had done most of the preparation himself. It is a stiff little volume, which can have given but scant consolation to Arthur's friends, but it was his only memorial aside from that at Clevedon since Trinity had politely refused the proposal for a tablet in the chapel, because Arthur had not been a scholar of the college.

During the autumn of 1834 Tennyson was near Clevedon; he went to the meeting of the Wye and the Severn, some fifteen miles away as the crow flies, and there wrote section XIX of *In Memoriam*. He wandered along the Wye, and at Tintern Abbey in 'the yellowing autumn-tide', as he stood looking through the ruined windows, full of the sense of the poignant rush of time, he composed 'Tears, Idle Tears', in its own way nearly as great a poem as Wordsworth's written on the same spot:

> Tears, idle tears, I know not what they mean,
> Tears from the depth of some divine despair
> Rise in the heart, and gather to the eyes,
> In looking on the happy Autumn-fields,
> And thinking of the days that are no more.
>
> Fresh as the first beam glittering on a sail,
> That brings our friends up from the underworld,
> Sad as the last which reddens over one
> That sinks with all we love below the verge;
> So sad, so fresh, the days that are no more.
>
> Ah, sad and strange as in dark summer dawns
> The earliest pipe of half-awakened birds
> To dying ears, when unto dying eyes
> The casement slowly grows a glimmering square;
> So sad, so strange, the days that are no more.
>
> Dear as remembered kisses after death,
> And sweet as those by hopeless fancy feigned
> On lips that are for others; deep as love,
> Deep as first love, and wild with all regret;
> O Death in Life, the days that are no more.

It is surprising that he did not go to Clevedon when he was so near, but no doubt he still felt the loss of Hallam too keenly to trust his own emotions if he were to see the tablet in the parish church.

On leaving the Hallams in July he had promised to bring Emily to them as soon as possible, but both he and Emily fell ill at Somersby. It was not until 13 October that he took her to East Molesey to introduce her to the family into which she had almost married. During the year following Arthur's death Emily and the Hallams had corresponded frequently, and Mrs Hallam had sent her a replica of the locket that Arthur had worn around his neck. Although both Emily and the Hallams were nervous about meeting at last, the visit went well and Emily was taken into the family. Three days after her arrival, Arthur's sister Ellen wrote in her diary: 'My dear Emily read to me this morning a little poem of Alfred's—a kind of ballad upon the death of King Arthur.' If this was the 'Morte d'Arthur', the description is a strange one. 'She reads very like him—slow, distinct & mournful.' Ellen found that Emily did not like to mention Arthur, even to his own family.

On 25 October the Hallams gave a large dinner party for Emily's twenty-third birthday, and among the guests was a 'Mr. Jesse', whose name appeared again on the guest list a month later, when Emily sang after dinner. Eight years later she married Richard Jesse, whom the Hallams disliked intensely; if they were responsible for introducing Emily to her future husband it was an irony they would not have appreciated. When the Hallams moved from East Molesey to Wimpole Street for the winter, she went with them, and then accepted an invitation to stay on for Christmas and into the New Year. Just before Christmas she went with Ellen and Julia to a ball, although Mrs Hallam disapproved of her going, presumably feeling that she should remain in mourning for Arthur. When she finally went back to Somersby in February, she had been with the Hallams four months and had been taken into the family almost as closely as if she had actually married Arthur.[11]

When Emily returned home she was so much better that the atmosphere in the Rectory lifted considerably. Christmas at Somersby had been a merry one, and John Heath had been there for the holidays, which Tennant, judging from his own experience, expected to be filled with parties and games. The end of 1834 marked the conclusion of Tennyson's worst grief over Hallam. Even that had been an anchor to which he could attach himself, and though his life was still disordered he was more ready to form new attachments.

While Emily was in London, Ellen Hallam taught her to waltz, and she introduced the dance to her family and friends at Somersby. We get a glimpse of life in the Rectory in the spring of 1835 from a letter Emily wrote to Ellen: 'We had a party to dinner last Thursday, and finished the day with dancing . . . there was a great deal of waltzing—a Miss Rawnsley who was here, is the lightest and most indefatigable dancer I ever saw,—she is a very nice, amiable girl, and so cheerful and happy, that it brings sunshine into one's heart, though it were gloomy before, to look at her. Alfred is delighted with her. I sometimes fancy she is the prototype of his "Airy Fairy Lilian." '[12]

Besides Sophy Rawnsley, with whom he kept up his brotherly affection, Tennyson saw other female visitors to Somersby that spring, including Emily Sellwood, with whom he sat on an iron seat in the garden under budding elm trees. Some years later he still remembered that she wore a silk pelisse and that he read aloud to her when he had just returned from London.

But Tennyson was still feeling friendless, and when he heard a description of a breakfast party the Hallams had given, at which Wordsworth and Rogers were guests, 'Alfred growled, as . . . Tennysons are apt to do sometimes, and said he was cut out from all society worth living for—he finished by venting his spleen unmercifully upon harmless, stout, foxhunting Lincolnshire Squires'.[13]

In March 1835 Samuel Turner died, releasing young Charles Tennyson at last from his awkward position at Tealby. He moved immediately to the big house in Caistor his great-uncle had left him, together with a life interest in properties at Caistor, Nettleton, Grasby, and Cabourne, which were enough to bring him an income of £400. Charles had also inherited the advowson of Grasby and nominated himself to the living. His grandfather offered him the living of Tealby, vacated by Turner's death, but Charles declined. To Eustace Tennyson, his cousin's move to Caistor seemed a good thing for the family at Bayons: 'I cannot help pitying him poor fellow, for he is the most good-natured fellow in the world, and I think he will kill himself soon.'[14] Happily, the change in his circumstances helped Charles to pull himself together, and during the next year or two he managed to break the opium habit for a time. In accordance with the wishes of his great-uncle he changed his name to Turner; if he had not been such a guileless man one would wonder whether he was glad to be totally rid of the name of Tennyson, for he did not incorporate it with Turner and he never used it again.

Charles's handsome three-storeyed Georgian house in the market-place of Caistor was the one where his grandmother had lived as a girl. Alfred described him to Brookfield as living in 'a wretched market town which looks more like the limit of the civilized world than Johnny Groat's house—about 9 miles from Tealby: he is however the first man in the place, an owner of books & pictures, a watercloset with a recumbent Venus in it, & a house with a stone front. The country about him is dreadful—barren rolling chalkwolds without a tree: he talks of travelling for three years, & afterwards of taking a wife.'[15] In the event he took spiritual care of Grasby, some three miles away, and by September he was engaged to Louisa Sellwood of Horncastle, the sister of Emily.

The lethargy with which the Tennysons seemed to accept whatever came their way was worrying to outsiders such as Mr Rawnsley, who wrote that 'They are all well at Somersby, but I wish they were earnest more either of fame or profit', then added almost enviously, 'but then, they are leading a *harmless* & *quiet* life, & this is what the Antient Poets & philosophers say is after all the highest state of permanent enjoyment'.[16]

But Alfred Tennyson was not in a state of enjoyment, and after Hallam's death he found himself unable to settle anywhere, least of all in Somersby. In February 1835 he had first proposed himself to Spedding as a guest at Mirehouse, on the banks of Lake Bassenthwaite, saying that he had sold his Chancellor's Medal for £15 and so had money to travel: 'I have an inclination to come and see you, and if possible to bring you back with me here. . . . I will come to you as Sheba came to Solomon.' Then, after Spedding's invitation had reached him, he changed his mind, begged off going to Mirehouse, and instead went to see the waves at Mablethorpe with his family during a week of high spring tide. When that failed to live up to expectations he took a flying trip of two days to Boulogne, and that too was unsatisfactory. In April he set off to join Edward FitzGerald, who was staying with the Speddings. The railway had not yet penetrated the Lake Country, and he took a stage-coach to Kendal, followed by a coach trip that began at 8 a.m., and arrived five hours later in Keswick, where he was only a few miles from Mirehouse, in the shadow of Skiddaw.

In the year following Hallam's death James Spedding had been nearly as upset as Tennyson, uncertain of what was to happen to him. Originally he had intended taking holy orders, but at Cambridge he realized that he had too many doubts to do so with a clear conscience. By nature he was a scholar, but he had failed twice to win a Cambridge fellowship, and now, at twenty-seven he still felt at a loose end about his future. His father wanted him to go into public life, an idea that did not interest him, and as much as possible he stayed at home in Mirehouse, reading, walking, training puppies, and generally trying to avoid discussions of his problems with his worried father.

Mr Spedding, who had retired from the Army, was a sensible Whig squire who farmed his Cumberland estate and was more interested in politics and the breeding of shorthorn cattle than in poetry. No doubt his faint distrust of poets themselves was sharpened by his memory of Shelley stalking about the Lake Country waving pistols; it had not been lulled by an acquaintance with the improvident Coleridge; and his old schoolfellow, Wordsworth, to whom family tradition says he had given money, struck him as singularly impractical. For all this he was generous and tolerant, with a quiet but strong sense of humour, and his doubts about poetry sprang from genuine perplexity rather than philistinism.

Although they had been introduced briefly in Cambridge, Tennyson and FitzGerald were no more than nodding acquaintances before meeting again at Mirehouse. FitzGerald was the cultured eccentric son of a rich family. He loved music as immoderately as Frederick Tennyson, with whom he kept up a correspondence on the subject, and his only financial extravagance was the constant purchase of bad pictures that he was always mistaking for masterpieces. Neither he nor his friends suspected that the poetry he wrote had the promise for the future of anything like his great version of the *Rubáiyát*. His face was lumpily formed, and he shambled along in clothes that always looked second-hand, but behind his shy and unpromising exterior was a sweet and loving nature, fierce only in his loyalty to his friends. His meeting at Mirehouse with Tennyson was the beginning of a lifelong friendship, more devoted on FitzGerald's part than on Tennyson's but necessary to them both. Until his death FitzGerald was to worry recurrently over whether Tennyson still counted him as a friend, but one random gleam of warmth from Tennyson would dissolve all his fears until the next time he felt he had been snubbed or neglected.

'Fitz', as he was invariably known, had been at school with Spedding, who was a distant relative, and he had a charming courtesy with his elders, so that Spedding's parents did not worry about his physical inertia or his vegetarianism as forms of eccentricity dangerous to James. In reaction to the grandeur of his own family, he hated ostentation or any kind of snobbishness, and the manifestation of either would draw his gentle reproof. Once in later years when he and Tennyson had listened to a common acquaintance talking of his titled friends, Fitz picked up a candle to go to bed, then turned at the door and said to Tennyson, 'I knew a Lord once, but he's dead.'[17] When they were both old men and FitzGerald had been hurt by Tennyson's neglect, the worst he could think of to say of him was that he lived in too grand a manner. Spedding called Fitz 'the Prince of Quietists', and said that 'Half the self-sacrifice, the self-denial, the moral resolution, which he exercises to keep himself easy, would amply furnish forth a martyr or a missionary. His tranquillity is like a pirated copy of the peace of God.'[18]

In April Mirehouse was still cold, and Emily heard from her brother that 'he admires the country near the lakes very much, but could dispense with the deluges of sapping rains. I understand the demon of vapours descends there in a perpetual drizzle.'[19] In compensation the larches on Skiddaw were just turning pale green, and the margin of the lake was coloured with bog-myrtle. Above all, the daffodils swept from the door of the house in a sheet of yellow to the lake, several hundred yards away. It was a perfect place to talk poetry, and the three young men did so constantly.

When the weather permitted, they would scull on the lake, and even in the rain they could take dogs and ramble over the fells. Outdoors or in Alfred wore his great cloak, either to keep off the rain or to pull up under his chin as he sat reading before the library fire, his feet on the fender, his book close to his near-sighted eyes. (See Plate V.) In lamenting the bad weather Spedding wrote, 'it must be a very capable and effective sun that shall make his soul rejoice and say "Ha! Ha! I am warm."'[20]

The Speddings kept country hours. Mr Spedding would go off on his cob immediately after breakfast and not return until two o'clock dinner, then he would disappear again until evening, when there was a 'serious tea', with 'many varieties of bread and cakes, with divers jams and marmalades, and this was the great time for talk, and the discussions in which the views of the younger generation were not always accepted without remark'.[21] Fitz, who hated political talk, would play chess with Mrs Spedding while the other men discussed the state of the world.

When the elder Speddings retired it was time for poetry. Usually it was read by Alfred out of the little red book in which he kept a record of the poems on which he was working, and often, while he read, Spedding would sketch him. Fitz remembered Alfred's speaking 'with a broad North-country Vowel—except the *u* in such words as *mute, brute*, which he pronounced like the thin French u. His Voice very deep, & deep-chested, but rather murmuring than mouthing; like the sound of a far Sea, or of a Pine-wood. His voice, I remember, greatly struck Carlyle when he first came to know him.' He read 'St. Simeon Stylites' with 'grotesque Grimness ... laughing aloud at times'. Tennyson preferred his own reading to that of Spedding, who he said sounded 'as if Bees were about his mouth'.[22]

Fitz and Spedding were good listeners, and they heard 'Dora', 'The Day-Dream', 'The Lord of Burleigh', and of course the 'Morte d'Arthur'. Tennyson seems to have made a few changes in this last poem at Mirehouse, for the local geography was deeply evocative of the poem's mood, and he frequently quoted it during the several weeks he was there. 'The Gardener's Daughter' was giving him trouble by being too 'full and rich', and he talked out with others the reasons for not pruning it further.

Keats and Milton he read as well, but particularly Wordsworth. Tennyson had passed within shouting distance of Wordsworth's house at Rydal in the coach to Keswick, and the sight of all those daffodils at Mirehouse must inevitably have reminded him of the older poet. The Speddings, too, would have spoken of him, for he was an occasional guest at Mirehouse. Tennyson had great admiration for Wordsworth, even if he could see some of his poetic weaknesses, and he referred to him as 'the dear old fellow'. On this one matter only he and FitzGerald disagreed constantly. Possibly in instinctive withdrawal from Tennyson's enthusiasm, Fitz would make fun of Wordsworth's lumpish solemnity, calling him 'the Daddy'. On another occasion Tennyson was to call Wordsworth's poetry 'thick-ancled', but he did not like the same kind of criticism from Fitz. Once Fitz spoke of his own brother-in-law and identified him as 'a Mr. Wilkinson, a clergyman'. Either Alfred or Fitz—they could never agree which it had been—proposed it as the perfection of a bad line from Wordsworth.

Although FitzGerald objected to what he thought of as patent preachiness in Wordsworth, he by no means disliked his poetry as much as he pretended, and even said that 'the vineyard of morality' should be 'the chief object of our cultivation: Wordsworth is first in the craft: but Tennyson does no little by raising and filling the brain with noble images and thoughts, which, if they do not direct us to our duty, purify and cleanse us from mean and vicious objects, and so prepare and fit us for the reception of the higher philosophy'.[23] But Fitz was shrewder and more sensitive than many of Tennyson's other friends, who worried that he was totally neglecting to till the vineyards of morality.

At Mirehouse the talk of poetry was so constant that Mr Spedding would say in wonder when he came in and found James and Alfred arguing, 'Well, Mr. F., and what is it? Mr. Tennyson reads, and Jem criticizes:—is that it?' His wife's perplexity is hinted at in a letter from her daughter-in-law after Fitz and Alfred had gone: 'I am so sorry I have missed seeing James's great Lion of a friend Mr A. Tennyson. I suppose you cannot take in a word of their mystical conversation.'[24]

In early May, after two or three weeks at Mirehouse, the three young men moved to the Salutation Inn at Ambleside for another week. Spedding, who had sketched Tennyson at Mirehouse sitting in his cloak before the fire, now drew him looking at a waterfall through his eye-glass, still wrapped in his cloak. Characteristically, Fitz made a quirky sketch of Tennyson from the rear, his hair a billowing, tangled mass of innocent of the comb (see Plate V).

When Spedding was called home for several days to attend to family business, Tennyson and FitzGerald stayed out their time in Ambleside. The atmosphere was easier once they were alone, because Tennyson had become increasingly annoyed at Spedding's 'trick of quiet banter that sometimes deranged one's equilibrium'. Fitz found himself constantly laughing happily at Tennyson's 'little humours and grumpinesses', seeing beyond them to the man they hid. He was disinclined to dispute any of Tennyson's statements, since he said he felt 'a sense of depression at times from the overshadowing of a so much more lofty intellect than my own'.[25] It was the kind of companionship in which Tennyson could relax well for at least a short time.

At Ambleside he was much concerned with the recasting of the 'Morte d'Arthur', and the possibility of adding an introduction and epilogue. He talked to Fitz about the sources of the poem, and once on Windermere, after catching a crab, he rested on his oars and repeated two lines:

> Nine years she wrought it, sitting in the deeps
> Upon the hidden bases of the hills.

'That is not bad, I think,' he added.[26] He and Fitz indulged in friendly foolishness, including the projection of a tragedy, *Gimblet, Prince of Dunkirk*. Another time he drew Somersby Rectory for Fitz, making it look considerably more stately than the original (see Plate V).

For all his companionship Tennyson was still full of Hallam, and it was undoubtedly his memory that often brought Shakespeare's sonnets vividly to mind. Henry Hallam, who may have been worried about their sexual undertone, thought it was 'impossible not to wish that Shakespeare had never written them'. Taking the opposite point of view, Tennyson told FitzGerald at Ambleside, 'Sometimes I think Shakespeare's Sonnets finer than his Plays——.' Then he added, 'which is of course absurd. For it is the knowledge of the Plays that makes the Sonnets so fine.'[27]

Despite Fitz's expressions of contempt, Tennyson continued to read a good bit of Wordsworth aloud, including 'Michael', which he had only begun to appreciate. *Yarrow Revisited* had just been published and it reached Ambleside while they were there. With his usual generosity Fitz forgot his own reservations and bought it for Alfred. The volume, with its affectionate inscription, is now in the Tennyson Research Centre.

Hardly a mile from where they were staying lived the author of the book. When he returned to Ambleside, Spedding tried to induce Tennyson to accompany him to Rydal Mount. 'He would and would not (sulky one),' Spedding told Thompson, 'although Wordsworth was hospitably minded towards him.' Nearly half a century later Fitz told Fanny Kemble, 'W. was then at his home: but Tennyson would not go to visit him: and of course I did not: nor even saw him.' Hallam Tennyson explained that his father did not wish to 'obtrude himself on the great man at Rydal'.[28] Shortly thereafter Fitz left the Lakes and Tennyson returned to Mirehouse for a brief stay.

There is, however, a minor mystery about the references to Tennyson's unwillingness to call on Wordsworth. In the visitors' book from Rydal Mount, now in Dove Cottage, under May 1835 are recorded the names of 'Mr. J. Spedding, Mirehouse' and 'Mr. A. Tennyson, London'. They are not signatures but copies, probably by Dora Wordsworth, in the same hand in which the rest of the book is copied.[29] There is no reason to doubt the authenticity of the entry, however.

It seems probable that Tennyson did not want to go to Rydal in the company of FitzGerald, fearing that he might later make fun of the man that Tennyson so admired. The call probably took place after Fitz had left Ambleside, when he would not be offended by being left out of the party. Spedding's letter to Thompson can be explained by the fact that FitzGerald and Thompson were close friends, and by Spedding's wish not to let Fitz know of the visit for fear of hurting his feelings. It is, of course, possible that Wordsworth was not at home when they called, but what both FitzGerald and Spedding had denied was the visit to Rydal, not the meeting between the poets.

There is one other bit of evidence about the visit, the record kept by Hallam Tennyson, when he was a Marlborough schoolboy, of his father's telling him of a visit to Rydal Mount and of the crusty old woman at the inn who said to him, 'Oh Mr Wordsworth. Theres never a body however far he be come, but knows Mr Wordsworths name.' Tennyson also told his son of climbing Loughrigg, looking down on Rydal, and thinking, 'Never was a poet more comfortably housed.' On 1 June 1835, about a fortnight after the departure of Fitz and Alfred, Spedding told Donne: 'I saw Wordsworth for a few hours not long ago.'[30]

Did Tennyson and Spedding go to see Wordsworth, then conceal their visit from FitzGerald? The evidence is incomplete, but it seems probable. The whole business would be unimportant were it not that a decade later a good deal was made of what was thought to be the first meeting between Tennyson and Wordsworth (although that description did not come from either of the poets). No doubt the initial denial of a meeting had been a generous fabrication to spare a friend pain, and with the passage of years it became one of those falsehoods to which it is almost impossible to confess.

One meeting about which there is no doubt, however, is that between Tennyson and Hartley Coleridge. The great poet's son was an eccentric little man with a large, red face like the sign of the Sun before a public house, which is precisely where it had become so red. They had dinner together in Ambleside, and Coleridge's enthusiasm mounted with each gin, until, after the fourth glass, he poured out his thanks to Spedding for introducing them. Then he turned to Tennyson and told him he was far too handsome to be a poet. He continued to talk volubly, vowed he would write to Tennyson, took his address, and let it slip from his hand and fall under the table. When he had recovered he wrote a sonnet to Tennyson, saying how long he had admired his poetry:

> Knowing thee now, a real earth-treading man,
> Not less I love thee, and no more I can.

After Alfred's departure Spedding described his visit to several friends. He was affectionately aware that Alfred was 'gruff and dyspeptic enough at times', but that his bad temper sprang from the fact that he was 'a man always discontented with the Present till it has become the Past, and then he yearns toward it, and worships it, and not only worships it, but is discontented because it is past'. Shrewdly, Spedding noted that Alfred was basically lacking in faith in his own powers: 'he seeks for strength not within but without, accusing the baseness of his lot in life and looking to outward circumstances far more than a great man ought to want of them, and certainly more than they will ever bring'.[31] It was an analysis that Spedding had no reason to revise for the rest of his life.

Fitz's delight in meeting Tennyson took the form of an offer of financial help, with a typical embarrassment at being caught out in kindness. He had heard Tennyson complain of poverty and asked if he might give him money. 'I vow to the Lord that I could not have a greater pleasure . . . I should not dare to say such a thing to a small man: but you are not a small man assuredly: and even if you do not make use of my offer, you will not be offended but put it to the right account. It is very difficult to persuade people in this world that one can part with a banknote without a pang. It is one of the most simple things I have ever done to talk thus to you, I believe: but here is an end; and be charitable to me.'

FitzGerald had an income of £800, and for some years he apparently contributed £300 annually to Tennyson. In 1844 Carlyle told Fitz of Tennyson: 'He said of you that you were a man from whom one could accept money; which was a proud saying; which you ought to bless heaven for.' Fitz's kindness at this stage makes it harder to understand Tennyson's neglect of him after Tennyson was the richer, more famous of the two.[32]

Fitz's offer of help was dated 2 July 1835; it must, therefore, have arrived at Somersby on the one day of Tennyson's life when he was most aware of his comparative poverty. On 4 July George Tennyson died at the age of eighty-five. He had been suffering from a miserable combination of gout (which Alfred said was unfair for a lifelong teetotaller) and an itching rash that covered his skin and nearly drove him mad. In his misery he lashed out at everyone around him, at last denouncing even his son Charles for not coming often enough to Usselby. Edwin Tennyson told his father that the old man had raved for at least an hour: 'I never saw him in such a rage. . . . He said . . . you neglected him when you knew his age & suffering.' Even in death he maintained his grip upon his son, for after a total reconciliation he died clutching his hand, saying pitifully, 'Charles, I am dying, help me.'[33]

There was no question of his being buried at Usselby. His remains were taken in state back to Tealby to be lowered into the family vault beside his wife, who had died ten years earlier. As his body passed through Market Rasen, sixty men on horseback joined the procession to follow to Tealby. That day all the windows in Rasen were closed in respect.

Charles had talent, as well as a prodigious appetite, for pageantry. On the day of the funeral 2,000 mourners came to Bayons to follow the body in a black cortège across the valley to the parish church, where the bell tolled at thirty-second intervals for fourteen hours. As chief mourner, Charles led the procession, followed by his sons in order of seniority. It was a grand spectacle, costing over £300 for mourning and refreshments, but in the procession there were several conspicuous absences, In spite of the vast numbers of persons there, the published lists show very few in attendance from the nobility and aristocracy with which Charles was so anxious to ally himself. And neither the Bournes nor the Somersby Tennysons were even represented, although they had been specifically invited.

Frederick Tennyson was in Corfu, and his brother Charles was said to be ill, but his indisposition was probably a diplomatic one, like those of his uncle and grandfather when Dr Tennyson died. Mrs Tennyson declined her invitation in a stiff little note. It is surprising that the Bayons family should have expected anything else, as it was only four years since her father-in-law and brother-in-law had found excuses not to attend her husband's funeral. All the pomp and outlay for old George's burial must have reminded her, too, that he had said it was too expensive even to take his son's body from Somersby to Tealby to be buried with the family.

In the original plan of the procession a place is indicated for only one member of the Somersby family, Alfred Tennyson. It is unlikely that he had ever intended to take part, but if he had he would surely have balked at the position indicated for him, at the very end of his uncle's family, walking with the youngest sons as if he came from a cadet branch. In any case, although he was the friendliest of the Somersby branch, he was not apt to co-operate with his uncle. Something of the contempt that he felt for him is indicated by his telling Milnes that he disliked 'afftly' as an abbreviation of 'affectionately' as the closing of a letter, since 'it looks like "affectedly", moreover Mr DEyncourt always writes it so'.[34]

Revenge is too strong a term for the reaction of the Somersby Tennysons, but their absence was a direct result of their own treatment at the death of the Rector, and it is easy to sympathize if they took some satisfaction in staying away in silent but public protest at Charles's new dignity as head of the family. By the time of the funeral they must have known, too, that their hopes for a large inheritance, which they had nourished in the face of all probability, were futile.

The reaction at Bayons was predictable. Ellen said her relatives had behaved shamefully, and Edwin, more forcefully and more crudely, wrote about the 'Somersby Family who really are quite hogs—not one of them came to the funeral'.[35] Nor did any of them call at Bayons afterwards. The reason for the absence of the Bournes is not certain, but their defection was evidently thought less offensive.

Old George left a large fortune, and according to his own lights (and those of his son Charles) it was fairly divided between Somersby and Bayons. In tacit recognition of the seniority of the Somersby branch, they received the land and fortune that had come to Mr Tennyson through entail or inheritance, while Charles was left everything his father had earned or made by purchase and speculation. This was essentially the disposition of his wealth that old George had always said he intended, and the Somersby Tennysons received precisely what Dr Tennyson would have got had he survived his father. As a theory it was perhaps fair financially, since Charles had helped his father in business matters as Dr Tennyson had not, but the real measure of old George's affection was that the younger son inherited the bulk of the fortune, while the senior branch received only the much smaller part their grandfather felt obliged to leave them.

It is misleading to speak of the financial disinheritance of George Clayton Tennyson's family, but that is how they regarded the matter and how Alfred Tennyson spoke of it to the end of his life. What they received was a large sum in total, but it seemed little enough when split between ten children and their mother.

Mrs Tennyson had hoped to receive at least a life tenancy of Usselby Manor, but she was left nothing directly in the will; Frederick's inheritance was charged with £200 a year maintenance for her during her lifetime.

As eldest son Frederick received the largest portion, most of it from a life interest in the Clayton estate at Grimsby; a capital sum of £3,000 was charged to his inheritance for the maintenance of his brother Edward, as well as the annuity for his mother. What was left was still a handsome legacy, however much Frederick might complain; in 1854 he listed his income as £800 a year.[36] Since Charles had been provided for by Samuel Turner's will, he inherited nothing from his grandfather.

As a result of Frederick's wrangling with his grandfather the old man had altered his will, to leave the manor at Grasby and an estate there to Alfred rather than Frederick. The combined value of Alfred's inheritance was probably more than £6,000. Although there were expenses chargeable to it the gross income was something over £500, and since he was also still getting his annual present of £100 from his aunt Russell he was actually in very comfortable circumstances. A few years later he lost most of his inheritance through bad investment, but it should not be forgotten that he was seldom, if-ever, in the desperately straitened circumstances that he claimed. When he was at his worst financially he still had a far larger income than Spedding, who earned but £150 at the Colonial Office, although he always envied Spedding's financial independence. The matter of how much money FitzGerald gave him, and during which years, is not clear. It seems reasonable, however, to suppose that Tennyson would not have accepted £300 from him in the years between 1835 and 1843 (the year he lost most of his inheritance), for that would have meant that Tennyson actually had more money than FitzGerald.

An improved estate at Scartho was sold for the benefit of the other seven children, for about £20,000, thus giving them each just under £3,000, not a large sum but sufficient to keep them.

Had Dr Tennyson lived to inherit the whole of the legacies that came to his family his portion would have seemed comfortable, but when divided it appeared negligible compared to Charles's inheritance of Tealby and all the rest of the manors, advowsons, and land scattered through Lincolnshire, as well as the personal estate. The truth is that what Dr Tennyson's family inherited was adequate to keep them comfortably for the rest of their lives, but it was far from the splendour of the style of Bayons.

The settlement made patent all the resentment between the two branches of the family. The Somersby family thought that undue influence had been brought to bear on the old man by their uncle Charles and his family, while the Bayons family despised their cousins for being ungrateful for what they had received. Mrs Charles Tennyson told her son George: 'I hear the family at Somersby are one and all much disappointed with their *handsome* increases of Property, but they expected more, and the girls very handsome fortunes besides. Some people are never satisfied!'[37]

Mrs Russell and Mrs Bourne received nothing further than their marriage settlements of £5,000 each. Mrs Russell had no need of more money, but Mrs Bourne had frequently complained during her father's lifetime about her portion, and this may explain why she did not attend his funeral.

Feelings ran so high that even those who thought they were left out fell to quarrelling. According to the elder Charles, Alfred had 'been so violent (tho' he gets the Manor of Grasby & an Estate there) that Mr. and Mrs. Bourne sent him away from Margate where he was with them'. 'What *a hog* that Alfred is,' said Charles's son Edwin, 'and what can you expect from a pig but a grunt.' Although he admitted he did not know Alfred, he did not hesitate to speak of him as 'a bloated ploughman'. The nature of his offence was not made specific, but Frederick thought that Mrs Bourne had caused it by her 'insufferable insolence' to him, and his aunt Russell said she believed him incapable of what was attributed to him.[38]

Family relations were made even more ticklish when the Somersby Tennysons realized that their uncle was instituting a petition to change his name when his father was scarcely cold, and that in doing so he was carrying out provisions in the old man's will that he had planned himself. On 31 July the royal licence was issued for him to take the name of d'Eyncourt 'in addition to and after that of Tennyson', and the following day there was a flurry of letters written from Bayons signed by 'C. Tennyson d'Eyncourt'. Edwin welcomed the change to keep them from being plain Tennysons: 'Besides which it will keep us in great measure clear of the Somersby Family.'[39]

It was surely malicious humour on the part of Frederick, not a desire to emulate his uncle, that made him circulate the rumour of his intention to change his own name to Tennyson d'Eyncourt, since he had a claim prior to that of his uncle. Then, when Bayons had worried sufficiently about that, he leaked the information that besides Tennyson d'Eyncourt he intended to assume Clayton forthwith, the name of the ancestress through whom the Tennyson d'Eyncourts claimed royal descent. His aunt Fanny was almost beside herself at the thought, after all the trouble her husband had taken to dissociate his family from Somersby.

His stay in Corfu had in no way helped Frederick's tact, and of all the Tennysons he won hands down in a contest for unpopularity at Bayons, although he seems to have been happily unaware that his boorishness might give offence. His cousin George called him a 'Northern bear', and Edwin said simply, '*What a beast that Frederick is.*'[40]

Frederick's teasing was only one manifestation of the resentment that he and his brothers and sisters felt over their uncle's change of name. Alfred's letters show how much he despised his uncle for pretentiousness, yet in another twenty years he had begun to assume without question his own descent from several royal houses, and when he received a peerage his first thought was to revive the ancient barony of d'Eyncourt, taking the style of Lord Tennyson d'Eyncourt. Was it a simple desire to accomplish what his uncle had never managed, or had he really forgotten the scorn with which he and his family greeted the lineage that Bernard Burke had conveniently cobbled up for his uncle after his change of name in 1835?

❋

CHAPTER XIV

ROSA BARING AND EMILY SELLWOOD, 1835–1837

BESIDES his new name, pedigree, arms, and crest, Charles Tennyson d'Eyncourt had schemes for a new Bayons Manor. Or, to be accurate, a very old Bayons, considerably more 'antient' than the original house, for at least part of it was to be contemporary with his new Norman ancestors. By the end of August his plans were ready for a dining-hall 'in the old College Hall style . . . like the Hall of a Manor House of Yore'.[1] Instead of tearing down the original house and its additions, he carefully encrusted them in a medieval shell (but with a sound modern slate roof). The house was to be an architectural emblem of his own family ambitions as the present gradually vanished under the accretions of an invented past.

As an addition to a modest manor-house, the dining-hall was spectacular in its dimensions, for it could seat 200. After such a beginning, there was no reason to stop, and for the next decade Charles put all his energy and a good deal of his money into the total rebuilding of Bayons. It became a fantastic mixture of monomaniacal pursuit of an elusive past and the deeply sensitive creation of a beautiful Romantic house. Everything that he had learned by helping the Russells rebuild Brancepeth was brought into play, combined with his one outstanding native ability, the architectural talent that it is not ridiculous to compare with the poetic genius of his nephew. Like the best architects of the day, interested in bringing back the plasticity of earlier building, he was something of a scholar. The exterior of the house became a sketch in stone of the history of building during the reigns of the Plantagenets and Tudors. It was unlike the eclectic buildings of the later part of the century, for where those often had Norman, Tudor, and French Renaissance details incongruously mingled on the same surface, Bayons was a collection of individual parts each purely of the period it was intended to represent, as if they had been added over the centuries to an ancient core. Bayons disappeared several years ago in a sad flash of dynamite, but if one can judge by the pictures of it, both verbal and visual, it was a brilliant realization of a dream of the medieval ages.

In all fairy-tale castles there must be an element of the improbable, and of that there was plenty in Bayons, sometimes going over the edge into sheer silliness. There were secret passages and a medieval oratory. A marvellous park was created on the hillside of Tealby Vale, with the trees that old George had planted now marching in maturity down to the lake at its foot; to repeat the theme of water, Charles had a moat dug to lap beneath the drawbridge that was the entrance to his castle. The moat was unwisely situated where no moat should be, high on the side of the hill, so that it had to be filled artificially, and water constantly leaked away down the slope as rats burrowed into the exposed retaining wall. The lake was stocked with exotic water birds, and herds of deer were imported to wander through the park, in picturesque contiguity to black-faced sheep. Then it was discovered that Charles's agents had bought only gelded rams, so that there were serious problems in keeping up the breed.

To give the visitor a complete tour of the six acres enclosed within the walls of Bayons, the entrance drive was designed to take him on a full quarter-mile spiral sweep from the moat, around the bailey, over the drawbridge, through the barbican, past or through the six great gates, in and out of courtyards, only to wind up some fifty yards from where he had started. Once the circuit was completed, the visitor entered a house full of portraits commissioned to show the royal progenitors who had been discovered for the Tennyson d'Eyncourts. Inside and out, the walls were carved with coats of arms, and in the corridors stood suits of armour fittingly bought from Mr Pratt of Jermyn Street in 1839, when he sold off the remnants of the Eglinton Tournament, that pathetically funny attempt to breathe new life into chivalry and jousting. The library contained a fine collection of early English chronicles purchased to add verisimilitude to the house. Even the footmen wore livery of ancient design, with light blue coats and gold lace on the collar.

The more obsessed Charles Tennyson d'Eyncourt became in spinning out the fiction implicit in his house, the more reminiscent he became of Dr Tennyson dreaming up hairbreadth adventures to give colour to a grey life. In both brothers there was a risky tendency to confuse fantasy and reality, and at times Charles was scarcely more rational in his dreams than poor George had been. What was so close to madness in both of them was, of course, nearly allied to the creative imagination of Alfred Tennyson, but unlike his father and uncle he was normally able to recognize the frontier between dream and waking. As Charles's mind became filled with the creation of his 'Castle as it is now called, from its Tower Turrets & battlements', and with the placing of corbels, portcullises, and barbicans, he sometimes forgot that he lived in an age when it was seldom necessary to repel the neighbours by force. In 1840 he wrote in a state of dangerous excitement to his son about changing the barbican, where he thought, 'we might do something of the nature of that which we have done at North Gate where we have made holes to pelt an enemy'.[2]

The whole splendid pile was a monument to a kind of historicism common in the nineteenth century, the belief that the spirit of the past could be revived by a recreation of its externals. Alfred Tennyson's narrative poetry often glances at the vulgar efforts of the newly rich to create tradition, and he obviously had at least some aspects of his uncle in mind, but when he came to build his own dream castle in Sussex it turned out to be a distant and diminished cousin of the archetypal Bayons. Indeed, in such poems as *The Idylls of the King* he displays closer kinship to his uncle than he knew, in his belief in the possibility of giving new life to a heroic past by making it a shell to encase the nineteenth century. In nothing did uncle and nephew seem more closely related than in their family passion for the past, and the poignancy of their longing was not made less by the brute fact that the particular segment of history for which they were nostalgic had never existed.

One of the most delightful features of Tealby Church is the charming series of Gothick family monuments lining its walls: to Charles Tennyson d'Eyncourt, his wife, parents, and children. It goes without saying that none of the Somersby Tennysons is commemorated there. When Tennyson d'Eyncourt put up the tablet to his father, the companion to that in memory of his mother, he paid back the Somersby relatives who had refused to come to the funeral of the Old Man of the Wolds. The long inscription, which says a great deal more about the son than the father, records that the old man LEFT SURVIVING HIS TWO DAUGHTERS, ELIZABETH AND MARY, AND HIS SON THE RIGHT HONOURABLE CHARLES TENNYSON, M.P. FOR LAMBETH, WHOM HE DIRECTED BY HIS WILL TO SUPERADD THE NAME OF D'EYNCOURT, IN ORDER TO COMMEMORATE HIS DESCENT FROM THE TWO ANCIENT FAMILIES WHO FORMERLY BORE THAT NAME AND TITLE. . . . THEIR

IX a. Tennyson c. 1849, by
Algernon Langton
Massingberd. The original
is badly faded.

b. Tennyson, January 1842.

X. Emily Tennyson, oil by G. F. Watts, 1862.

GRATEFUL SON PRAYS FOR THE GRACE TO WALK HUMBLY IN THEIR STEPS, AND PROVE HIS VENERATION FOR BOTH HIS PARENTS, BY STRIVING TO EMULATE THEIR VIRTUES. So far as any indication on the tablet goes, George Clayton Tennyson and his family might never have existed.

Half a century after his grandfather's death Tennyson still resented his grandfather and the tablet to his memory so deeply that in 'Locksley Hall Sixty Years After' he refers to the tomb in Tealby Church:

> Gone the tyrant of my youth, and mute below the chancel stones,
> All his virtues—I forgive them—black in white above his bones.

The monument was but one instance of Charles's compulsion to assert publicly that his father had directed him to change his name, for he knew that he had become the butt of spite and laughter in his pretensions. Even in the obituary notices of his father he managed to have mention made of the old man's condition about the inheritance of Usselby. The change of name combined with the neo-Plantagenet castle was too much to swallow for most of the Lincolnshire nobility and gentry whom he hoped to impress, and guests seem more often to have been imported from London than recruited from the neighbourhood. One of the most frequent visitors was Edward Bulwer, particularly after his separation from his contentious wife.

Poor Charles received abusive anonymous letters denying the legitimacy of his claims, and several newspapers publicly suggested the same thing, one going so far as to declare that he was mad. In 1836 his family was so chagrined over one particularly malicious story of his airs that for the first time in years they were too embarrassed to go to the Stuff Ball, the outstanding social event in the county. One paper said that young George was advertising that he was not responsible for his father's debts, since he was spending some £15,000 annually on the house. Worst of all was the story told gleefully around the county by Charles Anderson of Lea, near Gainsborough, that neighbours coming back from hunting had rung the bell at Bayons and been told by a page that 'The right honourable gentleman is walking on the barbican'.[3]

Beset as he was by ridicule and worry about the cost of what he was undertaking, Charles began to be paranoiac about being cheated, suspecting his servants and employees of dishonesty, feeling that he was being denied proper attention by his family, until he was nearly as persecuted and obsessional as his father before him. Even his children seemed to turn against him. Edwin, who had been helping him with the rebuilding of the house, hated the place and thought only of how to marry a girl rich enough to enable him to leave Tealby forever. If he were the owner of Bayons, he told his brother George, he would sell it '& cut the county altogether. It is a most beastly county compared with others.'[4] At last he became so abusive to his father that for some years he was unwelcome in the house that he so heartily disliked. All that Charles had hoped for and worked for all his life, everything that the rebuilt Bayons Manor was intended to represent, had lost its meaning.

On hearing of the division of old Mr Tennyson's property, Henry Hallam exclaimed, 'The damned scoundrel—then he has got the name and the money too!'[5] Had he known of the unhappiness the inheritance was to cause Charles, Hallam might have felt that a rough kind of justice was being done.

They were unlike each other in almost every other way, but Alfred Tennyson and his cousin Edwin had in common a deep need to escape Lincolnshire. For Edwin the county offered little scope for a life of licence; Alfred said its dullness came not from lack of dissipation but from the provincial stuffiness and unintellectual interests of the 'harmless, stout, foxhunting Lincolnshire Squires'. If he had ever had a wish to take a place among them, his comparative poverty would have made it impossible.

Even before his grandfather's death he had planned on moving, and his description of his residence in the visitors' book at Rydal Mount indicates that he may already have decided on London. 'I am going to live in or near London,' he wrote to Fitz after his grandfather's death, 'the equal dearth at once of books & men in this county, cooperating with petty miseries ten times worse to bear than good hard knocks of Providence have long rendered this part of the world distasteful to me.'[6] His need to escape the provinciality of Lincolnshire was further strenghtened at this time by an unhappy emotional involvement that assumed considerably greater symbolic importance for him than his own feelings in the matter merited.

On the very day in 1831 that Mr Rawnsley had had the duty of reading their father's will to Frederick, Charles, and Alfred, he happened upon Arthur Eden, Rosa Baring's stepfather, who had come to the vicinity to rent Harrington Hall, a pretty manor-house owned by the Cracrofts. In such a narrow circle as the families of the neighbourhood it was inevitable that the Tennysons should soon become acquainted with the Edens and Mrs Eden's unmarried daughters, Fanny, Georgina, and Rosa Baring; by the autumn of 1832 Emily Tennyson counted Rosa as a friend. The progress of the friendship was undoubtedly quickened by the loneliness of the Tennysons after their father's death and by the newness of the Edens to the neighbourhood. It is quite possible that the Tennyson daughters had been introduced to the Barings by the Cracrofts' cousin, Emily Sellwood, who would naturally have been asked to help the Barings meet new friends.

There could hardly have been a greater contrast between two girls of almost the same age than that between Emily Sellwood and Rosa Baring. Emily was shy, unworldly, invalid from a bad back ever since childhood, wanly pretty, and deeply religious. Rosa had been brought up among a rich and worldly aristocracy, she was well connected socially, with all the advantages that meant at the time, she was conventionally good-looking with bright blue eyes, a high colour, and a well-rounded, decidedly feminine figure. There is little solid evidence on which to base a conjecture about her character: it has frequently been said that she was shallow and flirtatious, cold at the very time that she was as sensual as her figure might suggest, but these estimates derive chiefly from the young women in Tennyson's poems who are said to be modelled upon her. It is a circuitous form of reasoning that is dangerous to rely upon.

Presumably Tennyson came to know Rosa Baring at the same time his sister did, in the autumn of 1832. Since there were so few young men with his good looks, intelligence, and literary reputation in the countryside, he met her often at parties at Somersby, Harrington, and elsewhere. There is little evidence that he felt more than casual friendship for her during the first two years of their acquaintance.[7]

As has been suggested, 'The Gardener's Daughter', which Tennyson began writing in the summer of 1833, may owe something to his acquaintance with Rosa, and he may have had her in mind when creating the eponymous character, Rose. Certainly, as Sir Charles Tennyson has suggested, the eroticism of the poem 'has a keener edge and a greater directness' than in any previous poem of Tennyson's, and this may have resulted from Hallam's engagement to Emily, which 'served to release in his friend emotions, which the exclusiveness of their early affection had tended to absorb'.[8] It was, however, a mild enough eroticism for a man of twenty-four.

The first poem known to be directly connected with Rosa Baring was written by Tennyson for her birthday, 23 September 1834:

> Thy rosy lips are soft and sweet,
> They fairy form is so complete,
> Thy motions are so airy free,
> Love lays his armour at thy feet
> And yields his bow to thee;
> Take any dart from out his quiver
> And pierce what heart thou wilt for ever.

There is little to distinguish these complimentary lines from the run of those to be found in the birthday book of any young lady of the time. Tennyson's lack of engagement is shown by the conventionality of his imagery, and it is surely not coincidental that he repeats 'fairy' and 'airy' from his joking verses to Sophy Rawnsley, 'Lilian'.

During the next two years Tennyson wrote a round dozen poems either directly to Rosa Baring or indirectly about her, with a rose as the central image. If we take the series at face value, it seems to record his infatuation with her, then the slow realization that she did not love him, that her attractions were only of the surface, and that her wealth and position stood between them as lovers:

> A rosy-coloured jewel, fit to make
> An emperor's signet-ring . . .
>
> But yet a jewel only made to shine,
> And icy-cold although 'tis rosy-clear—
>
> . . . ah! 'tis far too costly to be mine
>
> ('I lingered yet awhile to bend
> my way')

What is apparently the last of the poems that Tennyson wrote to Rosa, early in 1836, concludes with a bitter description of the vacuity beneath her beauty:

> A hand displayed with many a little art;
>   An eye that glances on her neighbour's dress;
>   A foot too often shown for my regard;
>   An angel's form—a waiting-woman's heart;
>   A perfect-featured face, expressionless,
>   Insipid, as the Queen upon a card.
>
> ('How thought you that this thing
> could captivate?')

At the same period he was also writing such poems as 'Lady Clara Vere de Vere', 'Lady Clare', and 'Dora'. The first of these is about a heartless coquette, 'daughter of a hundred Earls', who 'thought to break a country heart/For pastime', and who has yet to learn that 'Kind hearts are more than coronets,/And simple faith than Norman blood'. 'Lady Clare' echoes 'The Lord of Burleigh' in reversing the situation by making a magnanimous nobleman marry a simple girl. 'Dora' is concerned with the evil of arranged marriages.

The evidence from the poems might seem to be that Tennyson was in love with Rosa Baring, that her family was opposed to a match between them, and that he finally realized that he had been mistaken in loving her, since she was important to him only in a sensual way. That has been the tenor of most speculation about Rosa Baring ever since Ralph Rader first suggested her importance to Tennyson in his excellent little book about their relationship.

That Rosa was very attractive can hardly be doubted. John Rashdall recorded despairingly in his diary on 3 November 1834, after returning from Somersby, where he had taken leave of the Barings, who were going for a stay in London for the winter season: 'Rosa the prettiest & most elegant girl I ever was *intimate* with. I have parted from her probably for ever!'[9] Nor is there any reason to suspect that Tennyson's admiration for her at the outset was not genuine. All the same, since we must depend upon his poems so much, in the absence of letters or other direct evidence about his emotions, it is hard not to feel that there is something artificial, perhaps forced, about the sentiments and situations of the poems, precisely as there had been in the unsuccessful poems to young women in the volumes of 1830 and 1833. The loss of a beautiful young woman by a poor man because her parents want her to marry well is certainly a stock situation, and in the poems about Rosa Tennyson nearly always seems more inspired by traditional responses than by deep emotion.

But stock situations become so because they actually occur. In the years when he saw most of Rosa, which were those at the time of his grandfather's death, Tennyson was particularly aware of the forced limitation upon his choices imposed by his comparative poverty. He needed to look no further than his own family to see that parental permission for marriage was usually lacking unless there was plenty of money, and that when profit not passion finally dictated the choice of partner many marriages turned out badly. Emily had been prevented from marrying Hallam, Charles had been separated from the family governess as well as Miss Burton, and Frederick had been unable to marry Charlotte Bellingham.

The moral became more pointed when Frederick proposed again, in May 1836, to another wealthy young woman, this time his own cousin Julia Tennyson d'Eyncourt, apparently blissfully unaware that there was not another young man in the kingdom who would have been less welcome in that family. He told her he realized that his proposal was 'justified by no previous conversation or any very familiar habits of intimacy', but that he had loved her since he was a boy and had been afraid to express his feelings during his grandfather's lifetime. 'It is true that I once offered myself to another but it is not the less true that my heart was never really engaged to her, or to any one but yourself between whom & that person I vainly imagined that some resemblance existed.' He signed the letter, 'Your hoping yet trembling lover'. Gently, the amazed Julia refused him, assuring him that 'my feeling towards you altho' not so deep as the one you so flatteringly express for me has ever been one of kindness & affection'.[10]

At the time it is improbable that Alfred Tennyson would have seen the comic absurdity of his brother's proposal and rejection, or thought that the latter could have proceeded from anything but a concern for money. His grandfather's prudent match had certainly not led to happiness, and his uncle's life had been made miserable by a marriage for wealth. His cousin Edwin was openly looking for a wealthy bride, and another cousin, Emma Russell, had been turned into a thoughtless seeker for social pleasure by her marriage to Lord Boyne's heir. Love and marriage seemed to be of the market-place, and it is not surprising that Tennyson so often used the theme, as in 'Edwin Morris', 'Locksley Hall', and most importantly in *Maud*. No doubt the Edens (and Rosa) had never even considered him as a suitor, eligible or otherwise, but Tennyson's knowledge of the experience of his own family had conditioned him to see snubs and financial arrogance even when they did not exist.

The depth of Tennyson's sensual feelings for Rosa may have been as exaggerated in the telling as his sense of rejection by her. Surely no one who knows his poetry ever thought of it as unduly carnal or fleshly, and there is little reason to think that he was in immediate danger from that part of his nature. There is not the slightest evidence that he ever had any sexual experience with another person until his marriage at the age of forty-one, and he made at least one positive assertion that he had not so much as kissed a woman until 1850. Strange as that sounds to modern ears, such abstinence was probably common in the nineteenth century. Certainly, his statement is hardly evidence of an uncontrollable sexuality. When he was an old man he used to say of Burns that poets had stronger passions than other men, but that statement seems to have had little reference to himself. If a man without strong sexual drives feels a duty to fall in love, it is safest to choose a girl who is already cut off from his advances by other circumstances, as Rosa was. One suspects that the rather Puritanical attitude Tennyson took about sex during most of his life sprang from a distrust of what he did not know, rather than from much experience of it.

We can only conjecture about Tennyson's relations with Rosa Baring, but his love appears to have been more imaginary than actual, more dutiful than driving. What finally seems most persuasive is that in later years Rosa was quite unaware that Tennyson had ever entertained any particularly deep feelings for her.[11] Probably they had a mild flirtation, although certainly nothing like the touching scene invented by one recent biographer with Tennyson and Rosa 'discovered by her indignant relatives in each other's arms on the terrace of Harrington Hall'.[12] The knowledge that he was not even eligible as a suitor to Rosa was surely as galling to Tennyson as any actual rejection would have been. Finally, she became an emblem of everything that kept him from finding happiness in life. As Spedding had said of him, Tennyson was always 'accusing the baseness of his lot in life and looking to outward circumstances far more than a great man ought to want of them'.

What undeniably resulted from his acquaintance with Rosa were the re-enforcement of attitudes he already held, the background for a few later works such as *Maud*, and the dozen or so poems that he wrote about her from 1834 to 1836. These last are, quite simply, poor things. It is certainly wrong to judge the poet's sincerity solely by the quality of his poetry, but when a poet capable of great emotional depth chooses to write about actual situations or persons we may begin to question the quality of emotion that prompted him if the poems reflect pallid sentiments in conventional language. Tennyson was certainly capable of passion and originality in writing of his own emotions. One need look only at the gravity, maturity, and intensity of the poems written during the same years to express his sense of loss over Hallam: 'Ulysses', 'Tithonus', 'Morte d'Arthur', or the marmoreally controlled heartbreak of 'Break, break, break'. The difference between these poems and the inert ones written to Rosa Baring is that between major poetry and minor. This is not to over-emphasize the intensity of his feelings for Hallam, only to doubt the depth of his attachment to Rosa. If the 'Rose' poems indicate the actual course of his love for and subsequent disillusionment with Rosa, that love must have been a trivial one. If, as seems more probable, they reflect conventional sentiments about monetary barriers to love, using the figure of Rosa as a convenient symbol, we can understand their apparent lack of involvement with the young woman herself.

A clear indication that Tennyson realized how immature these poems were and how jejune his reactions to Rosa Baring is given by his plundering of them in 1854, when he was writing *Maud*. Practically every instance of his transference of a description of Rosa to a description of Maud occurs in the early sections of the poem when the anonymous narrator projects his own preconceptions on to Maud and wrongly assumes that she is 'faultily faultless, icily regular, splendidly null'. The girl whom he is describing has never really existed, and the hero then discovers that he has been using her as a mirror of his own neurotic prejudices, precisely as Tennyson had been doing with Rosa in real life.

Nor is it coincidental that of the longer poems Tennyson wrote about a young man in love with a girl of superior wealth and station, in no single one is the girl anything more than a stock figure who takes what personality she has from the reflection of the young man. If Tennyson had been writing about a girl with whom he was deeply in love and whom he was prevented from marrying, one would expect at least a trace of her personality to seep into the poems.

Of the poems apparently written with Rosa squarely in the forefront of Tennyson's mind, only one, 'The Roses on the Terrace', achieves anything like real success, and that was written half a century after the events of 1834–6. Significantly, there is no trace in it of pain or hurt, whether present or remembered. The emphasis is less on the heat of young love than on the tenderness of remembered emotion and on the telescoping of time and place, of Aldworth in the 1880s and perhaps Harrington in the 1830s, of the garden of Aldworth with the glimpse of a distant sea.

> Rose, on this terrace fifty years ago,
>   When I was in my June, you in your May,
> Two words, '*My* Rose' set all your face aglow,
>   And now that I am white, and you are gray,
> That blush of fifty years ago, my dear,
>   Blooms in the Past, but close to me today

> As this red rose, which on our terrace here
> Glows in the blue of fifty miles away.

This is a poem of serene old age not impetuous youth, so it is unfair to compare it to those written at Somersby, but it seems relevant that it was distance from Rose, not proximity, that truly inspired Tennyson. Nor can one believe that he would have published this poem had the memory of Harrington ever had any real power to hurt his wife of nearly forty years.

Argument from poetry to biography is tenuous at best, and it should be admitted that the thinness applies to disproof of a theory as much as to proof, so there can be no certainty about the matter of Rosa unless new evidence comes to light. It is true that Tennyson never published the poems he wrote about her in the two years after 1834, but the quality of the poems was as good a reason for suppressing them as any desire to hide the traces of an unsuccessful early love affair. In the poems Tennyson inadvertently reminds the reader of Romeo's infatuation with Rosa's namesake, Rosaline, as he goes through all the conventional agonies of frustrated passion without much basis in real feeling. Rosa Baring was certainly important to Tennyson, but as a representation of what he saw was wrong with his society rather than as a flesh-and-blood young woman with whom he was deeply in love.

In 1838 Rosa made a suitable marriage to Robert Shafto, a wealthy landowner in Yorkshire, but by then the Tennysons were gone from Somersby, and there is no indication that Alfred was even invited to the wedding. In 1835, when Tennyson talked of taking up residence in London, his decision was the result of deep ennui with everything that his family, his home, Lincolnshire, and even Rosa Baring had come to represent, rather than a necessity to fly from frustration in love.

As it turned out, Tennyson did not then move to London, either because he felt a duty to his mother to stay as head of the family or because his income seemed inadequate to live permanently in the city. As always, he compared his finances with those of wealthy friends, so that the money seemed a good bit less than it actually was. Instead of changing his residence he spent increasing amounts of time with friends in London, most often staying with Spedding in his new rooms at 60 Lincoln's Inn Fields. Tennyson had always smoked too much, and now he was drinking more than was prudent. Until near the end of his life, when he finally gave up port because of his gout, his drinking was a recurrent surprise to those who first met him, although he could drink steadily without seeming the worse for it. He said he needed alcohol as a stimulant, to keep him from lethargy, and he took it to overcome shyness when he was with strangers, but even in friendly company he sometimes drank too much. He could be amusing about his own habits, as on the evening in the autumn of 1835 that he spent convivially with Thackeray, Spedding, and FitzGerald at the Cock Tavern, one of his favourite resorts. After dinner they all squeezed into an omnibus. When another passenger came up, the conductor looked in and asked, 'Are you full inside?' 'Yes,' cried Tennyson ebulliently, 'the last glass did for me.'[13] On a later occasion Spedding told Milnes: 'Yesterday I dined with A.T. at the Cock Tavern, Temple Bar: we had two chops, one pickle, 2 cheeses, 1 pint of Stout, 1 pint of Port, and 3 cigars. When we had finished I had to take his regrets to the Kembles. He could not go, because he had the Influenza.'[14]

For at least one member of the Tennyson family the future looked promising. Alfred's brother Charles had managed to shake off the opium addiction that had plagued him since his miserable days as curate at Tealby, and by September 1835 he was engaged to Louisa, youngest of the Sellwood daughters from Horncastle. She was generally thought the prettiest of the sisters, she was intelligent, gentle, and pious, clearly an excellent choice for a parson's wife. The Tennysons and the Sellwoods had been friends for some years, and the approaching marriage brought them even closer, but as yet there was no indication that Alfred responded to the feelings that Emily Sellwood had entertained ever since the day they met in Holywell Wood.

Charles took Louisa to Switzerland for their honeymoon, then back to Caistor to the house left to him by Samuel Turner. Although he was lazy in most other ways, Charles was a conscientious parish clergyman, and he soon realized that they must move the three miles to Grasby to live among his flock. Louisa worked diligently with him, and the marriage should have been happy. Unfortunately, on his own wedding day, 24 May 1836, Charles had been so overtaken by nervousness that he took opium to calm himself, and within a short time he was as badly addicted as before. Louisa's care of him finally broke down her own mental stability, and for a dozen years they lived apart. In 1849 they were reunited, Charles finally conquered his addiction, and they lived devotedly, if eccentrically, together most of the rest of their lives. Both became extremely High Church, ascetic in their personal lives but generous to their parish. Louisa had intermittent periods of religious mania when her deep conviction of sin required her to be confined, but they were totally devoted to each other, and at Charles's death in 1879 she pined away and was dead within a month.

As groomsman to his brother, Alfred was naturally paired with Louisa's sister Emily. If one can believe his own sonnet on the occasion, he fell in love while Charles and Louisa were being married:

The Bridesmaid

O Bridesmaid, ere the happy knot was tied,
Thine eyes so wept that they could hardly see;
Thy sister smiled and said, 'No tears for me!
A happy bridesmaid makes a happy bride.'
And then, the couple standing side by side,
Love lighted down between them full of glee,
And over his left shoulder laughed at thee,
'O happy bridesmaid, make a happy bride.'
And all at once a pleasant truth I learned,
For while the tender service made thee weep,
I loved thee for the tear thou couldst not hide,
And prest thy hand, and knew the press returned,
And thought, 'My life is sick of single sleep:
O happy bridesmaid, make a happy bride!'

It is a curiously anaemic love poem, in which the emphasis falls on the verbal quibble of the repeated line rather than on the warmth of the poet's emotions that one expects in such an avowal. Above all, 'My life is sick of single sleep' is a bloodless statement of passion, even less convincing than the poems to Rosa Baring and succeeding only in making Emily seem an alternative to a hot-water bottle. The slack diction and jogging rhythm emphasize the emotional flaccidity. 'June Bracken and Heather' is proof of the beauty with which Tennyson could write of Emily, but it was written when he was an old man, the poetry of love grown from shared lives and gentle affection rather than from strong sexual attraction. It is difficult to resist the feeling that Rosa Baring, Sophy Rawnsley, even Emily Sellwood might not have been important in 1836 had Hallam's death not left such a vacuum of affection in Tennyson's life. Frederick once wrote of his brother Charles that he was 'not of a very ardent temperament',[15] and with equal justice he might have said the same of Alfred.

Tennyson was just turned twenty-seven, lonely and uncertain of his future. Emily's love for him was obvious, as well as her own loneliness as an unmarried eldest daughter. There are worse reasons for love and marriage than mutual need, and soon they were unofficially engaged.

It would be mistaken, however, to assume that the tender moment at the wedding of Charles and Louisa irrevocably swept Tennyson into an overwhelming love, for scarcely more than a fortnight later he was flirting mildly with Emily's cousin at the Sellwoods' own house, where Emily was acting as hostess for her widower father.

On 11 June Alfred, Frederick, and Mary went to dinner at Horncastle in company with the great Arctic explorer Sir John Franklin, who was Emily's uncle. Sir John was leaving soon for Tasmania, and he had come to Horncastle for the wedding before sailing. With him was his orphaned niece Catherine, who was meeting her Sellwood relatives for the first time. Miss Franklin's initial impression of Frederick and Alfred was of 'two very remarkable, tall, broad-chested men', both wearing their hair unfashionably long, 'quite out of the common in appearance, men whom you would speak of as more than *distinguished*, I should say, *noble* in appearance'. With them entered 'the most beautiful woman' she had ever seen, Mary Tennyson. Alfred was asked to take Catherine in to dinner, but through a servant's mistake they were separated at table. Her relief at not having to talk to him was replaced by the greater trial of sitting opposite to him and seeing him put his monocle into his eye in order to look hard at her. After a long inspection of her complexion he asked his neighbour in a gloomy undertone, 'Is she a Hindoo?'

When at last she made her escape to the drawing-room, Tennyson threw himself down across three chairs and lit his pipe. This 'vexed the soul of Sir John, who as an old naval officer held strong ideas about deference to seniors'. Later Catherine was asked to play the piano, and immediately Tennyson brought a chair to sit close to her, saying that he wanted to watch the sparkle of her jewels as her fingers moved over the keys. In flirtatious tribute to her dark good looks and to her garnets ('fit for an Eastern princess') he called her 'Zobeide'. His attempted gallantry only unnerved her, and she commented afterwards, 'I expect I played but ill.' The Tennysons had to return early to Somersby and there was little time for talk, but she 'thought them very remarkable looking people tho' certainly formidable in their unconventional manner'.[16]

Emily Sellwood left no record of what she thought as she watched Tennyson's eyes attentively following her cousin's hands on the keyboard, remembering that he had pressed her own less than three weeks before and that she had returned the squeeze. She and Catherine were to become as close as sisters, and in 1850 Catherine helped to bring Emily and Tennyson together for their long-delayed marriage, but Emily would have been scarcely less than angelic had she felt no jealousy on this occasion.

Since practically all the correspondence of Emily and Alfred was destroyed after Tennyson's death, our knowledge of their protracted courtship between 1836 and their marriage in 1850 is sketchy. By 1837 their engagement had been accepted by both families, and during the next two or three years they occasionally visited each other's house. Not much more is certain.

The beautiful Mary Tennyson was now engaged to John Heath, her brother's friend from Cambridge, but there was no immediate prospect of their marriage. Frederick had taken Julia's refusal with no more apparent concern than he had received Charlotte Bellingham's. With little promise of marrying wealth ahead of him, he set out for Italy, where he stayed until 1859. The rate of exchange made possible a luxurious life there on his inheritance, indulging his taste for music and painting.

The Somersby household appeared to be breaking up, and at the end of 1836 they knew they would have to vacate the Rectory for young Mr Burton upon his marriage. Alfred's first impulse was to join Frederick in Italy, a move which his uncle's family welcomed. Mrs Tennyson d'Eyncourt wrote inaccurately to her son George: 'Charles Turner is going to change his living for one in the South of England. Alfred & one of the others (I do not remember who) are going abroad, but of their destination I am ignorant, & the rest are all going to live in Devonshire. Tant mieux.' The thought of Italy made her husband add a postscript showing that he was beginning to worry about the expense of Bayons: 'what a donkey I am to build a chateau when Palaces are to be had for an old song in such a climate & place as that'.[17] It took several months for them to find a suitable house, but in the end Alfred stayed in England to join his family in Essex.

Amidst all his worries Tennyson continued writing and showing his poems to his friends; according to John Heath he intended soon to be 'father to two volumes of Poems', but the project lapsed, largely because of the previous hostility of the reviewers. Although he professed not to notice them, he took their criticism to heart and continued to revise the poems of the 1833 edition extensively.

Wilson was still taking passing slaps at him in *Blackwood's*, showing how little Tennyson's abject letter had appeased him. What Tennyson should have been able to take pride in, however, was the intelligent article by John Stuart Mill in July 1835 in the *London and Westminster Review*. Mill began by demolishing Wilson and Croker and their reviews, characterizing the former as flippant and the second as cynical, hackneyed, and thoroughly disgraceful. He then singled out Tennyson's great 'power of *creating* scenery, in keeping with some state of human feeling; so fitted to it as to be the embodied symbol of it, and to summon up the state of feeling itself, with a force not to be surpassed by anything but reality'. These scenes, he said, were 'not mere pictures, but states of emotion, embodied in sensuous imagery'.

As one might expect, Mill felt that Tennyson should cultivate his rational powers in order to discipline 'the materials of his imagination', to place his 'thoughts in a strong light before the intellect', and thus give form to his feelings. Otherwise, he was in danger of taking the easy and unphilosophical approach of 'embracing as truth, not the conclusions which are recommended by the strongest evidence, but those which have the most poetical appearance'. It was sensible advice, since Mill saw that Tennyson could best improve his work by beginning with basics; it was unlike the admonitions of the Apostles, who thought there would automatically be more depth in his poetry if he would only change the subjects to political or philosophical topics. Indeed, Mill noticed some of the political poems as the most juvenile of the entire volume. Like Coleridge, he mentioned metrical awkwardness, but all his adverse criticism was subsumed in the belief that Tennyson 'would secure to himself the high place in our poetic literature for which so many of the qualifications are already his own'. As proof he printed a number of poems in full, including 'Mariana' and 'The Lady of Shalott'.

It was a review that went far to vindicate his genius against the barbs of Wilson, Croker, and Bulwer, but Tennyson was too absorbed in his own troubles to be comforted. When first he heard that Mill was working on the review, he told Spedding, 'it is the last thing I wish for, and I would that you or some other who may be friends of Mill would hint as much to him. *I do not wish to be dragged forward again in any shape before the reading public at present*, particularly on the score of my old poems, most of which I have so corrected . . . as to make them much less imperfect . . .'

He did, however, consent to publish 'St. Agnes', which appeared in November 1836 in the *Keepsake*, an annual edited by Lady Emmeline Stuart Wortley. Shortly thereafter Milnes asked for a contribution to another volume, *The Tribute*, edited by the Marquis of Northampton.

'Three summers back,' Tennyson replied, 'provoked by the incivility of editors, I swore an oath that I would never again have to do with their vapid books, and I brake it in the sweet face of Heaven when I wrote for Lady What's-her-name Wortley. But then her sister wrote to Brookfield and said she (Lady W.) was beautiful, so I could not help it.' But now he intended to keep his oath. 'To write for people with prefixes to their names is to milk he-goats; there is neither honour nor profit.'

Milnes, who was irritated because he would not be able to oblige Lord Northampton and also because Tennyson had been proving difficult about accepting an invitation to Fryston, took offence at the letter; more than half in earnest he accused Tennyson of 'insulting irony' and 'piscatory vanity'. He also threatened to give his copy of 'Anacaona' to Lord Northampton for publication if Tennyson refused to send anything else.

With the emollient good humour he could summon up too rarely, Tennyson apologized, obliquely indicating that part of his unwillingness to publish was due to the impending move of his family: 'I & all my people are going to leave this place shortly—never to return—I have much upon my hands.' He said he was certainly unaware of the reason for Milnes's taking offence. 'Why what in the name of all the powers, my dear Richard, makes you run me down in this fashion? Now is my nose out of joint, now is my tail not only curled so tight as to lift me off my hind legs like Alfred Crowquill's poodle, but fairly between them. . . . What has so jaundiced your good-natured eyes as to make them mistake harmless banter for *insulting* irony: harsh terms applicable only to Lytton Bulwer, who, big as he is, sits to all posterity astride upon the nipple of literary Dandyism, & "takes her milk for gall". . . . Had I spoken the same things to you, laughingly, in my chair, & with my own emphasis, you would have seen what they really meant, but coming to read them, peradventure, in a fit of indigestion, or with a slight matutinal headache after your Apostolic symposium, you subject them to such misinterpretation as, if I had not sworn to be true friend to you till my latest death-ruckle, would have gone far to make me indignant.' Then he promised Milnes not only the desired poem but others from Charles and Frederick: 'see now whether I am not doing my best for you, & whether you had any occasion to threaten me with that black b——— Anacaona & her cocoa-shadowed *coves* of niggers—I cannot have her strolling about the land in this way—it is neither good for her reputation nor mine . . .'[18]

His contribution was 'Oh! that 'twere possible', which he had been tinkering with ever since he began writing it shortly after Hallam's death. Getting it into shape for Milnes gave him infinite trouble, and it was not totally finished until it was used as the germ of *Maud* nearly twenty years later.

His reluctance either to publish or to accept invitations prompted George Darley to ask Milnes, 'But what can T. have to drown him in the slough of despond, as you tell me, if he retain the free use of his faculties? . . . But what can be the worm at Tennyson's heart? Is he in the flames, furies, & tortures, agonies & excruciations of the "tender passion"?'[19]

※

CHAPTER XV

MATTHEW ALLEN AND THOMAS CARLYLE, 1837–1838

THE move from Somersby turned out to be almost wholly Alfred Tennyson's responsibility. With his elder brothers gone from home, he had to make all the decisions, since his mother's impractical vagueness was worse than useless. In 1837 he spent most of March, April, and May in and around London, choosing a house in Epping Forest, then single-handedly buying cheap and attractive furnishings for it. Beech Hill House in High Beech, close to Loughton, was some twelve miles from the centre of London, too near to be rural, too far for urban life. Still, he had the chance to get to the city, which he found increasingly necessary; the rest of his life he tried to live at some distance from its distractions but close enough to allow him to rub off the rust that accumulated when he was away too long.

During that spring he shuttled between High Beech and London, staying part of the time with Spedding, then taking rooms at 12 Mornington Crescent, in Hampstead. In the correspondence of his friends there are glimpses of him reading 'The Two Voices' in Edmund Lushington's rooms, or smoking with the Lushington brothers, Milnes, Monteith, Venables, Spedding, Brookfield, or Frederick Pollock. There were frequent visits to the Cock in the Strand and attendance at a production based on *The Rape of the Lock*, with 'lumpish sylphs hanging plumb-heavy over the toilette'.[1]

It was an unsatisfactory life, partially reflected in 'Will Waterproof's Lyrical Monologue', set at the Cock. With half-humorous self-deprecation he faces his own poetic failures, confronted with the solid reality of the head-waiter before whom

> We fret, we fume, would shift our skins,
>   Would quarrel with our lot;
> Thy care is, under polished tins,
>   To serve the hot-and-hot.

The poem owes a good bit to Pope in the transformation of the 'plump head-waiter' into a latter-day Ganymede borne in the clutch of the Cock to be dropped among the chops and porter, and in its invocation of the Muse by successive pints of port. When the wine is red, 'High over roaring Temple-bar', the poet can

> look at all things as they are,
> But through a kind of glory.

When his glass is empty, he becomes 'maudlin-moral', and

> The truth, that flies the flowing can,
> Will haunt the vacant cup.

Beneath the lightness of the poem lie layers of desperation.

According to FitzGerald, the head-waiter was offended by his own characterization: 'Had Mr. Tennyson dined oftener there, he would not have minded it so much,' he said. FitzGerald, not a *habitué* of the Cock, remembered that 'AT's chief Dinner-resort in those ante-laureate Days was Bertolini's at the Newton's Head close to Leicester Square. We sometimes called it *Dirtolini*'s; but not seriously: for the Place was clean as well as very cheap, & the Cookery good for the Price. Bertolini himself, who came to take the money at the end of the Feast, was a grave & polite man.'[2]

Tennyson's reputation was already sufficient for established men of letters to be anxious to know him. In 1835 Leigh Hunt had retailed Thomas Carlyle's hope of meeting him, and though nothing had come of it at the time, Hunt renewed the invitation in the summer of 1837. Since they were holding an auction at Somersby, Tennyson wrote: 'I was obliged to leave town on the day after that when I was to have drunk tea with you, seen Carlyle, & tumbled your books.' In response to Hunt's request for a fuller biographical account, he wrote: 'I have no life to give—for mine has been one of feelings not of actions . . .'[3]

Although he failed then to meet Carlyle, who was to play such a large part in his later life, he did renew his acquaintance with old Samuel Rogers. James Spedding wrote to his mother that 'A. Tennyson is in Town and appears to be very well—he carries about a small baccy box and a cutty pipe, and writes down no poetry, but his mind makes it in great abundance. He and the poet Rogers, who is reputed one of the most accomplished men in London for wit and taste, have become acquainted and seem to have taken a great fancy to each other.'[4]

During the next decade Rogers and Tennyson saw each other often, nd Rogers did all he could to help the younger poet, asking only that Tennyson give admiration in return. Once they were walking arm-in-arm, while Tennyson spoke of how few writers could be sure of immortality for their own works. Upon that Rogers squeezed his arm and said, 'I am sure of it.' Another time he challenged Tennyson, who had been praising one of his poems, 'Repeat a passage—ha, you can't.' And at the moment Tennyson could not.[5] In spite of such setbacks Tennyson remained a favourite of the ugly little man whom Frederick Locker-Lampson described as 'a wrinkled Maecenas'. He frequently went to St. James's Place for the half-day-long breakfasts at which Rogers assembled his lions among the Egyptian antiquities and Etruscan vases. If one of the guests asked if he might show a friend the Raphael or the Giorgione upstairs, he would acquiesce with a courtly bow, saying with overdone politeness, 'They are yours!'[6]

Most of literary London streamed through Rogers's house. The brilliance of the conversation was such that when Spedding had described one breakfast to his mother, she answered: 'You make one long to breakfast with Rogers or even to put one's head in for a minute amongst such delights.'[7] As Rogers's guest Tennyson met writers of an earlier generation for the first time, among them Thomas Moore, who liked to gossip with Rogers about their old friend Byron. Tennyson admired some of Byron's poetry, but he had come to think the man unpleasant and affected; it was a far cry from the day in 1824 when the fifteen-year-old Alfred had run weeping into the woods at Somersby and despairingly carved 'Byron is dead' into the sandstone. One story he heard at Rogers's table was that on his wedding night Byron had awakened to see a lamp shining through a red curtain; 'Am I in hell?' he shouted. Rogers said that he had once invited Byron to dinner but his guest took nothing but a biscuit and a bottle of soda water. It was only later that Rogers found that he had 'gone to a tavern and had a jolly good dinner'. Tennyson used to repeat the story, adding indignantly, 'What monstrous affectation!' He was equally incensed at Moore's story of Byron's saying when he heard of Wellington's victory at Waterloo, 'I am damned sorry to hear it!!'[8] With his strong belief in the privacy of writers' lives, Tennyson agreed that it was right of Moore to destroy Byron's scandalous memoirs. Once as Tennyson listened intently and silently to Moore talking of Byron, Rogers said acidly, 'I suppose, Mr. Tennyson, we shall hear your voice as soon as Mr. Moore has gone.'[9]

According to Tennyson it was also at Rogers's breakfast table that he met Gladstone, of whom he had been hearing ever since first he knew Hallam in 1829. Gladstone and Tennyson each thought he had been Hallam's best friend, and until the end of their lives there was an odd undercurrent of jealousy in their relations, although they felt real mutual admiration and publicly spoke well of each other. Something of their uneasiness is shown by the fact that it had taken four years since Hallam's death for them to meet. Gladstone's own memory of their meeting in 1837 was that Tennyson came to call on him in Carlton Gardens, 'an unexpected honour, for I had no other tie with him than having been in earlier life the friend of his friend'. Certainly they met again at Rogers's house in 1839 at breakfast, when Gladstone noted in his diary that he had brought Tennyson home with him. They maintained regular social intercourse until Tennyson's death, but they frequently found something over which to differ when they met, and it was more than political belief that divided them.

The gregarious Richard Monckton Milnes, now MP for Pontefract, was beginning his own rival series of breakfasts in his rooms in Pall Mall; they were not yet so famous as those of Rogers but were soon to eclipse them. Among his guests he naturally included Tennyson. Frederick Pollock recorded that at Milnes's 'Young England' evenings he habitually met Gladstone, Spedding, Tennyson, Kinglake, Thirlwall, and even Carlyle.

From all this activity High Beech seemed separated by more than a mere dozen miles. Beech Hill was a large house set in its own walled park on an eminence, with a fine view of Waltham Abbey, but Tennyson was soon referring to it as 'that cockney residence'. With greenhouses, walled gardens, an ornamental lake, gardeners to care for them, three women and a liveried man indoors, it was surely an extravagant house to run, for the Tennysons seldom succeeded in contracting their expectations of the minimum style in which they could live. Understandably, they felt pinched for money, and since Tennyson took this as the norm for his own life he naturally felt he could not afford to marry.

However much he wanted to see the last of Lincolnshire, he was overcome with sorrow at leaving the only home he had ever known, where his boyhood had been passed, where his father had died, above all where he had spent so many hours with Arthur Hallam. Mixed with this was the melancholy knowledge that in the wolds and valleys life would continue without him, and that in time even the memory of his twenty-eight years there would disappear from that green world:

> Unwatched, the garden bough shall sway,
>   The tender blossom flutter down,
>   Unloved, that beech will gather brown,
> This maple burn itself away;
>
> Unloved, the sun-flower, shining fair,
>   Ray round with flames her disk of seed,
>   And many a rose-carnation feed
> With summer spice the humming air;
>
>   *   *   *
>
> As year by year the labourer tills
>   His wonted glebe, or lops the glades;
>   And year by year our memory fades
> From all the circle of the hills.
>
>   (*In Memoriam*, CI)

After clearing out of Somersby Rectory the Tennysons visited their old friends in the countryside before the actual move to Essex. Mary, Cecilia, and Alfred got their brother Charles to drive them around in his phaeton; of their farewell visit to Dalby their aunt Bourne wrote caustically that 'they came at *ten* o'clock at night, wanted supper etcetera, etcetera, & were proceeding that night to Rawnsleys! Natural affection is not easily repulsed. I felt gratified by their *short* visit & late attention.' With apparent pleasure she added, 'I have never heard of them since.'[10]

The family trip to High Beech was characteristically disorganized. Cecilia carried her dog Ariel on her lap in the coach from Spilsby to Waltham Cross, where they took a chaise at five in the morning for Beech Hill. Their manservant failed to show up to direct them to the house, and they were driven miles out of their way to alarm a pair of spinsters by ringing the bell of the wrong house; after repeated efforts they convinced the postboy that their name was not Trundown, and at last reached the right house. They were delighted with the creeper-covered verandah and the simple thatched park lodge. Opposite them stood the house of the owner of Beech Hill, Sergeant Arabin, a merry little man whose wife was related to Lincolnshire friends of the Tennysons.

'It will be a long time before I shall know people and things here,' wrote Cecilia, 'every thing appears so strange to me.' She and Alfred walked in Epping Forest and were disappointed to find that many of the trees were now only stumps, 'shooting out here and there a little green'. The country was 'rather flat', but she bravely insisted that 'still there is a grandeur about it'.[11] In the days to come Tennyson was to walk more and more among the disconsolate 'stunts and stubs' of the Forest, alone except for his bad-tempered mastiff, or with Horatio on his daily walk at noon, or leading Cecilia's black pony. In the winter the pond froze and he would swoop around it on his Lincolnshire skates, his blue cloak billowing out behind him as he cut endless lonely figures. Often he walked up and down the house reciting poetry to himself, shaping it to copy down later in his red-curtained, bay-windowed study above the dining-room.

Predictably, once he had escaped Lincolnshire he began longing for it again. 'You hope our change of residence is for the better,' he wrote to Mrs Rawnsley. 'The only advantage in it is that one gets up to London oftener. The people are sufficiently hospitable, but it is not in a good old-fashioned way, so as to do one's feelings any good. Large set dinners with stores of venison and champagne are very good things of their kind, but one wants something more; and Mrs. Arabin seems to me the only person about who speaks and acts as an honest and true nature dictates: all else is artificial, frozen, cold, and lifeless.'[12] In one of his letters to Emily Sellwood he complained of having 'nothing but that muddy pond in prospect', and the 'two little sharp-barking dogs' of his sisters to listen to. 'Perhaps I am coming to the Lincolnshire coast, but I scarcely know. The journey is so expensive and I am so poor.' There is something a little chilling about the recurrent references to poverty in his letters to Emily, almost as if to convince both her and himself that marriage was impossible. Neither his life at High Beech nor his visits elsewhere in England suggest that he was unable to travel when he wanted to do so, and we know that he had an income that would have been more than adequate on which to marry for such friends of his as Brookfield or Tennant.

According to his son he did make frequent trips to Lincolnshire, staying with either the Sellwoods or his brother Charles. It was accepted by both the Sellwoods and the Tennysons that he and Emily were 'quasi-engaged', but there was no prospect of a wedding in the near future. Money was named as the chief obstacle, but part of Tennyson's apparent reluctance may have sprung from worry over Emily's illness. She was so feeble that Cecilia Tennyson described another friend (thought 'to be in a consumption') as being 'in a very very weak state of health indeed almost—nay I think quite—as weak as Emily Sellwood'.[13] None the less, Emily came on at least one occasion to stay at Beech Hill, and Alfred went to Horncastle when he could.

Mrs Tennyson hated to have Alfred absent from Beech Hill, now that she had come to lean on him so much, and any long trips were out of the question for him. 'My mother is afraid if I go to Town, even for a night,' he wrote; 'how could they get on without me for months?'[14] During one thunderstorm Alfred went to reassure her and found her grovelling on the floor of her room, crying and threatening to leave the house forever.

Further family trouble came in 1837 with the termination of Mary's engagement. 'Mary is become *serious* they *say*,' wrote Mrs Bourne, '& *they say* that Heath to whom she was engaged deserted her in consequence. . . . if she has found this pearl of great price it is a *gift* above everything the world calls good or great.' Even with her new religious seriousness Mary was deeply hurt, and she was said to have lost her beauty in grief. Shortly thereafter she was 'dreadfully torn & mangled' by the mastiff.[15] It was perhaps the effect of her double disaster that made her increasingly absorbed in Swedenborgianism and in all kinds of spiritualism and mesmerism, interests that she shared with Frederick. John Heath was generally held to have behaved badly in breaking the engagement, and Mary became so bitterly antagonistic to men that she did not marry for another fourteen years. She now settled down with Emily in joint spinsterhood. Matilda had never been totally normal, according to family tradition because she had fallen head first into a coal-scuttle when a child, and it began to look as if Cecilia would be the only one of the sisters who might marry. For Alfred it all meant the increase of responsibility for which he was not equipped.

Not that everything at Beech Hill was lugubrious. After Mary's disappointment she went to Guernsey for some months with Anne Sellwood, who shared her sister's bad health and had been 'advised to bathe to strengthen her Spine'. Cecilia wrote to Susan Haddelsey about their departure, with indifferent spelling and almost no punctuation: 'The night before they went we had some wild fun we sat up till one oclock Alfred amusing us all the time by taking different caracters, he made us laugh so much you should have heard him would have amused you so.'[16]

But the laughter was too infrequent, and his remedy was to escape to London, 'to rub the rust from off him'. He would set off by coach in the evening, with 'the light of London flaring like a dreary dawn' before him, but even then he would be overcome by worry about his family, so that instead of remaining he would walk the twelve miles home, often arriving scarcely before daybreak. After living a year or so in High Beech he gradually induced his family to go to London too, and they shared his lodgings in Mornington Crescent, where they would take some of their own servants to help the keeper of the house. It was not the escape from the family that he needed, but it did allow him to get to London for longer periods of time.

In his rambles through the Forest Tennyson occasionally came across other regular walkers from High Beech, most of them scarcely more self-absorbed than he. They were patients from the nearby insane asylum run by Dr Matthew Allen, a Scotsman who had moved there in 1825. Allen was an intelligent, likable man with very advanced and merciful theories about handling the insane, he bubbled with enthusiasm, and he made friends easily. Unfortunately, for all his admirable qualities, he was also a scoundrel, if the phrase is accurate for someone who was in frequent hot water because he was more interested in the excitement of the various projects he was involved in than he was in their legality. He had twice been in prison, but since coming to High Beech he seemed a model citizen. His medical qualifications were thin, but he knew a good bit from practical experience with the insane, and in 1837, when the Tennysons moved to Essex, he published his daringly original book, *Essay on the Classification of the Insane*.

Allen advocated a minimum of restraint in treating disturbed persons, and he did not believe in the use of strait-waistcoats (although he did put desperate patients into small dark cupboards until they were recovered). Instead of restraint he believed in healthy amusement to keep the patient's mind busy. In High Beech he had three houses, Fair Mead for men, Springfield for women, and Leopard's Hill Lodge for the most severe cases. In each the front room was fitted up like that of an ordinary house, with games and adequate facilities to receive visitors. The inmates were encouraged to do manual labour, to take unsupervised walks, and to tire themselves with exercise but to shun books. Few patients tried to escape from Allen's benevolent surveillance.

One patient whom Tennyson must often have seen walking sadly in the stumpy woods was the Northamptonshire poet John Clare, who was committed the year that the Tennyson came to High Beech. When he arrived Clare thought it a beautiful place, but by 1841, when he ran away, he was calling it 'this Hell of a Madhouse'. But it was homesickness, not his treatment, that he hated, and he remained devoted to Allen. In his walks Clare was often accompanied by another patient, the son of Tennyson's acquaintance Thomas Campbell.

Allen was one of the first doctors in the country to encourage voluntary patients, those who realized that they needed care in order to keep from becoming more seriously deranged. Septimus Tennyson was a voluntary patient in Fair Mead for several stays of varying length, and Alfred stayed there occasionally, although on what terms we no longer know. It may be that Tennyson and Allen met through Septimus's first voluntary admission, apparently within a year of the Tennysons' arrival at High Beech. The two men already had several literary friends in common, and Allen had long been a friend of Carlyle.

There was no stigma to being a voluntary patient, and even Jane Carlyle said Allen's asylum was a place to which any sane person would be delighted to be admitted. She was so taken with the houses hung with roses and grapes, with the gardens and the air of general freedom that she went there to stay several days in 1831. Allen had earlier suggested to Thomas Carlyle that he might like to live there permanently, at an annual cost of £40 for his keep and that of a horse. Wisely, Carlyle declined the invitation, feeling that he had sufficient access to insanity in the general folly of the world; besides, he somewhat distrusted Allen as deficient in perseverance.

Through his friendship with Allen, Tennyson was to learn most of what he knew of madhouses, which loom so large in *Maud*. He was probably also made even more painfully aware of his own lack of solid mental balance and turned further towards hypochondria. Certainly, he was to lose almost all his little capital through trusting Allen too well.

Any detailed records of Tennyson's health between 1839 and 1850 have disappeared, so that we can only speculate about what ailed him so badly during those years and why he had to retreat first to Fair Mead and then, in the 1840s, after he had broken with Allen, to at least three different establishments offering the 'water cure'. His recurrent breakdowns were connected with the inherent melancholia and neuroticism of his family, the Tennysonian 'black blood', but beyond that it seems clear that his worries sprang from the epilepsy from which his father, his uncle Charles, and his cousin George all suffered, and to which two or more of his brothers may also have been prey.

The 'waking trances' into which he had fallen ever since boyhood, and the abstracted sadness that used to drive him forth from parties and take 'all the pleasure' from his blood obviously had a deeply traumatic effect upon him. What is remarkable is that though they afflicted him during boyhood and young manhood, there is no indication that he ever mentioned them until he was much older, when he could look back on them as springing from perfectly innocuous causes, quite unconnected with epilepsy. Probably he talked about them to Arthur Hallam, but otherwise he kept them to himself out of the shame that epilepsy then evoked.

At about the time Tennyson was getting to know Allen, his uncle Charles apparently had a recurrence of his own epilepsy: 'I had scarcely finished my letter yesterday,' he told his son Edwin, 'before I was attacked by one of my old spasms. It did not produce insensibility—but has left me weak today—.'[17]

Charles Tennyson d'Eyncourt was having other problems as well. The whole rebuilding of Bayons was undertaken with the idea that it would finally be fulfilled by a title bestowed on the family, but so far the Prime Minister had been singularly unresponsive to hints. His hopes were revived with the accession of Victoria, since it seemed natural that she should reward Charles on the occasion of her coronation. In August 1837 Charles wrote complacently to his son George: 'All the Papers have said they are to make me a Peer. I have heard nothing of it & have no reason to think such a thing will be offered, altho' it isnt perhaps improbable.'[18] His son thought '"Lovell and Eyncourt" would sound very well', and the title was almost certain to secure a suitable embassy for Charles, perhaps Munich. But the months passed without word until April 1838, when they heard at last that Melbourne had disregarded the nudges given to him by Charles's friends and relatives and was not disposed to grant a peerage. Again in 1840 and 1841 Charles bombarded an unwilling Melbourne with suggestions for a peerage and a suitable title, without which Bayons would be only a hollow triumph, but there was no response.

The cruellest irony of all was one of which he knew nothing. His beloved daughter Julia, who had so properly refused her cousin's proposal, was in love with another man even more unsuitable than Frederick: Edward Bulwer, Alfred's tormentor and by now Charles's best friend, a man of known profligacy, still married but seperated from his wife. Charles had instigated the friendship in the first place and had brought Bulwer to Bayons, and now that friendship was to be responsible for the wreck of the life of his daughter.

*   *   *

In March 1838 Tennyson spent a week in Cambridge, looking well and in good spirits, 'but complaining of nervousness,' wrote Blakesley. 'How should he do otherwise, seeing that he smokes the strongest and most stinking tobacco out of a small blackened clay pipe on an average nine hours every day? He went off to-day by the Wisbeach to Epping, where he complains that there are no sounds of Nature and no society; equally a want of birds and men.'[19] Before long he was off again to London, where he took lodgings in Norfolk Street, the Strand. Although he often stayed in Mornington Crescent with his family, during the next dozen years he dated his letters from as many different addresses. The income from his inheritance allowed him to travel as he wished, but he tried to economize on respectable living quarters, which meant little to him. Frequently he slept on a sofa or spare bed in the rooms of a friend.

'We have had Alfred Tennyson here,' the faithful Fitz wrote from London, 'very droll, and very wayward: and much sitting up of nights till two and three in the morning with pipes in our mouths: at which good hour we would get Alfred to give us some of his magic music, which he does between growling and smoking; and so to bed. All this has not cured my Influenza as you may imagine: but these hours shall be remembered long after the Influenza is forgotten.'[20]

The following year he wrote of having 'Alfred Tennyson up with me here, and to-day I give a dinner to him and two or three others—It is just ordered; soles, two boiled fowls, and an Apple Tart—cheese &c. After this plenty of smoking.' Two days later he finished the letter to Bernard Barton, feeling 'still more smoke dried and two-o'clock-in-the-morning-fuddled than before'. Tennyson's late hours and pipes could be fatiguing to other hosts than Fitz, since most of them were unable to sleep in the morning as Tennyson did; the news of his coming was the occasion for mixed anticipation and apprehension. FitzGerald was probably not more than half-joking when another time he wrote: 'Alfred Tennyson has written to announce he will pay me a visit here: and I have written back to stipulate that it shall be a very short one.' When Tennyson stayed too long with Fitz they would 'squabble and growl like dogs at each other'; when he was gone Fitz missed him terribly.[21]

FitzGerald persuaded Tennyson to sit to Samuel Laurence for his earliest and most famous portrait in oils. The painter and poet got on well, although Laurence used to say that Tennyson was the strongest-minded man he had ever met. Fitz greatly admired Tennyson's arrogant, masculine good looks before he grew a beard (while still a 'shorn Apollo') and insisted that Laurence's portrait was the only one he ever cared to have, although he agreed that it failed somewhat in the mouth, 'which A.T. said was "blubber-lipt"'.[22] The picture now hangs in the National Portrait Gallery, but it is no longer Tennyson as Fitz loved him, since after Tennyson's death it was partly repainted (and tamed) by Burne-Jones at the request of Hallam and Emily Tennyson, to whom FitzGerald had given it (see Plate VIII).

Some of Tennyson's uncouth rustic manners needed burnishing for London. When dining with Venables and Brookfield at the Reform Club, he put his feet on the table and kept them there in spite of his friends' remonstrances. At last one of them said, 'Take care, Alfred, they will think you are Longfellow.' The feet were removed without further ado.[23]

More and more his friends were now married, and he became a solitary *habitué* of their firesides. In 1838 the Thackerays took a house in Coram Street, opposite John Allen and his wife. Tennyson was often in and out of both houses, and for a time treated Allen's house almost as his own, sitting for silent hours in front of the fire, brooding abstractedly over the polish of the lines he composed in his head. When he read he would comment on the book before him, spreading out his huge hands to the flames to emphasize his point. He loved, too, to tell horror stories to frighten Mrs Allen, whose sensibilities were near to the surface, but he never did so with malice.

Thackeray found Tennyson a little earnest at times, and Tennyson thought Thackeray's 'outer husk . . . cynical', although he never lost sight of the kindliness of the inner man, 'with a heart of true flesh & blood'. Once when Tennyson was holding forth at his table, Thackeray suddenly exclaimed, 'Well Alfred you do talk damn'd well', and to the end of his days he claimed Tennyson as the wisest man he had ever known. 'Alfred Tennyson, if he can't make you like him, will make you admire him,' he told Mrs Procter, 'he seems to me to have the cachet of a great man. His conversation is often delightful, I think, full of breadth manliness and humour: he reads all sorts of things, swallows them and digests them like a great poetical boa-constrictor as he is. . . . Perhaps it is [his] great big yellow face and growling voice that has had an impression on me. Manliness and simplicity of manner go a great way with me . . .'[24]

Thackeray stayed at least once at Beech Hill, showing the esteem in which Tennyson held him. It is curious how few of his friends seem to have been invited there, probably because he disliked the house, or perhaps because of the confusion of the household. From his departure from Somersby until his marriage there is little indication that he tried to repay any of the hospitality so often extended to him in London.

One of Tennyson's admirers whom he had not yet met was Elizabeth Barrett, whom Leigh Hunt described as 'a fair and no unworthy imitator of yours'. Both her own romantic interest in him and the degree to which he was being generally talked about are shown by the eagerness of a letter to Miss Mitford in 1839: 'Is Alfred Tennyson among your personal acquaintances? I heard of him the other day as having an unduly large head, handsome features, and a fathoming eye—and that they had all settled into a cottage in Devonshire where he smoked and composed poems all day . . . and [that he was] separating from his family *because they distracted him*.'[25] The haze of mystery about Tennyson as he moved unheralded in and out of town contributed to the curiosity so many literary people felt about him. His unexpected appearances on the social scene also helped to cast him in the unlikely role of lion and man-about-town.

It was probably in 1838 that he at last met Thomas Carlyle; both the date and the circumstances of their meeting are uncertain. It has been suggested that Matthew Allen introduced them in 1840, but it is more likely that they were introduced by James Spedding, who had met Carlyle late in 1837. There were other opportunities for them to meet, since both were members of the Sterling Club, called after John Sterling, the former Apostle, from whom Carlyle had heard much of Tennyson.

Carlyle was fourteen years older than Tennyson, and his reputation had already been secured in 1837 on the publication of *The French Revolution*. It was a somewhat improbable friendship of two difficult men, but from the first it went well. 'He seemed to take a fancy to me,' Tennyson said laconically.[26] Carlyle had no feeling for English poetry and thought that Tennyson was wasting his talents, while Tennyson thought that Carlyle's Scottish-Germanic fulminations were frequently only a disguise for bad temper. All the same they brought out the best in each other, and there was hardly another friend of Tennyson's with whom he was ever so much at ease except Hallam. The two men would smoke together, talking, more often sitting in silent communication in the fumes. In later years as Tennyson became increasingly impatient with nonsense from other men he usually managed to keep philosophic calm with Carlyle, and they quietly enjoyed each other's provincial humour.

Like most others who met Tennyson at the time, Carlyle was captured by his physical beauty, and with his own unrivalled ability to dash off a vivid picture of others he twice described Tennyson in unforgettable detail. The first time was in 1840, when he wrote of him: 'A fine large-featured, dim-eyed, bronze-colored, shaggy-headed man is Alfred; dusty, smoky, free-and-easy: who swims, outwardly and inwardly, with great composure in an inarticulate element as of tranquil chaos and tobacco smoke; great now and then when he does emerge: a most restful, brotherly, solidhearted man.'[27]

When he had known him longer, he sketched Tennyson for Emerson in a few broad strokes: 'One of the finest looking men in the world. A great shock of rough dusty-dark hair; bright-laughing hazel eyes; massive aquiline face, most massive yet most delicate, of sallow brown complexion, almost Indian-looking; clothes cynically loose, free-and-easy;—smokes infinite tobacco. His voice is musical metallic,—fit for loud laughter and piercing wail, and all that may lie between; speech and speculation free and plenteous: I do not meet, in these late decades, such company over a pipe!—We shall see what he will grow to. He is often unwell; very chaotic,—his way is thro' Chaos and the Bottomless and Pathless; not handy for making out many miles upon.' With language like that at his fingertips, it is hard to see why Carlyle so disliked poetry; he was, as Tennyson observed, 'a poet to whom Nature has denied the faculty of verse'.[28]

When they met, Tennyson was assiduously revising the poems in the 1833 volume, an exercise that Carlyle considered useless, particularly when the poems were on classical subjects. One evening at Bath House, Lord Ashburton's London residence, Carlyle introduced Tennyson to Sir John Simeon, and described Tennyson to him as 'sitting on a dung-heap among innumerable dead dogs'. Years later Tennyson teased him about the remark, and Carlyle replied with amusement, 'Eh! that was not a very luminous description of you.' The Ashburtons, relatives of Rosa Baring, were the parents of Tennyson's friend William Baring, who was also a member of the Sterling Club. During the next two decades Tennyson was occasionally entertained at Bath

House, and it was there that he refused Milnes's offer of an introduction to his hero, the Duke of Wellington. Tennyson tore himself away, saying roughly, 'What the devil do you suppose the Duke wants to see me for?'[29]

Jane Carlyle was nearly as fond as her husband of Tennyson, although she had to put up with his curious shyness with women and to sit in stupefying clouds of smoke while Tennyson expounded the advantages of drying tobacco before use and her husband insisted that it should be moistened. Like her husband she was very much impressed with his appearance, and she was sure that any woman would fall 'in love with him on the spot, unless she be made absolutely of ice'.[30] In time Tennyson became so intimate with the Carlyles that his clay pipe was kept for him in a special niche of the garden wall, and he would call at all hours at Cheyne Row with no warning of his coming.

❊

CHAPTER XVI

BREAK WITH EMILY SELLWOOD,
1838–1842

THE immutable, rock-hard core of Tennyson's existence was the need to create poetry, whether in High Beech, Cambridge, or London, and to that end he had to escape a too-absorbing social life. 'I require quiet, and myself to myself, more than any man when I write,' he told Emily Sellwood rather forbiddingly. In the autumn of 1838 he went alone to Torquay, where he wrote 'Audley Court', which he said was partly suggested by Abbey Park, in what was then 'the loveliest sea village in England'. A solitary trip to Wales in 1839 brought him disappointment in Aberystwyth, 'the Cambrian Brighton', for he found nothing worth the journey, 'always excepting the Welsh-women's hats which look very comical to an English eye'. Because it reminded him of Mablethorpe, he liked Barmouth considerably better, and the Llanberis lakes, 'the most beautiful thing I saw this time in Wales', inspired him to write 'Edwin Morris'.

In spite of these poems the spate that had borne him along for years was beginning to slacken. His insistence on quiet and solitude was part of a search for renewed poetic inspiration, in itself an unconfessed awareness that the stream was neither so swift nor so deep as it had once been. Hallam's death had been excruciating, but it had wonderfully sharpened his emotions, and now that his grief was ameliorated the irresistible, almost ruthless drive to creation was also lessened. Some of his reluctance to publish the poems he had already composed sprang from an inarticulate fear that if he were to relinquish them he would be left with nothing. Rather than commit them to print, he preferred to polish them endlessly.

His distaste for publishing applied as well to non-poetical writing. Early in 1839 his sister wrote that Alfred 'tells us that Moxon the publisher has just offered him sixty pounds, if he will write a preface to the life of Beaumont and Fletcher, I do not think he will undertake it—I wish he would, even if it were but for the sordid pelf, for I am sure

XI. Emily Tennyson, c. 1863.

XII. Farringford c. 1894.

his affairs are not sufficiently flourishing to reject such an offer without thinking twice about it.'[1]

Nor were his friends successful in urging him to publish. 'Tennyson composes every day,' wrote Milnes, 'but nothing will persuade him to print, or even write it down.' For a time it appeared that he had begun to relent, and early in 1838 FitzGerald announced 'a forthcoming volume by A. Tennyson, but this genius appears so sturdily indifferent to fame and so abhorrent of trouble [that] his friends can only hope to overcome by the help of an oak stick.' But it was no use; a year later Fitz was writing plaintively: 'I want A.T. to publish another volume: as all his friends do: especially Moxon, who has been calling on him for the last 2 years for a new edition of his old volumes: but he is too lazy and wayward to put his hand to the business—He has got fine things in a large Butcher's Account Book that now lies in my room . . .'[2]

The impetus for Tennyson to break his long silence finally came not from his friends but from the United States. Foreign authors were still unprotected there by copyright, so that their works could be published without payment of royalties. His 1833 poems had been copied out by hand and passed around the admiring literary world of Boston. In 1838 Emerson had persuaded C. C. Little and Co. to publish an edition, but nothing then came of the plan. On Christmas Day 1840 C. S. Wheeler wrote to Tennyson, asking for his permission to undertake an American edition. When the letter arrived, Tennyson reported to the persistent Fitz: 'You bore me about my book; so does a letter just received from America, threatening, tho' in the civilest terms, that, if I will not publish in England, they will do it for me in that land of freemen. Damn!'[3] He knew that if he did not co-operate the American edition would contain the uncorrected versions from the 1833 volume, so he reluctantly agreed to prepare a two-volume edition for Moxon, containing revised poems from the old edition as well as new ones. In return for early copies W. D. Ticknor paid £150, probably the first time an American publisher ever paid an English poet.

Tennyson's trip to Wales in 1839 was connected with his impending separation from Emily Sellwood as well as with his need to write. Since most of their correspondence of the period was burnt by their son at Tennyson's direction, the evidence about their ten-year separation is necessarily fragmentary. In November 1838 Emily had stayed for some time at Beech Hill, where she walked with the Tennyson daughters in the cold, damp woods while Alfred, who was seldom seen on horseback otherwise, rode in the Forest with Horatio. One evening Emily and Alfred stayed up to see a sky of meteors and a magnificent aurora that made everything in her room look rose-coloured. It was a successful visit, and by now she was almost one of the family; two months later Emily Tennyson stayed with her in Horncastle.

But by the autumn of 1839 a serious rupture had occurred between the two families because of Charles Turner's apparently hopeless addiction to opium and his consequent separation from Louisa. The relations between Tennyson and Emily Sellwood thereafter are hard to assess: his letters for nearly another year constantly assured her of his love and called her his 'dearest—dearest', but it is clear that he was beginning to detach himself from the engagement and that Emily was being made miserable.

In the library of Wellesley College is a pitiful letter (undated but apparently of October 1839) in which Emily pleaded almost hysterically with Emily Tennyson, who she feared no longer wanted to correspond with her. She was afraid that the difficulty between Louisa and Charles would mean that all communication between the two families would stop. To avert that possibility she insisted that Louisa still loved Charles and was as fond as ever of Emily Tennyson. 'From my heart I thank you for having made that painful effort to write to me. I hope I shall not drive thee to it again.' In asking Emily Tennyson to write, she said she had been acting from 'a selfish fear lest thy love for me had departed; a selfish desire to have those anxieties relieved which sprang from my interest in another—'. By now she apparently could not write directly of her feelings to Alfred but depended upon his sister to relay them. 'Wilt thou not go with Alfred into Wales? Thou knowest I am very jealous, that he is thine own brother and thou mayst go. And would he not cheer thee and would not Mountains and free air cheer you both.[4]

On October Tennyson answered her directly:

Knowest thou that I am pleased with thee for feeling moments of jealousy about Glenthorne. I can't very well say why I am pleased. I suppose because it is a proof of thy love, dearest . . . but certain it is that I am gratified by thy jealousy. I hope to have a nice summery letter from thee enclosing full forgiveness for all my bantering & grumbling. Farewell—dearest—dearest—trust in me always & trust me always thine AT[5]

It would seem a sufficiently loving letter with little to alarm Emily were it not for the exhortation to trust him, which sounds as if there had been trouble. This last sentence throws a more ominous light on the fragment previously quoted: 'I require quiet, and myself to myself, more than any man when I write.' Probably Emily regarded his trip to Wales as not only flight from the distractions of London but also as an oblique warning of his inability to marry her. The impression is strengthened by the existing fragment of a letter, probably of 9 January 1840, in which he told her either that their engagement was at an end or that they would be unable to marry for a long time, while once more urging her to trust him:

How should this dependence on thy state coexist with my flying from thee? Ask not, believe that it does. Tis true, I fly thee for my good, perhaps for thine, at any rate for thine if mine is thine. If thou knewest why I fly thee there is nothing thou would'st more wish for than that I should fly thee. Sayest thou 'are we to meet no more?' I answer I know not the word nor will know it. I neither know it nor believe it. The immortality of man disdains & rejects it—the immortality of man to which the cycles & the aeons are as hours & as days.[6]

All the talk of immortality and aeons sounds like irrelevant cold comfort, and without further context it seems a perplexing, almost callous letter, breaking their engagement without giving the reason, while continuing to protest his love for her. Total separation would seem far kinder. Tennyson was not hard or deliberately cruel, but when he was frightened or was unable to deal with a situation he was sometimes unaware of how much he could wound others. Even the deep tenderness he felt for Emily was not enough to prompt him to comfort her when he felt trapped.

In the summer of 1840, according to their son, 'all correspondence between Alfred Tennyson and Emily Sellwood was forbidden; since there seemed to be no prospect of their ever being married' because of Tennyson's poverty. Tennyson used to say that his ideal life was to be 'a country squireen who lived on about eight hundred pounds a year quietly, with his wife and family'.[7] In 1840, when he had the interest from his inheritance as well as his annual gift of £100 from Mrs Russell and perhaps something from FitzGerald, his income was not too far off his ideal. He was beginning to sell the property left to him by his grandfather, and no doubt he was helping with the expenses of his mother's household, but he still had sufficient to marry had he wished to do so. In any case, poverty was nothing that he would have had to conceal from Emily, nor would it have made her anxious for him to fly from her, as he suggested. The reason for his withdrawal from the engagement must be sought elsewhere.

His own lack of physical ardour may have influenced his decision, and perhaps an inarticulate but understandable desire simply to escape the ties of marriage; certainly, the breakdown of Charles Turner contributed to it. The last has frequently been given as the reason why Mr Sellwood finally put his foot down and stopped the correspondence, but this misses the central point that it was Tennyson who broke off the engagement, probably fearing marriage and paternity because of his own inheritance of mental instability. This was indeed a reason that would have made Emily think it better for him to break the engagement, and it was also something that we can understand he was reluctant to tell her. Mr Sellwood was no doubt wary of further connections by marriage with the Tennysons, but in finally forbidding further correspondence he was only trying to make the break clean and protect his daughter from the miserable uncertainty of Alfred's vacillations. Emily's mother had been jilted before her engagement to Mr Sellwood, and he wanted to save Emily from a repetition of her mother's anguish.

In the account of her youth and the early days of her marriage that she wrote for her sons, Emily implied that the break came about because Tennyson had lost his inheritance, but that was only an evasion of the truth, for the estrangement antedated Tennyson's financial troubles by some two years. If she ever totally understood why Tennyson had broken off the engagement (or indeed if Tennyson himself ever understood the whole business clearly), it was certainly nothing that she would have told her sons, since it seemed to reflect poorly upon their father.

Tennyson's version, according to his brother Charles, was 'that his monetary position did not improve as he expected . . . and from a sense of honour, though sorely against the grain, [he] came to think that under the circumstances it was unjust and unfair in him to hold the lady bound, and that he ought to set her free. His mother had such a high opinion of his choice that she offered to share her jointure with him to enable him to marry. This, however, Alfred refused as being unjust to his brothers & sisters. So by mutual and friendly consent the engagement was broken.'

Tennyson's brothers and sisters, however, believed that it was his 'morbid doubts' and 'shilly-shallying' that caused the break, not Sellwood's disapproval. In 1850 Tennyson went to Charles and 'assured him that all in the past that had laid him open to such misinterpretation had been done solely in the interests of [Emily]—was on his part a sacrifice of self-renunciation'. Charles believed that Alfred had continued to love her, 'and that but from an overstrained morbid scrupulousness as to what he conceived to be duty, he might have been content to wait—and so both might have been spared much suffering'.[8]

Even though Tennyson was extreme in his reticence about his own affairs, it is extraordinary that none of his close friends such as Spedding or Carlyle had ever heard the slightest mention of Emily Sellwood all during the 1840s and did not even know her name when they were married; it is not obvious testimony to the depth of his love for her or the extremity of his anguish during the decade. The reasons he advanced for breaking with Emily were not the whole truth, but he was not deliberately lying: the formulation in words of one's own emotions is difficult, even for a poet.

Since his whole existence was so dominated by poetry and its composition, he may also in part have been unconsciously motivated by the failure of his love for her to result in the flood of emotions that produced great poetry. Not that he would deliberately have judged his love by that standard, but he could scarcely have failed to see that their attachment had had scant poetical result, less even than his feelings for Rosa Baring had produced.

Whatever the complex reasons for the estrangement may have been, Emily and Alfred no longer corresponded after 1840 or saw one another, but they occasionally had news through Tennyson's sisters, with whom Emily assiduously kept in touch. After Emily Tennyson married Richard Jesse, her friendship with Emily Sellwood slackened, but Cecilia became progressively more attached to her brother's former fiancée.

In 1842 Emily's cousin Catherine Franklin, who had been living with the Sellwoods, married Drummond Rawnsley. Then, after her sister Anne's marriage, Emily was left alone in the big house in Horncastle with her father, whom she idolized. When he was in bad temper she sang to him; he read history to her; and they took daily walks with her leaning on his arm. The wind from the Fens bothered her lungs, and she believed that she was developing consumption. Then a large terracotta vase fell on her arm and crippled it so that she could no longer play the piano well, nor could she write a very legible hand. The bright blue dresses to match her eyes, which she had loved to wear, were put away, and she took to soft, flowing robes in sober shades of grey, plum, or violet, more suitable to her spinsterhood.

Her youth was gone, and when she was thirty in 1843 she wrote to her sister Anne, who had been travelling on the Continent: 'Right glad am I to hear you speak so ecstatically of mountain glories. They were the dreams of my childhood and youth but I suppose I have grown somewhat prematurely old, for I am no longer beckoned by snow capt giants, summoned by them in tones irresistible; such is only the fate of the young in years or the young in heart though aged in days.'[9] They sound like an echo of the words of Alfred's Mariana immured in her moated grange.

Through the weary decade before she was to marry Alfred she seems to have thought of herself as one-sidedly but irrevocably betrothed to him with no hope of marriage; it was far worse than no engagement at all, for she would not even have considered marrying anyone else. There are several indications that Alfred thought of marriage elsewhere (he apparently had no particular woman in mind), but Emily's fidelity was complete. 'I like not, nor have I as far as human eyes can see, any reason to like long engagements,' she wrote after her marriage.[10] It was a phrase that was to resound through her correspondence for the rest of her life.

* * *

Tennyson's health, which was already bad enough, was further affected early in 1840 by his worry over the impending break with Emily. Although FitzGerald sometimes stipulated that he was not to stay long, Tennyson knew he could depend upon hospitality in Charlotte Street when he was in bad shape. How shaky his condition was in the period between his breaking the engagement and the final interdiction upon his correspondence with Emily is suggested by a letter from Fitz on 17 February 1840: 'When I got back to my lodgings, I found A. Tennyson installed in them: he has been here ever since in a very uneasy state: being really ill, in a nervous way: what with an hereditary tenderness of nerve, and having spoiled what strength he had by incessant smoking &c.—I have also made him very out of sorts by desiring a truce from complaints and complaining—Poor fellow: he is quite magnanimous, and noble natured, with no meanness or vanity or affectation of any kind whatever—but very perverse, according to the nature of his illness—So much for Poets, who, one must allow, are many of them a somewhat tetchy race—.'[11] After staying for some time with Fitz, Tennyson went to join his mother in Cheltenham; she reported from there that both he and his brother Charles were improving in health, but it is improbable that she yet knew about the breaking of his engagement, or of his worry about it.

Mrs Tennyson, who had been ill, was in Cheltenham to be out of the way of yet another family move, which she was unable to manage herself. With the exception of Alfred, most of the others had liked Beech Hill, but it was large and expensive to run, and a physician had suggested that their collective health would be improved by a removal to Tunbridge Wells, where 'the air is so dry and the place so high that it just the thing for a Tennyson'.[12]

Alfred took against the town at once and particularly disliked 5 Grove Hill, 'a mere mousetrap' that was too cramped for all his books, but at least he was within easy reach of London. When he first arrived in his new home he went riding, but four hours in rain on an animal of which he was not fond in the first place gave him 'a disgust which is not yet overcome', his sister Emily said. 'We shall not allow him to continue in this restful state, because the country is beautiful & it is a pity he should not see it—so infinitely better than smoking so much.'[13]

As usual Alfred refused to see that smoking had anything to do with the matter. His bad health, he wrote to Tennant, came from their location, 'which is my abomination'. The London doctor had 'said it was the only place in England for the Tennyson constitution: the sequel is that they are half killed by the tenuity of the atmosphere and the presence of steel more or less in earth, air and water. I have sometimes tried to persuade them to live abroad but without effect . . .'. Within a few months he was beginning to think of moving once more.

What FitzGerald called hereditary tenderness of nerve and Tennyson later called hypochondria combined with financial worries and chagrin over the impending breach with Emily Sellwood to drive him forth in the spring of 1840 in another outburst of aimless wandering about the country. Just before the move to Tunbridge Wells he went to stay for a time with Charles, alone in Grasby. He also went to Horncastle, where some of Emily's relatives were apparently rude to him about the breaking of his engagement, in the belief that he was jilting Emily. 'Of all horrors a little country town seems to me to be the greatest,' he wrote at the time, and five years later, when he had received a flattering letter from the Prime Minister, his chief wish was that 'certain crones in or about Horncastle' who had been 'causelessly bitter against me & mine' might read what Peel had said.[14]

On the return journey from Lincolnshire Tennyson was driving into Warwick in a slow mail-coach, and by chance happened to have his glass in his eye when they passed FitzGerald walking in the direction of Leamington. Tennyson stopped the coach, hailed Fitz, who climbed in beside him, and went to the George Hotel, where they stayed the night. The next day they went to Kenilworth and tumbled about its ruins for three hours, with Scott as their lure, but Tennyson was disappointed in his expectations of grander, more august remains. In one of his last letters to Emily for nearly ten years, he said that he was afraid that he might not have enough money to stay over a night or two to see Warwick Castle, since 'it is very expensive being at an inn'. In spite of his professed poverty he managed to stay, but even the gardens and the views of Warwick were less impressive than two great portraits by Rembrandt and Titian.

On a trip to Stratford Fitz was most moved by the footpath to Shottery and Anne Hathaway's cottage, thinking of the times that Shakespeare had so often followed the same route. Tennyson was overcome 'with a sort of enthusiasm' when he went into the room where Shakespeare was born, seized his pencil, and scribbled his name on the wall with the thousands of others already there. 'I was a little ashamed of it afterwards,' he confessed.

Shortly thereafter he wrote to Emily telling her of the trip, then the correspondence stopped for a decade. There must have been a final letter, but it has disappeared.

At the end of June he went to Southampton to spend three days with Brookfield and his fiancée Jane Elton, who was Arthur Hallam's cousin. If Tennyson had been seeking reassurance about his ability to afford marriage, he could have looked to Brookfield and Jane Elton, who were planning to marry on Brookfield's income of £190 as a curate; it was minimal but adequate to provide for the daughter of a wealthy baronet. Had Tennyson really wished to marry, the Sellwoods would surely have demanded no more of him financially than the Eltons did of Brookfield, who was far poorer than Tennyson. To be sure the Brookfields later came to marital grief but not because of poverty. At about this time Elizabeth Hallam, aunt of both Jane Elton and Arthur Hallam, died and left £500 to Tennyson.

When he left Southampton Tennyson murmured vaguely about going to Le Havre but never got up the energy to board a ship. During the summer he made his first stay at Park House, the home of the Lushingtons near Maidstone. It was to have important consequences, for Tennyson liked the neighbourhood, as well as the Lushingtons, and decided on moving there. Edmund Lushington accompanied him back to Tunbridge Wells for a short visit, and there he met Cecilia, to whom he was to be married within two years. Mrs Tennyson and two of her daughters went with Tennyson on a return trip to Park House, from which they made expeditions looking for another home.

The best summary of Tennyson's unpremeditated, snipe-like darts around the country was that of Spedding, who wrote in amusement at the end of August: 'Alfred Tennyson has reappeared, and is going to-day or to-morrow to Florence, or to Killarney, or to Madeira, or to some place where some ship is going—he does not know where. He has been on a visit to a madhouse for the last fortnight (not as a patient), and has been delighted with the mad people, whom he reports the most agreeable and the most reasonable persons he has met with. The keeper is Dr. Allen . . . with whom he has been greatly taken.' Of Tennyson's stay at Fair Mead Fitz wrote drily, 'He did not want this to finish his education, I think.'[15]

The ostensible reason for Tennyson's return to High Beech was to visit his brother Septimus, who had been a voluntary patient there since the family moved to Tunbridge Wells. 'Sep', as the family knew him, remained there, comfortably ensconced in his own room, for some three years, although he seems to have left for short periods during that time. In 1840, when Alfred made his first stay in Fair Mead, his own precarious state of mental balance suggests that his status was somewhere between outright patient and paying guest. Once, when he was having luncheon with Allen and some of the other patients, Allen was called from the room. Immediately a patient seized a knife and brandished it threateningly at Tennyson. Fixing his gaze on Tennyson's monocle, he demanded, 'Why do you wear that glass thing in your eye?' With commendable composure Tennyson responded, 'Vanity, my dear Sir, sheer vanity.' The splendidly irrelevant reply so satisfied the lunatic that he resumed his seat and his calm. When he could afford to look back with equanimity on his fears of insanity, Tennyson described his stay with Allen as a 'study of the ravings of the demented at firsthand',[16] but it sprang from needs much more immediate than that.

After Tennyson had gone, Allen wrote to him, 'I have been very sad since we parted, and I can hardly tell why, unless it were because you were so out of spirits. I hope by this time that your family circle has taken them all away & that you are now as happy as I can wish you to be.'[17] If the visit to Allen's establishment helped to restore Tennyson's equilibrium temporarily, it was also to be the beginning of the longest and most serious threat to his sanity during his life.

Tennyson was much taken with his 'mad doctor', and within a fortnight he had met him in London and accompanied him to make a call in Cheyne Row. Carlyle was out, but they made themselves at home in the garden. During the late summer and autumn of 1840 they frequently saw each other, and gradually Allen told Tennyson about the plan he had for becoming so rich that he would no longer have to run an insane asylum.

In hindsight the scheme to make wood carvings by steam-driven machines seems a peculiarly Victorian project. By providing decoration for the homes of those too poor to hire craftsmen, it would help the democratization of art by using the efficiency of the industrial age. Allen's ebullience must have been attractive to Tennyson when he was in such a depressed state, and when he offered Alfred a chance to become rich with him, the lure of wealth was too much.

On 23 November 1840 Tennyson paid over £900 to Allen, for which he received in return an insurance policy of £2,000 on Allen's life; more insurance was to be taken out if Tennyson gave him more money. Two days later a memorandum of agreement between them was drawn up: Tennyson was to make up the initial payment to £1,000, then when the sale of his holdings from his grandfather's will was completed, Allen was to receive another £2,000, and both sums were to draw five per cent interest; a further £100 was to be paid to Tennyson annually beyond the interest. In addition to the insurance Tennyson was to receive a bond for £3,000 and the mortgage upon Fair Mead. Whether these two last were ever turned over to Tennyson is problematical; in any case, by the time he could have collected on them Allen was bankrupt and they would have been valueless.

The arrangements make Tennyson sound more business-like than has usually been assumed; presumably they would have been adequate had Allen been all that he appeared to Tennyson and all that he probably thought himself. To Tennyson he seemed charitable in sharing the golden opportunity, but Allen was in need of money to pay the owner of the process, a Mr Wood. Throughout the rest of 1840 and 1841 there were occasional difficulties, but the future seemed so bright that Tennyson acquiesced when Allen suggested that more of the

Tennysons might like to buy into the scheme, which he had grandly
named 'Pyroglyphs'. (He later changed it to 'The Patent Method of
Carving in Solid Wood', as more comprehensible.)

Henry and Frank Lushington in 1841 made a visit to High Beech to
see Alfred when he was staying there. As Henry said, they 'passed a
very tranquil night among the madmen. From all I can see, they are . . .
if anything better than ourselves. Dr. Allen's mania did not break out
much,—unless it was on the subject of wood carving.'[18] Because he so
hated Tunbridge Wells Tennyson entertained a few friends at Fair
Mead as he never did at home.

Mrs Tennyson sent word of the splendid progress of the carving
scheme to her apprehensive sister Mary Anne Fytche, telling of the
flow of orders for ornaments for churches, organs and chairs; there
was to be a 'Lecture at the Royal Society on this beautiful discovery . . .
the returns are so rapid, they talk of a dividend already'.[19] Tennyson's
four sisters were eager to have their own property sold, so that they
could invest as well; they wrote indignant letters to their uncle
Charles, who acted as their guardian, demanding that he surrender the
deeds to their property. When he understandably questioned the
financial stability of Allen's company they sent him a long and insulting joint letter in which they said they had been writing for three
months without receiving a satisfactory answer. The manner of the
letter sounds as if they were addressing a peculating tradesman rather
than an uncle anxious to protect their investment: 'We have been told
by those who understand the matter, that we are *shamefully
treated*. . . . We are sadly afraid that the delay is on purpose, you do
not deal openly with us. . . . Will you be sorry that we should be a little
richer than we have been, or what is it that you object to?'[20] It was, of
course, Allen who had been suggesting that their uncle was acting
shamefully. Emily, who was better off than the others because of her
allowance from old Mr Hallam, finally backed out of investing with
Allen, but the other three girls put up £4,000 in equal shares. Mrs
Tennyson and Charles Turner also invested, but it is probable that
they supplied no more than £1,000 between them.

All this was insufficient for Allen when his affairs began turning
sour, and he tried to wheedle Frederick Tennyson into joining the rest
of the family, saying that his financial advisers were of the opinion that
an investment of £3,000 would be worth £10,000 by the end of the
year and that in five years it would be worth that annually. Allen
probably believed what he was saying, but he used all the standard

tricks of the confidence man, threatening that the opportunity would soon pass and that there were plenty of other investors ready to buy in at the slightest opportunity.

It was obvious enough to outsiders that the Tennysons were going to lose their money. Venables, Henry Lushington, and other lawyers were all doubtful of Allen, and Fitz, predictably gloomy, thought that Allen was madder than his own patients. 'Depend on it, all the world is right about Dr. Allen,' he wrote to Frederick: 'he is not a man to be trusted. But you Tennyson's [*sic*] have the obstinacy of mules.' But Fitz had cried wolf too often for Alfred, who was so worried he did not want to hear anyone else's doubts. In the autumn of 1841 Fitz once more wrote to Frederick: 'I much fear for poor Alfred's money. There is a providence over fools and drunkards but not over poets, I fear.'[21] Throughout 1841 and the early part of 1842 Alfred was able to tell himself that all would be well, whatever anyone else might say.

The more he pushed his financial worries out of his consciousness, the more Tennyson's illnesses increased, and their incidence in turn made him more morbidly unable to remain in one spot. During 1841 and 1842 he moved around England as if possessed; in January 1841 he was in London, staying with Fitz, the following month in Mablethorpe hiding among the dunes, communicating with the outside world only through the itinerant muffin-man who visited that deserted resort. He hated to go to the family house in Tunbridge Wells, and when he was not in London he was most often found under treatment by Allen in High Beech. In August 1841 Spedding told a correspondent who had asked Tennyson's whereabouts: 'When I last saw him (which was a fortnight or 3 weeks ago) he talked of going to Ambleside or some quiet place in the lake district—he and his MSS.—that he might prepare them for the press. Another friend, who saw him two or thre hours after he parted from me, said he was then talking of going into Wales. What part of the world he may have talked of when he reached the Coach-office, I cannot guess, nor (wh. is still another question) what part he ultimately arrived at. All I can say is that I think he is *not* likely to be either in Wales or in Ambleside. For the rest of the globe—that portion of it at least wh. lies within 3 weeks journey of London—I do not know that there is any one place where I should expect to find him rather than another.'[22] The truth of the matter was that Tennyson was then off for a solitary trip of some weeks to Rotterdam and Amsterdam. Lonely and ill, he wandered ceaselessly, so that his friends were constantly writing to each other to inquire about his whereabouts.

Even in London it was almost impossible to trace him. When he stayed with FitzGerald in Charlotte Street, he would sit on the sofa working on his poems in a filthy vellum book as he smoked the pipe that so offended Fitz. When he was with Spedding in Lincoln's Inn Fields, he would wander over to 1 Mitre Court Buildings in the Temple, where Henry Lushington and Venables shared top-floor rooms. If there was a light in the window he would go upstairs, confident of finding a group of Cambridge men with whom he could smoke and talk in unbuttoned friendliness until the flare of the closing fireworks at the Surrey Gardens signalled the end of the evening. It was there he first met the Irish poet, Aubrey de Vere, who was pleased at the air of informality, so that only Christian names were used, even by the newest of acquaintances. Years later de Vere remembered Tennyson's 'large dark eyes, generally dreamy but with an occasional gleam of imaginative alertness, the dusky, almost Spanish complexion, the high-built head and the massive abundance of curling hair like the finest and blackest silk'.

In spite of his romantic appearance, Tennyson was beginning to look seedy and worn. At one of Milnes's breakfasts in March 1841 he met the ubiquitous Henry Crabb Robinson, in a company that included B. W. Procter ('Barry Cornwall') and his wife, John Kenyon, and Robert Browning, 'author of unreadable books'. It was the first meeting of the two greatest Victorian poets, and though they did not immediately become intimate Tennyson and Browning were to be on the friendliest of terms during the rest of their lives, providing a model of what such a relationship should be, even if they did not entirely like each other's poetry. Tennyson himself was so unkempt at the breakfast that Crabb Robinson said he looked like 'a bandit of genius'. Shortly thereafter he again met Catherine Franklin, the young lady with whom he had flirted at the home of her cousin, Emily Sellwood. She said he looked 'very much like the old man of the sea, as if seaweed might cling to him, unkempt and unbrushed and altogether forlorn as to the outer man'.[23] Tennyson had never been careful of his appearance, but now he was beginning to resemble the tramp he was in danger of becoming.

His poetry, which had always been the one solid anchor to order in his existence, probably saved him at this time. He now had the assurance that it was to be published in 1842, and after his return from

Holland the preparation of the manuscript gave him a necessary occupation, much as he hated the task. It was to be his first major publication in ten years, now to be undertaken without the advice and loving help of Arthur Hallam. Although it necessarily brought back sad memories, it also marked another stage in the liberation from the grief that had gripped him for so long. Hallam's memory was to remain always fresh, but after this it was a comfort not a clog to the spirit.

A more overt indication that life had to continue even after the death of Hallam was the engagement in September 1841 of Emily Tennyson to Richard Jesse, a lieutenant in the Navy. It was probably at the dinner table of the Hallams in 1834 that Emily had met her future husband, but the family reacted badly when they heard the news. 'Only *conceive* Emily Tennyson (I really can hardly even now believe it) Emily Tennyson is actually going to be married—and to whom after such a man as Arthur Hallam,' wrote Hallam's cousin Jane Elton. 'To a boy in the Navy, *supposed* to be a Midshipman. . . . I feel so distressed about this, really it quite *hurts* me, I had such a romantic adoration for her, looked at her with such pity, and now all my feeling about her is bouleversé—and Alfred Tennyson falls headlong into the abyss with her—but I cannot think he would like her to marry.' To the disgust of the female Hallams and Eltons, Emily told Julia Hallam that she had to think of her own unprotected state should her mother die. Jane Elton said that 'her £300 per annum was expressly intended to render her quite independent, and of course, to obviate her marrying merely for a comfortable home'.[24] Henry Hallam's more generous reaction was to continue Emily's allowance after her marriage, rather than trying to enforce an unnatural fidelity to his dead son.

Richard Jesse was a brave and singularly handsome man, but the Hallams were right in thinking he was not the equal of Arthur. In particular he was cursed with a compulsion to constant chatter, and after his marriage Alfred used to leave home on pretended errands when the Jesses were expected. It must have been a trial to Jesse when Emily named their first son Arthur Henry Hallam Jesse, but aside from that she seems never to have marred their marriage by repining over Hallam's death. Others than the Eltons and Hallams were surprised by the name: Elizabeth Barrett thought Emily was 'a very radically prosaic sister for the great poet . . . What a disgrace to womanhood! . . . to marry at all—bad!—to keep the annuity, having married—worse! to conglomerate & perpetuate the infidelity & indelicacy, by giving the sacred name to the offspring of the "lubberly lieutenant"—worst of all!!'[25]

As she grew older Emily Jesse became more eccentric, devoted to animals and spiritualism and worrying guests at her brother's table by her habit of feeding alternate mouthfuls to the pet dog in her lap and the raven tethered to her wrist. Like her husband she sometimes talked without ceasing until her auditors were nearly demented. But since all Tennysons grew increasingly odd with the years, her eccentricity cannot be entirely blamed on her husband.

One charming story was told of their marriage. Towards the end of her life she attended a seance with her husband, where her contact with the spiritual world announced that in afterlife she would join Arthur Hallam eternally. 'I consider that an extremely unfair arrangement and shall have nothing to do with it,' she exclaimed indignantly to her husband. 'We have been through bad times together in this world and I consider it only decent to share our good times, presuming we have them, in the next.'[26]

After her marriage Emily was totally unable to remember when Arthur's sister Julia asked her the name of the ship on which his body had been brought home. 'I cannot remember having heard the name, between ourselves, how little does it matter,' she wrote to Alfred. As an old woman she had so forgotten her former life that she got rid of the copy of Arthur Hallam's *Remains* given to her by old Mr Hallam, and Hallam Tennyson was irritated to have to buy it from a Brighton bookseller for six guineas.[27]

Emily's forgetfulness was a more healthy reaction than Alfred's remembrance of every detail of his friendship with Arthur. But whatever his reservations may have been about Jesse, he in no way resisted the marriage, and he gave the bride away at the wedding in January 1842. It is worth noting, however, that it was not this wedding but that of Cecilia Tennyson and Edmund Lushington in the autumn of 1842 that Tennyson used as the symbolic end of mourning for Hallam and the augury of the future in *In Memoriam*. This disjunction of characters gives a slightly odd flavour to the conclusion, but apparently even Alfred felt there was something faintly disloyal in Emily's marriage, so that it would not have been a fitting close to the poem.

At the end of 1841 the Tennysons had moved from Tunbridge Wells to Boxley Hall, some two miles from the Lushingtons' house, Park House, near Maidstone. There they had a much bigger house than the one in Tunbridge Wells, and Alfred made it his home as he had not the other. Best of all was the proximity to the Lushingtons, who could be reached by their own short cut through the fields. After the arrival of the Tennysons at Boxley, it did not take long for Edmund Lushington and Cecilia to become engaged. He was professor of Greek at Glasgow, and there were two brothers and four sisters still at home in Park House. Charles Turner officiated at the wedding, a few days after Cecilia's twenty-fifth birthday in October 1842, and Alfred gave away the bride. Once Arthur Hallam had hoped to establish a hearthside at which the Tennysons could feel a second home, but it was destined to be Park House at which they all congregated for the rest of their lives, sometimes to the inconvenience of the Lushingtons.

Frederick had been married since 1838, living in Florence with his Sienese wife. Although Charles's marriage was in disrepair, there was hope it could be salvaged. With the weddings of Emily and Cecilia, all the Tennysons closest to Hallam except Mary and Alfred were now married.

✵

CHAPTER XVII

FINANCIAL DISASTER,
1842–1843

TENNYSON'S distraught state made him peculiarly vulnerable to mishaps that would not have bothered him if he had been in more robust emotional condition. After the wedding of Emily and Richard Jesse he brought his other sisters to London, and the lodgings they took turned out to be the home of a violent madman, who woke them in the middle of the night with cries of murder, which were stilled only by putting him into a strait-waistcoat. The incident so upset Tennyson that he had to go to Fair Mead for a month of treatment by Allen. There the news of the wood-carving scheme was still reassuring.

By the beginning of March 1842 he was able to come back to London to work at the preparation of his poems for publication. He stayed with Spedding, who patiently advised him about revisions and helped him smooth out the rough spots. Fitz was anxious to help, too, but Tennyson was hesitant about taking his advice, since Fitz was uanble to hide completely his growing disenchantment with the direction he thought Tennyson's poetry was taking. In spite of his reservations about the poems Fitz dragged Tennyson off 'with violence to Moxon' at the beginning of March to settle the details of publication.

There were few publishers who would have understood Tennyson so well as Moxon, or who would have put up with so much in his hesitant attitude towards publication. As a poet who had suffered from them he understood Tennyson's nervousness about the reviewers. Although he did so little advertising that Leigh Hunt called him 'not a publisher but a *secreter* of books',[1] the standard of what he published was so high that he could usually get it reviewed by reputable periodicals even if he could not guarantee favourable criticism. In other ways he took such good care of Tennyson that he seemed to their friends to spoil him: he borrowed books for his use from the London Library, he frequently invited him to dinner to meet members of the literary coterie who might be useful to him, he arranged his schedule and tried to get him to appointments on time, and he acted as banker for the small accounts that Tennyson ran up and forgot to pay. When Tennyson went off to Mablethorpe to gloom with no company save the two live starfish he claimed to have seen there, Moxon sent him bundles of magazines and books.

Until Moxon's early death he and Tennyson had an almost flawless relationship as publisher and poet, one that was rewarding both financially and artistically. Not everyone saw the best side of Moxon, and Carlyle, for one, thought him an ambitious and avaricious man who barely avoided open dishonesty; beneath his civility was a calculation that Carlyle said made him look at others 'with the eye of a famished hound crushing a stolen bone'.[2] Nevertheless, their association was one of the luckiest of Tennyson's life.

In the spring of 1842 Tennyson was in a bad state of anxiety over the poems, some of which he had been tinkering with for more than ten years. Few of them were really new; they had all been written by 1840 and Tennyson had completed little since then. When he had the poems assembled, he was convinced of their excellence, but he was still worried about the reviewers. A fortnight after he and Moxon had arranged the publication, he received his first proofs and immediately lost his confidence; according to Fitz, when he saw them 'in hard print' he thought them detestable and wished 'he had never been persuaded to print'. Loyally, Fitz said that 'with all his faults, he will publish such a volume as has not been published since the time of Keats: and which, once published, will never be suffered to die'.[3] As Tennyson sat correcting proofs, he would tear the original manuscripts into long strips to use in lighting his pipe; the ones that have survived were retrieved from the fire by FitzGerald, who gave them to Trinity College.

When the first proofs were all corrected, Fitz took Tennyson off to Dulwich, predicting gloomily that 'when we get there of course the Gallery will be shut because of Easter. Well, then we shall go in a bad humour to dine at a tavern: get heartily sick of each other: and so back to town.' As they walked through the meadows to the gallery they talked of divinity, eternal life, design in the creation of the world, and the meaning of suicide. Recently Tennyson had said, 'I would rather know I was to be damned eternally than not to know that I was to live eternally.' All his troubles had made him hungry for belief in divine order, and once in St. Paul's he had said defiantly, 'This is a Symbol that man is immortal.' Near Dulwich he picked a daisy and brought its crimson-tipped petals near his myopic eyes. 'Does not this [suggest] a thinking Artificer,' he asked Fitz pleadingly, 'one who wishes to ornament?'⁴

When Tennyson was at his most depressed Fitz would walk him all around London, taking him to picture auctions to buy fly-blown daubs, reassuring him about the poetry, listening to his irritable doubts, best of all giving him silent love. Once he took him on a trip by steamer down the river to Gravesend, and on board the boat Tennyson sat for a silhouette-maker. Fitz pocketed the result and kept it; 'though not inaccurate of outline', it seemed to give 'one the idea of a respectable apprentice'⁵ (see Plate IX).

With all his stubborn, tactless honesty Fitz felt impelled to indicate his doubts about some of Tennyson's poems, and the first hair-line crack developed in their friendship, one that was to widen over the years. Something of this is implicit in Tennyson's tetchy plea: 'Don't abuse my book: you can't hate it more than I do, but it does me no good to hear it abused; if it is bad, you & others are to blame who continually urged me to publish. Not for my sake but yours did I consent to submit my papers to the herd—d——m 'em! & all reproach comes too late.'⁶

For all Tennyson's worries, the two-volume *Poems* of 1842, published on 14 May, eventually became the best loved of his miscellaneous collections. The first volume contained a selection of poems from 1833, most of them extensively and skilfully revised. In particular 'Œnone', 'The Lady of Shalott', 'The Palace of Art', and 'The Lotos-Eaters' were radically changed, and it is in their later form that they have descended to modern readers. The second volume was composed of poems published for the first time. Among these are some of Tennyson's finest poems: 'Ulysses', 'Break, break, break', and the 'Morte d'Arthur', all largely inspired by the death of Arthur Hallam and all among the glories of nineteenth-century English poetry. His growing interest in the Arthurian legend is reflected in 'Sir Launcelot and Queen Guinevere', 'Sir Galahad', and of course 'Morte d'Arthur'. 'The Vision of Sin' is Tennyson's first attempt to deal with the full destructive power of unbridled sexuality, and it is noticeable that his distrust of it is responsible for poetry of considerably greater power than any of his love poems had yet been. 'The Two Voices' is a dialogue between suicide and stoicism, begun during Hallam's lifetime but undoubtedly influenced by his death. It is more mature than the earlier poem on the same theme, 'Supposed Confessions of a Second-Rate Sensitive Mind', but there is still a fatal division in Tennyson's allegiance that makes for ambivalent diction over which the reader stumbles for meaning and which makes him suspect that Tennyson stumbled too in his alleged choice of joy and life rather than death.

A more fertile division of mind lies behind the dramatic monologue 'St. Simeon Stylites', which was inspired by the hoary paradox of asceticism, that it takes its vitality from a perverse love of what it seeks to suppress. The speaker is a welter of contrarieties to match: sinning and saintlike, overweeningly arrogant and pathetically frightened, comic and oddly dignified. It is one of the best pieces of characterization in Tennyson's poetry, and its power derives from the imagined similarities of the poet to the protagonist, so that the differences between the consciousness of the Victorian poet and that of the fifth-century Syrian are only on the surface. As always, Tennyson wrote most convincingly of the psyche of someone like himself. Like the saint, he was deeply unhappy and felt diseased, ageing, guilt-ridden, isolated, and dirty, at the very time that he was full of aspirations to immortality. The ambiguity that in 'The Two Voices' seems Tennyson's confused inability to make up his mind is here transformed into a strong statement on the dual nature of man. Into the pillar-hermit Tennyson put all his distrust of asceticism and by objectifying his own failings made him into a figure at whom he could laugh without pain to himself.

In the 1842 *Poems* is another group of poems dealing more specifically with modern English life than Tennyson was yet used to writing, and over them critical opinion has probably been more divided than over any others; they include 'The Gardener's Daughter', the revision of 'The Miller's Daughter', 'The May Queen', 'Dora', 'Walking to the Mail', 'Audley Court', and most popular of them all, 'Locksley Hall', which Rogers claimed Shakespeare could not have done better. They show Tennyson's determination to prove that he was not insulated from contemporary sensibility; 'English Idyls' he was to call them, indicating his attempt to domesticate the classical form. As sketches they are half-way between static pictures and narrative. For many of Tennyson's contemporaries they were deeply appealing, and their success in part determined the course of his art in the future. Lately there has been a renewal of interest in them, and one recent critic has made a good case for them as 'works of a subtle and delicate art. . . . among the finest of Tennyson's poems, certainly the most neglected in proportion to their merit of all of Tennyson's works.'[7] Ever since their publication, however, some readers have felt that Tennyson's attempts to reproduce contemporary life accord poorly with the form, with the curious result that he seems less at home with his own day than with antiquity. Certainly, one must have a strong sense of 'period' to appreciate them, and though they have the authentic Victorian feeling they seldom have the extra resonance to lift their appeal beyond the antiquarian; even the most enthusiastic admirer could not claim that they still speak directly to most readers. Here, as in his later works, one feels that the more Tennyson attempted to be up-to-date, the more his poetry has dated.

Whatever reservations there may be about individual poems, the new volumes marked Tennyson as the outstanding poet of his generation, a position that had been in doubt. From 1842 onward there was still adverse criticism of his work, but he could no longer be ignored. The reviews began appearing a fortnight after the publication of the *Poems*. Four were written by former Apostles: Francis Garden (*Christian Remembrancer*), Milnes (*Westminster*), Sterling (*Quarterly*), and Spedding (*Edinburgh*). Naturally, all were warmly enthusiastic and all urged that Tennyson unite himself more closely with the thought of his own day, to teach rather than merely delight: it was good Apostolic doctrine.

The most remarkable indication of the change in Tennyson's reputation was that Sterling had been asked to write about the *Poems* in the *Quarterly Review*, in which Tennyson had been so badly treated by Croker a decade earlier. The *Quarterly*'s editor, Lockhart, was apparently repentant about the Croker attack, and he invited Sterling to review any book of his choice, knowing full well that he would pick Tennyson's. Lockhart specified that Sterling should not antagonize Croker by deliberately praising any poem that Croker had damned in the earlier review. That did not, however, keep Sterling from writing a very flattering review in the September issue, nor did it keep Croker from being so offended that he nearly severed his connection with the *Quarterly*.

Sterling was shrewd about Tennyson's weaknesses and strengths, and he wrote privately that the new volumes were 'beautiful but have hardly as much substance as we would have hoped for after 10 years' silence. But his fancy is exquisite.' To John Stuart Mill he said that there was some doubt whether Tennyson 'could conceive a serious character, but as a lyrical and specially a descriptive poet & writer of eclogues he is quite in the front rank of our countrymen'.[8]

Even such mild private reservations he kept out of the review itself, but since he preferred 'the modern & democratic poems' to the 'mythologic', he allowed himself to speak somewhat coolly of 'Morte d'Arthur', calling it 'less costly jewel-work, with fewer broad flashes of passionate imagery, than some others, and not compensating for this inferiority by any stronger human interest. The miraculous legend of "Excalibur" does not come very near to us, and as reproduced by any modern writer must be a mere ingenious exercise of fancy.' Tennyson, who was neurotically susceptible to criticism, neglected the general praise in which the remark was buried, and morbidly concentrated on Sterling's lack of enthusiasm for this poem. He was especially sensitive because he had gone to great pains to frame the poem in a modern setting, 'The Epic', hoping thus to indicate its relevance to contemporary problems and to avoid Sterling's kind of criticism. Later he claimed that he had worried so much over the review that it had been the death of his ambition at the time to write an Arthurian epic of the standard twelve books. 'I had it all in my mind,' he said a quarter of a century later, 'could have done it without any trouble.'⁹ For all his tender nerves, it is probable that Sterling had only made patent what Tennyson sensed for himself, that he was not ready for an undertaking of such magnitude; nor it is it likely that the poem was in the state of readiness he claimed.

There were some twenty reviews before the end of 1842, most of them favourable, and sales went satisfactorily. Sales were good in Cambridge, and by the beginning of the Michaelmas term in Oxford Tennyson's 'name was on everyone's lips, his poems discussed, criticised, interpreted; portions of them were repeatedly set for translation into Latin or Greek verse'. By September some 500 copies had been sold, although Moxon claimed that otherwise poetry simply did not sell. He turned down Elizabeth Barrett's poems for publication, Milnes's works were at a standstill, Wordsworth's were only beginning to make their way, and only Tennyson might be said to be successful.

Even being turned down by Moxon when he was publishing Tennyson did not lessen Elizabeth Barrett's admiration of the poems. 'I think such a godship of Tennyson!' she exclaimed when she read them. When she heard that Tennyson had said, 'There is only one female poet whom I wish to see—& that is Miss Barrett', she was so happy that she declared she was 'ready to kiss his shoetyes any day'. None the less she spotted one grave flaw in his poetry: 'He has not flesh and blood enough to be sensual—his forms are too obviously on the surface to wear pulses. His representation of beauty . . . is rather the fantasma of beauty, than the thing. You can no more touch or clasp it, than beauty in a dream. It is not less beautiful, for *that*; but less sensual it *is* . . .'[10] She had accurately sensed the deep lack of sexuality that sometimes made Tennyson's poetry seem a touch pallid.

Unlike most of the reviewers, Robert Browning hated the revisions of the older poems: 'The alterations are insane. *Whatever* is touched is spoiled. There is some woeful mental infirmity in the man.' Kemble echoed Browning in saying that 'the worst of the man is, that he rubs & scrubs and polishes till he gets half the bloom off. . . . I know that the villain has sublimed away some of the Gardener's Daughter, for which may he be circumcised!'[11]

Carlyle had most of his philistine objections swept away when he read the volumes. 'Truly it is long since in any English book, Poetry or Prose, I have felt the pulse of a real man's heart as I do in this same. A right valiant, true fighting, victorious heart; strong as a lion's, yet gentle, loving and full of music,' he wrote to Tennyson. He quoted three lines from 'Ulysses':

> It may be that the gulfs will wash us down;
> It may be we shall touch the Happy Isles
> And see the great Achilles, whom we knew.

'These lines do not make me weep, but there is in me what would fill whole Lachrymatories as I read.' For all Carlyle's aversion to poetry, it was a truer judgement on the lines than Thackeray's (see p. 190). Sterling, who was amused at his improbable interest in a poet, reported to Tennyson that Carlyle had said more in his 'praise than in any one's except Cromwell & an American Backwoodsman who has killed 30 or 40 people with a bowie-knife & since run away to Texas'.[12]

FitzGerald was afraid that some of the trifles in the books that should have disappeared before printing would put off the reviewers: 'Alfred, whatever he may think, cannot trifle—many are the disputes we have had about his powers of badinage, compliment, waltzing, etc. His smile is rather a grim one.'[13] Neither lightness nor wit was ever Tennyson's strong point.

When all reservations are taken into account, the 1842 *Poems* were still a magnificent achievement, and Edgar Allan Poe was near the mark when he said that by his reaction to the 'Morte d'Arthur' or 'Œnone' he could test any man's sense of the ideal. 'I am not sure that Tennyson is not the greatest of poets.'[14]

Although the early reviews were less enthusiastic than some of the later ones, they were so encouraging that Tennyson should have been cheered, but he was so depressed that he asked Moxon to forward only the totally favourable ones. He was passing through a period of creative dryness, common enough for most writers but rare for him. Almost all that he could bring himself to compose were occasional poems on Hallam's death, what he called his 'Elegies'. As he waited for more complimentary reviews, he walked on the shore in Torquay and Eastbourne, then he visited the Lushingtons at Park House, and finally in September he went to western Ireland at the invitation of Aubrey de Vere. Typically, however, he and de Vere were unable to find each other in London at the time they had agreed to leave, and Tennyson set off by himself for a lonely fortnight, wandering from Limerick and Killarney down to Cork, on the way visiting the Ballybunion caves, of which de Vere had told him. The rough weather kept him out of the best of them, but the ocean had its usual therapeutic effect for a short time. At Ballybunion he thought of the lines that he kept in his head for fourteen years until he found a place for them as a striking metaphor in 'Merlin and Vivien':

> So dark a forethought roll'd about his brain,
> As on a dull day in an Ocean cave
> The blind wave feeling round his long sea-hall
> In silence.

It was only a momentary respite from the troubles from which he had been trying to escape by the Irish trip. The favourable reception of his poems seemed something that might never be repeated unless he recovered his poetic fertility, and behind everything else loomed the spectre of financial ruin. On the day of his arrival in Ireland he had written to Edmund Lushington: '500 of my books are sold—according to Moxon's brother I have made a sensation—I wish the woodworks would make a sensation! . . . What with ruin in the distance and Hypochondriacs in the foreground I feel very crazy. God help us all.'[15]

The crash of the woodworking scheme had come about with a frightening rapidity. Only a few months before, he had been able to give Mr Rawnsley a blithe answer to the question of how it progressed: 'Why very well, only we are not a company yet—there has been so much talkee talkee, as the niggers say, & so little settled.'[16] There had been difficulty about machinery and workmen, but he still believed the project to be so sound that he had offered Rawnsley the chance to buy shares.

By the late summer of 1842 he was trying to get out of his association with Allen. Mary Tennyson said that since Allen kept insisting he had three takers for every available share, it might be better if he were to sell those she and her sisters owned. 'It would relieve Alfred's mind very much—he fidgets himself to death; I am afraid sometimes he will bring on again the complaint he has suffered from in London not long ago, & which he has been told is dangerous as it might at last reach the heart. . . . I shall always feel that Dr Allen intended to do us a kindness but we are not the people to keep peaceful & quiet minds under a state of uncertainty & suspense.'[17] There is no clear indication of what Alfred's complaint was, but it was probably connected with the illness to which he was to succumb the following year.

Tennyson's worry over Allen's collapse was so intense that he returned to England, where he found that Allen had been attempting to get money from the credulous Septimus, who was still staying at Fair Mead, and that he had already succeeded in turning Sep against the rest of the family. Charles now had to help support his mother and sisters, and to Mrs Allen Alfred described himself as 'a penniless beggar and deeply in debt besides. . . . What I have felt and suffered may rest unmentioned, but I entreat you, if you have any regard for your husband's honour to do all in your power to prevent him making another victim of my family.'[18]

Tennyson had invested all the proceeds from the sale of his inherited property, which had apparently been badly managed, since it had originally been worth twice the £3,000 he turned over to Allen. In addition he had put in the £500 he had inherited from Miss Hallam. At the end of 1842 there was no longer any pretence of friendliness with the Allens, and little chance that anything could ever be retrieved of the £8,000 the Tennyson family had so hopefully invested in the scheme.

In the spring of 1843 Frederick returned from Florence in connection with the family's dealings with Allen. He had always had the hottest of the Tennyson tempers, and he was seldom reluctant to make a point by force, as his threats of physical violence to his father showed. FitzGerald, in trying to imagine Frederick's reaction to an Italian overcharging him, once remembered how he used to offer to 'mash' cabmen who argued with him. After Frederick met Allen, the 'mad doctor' complained that he had been the victim of 'assaults'; whether Frederick's attacks were physical or verbal is not clear, but they were enough to make Allen grovel. 'I have done all that is possible for man to do to save your family,' he assured Frederick, 'and I have *utterly ruined myself* in the attempt. . . . Every stick and stave is to be sold to pay A.T. *this day*—and yet people boast! I ail! and I suffer! and I die!'[19] All his melodramatic protestations produced no money, and the life insurance policy and deeds that he had given Alfred earlier were apparently invalid, so that Tennyson said he was left penniless. Generously, Edmund Lushington gave Alfred another policy of £2,000 on Allen's life and paid the premiums of £80 himself. Allen was suffering from heart trouble, but the Tennysons apparently did not know that. They were left feeling morally dispossessed, not wanting to realize that what would best serve them was Allen's death.

Charles continued to help the family, Mrs Russell still sent frequent generous gifts of money, and Mrs Tennyson had her jointure of £200 a year. Had the Tennysons been capable of real economy, they could have lived comfortably. As it was, the best they could think of was to cast about for a smaller house than Boxley, although even that seemed difficult, since Horatio had come home from Australia, where he had lost his own inheritance in an abortive scheme to make a fortune by farming.

It was presumably at this juncture in 1843 that FitzGerald began giving Tennyson £300 annually; a year later Carlyle spoke to him of Tennyson's gratitude (see p. 204). Apparently it never occurred seriously to Tennyson that he might take any employment, although Carlyle and Fitz were constantly assuring him that his poetry would be vastly improved if he had some other occupation. An argument on the point would have been graceless at best while accepting Fitz's help, but it was hard to swallow the advice from a man like FitzGerald who had never done a day's work in his life.

At the bottom of a common attitude like that of Carlyle and Fitz-Gerald lay a covert disbelief in the value of poetry, an assumption that it could occupy no more than a segment of the mind of a reasonable man. Because he was physically, and sometimes intellectually, slothful, Tennyson was constantly being confronted by those who thought he would be better occupied by taking more conventional employment and leaving poetry for his hours of leisure.* Had he taken the advice of such counsellors, Tennyson would never have written any more poetry, for with him it was the whole concentration of a life or it was

* Did anyone ever believe that Matthew Arnold's poetry was improved by his work as Inspector of Schools?

nothing. Behind the pressure of his friends to get him to publish it was easy to see a worried desire for something as palpable as the weight and feel of a book, tangible proof that all Tennyson's hours of composition were not totally wasted. It is not surprising that the attitude sometimes infected Tennyson himself, and that when he ran dry poetically, as he had done since 1840, he should become grumpy, anxious, morbid. Part of his desire to meet Elizabeth Barrett sprang from her encouragement in a review of Wordsworth's last book of poetry in 1842, when she found hope for poetry's survival in the stubborn insistence of Wordsworth, Browning, and Tennyson on devoting the entirety of their lives to writing, rather than being 'mere parenthetical poets'. But Miss Barrett's point of view was rare, her enunciation of it perhaps unique.

In March 1843, at the time when Allen's woodworking scheme was in its last throes, Robert Southey died, leaving the position of Poet Laureate vacant. The post no longer had much definable function, and there was considerable feeling that it should be done away with. 'I think the place of Court Poet ought to be abolished with that of Court Fool!' wrote Charlotte Williams-Wynn, echoing the opinion of many others. To some of Tennyson's friends, however, it seemed that the combination of the residual honour of the post and the stipend of over £100 might serve to keep him from a total breakdown. Barry Cornwall suggested to Fanny Kemble that she write to Lord Francis Egerton to solicit the Laureateship. Lord Francis, who felt that the post would 'receive more honour than it can give', forwarded the petition to Lord De la Warr, the Queen's adviser on the appointment. De la Warr told Egerton that the post had already been offered to Wordsworth.[20]

It has usually been assumed that Tennyson knew nothing of the negotiations on his behalf, but another possibility is suggested in a letter written by Lord Francis to the Prime Minister before Wordsworth's name was announced. Egerton wrote to tell Peel that the salary of the post would save Tennyson from absolute starvation, but he wanted to make it clear that he was not soliciting a favour for a personal friend, that he had never so much as seen Tennyson, and that Tennyson had no idea that Egerton was even aware of his 'wishes or difficulties'.[21] The single word 'wishes' is slender evidence, but it suggests that Tennyson was party to the instigations of Barry Cornwall and Fanny Kemble; if so, his failure must have been a further blow to his battered self-esteem. As consolation, Peel offered a sum of money out of public funds to help Tennyson with his immediate difficulties, but this he refused.

Every prospect was black for Tennyson, as he made clear to his friends: 'I have drunk one of those bitter drafts out of the cup of life, which go near to make men hate the world they move in.' Since at the time he insisted so vehemently on his total penury, it is easy to over-estimate his financial difficulties, real though they were. His vanished income, which had seemed little enough when he had it, now represented wealth indeed, and like all his family he had sufficiently grand ideas of how much he needed. But at the time he probably had £300 from FitzGerald and his usual £100 from his faithful aunt Russell; in addition he had the income from his poems, which in 1846 Browning estimated at £178, presumably not far different from his royalties in 1843 and by itself adequate to live on, Browning thought, if not exactly handsome. Tennyson was always neurotic about money, sure he was going to starve when it was scarce, concerned to hang on to it when it was plentiful, and his statements about his own destitution must be accepted with caution. 'I am such a poor devil now I am afraid I shall very rarely see you,' he wrote to Fitz. 'No more trips to London & living in lodgings, [but] hard penury & battle with my lot.'[22] As he so often did when pressed for money, he threatened to move to Italy and live well on eight shillings a day. But he must have had £500–600 a year.

Not that Tennyson was deliberately telling his friends anything but the truth when he went on about his poverty: his bad health and nervousness only increased his natural tendency to think he was in imminent danger of starvation, and the multiplication of his complaints was as much a symptom as a cause of his condition. But deep beneath the layers of morbidity was a healthy instinct of self-preservation, which would have prevented him from refusing Peel's offer of financial help had he been in the straits his friends thought he was.

At the time of his disappointment over the Laureateship Tennyson for the first time met the great writer who already bestrode Victorian fiction as he was to dominate the poetry of the period. Charles Dickens had been deeply impressed with the 1842 *Poems*, and early in March 1843 he sent Tennyson a set of his own works with a note testifying to 'the love I bear you as a man whose writings enlist my whole heart and nature in admiration of their Truth and Beauty'. On 27 April Dickens entertained a remarkable trio of guests at his house in

Devonshire Terrace: Thackeray, FitzGerald, and Tennyson, the latter two probably meeting their host for the first time. They all went for a drive before dinner, but unfortunately there is no record of their conversation nor even of which of his guests sat beside Dickens in the carriage. Luckily, there were no mishaps, no broken axles, no runaway horse; had there been, the entire course of Victorian literature might have been changed. Dickens was modest and affable, 'seeming to wish any one to show off rather then himself'.[23] After dinner the four men had a round game at cards as they drank mulled claret. In deference to FitzGerald's interests, they all talked of the poetry of Crabbe. Dickens and Tennyson liked each other greatly and remained good, though not intimate, friends until Dickens's death. In their relations there was often a touch of hesitation, particularly on Tennyson's side, and it is tempting to think it was due in part to the extraordinary facial resemblance of the two men, especially after Tennyson grew a beard. It was somehow unnervingly fitting that the two literary giants of the age should be so alike that people seeing them together inevitably remarked on the resemblance; for the men themselves it was too like catching a sudden glimpse of one's self in a glass, and it is certain that Tennyson found it disturbing, much as he liked Dickens.

Rather less successful was the meeting of Tennyson and his brother Charles with Henry Taylor at the house of old Rogers. Taylor was already well known for his poetic dramas, in particular *Philip van Artevelde*, which many of his contemporaries thought a work of genius. He could be blindingly complacent, and perhaps he was condescending on that occasion to the younger poet, or perhaps Tennyson was rubbed by the thought of the other man's 'meridian splendour and glory', for he thought Taylor guilty of 'extreme insolence'.[24] After Tennyson moved to the Isle of Wight he frequently saw Taylor with Julia Margaret Cameron, but it took years of acquaintance for him to accept Taylor, and then he never moved far beyond tolerance.

However unsatisfactory some of his friends thought it as a career, Alfred's single-minded devotion to poetry seemed remarkably sensible compared to the lives of his brothers. It was now the turn of Arthur to come to grief. He could find nothing to interest him and so had fallen to drinking. In September 1842 he had been driven home to Boxley 'in a state of deep intoxication', and he then proceeded to terrify the family 'till near one o'clock by his epileptic howlings &c.'.[25] On another occasion he went to his uncle Charles's house while drunk and had to be sent back by carriage. In the spring of 1843 he became a voluntary patient in a Scottish asylum, intending to stay at least a year to cure his addiction, but after six months he left the hospital, still not cured, and went off to Italy to live with Frederick, having borrowed money from his uncle Charles for the journey.

For a decade Edward Tennyson had been locked away in York, as he was to be for the rest of his life; Septimus was apparently still under treatment in High Beech, although the rest of the family had broken with Allen; and Alfred had been at least an intermittent patient of Allen's. Arthur's confinement made a total of four of the brothers who are known to have been in asylums, and it is certainly possible that Charles was confined during the worst of his drug addiction, although no details survive of his treatment. It was beginning to look as if there were a compulsion among Dr Tennyson's sons to re-enact the grim ritual of his last days.

Alfred complained to Fitz of not having 'had a good day, a perfect white day, for years'. To another friend he said that 'his waking hours in the morning were very miserable ones & he used to ask himself, "how am I to get through the day."' All during 1843 his health and spirits deteriorated, and the few friends he saw commented sadly on his hypochondria. Neither stays by the sea in Mablethorpe and St. Leonards nor a rest at Park House did him any good, and he became so nervous that his dwindling correspondence almost ceased. When he had to write a letter about the defunct woodworking scheme, he confessed that it 'threw me into a kind of convulsion. I went thro' Hell.'[26]

It was perhaps the example of Septimus and Arthur in becoming voluntary patients (as well as the memory of Arthur's 'epileptic howlings') that at the end of 1843 gave Alfred the idea of committing himself for treatment. In November or early December the entire family moved from the too-expensive Boxley house to Cheltenham, where most of them had already fled at one time or another during periods of crisis. Fitz saw Tennyson 'in transitu' and thought he had 'never seen him so hopeless. . . . Are our poetical nerves to come to this. Must a man vegetate like a beast to keep himself well & hopeful. I doubt poets are an illstarred race—that is poets who deal in their own susceptibilities. Yet Alfred might be fairly well if he would do as he should, but that again he does not do for the very reason he is a poet.'[27]

Mrs Tennyson and those children still at home took a 'nasty house in Bellevue Place' in Cheltenham. On the last day of 1843 Elizabeth

Barrett reported inaccurately that 'Tennyson is dancing the polka and smoking cloud upon cloud at Cheltenham'.[28] The truth was a good deal less pleasant: after settling his family he had gone to the neighbouring village of Prestbury, there to begin the cure at a water establishment, and there was no more dancing and very little smoking for more than half a year.

❉

CHAPTER XVIII

EMOTIONAL BREAKDOWN, 1844–1845

To stay in High Beech for treatment was out of the question after Tennyson's break with Allen, but to go to another asylum would have presented difficulties of a different kind. In the period since Arthur had gone to Scotland there had been rumblings of discontent among the medical profession about the voluntary admission to hospitals of 'low-spirited' or 'desponding' persons as boarders. In 1844 the Metropolitan Commissioners in Lunacy decided it was a bad practice because it could be used as a subterfuge for receiving into hospital 'as nervous those who are manifestly of unsound mind',[1] and in 1845 voluntary committal to mental hospitals became illegal. Hydropathic establishments, however, were not recognized as hospitals, and hence patients could enter at will without the stigma of being certified as of unsound mind. For that reason Tennyson, who of course did not think of himself as insane, was to be a patient in various water establishments for the next five years.

This was almost certainly Tennyson's first stay in such an establishment.[2] The process of cure by water, which had been commenced in Gräfenberg by a talented but uneducated farmer's son, Vincenz Priessnitz, had been imported from Austria to England early in the 1840s. A logical outcome of the Romantic mode of thought, it seems today very like something developed in our own century by the ecological movement. Its basic tenet was that drugs were harmful and that the best the medical profession could do was to assist Nature in her own cure of disease, chiefly by the application both internally and externally of that most sovereign natural remedy, water.

Most practitioners believed that chronic disease was due to impure or inadequately circulated blood engorging the internal organs. Impurities could be got rid of by excretion and sweating and also by the more dramatic method of inducing fever, skin eruption, and boils, known as 'crises'. These were encouraged by sitz-baths, jets of water, and the 'great douche', an overpowering fall of cold water from a twenty-foot-high cistern emptied through a tapered pipe on to the back and body of the (usually) uncomplaining patient. The commonest but most drastic method involved rolling the naked patient in a wet sheet laid on two blankets, which were then folded around him until he was powerless to move. Horatio Tennyson, who was a patient at Prestbury in 1844 at the end of Alfred's stay there, said that the mysteries of the cold water cure 'chiefly consist in a series of packings & unpackings. You are packed in a wet sheet 2 or 3 times a day & each time on coming out you are plunged into a cold bath after which you have a wet bandage tightly bound around your waist, you are also occasionally thawed & dissolved into a dew by being swathed in 3 or 4 blankets on the removal of which, greatly to your disgust you are again plunged into stinging cold water with a variety of others things too numerous to particularize.'[3]

Copious quantities of water were drunk to assist the kidneys and bowels, and the patients were made to walk long distances whatever the weather. Smoking and drinking were forbidden during the treatment, which made the patients unpopular with hotel-keepers and publicans in the locality, but social life in the 'hydropathics' was encouraged during the times patients were not being immersed. The combination of treatment and social activity increased the popularity of the establishments, so that a stay in some of them had the same attraction as a visit to a spa. Among the eminent patrons of the various hydropathics, some of whom Tennyson probably encouraged in attendance, were Thackeray, Dickens, Carlyle (who found 'water, taken as a medicine, to be the most destructive drug I had ever tried'),[4] Darwin, Florence Nightingale, and Bulwer-Lytton, who wrote about his experiences in *Confessions of a Water-Patient* (1845). Some of the recorded cures besides those more to be expected were of corns, baldness, near-sightedness, and sterility in middle-aged couples.

According to Tennyson the Prestbury establishment was 'the only one in England conducted on pure Priessnitzean principles', since the originator's nephew ran the cure. At the beginning of February Tennyson had 'had four crises (one larger than had been seen for two or three years in Gräfenberg indeed I believe the largest but one that has been seen) much poison has come out of me which no physic ever would have brought to light'. His mild boasting about the size of the eruptions is reminiscent of Dr Tennyson's claims about the severity of his own symptoms. Priessnitz gave Tennyson hopes of a cure by the end of March, but it was not until July that he was able to leave the 'hydro', after some seven months of treatment. As Horatio told his uncle, 'it is rather expensive, but not so much so as constantly taking medicine'.[5]

Since hydropathics were not mental hospitals but were chiefly intended to treat the body, many practitioners, including the elder Priessnitz, discouraged the admission of epileptics because they could not undertake a cure of the disease, although cold baths and packings were thought to relieve the worst of the symptoms. Rather surprisingly, 'hypochondriacs' were encouraged to come. Of all diseases gout had the most favourable prognosis, its cure apparently presenting no problems to water practitioners.

The inevitable question is what the specific nature of the complaint was for which Tennyson had treatment in Prestbury and for which he went at least three times to other water establishments. The answer must be conjectural because so much evidence was destroyed. Hallam Tennyson glides briefly over the whole matter of the water cure, saying of the period after the collapse of Dr Allen's scheme: 'Then followed a season of real hardship, and many trials for my father and mother, since marriage seemed to be further off than ever. So severe a hypochondria set in upon him that his friends despaired of his life.'

In Memoriam, published in 1850, the year of his marriage, is in large part concerned with the meaning of trances, whether they are malign in nature or whether they are genuine pathways to supra-sensory knowledge, and the conclusion is of course that they can be the latter. *The Princess* originally appeared in 1847; four years later, in the third edition, Tennyson added the curious and puzzling passages about the 'weird seizures' of the Prince, cataleptic or epileptic spells inherited from his family, 'An old and strange affection of the house', that actually threaten his life and from which he is released by his love of Princess Ida. *Maud*, written in 1854, is about the recovery of the narrator from insane ravings and fits like those of his father before him; he is redeemed by devotion to things exterior to himself: his love of Maud, and the alliance of his will with that of his country by embracing 'the purpose of God, and the doom assigned'. It can hardly be coincidental that these major poems, all three of which were begun in the 1830s or 1840s, are so saturated with references to the fear of fits and trances, followed by either recovery from them or the discovery that they are not malign in their effect. No single one of them is wholly autobiographical, but they do indicate how preoccupied Tennyson was in middle life with descent into mental illness and subsequent recovery, bringing with it a wider knowledge.

In writing of the 'blind haze' that falls upon Arthur in the *Idylls of the King*, Valerie Pitt remarks that 'it is clear that Tennyson was in some way afraid of' the mist that descends upon him. Of the 'weird seizures' in *The Princess* she shrewdly guesses 'that experience of this kind troubled Tennyson in the nervous illness from which he suffered in the early eighteen-forties'.[6] Until now, however, the meagre evidence has not been pieced together to substantiate her conjecture.

After 1848 Tennyson stopped taking hydropathic treatment and apparently never again suffered from the kind of 'hypochondria' that had led him to it in the first place. Thereafter he also began referring openly, for the first time, to his own trances, which he ascribed either to gout or to his passing voluntarily into an extra-sensory state through a form of self-hypnotism or meditation. Within a year after his last visit to a water establishment he resumed the engagement that had begun thirteen years earlier and had been broken for nearly a decade.

There is no positive proof of the nature of Tennyson's ailments and of how they disappeared, but the conjunction of events makes it seem almost certain that he underwent treatment at High Beech, Prestbury, Umberslade, and Malvern under the impression that he was suffering from inherited epilepsy because of the fits and trances that so closely resembled the 'petit mal' from which other members of his family suffered. Because of the reluctance of practitioners to admit epileptics to hydropathic establishments, as well as the shame connected with the disease, he told none of his friends about it, preferring to call it hypochondria. Marriage seemed out of the question because of the danger of passing the disease on to his children, besides the almost inevitable dissolution of mind that seemed the end of the disease.

In 1848, on his second visit to Malvern, he was under the care of Dr James Gully, who specialized in the cure of gout. After that time Tennyson seems to have believed that the true cause of his trances was indeed an inherited disease but that it was purely physical in nature not mental, that it was gout not epilepsy.

There is just enough likeness between epilepsy and gout for this to have been a reasonable supposition. The onset of gout attacks is sometimes accompanied by the stimulation of the imagination that is like the 'aura' that usually gives warning to victims of epilepsy of the imminence of a seizure. Sir Victor Pritchett, for example, writing of the recurrences of gout that he suffered from as a young man, tells us that immediately before they begin, 'one is in a state of startling illumination and euphoria, as happens—according to Dostoevsky—before the attack of epilepsy'. As an old man Tennyson spoke of his own trances as 'not a confused state but the clearest of the clearest, the surest of the surest, utterly beyond words'. But it was only after he had been released from the fear of epilepsy that he could forget the terror they had once inspired and speak of them as if they were beneficent or at worst innocuous. In time he even professed to think that he had imagined them altogether. In the last decade of his life, when he had lost the ability to pass into a trance, he told his son: 'I used from having early read in my father's library a great number of medical books to fancy that I had all the diseases in the world, like a medical student.'[7]

After 1848 his depressions and mental anxiety were certainly not finished, but one of his chief worries was over. The breaking of his engagement and the loss of his patrimony were not unimportant, but they, as well as the 'black blood' of the Tennysons, were but part of a deeper anguish plaguing Tennyson, the fear that his life would end as his father's had done and as his uncle's threatened to do.

But this is to anticipate 1848 and the treatment by Dr Gully. Tennyson stayed miserably on at Prestbury until July 1844. The discomfort of the treatment is described in a letter to Fitz when he had been there a month or two: 'Of all the uncomfortable ways of living sure an hydropathical is the worst: no reading by candlelight, no going near a fire, no tea, no coffee, perpetual wet sheet & cold bath & alternation from hot to cold: however I have much faith in it.'[8]

When he went for his prescribed walks he would be followed by the village boys of Prestbury, shouting derisively, 'Shiver and shake'. They so worried him that when he left the establishment he could still be overcome by nervousness at the mere thought of passing through Prestbury.

Tennyson took excursions away from the water establishment during the treatment, and he kept hoping that he would not have to return to Prestbury. In the spring of 1844 he wrote to his aunt Russell: 'I am not yet cured, as the recurrences of old symptoms sufficiently testifies: it is a terribly long process but then what price is too high for health, & health of mind is so involved with health of body.'[9]

By July he was sufficiently well to stay some time with his mother in Cheltenham and to go to Wales, where he went up Snowdon three times. But he still intended to return to Prestbury after a brief trip to London to see friends and look at pictures: 'I shall have to go into the system again and carry it out to the end,' he wrote to Edmund Lushington. 'It is true I had ten crises but I am not cured, tho' I do not doubt of the efficiency of the treatment in most cases, having *seen* most marvellous cures performed. . . . I have seen no Art, and my soul thirsts for it, for a year.'

Tennyson's determination to return to Prestbury for the completion of his cure went the way of most of his resolutions. In London he stayed in Henry Lushington's rooms, and the day or two he had planned on being there stretched to a week. To some friends he professed to be quite recovered, but within a few days he was down again with a bad fever. After taking no food but the juice of eighteen lemons for three days, he was well enough to leave London, although his knees were 'miserably imbecile'. Rather than return to Prestbury he packed enough clothes for an overnight visit to Park House, and in mid-September Lushington reported that he had been there for five weeks with 'every prospect of indefinite prolongation thereof. He certainly seems to have derived some benefit from the water treatment, or its concomitants. Yet he has been very unwell during the last three days. Indeed if one of the *earlier* set of Apostles were to heal him for the time ever so completely, he could not continue well, as long as he paid so little attention to their words of healing: "Arise *and walk*." How can a man with such great natural strength of body live so indolently, & be well?'[10]

Tennyson was too exhausted from his illness and its treatment to do much more than exist; poetry was generally out of the question, except that even in the depths of illness and fatigue he felt compelled to write his 'elegies' about Hallam. He stayed on at Park House until October, then he went back to London, where his strength was soon depleted again. His weakness brought very near the surface the turbulent emotions that he normally kept under control. At Park House Savile Morton thought he had 'never met a heart so large and full of love'. In Chelsea Tennyson spent a memorable day with the Carlyles, who sent him off that night with 'Macpherson's Farewell', the tune composed and played on his way to the gallows by a Highland robber, who dies without kinsman or friend. As Carlyle told the story, 'Alfred's face grew darker, and I saw his lip slightly quivering'. It would be impossible to unpick the complex emotions behind the quivering lip, but one of them was surely Tennyson's desperate awareness of the vortex of loneliness into which he was being swept. Carlyle had often noticed that Tennyson kept to himself, even in London, and described him at this time as 'a man solitary and sad, as certain men are, dwelling in an element of gloom'.[11]

The only thing that could restore him to a moderately even keel was some piece of unexpected good fortune. This came about through the misfortunes of another: in the first days of the New Year, 1845, Matthew Allen died suddenly of a heart attack. The day after he heard the news Tennyson went to London, heading directly to FitzGerald. 'Dr. Allen, who had half swindled his money, is dead,' wrote Fitz: 'and A.T. having a life insurance, and Policy, on him, will now, I hope retrieve the greater part of his fortune again. Apollo certainly did this: shooting one of his swift arrows at the heart of the Doctor; whose perfectly heartless conduct certainly upset A.T.'s nerves in the first instance.'[12]

Tennyson received £2,000 from his policy, less than he had lost but enough to make him feel more prosperous after his financial worries of the past three or four years. The speed with which he went to Fitz suggests that he wanted to tell his friend that he would no longer need the money that Fitz had been giving him. On the strength of what he had received, Tennyson was able to take lodgings in London for nearly the whole of 1845. Although he still was withdrawn occasionally, he threw himself into active social life again, and with his gradual reassumption of the ties of friendship his health quickly improved. There was no single person central to his life, as Hallam had been or Emily Sellwood had promised to be, and more importantly there was no one for whom he was uniquely necessary, so that all the proffers of love and friendship made to him were inadequate, since they finally were only invitations to the perimeters of the affections of others. As the year went on, he talked more openly of how much he wished he were married, but he seems either to have almost forgotten Emily or to have believed no longer in the possibility of their marriage.

On Tennyson's arrival in London after Allen's death, Fitz was so worried about his health that he called him 'a valetudinarian almost:—not in the effeminate way; but yet in as bad a man's way. Alas for it, that great thoughts are to be lapped in such weakness.' A few weeks later Fitz was pleased with the improvement in his health in spite of his continued smoking. 'The water business would do him good if he gave it fair chances—but he smokes, & drinks a bottle of wine a day. He looks however twice as well as he did a year ago: & is certainly in better spirits.'[13] The improvement was commented on by most of those who knew him.

For so long Tennyson had behaved as if poverty-stricken that it was difficult for him to think that he was in reasonable financial circumstances, nor could his friends believe that he was, after being told so long of his penury. When Carlyle heard of the insurance from Allen's death, he said, 'I wish he would straightway buy himself an annuity with it.' Carlyle was one of a group who had been scheming to get a pension from the Civil List for Tennyson; some of the others were Rogers, Milnes, Henry Hallam, and William Howitt. At the end of 1844 Howitt's brother Richard, himself a minor poet, asked Lady Peel to urge Tennyson's worth on her husband; Howitt had 'heard that the Poet had unfortunately lost his little property: that he was in a dreadful state of depression; and that it was feared by his friends his mind would quite sink under his misfortunes'.[14]

Hallam and Gladstone both wrote to Peel in support of the suggestion, the latter saying that though Tennyson was 'a great poet, he can hardly become a popular & is much more likely to be a starving one'. Peel was unable to grant a pension, but he offered relief of £200, with the understanding that it was not renewable. As he had done the first time that he was offered a flat payment, Tennyson declined politely, probably out of natural reluctance to take charity, perhaps stiffened by a feeling that the offer was inadequate. When Hallam sent Tennyson's refusal to Peel, he had to admit that Howitt had exaggerated Tennyson's poverty: 'he is not destitute of means, though less considerable than his position in society requires for competence'.[15] It was a far more accurate statement of Tennyson's circumstances than most of those made by either his friends or himself.

By now Tennyson was something of a lion. On 26 January 1845 he was invited by Samuel Rogers to a dinner for eight. When they entered the dining-room, there were no candles on the table, the light all being directed at the walls and the pictures. Sydney Smith had once said acidly of dining there that there was 'a flock of light on all above, and below nothing but darkness and gnashing of teeth'. The other guests were Moxon, Henry Crabb Robinson, Spedding, Henry Lushington, and the dramatist James Kenny. Tennyson was seated between Crabb Robinson and the empty chair kept for the last guest, who had not appeared when dinner began. Crabb Robinson, who thought Tennyson 'by far the most eminent of the young poets', had a long chat with him about Goethe and Schiller: 'He was searching in his questions. . . . a fine fellow in his physique, almost as powerful and rough as Whewell.' Lushington and Spedding he thought particularly refined in manner, and all three young men ('belonging to literary Young England') brilliant conversationalists. Half-way through dinner the last guest arrived, and Rogers got up to escort her to the table, where she sat next to Tennyson. It was the 'much eulogized and calumniated Honourable Mrs. [Caroline] Norton', one of the three beautiful daughters of the playwright Sheridan. Because of the notoriety of her unhappy marriage and her independent career as a novelist, her 'position in society was to a great degree imperilled'. She immediately joined the conversation 'with an ease and spirit that showed her quite used to society'.

Either because of her compromised reputation or because he thought it inappropriate for her to have dinner with seven men, Tennyson disliked her at sight. Rogers had asked her as a special treat for Tennyson, and when she left the dining-room he asked what he thought of her, to which Tennyson answered that 'he felt as if a serpent had just dropped off' and that he had 'shuddered sitting by her side'. It was, in Crabb Robinson's understatement, 'a strange remark from a young man', but typical of Tennyson's rather priggish attitude, before his marriage, towards *déclassée* women; one of the liberalizing effects of his wife was that he became less censorious in such matters. A decade later Mrs Norton said that his behaviour at Rogers's table had been so offensive that she would like nothing better than 'to see all the Tennysons hung up in a row'.[16] Only after it had become apparent to him that she was the intimate of such impeccable members of society as the Duchess of Argyll did Mrs Norton and Tennyson become friends.

One woman with whom Tennyson got on well immediately was Mrs Carlyle, and it is suggestive that he spent an evening with her later in the same week he met Mrs Norton, almost as if to cleanse his memory of the Rogers party. Jane Carlyle was at home alone, dozing in front of the fire as she waited for her husband to come back from dinner, when to her surprise she heard a carriage draw up in the quiet street. Tennyson had brought Moxon to call; Jane could only be sensible of her husband's 'misfortune in having missed the man he likes best'. She noticed how embarrassed Tennyson was 'with women alone—for he entertains at one and the same moment a feeling of almost adoration for them and an ineffable contempt! adoration I suppose for what they *might be*—contempt for what they *are*!' To make him forget her 'womanness', she did as Carlyle had so often done, getting out pipes and tobacco with brandy and water 'with a deluge of *tea* over and above'. To her delight he smoked on 'for *three* mortal hours!—talking like an angel—only exactly as if he were talking with a clever *man*—which—being a thing I am not used to—men always adapting their conversation to what they *take to be* a woman's taste—strained me to a terrible pitch of intellectuality'. When Carlyle arrived home at midnight he found her alone, reliving the evening 'in an atmosphere of tobacco so thick that you might have cut it with a knife'.[17]

It was eight months before she saw Tennyson again, and then it was at private theatricals that Dickens and Forster got up for their friends. Tennyson, who had been in Cheltenham, came up to London especially for the party, which included Lady Blessington, Count D'Orsay, the Duke of Devonshire, Browning, and Macready. During the interval Tennyson morosely retired from the glitter of the guests into a long dim passage, where Jane Carlyle came across him 'leant to the wall, with his head touching the ceiling like a caryatid', apparently fast asleep in that awkward position: '"Alfred Tennyson!" I exclaimed in joyful surprise. "Well!" said he, taking the hand I held out to him, and forgetting to let it go again. "I did not know you were in town," said I. "I should like to know who you are," said he: "I know that I know you, but I cannot tell your name."'. To her embarrassment Mrs Carlyle had to identify herself to the sleepy poet, but he redeemed himself by saying that he intended to call on her, even though Carlyle was in Scotland. The next evening he arrived by cab and talked to her until eleven. The exertion of giving him tea drove away Jane's headache, assisted by 'a little feminine vanity at having inspired such a man with the energy to take a cab on his own responsibility, and to throw himself on providence for getting away again!' Her mild irony does not conceal the fact that neither his failure to recognize her nor his overwhelming indolence lessened his attraction for Jane Carlyle, and she put herself out to be agreeable to him. He liked to be with women who fenced conversationally, but his initial pleasure frequently rubbed off on longer acquaintance. After her death he told a friend that Mrs Carlyle was 'a most charming, witty converser, but often sarcastic'.[18]

It is significant that Jane Carlyle found him at his best when treating her like a man, for the society in which he moved was essentially masculine. It was not until after his marriage that Tennyson learned to talk with women without either assuming that a clever mind was masculine at bottom or flirting in the elephantine manner he seemed to think proper for intercourse with unintellectual women. There is little indication that he felt a more serious attraction to any woman during the 1840s. His feelings about Emily Sellwood are hard to reconstruct, but one remark to Lady Harriet Baring, reported by Mrs Carlyle, indicates that he no longer considered himself engaged, however tenuously: 'Lady Harriet told me that he wanted to marry; "must have a woman to live beside; would *prefer a lady*, but—cannot afford one; and so must marry a maidservant." ' Recognizing the lack of conviction behind the statement, Mrs Henry Taylor wryly offered to 'write him on behalf of their housemaid, who was quite a superior character in her way'.[19]

Another time he was growling to de Vere that 'he could no longer bear to be knocked about the world, and that he must marry and find love and peace or die. . . . He complained much about growing old, and said he cared nothing for fame, and that his life was all thrown away for want of a competence and retirement. Said that no one had been so much harassed by anxiety and trouble as himself.' De Vere, like all of Tennyson's friends, had heard the refrain often enough before and responded rather shortly by saying that it was simply a matter of wanting 'occupation, a wife, and orthodox principles, which he took well'.[20]

The question that springs spontaneously to a twentieth-century reader's mind concerns the nature of Tennyson's sexual life, since by 1845 he was thirty-six years old. The best clue is found in his conversation many years later with Laura Gurney, when he said that his 'great aim had been never to write a single word that an Eton boy could not read aloud to his sister; and another thing he said to me when we were talking of romance, was that he had never kissed a woman, in love, except his wife'.[21] It was an extraordinary thing to say, with some odd implications. The second part of the statement was clearly meant to convey that until his marriage he had been as innocent of sexual activity as his poetry was free of innuendo. But since it is difficult for most of us to imagine a man's keeping his virginity until the age of forty-one, it is tempting to try to get around that part of what he said, to evade its clear meaning by equivocal readings of the words. But the simple fact is that Laura Gurney, who recognized such possibilities clearly enough, was so impressed with his sincerity and simplicity that she believed he was telling the plainest of truths. He had no reason to make such a statement if it was intended only as an evasion of the truth, and, as she indicated, he was not joking, since he had little sense of humour about such matters. The sexual naïveté of much of his poetry validates the first part of the statement, which in turn seems to confirm the second. The thirty-six-year-old Tennyson in 1845 would have been most unusual if he had never had any sexual promptings, but probably they were more undemanding than in most men. The lack of urgency in his feelings and the deficiency of his experience were undoubtedly behind his tight-lipped attitude towards women like Mrs Norton.

Several of Tennyson's contemporaries wondered why he had not yet married, and it was occasionally rumoured that he had done so secretly. Elizabeth Barrett heard such a report in June 1845 and said that 'if he has found a princess dowered with "fine gold," under "a silken coverlid," . . . why so much the better,—at least so I hope! She must condescend to the smoke . . . but the smoke is said to be so essentially Tennysonian that he couldn't be supposed to rhyme without it.'[22]

The whole problem of the relations between the sexes was much in Tennyson's mind during 1845, for he had begun in earnest a long poem about the place of women in society, asking what their rights were and considering the basic question of the nature of the education they should receive. According to his son, Tennyson had discussed the problems of the poem with Emily Sellwood some years before this, while they were still engaged, and he may even have written small parts of it at the end of the 1830s. But with the improvement in his health after the restoration of his money from Allen, Tennyson had set himself to the long-deferred task. He believed the sexes had equal potentialities, but he was deeply aware of the many injustices to women. In part he was determined to show that he was concerned with contemporary issues and that he was capable of a great deal more than the 'foolish facility' that one reviewer had found in his poetry. In April he read some of 'The University of Women' to Aubrey de Vere and Tom Taylor. By June he had completed 200 lines of it, and 'in the hottest part of the summer' he went to Eastbourne, where he read the first part of the poem to Edmund Lushington. Contrary to his usual practice, he said little about it to others, and since he was publishing nothing there were rumours that he had given up poetry, but it was to be his major work during the next two years, before it finally became *The Princess*. Although there is nowhere in the completed poem any recognizable reference to Mrs Carlyle, some of Tennyson's attitudes towards high-minded, independent women may have derived from the long evenings in Cheyne Row, either talking alone to Jane Carlyle or hearing her oblique comments upon the subjects he and her husband were discussing.

With the improvement in his finances, Tennyson took more part in the literary life of London. During April and May 1845 the journal of Aubrey de Vere and the letters of Brookfield, to name only two sources, list evening after evening when Tennyson was in company with Thackeray, Venables, Tom Taylor, the Spring-Rices, Lord Ebrington, Merivale, Moxon, Henry Lushington, the Hallams, Fitz-Gerald, Kinglake, and others. Usually the entries have some such ending as 'We smoked till nearly two. A *most* agreeable evening', or 'I got home after two, and spent a quarter of an hour knocking before I could get in'.[23] In such small groups Tennyson's conversational brilliance and charm came out, as it never did in larger, more formal gatherings. The adjectives that recur in the accounts of his stay in London are 'jolly', 'merry', 'agreeable'.

Not all his friends shared his enthusiasm for late hours. 'I have still been sitting up very late,' wrote Aubrey de Vere. 'There is but one person in London for whom I would do this. . . . Who is that person—a lady? Certainly, if as old Coleridge said, every true Poet is inclusively woman, but not the worse man on that account—Alfred Tennyson.'[24]

No wonder that Elizabeth Barrett understood that Tennyson liked London 'beyond all places'. Without knowledge of, and occasionally without care for, what was to happen to him in the future, he was living in what George Darley described as 'a kind of genteel vagrancy'.

❄

CHAPTER XIX

CIVIL LIST PENSION AND 'THE NEW TIMON', 1845–1846

In the spring of 1845 Tennyson formed a new friendship with Wordsworth. It was never intimate, but it had considerable symbolic importance for him. The two men had presumably been together at Rydal Mount ten years earlier when Tennyson went there with Spedding, but since then they had not met. Wordsworth, however, did continue a mild interest in the works of the younger poet without getting to know them well. In March 1845 de Vere spent some days at Rydal and read aloud two of Tennyson's poems picked to appeal to Wordsworth for their patriotic sentiments and metrical regularity, 'Of old sat Freedom on the heights' and 'You ask me, why, though ill at ease'. When de Vere had finished reading, Wordsworth said reluctantly, 'I must acknowledge that those two poems are very solid and noble in thought. Their diction also seems singularly stately.'

In April Wordsworth was in London for presentation to the Queen as Poet Laureate, staying for several days with Moxon, then with his Quaker friend Samuel Hoare in Hampstead. Rogers offered to lend a court suit to Wordsworth, although he was some six or seven inches shorter than the new Poet Laureate.

In the weeks after the dinner with Mrs Norton, Tennyson had fallen out with Rogers 'one wet day in Pall Mall', when, as Tennyson remembered, he had said something that offended Rogers, and 'his face flushed and he plucked his arm out of mine and told me I was "affecting the smart"'. To avoid meeting him, Tennyson kept away from Moxon's house while Wordsworth stayed there, but it seemed safe to call at Mr Hoare's. One afternoon early in May Tennyson asked de Vere to accompany him to Hampstead; 'mind you do not tell Rogers,' he warned him, 'or he will be displeased at my being in London and not going to see him.' From de Vere's account, he seems not to have realized that Wordsworth and Tennyson had met before.

When they knocked at the door of The Hill, it was opened by Rogers, with Wordsworth at his side. Wrinkling up his ancient face, Rogers said drily, 'Ah, you did not come up the hill to see me!'

Generously, Rogers allowed Wordsworth and Tennyson to talk alone while he conversed with de Vere. As they walked back to London, Tennyson complained to de Vere of Wordsworth's coldness and said that he had tried in vain to interest him by telling of a tropical island where the trees on coming into leaf were a vivid scarlet, 'one flush all over the island. . . . It would not do. I could not inflame his imagination in the least!'

It was an inauspicious start, but two days later they were both at Moxon's dinner table, and Wordsworth was much warmer than before, entertaining them with an account of his presentation to the Queen. On a further meeting, once more at Moxon's, Wordsworth completed his conquest of Tennyson. Going into the dining-room, he turned to the younger poet, took his arm, and said, 'Come, brother bard, to dinner.' They sat opposite each other at table, and at first Tennyson still felt some resentment over Wordsworth's behaviour at Mr Hoare's, then as he watched the white-haired old poet he reminded himself that it was the author of 'Tintern Abbey' across from him. Thinking of the 'other poems which he had delighted in since boyhood, he could not help a strange feeling of affection for him which strengthened by degrees'.

After dinner Wordsworth followed the ladies to the drawing-room, leaving the other men at the table. Tennyson, who had a later engagement, was increasingly nervous and kept muttering that he must leave. At last he could stand it no longer, and when Wordsworth was brought back by Moxon, Tennyson went up to him and led him into the shadows at the edge of the room. There, speaking in a low voice full of emotion, as he later told it, he had 'at last, in the dark, said something of the pleasure he had had from Mr. Wordsworth's writings, and . . . the old poet had taken his hand, and replied with some expressions equally kind and complimentary'.

In de Vere's memory Wordsworth had never looked so pleased, and from then on the two poets thought of each other with affection as well as admiration. From reluctant approval of Tennyson, Wordsworth moved to the flat assertion that 'he is decidedly the first of our living poets'. It was an emblematic handing on of the sceptre from the Romantic poet to the Victorian forty years his junior, and it was totally appropriate that when Tennyson succeeded as Poet Laureate he was presented to the Queen in the same court suit, once more groaning at the seams, that Wordsworth had borrowed from Rogers in 1845.[1]

Long afterwards, Tennyson spoke of the evening at Moxon's as a deeply symbolic occasion, and he would often show how aware he was of the parallels between his own life and Wordsworth's by such remarks as that in 1888 to Gordon Wordsworth, who said that his grandfather had been eighty when he died. 'One more year,' said Tennyson contemplatively.[2] His continued regard for Wordsworth was shown by the half-life-size statue of him that stood in the drawing-room at Farringford.

Yet it was not in the nature of the two poets to remain constantly appreciative of each other. Tennyson frequently asserted that Wordsworth was the greatest poet of the century, but he could also be annoyed by what he considered prolixity, dryness, and prosodic gracelessness in Wordsworth. Finally, however, he admitted, 'He seems to have been always before one in observation of Nature.' For his part, Wordsworth still found Tennyson's poetry irregular and often affected, although he once told him, 'I have been endeavouring all my life to write a pastoral like your "Dora" and have not succeeded.' Few admirers of either poet would regret his lack of success. For all their shared devotion to nature, they were very different in their perceptions, a point illustrated by Tennyson's saying that in the future balloons would be fixed at the bottom of high mountains so as to take people to the top for the views. At the time Wordsworth merely grunted in disagreement, but the remark evidently still rankled in his memory when he wrote that Tennyson was 'not much in sympathy with what I should myself most value in my attempts, viz. the spirituality with which I have endeavoured to invest the material Universe'.[3]

Tennyson's undeniable poetic achievement made it imperative for his friends to renew their efforts to relieve the poverty in which he thought he was struggling. Wordsworth was receiving a pension of £300 from the Civil List, and Carlyle, whose ideas about money were less grandiose than those of Tennyson, thought Tennyson should be offered £150. Carlyle liked to think that the entire idea of a pension had been his own, and the story is well known, though possibly apocryphal, of how he had been urging Milnes to secure it for Tennyson, until at last Milnes protested that his parliamentary constituency would be offended, since they knew nothing of Tennyson or of his poetry and would think that he was a poor relative to Milnes. Solemnly, Carlyle answered, 'Richard Milnes, on the Day of Judgment, when the Lord asks you why you didn't get that pension for Alfred Tennyson, it will not do to lay the blame on your constituents; it is *you* that will be damned.' The story is true in spirit if not fact.

The other major contender for the available pension was Sheridan Knowles, a poverty-stricken playwright whose name is now forgotten. Milnes wrote to Peel to tell him that if the pension was a matter of pure charity he should give it to Knowles, but that if he wished to benefit literature and the nation at large by giving it to Tennyson, he would ensure the continuance of great poetry.

In fact, it was Henry Hallam who finally worried away at Peel until at last he granted the pension to Tennyson. Wordsworth and Rogers also wrote on his behalf. Rogers, who generously forgot about his own fallings out with Tennyson, wrote that he was 'by many thought unfit for a pension; but he has many infirmities, such as to you I hope will be ever unknown, and such as to make him utterly incapable of supporting himself. Of his genius I need say nothing, and have only to wish that I could always understand him.' At the end of his life, some thirty years after the death of Rogers, Tennyson came across the letter reprinted in a book about himself. Without stopping to consider the kindness that lay behind the letter, he underlined 'infirmities' in the text and wrote in the margin: 'No truer comment cd. be made than this on my favourite adage "every man imputes himself." My good old friend had many infirmities. What mine were, I know not, except short sight & hypochondria be infirmities. . . . I dare say old Rogers meant it all for the best. . . . Peace be with him! often bitter, but very kindly at heart.'[4] Tennyson's reaction was an excessive one to an apparently innocent attempt to help him, doubly difficult to understand after so many years had passed. Presumably he was angry because he thought that Rogers had got wind of his congenital illness and had been indiscreet enough to mention it. There is no evidence that Rogers meant anything of the sort, but the annotation shows how concerned Tennyson was, even as an old man, to deny his real and imagined illnesses before his marriage.

At the end of September Peel wrote to offer Tennyson an annual pension of £200. Tennyson did not receive the letter for some days, and when he did he accepted gratefully without thinking twice about the matter.

In no serious way could Tennyson have thought he was poor once he had received the pension. If, as seems probable, he was no longer receiving any money from FitzGerald, he still had some £500–700 annually, if one takes into account the income from his capital, earnings from poetry, the pension, and £100 from his aunt Russell. It was a sum equal to the benefices of only the most luxuriously provided clergymen of the day, and well beyond the dreams of most small professional men. £600 had been the amount that a rich man like Henry Hallam thought proper to allow his favourite son to maintain a household, and his representation to Peel about Tennyson's circumstances makes it probable that he knew Tennyson was in command of a similar amount. Most of Tennyson's other friends, however, must have had little idea of his income. Even with our knowledge of Tennyson's genius and the fact that Sheridan Knowles is now forgotten, it is still slightly disturbing that the poorer man was passed over in favour of one in comfortable circumstances. It is easy to sympathize with his contemporaries who thought the wrong man had been given the pension.

Even more understandable is the resentment by other literary men of the fact that Tennyson kept his pension until his death. For forty-seven years he received the money, even when he was making more than £10,000 p.a. from his poetry. In all he had nearly £10,000 from the Civil List, while poorer authors had to be denied. His own justification was that he was so often asked for money by impecunious writers that he needed it to provide the charity, but that is an evasion of the central issue, and in any case he was not renowned for his generosity in such instances. 'I think it is very hard that I am obliged to subscribe to all the bad poets,' he wrote some years later, '. . . and I do not believe that old Wordey payed any attention to such. He was far too canny.'[5] Wordsworth, it is true, also kept his pension until his death, but that was a matter of only eight years and he was never a wealthy man, as Tennyson certainly became. But Tennyson had inherited the attitudes to money that filled Somersby Rectory, and perhaps he was afraid that he might one day be as unable to provide for himself as poor Edward, locked away in York. It must be remembered, too, that it was natural for him to compare his own financial position to that of wealthy friends like Hallam, Milnes, Spedding, FitzGerald, de Vere, Lushington, or even the inordinately rich Monteith, rather than those like Tennant or Brookfield, who had to worry where the next penny was coming from. His attitude towards money was far more like that of the Tennyson d'Eyncourts or that of the Old Man of the Wolds than he would have liked to think.

In response to the congratulations of T. H. Rawnsley, Tennyson wrote in a curiously self-exculpating way about the pension, a word that he said 'sticks in my gizzard'. At least, said he, 'I have done nothing slavish to get it: I never even solicited for it either by myself or thro' others. . . . Peel tells me that I need not by it be fettered in the public expression of any opinion I choose to take up so if I take a pique against the Queen or the court, or Peel himself, I may, if I will, bully them with as much freedom tho' not perhaps quite so gracefully, as if I were still unpensioned. . . . I doubt not that I shall meet with all manner of livor, scandal, & heartburning, small literary men whose letters perhaps I have never answered, bustling up & indignant that they are past by—they!!'[6] His last gloomy prognostication was more accurate than he could have guessed.

Like most of Tennyson's friends, Carlyle was delighted at the news, though he expressed his pleasure in typically dour fashion: 'Poor Alfred, may it do him good;—"a Wife to keep him unaisy," will be attainable now, if his thoughts tend that way.' But in 1845 Tennyson's thoughts did not so tend. A few months later when Bernard Barton was given a pension of £100, Tennyson wrote to Fitz to say that he was almost reconciled to his own pension. 'Certainly I am twice a Barton in verse.'[7]

Even a writer as friendly as William Howitt, who knew that his brother had interceded with Lady Peel on Tennyson's behalf, was like the constituents that Milnes feared in thinking that the pension was the result of familial influence, but he put it down to Tennyson's 'uncle in parliament'. Charles Tennyson d'Eyncourt, who still thought but poorly of Alfred's poetic talents, certainly had nothing to do with the pension; in fact it was probably through his resentment of it that one of the worst of all attacks on Tennyson came about.

But even more painful things were happening to Tennyson d'Eyncourt than the news of the unfair reward his nephew was receiving. The Tennyson family had always been staunchly anti-Catholic, like many of the predominantly Evangelical church-goers of East Anglia. To Tennyson d'Eyncourt's dismay, his eldest daughter Julia had for some time been turning unsuitably religious, her churchmanship moving progressively higher, until at last she announced her wish to become a Roman Catholic convert. On the face of it, this might seem a logical extension of the medieval aspirations of her father, but that was not how he viewed the matter, and his first reaction was to tell her that if she changed her religion she would have to change her residence as well, and that she could then consider herself as no longer belonging to the family. For all his fury, he loved Julia, and after protestations from his friends he at last agreed to let her stay in the family and even allowed her the use of the oratory at Bayons. The Bournes at Dalby were so horrified at the proceedings that they protected their Calvinist principles by cutting themselves off entirely from the Bayons relatives.

Worse still, the county, which had delighted for years in telling stories of the absurdities of the Tennyson d'Eyncourts, now began speculating that the entire family was turning Roman Catholic, and that the oratory had been secretly designed as a Popish chapel from the beginning. Time had not softened the laughter at the grandeur of Bayons and the pretensions of its owner. Colonel Cracroft of Hackthorn Hall went to see the house and wrote in his diary: 'But *that* an old baronial hall; and the owner the second son of a Market Rasen attorney! It is too absurd.'[8] Charles Tennyson d'Eyncourt knew that the amassing of his fortune, the even more sizable piling up of Bayons, and the Frenchifying of his name had all made him a figure of fun in Lincolnshire; if there was one thing that would make him more laughable, it was the belief that they were all turning Roman Catholic. It seemed unfair that this should be happening to him while his lethargic, untalented nephew became increasingly famous and was now actually rewarded by the Government for his second-rate poetry. In any case, Alfred had received a large sum of money from his grandfather's estate, which he had promptly invested imprudently, so that there was no reason for him to get a pension. All this Charles Tennyson d'Eyncourt told to his intimate friend Edward Bulwer-Lytton, whom he repeatedly consulted over his troubles with Julia. Bulwer-Lytton told her worried father that he had tried hard to keep Julia from changing her religion and had at one point exacted an assurance that she would not become a Roman Catholic, but now she had broken her promise.

Shortly after the news of the pension first appeared, Bulwer was staying at Bayons, writing a long satirical poem, 'The New Timon', which was to be published at the end of the year. Almost certainly Charles Tennyson d'Eyncourt had no idea of the contents of the poem until it appeared, for he was not a malicious man in spite of disliking his nephew, and he would not deliberately have given Bulwer ammunition for a public attack upon Alfred. None the less, he must have talked a good bit about his nephew, and Bulwer said to the younger Tennyson d'Eyncourts, 'How I shd. like to know your cousin, Alfred.'[9]

In January 1846 Tennyson was staying at Cheltenham, bored with what he called a 'polka-parson-worshipping place', with 'pumps and pumprooms, chalybeates, quadrilles'. He went one day into the book-club of which he was a member and there found a paper folded down so that the first words to meet his eyes were, 'see how Sir Edward tickles up poetasters & their patrons'. It was a reprint of the second part of 'The New Timon', and the editor was calling attention to its most offensive section. Although the poem was published anonymously, the editor's heading made it clear how easily recognizable Bulwer's style was. It was a repetition of many of the most offensive parts of what had appeared in the *New Monthly* of January 1833, so much like the earlier attack that Tennyson called it a mere 'versification' of Bulwer's review.[10] This time, however, Bulwer's malice was inadequately hidden behind a pious mask of pity for poor Knowles, who had been done out of a pension:

> Not mine, not mine, (O Muse forbid!) the boon
> Of borrowed notes, the mock-bird's modish tune,
> The jingling medley of purloin'd conceits,
> Outbabying Wordsworth, and outglittering Keates,
> Where all the airs of patchwork-pastoral chime
> To drowsy ears in Tennysonian rhyme!
>   . . .
> Let School-Miss Alfred vent her chaste delight
> On 'darling little rooms so warm and bright!'
> Chaunt, 'I'm aweary,' in infectious strain,
> And catch her 'blue fly singing i' the pane.'
> Tho' praised by Critics, tho' adored by Blues,
> Tho' Peel with pudding plump the puling Muse,
> Tho' Theban taste the Saxon's purse controuls,
> And pensions Tennyson, while starves a Knowles,
> Rather, be thou, my poor Pierian Maid,
> Decent at least, in Hayley's weeds array'd,
> Than patch with frippery every tinsel line,
> And flaunt, admired, the Rag Fair of the Nine!

In a note to the poem Bulwer reprinted part of 'O Darling Room', which Tennyson had been trying to forget ever since its publication in 1832. Bulwer also said that Tennyson came from a wealthy family and was in the prime of life without wife or children, and now was 'quartered on the public purse'.

To add to the pain of the attack, Tennyson knew that Bulwer was his uncle's best friend, that he frequented Bayons, and that much of his misleading information must have come from the Tennyson d'Eyn-courts. But Bulwer on his own also represented everything that Tennyson loathed, both as a writer and as a man. As Thackeray had said, his literary taste was slight, and he 'had made the very most of a very shallow soil'. Tennyson thought the best of his works was his novel of 1828, *Pelham, or The Adventures of a Gentleman*, in spite of the fact that Pelham 'is not a gentleman, no more is he'.[11] Bulwer touched up his face with make-up, dyed his hair and beard a bright red, and on at least one occasion came to Little Holland House leading twelve French poodles, with their hair and his own coiffed to match. He was a joke in society for his chamois-tipped pink boots with three-inch cork heels to give him height. George Eliot used to tell how he would deliberately put on untidy clothes and saunter down the street until he met a friend, talk to him, then hurry home to dress himself sumptuously before calling on his friend in splendour. He was a very easy man to despise, but he was not a fool.

Tennyson went immediately to John Forster, a close friend of Bulwer, to ask whether his own suspicions about the authorship of 'The New Timon' were correct. Forster thought they were, for he had written the previous month to Bulwer, hinting at the authorship without directly asking Bulwer whether he had written the poem. When Tennyson came to him, Forster showed him a letter from Bulwer in reply to his own: 'I do not know what you mean by the New poem which is either by BL—or—By BL—do you mean me—I am innocent. What poem is it? Not I suppose the Modern Timon which I saw just before leaving England at Lady Blessington's & afterwards glanced over at Home—I believe it is by [Sir James Weir] Hogg—MP for Beverly—at least so I heard at Paris. I was in too great a hurry to do more than glance at it. It seemed to me clever & Crabbe like.'[12]

Neither the deliberate use of the wrong title nor the bald-faced lie that it was designed to support fooled Forster and Tennyson. In fury Tennyson sat down and wrote 'The New Timon, and the Poets', a reply to Bulwer. Apparently he wrote it without thought of publication, but he gave it to Forster, asking him, 'in his sense of the littleness of revenge', to destroy the lines after reading them. According to W. C. Macready, Forster said that 'justice was more dear than friendship to him', offered to publish them, and so convinced Tennyson that they should be made public.[13] On 28 February 1846 the poem appeared in *Punch*. Tennyson begins by comparing Bulwer with Shakespeare's Timon:

I *thought* we knew him: What, it's you,
    The padded man—that wears the stays—

Who killed the girls and thrilled the boys,
    With dandy pathos when you wrote,
A Lion, you, that made a noise,
    And shook a mane en papillotes. [curling papers]

And once you tried the Muses too;
    You failed, Sir: therefore now you turn,
You fall on those who are to you,
    As Captain is to Subaltern.

            . . .

What profits now to understand
    The merits of a spotless shirt—
A dapper boot—a little hand—
    If half the little soul is dirt?

You talk of tinsel! why we see
    The old mark of rouge upon your cheeks.
You prate of Nature! you are he
    That spilt his life about the cliques.

A Timon you! Nay, nay, for shame:
    It looks too arrogant a jest—
The fierce old man—to take *his* name
    You bandbox. Off, and let him rest.

It lacks the wit of good invective, but it rings with anger, and that probably counted for more in this case since it made it clear that Tennyson was responding to grossly unfair treatment. Within a few weeks several newspapers and magazines had come to Tennyson's defence, and though Bulwer still disavowed the poem the reviews and articles were in no doubt who the author was, and the identification was not to Bulwer's credit. The writer in the *Eclectic Review* said scathingly, 'Little dogs at the foot of Mount Parnassus, as here manifest, will still bark at the moon.'[14] Bulwer's malice had exploded in his own face, ending in a triumphant vindication of Tennyson.

Tennyson's initial anger quickly subsided, and he regretted that his squib had found its way into print. Almost immediately he sent a brief poem, 'Literary Squabbles', to be published in *Punch* the following week, deprecating the spite of 'poetasters' but admitting that lack of charity infected his own reaction:

Surely, after all,
The noblest answer unto such
Is perfect stillness when they brawl.

For all his advocacy of charity, he found it impossible to resist signing the poem 'Alcibiades', the name of the philosopher who reads aloud the misanthropic epitaph composed by Timon of Athens for himself. In later years, when he had become increasingly ashamed of the initial poem, Tennyson was to declare that he did not even know that Forster was publishing it in *Punch*.

Bulwer, who knew when he was beaten, could now not afford to admit that he had written the poem, and he wrote once more to Forster, blaming him for the rumour that Bulwer was its author and asking him to repair the damage done. He professed to be unable to understand how he of all men, who had been so 'generally kind & good natured to all literary men whom I could help', should be so slandered. 'I am not in the habit of writing anonymously. . . . I have nothing to do with the poem one way or the other . . . You have my decided & peremptory authority to deny the report.'[15]

Even to the family at Bayons Bulwer seems to have denied any connection with the offensive poem. George Tennyson d'Eyncourt, after a stay of ten days at Knebworth, wrote to Frederick telling him that he had talked to Bulwer: 'I can say that he is *not* the author of the New Timon.'[16] It was not until a year later that Bulwer finally came clean when Forster advised him that it would be unwise to sign his new poem 'King Arthur' as the work of 'the Author of the N.T.'.

In subsequent editions of the 'The New Timon' Bulwer expunged the offending passages, and he never again attacked Tennyson publicly, but his private opinion of him remained unchanged, as 'a poet adapted to a mixed audience of school-girls and Oxford dons', who was full of 'vulgarities and conceits'.[17] No doubt he was influenced by the memory of the licking he had taken. One suspects, too, that Tennyson's own interest in the Arthurian legend was not lessened by the knowledge that he was going 'King Arthur' one better when he published the *Idylls of the King*. The affair of 'The New Timon' shows the growing acceptance of Tennyson as the coming poet of his age, an acceptance that four years later had become something like deification.

Charles Tennyson d'Eyncourt's sympathies in the quarrel between Bulwer and Tennyson are clearly shown in the continuance and increasing warmth of his friendship with Bulwer, to whom he turned for comfort in 1846 when his daughter Julia announced her intention of going to France to enter a convent. Characteristically, her father tried to turn his bitter disappointment into a glorification of his lineage. In the little French town of Aincourt he bought a large house, which he proceeded to improve, with the idea that Julia, instead of taking vows as a nun, might there live a life of contemplative retirement with a chaperone. No doubt he had the sincerest intention of benefiting Julia (although it was far from what she had in mind), but it was surely more than coincidental that the town in which he proposed to establish her was the seat of his Eyncourt ancestors and the source of his new surname. After several changes of convent, Julia at last became a postulant in 1848 and ended her life as a secluded nun in Coventry. Charles spent much of the rest of his life in Aincourt, reinforcing his imagined ties with the origins of his forebears. With the pathetic self-importance he never learned to hide, he used to announced proudly on leaving for Normandy that he was going to take up residence in his château there.

What Charles Tennyson d'Eyncourt never knew was that Julia's retreat into religion was the result of the gentle rebuff she had received when she declared her love to Edward Bulwer-Lytton. He was still married, though he did not live with his wife, and she surely knew that at best she could only be another in the succession of his mistresses. In the Lytton family papers is the touching letter she wrote when she had recovered her composure after receiving Bulwer's reply. In it she expresses her regret at having exposed her own love, and though his reply has caused her pain, she thanks Bulwer for having led her to religion for consolation. If Alfred Tennyson had been malicious, he could not have devised a more painful revenge upon his uncle for the comfort that he had given to the man who so crudely attacked his nephew.

✿

CHAPTER XX

THE PRINCESS,
1846–1847

DURING January 1846, while Bulwer's attack on him was appearing, Tennyson went to London, and as usual when his emotional state was at its lowest he fell ill again, this time with a severe internal attack that Elizabeth Barrett said did not put him 'precisely in danger . . . but the complaint may *run* into danger'. Fitz found him 'in a ricketty state of body; brought on wholly by neglect, etc., but in fair spirits'.[1] In spite of his illness Tennyson continued working hard at *The Princess*, talking about it to his friends and reading them portions. On one inauspicious evening he recited aloud to Fitz, who was tired from a day's pleasures in London, began nodding at what he considered the monotony of the poem, then fell fast asleep. After such implicit criticism, Tennyson was not surprised that his old friend thoroughly disliked the poem when it had been published.

Even Elizabeth Barrett, fervent as she was in her admiration of Tennyson, was not happy when she heard he was writing a poem 'in blank verse & a fairy tale, & called the "University," the university-members being all females. . . . Now isn't the world too old & fond of steam, for blank verse poems, in ever so many books, to be written on the fairies?'[2] Writing poetry was therapeutically important for Tennyson when he was ill, but that was not necessarily the time at which his judgement of his own work was at its keenest, and it is possible that some of the shapelessness of *The Princess* is due to his ill-health during its composition.

Miss Barrett had still not met Tennyson, although Browning had done so, and in May the two men were together again at Moxon's table, to Browning's delight. They were in company with Joseph Severn, who had been with Keats at his lonely death in Rome, but instead of speaking of Keats Tennyson put questions about Shelley, whom he knew Browning loved. Browning found the way that Moxon took care of Tennyson 'the charmingest thing imaginable, and he seems to need it all . . . being in truth but a LONG, hazy kind of man, at least just before dinner—yet there is something "naif" about him, too—the genius you see, too'.[3] No doubt their pleasure in each other would have led on immediately to a closer friendship between the two poets had Browning not been within three months of his elopement with Elizabeth Barrett to Italy. It was not until 1851 that he again met Tennyson, in Paris, when they were both accompanied by their wives.

In truth neither much cared for the other's poetry, and by the time they had both achieved wide fame there was a touch of poetic jealousy in their relations, although they never allowed it to interfere with the personal courtesy and generosity with which they treated each other. They were certainly the two outstanding poets of their day, and Browning constantly spoke warmly of Tennyson's poetry, but Tennyson often had to swallow hard before going beyond his distaste for Browning's cacophony. His dislike of Browning's poetry was of long standing. He had read *Sordello* in 1840, on the appearance of that perplexing work, and said that there were only two lines in the entire poem that he understood, the opening and closing lines: 'Who will may hear Sordello's story told', and 'Who would has heard Sordello's story told'. Unfortunately, he added, both lines were lies.[4]

When Browning returned to live in England after his wife's death in 1861, he began a new life of social activity of a kind that Tennyson disliked; when Browning was invited to stay with the Tennysons he seemed always to find that he was previously engaged. The two men were genuinely fond of each other, but their affection was preserved by their not spending too much time together.

Charles Dickens would have liked more intimacy with Tennyson than he was ever permitted; more than Tennyson's habitual lethargy lay behind his lack of response to Dickens's overtures. On 21 April 1846 Tennyson stood as godfather to Dicken's son Alfred D'Orsay Tennyson Dickens, whose other godfather was the famous dandy Alfred, Count D'Orsay, making it probable, said Elizabeth Barrett, that the child would be 'half a poet and half a "paletot".' Shortly thereafter, when Tennyson was dining at Dickens's house, Dickens invited him to share a house that summer in Switzerland, where he was going to work on *Dombey and Son*. 'If I went,' said Tennyson afterwards, 'I should be entreating him to dismiss his sentimentality, & so we should quarrel & part, & never see one another any more. It was better to decline—& I have declined.'[5] In spite of his refusal of the invitation, it had suggested a destination that year for the restless Tennyson.

Dickens's liking for Tennyson did not please John Forster, who thought of the novelist as his particular property and regarded him as a much greater celebrity than Tennyson. Once, when Tennyson and Dickens were talking, Forster ('a rude peacocking man') came into the room and offensively ordered Tennyson to 'Get out, sir'.[6] His boorishness must unaccountably have amused Tennyson, for it caused no definite break in their tenuous relations.

There were already a few flaws in his friendship with Carlyle as the two became more critical of one another. Carlyle, who had frequently told Tennyson that he was a Life Guardsman spoiled by poetry, began innocently inventing stories that fitted his conception of Tennyson as a great man sadly misguided. He once told the visiting American Margaret Fuller that Tennyson wrote in verse 'because the schoolmasters had taught him that it was great to do so, and had thus, unfortunately, been turned from the true path for a man'.[7] And since writing poetry did not fit his idea of work, he thought Tennyson was even lazier than he was, insisting that he had to be urged to go collect his pension.

Understandably, Tennyson was rubbed the wrong way by such stories. On one occasion Carlyle said, 'He wants a *task*; and, alas, that of spinning rhymes, and naming it "Art" and "high Art", in a time like ours, will never furnish him.' When Tennyson read the printed version of the remark he underlined 'high Art' and wrote in the margin, 'I never in my life spoke of High Art.' Increasingly their conversations became debates, and in May 1846 Fitz wrote of one evening when the 'two discussed the merits of this world, and the next, till I wished myself out of *this*, at any rate. Carlyle gets more wild, savage, and unreasonable every day; and, I do believe, will turn mad.' During that spring Carlyle and Tennyson spent many nights walking the streets of London, inveighing against its invasion by a constantly growing mass of humanity. A year later Tennyson said of the older man, 'You would like him for one day, but get tired of him, so vehement and destructive.'[8] But Tennyson never dropped him, as he would have done another man who worried him so much.

Rather more to Tennyson's taste was the scene in a cab leaving a meeting of the Society of Authors, of which Serjeant Talfourd was president. As Tennyson liked to tell it: 'I happened to say to my neighbour "I wonder which of us will be alive 500 years hence" on which Talfourd burst forth into a speech about me saying "I was the one likely to live!" . . . I drove away afterwards with old Douglas Jerrold who fell on his knees, seized me by the hand and kissed it and kissed it and said "I haven't the smallest doubt that *you* are the one who will live five hundred years."[9] Tennyson tried to make a joke of the incident when he spoke of it, but he was still telling the story with undiminished pleasure forty years later, not recognizing that his attitude was exactly that of which he had been so contemptuous in Samuel Rogers.

Tennyson's miserably thin skin and his liking for heavy flattery, which made him unhappy with criticism from FitzGerald and Carlyle, often led him into friendships with second-rate men on the fringes of the literary world. For years he had found uncritical affection among men of his own calibre in the Apostles, but now he sought it among those whom once he would have considered unworthy. At heart he was ashamed of his willingness to accept mediocrity, and he took out his self-disgust on the younger men, using them for his own convenience and rewarding them with contempt when the mood was upon him. Some of them were ready to put up with his treatment for the privilege, even the worldly advantage, of associating with an authentic genius, although most of them were genuinely fond of him. Over the years there was a procession of such friends as Francis Palgrave, William Allingham, Thomas Woolner, James Knowles, and lesser men. Tennyson would allow them to entertain him when he was in London, or act as errand boys, walking companions, and sounding-boards for his ideas about poetry. There is no indication that he was often cynical about, or even totally conscious of what he was doing, but most of the relationships seem to have sprung from motives that were not wholly admirable on either side. It was a sad come-down from the days of Arthur Hallam. There is nothing unusual about a love of adulation, but it kept Tennyson from the kind of healthy criticism by an equal that his poetry needed.

The first of these young followers was Coventry Patmore, whom he saw a great deal of in 1846. Patmore had hopes of establishing himself as a poet, in spite of the bad reviews he had received for his first volume in 1844. He had modelled his poetry upon that of Tennyson to such effect that it was thought by many that 'Coventry Patmore' was the nom de plume of Tennyson himself. Patmore was lonely (he was not to marry 'The Angel in the House' until 1847) and unhappy with his work as an assistant in the printed book department of the British Museum. At twenty-three he was much junior to Tennyson in years and experience, and he adapted his own life to suit the other's, taking over Carlyle's place as Tennyson's companion on those circuitous nocturnal rambles when they walked through the city, talking until dawn broke. Unlike some of those who succeeded him as Tennyson's squire, Patmore had a truculent independence of his own and resented Tennyson's patronizing at the very time that he courted it. Matters between them were not made easier by Tennyson's bluntness about deficiencies in Patmore's poetry, such as the one line that he said 'seems to me hammered up out of old nail-heads'.[10] Their intimacy slackened after Patmore's marriage, so that they saw less of each other, although they did not break totally until the 1880s. The *Dictionary of National Biography* describes Patmore as 'haughty, imperious, combative, sardonic . . . at the same time sensitive, susceptible, and capable of deep tenderness'. With a change of names the description would fit Tennyson aptly; with such likeness of temperament it is no wonder that their mutual regard lessened soon after its intense beginning.

Tennyson spent most of the first half of 1846 in London. His loneliness and recurrent worry over his health made him unhappy there, but the alternative of spending the time with his family in Cheltenham was unthinkable. He spoke of returning to Italy with Frederick, who was visiting England, then had his usual difficulty in making up his mind, and the opportunity passed. Then he decided to go to Switzerland, as Dickens had suggested, but with Moxon as travelling companion. Once more he found trouble in getting himself ready, and instead of setting out with Moxon he went to the Isle of Wight in June, probably for the first time. One of his companions on the island was Edmund Peel, cousin of Sir Robert, who was an amateur poet and lover of Tennyson's works. Together they wandered over the southern downs of the island and rowed around the Needles. When Tennyson was looking for a house near London after his marriage, it was Peel who helped him find it; then, after that house proved unsatisfactory, it was the memory of the trip to the Isle of Wight that led Tennyson to Farringford, with which his name has been associated ever since.

On his return to the mainland Tennyson spent some weeks at Park House while he waited to leave with Moxon. Tennyson, who had what amounted to a fetish about accuracy in his poems, was checking details of the Lushingtons' house and park for *The Princess*, which opens with a description of a fête he had attended there four years before. The Lushingtons were hospitable, and it never occurred to Tennyson that his presence, for whatever length of time he chose to stay, might be inconvenient for his hosts.

At last, on the first of August, he set out for Switzerland with Moxon. During part of the trip he kept a lively and amusing journal, of which the first two days are a fair sample:

A. 1 Arrived at Ramsgate—cold bath—slept at a fishmongers—
A. 2 M. likewise—up at four to go by Princess Maude—picturesque sunrise from pier—[Englishman] with moustache told us of festival at Bruges. M. sickish. I go down into fore-cabin & get the very worst breakfast I ever had in my life—arrival at Ostende—order from Belgian King that no passports need be shown—inhuman conduct & supererogatory fury of porters—we lose our presence of mind & run for it—but there is plenty of time—2d class—arrive at Bruges—went to Hotel de Blé recommended by moustached Englishman, missing the conveyance whitherward which marked with gilt letters 'Fleur de Blé' rolled by us as we neared our Hotel—great rejoicings of the people & hero-worship . . . dinner in Salle—not very good, affected Englishwoman whom I took for Belge or German opposite—go to bed—hot nervous night with me—man hemm'd overhead enough to shake the walls of Jericho—call'd too soon—off to Gant . . .[11]

As Jerome Buckley has noticed, the journal indicates 'the vividness with which every raw impression, every sound and sight, registered itself on an open consciousness and so became the potential substance of a refined and concentrated imagery'.[12] Cheek by jowl with the terse perceptions of the mountains he had gone to see is Tennyson's irritation with the cold baths, paper-thin walls, fleas, bad beer, vulgar companions, surly servants, and constant thieving that were the lot of travellers a century ago.

Unfortunately, Moxon proved to have a poor head for heights and had to hold on to the arm of their guide, so that Tennyson went on alone, with no one on whom he could test the immediacy of his impressions, which was a large part of what he had wanted in a travelling companion. As Tennyson's publisher and senior by some eight years, Moxon was hardly one of the young men on whom Tennyson became accustomed to lean, but he was expected to fulfil some of the same functions of courier and listener.

It was largely an uneventful trip as they went down the Rhine, where Nonnenwerth and Drachenfels brought 'sad recollections' of his earlier journey with Hallam. In Switzerland the mountains were disappointing; when he 'saw Blanc, he was very sulky—kept his Nightcap on—doff'd it one morning when I was knocked up out of bed to look at him at four o'clock—the glance I gave did not by any means repay me for the toil of travelling to see him'.[13] Two of the 'stateliest bits of

landskip' that Tennyson had ever seen were the valley of Läuterbrun-
nen and a view of the Bernese Alps. The most important result of his
visual impressions was the love lyric he later planted in *The Princess*,
in which the shepherd implores the maiden to forsake her virginal
fastnesses:

> Come down, O maid, from yonder mountain height:
> What pleasure lives in height (the shepherd sang)
> In height and cold, the splendour of the hills?
> But cease to move so near the Heavens, and cease
> To glide a sunbeam by the blasted Pine,
> To sit a star upon the sparkling spire;
> And come, for Love is of the valley, come,
> For Love is of the valley, come thou down
> And find him; by the happy threshold, he,
> Or hand in hand with Plenty in the maize,
> Or red with spirted purple of the vats,
> Or foxlike in the vine; nor cares to walk
> With Death and Morning on the silver horns,
> Nor wilt thou snare him in the white ravine,
> Nor find him dropt upon the firths of ice,
> That huddling slant in furrow-cloven falls
> To roll the torrent out of dusky doors:
> But follow; let the torrent dance thee down
> To find him in the valley; let the wild
> Lean-headed Eagles yelp alone, and leave
> The monstrous ledges there to slope, and spill
> Their thousand wreaths of dangling water-smoke,
> That like a broken purpose waste in air:
> So waste not thou; but come; for all the vales
> Await thee; azure pillars of the hearth
> Arise to thee; the children call, and I
> Thy shepherd pipe, and sweet is every sound,
> Sweeter thy voice, but every sound is sweet;
> Myriads of rivulets hurrying through the lawn,
> The moan of doves in immemorial elms,
> And murmuring of innumerable bees.

The lonely heights of the mountains, in all their barren majesty and
splendour, are set against the melody and fertility of the valley, and the
whole lyric becomes the invocation of the shepherd to the maid to
leave the isolation of the heights for the teeming life below. Much of
the poem rings with echoes of his stay with Hallam in Cauteretz, when

together they heard the yelp of the lean-headed eagles and saw the blasted pine and the wreaths of dangling water-smoke like lawn that became the germ of 'The Lotos-Eaters': the streams that 'like a downward smoke,/Slow-dropping veils of thinnest lawn, did go'. Even at the most superficial level one can see how the loneliness of the Swiss trip brought back the contrasting memory of the companionable summer of 1830 in the Pyrenees. Yet there is an oddity about the poem which indicates that Tennyson was at last beginning to detach himself from the past and to ally himself with the life around him: although the memory of Hallam and his connection with the valley of Cauteretz remain potent, many of the echoes of 1830 are now connected with the sterility of the heights, with death and the past, those things which must be put behind. It is as if Tennyson, at least unconsciously, was preparing himself to embrace hope not regret. Everything that the Pyrenees represented for him about his affection for Hallam, when Love was of the valley of Cauteretz, was to retain its intensity for the rest of his life, but he could finally put it in its proper place.

Tennyson wanted to call on old Mr Hallam, who had taken a house in Lausanne, and while there he and Moxon intended to visit Dickens. On the evening of 23 August Dickens saw two travel-stained men arriving at the door of his house, Rosemont, the elder of them looking rather peculiar in a limp straw hat. Tennyson and Moxon had already dined aboard the steamer from Geneva, and Dickens gave them 'some fine wine, and cigars innumerable', which Tennyson so enjoyed that he quickly felt at home. Dickens found Moxon 'snobbish, but pleased and good-natured'; he may have been put off by the hat, for he thought him 'an odd companion for a man of genius'.[14]

During the trip Tennyson once said petulantly, 'Moxon, you have made me very unhappy by something you said to me at Lucerne.' For days he had been brooding over his companion's tactless remark, 'Why Tennyson you will be bald as Spedding before long.' As soon as they were back in England, 'he put himself under a Mrs. Parker . . . who rubs his head and pulls out dead hairs . . . besides cosmetics *ad libitum*'. Jane Brookfield thought that Mr Hallam's own 'hair would bristle up at the idea of the Queen's pension being spent in this manner' at ten shillings an hour, but Tennyson's 'hair is such an integral part of his appearance it would be a great pity he should lose it'.[15] Tennyson, who was vain about his looks in spite of his careless dress and intermittent cleanliness, insisted to the end of his life that his

I hate the dreadful
hollow behind
the little wood

27 Sept. 1855

XIII. Tennyson reading *Maud*, 27 September 1855,
by D. G. Rossetti.

a

b

c

XIV. 3 drawings of Tennyson, c. 1855, by Richard Doyle.

hair was neither thin nor grey, when the contrary evidence was only too apparent.

The return Channel crossing was rough, and Moxon had to retire to his bed again. Tennyson prided himself on being a good sailor, but he was 'sick as a dog . . . no doubt owing to the passage—if it was not to standing at the Custom House'.[16]

After coming back to England Tennyson concentrated on finishing *The Princess* for publication in 1847, but he felt very unsure about the poem. By late spring of 1847 he had worried himself into such a state that he had to go off again to a water establishment for the cure. It is probable that he was no longer suffering so severely from the trances that had bothered him earlier and that it was general nervousness for which he needed treatment. Umberslade Hall, south of Birmingham, near the village of Tanworth, was run on less strict lines than Prestbury, and the doctor in charge of the establishment, Edward Johnson, allowed Tennyson more time to himself than Priessnitz had done. Certainly, it was pleasanter to take his constitutional walks, for he could stay within the fine old park surrounding the mansion where he was quartered, rather than going through the streets followed by jeering urchins as he had been forced to do in Prestbury.

At Umberslade he was correcting proofs for *The Princess*, but he was still undecided about when it should be published. There was a general election scheduled for the autumn, and it seemed unwise to launch a major poem at a time when public attention would be so firmly focused elsewhere. Probably Tennyson's worry about the publication date was indicative of a deeper uncertainty about the poem, for it was finally published on Christmas Day 1847, a date surely as ill-calculated for public notice as any during an election.

On leaving Umberslade he stayed at Park House, which he was beginning to use as a regular convalescent home. One of the Lushingtons finally admitted to Brookfield that the 'Tennyson habit of coming unwashed and staying unbidden was, is, and will be the great burthen and calamity of the Lushington existence, socially considered'.[17] It shows both the kindness of the Lushingtons and the social unawareness of Tennyson that he never knew how they felt about his visits.

His illness that summer was to result in his becoming known to another family with consequences so profound as to affect the rest of his life. The circumstances are not clear, since the only record is a brief paragraph in *The Times* of 9 August 1847, copied from the *Cork Constitution*:

ROYAL COMPLIMENT TO THE POET TENNYSON—

It was but the other day that Her Majesty and Prince Albert evinced their contempt for the fashionable and dissipated fools of Esher in a very marked manner for their deadness to the value of the society of a man of high intellect and accomplished mind. Alfred Tennyson, the poet, had been sojourning at Esher in bad health. No one thought it worth his while to call on him or to solicit his acquaintance. The Queen and Prince, hearing of it, paid their respects to him without delay. No sooner was this known, than Tennyson was inundated with cards and invitations. The cards he returned, the invitations he declined.

There is apparently no other evidence that Tennyson was in Esher that summer, although he was certainly not far away, and the tone of the note is so spiteful that it is initially tempting to dismiss it as an Irish attack on the suburban snobbishness of the English. It may seem most improbable that the Queen and Prince should pay their respects to one of her subjects whom they had never even met, but we know that the Prince came unannounced to Farringford some years later, simply knocking on the door and asking to see Tennyson, then saying that he intended to bring the Queen to Farringford in a few days. It is documented evidence of even greater Royal informality that makes the Esher story seem credible. 'Paid their respects' probably indicates that a note or card was left for Tennyson, not that they called in person, but the Prince did so at Farringford, and the contents of Tennyson's dream at the time of his appointment as Poet Laureate may have been a reshuffling of past experience, with the Queen and Prince appearing in person to see him. At the end of June 1847 the Queen and the Court were at Claremont, her house in Esher, which would certainly explain the mention of that town.

The details of the newspaper account are probably inaccurate, and the whole matter remains obscure, but in the absence of contrary evidence it is probable that Victoria and Albert took some kind of informal notice of Tennyson in the summer of 1847. If so, it helps explain how Tennyson was picked as Poet Laureate and why the Royal family felt sufficiently familiar with him to visit Farringford so easily.

At the end of the summer Tennyson went to Mablethorpe to finish reading proofs of *The Princess*, then in the autumn he returned to London. Henry Lushington had gone off to Malta as secretary to the government there, and Venables, who kept on their rooms in the Temple, seemed less welcoming than Lushington, so that Tennyson felt he must find other quarters. He moved from one sordid hotel to another in the vicinity of Leicester Square, living, as Fitz said, among 'fleas and foreigners'. In December, just before the publication of *The Princess*, he settled for some months in respectable lodgings in Ebury Street.

The version of *The Princess: A Medley* that appeared on 25 December was considerably different from the one known today because Tennyson tinkered with it constantly for three or four years after its initial production, changing it more than any other major poem of his, attempting to make its central themes more comprehensible. It was his first long poem, and it shows baldly his fundamental problem of believing that basically disparate material could be fused if only it had enough connective tissue added. When he wrote short lyrics they sprang out of the associations that naturally grouped themselves around a phrase or situation, but his method of writing long poems was to assemble discrete sections, then to try to find a common link between them; it was the reverse of organic poetry and in only two cases did he create the special circumstances that imposed meaning upon discontinuity: *In Memoriam* and *Maud*. The sub-title of *The Princess* is both an accurate description of the heterogeneous nature of the elements of the poem and a self-defensive attempt to disarm criticism by acknowledging its lack of unity.

On one level, that of plot, the poem is straightforward enough, with the clearest narrative of any of Tennyson's long poems; the uncertainty is in the tone and in the inconstancy of theme. The frame is provided by an outing of the Mechanics' Institute held in the thinly disguised grounds of Park House, where the workmen are entertained by scientific tricks and toys, 'so that sport/Went hand in hand with Science'. The son of the house reminisces with six friends about their college life, which makes his sister Lilia wish that women had their own university. The seven young men agree to tell a story of such a university, each taking a turn at being the hero, the Prince. By the diversity of styles so intimated Tennyson was once more protecting himself against a charge of inconsistency of tone and style, but the truth was hit on by FitzGerald, who said that there was 'no indication of any change of speaker in the cantos', and that they seemed to be 'all of the Tennyson family'.[18]

The interior story told by the several narrators is of the Prince, betrothed since childhood to Princess Ida. When she refuses to honour her engagement she founds a female university in a remote house owned by her father, to which the Prince goes to find her. He and two friends disguise themselves in girls' clothing and become undergraduates. When their sex is discovered, the Prince pleads his love for Ida, but she remains obdurate in renouncing marriage. The lives of the young men are in danger until the Princess's father is taken hostage by the father of the Prince. A tournament is held to decide the issue, and the Prince and his two friends are wounded. At this the university is turned into an infirmary and the young ladies into nurses. Ida's scorn of men is melted by pity for the Prince, and she happily agrees to marry him.

The story begins light-heartedly as a burlesque of women's education, with a direct inversion of all the accepted roles for men, now taken by women. At Lilia's suggestion it turns serious for the battles and for the conversion of Princess Ida. Lilia is touched by the ending of the story, but whether it is sufficient to change her mind is left in doubt when the Institute outing breaks up; all are left pondering the future.

In spite of the feudal trappings of the tournament, the poem is not a fairy tale, as Miss Barrett feared, but Tennyson's attempt to deal with a thoroughly contemporary problem, that of the education of women in Victorian England. In part it was his answer to those critics who felt he was too removed from the intellectual questions of his day. One of his recurrent problems was how to make clear the relevance of the past to the present; in this poem the setting is a deliberate attempt to show the seamless continuity of time, with modern scientific gadgets set in 'Vivian Place', in whose park stand 'A Gothic ruin and a Grecian house'. A more subtle indication of the same idea is the lyric later inserted between sections III and IV of the poem, 'The splendour falls on castle walls'.

But Tennyson was not temperamentally equipped to deal with educational theory, for his interest was in individual emotions, and what was a serious problem to his contemporaries is not treated seriously in the poem. The university is presented as little more than a second-rate girls' school whose pupils spend most of their time patting peacocks, tossing a ball across a fountain, and changing the pastel academic gowns whose colours appear to be chosen by each girl for their suitability to her own complexion. As one would expect in such an institution, there is an impressive list of lectures, but the chief example given glances at so many diverse subjects that it seems a potted history of the world set forth in an hour. The science taught there inevitably reminds the reader of the outing of the Mechanics'

Institute, in which science is ignobly reduced to an amusement. Few of the young ladies, one suspects, would be very well equipped to sit an entrance examination to Girton or Somerville. Through their pretty ranks strides their Head, the fiercely Amazonian Ida. The whole subject of female education has been so trivialized as almost to dismiss its seriousness. In 1884 when W. S. Gilbert was writing his burlesque of the poem, *Princess Ida*, he had little about the university to change to suit a farcical musical treatment.

With Ida's conversion to love at the end of the poem the whole project of female education has been quietly forgotten, for it has been transmuted into the consideration of the relation between the sexes and that in turn has melted into the very personal question of Ida's femininity, so that Tennyson has successfully avoided the problem that he proposed for himself. Even Ida's personality receives its most potent statement not in plot but in the lyrics that thread through the story. It is almost as if Tennyson's deepest allegiance to lyricism had subverted his deliberate attempt to transcend it.

The change from the light-hearted beginning of the poem to the solemnity of the ending has plenty of precedent and would be unimportant if it were not that the mock-heroic posturings of the first sections inevitably colour the reader's reactions to the version of the Turandot legend that succeeds them, so that it is hard to take Princess Ida as seriously as Tennyson intends. In self-exculpation at the end of the poem, Tennyson says in the person of the narrator that by trying to mediate between the mockers and the realists,

> I moved as in a strange diagonal,
> And maybe neither pleased myself nor them.

Tennyson's attitudes to the position of women in the modern world are easy enough to trace. At one extreme is the cynically sexual opinion of the Prince's father:

> Man is the hunter; woman is his game:
> The sleek and shining creatures of the chase,
> We hunt them for the beauty of their skins;
> They love us for it, and we ride them down.

Opposed to this is Ida's belief that women can do everything that men can, and better. Tennyson is constantly suggesting that in taking on masculine attributes women are unknowingly paying tribute to the superiority of men, and that the only way the sexes can ever achieve equality is for each of them to develop its own potentiality to the full.

Ida has to give up her masculine hardness to find fulfilment, just as the Prince has to put off his feminine garments in order to become a whole man.

But Tennyson would not be himself as a poet if his best means of persuasion were discursive. One way in which he advances his argument is by the gradually changing meaning of language and metaphor. One example occurs at the beginning of the poem when Ida says that lack of knowledge has kept women from growing into maturity, and that 'they must lose the child, assume/The woman'. Initially it seems a simple statement of her feminist beliefs, then the reader begins to look beyond her intended meaning and to recognize that it may also mean that a denial of her own nature causes woman to be deprived of motherhood and of the love of children that is the civilizing portion of both man's and woman's nature. Finally, losing the child to 'assume the woman' suggests that the unmaternal woman is only assuming the name of woman, precisely as she would assume a disguise. The phrase has come to mean exactly the opposite of what Ida first intended.

Ida's transformation is forecast by her reading 'Come down, O maid', with its suggestions of the richness of marriage, and by the even more explicitly sexual symbolism of the other lyric she reads over the half-conscious Prince:

> Now sleeps the crimson petal, now the white;
> Nor waves the cypress in the palace walk;
> Nor winks the gold fin in the porphyry font:
> The fire-fly wakens: waken thou with me.
>
> Now droops the milkwhite peacock like a ghost,
> And like a ghost she glimmers on to me.
>
> Now lies the Earth all Danaë to the stars,
> And all thy heart lies open unto me.
>
> Now slides the silent meteor on, and leaves
> A shining furrow, as thy thoughts in me.
>
> Now folds the lily all her sweetness up,
> And slips into the bosom of the lake:
> So fold thyself, my dearest, thou, and slip
> Into my bosom and be lost in me.

Indeed, these two lyrics are so complete in their suggestion that what succeeds them is almost anti-climactic.

Both in the lyrics that carry forward the emotional burden of the action and in the blank verse of the narrative proper Tennyson displays the technical ease and virtuosity of a great poet. It is difficult to quarrel with his opinion that this was some of the best blank verse he ever wrote, particularly in such passages as that describing the Prince's circuitous route to his father's camp:

> one, that clashed in arms,
> By glimmering lanes and walls of canvas led
> Threading the soldier-city, till we heard
> The drowsy folds of our great ensign shake
> From blazon'd lions o'er the imperial tent
> Whispers of war.

In 1850 Tennyson added the six songs that stand between the sections of the poem, in order to make clearer the emblematic importance of the child as the harmony of the sexes. Later that year, on his honeymoon, he began writing the sections on the Prince's inherited 'weird seizures' which have so worried critics ever since. Part of his intention was to show that love and marriage reconcile the real and the apparent, the actual and the ideal, so that a split vision is no longer necessary in an integrated personality. Beyond that, however, many readers have suspected that the seizures have a personal meaning for the poet that never quite gets into solution in the poem. Surely, Princess Ida's cure of the Prince glances obliquely at the power of Emily Sellwood's love for Alfred Tennyson; in addition his recovery seems to bear testimony to Tennyson's own recovery from the fear of trance and epilepsy. Undeniably, this part of the poem is slightly awkward, but we can see from it how Tennyson tried to magnify the meaning of his own experience to that of the condition of other men.

The emotional strain of preparing the poem for press when he was so unsure about it was too much for Tennyson, and while he was waiting for it to appear he had briefly to undergo water treatment once more, but he did not return this time to either Prestbury or Umberslade. On 7 December 1847 his mother and his aunt Fytche wrote to Frederick about Malvern, where they had been staying with Mrs Russell while she was being treated by hydropathy. 'Alfred has been spending a short time with us, he has been in the water cure at Malvern with Dr Gully who is a very clever man. He talks of going to Rome after Christmas . . .'[19] As usual, the talk of going abroad was no more than that.

There is scant record of Tennyson's stay this time in Malvern, but he was obviously much impressed by Dr Gully, who sensibly told him that his troubles came from his own self-indulgence rather than from inherited epilepsy, and that 'he wd. probably have some Paralysis at about 55: but, if he went on smoking, *sooner*'.[20] With that warning rining in his ears he went back to London to his lodgings in Ebury Street, almost directly across from the Brookfields, of whom he saw a good bit at this time.

CHAPTER XXI

FINANCIAL SECURITY AND MARRIAGE, 1848–1850

THE early reviews of *The Princess* were divided in appreciation, most of them praising its extraordinary beauty while deploring a feeling of emptiness at its heart. Tennyson was by now so well known that the pleasure of discovering a major poet had been exhausted, and the reviewers instead grumbled that he had not yet developed into what he ought to be. But there was no agreement on what that was, except that some of them thought it was time he put on the robes of a prophet and told the age how to conduct itself. The grumbling was in itself implicit recognition of his stature as a poet, but Tennyson, with his abnormal sensitivity to reviews, was greatly disappointed, even though he had said bravely enough before publication that he did not expect the poem to be popular. All the same, the first edition was sold out within a month or two, and by 1851 there had been four editions.

As he had expected, Fitz's reaction was one of disappointment at the waste of Tennyson's poetic powers on a 'grotesque abortion' at a time when he should be at the peak of his creativity. With his usual bluntness Carlyle said simply that the poem had 'everything but common-sense'. The reaction from Bayons was not unexpected: Ellen Tennyson d'Eyncourt wrote to her father that 'Alfred Tennysons new Poem called "The Princess" is just published—but Emma says it contains but little beauty'.[1] Since her letter was written only six days after the publication date it at least shows how anxious the family were to hear about the works of the relative who seemed so unaccountably popular.

In his relaxed moments Tennyson had a splendid sense of humour about himself, but it was seldom in evidence when his poetry was attacked. One pleasant record of his reactions to the disappointment of his friends and reviewers was his casual remark at a London dinner table at the time: 'I don't think that since Shakespeare there has been such a master of the English language as I.' When the other guests looked embarrassed he continued calmly, 'To be sure, I've got nothing to say.'² Had he always been able to laugh at himself in this way, he would have been a far happier man.

Like most writers, Tennyson was thinking of the next work by the time the last was published; at the beginning of 1848 he was turning back to the gigantic project that he had already deserted twice, his treatment of the Arthurian legend. He felt the need of time to himself to prepare for such a work, but it was impossible for him to resist the stroking of his vanity that came with the incessant invitations pouring into his Ebury Street lodgings. They arrived in acknowledgement of his increasing fame, but also because he was delightful but eccentric as either guest or host. When he was entertaining, no trouble was too much. Once, when he was giving a dinner party for the Brookfields and Lady Duff Gordon, he rearranged his entire set of rooms in order to give the ladies a retiring room and brought in a cook and servants to supplement those of his landlady. It is a mark of his charm that he became a friend of Lady Duff Gordon at all after his odd behaviour when they were introduced. She used to tell, not without malice, how on their first meeting he lay at full length on the carpet, then rolled himself over to her and said, 'Will you please to put your foot on me for a stool.'³ Only a man of considerable magnetism could have got away with behaviour of that sort in a Victorian drawing-room.

Early in January 1848 he went off to Ireland to stay with Aubrey de Vere, whom he had missed on his visit to Ireland in 1842. Before accepting the invitation he set conditions about his stay: there was to be no mention of Irish distress, he was not to be expected downstairs for breakfast, he was to be allowed half the day alone for writing, and he might smoke in the house. When de Vere agreed, they set out for Curragh Chase, the de Vere house in County Limerick.

The eccentricities of behaviour that passed muster in Lincolnshire and even in the more relaxed circles of London seemed very odd in the stiff provincial society of western Ireland, and Tennyson proved an awkward guest, growling at whatever he disapproved of and becoming truculently English among the Irish. For all that, de Vere found himself 'growing very much attached to him', and in looking at his guest he 'felt all at once such an affection for him as made his noble face look very dim and misty'. Tennyson talked to de Vere of how badly he wanted to marry, but he did not mention Emily Sellwood's name, and few of his friends had ever heard of her before their marriage. De Vere judged that he would 'not be right until he has some one to love him exclusively'.⁴

De Vere had lured Tennyson with the promise of waves that would make those of Beachy Head or Mablethorpe or Cornwall look paltry, and after leaving Curragh he went to the island of Valencia to stay with the old Knight of Kerry on the western extremity of Ireland, where the waves seemed to pound in from thousands of miles away. Staring out at the ocean, Tennyson said that all the revolutions of Europe that were lit in 1848 had dwindled into irrelevance.

On his way home he stopped at the lake of Killarney and there heard a bugler playing by a ruined castle, the echoes continuing until he had heard nine of them, the 'last like a chant of angels in the sky'.[5] At the time Tennyson was writing the poems that were to be put between the sections of *The Princess*, and the echoes of Killarney became the germ of 'The splendour falls'.

He had been in Ireland about three months, and when he returned to London he plunged with his old vigour into the round of London social life, naturally wearing himself out again. He professed to long for a solitary 'pint of pale ale and a chop' rather than being 'be-dined usque ad nauseam', but it was difficult to resist the invitations.

One evening typical of many that spring was spent at Patmore's house, where the other guest of honour was the American writer Emerson, who was in London on his way to France. At dinner Tennyson told wild stories of his Irish stay. Emerson found him 'cultivated, quite unaffected . . . [with] the air of one who is accustomed to be petted and indulged by those he lives with'. After dinner they all set off for Brookfield's, with Tennyson riding outside on the box of the omnibus. Brookfield told Emerson that Tennyson would probably go with him to France if pressed. 'That is the way we do with him. We tell him, he must go, & he goes. But you will find him heavy to carry.' Unexpectedly, Tennyson suggested Italy instead, but Emerson (perhaps worried by Brookfield's comments) was resolute for France. Subsequently he visited Tennyson in his lodgings, where their conversation proved disappointing to him.[6] It is interesting to speculate on what a joint trip would have been like; Tennyson was somewhat anti-American, and a continued draught of the clear cold water of Emerson's New England discourse would either have driven him mad or have cured him of his prejudices.

Because of its Celtic background on the coasts of Ireland, Wales, Cornwall, and Brittany, the Arthurian myth was always intimately connected in Tennyson's mind with the sea, a connection that is borne out by the imagery of the *Idylls of the King*, in which, according to the

Concordance to Tennyson's works, 'sea' occurs forty-four times and 'waves' eighteen. It had been his wish to spend the previous winter ' "alone with God," on the rocky coast of Cornwall, beside the wintry sea', saturating himself in the atmosphere of the Arthurian country.[7] At the end of May 1848 he finally went to Cornwall; on the night of his arrival in Bude he cried out, 'Where is the sea? Show me the sea', and foolishly running out in the dark fell over a wall to the 'fanged cobbles' six feet below, gashing his leg so badly it did not heal for six weeks.

Two days later he was taken by his doctor to meet his brother-in-law, the Cornish poet Robert Stephen Hawker, Rector of Morwenstow. Tennyson hobbled up a cliff with Hawker to sit with Tintagel in full sight while he spoke of the purpose of his trip. 'He is about to conceive a Poem—the Hero King Arthur—the Scenery in part the vanished Land of Lyonesse, between the Mainland and the Scilly Isles.'

Hawker called Tennyson 'a tall swarthy Spanish-looking man, with an eye like a sword', and he was startled by the Spanish cloak and wide-brimmed hat that Tennyson wore. It is hard to imagine how anyone's clothes could have surprised Hawker, who habitually wore a purple cassock, a blue fisherman's jersey with a red cross knitted at the spot where Christ's side had been pierced by the centurion's spear, hessian boots, and a round brimless hat like those of the Greek clergy. In a county full of eccentric clergymen he was surely the strangest, with a nature compounded of kindness, excessive affection for animals, heroism in saving the shipwrecked, practical joking, poetical mysticism, and simple piety.

Over the bottle at dinner Tennyson admitted that 'his chief reliance for bodily force was on Wine', and, said Hawker, 'I should conceive he yielded to the conqueror of Ariadne ever and anon'.[8]

From Morwenstow Tennyson went to Tintagel, then spent another six weeks moving slowly around Cornwall, chiefly in the coastal villages, swimming, stopping at inns for beer and a pipe, seeing the lighthouses on the Lizard ('two southern eyes of England'), trying endlessly to find words to describe the swing of the sea. And everywhere he kept a brief journal. On 6 July, for example: 'Went to Land's End by Logan rock, leaden-backed mews wailing on cliff, one with two young ones. Mist. Great yellow flare just before sunset. Funeral. Land's End and Life's End.'

He spent one evening and the whole of the following day with the Rundle family in the country house where they were staying near Plymouth. The daughter of the house wrote a long account of his conversation, in which he was given his head, with no one to rival him. As he became increasingly confident it was splendid talk, ranging from the Ichthyosaurus to Goethe, from eating gooseberries to *Revelations*. After hours of talking, he surprised them by saying, 'You would not think me a shy man, but I am always shy with false or conventional people.' Miss Rundle took it all down in a transcription that occupies four pages of miniscule type in Hallam Tennyson's biography of his father. Tennyson's laconic comment on the two days was written in his Plymouth hotel: 'Flea'd at night.'[9]

Tennyson left Cornwall in the middle of July, then became a patient once more in Dr Gully's establishment in Malvern. He spent at least one and perhaps as many as three months there, and by autumn his treatment was finished. This was his last water treatment, after which he seems to have regarded himself as cured.

Dr Gully had doubtless made it clear to Tennyson in his earlier stay in Malvern that his illness was not inherited epilepsy. Gully was surely also the source of Tennyson's reiterated statement that the root of his troubles was gout. The supposition is strengthened by Gully's drastic curtailment of his drinking. As Hawker had noticed at Morwenstow and Fitz had often remarked, alcohol had become increasingly necessary to Tennyson. Patmore said that he needed at least a bottle of port daily for stimulation, although he was not particular about its quality but simply bought whatever was available at the nearest public house. Gully allowed his patients nothing to drink at Malvern, and when Tennyson left he was under orders to have no more than two glasses daily, which sounds like the standard contemporary treatment for gout. However, marriage was now possible, since he need not worry about passing on the family epilepsy to his children. Furthermore, a wife could be of great help in keeping him from drinking too much.

In the more than seven years since the interruption of their engagement, little had happened to Emily Sellwood except that she had begun to believe that the cold winds of Lincolnshire were giving her consumption, and in 1847 she and her father had moved to Hale Place near Farnham in search of milder surroundings. The breaking of Lincolnshire ties seemed appropriate, since it was improbable that she and Alfred would ever marry. For a time Louisa Turner, who had suffered a mental breakdown during her estrangement from Charles, lived with Emily and her father. In all that time Emily had probably seen Tennyson only once, by accident in early 1848 at Park House, when both she and the Lushingtons believed that he had gone to Italy.

'Your father appeared unexpectedly before breakfast,' she later told her sons. 'I returned home to Hale as soon after as I could.'[10]

The strong new erotic tone of *The Princess* suggests that marriage had finally become necessary to Tennyson, and some time after its publication, presumably after he had seen her at Park House, he wrote to Emily to ask her to end her years of waiting. But she refused in spite of still loving him. H. D. Rawnsley, on whose authority the story of the renewed proposal rests, suggests that she was doubtful about the possibility of reconciling the differences in their religious opinions. Edmund Lushington, however, believed that the bar to their marriage was only financial, and he offered to give up his carriage and horses in order to help them, but they refused, as they had earlier declined Tennyson's mother's offer of help. Neither of these sounds like a compelling reason for Emily's refusal, but whatever the truth of it may have been Tennyson did not take it as irrevocable and in 1849 he renewed his suit.

After leaving Malvern he spent more time than usual in Cheltenham, largely because he hated to neglect his mother, but he lived a life somewhat apart from his family, confining most of his home activity to reading, smoking, and talking among the litter of books in the study at the top of the St. James's Square house. Mrs Tennyson had come under the influence of the apocalyptic teachings of Dr John Cumming, and Alfred would tease her about her beliefs. If she was pressed too far, the tears sprang to her eyes, at which he would say with tenderness, 'Dam your eyes, mother, dam your eyes!' Inevitably he called her pet monkey St. Simeon Stylites, since it loved to perch on a pole in the garden. In spite of his teasing of his mother he was becoming more concerned with religion himself, possibly spurred on by Emily Sellwood's exemplary piety. 'It is rugging at my heart,' he would say of Christianity. But Emily had been right if she worried about his orthodoxy, for he was certainly no regular church-goer, and so far almost all that he could accept completely was a belief in personal immortality, without which he could see no purpose in life.

He took long walks to forget the provinciality of Cheltenham, and on one occasion even proposed to escape it by a balloon ascent from Montepelier Gardens, but when his mother and sisters heard of his 'mad resolve' they were so unhappy that he had to give it up.[11]

It is probable that another form of escape from the boredom of Cheltenham was drink. By November, when he was back in London, FitzGerald wrote that he 'now drinks a bottle of wine a day, and smokes as before; a sure way to throw back in a week or two all the benefit (if benefit there were) which resulted from many weeks of privation and penance—'. To be sure, Fitz took a gloomy pleasure in noting the slow dissolution of one of the few men he knew who was more undisciplined than himself, and he may have exaggerated at times, but there is real despair in another letter he wrote then about Tennyson's being 'half-cured, or half-destroyed'; he had 'gone to a new Doctor who gives him iron pills; and altogether this really great man thinks more about his bowels and nerves than about the Laureate wreath he was born to inherit. . . . I believe the trumpet can wake Tennyson no longer to do *great* deeds . . . how are we to expect heroic poems from a valetudinary?'[12]

Despite Fitz's mopishness over him, Tennyson's affairs had begun to improve greatly before the end of 1848. First of all, there was renewed hope for his family. Charles Turner now seemed to be in control of his opium addiction, and Louisa was apparently recovered from her mental breakdown; within the year they were happily reunited, to live together most of the time until their deaths within a month of each other thirty-one years later. Frederick, who was always improvident with his inheritance, had invested in railway shares, and with the collapse of their value in the panic of the summer of 1848 he had to borrow heavily from his sisters and brothers, including Alfred, to repay obligations to the Lincoln bank. To get the money, his sisters demanded it with their usual peremptoriness of their uncle Charles, who found himself embarrassed to return it, even though his income was now at least £3,000 more than it had been when he first inherited. But while he was at his lowest there was a dramatic reversal of Frederick's fortunes when the new docks at Grimsby were built on land that he owned, so that by the middle of 1849 he was once more in comfortable circumstances.

Financially, the advance in Alfred's fortunes was much smaller, but it was at least as unexpected. The second edition of *The Princess* was selling well, since the later reviews had been enthusiastic, but there was little reason to believe that the poem would ever make him independent. In either December 1848 or, more probably, January 1849*,

---

*There is a good deal of contradictory, apparently irreconcilable evidence about the date when Moxon made his offer to publish *In Memoriam*, how much the offer was, and when Tennyson renewed his suit of Emily Sellwood. Most of it is summarized by W. D. Paden in 'A Note on the Variants of *In Memoriam* and *Lucretius*'; Joseph Sendry; and Susan Shatto and Marian Shaw, to whom I am particularly indebted. There is no room here to rehearse the arguments, but the present account is what

Moxon was visiting Alfred, according to Charles Turner, and asked, 'if he had been writing anything of late, with a view to issuing a vol. for him. On which Alfred said emphatically "No." Moxon then said surely you have not been idle? Alfred said that he had been writing for his own relief & private satisfaction some things that the public would have no interest in, and would not care to see. Moxon asked to see the Ms. It was "In Memoriam". Moxon was delighted, &, to Alfreds utter astonishment, offered to publish it and to hand him a cheque to a/c on the spot. (If my memory serves me I think the amt. was £300.)'[13]

Frederick's recovery of his fortune and Charles's return to his cure at Grasby meant that the family finances were no longer anything about which Alfred had to worry, and Moxon's offer indicated that he could now count on a real competence from his writing. According to Hallam Tennyson, Moxon also offered to guarantee a small annual income if he were allowed to publish Tennyson exclusively.

Tennyson still had cold feet about the publication of these, the most nakedly personal poems he had ever written, and rather than accept the offer at once he decided to have trial copies set up and distributed to his closest friends for comment, with strict injunctions of secrecy. He had already read many of the individual sections aloud in the long smoke-filled evenings with cronies in London, sometimes with his voice breaking and the tears streaking secretly down his face. Now he felt sufficiently composed to allow more dispassionate criticism than would have been possible at the readings.

At the end of 1848 he had been staying in Venables' chambers in Mitre Court, but the woman in charge was constantly out at her Roman Catholic chapel, the chimney smoked, and the lock was broken, so that he dared not go out and leave the rooms unattended. Early in 1849 he fled to the Isle of Wight for some three or four weeks, and while there he discovered that he had left the manuscript of the 'Elegies' in the cupboard where he kept his tea and bread and butter in Mitre Court. He wrote to Patmore and asked him to stop on his way to work at the British Museum, and to retrieve the 'butcher's account book' in which the poems were written. He was not particularly worried, since there were other copies of the poems and he had most of

---

seems to me the most probable and sensible ordering of the events; new evidence, however, might change some of the details. Much of the confusion in chronology was no doubt introduced deliberately by Hallam Tennyson to hide the fact that his parents were not married for a year and a half after the last possible financial barriers to their union had been removed.

them by memory. Characteristically, Patmore hurried to Mitre Court and excitedly demanded to search the cupboard. 'The landlady assured me that no such book had been left there, and objected to my going to see; but I insisted, and, pushing by her, ran upstairs and found the manuscript.'[14] Patmore, who could create a good bit of drama with little or no material, told his friends that Tennyson 'had no other copy, and he never remembers his verses'.

Mrs Patmore copied out the poems for the trial edition, and Tennyson let her and her husband keep the original book, reminding them both that its contents were not to be shown to anyone else. In August 1849, when William Allingham was at their house, Patmore could not resist saying mysteriously, 'I have in this room perhaps the greatest literary treasure in England—the manuscript of Tennyson's *next poem*', adding that he had 'found it by chance'. He took it from a cabinet and flipped the pages before Allingham's curious eyes without allowing him to read them, and would not even reveal the name of the poem, although he insisted it was Tennyson's best work.[15] It was lack of knowledge not conscientiousness, however, that kept him from giving the name, since Tennyson had not yet decided on one.

Tennyson himself had no hesitation about showing the poem, even to casual acquaintances like Francis Palgrave, to whom he read it two days after their first meeting. But it was his own secret, and no matter how often he gave it away he hated having others mention it. By November Patmore had presumably decided the prohibition no longer held, and he showed the poems to William Rossetti. Tennyson was unhappy when he heard how free Patmore was with the poems, and that is presumably part of the reason he asked for the return of the manuscript. None of this helped relations between the two men, nor did Mrs Patmore's irritating habit of referring familiarly to Tennyson in conversation as if he were one of her best friends. It was not long before Patmore was feeling the itch of disenchantment with Tennyson, suggesting that Browning was a better poet, and believing that he had been mistaken in his first impressions of Tennyson, when he 'used to follow him about like a dog'.[16]

There were plenty of other candidates for the place he was vacating. Palgrave was only too ardent in his enthusiasm. He met Tennyson at Brookfield's and was invited to his lodgings in Hampstead. Palgrave, who had been assistant private secretary to Gladstone, was a self-assertive little man with a cast in his eye, not long down from Oxford. Two days after meeting Tennyson he went to Hampstead and 'with a

mixed sense of fear and delight (almost as if about to make a proposal), I accordingly climbed to the upper floor of his lodgings'. In his
recollections of the visit Palgrave said that he had 'a dim perception
that the man was even greater than the work: a perception, as the years
went by, to be revealed how clearly! and, I trust, to be recognized
throughout these memorials, like the deep rich bass note of the violon-
cello, supporting the melodies above it'. Such unclouded adoration of
himself and such unqualified enthusiasm for his poetry was more
important to Tennyson than a sensible prose style, and for years he
allowed Palgrave to follow him around and perform unpleasant tasks.
Only a man of monumental insensitivity or incredible masochistic
leanings could have failed to notice Tennyson's contempt and to have
given up the friendship, but Palgrave persisted, and before the end of
his life Tennyson had become so accustomed to him and his purple
prose that he felt gratitude and even reluctant affection for the younger
man, so perhaps Palgrave had been right all along in believing that he
was necessary to Tennyson.

Two other young men who made their first acquaintance with him
at this time were Thomas Woolner and Edward Lear. Woolner, who
was already making his name as a Pre-Raphaelite sculptor, met Tennyson first in 1848 and was immediately fascinated by his massive
head. Woolner was acquainted with Patmore and through him tried to
get Tennyson to sit for a bust. 'Patmore says Tennyson is too lazy to go
to Woolner's for his portrait, but will be at home for him any evening
he may call,' wrote William Rossetti.[17] It was not until Tennyson's
honeymoon in 1850 that Woolner finally got him as a subject, and
after that their acquaintance ripened into friendship.

Lear was a friend of the Lushingtons, and in particular of Franklin
Lushington, for whom he felt deep love, undoubtedly homosexual at
the root. He first met Tennyson in June 1849 at Park House, where he
was an uncertain guest, overwhelmed by the hordes of Lushingtons
and always afraid of being in the way. He was as gentle, unpredictable,
and shy as his verse suggests, and ready to respond warmly to the
slightest overture of affection. Tennyson and Lear had in common one
deep fear of which each was probably unaware in the other during all
the time they were friends: the fear of epilepsy. With Lear, however,
the disease was a terrible actuality that struck unpredictably but
inevitably, sometimes as often as two days out of three. His deep
shame over the disease and his desperate anxiety to conceal it only
contributed to his innate uneasiness, and he led a tormented life from

which he tried to escape by the gaiety of his writing and the tumultuous warmth he returned at the least encouragement from another. He and Tennyson got on well enough, but Tennyson never felt a tithe of the affection that Lear did. After Tennyson's marriage Lear found that his real affinity in the family was with Emily, who became half-mother, half-sister to him. She must have known the tendency of his love for Lushington, but it never bothered her, and she answered his sad letters with reassuring warmth. His increasing affection for Emily made him unduly and unfairly critical of Tennyson's treatment of her, so that a stay with them was agonizing as he chafed over the hurt he imagined she must be feeling, yet knowing in his heart that both the Tennysons provided the family he otherwise lacked. Like Lear, Woolner finally became even more attached to Emily than to Alfred, and the two men provided for her the safe, almost maternally flirtatious relationships with other men that a happily married and deeply conventional woman could undertake.

Another young artist who wanted at this time to make Tennyson's acquaintance was Dante Gabriel Rossetti, but after he met him in October 1849 he became progressively disillusioned with the man, and as he did his admiration for Tennyson's poetry lessened too. Tennyson said of some of Rossetti's early poems that they had 'Cockney rhymes', which did little to endear him to the other. Rossetti, whose sensitive nose as often detected imagined affectation as real, thought Tennyson artificial, and by 1855 he had lost practically all admiration for him.

By now most of Tennyson's old friends were busy with their families and professions, so that travelling companions were harder to find, and as yet none of the young men seemed suitable. In September Tennyson went on a solitary trip to Scotland, but it was not a total success. He stayed in Edinburgh with Francis Garden and his wife, whom he delighted by calling by her Christian name. He and the Gardens, Milnes, and Frederick Pollock had a brief stay at the magnificent house of the Monteiths at Carstairs, then he went off to be by himself in the little village of Millport, but he was driven from there by an outbreak of cholera. On the coach to the Highlands he indulged himself in the innocent vanity of talking with one of his fellow passengers about Tennyson's poetry without revealing who he was until the end of the trip, when he announced his name to the incredulous delight of the other. On the way home he stopped in Ayrshire to visit the Burns country as homage to one of the poets whom he most loved. As

Tintern Abbey had once overcome him with the 'passion of the past' while he thought of Hallam, so he was now suddenly stricken by the associations with Burns: 'When I was sitting by the banks of the Doon—I don't know why—I wasn't in the least spoony—not thinking of Burns (but of the lapsing of the Ages)—when all of a sudden I gave way to a passion of tears.'[18] It is in the lonely moments of life that one is most overwhelmed by the swiftness of the years. And Tennyson was desperately lonely.

In an attempt to soothe his companionless state he went to Lincolnshire in November, and there he was so fêted that he had to postpone his return to London. One Sunday evening he went to dinner at Halton Holgate with his old friends the Rawnsleys, who had staying with them their daugher Sophy Elmhirst and her husband, as well as Colonel and Mrs Weston Cracroft of Hackthorn Hall. In his diary Colonel Cracroft left his impressions of the evening: 'Alfred Tennyson the Poet dined with us. When he lights up his face is almost fine, but his expression coarse when unexcited. On the whole his features coarse, and complexion dirty and sallow—he wears spectacles—conversation agreeable. I was amused when the Poet put his feet up on the sofa and Mrs Rawnsley, careful soul, whom I had observed to grow fidgetty, all of a sudden quietly warned him off.'

In spite of his surprise at Tennyson's manners, Cracroft was pleased with his lively talk and the way he could entertain the whole table. The next day, however, he met Tennyson again at Raithby, and found him 'a scrubby looking fellow by daylight—dress no way neat—in short a poet'. Shortly after that he met Mary Tennyson and liked her 'noble countenance'; a few years later he found Frederick 'a very silent and therefore not very interesting individual, but not quite so dirty looking as the Poet brother'.[19]

Some of Cracroft's disapproving interest in the Tennysons may have sprung from the knowledge that his cousin had been engaged some years before to Alfred, who had then broken the engagement. It is improbable that he would have been pleased had he known that, when they met, Tennyson was already planning the renewal of his suit to Emily Sellwood and within a week was to be in communication with her. It was probably during this trip to Lincolnshire that Tennyson visited Gunby Hall, where he was sketched with a clay pipe by Algernon Langton Massingberd. (See Plate IX.)

On 24 November, immediately after his return to London, Tennyson made another attempt to cure his solitude finally. The evidence is

convincing that he sent a carefully copied pair of alternative versions
of 'Sweet and low' to Emily Sellwood, asking her to choose between
them for the new edition of *The Princess* with its intercalated songs.[20]
The letter she wrote on returning the verses has not survived, but it
gave him renewed hope that she was not opposed to marrying him. His
grandson has written that Tennyson stayed in Farnham, seeing the
Sellwoods, in 1849 'when relations were resumed',[21] which was presumably after she had returned the poem. If so, Tennyson seems not to
have spoken directly about renewing their engagement, although his
presence at Hale Place must have been difficult to explain in other
terms. The indications he received of Emily's feelings were encouraging despite all the years that had passed, and he intended to propose
again before the end of 1849.

Early in December he took chambers in the same house as John
Forster in Lincoln's Inn Fields, then he somewhat mysteriously disappeared from London. On 13 December William Rossetti wrote that
'He is to leave London shortly for a little while, and to return about
Christmas'. Five days later he noted that 'Tennyson has left town, and
will not be back until Sunday, when he thinks of remaining for a
month or so longer'.[22]

Tennyson's destination is revealed in a letter to Drummond Rawnsley saying that he intended to come to Shiplake in mid-December.[23]
What he surely had in mind was to find out from the Rawnsleys what
they knew of Emily's feelings, and to get back into the good graces of
Catherine Rawnsley, who thought with reason that he had behaved
badly in breaking with Emily in 1840. He must have lost his nerve
about speaking to Mrs Rawnsley, however, for on Christmas Day he
sent her a short note: 'I have made up my mind to marry in about a
month. I have much to do & to settle in the mean time. Pray keep this
thing secret. I do not mean even my own family to know. You gave me
a cold shake of the hand when I came away. You should have given me
a warm one.'[24]

In the absence of the letters between Tennyson and Emily before
their marriage what then happened may never be known exactly.
Perhaps Tennyson got cold feet again, for they were epidemic with him
now, and never proposed at all. More probably, Emily refused him
again, insisting upon a settlement of their religious differences. If so,
her refusal had the effect she wanted, the strengthening of Tennyson's
wavering resolution to marry.

While he considered other ways to make Emily change her mind, he completed the revisions of *The Princess*, a new edition of which was published in February 1850 containing the version of 'Sweet and low' that Emily had chosen. Then he set to work in earnest on the 'Elegies'. His task was complicated by losing his manuscripts a second time. A 'domestic thief' stole a quantity of poems from his lodgings,[25] but there was no serious harm done since the original manuscripts had been copied already. It was presumably then that he asked the Patmores to return to him the manuscript that they had been showing too openly. At last, in mid-March 1850 Moxon printed a private trial run of the still untitled poems, which bore the dedication, 'IN MEMORIAM A.H.H. OBIIT MDCCCXXXIII'.

Tennyson sent copies of the poems to his closest friends; there are only three still extant, since he was fierce about demanding that they should not be preserved. In the copy that he gave to Edmund Lushington he wrote: 'Essentially & inconceivably private till its later tho longer brother appear then to die the death by Fire! Mind! A.T.' Lushington followed his instructions, but he kept the warning and pasted it into his copy of the first edition of *In Memoriam*.[26] Venables and de Vere were less obedient. Two persons who rather unexpectedly did not receive copies were FitzGerald and Gladstone. Fitz's lack of enthusiasm over *The Princess* had nettled Tennyson, particularly when Fitz insisted on telling his friends that even the lyrics inserted into the new edition lacked 'the old champagne flavour' and that 'the old vintage of his earlier days' was far superior. There seemed little reason to give him further material for contempt. When Fitz finally read *In Memoriam* he found it monotonous, with an 'air of being evolved by a Poetical Machine of the highest order'.[27] No doubt his dislike was sharpened by his not having been asked to look at a trial copy.

To Gladstone Tennyson sent neither trial printing nor the first edition of the poem. In spite of their surface friendliness, there was always a buried rivalry between them over their feelings for Arthur Hallam, and Tennyson's negligence about sending the poem is tacit evidence that he believed Gladstone had been far less important in Hallam's life than Tennyson himself.

Two copies it would be instructive to see were those sent to Spedding and Drummond Rawnsley. Spedding had been insistent that the poems be published, and Tennyson allowed him to go over them carefully, making corrections and suggestions. He was so thorough that Tennyson said he had 'overhauled' them. The surviving manuscript in Trinity College no longer supports such a statement, since most of Spedding's remaining suggestions are minor verbal changes and alterations of punctuation. It is reasonable to suppose that some of the overhauling took place on the trial copy given to Spedding, but it has disappeared.

The other most important copy, that sent to Rawnsley, had biographical rather than poetical significance. Because relations between Tennyson and Emily Sellwood were still tentative, Tennyson sent a copy of the trial issue to the Rawnsleys, to be turned over to Emily for inspection. It is worth noting that one part of the poem that was apparently written especially for the trial issue was the 'Prologue', which has stood at the head of the poem ever since, clearly dated '1849' as if it had been written after Emily's refusal of Tennyson. It is not out of character with the rest of the poem, but it is more transparently Christian than any other section, reflecting Tennyson's increasing absorption with what had been 'rugging' at his heart. It may be, as has been suggested, that it was written especially to convince Emily of his essentially Christian beliefs. If so, it served its purpose well. The copy reached her within a few days after being printed, and on 30 March 1850 she returned it to the Rawnsleys. Two days later she wrote an unaddressed, unsigned note to be sent to Tennyson:

Katie told me the poems might be kept until Saturday. I hope I shall not have occasioned any inconvenience by keeping them to the limit of the time; and if I have I must be forgiven, for I cannot willingly part from what is so precious. The thanks I would say for them and for the faith in me which has trusted them to me must be thought for me, I cannot write them. I have read the poems through and through and through and to me they were and they are ever more and more a spirit monument grand and beautiful, in whose presence I feel admiration and delight, not unmixed with awe. The happiest possible end to this labour of love! But think not its fruits shall so soon perish, for they are life in life, and they shall live, and as years go on be only the more fully known and loved and reverenced for what they are.

So says a true seer. Can anyone guess the name of this seer? After such big words shall I put anything about my own little I?—that I am the happier for having seen these poems and that I hope I shall be the better too.[28]

'I cannot say what I feel,' she told Catherine Rawnsley, worrying that it might not be specific enough. But the import is clear enough to a casual reader, let alone Tennyson, who was waiting for her answer. He took it for what it was, her admission that she still loved him and was now ready to marry him if he still wished. The 'true seer' to whom she referred was Charles Kingsley, a friend of Rawnsley's. According to her son, 'An urgent message from Charles Kingsley, whose living at Eversley was within a drive of Shiplake, did more than anything to encourage her, and after ten years of separation their engagement was renewed'.[29] There is no proof of Tennyson's ever having met Kingsley before this, although they may have been together at Shiplake the previous December. Kingsley, one of the most extravagantly uxorious men of the century, had been married six years, and he constantly recommended the joys of conjugal love to his friends. Emily's somewhat coy question, 'Can anyone guess the name of this seer?' suggests that she may have thought Tennyson had put him up to the message, but it is hard to believe that a man as private as Tennyson would have allowed a casual acquaintance to intervene in his courtship. Yet Tennyson's gratitude was such that the two men remained close for some years until their friendship cooled briefly when Tennyson thought he was being parodied in one of Kingsley's novels.

Charles Turner, too, interceded on Tennyson's behalf, but since he knew his brother better than Kingsley did what bothered him was the fear that even now Alfred might change his mind. He said 'he could easily bring about a meeting but would not move an inch in the matter till he was satisfied that Alfred had firmly made up his mind to go through with it, and that there were to be no more morbid doubts, conscientious changes, shilly-shallying and such like nonsense'. When he felt convinced of Alfred's constancy, he spoke to his sister-in-law and to old Mr Sellwood, then Emily and Alfred were brought together at Shiplake in May, and the decade-long rupture in their engagement was healed. Even so, Charles said, 'after what happened before, we kept a strict eye upon him, in case he should take it into his head to bolt!!!'[30] Alfred immediately took out a licence on 15 May, almost as if to convince himself that the matter was settled. But he had left himself one last loophole, for a special licence gave him freedom about the time and place of the wedding, as having the banns read would not have done, and it is presumably for this reason that the marriage finally took place at Shiplake rather than in the Sellwoods' parish church.

Once the marriage was finally agreed upon, Emily characteristically began helping Alfred with his work. He had planned on calling the new poem *Fragments of an Elegy*, but she convinced him (correctly, it seems in hindsight) that the dedication itself could stand as a better title. On 1 June 1850 Moxon published the anonymous *In Memoriam*

A.H.H.Obiit MDCCCXXXIII. Less than a fortnight later, on 13 June, Alfred Tennyson and Emily Sellwood were married by Drummond Rawnsley at Shiplake Church.

It all sounds easier than it was. Charles Turner had been right in worrying about Alfred's readiness for marriage. He was neither the first nor the last man in history to find the married state more attractive when it seemed distant or even impossible than when it was imminent, and now he began presenting new difficulties. There was no longer any possibility of saying that he could not afford to marry, and the threat of epilepsy had been removed, but the loss of freedom that nearly everyone worries about in marriage still haunted him. Even after he had the licence Catherine Rawnsley had trouble getting him to set a firm date; she needed to know when the cake was to be ready, and she was arranging to supplement his store of shirts, the dirtiness of which had been the subject of comment by his friends ever since Cambridge, but he continued to plead he was too busy to fix a day. Nor could the Lushingtons force him into a decision. At last, at the beginning of June, he wrote to Mrs Rawnsley: 'It is settled for the 13th, so the shirts may be gone on with.' To his mother he wrote that he 'should have written to let her know earlier, but that he did not know himself till just at the last, as he could not make up his mind'. His sister Mary, who took a gloomy view of the whole proceedings, sympathized with him: 'poor thing, I dare say he is miserable enough at times, thinking of what he is about to do'.[31]

Tennyson was forty-one years old, but his behaviour was that of a hesitant boy. Yet boys can finally be pushed into decisions, and he had at last been unable to resist the combined moral pressure of the Rawnsleys, the Lushingtons, the Turners, Mr Sellwood, Kingsley, and above all the gentle, unspoken obduracy of Emily Sellwood.

Perhaps Tennyson himself felt that he was marrying in recognition of Emily's fidelity rather than his own love: in a letter written immediately after the wedding he described her as a lady 'who has loved me for 14 years without variableness (or any shadow of turning.)'[32] In the letter he praises her nature, but the absence of any statement of his own feelings considerably lowers its temperature.

When his resistance had finally collapsed he gave in with a good grace, not allowing himself to think about the matter again. We do not know whether the shirts were finished, but the wedding-cake was not ready, there was no time to assemble most of the families, and Emily had neither white dress nor gloves. But it might have been risky to postpone the ceremony any longer, for fear the bridegroom would find new reasons for not being there.

Tennyson spent the night before the wedding with the Rawnsleys, while Emily stayed nearby. Mrs Rawnsley's old nurse helped her dress in silvery blue silk, a white bonnet with white ribbons, and a white veil with lace over her shoulders. Just before the ceremony Alfred went into the garden of the Rectory and picked a bouquet for her to carry. To the surprise of the Rawnsleys he was well dressed and clean himself, and in his buttonhole he wore a white satin rosette. There were only a half-dozen guests, since the date had been decided on so quickly that none of the Tennysons except Cecilia and Edmund Lushington were able to attend. It was Lushington who produced the ring, which he had rightly guessed Tennyson would forget. But all went smoothly in spite of the haste, and to the delight of the others Tennyson pronounced it the nicest wedding he had ever been at.

The Rawnsleys had asked the bridal pair to spend their honeymoon at Shiplake, but Emily said at once that she would prefer a short trip. They spent the wedding night at Pangbourne, and the next day Tennyson wrote to Sophy Elmhirst:

> My dear Sophy
>   We seem to get on very well together.
> I have not beaten her yet.
>   ever yours affectionately
>   AT.[33]

Once the wedding was over Tennyson found himself at ease in a way he had never been before. 'The peace of God came into my life before the altar when I wedded her,' he said. In spite of his having resisted so long, there is no reason to think that he ever regretted his marriage for a moment. It was the end of his lonely wanderings, his frequent feelings of being an outsider at the hearths of his friends, and it finished the worst of his depressions and melancholia. He had deep respect for Emily's religious feelings, and she was the first person after Hallam whose instincts about his own poetry he trusted almost totally. Since her taste in poetry was more than a little conventional, it has often been suggested that her influence tamed his poetic genius and turned him from a rebellious Romantic into a conforming Victorian. Certainly, his poetry did change considerably after his marriage, not always for the better, and she probably did nothing to encourage him to experiment, but there was little in the alteration of his poetry that cannot be ascribed as easily to advancing age as to Emily's influence. What is certain is that she brought a new order into his life without which he could hardly have continued his existence. For the first time his letters were answered, his bills paid, his friends entertained, his meals on time, and his clothes moderately clean. Dull achievements, perhaps, but they relieved him of the necessity of thinking of such things himself.

His relationship with Emily inevitably brings to mind that with his mother when he was a boy, for the two women were alike in being gentle, delicate, rather ethereal and unphysical in manner, calling forth Tennyson's innately chivalrous attitude to women. In later years he pulled Emily around in a chair, just as he had pulled his mother when he was young. But beneath her delicate profile and saintly expression Emily Tennyson had a will of steel quite unlike that of her mother-in-law. Her will drove her into undertaking many things that her frail constitution would have denied to a less dedicated woman, and it constantly stiffened Alfred's backbone when that was necessary. Most of his friends were charmed by her, although some like Fitz-Gerald thought that she stood too protectively between them and Alfred. Because of her ill-health she was unable to accept many invitations for both of them, but she tried to make up for that by constantly filling the house with men of widely differing kinds of mind for Alfred to talk to. With the rest of the Tennyson family she was only moderately successful; her mother-in-law, Cecilia, Charles, and Matilda were fond of her, but Frederick and Mary both thought she was too ambitious socially and financially, for Alfred if not for herself.

At the time of their marriage Tennyson was forty-one, she was thirty-seven. As his earlier life would have suggested, it was almost certainly not a passionate marriage. His choice of an invalid wife approaching middle age was no indication of overwhelming sexuality. Before their marriage Emily had frequently been confined to a sofa by spinal trouble, and her affliction worsened afterwards. There was surely a physical cause of her increasing illness, but it is hard to avoid the suspicion that it was also connected psychologically with a dislike for or difficulty with sex. Certainly, within a short time after their marriage they habitually went to bed at different hours, and during much of their life together they occupied separate bedrooms. None of it conclusive evidence, but it does not suggest deep passion. There was plenty of tenderness, however, and great affection; their letters to one another could not have been written had they not loved each other deeply. The nature of the marriage may have been unexpected, but it was successful. When Emily Tennyson died four years after Alfred, it was touchingly appropriate that almost her last words were: 'I have tried to be a good wife.'[34]

CHAPTER XXII

✵

THE GOLDEN YEAR: *IN MEMORIAM* AND THE LAUREATESHIP, 1850

'MARRIED!! is it possible?' wrote the incredulous de Vere. 'Well I do most heartily wish you all happiness in your marriage: but I want to hear something more about it than the bare fact. Spedding who gave me the news was not even certain of the lady's name. Who is she & have you known her long, & how long has the marriage been determined on, & why did you keep it so close & not say a word about it to any of your friends?' His startled pleasure was typical of the reaction of Tennyson's friends, although some of them shared the bridegroom's fear that he had been unmarried so long he had 'crystallized into batchlerhood beyond redemption'.[1]

Tennyson's secrecy about his marriage disturbed at least two of his friends. Venables wrote enigmatically in his journal that the wedding was 'A strange piece of news. It would once have given me extreme pleasure—but now like all other things it has drawbacks.'[2] John Forster, who was less interested in the fact of Tennyson's marriage than in being able to gossip about it himself, was furious, since Tennyson had 'held his peace' when Forster specifically asked his intentions only a few days before the event. All that Forster had to go on was rumour: 'Alfred's wife has had indifferent health, and indeed (like the lady Browning married) has passed half her life hitherto on the sofa—but marriage is often a restorer; at least has proved so in Miss Barrett's case, and may be expected to be no less so in this. . . . The only anecdote told, in connection with any public announcement of the affair, was mentioned to me on Sunday by Lushington, who says that Alfred will gladly give 7/6 out of his limited income (for a married man) to every penny-a-liner who will keep it *out of the papers*.'[3] Tennyson was able to placate Forster only by telling him that it had all taken place so suddenly that even his family had known almost nothing of it.

Mary Tennyson, who was also nettled that she had been told so little of the marriage beforehand, and perhaps that she had not been invited to the ceremony, took notice of the wedding with her habitual gloom, changing the day of the wedding and the weather to fit her forebodings: 'Well, all is over. . . . *Friday*, [actually Thursday] *and raining*, about which I feel very superstitious. . . . Emily looked bright, they say. . . . I hope they will be happy, but I feel very doubtful about it.'[4] Most of the family were more charitable. Charles Turner sent his delighted 'good wishes in crowds' to his 'dear Double sister & long-single brother',[5] and Mrs Russell characteristically enclosed £50 with her invitation to use Brancepeth for the honeymoon.

Milnes offered them a wing of Fryston, but they instead accepted the invitation of Mr and Mrs James Marshall (she was the sister of Stephen Spring-Rice, whom Tennyson had known at Cambridge) to spend some time in Tent Lodge on the edge of the grounds of Monk Coniston, the Marshalls' house overlooking Coniston Water.

They made their way to the Lakes slowly, going first to Weston-super-Mare, from which they took a day's excursion to Clevedon at Emily's request, to call on the Eltons in Clevedon Court and to see the tablet to Arthur Hallam's memory in the parish church. It was apparently Tennyson's first visit to Hallam's tomb, although he had been near it several times since Hallam's death in 1833. He is said to have stayed in Clevedon Court in 1839, and on at least one occasion, in 1845, he stayed only three or four miles away with old Mr Hallam. It is surprising that he should not have seen the tomb before, but perhaps the memory of his dead friend would have been too painful until it was partially exorcized by his own marriage. Emily Tennyson was shrewd enough to know that Hallam's memory could become their joint property if they saw his tomb together. 'It seemed a kind of consecration to go there,' she said.

They went on to Devonshire and Exmoor, then to Glastonbury with its Arthurian associations and the refectory built by John de Selwode, 'of the same name and race' as Emily. Their progress took them through Clifton and Bath to Cheltenham to pay their respects to Mrs Tennyson, then to the Lake Country. Their first visit in the Lakes was to Mirehouse, where Emily met James Spedding, who with his usual pawky humour had brought all the old socks that Tennyson had discarded in his London bachelor lodgings and laid them out on the Tennysons' bed, with their holes showing, as mute evidence of the change in his friend's fortunes.

At Tent Lodge Emily had her initiation into the circle that surrounded Tennyson. The Marshalls, who were part of a huge family network of enormously wealthy linen manufacturers, loved having literary and artistic guests: 'Sir, we keeps a Poet,' said Carlyle sarcastically of them.[6] Besides Carlyle, Venables, de Vere (who was related to Mrs Marshall), Woolner, Patmore, Franklin Lushington, Lear, and Matthew Arnold ('then in the hey-day of youth') all came to stay with the Marshalls or to meet Tennyson's bride. They rowed and walked, drove to see Wordsworth's house at Rydal, 'but did not go in'. On one splendid August day Tennyson and Patmore climbed Coniston Old Man, and though the ascent of the mountain took five hours they thought the labour worthwhile as they stood at the top looking through the rents in the stormy skies at Westmoreland, Lancashire, and Yorkshire spread out before them. To keep up their strength they resorted more and more frequently to the bottle they had with them, got 'rather glorious', and raced unsteadily down the mountain 'six times faster than we had ascended'.[7]

Meeting so many of Alfred's old friends was something of an ordeal for Emily, but she managed to charm them. De Vere in particular was pleased to see that 'her great and constant desire is to make her husband more religious', and he had 'never before had half so much pleasure in Alfred's society. He is far happier than I ever saw him before; and his "wrath against the world" is proportionately mitigated.'[8] Though de Vere thought Alfred was gravitating towards more orthodox Christianity, Tennyson disappointed Emily by refusing to attend church, but on at least one wet Sunday he read aloud prayers, lessons, and a sermon by F. D. Maurice.

It was the other side of Emily's nature, her gritty independence, that won over Carlyle. Only a month or two before their wedding he had told his brother that Tennyson was looking 'very mouldery and dilapidated . . . does nothing but travel in railways and dine; his "work-arm" seemingly as good as broken'. He knew that it would take a woman of character to handle Tennyson. His first meeting with Emily was frightening for her, as he stood scanning her from head to foot before shaking her hand. At dinner he grumbled until she could stand it no longer, and though she saw Alfred looking apprehensively at her she finally said in response to one of his more outrageous statements, 'Mr Carlyle, you know that that is not sane.' It may have reminded him of Jane, for he was delighted. The next day he called again, and when he heard her cough he quietly went and closed the window behind her. 'The first glance of her is the least favourable,' he wrote to his wife. 'A freckly *round*-faced woman, rather tallish and without shape, a slight lisp too: something very *kleinstädtisch* and unpromising at the first glance; but she lights up bright glittering blue eyes when you speak to her; has wit, has sense, and were it not that she seems so very delicate in health, "sick *without* a disorder," I should augur well of Tennyson's adventure.'[9]

As his friends noticed, Emily constantly encouraged Alfred to get on with the composition of his poetry, and at Coniston she would send him out on long walks so that he might have time alone. Appropriately enough, he was composing the new sections of *The Princess*, the recovery of the Prince from the 'weird seizures', which were completed and written out the following January. His concentration was so intense that he would often pass the entrance to Tent Lodge until Emily had the gatepost painted white to catch his attention.

The only unpleasantness on his honeymoon was the receipt of a clipping from an American newspaper expressing the 'hope now that Mr Tennyson is married and has returned to his native lakes, that he will give up opium'.[10] It was a libel that was to haunt him all of his life and that even today still crops up occasionally. Presumably it derived ultimately from a confusion with the weakness of his father and his brother Charles. It was particularly unpleasant because it was the kind of rumour to which he could make no reply.

When they left Coniston on 14 October for Cheltenham, they travelled with Matthew Arnold. Neither poet left any record of their meeting and trip, which is perhaps as well, since they were never friendly, although they had qualified admiration for each other's works. The Marshalls had invited the Tennysons to make Tent Lodge their permanent home, and Lord Ashburton offered them a house he was buying in Croydon, for a peppercorn rent, but they declined both offers. At first they intended to live in Cheltenham with Mrs Tennyson and the rest of the family, taking a larger house into which they would all fit. But by now Emily was pregnant, and fortunately they realized that joint tenancy of a house was a risky procedure, particularly when the family involved was as volatile as the Tennysons. Instead they went to their usual refuge, Park House, to stay with the Lushingtons while Alfred looked for a house not too distant from London.

In the accounts of Tennyson's honeymoon there is one conspicuous absence: in none of them is there any mention of his growling about the reviews of his new poem. The reason is not far to seek: he was

XV. Self-portraits by Tennyson.

XVI. Tennyson, 1856, medallion by Thomas Woolner.

inclined to notice only those that he thought were hostile, although that might include any that was less than totally laudatory, but the notices of *In Memoriam* were almost unanimously favourable, many of them full of unqualified praise. The major modern book about the reviews of Tennyson's works lists some forty that appeared between the time of his wedding and the end of his honeymoon,[11] and the chapter on *In Memoriam* is quite properly called 'The Pinnacle of Success'. The poem was a triumph, both critical and popular, of a kind that is almost without parallel. Before the Tennysons left Tent Lodge, only four months after publication, there were already plans for the fourth edition. Any doubt of Tennyson's being the major living poet was no longer possible, and many of the reviewers had no hesitation in saying that the new poem made him the equal of Milton and of Wordsworth, who had died a little more than a month before its publication. The poem had appeared anonymously, but on the day of publication the *Publishers' Circular* announced it as the work of Tennyson. If this was a deliberate mistake by Moxon it hardly mattered, for rumours of the authorship had leaked out even before publication. Tennyson was apparently not upset by the announcement, but during his lifetime he never allowed an edition to appear with his name on the title-page.

Any attempt to come to terms with what is often called the most representative single Victorian work of art must stress three major and obvious points. *In Memoriam* was written intermittently over a period of nearly seventeen years, with no initial attempt to impose order on the lyrics that ultimately made up the whole poem. It was begun and continued for many years with no thought of publication. In spite of the dedication and title the poem is about Alfred Tennyson and his reactions to Arthur Hallam's death, not about Hallam himself. All three of these facts are crucial in understanding what the poem finally became.

In the most frequently quoted opinion of our century on the work, T. S. Eliot said that it was a single poem constructed by joining 'lyrics, which have only the unity and continuity of a diary, the concentrated diary of a man confessing himself'.[12] True enough, for diaries take the shape of their writers' minds rather than that of an accepted literary form, and as reflections of those minds they make unexpected leaps, unexplained transitions that may be baffling to others. This we can easily accept when the diary is published posthumously. The difficulty arises when the author chooses to publish it himself, as Tennyson did, for then the reader may expect that the connections will be filled in and a pattern imposed upon the whole.

In part Tennyson did attempt before publication to give a coherence to his lyrics that was not there from the beginning, but the residual difficulties in the poem are clearly indicated in what he told James Knowles was the 'general way of its being written . . . if there were a blank space I would put in a poem'.[13] Even when allowances are made for his tendency to shrug off answers to the inquisition of Knowles, this still remains a procedure that does not guarantee smooth continuity.

Another difficulty in looking at the poem as a diary is that the reader might fairly expect that the diary would always be a record of the mind of the author himself, but Tennyson was almost vehement in denying that it represented only his own emotions and thoughts about Hallam's death: 'It must be remembered that this is a poem, *not* an actual biography. . . . "I" is not always the author speaking of himself, but the voice of the human race speaking thro' him.' But what are we to make, then, of the constant references to 'Arthur', to the funeral trip from Vienna and burial in Clevedon, to the marriage of Charles and Louisa Turner, to that of Edmund and Cecilia Lushington, to the meetings of the Apostles and the shape of Arthur's head, to the grief of Emily, to the move from Somersby to Beech Hill, and dozens of other details straight from life? These are sandwiched in among general and philosophical statements with no warning of the movement from one to the other.

And if we look at the ideas themselves, what are the informing ones? Immortality, geology, evolution, theology, poetry, the relation of man to nature, the future of England: each of these, and as many more, has been advanced at one time or another as the dominant theme of the poem.

The precedents for the poem are equally diverse, and one recent book has suggested that Tennyson drew upon Theocritus, Horace, Catullus, Ovid, Moschus, Milton, Shelley, Petrarch, Shakespeare, Keats, Lucretius, Goethe, Lyell, Chambers, Paley, Dante, and so many other sources that the wonder is he could even link them, let alone fuse them into unity.[14] There are pastoral poems, propemtika, Pre-Raphaelite vignettes, epicedia, epithalamia, and Christian hymns all thrown together.

With this wealth, or welter, to consider, it is not surprising that so many modern critics have tried to hack out clear paths through the foliage for others to follow, even when they have had to reduce the poem considerably in so doing. Too many of them have quoted Eliot without quite believing what he wrote, that the poem owes what unity it has to the experience of one mind, however diverse that experience is. For the Victorians the wealth of detail, even of clutter (their name for it was luxuriance), was no problem, and they could appreciate it without demanding a rigid pattern in its organization. Tennyson's wonderful amalgam of forms, ideas, sources, and viewpoints seems very much of its period, and it is easy to see that it springs from the same impulses towards diversity that led his uncle Charles to build Bayons Manor in a mixture of styles from several centuries, the same yearning to connect the present to the past by casting contemporary ideas in ancient forms.

To vary the metaphor further, the form of the poem, although analogous to architecture, is probably even closer to that of one of the great Romantic parks planted by Capability Brown or Humphry Repton. 'An old park is my delight,' said Tennyson, 'and I could tumble about it for ever.' In such parks deliberate carelessness is imposed upon pre-existing order, asymmetry set against balance, harmony given the look of nature, and artifice disguised; there is indeed design, but there is no one place where it all becomes apparent, for it is a design of discontinuity. Broad avenues and vistas strike through the parks, just as the major consideration of immortality drives through the poem. But there are also side alleys and subsidiary rides leading off the main avenues into culs-de-sac, as the references to grief, religion, the function of poetry, the relevance of evolution, diverge from immortality and return to it. Most importantly, however, for the likeness, both Romantic parks and *In Memoriam* must be appreciated for local, momentary pleasures, where elaborately casual plantings lead to unexpected views and relationships that are apparently divorced from a central plan, where small and nearly self-contained areas suddenly reveal themselves. To attempt a wholly logical, diagrammatic philosophical ordering of the poem is like making an aerial photo of a park that is intended to be seen as a constantly unfolding succession of views, never perceived in totality. To look at only the broad avenues is to miss the essence of the design, as well as to miss the pleasures of local experience.

Not, of course, that Tennyson planned it that way from the beginning. Had he been taking the advice of his friends and critics who wanted him to confront the great social, political, and philosophical problems of the age directly he would undoubtedly have worked from a far more formal plan, but it would have produced a far more limited poem. Trying, as he so often did, to give some shape to what he had previously written, he wisely did not attempt to harden the pattern of what was already there. The vacillations of mood, the changes of consideration are precisely what convey the sense of a grieving, questioning, intelligent mind trying to cope with the questions inevitably set by the death of a loved one. Tennyson had little sense of narrative, but he had a strong sense of character so long as it was his own, and that character comes across directly in the waverings of mood, so wildly aberrant at first, slowly stiffening as he learns the meaning of his experience. And it is that character that is the shape of the poem.

There are artists who look outside themselves to the experiences of others, to the mass of observed mankind for their knowledge of the world, and there are those who constantly bore deeper into their own entrails in order to understand what lies about them. The latter is probably the tendency of a majority of lyric poets, and it was certainly the method of Tennyson. It is when he is most personal, when he is either looking directly at his own experience or when he is projecting himself into feelings closely akin to his own that he finds the original poetic counters to convey them; it is when he tries too hard to generalize that he is apt to stumble into borrowed situations and hackneyed diction that make him seem momentarily sentimental.

This is not to deny Tennyson the use of speculation upon intellectual concerns of his day, for they were part of his thinking. He has, for instance, often been praised for the exactness of his knowledge of evolution in its pre-Darwinian stages, which came from his voluminous if unsystematized reading; but it is praise that might have been extended to thousands of other educated Victorians, for he remained only an intelligent amateur of science, as he did at theology, philosophy, and politics. Where he was never anything but totally professional was in the analysis of his own perceptions through the use of exact language. For example, one of the great lyrics of *In Memoriam* is that in which the narrator is contemplating his own return to relative peace, even though the knowledge that Hallam's body is silently coming home by sea is only precariously pushed into the subconscious. What begins as a beautiful landscape poem is suddenly fused into greatness by what initially seems little more than a verbal quibble:

Calm is the morn without a sound,
　　Calm as to suit a calmer grief,
　　And only through the faded leaf
The chestnut pattering to the ground:

Calm and deep peace on this high wold,
　　And on these dews that drench the furze,
　　And all the silvery gossamers
That twinkle into green and gold:

Calm and still light on yon great plain
　　That sweeps with all its autumn bowers,
　　And crowded farms and lessening towers,
To mingle with the bounding main:

Calm and deep peace in this wide air,
　　These leaves that redden to the fall;
　　And in my heart, if calm at all,
If any calm, a calm despair:

Calm on the seas, and silver sleep,
　　And waves that sway themselves in rest,
　　And dead calm in that noble breast
Which heaves but with the heaving deep.　　　　　(XI)

The sudden jolt of recognizing the reality behind the inert and unconsidered metaphor 'dead calm' is a heart-stopping moment as one confronts the stopped heart. The shock of discovery turns back upon itself to reveal the droop to death that has, all along, been implicit in the calm of the reddening or the faded leaf, the falling chestnut, the autumnal bowers that become the emblems of the imperfectly submerged grief of the narrator. It is an aesthetic, almost intuitive mode of perception.

But the whole of *In Memoriam* is Tennyson's tribute to the powers of intuition and the denial of the ability of unaided rational argument to settle most of the important questions about life and death. As the poet learns to respect the powers of intuition, he learns not to fear the trances and dreams that occur with increasing intensity and truth through the poem. Yet even in this most intensely private experience, a complete withdrawal from externals, his understanding paradoxically broadens out to accept Hallam's death as a process of becoming, then to ally himself with all mankind, and to look to the future with confidence.

As he discovers the limits of the abstractions of science he progressively recognizes the power of the loving heart to penetrate to understanding, from which pure intellect is excluded. Tennyson does not discount the importance of the codifying intelligence, but he marks its limits; abstractions cannot deal with the totality of man. Evolution has meaning for the poet only as it evolves into metaphor, a method of dealing with changing reality that recalls by its language the image of Prospero creating the great globe:

> There rolls the deep where grew the tree.
> O earth, what changes hast thou seen!
> There where the long street roars, hath been
> The stillness of the central sea.
>
> The hills are shadows, and they flow
> From form to form, and nothing stands;
> They melt like mist, the solid lands,
> Like clouds they shape themselves and go.
>
> But in my spirit will I dwell,
> And dream my dream, and hold it true;
> For though my lips may breathe adieu,
> I cannot think the thing farewell.   (CXXIII)

For Tennyson evolution seemed the attempt of science to deal with the problem that lay at the heart of his own religious speculation: what to make of purpose in a natural world where death is the norm. In considering immortality he instinctively went to nature for his metaphors, and it is in this sense that *In Memoriam* is a great nature poem, for it is largely about the perceptual interchange between man and nature.

Both as man and as poet Tennyson habitually resorted to nature, and there are splendid evocations of landscape in the poem, but they are different from the 'word-painting' that the Victorians so loved, even though many of his readers admired him chiefly for his faithful adherence to literal detail and its recreation. What Tennyson is largely concerned with in this poem is whether there is hostility or friendship between man and nature. At one extreme he postulates that man must forsake his own identity in order to dissolve into and to become one with nature. The attitude is implicit in a lyric like the first of the pair concerned with the old yew tree in the churchyard, where he sees the meaning of his emotions expressed by nature, with the tree's roots taking nourishment from the bones beneath it to become a fitting symbol for his own absorption with death:

> And gazing on thee, sullen tree,
>   Sick for thy stubborn hardihood,
>   I seem to fail from out of my blood
> And grow incorporate into thee.   (II)

It is a way of finding significance in nature, but it denies the autonomy of man's imagination. The opposite way of seeing meaning in his surroundings is illustrated when the poet goes to the Wimpole Street house of the Hallams at dawn; rather than growing incorporate into the townscape around him he recasts the first rays of morning light in the frame of his own imagination:

> He is not here; but far away
>   The noise of life begins again,
>   And ghastly through the drizzling rain
> On the bald street breaks the blank day.   (VII)

But in this case the imagination of grief distorts the reality of nature. It is when there is an easy interchange of influence between man and nature that harmony is achieved. In the peace of a Somersby evening with the unflickering candles burning below the wheeling bats, the poet's trust in the external world increases until man and nature reach out to each other as the poet and his friends sing

> old songs that pealed
> From knoll to knoll, where, couched at ease,
>   The white kine glimmered, and the trees
> Laid their dark arms about the field.   (XCV)

It is after this unity with nature that he is first able to rely upon the validity of the trance into which he falls.

In the extended moon image of the 'Epilogue' the beneficence of the night calms the poet, and in turn the hard-won tranquillity of his emotions affects the way that he sees the moon. Both the soothing effect of nature and the subjective quality of his vision are hinted at in the serenity of the passage, which is an apt one for the ending of the poem, after the wedding of his sister, before his prognostication of the 'one far-off divine event, / To which the whole creation moves'.

> Dumb is that tower which spake so loud,
> And high in heaven the streaming cloud,
>   And on the downs a rising fire:

And rise, O moon, from yonder down,
　　Till over down and over dale
　　All night the shining vapour sail
And pass the silent-lighted town,

The white-faced halls, the glancing rills,
　　And catch at every mountain head,
　　And o'er the friths that branch and spread
Their sleeping silver through the hills;

And touch with shade the bridal doors,
　　With tender gloom the roof, the wall;
　　And breaking let the splendour fall
To spangle all the happy shores

By which they rest, and ocean sounds . . .

This passage might stand in itself as partial answer to T. S. Eliot's dictum about the poem that has been so often echoed: 'It is not religious because of the quality of its faith, but because of the quality of its doubt. Its faith is a poor thing, but its doubt is a very intense experience.'[15] If dramatic intensity is the sole measure of quality, Eliot was undoubtedly right, since fear is intrinsically more dramatic than serenity, doubt more so than faith in which tensions are already brought to resolution. Surely, however, what is in question is not the quality of Tennyson's doubt or belief but the quality of his expression of them: in short, whether they are adequately embodied in the poetry. Drama is not all in lyric poetry, particularly in the poetry of nature, and Tennyson as often finds the perfect counterpart for human emotion and religious experience in tranquil beauty as in the troubled elements. The doubt in the poem is certainly intense, but the poetry of serene faith is far from 'a poor thing'. When wild weather reminds him of the dangers facing the ship bringing Hallam's body, his fears and doubts are recast as a storm:

Tonight the winds begin to rise
　　And roar from yonder dropping day:
　　The last red leaf is whirled away,
The rooks are blown about the skies;

The forest cracked, the waters curled,
　　The cattle huddled on the lea;
　　And wildly dashed on tower and tree
The sunbeam strikes along the world:

*　*　*

> The wild unrest that lives in woe
> Would dote and pore on yonder cloud
>
> That rises upward always higher,
> And onwards drags a labouring breast,
> And topples round the dreary west,
> A looming bastion fringed with fire.   (xv)

But it is with equal effectiveness that the memory of Arthur's visits to Somersby is conjured up by the peace of a summer night that reflects the profound order of nature:

> Witch-elms that counterchange the floor
> Of this flat lawn with dusk and bright;
> And thou, with all thy breadth and height
> Of foliage, towering sycamore;
>
> How often, hither wandering down
> My Arthur found your shadows fair,
> And shook to all the liberal air
> The dust and din and steam of town:
>
> *   *   *
>
> We talked: the stream beneath us ran,
> The wine-flask lying couched in moss,
>
> Or cooled within the glooming wave;
> And last, returning from afar,
> Before the crimson-circled star
> Had fallen into her father's grave,
>
> And brushing ankle-deep in flowers,
> We heard behind the woodbine veil
> The milk that bubbled in the pail,
> And buzzings of the honied hours.   (LXXXIX)

In metaphorical statements of this quality it is surely unnecessary to choose between those expressing faith and those expressing doubt, since both seem part of an overwhelming experience.

*   *   *

In October 1850 when Alfred and Emily returned to the south of England after their extended honeymoon, Tennyson's reputation had totally changed since their wedding four months before. In June he had been a promising poet, greatly admired by other poets but not yet a widely popular figure. By the end of his honeymoon the publication of

In Memoriam had made him easily the most famous poet in England, and Dickens was the only literary man of any kind whose fame excelled his.

Tennyson was not particularly vain about his success, but it would have been unnatural if it had not affected him. He had inherited the ideas of his father and uncle about the style in which the Tennyson family ought to live, and his specifications for the house that he and Emily needed gradually expanded to accommodate his reputation. Emily insisted on large and airy rooms, while Alfred, as Walter White noted, 'is difficult to please in the matter of a house, he must have all the upper part to himself, for a study and smoking-room, etc., and to avoid noise above his head and indoor privacy, as he is accustomed while composing to walk up and down his room loudly reciting the flowing thoughts'.[16] By the standards of Bayons, which Tennyson was accustomed to apply to himself, it was little enough, but it was a marked contrast to the recent days when he had loudly proclaimed his poverty and moved from sofa to extra bed in the chambers of his friends. In the event of renting, rather than buying a house, he was willing to go to an upper limit of £60 annually. Ideally, he wanted to be within striking distance of London without living in the metropolis itself.

While they looked for a house, he and Emily stayed at Park House. After three months of pregnancy she was already too indisposed to accompany him in house-hunting; he hated going by himself, and asked the help of a number of his friends in finding a suitable place. There was another matter also bothering him at the time, and he had been thinking of it since Wordsworth's death in April. The post of Poet Laureate was now empty, and there was a strong possibility that it would be offered to him.

In spite of rumours that he was being considered he disclaimed any such possibility, as well as any ambition of his own for the post. Only four days after the death of Wordsworth the *Spectator* had said there were two major candidates, 'both basking in the sunshine of royal favour'. Tennyson took this to refer to himself and Leigh Hunt, as both held Civil List pensions, and he assured Forster unequivocally that he hoped Hunt would be successful.[17] But he could hardly have said, without immodesty, that he expected to be named, particularly to Forster who was a notorious gossip. It was thought that Hunt's religious views would make him unacceptable for a court post, but Hunt could not see the force of that argument himself.

On 8 May 1850 the Prince Consort wrote personally to Samuel Rogers, offering the position to him, but Rogers, who had wanted all his life to be Poet Laureate, had to decline because at eighty-seven he was nothing but 'a shadow so soon to depart'.[18] *The Times* proposed that the post should be done away with, since it would be difficult to find a replacement of the stature of Wordsworth or Southey, but the suggestion met with little general favour. With Rogers out of the way the race was an open one, with Hunt, Henry Taylor, Sheridan Knowles (who by now had the pension that Bulwer said Tennyson had deprived him of) and Elizabeth Browning at the post. She was the favourite of the party that felt a Queen Regnant should have a feminine Laureate. There were some other outsiders, like Robert Browning and Tennyson's old enemy Professor Wilson ('Christopher North'), but after the publication of *In Memoriam* Tennyson was the odds-on favourite.

In September Lord John Russell, the Prime Minister, submitted to the Queen the names of Taylor, Knowles, Wilson, and Tennyson. The Prince Consort was his wife's adviser on poetry, as on most other subjects. We know from the courtesy paid to him by the Queen and her Consort in 1847 that the Prince was already an admirer of Tennyson, and Hallam Tennyson's biography indicates that Albert had been deeply impressed by *In Memoriam*, which finally made up his mind. After Lord John had made discreet inquiries about Tennyson's character, a letter was dispatched to Park House on 5 November, inviting him to become Poet Laureate.

Tennyson used to assure his family and friends that he 'had not any expectation of the Laureateship, or any thought upon the subject', but his letter to Forster indicates that he was not quite truthful in saying so, however slight he thought his chances of success were. In any case, he would have had to be singularly insensitive to his reputation (which he certainly was not) to miss the speculation in the press about his chances. It was not dishonesty that prompted his disavowal but deep diffidence of the sort that made him assert all his life that he accepted his pension, his Oxford honorary degree a few years later, and the Laureateship on this occasion only at the urging of his friends.

Proof that his thoughts were actually very much with the Laureateship is given by the dream he had the night before the letter arrived. In the dream the Queen and the Prince came to call on him at his mother's house (perhaps as they had done at Esher) and were very gracious to him, the Prince going so far as to kiss him, to which his response was

'Very kind but very German'. When he woke in the morning he told Emily about the dream before the mail was brought to them in the bedroom. After opening the letter, he said, he had trouble all day in deciding whether to accept; 'at the last I wrote two letters, one accepting and one declining, and threw them on the table, and settled to decide which I would send after my dinner and bottle of port'.[19] It is probable that he consulted at least one friend as well as the port bottle, for he used to say that it was Venables, then staying at Park House, who tipped the scales by assuring him solemnly that if he accepted, he would, as Laureate, always be offered the liver-wing of a fowl when dining out. He was somewhat worried by the knowledge that the post was now worth little more than £100, all of which would be swallowed up the first year by the price of the patent and the court dress, so that he would have nothing to lay by for the 'heir to nothing' that Emily was expecting the following spring. But it is improbable that there had ever been any serious doubt of his acceptance.

Tennyson took the duties of the Poet Laureate seriously, although he was no longer required to celebrate the birthday of the Sovereign or even to commemorate great public occasions in verse as his predecessors had been. He believed that his acceptance morally obliged him not to oppose the Queen, either publicly or privately, and above that it seemed to him reasonable that she should occasionally ask him to solemnize an event by his craft. It was, after all, a position that put him in direct succession to Chaucer, Spenser, Jonson, Dryden, and Wordsworth. Although he was to write no masterpieces to order, the level of his official poetry was at least as high as the average set by other Poets Laureate. It is, however, the name of Tennyson that has ever since been associated pre-eminently with the position, not in reality for his poetry but because he was to embody so well the idea held by both Victoria and her subjects of what a poet should be, so that in time he became as much an emblem of the age as the Queen for whom it was named.

His later friendship with the Queen and the Royal Family could not have ripened so easily had he not been Poet Laureate, but otherwise the advantages were largely peripheral, except for the privilege of not having to serve on a jury because he was a member of the Household, in theory on call at any moment by Her Majesty. It was an exemption he claimed at least once.

An immediate and real drawback to his position became apparent after the announcement of the appointment, as each of 'the two hundred million poets of Great Britain' felt free to send him verses for criticism and advice, almost always without return postage; as he said, 'no man ever thinks of sending me a book of prose, hardly ever. I am like a man receiving perpetual parcels of currants and raisins and barley sugar, and never a piece of bread.'[20] As far as possible he tried to answer, or rather to have Emily answer, most of those who had sent their works, but the volume was so great that his comments, and even the names of the other poets, sometimes got mixed up.

There was almost universal agreement on Tennyson's suitability as Laureate. Leigh Hunt gulped down his disappointment and wrote his congratulations on the Queen's choice, to which Tennyson would bring 'abundance of honour & glory. I never, thank God, wished anything but happiness to persons more fortunate than myself, however I might have looked to see the ball rolling to my side.' When Thackeray expressed his delight to Tennyson, he added, 'A Laureate indeed without guile'.[21]

Henry Taylor, with hardly more than a glint of malice, passed on Sir Edmund Head's astonishment at the appointment, 'conceiving that Tennyson was little known, and that his claims would not be generally recognised'. Taylor found it difficult to understand how anyone but himself could have been made Laureate, but he had to admit that 5,000 copies of *In Memoriam* had been sold, of Wordsworth's *Prelude* fewer than 2,000: 'I suppose there is hardly ever more than one poet *flourishing* at a time, as there is only one Prima Donna.'[22]

There was a little opposition to Tennyson from the relatives of his predecessor. Alfred Ainger said 'that some of the Wordsworth family had been furious when so inconsiderable a person as Tennyson succeeded their illustrious relative, whose own elevation to the Laureateship had been just as unfavourably regarded in some quarters'.[23]

It was pleasant to have no public insult from one quarter where it might have been expected. Bulwer-Lytton presumably remembered his painful tumbling five years earlier, for he made no public comment, although he still hated Tennyson's poetry. It was a feeling shared by his friend Charles Tennyson d'Eyncourt, and Tealby was loud with the gnashing of teeth, particularly since Tennyson d'Eyncourt already had in hand an elegy to show that not all members of the family wrote 'horrid rubbish'. The poem was in memory of his son Eustace, who had died eight years earlier, and it was intended to shed honour on both Eustace and the family from which he had sprung, as well as to provide an example for Alfred. Tennyson d'Eyncourt had been showing his completed 750 lines to his literary friends, and they had presumably been approved by Bulwer-Lytton. *In Memoriam* and its success came as an unpleasant surprise, for Alfred seemed to have anticipated his uncle's triumph. Five days after its publication Clara Tennyson d'Eyncourt wrote to her father to reassure him and to reinforce John Forster's opinion of *Eustace*: '"A prophet was never without honour save in his own Country" &c. Print yr. poem by all means—Forster must be a very good judge, tho' he does admire Alfred Tennyson's verses, at any rate, he evidently sides with the popular taste.'[24] For the next few months Charles Tennyson d'Eyncourt worked to get the poem in shape for publication before the end of the year.

The middle section of the poem is devoted to a description of a grand banquet in Bayons before Eustace's departure for the West Indies, where he was to die. His father's sorrow over Eustace's death and his own pride in his home are touchingly and amateurishly evident, and the morality with which the poem is interlaid is unimpeachable, but in spite of the forests of exclamation marks intended to give it immediacy the verse is so pedestrian that the reader's sympathy with the author is of a kind he never intended. The volume, which must have been subsidized by the Tennyson d'Eyncourts, is a beautiful production, with engravings of Bayons inside and out, making it look grander than it did in reality (see Plate VII). In an attempt to indicate the unity of the more respectable members of the family, Charles asked Elizabeth Russell for permission to dedicate the poem to her because of her kindness at the time of Eustace's death and because of her interest in poetry. Actually, it may have been that very love of poetry that made her decline the honour. Rather than hurt his feelings by a direct refusal, however, she suggested that since he had two sisters such a dedication might offend Mrs Bourne. In spite of her attempts to get out of it, the book was finally dedicated to her.

One of the most genial aspects of Tennyson was that though he disliked his uncle he seldom showed any resentment or took any apparent pleasure in his discomfiture. The worst that he ever said of *Eustace* was that 'It was written by an uncle of mine who fancied himself a Poet, and was—a considerable humbug'.[25]

By the end of 1850 Tennyson could well afford to be generous. The year that had just finished was the miraculous one of his marriage, *In Memoriam*, and the Laureateship: the pivotal year of his life, half of which was now over. Half the century was finished, too, and the second part of each was to bring a whole new existence to Tennyson, a fame and respectability that were in utter contrast to his untidy, vagrant earlier years of obscurity, and perhaps even harder to deal with gracefully than they had been.

✳

CHAPTER XXIII

LITERARY LONDON,
1851–1852

IN mid-January 1851, seven months after their marriage, Emily and Alfred Tennyson moved into the first house of their own, 'The Hill', in Warninglid some five miles from Horsham. They both preferred an old house, and this was a pretty one with a good view of the South Downs. From Hale Mr Sellwood had let them take the cook, Mrs Milnes, and as housemaid her sister Matilda, to help set out their scanty furniture; they were to get more servants locally. In the event, they never did, for the house was a total disaster. Alfred set out for a long walk before breakfast on their first day and returned full of pleasure at all the birdsong he had heard. At lunchtime the dining-room, Alfred's study, and their bedrooms had all been made snug, and they congratulated themselves on their choice. By mid-afternoon the breezes off the downs had turned into a howling wind that swept them out of the dining-room; when they moved to the study, the chimney smoked so badly that they had to retreat to their bedroom; and that night part of the wall in their bedroom was blown in, so that the rain poured upon them in bed, and they finally had to get up and read aloud to each other for the rest of the night.

By morning they had decided to move, even though they had to pay £85 for buying out their lease. Emily repacked while Alfred wrote down the last of the sections on the 'weird seizures' for the new edition of *The Princess*. With Milnes and her 'yard-wand' to measure the rooms he began once more looking at houses, but none in the vicinity was suitable. Workmen were got in to make 'The Hill' minimally habitable until they could find another place, but even so it proved impossible to live in and less than a fortnight after arriving they set out over the muddy road by which they had come. Alfred drew Emily two miles in a wheeled garden-chair, since she was not supposed to walk because of her pregnancy. As quickly as possible they took themselves to the Rawnsleys at Shiplake and began looking for houses.

When they concluded that there was no reasonable house near

Shiplake they set out for their usual refuge, Park House. To make the journey easier for Emily they stopped for a night at an inn, where she fell down a step. 'I had such a bad sprain', she wrote, 'that I could not get up & had to go to bed & for a time was very ill indeed.'[1] Their first fear, of course, was for the unborn child, since Emily was nearly thirty-eight years old and frail. It was imperative that they settle soon.

Almost the first house Tennyson saw when he was looking nearer London was suggested to him by both Edmund Peel and the Henry Taylors: Chapel House, Montpelier Row, Twickenham, at the end of a fine early eighteenth-century row near the river, originally built for members of the Court. It was spacious, the upper rooms all had beautiful views of the river and of the park of Marble Hill in front, and to the rear the grounds of Orleans House, belonging to the Duc d'Aumale. Tennyson liked it, and he could easily afford the £50 annual rent, but he unfortunately did not agree on the spot; when he returned later in the day it was taken. A month later the original agreement fell through so that the house was once more available, and this time he immediately signed a five-year lease without waiting for Emily to see it, only assuring her that the rooms were all high enough for her beds. It is still a beautiful house, with a grand oak staircase in the entrance-hall, fine carving, and a splendid drawing-room. There was a smaller study looking down the long garden that separated the house from the small chapel that gave the place its name, and there was plenty of room for guests and servants. What seemed an additional advantage was that, although Twickenham was then very rural, it was only eleven miles from the centre of London with an express train every eleven minutes.

While waiting for the house to be put in readiness, Alfred went to London to be presented as Poet Laureate to the Queen at her levee, on 26 February. He was worried about money because of the costs of moving; he refused to buy his own court dress for the occasion, and though he drove all over London he was unable to hire any, and so had put off attendance. When Samuel Rogers heard of his dilemma he offered his own court dress, that which Wordsworth had worn on a similar occasion six years earlier, and which 'had been promised to the Wordsworth family as an heir-loom'. The coat was a good fit, 'but about other parts of the dress there was some anxiety, as they had not been tried on'.[2] Tennyson was taller than Wordsworth and a good bit heavier in the hips and legs; since he was some eight inches taller than Rogers he was naturally apprehensive about the prospect of bowing

before the Queen to kiss her hand. All the Tennysons, in particular
Frederick, Septimus, and Alfred, had enormous calves of which they
were inordinately proud, so that he clearly had to wear his own black
silk stockings. After he had tried on the dress he went in ingenuous
pleasure to see Thackeray, who wrote that he had 'just been here much
excited about his court dress and sword (he says his legs are very good
but we know what the Psalms say on that subject)* and as much
pleased and innocent about it as a girl or a page'.[3]

A fortnight later he was finally presented to the Queen by Lord
Monteagle. There was an initial hitch, when he absent-mindedly
blundered into the Royal circle and was motioned back by Lord
Breadalbane, whom he saw but dimly. In a loud voice he said, 'Surely
Her Majesty might keep her flunkeys in better order.' Without mishap
he made his bow over the Queen's hand, kissed it, and then sent a brief
message of reassurance to Emily to tell her that all had gone well and
that 'the inexpressibles were not hopelessly tight'.[4] Symbolically, as
well as literally, he had now taken Wordsworth's place as first poet of
the Queen's realm. The Royal post also meant that he automatically
began moving in circles that had not been easily available to him
before. Within a few days Lord Monteagle, Stephen Spring-Rice's
father, had entertained him, and he had met Sir Alexander Duff
Gordon; Sir George Grey; the Prime Minister, Lord John Russell; and
the Duke of Argyll, who was to become one of his most constant, if not
exactly intimate, friends for the rest of his life.

Even more convincing evidence of his new position in society was
the offer in June of the Queen's box at the Crystal Palace, presumably
through the offices of the Prince Consort who knew of his scientific
interests. Unfortunately, there is no record of his opinion of the Great
Exhibition.

A few days before his presentation to the Queen he had been asked
to be one of the fifty stewards and 600 guests at the grand farewell
banquet on Macready's retirement, taking his place among Thackeray, Forster, Dickens, and the other leading literary men of the day.
Forster, proposing a toast to 'Dramatic Literature', held up a piece of
paper which he said contained a sonnet in tribute to Macready by the
Poet Laureate, and to cheers he read it aloud. When Dickens made an
entrance wearing a brass-buttoned blue coat with silk facings, a waist-
coat of satin, and a heavily embroidered shirt, Thackeray murmured,

---

* He hath no pleasure in the strength of an horse; neither delighteth he in any man's
legs.' (Psalm 147:10, *Book of Common Prayer.*)

'The beggar is as beautiful as a butterfly, especially about the shirt-front.'[5] More charitably, Tennyson stifled his own emotions about seeing Bulwer-Lytton in the chair and his own uncle Charles as one of the other stewards.

As so often happened with Tennyson, catastrophe and disillusionment set in just when everything seemed at its peak. Although he had the run of the Peels' park at Marble Hill, he found Twickenham confining and suburban, his constitutionals mere 'dirty walks and alas without pleasure',[6] so that Warninglid began retrospectively to seem pleasant. The low-lying land beside the river was damp, and he complained of the smell of cabbage from nearby market-gardens. Even the distance from London, which at first had seemed to prove the sincerity of guests willing to come so far, now seemed too easy for casual visitors.

Worst of all, on Easter Sunday, when Emily's pregnancy had come to term, the male child was born dead, strangled by the cord at birth, just as the organ in the chapel at the foot of the garden began to play. The doctor said that its death was the result of Emily's fall at the inn after leaving Shiplake, and that its very health and size had contributed to her difficulties. For several days she wavered between death and life before recovering. Tennyson could not forget the alabaster perfection of the little corpse as it was dressed for burial, and he wrote compulsively to friend after friend to tell them of the death of his son. He was assured that if Emily had another child there was no reason to believe that it would not be born normally, but the infant's death haunted him all his life, so that when he was ill forty years later he wept as he 'talked about his firstborn, & broke down describing the fists clenched as if in a struggle for life'.[7]

Beautiful as it was, Chapel House was too linked to misfortune ever to become dear to the Tennysons, and though they had taken a lease of it they began to think of moving again. In the meantime, when Emily seemed sufficiently fit, they set out for Italy for her convalescence.

The hardships of nineteenth-century travellers would be arduous even with modern conveyance, but they apparently thought little of the difficulties facing them. One wonders how beneficial it all was for Emily, even though they tried to take the trip slowly. Their first stop was for four days in Paris, part of which they spent with Cecilia and Edmund Lushington. Tennyson went to the Louvre, and while there he was spotted by Robert and Elizabeth Browning, who were on their way from Florence to London. Browning thought he knew Tennyson too slightly to accost him in public, and held back to watch him sign the visitors' book; when he had gone, the Brownings immediately examined it and saw the signature of 'A. Tennyson, Rentier'. On their return to their rooms they found Tennyson's invitation to tea in the nearby Hôtel de Douvres. Mrs Browning was 'tired half to death' from the Louvre, but she rose from the sofa 'in a decided state of resurrection' and went with Robert to see the Tennysons. It was the first time Browning and Tennyson had ever talked except in general conversation at other men's tables, and they found themselves easy at once. Elizabeth Browning liked Emily's 'gentlest of smiles' and her soft, winning ways; Emily loved Mrs Browning's 'great spirit-eyes'. Tennyson was beginning to find out how much closer he could be brought to other men when their wives felt mutual regard. Mrs Browning had been even older than Emily when she married, and she could sympathize with Emily's sorrow over the loss of her child, since she had lost several infants of her own before the birth of Pen Browning. Both women were partial invalids, as Forster said, but marriage had been invigorating for them. They thought at once of themselves as almost sisters.

Browning gave Tennyson advice about Italy, suggesting Bagni di Lucca rather than Lake Como for the bulk of their stay. In turn Tennyson warned that England was changed and vulgar, that he was flying it himself to get away 'from the dirty hands of his worshippers', and that he was hoping to be quite unnoticed in Italy if that were possible. Wryly, Mrs Browning, who knew there was small chance her husband would be mobbed by adoring throngs in England, said 'that there was not zeal enough for literature among the English of Florence to persecute anybody by over-worship'. After tea Tennyson pulled out his clay pipe and lit it, with little more than a formal word to be sure it would not throw the Brownings 'into fits'.

There were several more meetings before the Tennysons left, each of them increasing the Brownings' sense of Tennyson's greatness and shy simplicity. He gave them a note to the servants at Twickenham, so that they might use the house if they wished for as long as they stayed in England. The Brownings were 'pleased and touched to the heart', and on parting gave Alfred and Emily identical little nosegays of artificial flowers 'arranged in a sort of Grecian pattern.' The wives kissed, and both were touched by the affectionate response, although each insisted that the other had made the first move towards embracing.[8]

As the last meeting between Tennyson and Browning had done a few years before, this looked like the beginning of a deep friendship, but it never came to that. Within a year Tennyson was complaining of Browning's flamboyant manners, and it did not take long for Browning to feel uneasily that the Laureate was too uncharitable to his own poetry, for Tennyson thought it totally lacking in music. Carlyle put the matter bluntly and crudely: 'Alfred knows how to jingle, but Browning does not.' Tennyson took far less trouble to be polite than Browning did, but his friends thought this a mark of his unspoiled natural nobility. Patmore, for one, said that Tennyson was the 'greatest *man* he ever came in contact with . . . perfectly sincere and frank, never paying uncandid compliments. Browning takes more pains to please, and is altogether more a man of the world.'⁹

The Tennysons moved slowly southward through Monaco, arriving in Genoa in mid-August, going through La Spezia to Bagni di Lucca, where they spent some time with Tennyson's old friend Francis Garden, who had come there from Rome for the sake of his wife, who was suffering from consumption. Emily Tennyson was always a great deal more apprehensive about the food, cleanliness, and morals of foreigners than Alfred, and she was greatly put off by the religion of the Italians, although she was convinced they were all on the verge of turning Protestant. All the same she was touched when priests twice bowed to them on the street, 'a sort of acknowledgment of universal brotherhood. Do not think from this I am likely to turn Romanist', she wrote to her mother-in-law. She and Alfred sat in a darkened room most of the time, wearing veils against the flies and mosquitoes, and since Italian food was clearly not to be trusted, she said that they ate 'little bits of rather tough meat plainly roasted, & we get on very well for we can always make up with peaches'.¹⁰ But the fleas finally drove them on after three weeks in Bagni di Lucca.

The first place not to disappoint them was Florence, where they stayed with Frederick and his Italian wife in their grand Villa Torregiani, which was said to have been designed by Michelangelo. Emily was embarrassed that Maria Tennyson sat at the head of the table without understanding a word of the English in which they chattered. Mrs Trollope called on them, and she turned out to be 'a kind motherly sort of body & not at all coarse as one would expect from her works'.¹¹

After ten days with Frederick they started home again, largely because Alfred was worried for Emily if they should be caught in the civil unrest plaguing Italy. Her chief worry was that Alfred might not have another chance to see the country. When he returned to England he complained there of the difficulty of finding proper English tobacco in Florence, and the story was told cynically around London that it was only the shortage of shag that had caused his return. They went through Milan and Como, then to Switzerland through the Splügen pass. Near its highest point Alfred picked a flower for Emily. The trip had been a success scenically, but Emily was vastly relieved to be home again, as she always was after being abroad.

Two years later Alfred was in Edinburgh, found the flower pressed in a book he was reading, and wrote a charming verse epistle, 'The Daisy', about the remembered beauties of Italy:

> O love, what hours were thine and mine,
> In lands of palm and southern pine;
>   In lands of palm, of orange-blossom,
> Of olive, aloe, and maize and vine.
>
> *   *   *
>
> How richly down the rocky dell
> The torrent vineyard streaming fell
>   To meet the sun and sunny waters,
> That only heaved with a summer swell.
>
> *   *   *
>
> O Milan, O the changing quires,
> The giant windows' blazoned fires,
>   The height, the space, the gloom, the glory!
> A mount of marble, a hundred spires!
>
> I climbed the roofs at break of day;
> Sun-smitten Alps before me lay.
>   I stood among the silent statues,
> And statued pinnacles, mute as they.
>
> *   *   *
>
> I found, though crushed to hard and dry,
> This nurseling of another sky
>   Still in the little book you lent me,
> And where you tenderly laid it by:
>
> And I forgot the clouded Forth,
> The gloom that saddens Heaven and Earth,
>   The bitter east, the misty summer
> And gray metropolis of the North.

Ever after his first miraculous trip abroad with Arthur Hallam, Tennyson loved foreign travel, but he knew that Emily did not, and the rest of their married life was complicated for him by the choice between leaving her behind or making her uncomfortable by taking her from home.

Once back in Twickenham, Tennyson resumed his acquaintance in literary London. Living eleven miles away from the metropolis, he had to make a special effort to see his friends. The world is divided between those who are good hosts and those who are natural guests. Certainly Tennyson found it easier to be a guest than to entertain his friends. For years he had moved in on Fitz or Spedding or Forster or the Lushingtons quite casually, or gone without invitation to Park House; he now began to realize how disruptive guests could be, both to his own work and to the household. All the same, he learned in time to be a good host, so long as the stay of his guests was not prolonged. Usually new acquaintances found him a bit forbidding on first meeting, but if they proved interesting he would invite them to stay for dinner and the evening.

In June 1851 he had made the acquaintance of two young literary men, one of whom was to remain a friend until death while the other was soon disillusioned with Tennyson. The latter of these was a touchy, opinionated, charming young man only twenty-three years old, George Meredith, who had just published his first volume of poems, a copy of which he had sent to Tennyson. Although he often did not acknowledge unsolicited books of poems, Tennyson had been so impressed with this that he wrote to say how much he liked it. In reply Meredith said that his chief ambition in publishing the poems was to obtain Tennyson's praise. The little volume, with Meredith's inscription, is now in the Tennyson Research Centre, and it falls open naturally to 'Love in the Valley', which Meredith used to say Tennyson was the first person to admire. He told Meredith that he had been going up and down stairs repeating it, and that he had told Emily he wished he had written it. In conclusion he invited Meredith to Twickenham.

In later years Meredith was mischievous about Tennyson, so that his stories are suspect, but if we can believe him he did not go to Twickenham but met Tennyson for the first time when they were staying in the same country house. He arrived too late to see him the first night, but when he got up for an early walk the next morning he found Tennyson ahead of him, standing silently by a stream. When he finally took notice of the young man, he said in greeting, 'George Gilfillan should not have said I was not a great poet.' Meredith knew that the critic in question was not taken seriously, and asked, 'What possible importance can have what such a worm writes about you?' Tennyson considered for a time, then repeated glumly, 'But he should not have said that I am not a great poet.' Meredith used to tell the story with great shouts of laughter, adding, 'And after that I never wanted to see him again.' Tennyson kept his admiration for Meredith's poetry, but he used to say that reading his novels was like 'wading through glue'.[12]

A far more successful meeting in 1851 was that with William Allingham, a young poet who had just moved to London from his native Ireland; like Meredith he had sent his first volume of verse to Tennyson and was anxious to meet the great man. Patmore arranged for him to go to Twickenham at the end of June. When Tennyson walked into the room where he was sitting Allingham was surprised to find him looking much older than his age, because of his short sight, hollow cheeks, and an unhealthy grey pallor of the skin. He was stooped, obviously very tired, and carelessly dressed. But it was all redeemed when he began talking of Allingham's poetry, criticizing, praising, finally reading it aloud to its author. 'The pieces never seemed to me so good before or since', Allingham wrote. Emily invited him to dinner, and he accepted with alacrity. Tennyson talked of 'Love in the Valley' and how he liked it, and Allingham recited Poe's 'The Raven', which Tennyson did not know. After dinner the Patmores came in, and when they had drunk their port the three poets went to the study to smoke while Tennyson talked well about his belief in immortality. It was a memorable evening for Allingham, who felt as if he 'had been familiar for years with this great and simple man'.[13] Allingham kept a diary over the next four decades, which is perhaps the closest record of what Tennyson's conversation and company was like, for he could talk at length with the younger man, unafraid of being interrupted. Allingham was careful never to show any disapproval of Tennyson, and indeed felt but little. The relationship of master and pupil was tacitly accepted on both sides, the basis on which Tennyson kept most of his friendships over the years.

As relationships tended to lose suppleness in time, so did the pattern of entertainment provided by the Tennysons, until it had gradually become almost inviolable. Allingham's evening was to be repeated with minor variations hundreds of times at Farringford and at Aldworth until Tennyson's death four decades later.

At the end of 1851 Emily was expecting another baby. As in her other pregnancies, the early stages were difficult, making her unhappy with Twickenham and unreasonably nervous when Alfred was away from home. Concern about her contributed to Alfred's unsettled state at the beginning of 1852 and no doubt exacerbated his worries about the possibility of a French invasion after Louis Napoleon's *coup d'état*. The excitable Coventry Patmore, 'thinking that an ounce of action might be worth a ton of talk', organized a club of his fellow employees at the British Museum as volunteer riflemen to repel the invaders. He succeeded in making Emily as militant as Alfred became, and they each contributed £5 to the club.[14] In addition Alfred wrote a series of seven poems in January and February 1852 that any admirer would wish had never seen light. A few of their over-punctuated titles tell the story: 'Rifle Clubs!!!', 'Britons, Guard Your Own', 'Hands All Round!'. In them Tennyson slips across the narrow line dividing ardent patriotism from hysteria, proclaiming his dislike of the French, shrilly urging England to 'Arm, arm, arm!', and succeeding only in manifesting the hollow belligerence of the unmartial man caught up in blind chauvinism. Aware that his position as Poet Laureate put him in a peculiar position for promulgating such a point of view, Tennyson published the poems in several different periodicals, either anonymously or pseudonymously. The best that can be said of them is that they contributed to the writing of *Maud* three years later.

At the beginning of April 1852 he took Emily to Malvern to stay with the Vicar, his old Lincolnshire friend John Rashdall, while they unsuccessfully looked for a house in the remoter hills of Worcestershire and Gloucestershire. They were in the West Country more than two months, finishing their trip at Cheltenham with Tennyson's mother, in time to bid his sister Mary farewell as she and her new husband set out for Antigua, where he was to stay in the Judicial Service for thirty years. Mary had displayed a thoroughly Tennysonian contempt for convention when she unexpectedly married Alan Ker, a penniless Cheltenham barrister; she simply walked in and announced to her startled family, 'I'm married.' Alfred's gloomy predictions about her marriage strangely recall her dark prognostications about his own: 'Ker has borrowed Mary's principal for a start in life,' he wrote to Emily, 'a bad enough look-out.'[15] Tennyson gradually drifted away from most of his family after marriage, but the Kers in particular disliked Emily and felt that she was snobbish and overly ambitious for Alfred.

The Tennysons were back in Twickenham in mid-June, still having found no house. Emily was expecting the baby in two months' time, and they had to give up the search temporarily. Tennyson had been home little more than a fortnight when he went away again, this time for more than three weeks, to wander around Yorkshire. He was suffering from the hay fever that plagued him all his adult life, and it was alleviated by the sea air when he went to Whitby and Scarborough. It was a pleasant, uneventful trip, with no worries save a letter forwarded by Emily in which a fellow poet asked him for money, which he refused, thinking it an impertinence. 'Besides this kind of demand (if it be found that I respond to such claims) is likely to increase'.[16] On the return journey he went to Crowland Abbey, then stayed with the Turners in the new vicarage they had built at Grasby.

While he was away Emily had the company of Matilda Tennyson, her own father, and the Welds, but it was peculiar that Alfred should have gone away when the baby's arrival was imminent, particularly when Emily's previous pregnancy had terminated so sadly. Tennyson always needed to move around a good bit, and the trip seems to have been the result of his feelings of imprisonment in his new life of domesticity. Not that he would have wanted to exchange it for bachelorhood, but the cares of a house and approaching paternity could be oppressive. Just before leaving for Yorkshire, he had confessed to Woolner, who was going to Australia, 'that were it not for Mrs. T. he should go himself'.[17]

He was back in Twickenham at the beginning of August which should have left plenty of time for Emily's confinement, but the baby was more than a week early, arriving unexpectedly on 11 August, just when the doctor had gone out after assuring Emily that the birth was well in the future. Later Emily was ill again, and finally she had to give up nursing the baby. She was thirty-nine, Alfred forty-three, and they became as doting as middle-aged parents normally are with their first child. Although he told Venables in mock deprecation that the baby boy looked like a brickfaced monkey, Alfred loved holding it and listening to its cries, like the bleat of a new-born lamb. 'I do like men who are not ashamed to be happy beside a cradle,' said Elizabeth Browning.[18]

Hallam Tennyson was christened on 5 October at Twickenham, with a large party afterwards at Chapel House. His godfathers were old Mr Hallam and F. D. Maurice, who was picked expressly by Emily as an antidote to such free-thinking friends of Alfred's as James Spedding, whom she addressed with leaden playfulness as a 'naughty infidel', thinly disguising her disapproval. Many of the guests were surprised that Mr Hallam, who was very infirm, had been able to come, but he made the effort because of his constantly deepening affection for Alfred. He liked to say that the baby had been named Hallam, in spite of Emily's wish to call him Alfred, for fear that he might turn out a fool. During the christening Robert Browning held the infant, happily bouncing it in the air.

Besides the two godfathers and Browning (who would not let his wife venture outside their own house because of the cold wind), the guests included Palgrave, Jane Carlyle (in wickedly funny form in her husband's absence), the Brookfields, Henry Taylor, Thackeray, Venables, and Louisa and Charles Turner. Spedding was not there. For the guests, among whom poets were 'as thick as blackberries', Emily had provided a haunch of venison sent by Drummond Rawnsley, peaches, and 'the best champagne we could get'. When the others had gone, Tennyson took Browning, Palgrave, and Robert Morier up to his study, where they argued over their port and whisky until one a.m. When he got home, Browning told Elizabeth that it had been 'a brilliant breakfast' and that Tennyson had been very kind. But Browning's manners, particularly the assumption that he could hold a baby better than its father, had irritated Tennyson, who said of him afterwards: 'how he did flourish about when he was here!'[19]

Once there had been deep opposition between Tennyson and Henry Hallam, but by now Alfred was almost a son to the old man. His last and worst blow had been in 1850, when young Henry Hallam unexpectedly died in Italy, as Arthur had done in Vienna, leaving Julia the sole survivor of the original eleven children. The contentiousness of which Sydney Smith had so often complained had been replaced by warm affection, with gratitude when it was returned. Having Alfred as close to London as Twickenham meant a great deal to him, and he occasionally drove down to Chapel House. Once he arrived unexpectedly in his carriage with Julia and Jane Brookfield, to find Alfred and Emily weeding in the garden. When their guests refused an invitation to stay overnight, the Tennysons pressed on them a large tin of pineapple sugar-candy. Julia sampled it with pleasure, but her father 'refused with a grand air', then in the carriage driving back to London he devoured the rest of it, 'confessing that he thought 'twould be childish to eat it before the Tennysons'.[20]

On 14 September 1852 the Duke of Wellington died. Richard Monckton Milnes, who knew Tennyson's disinclination to flatter the Royal Family and probably also remembered his bad temper some years before when asked to write for 'people with prefixes to their names', inquired two days after Wellington's death, 'Will you think "the Duke"—worth writing about? That is a kind of royalty you need not disdain to commemorate.' Tennyson had refused Milnes's offer to introduce him at Bath House, and he had only once seen the Duke in person, in St. James's Park, when he had lifted his hat and been acknowledged with a curt salute from Wellington. But the old soldier was one of his greatest heroes, and he hardly needed the suggestion. Strictly speaking, the *Ode on the Death of the Duke of Wellington* was not written as Poet Laureate, since it was not requested by the Queen and had no official publication, but Tennyson none the less felt that it was his public duty. 'I wrote it because it was expected of me to write,' he told his aunt Russell.[21]

The *Ode* gave him a good bit of trouble, but he had it ready by the end of October, and he came to London to sell it to a publisher. As Jacksons of Louth had discovered when they were publishing *Poems by Two Brothers*, Tennyson was surprisingly shrewd about payment for his poetry. The *Ode* was a labour of love, but he had every intention of getting hard cash for it. John Parker offered him £150 for an edition of 10,000 copies at a shilling each; 'Tennyson will accept this', wrote Walter White, 'if Moxon, to whom he went forthwith, is less liberal in his offer.'[22] With a definite sum to discuss, Tennyson was in a good position, and Moxon had to offer him £200 for the same number of copies to be sold at two shillings, with the rate to apply to any further printings, of which there was one a few months later. It first appeared on 16 November, two days before Wellington's funeral, in time to be hawked rather indecorously to the crowds at St. Paul's. Tennyson went to London to see the procession but did not go to the Cathedral.

Like the poems on the French threat earlier that year, the *Ode* celebrates the martial supremacy of England, as well as the person of Wellington, but with the important difference that the emphasis is on honouring heroism rather than inciting to fight. The result is a gravity, occasionally a nobility, that the other poems of 1852 totally lack. As was to be expected from earlier works, Tennyson was surest in the poem when dealing with specific detail, as in the recreation of the rhythm of the funeral procession in the opening stanzas (much of it comes from the reworked second edition):

> Bury the Great Duke
> With an empire's lamentation,
> Let us bury the Great Duke
> To the noise of the mourning of a mighty nation,
> Mourning when their leaders fall,
> Warriors carry the warrior's pall,
> And sorrow darkens hamlet and hall.

> Where shall we lay the man whom we deplore?
> Here, in streaming London's central roar.
> Let the sound of those he wrought for,
> And the feet of those he fought for,
> Echo round his bones for evermore.

It is when he has to shift to more abstract matters that Tennyson comes unstuck, as in the celebration of Wellington's place in history. Repetition is nearly always for him a sign of lack of certainty:

> O peace, it is a day of pain
> For one, upon whose hand and heart and brain
> Once the weight and fate of Europe hung.

There is insufficient difference between hand and heart and brain, any one of which might stand for the fatefulness of the Duke's personal qualities; 'weight' and 'fate' seem arbitrarily linked for rhyme not meaning, when either would do by itself. Tennyson is trying by reiteration to achieve apotheosis, but the effect is dangerously close to padding.

In spite of its faults the poem is one of the most successful he ever wrote with the intention of speaking for a whole country, and it does achieve the difficult fusion of the personal and the heroic that makes one man the symbol of a realm. At the time it was only a mild success with the critics, although it has in our own century achieved a reputation that it did not have on first publication.

CHAPTER XXIV

FARRINGFORD AND *MAUD*, 1852–1855

ALTHOUGH they had not yet found a house, by the end of October 1852 the Tennysons felt obliged at any cost to escape the damp, mists, and bad drains of Twickenham. When they heard that Lord Howard de Walden was willing to let Seaford House, half-way between Eastbourne and Brighton, they took it until after the New Year at £2 a week, furnished. The gardens were still in flower, when everything at Twickenham had been killed by frost. There were good views of both sea and downs, and Alfred loved the thunder of the waves on the shingle. Previously they had thought little of living near the sea, but now it seemed obvious to do so.

While they were in the area, Tennyson went to Eversley in Hampshire, at the invitation of the Rector, Charles Kingsley, who had found a Jacobean farmhouse he thought would suit them. Tennyson enjoyed his pipes and conversation with Kingsley and would have liked to live near enough to have them frequently, but the northward aspect of the house and the constant damp from the springs on which it was built made him decide against it. There were abortive excursions to see other houses in the spring of 1853, but nothing else was quite right after a taste of living by the sea.

Once back in Twickenham, Tennyson's health seemed to be deteriorating. His friends noticed that he was drinking a good deal and that he could not settle down to composing poetry. That spring he had to have some of his teeth extracted and to be fitted with false ones. He had trouble with them for a long time; his plates never fitted well and were responsible in part for the dour, unsmiling aspect of many of the later paintings and photographs of him. It was probably to hide the changed shape of his mouth that in 1855 he began to grow the beard and moustache that were so characteristic in later life.

Both her own ill health and the responsibility of the baby made it difficult for Emily to accept engagements with Alfred. For a time he hardly went to London except on business, although he did find time occasionally to go to the Cosmopolitan Club, which had been founded the year before as a meeting place for a set of youngish men that included such artistic friends as Venables, Palgrave, Spedding, Brookfield, Milnes, Browning, Thackeray, Holman Hunt, and G. F. Watts, as well as many politicians. They met in Charles Street, Berkeley Square, in a curious windowless room, belonging to an auctioneer, that had been Watts's studio. The club provided no meals and was opened for informal smoking only an hour or two before midnight, at a time when members could come in after dinner parties or the House. It was a brilliant group, 'the arcanum & the Parnassus of literary swells'. One evening in March 1853 Tennyson was there with a company so scintillating that Henry Reeve wrote: 'I don't know any other room in London which could contain such a force of men.'[1]

Even in a group whose chief excuse was smoking, Tennyson's addiction to tobacco was remarkable. Lord Lansdowne used to tell how, as a young man, he was asked at the Cosmopolitan by Tennyson whether he smoked. When he admitted that he did not, Tennyson said, 'Oh, you make a great mistake. Now, begin tonight. You shall begin by taking a pull at *my* pipe.' With that he took the blackened clay from his own lips and offered it to Lansdowne, who eyed with trepidation the nicotine dripping from the mouthpiece. 'I could not resist his eye, and I did as I was told,' he would say with a shudder of recollection. 'But it did not induce me to begin the regular habit of smoking.'[2]

Tennyson was asked to join many clubs, and he was a member of several, but he was not essentially clubbable, for he was at his best with a few friends rather than in a large group. At the Cosmopolitan where he and 'some great man of Darmstadt' were the only two honorary members, he smoked much and spoke little.

At the end of July 1853 Tennyson took Emily and Hallam to the north for a holiday. They intended to explore Yorkshire, then go on to stay at Carstairs, the Monteith house near Glasgow, from which Tennyson would continue for several weeks in the Highlands while Emily, who was pregnant again, went back to Grasby in time for Hallam's first birthday to be celebrated with the Turners. Accompanying them was Palgrave on his first trip with Tennyson, in polysyllabic bliss at the idea of travelling with the Poet Laureate. At Richmond in Yorkshire Emily fell ill, or, as Palgrave put it, 'that devoted wife whom one cannot think of, and can hardly write of, without some admiring prefix, found herself unable to bear the fatigue further'. She took Hallam directly to Grasby, while Tennyson and Palgrave went on.

Palgrave was already proving himself too assiduous in his care of Tennyson, who finally had to stipulate that he have time alone to smoke, think, and look at the view. Trembling with solicitous anticipation, Palgrave would wait behind a 'sheltering rock or covert' until the signal was given for him to rejoin Tennyson. 'It is not, however, to be hence inferred,' said Palgrave, 'that my dear and honoured companion had anything which would be correctly termed a recluse, exclusive disposition.' Palgrave also liked a more careful itinerary than was habitual with Tennyson, who put off all plans by saying, 'We will talk after to-morrow's after-breakfast pipe.' In Edinburgh they separated for a time, while Tennyson went to stay in old-fashioned comfort at Carstairs. Palgrave, he told Emily, 'accused me at parting of a Goethe-like coldness and indifference to friends. I really believe he has a liking for me which he thinks is not fully returned.'[3]

When Tennyson rejoined Palgrave at Ardtonish in Morvern, things went better, for they were with friends of Palgrave, who in company hid his zeal to be with Tennyson every moment. The trip to the Highlands, however, had to be cancelled because of a sudden illness that sent Tennyson off to Edinburgh, where he stayed for three weeks, chiefly seeing Ludovic Colquhoun, with whom he had been friendly ever since they met 'under hydropathic circumstances' at Umberslade, where they talked as they sat soaking with reddening 'spines & posteriors' in Dr Johnson's baths. Palgrave's journal does not suggest that he was invited to stay with Tennyson in Edinburgh, and Tennyson probably welcomed a temporary escape.

After their return to Twickenham, Tennyson went to the Isle of Wight to visit James White of Bonchurch, with whom he had stayed in 1846. Once more he was looking for a house by the sea, and the then totally secluded island was a better place to find one than the more fashionable south coast. While in Bonchurch Tennyson heard of a house called Farringford, near the little village of Freshwater at the western end of the island. 'He went and found it looking rather wretched, with wet leaves trampled into the lawns.' None the less he asked Emily to see it, as her journal records. 'The railway did not go further than Brockenhurst then and the steamer, when there was one, from Lymington felt itself in no way bound to wait for the omnibus which brought as many of the passengers as it could from the train. We crossed in a rowing boat. It was a still November evening. One dark heron flew over the Solent backed by a Daffodil sky. We went to Lambert's, then Plumbly's Hotel & smaller than now. Next day we went to Farringford & looking from the drawing-room window I thought "I must have that view", and I said so to him when alone.'[4] The rent for the house was exactly what they had paid for Seaford House, £2 a week, furnished. On 11 November 1853 Tennyson wrote to agree to a three-year lease with an option to buy at its conclusion, which would be almost coincident with the end of their lease on the house in Twickenham. The remainder of the lease of Chapel House he turned over to his mother, who moved there from Cheltenham, bringing with her Matilda, Septimus, Arthur, and Horatio, the still unmarried children. Presumably Tennyson thought they were all more immune to damp, floods, and bad drains than he and Emily.

On 24 November they took their leave of Twickenham and arrived at Lymington, where they slept, for even in their eagerness to be in their new home they were afraid to take Hallam in a rowing-boat. Early the following morning, before the mists had lifted, they arrived at Farringford. 'Two of the servants on seeing it burst into tears saying they could never live in such a lonely place.'[5] But their weeping could not spoil the pleasure of Alfred and Emily in their arrival at the house that was to be the family home for nearly a century.

Farringford is not on the shore, where they had hoped to find a house, but it is within sight, sound, and smell of the sea, and the lawn is often white with gulls that have flown in sideways on the wind over the downs that protect the house from Channel gales. It was a miniature Georgian country house built in 1806 and considerably enlarged four years later, so that it had about fifteen rooms when the Tennysons first saw it. During the enlargement it had been decorated with charming Gothick parapets and wood-mullioned windows imitating stone tracery. The decoration was almost exactly contemporary with that added to Somersby Rectory, and it is not surprising that it was reminiscent of Tennyson's boyhood home, the last place he had lived permanently until now. Like his father and uncle, Tennyson greatly preferred the Gothic style to the classical, and all three houses most closely connected with him, Somersby, Farringford, and Aldworth, were neo-Gothic in building or decoration. 'It is like blank verse,' he said, 'it will suit the humblest cottage and the grandest cathedral. It has more mystery than the classic.'[6] It sounds like an echo from Ruskin or Charles Tennyson d'Eyncourt.

The walls of Farringford were covered in creeper that in time nearly buried the house, which was dark inside because of the trees so close to the windows. There were, however, splendid views of the Solent to the north and over Freshwater Bay to the south-east. Only a few minutes walk from the house were the great chalk cliffs of the downs, towering 500 feet above the rocks rounding away westward to the Needles. The springy turf on the top of the downs was kept cropped by sheep, and the cliffs were alive with sea-birds. It all seemed light years away from London and was so remote in actuality that the porter on the dock at Yarmouth used to shout to passengers for Lymington, 'This way to England!'

In spite of his love of the seclusion of the island, Tennyson sometimes badly missed London and his friends. Emily, who could happily have gone on for years without seeing anyone else, was aware of this and tried to maintain a constant flow of guests across the Solent, to keep Alfred contented with their new home. She kept a good table for her guests, and she would put up as many as the house would hold, sending the overflow down the hill to the little hotel at Freshwater. There was great care taken for the guests' comfort, but there was little doubt about whose benefit the entertainment was for. Tennyson quickly developed his own habitual schedule at Farringford, which was useful in giving him regular times for composing poetry, and guests were expected to fit their activities into his routine. He normally ate early breakfast alone in his room and then sat either there or in his study thinking about his verses. Occasionally he would join a guest at breakfast without eating himself, keeping his hat on in silent witness of his intention to leave soon. Rain or shine, before lunch there would be at least a two-hour walk, in which he was usually accompanied by the younger guests who could keep up with his rapid shuffle. In the afternoon there was another long walk, during which he would talk about what he had just written. Dinner was between 5 and 6.30, although the clocks were so inaccurate that it was hardly a fixed feast, and it was simple, to suit the host's tastes. Most often there was a roast, carved at table, as frequently by Emily as Alfred; it was accompanied by claret, on which the Tennysons like to economize, occasionally drawing wry remarks from the guests when recording their stay. A curious habit was observed, copied either from the combination rooms of Cambridge or from the old-fashioned household at Carstairs, where Tennyson had often seen the Monteiths move from the dining table for dessert. At Farringford everyone withdrew to a little ante-room for dessert, where port was taken when the ladies had gone. Afterwards Tennyson would go up to his study under the eaves for an hour or so, during which he worked again on his poetry. Emily would entertain the guests while lying on the sofa in the drawing-room, until Alfred came down and took the men upstairs for a smoke and a talk about poetry. When they reappeared for tea, Tennyson would often read his own poetry aloud to the company, sometimes for as long as two or three hours. If the party was small, the reading was in the study so that Emily could go to bed. There were only minor variations in this routine, which made it easy for guests to discover how much time they were expected to spend with their host, but it was so centred on Tennyson and his poetry that some of his friends soon found excuses not to make the crossing to the island. In spite of frequent invitations neither Browning nor Carlyle ever stayed at Farringford; as late as 1867 Emily complained that Spedding had never been there, Fitzgerald apparently never returned after his first stay, and eventually even the most constant of friends like Edward Lear began sending their regrets.

As soon as she could, Emily increased the staff, until at last there were a butler, housekeeper, cook, lady's maid, several parlour and kitchen maids, and a page inside the house, with gardeners, coachman (this much later), and grooms outside. When Tennyson bought the neighbouring farmland, he added farm labourers and a shepherd. There was a nurse for the children when young, then a succession of recent university graduates as tutors.

Although so much of her life at Farringford was spent lying on a sofa, Emily Tennyson kept the house comfortable by a strict surveillance of the staff. In the Tennyson Research Centre is a copy of her 'general orders' for the domestics. It is a detailed description of what was expected of them, beginning with 'Be downstairs at half past six o'clock. Move quietly', until their 'Needle-work after dinner' and the stern injunction, 'Do not go out without leave.' After a few initial catastrophes with insolent staff, Emily was generally loved by those who worked for them, as was Alfred, although he worried unduly about not having their respect.

It sounds a grand household for a man who only four years before had been forced to beg beds of his friends and two years before had said he could not afford court dress to be presented to the Queen. On the very day he agreed to take the house he asked Moxon to send him £400 that was already owed to him, and £600 to be paid the following March. 'Why I did it?' he asked. 'Because by buying safe debentures in the East Lincolnshire Line for two thousand five hundred pounds, with that and five hundred a year I think we ought to get on.' Tennyson's son assumed that the 'five hundred a year' referred to his earnings from poetry, but it was actually the income from his inheritance. In 1853 his income from his work was £1,658, and three years later it was more than £2,000, a truly startling amount for a poet to earn. To his income from his poetry must be added the £500 from his inheritance, the small amount that Emily had brought to the marriage, slightly over £100 from the Laureateship, his pension of £200, and the £100 that he still got annually from his aunt Russell: in 1853 a total well in excess of £2,500. He had little capital, but he had the income of a rich man, a fact that he carefully concealed. Probably even Emily never knew how much money he made, as many other Victorian wives never knew their husband's incomes. 'I think we ought to get on' was a considerable understatement.

The belief that he was a poor man, which Tennyson had been fostering for so many years, was beginning to take on a slightly selfish quality that some of his relatives and friends resented. Only a few months after moving to Farringford, he acknowledged a cheque from his aunt, saying that it was 'most welcome, however some one (I know not who, perhaps that cackling fellow, Jesse) may have been dilating to you about my elegant sufficiency. If I were to die tomorrow I could only leave my wife &, now two, sons £150 per ann. in railway shares: that is surely no great matter: meantime my books make money but who can guarantee that they will continue to do so. A new name, & such must arise sooner or later, may throw me out of the market: even a Russian war (for books are nearly as sensitive as the funds) may go far to knock my profits on the head.'[7] Tennyson's unwillingness to buy court dress in 1851 was paralleled years later by his borrowing robes to take his seat in the House of Lords. He was constantly pleading poverty: he even managed to get out of the expenses of taking a peerage when he was a rich man, he worried over the subscriptions to the various clubs to which he belonged, and it seems probable that he was an honorary member of the Cosmopolitan because he had said that he could not otherwise afford to belong.

Tennyson's attitude towards money was the same as that of his father, who had learned it from the Old Man of the Wolds. Alfred's grandfather undoubtedly had a broad streak of meanness that made him stingy with everyone except his son Charles. Dr Tennyson was not mean, but he was so improvident that the result was the same, for he was in a constant state of worry that his outlay would far exceed his income, which made him ungenerous to his wife and family. With

these two as his primary models in his immediate family, it is understandable why Tennyson so often pleaded poverty, for he sincerely
thought that his financial demands were far more than anyone else
could possibly comprehend, and that he was perpetually on the brink
of disaster. There is no reason to doubt that he honestly believed for
many years that he was too poor to ask Emily Sellwood to marry him,
but it was a belief that would have been exploded by either a rational
examination of his situation or an overwhelming desire to marry.
What was perhaps the least attractive aspect of his whole attitude was
his willingness to take money from others, FitzGerald and his aunt
Russell for example, and his keeping, when he was the best-paid
literary man in England, the government pension intended for relief
from financial misery.

Emily Tennyson gave birth to another son on 16 March 1854. It had
been a difficult pregnancy, and she was so ill afterwards that she was
unable to walk for more than a month. Tennyson, who had first
attempted mesmerism in Malvern at the request of a local doctor, now
employed it upon Emily with great success. There were no more
children, for she was now nearly forty-one and it would have been
foolhardy to have more.* According to Emily, Alfred was watching
the stars from his study when he heard that the baby was born,
'and saw Mars in the Lion culminating. This afterwards determined
us to give our baby the name of Lionel—a family name before
proposed among others.' What Tennyson had in mind, of course,
was England's declaration of war on Russia. In *Maud* he turned
the phrase into the hero's vision of hope when he 'pointed to
Mars/As he glowed like a ruddy shield on the Lion's breast'. Emily's
assumption that Lionel was a family name indicates that she by now
believed in the splendid but faked pedigree that Charles Tennyson
d'Eyncourt had paid Bernard Burke to make for the family,
tracing their descent from Lionel, Duke of Clarence and son of
Edward III. Alfred's brothers and sisters thought Emily rather
snobbish, and it would be tempting to regard this as an innocent
example of her pretension that Alfred did not share, were it not that he
said of his family some years later: 'I have myself never made a study of
my ancestry but those who have tell me that thro' my great grandmother one of the Lascelles Claytons and thro' Jane Pitt a still remoter

---

* There have been suggestions that she bore one more son in the 1860s, who did not
survive infancy, but the total absence of records of such a birth makes the story
extremely improbable, as well as her age by then.

grandmother I am doubly descended from Plantagenets (Lionel Duke of Clarence and John of Lancaster) and this thro' branches of the Barons d'Eyncourt.'[8] He had come a long way from the old days at Somersby when they all laughed at the airs of his uncle Charles; the aristocratic shrugging off of detailed knowledge of his ancestry could well have come from the mouth of the Right Honourable gentleman walking on his barbican at Tealby.

Tennyson was wrong in thinking that Lionel might be a soldier when he was grown, but he was certainly a rebel against most of what his family stood for. 'I dont think the younger one will turn out such a noble child as Hallam but who can tell,' wrote Tennyson. Hallam was to become a highly conventional man, obedient, careful, devoted to his parents almost beyond credibility. Lionel was far more interesting, with some poetic ability, a mercurial personality, a talent for getting into scrapes, and a charm that his elder brother never had. The headmaster of their first school correctly described them: 'Lionel the more brilliant, Hallam by far the more accurate'.[9]

As middle-aged parents, Emily and Alfred were excessively devoted to both their children, but it seems clear from their letters that Hallam was the favourite from the beginning and that Lionel was a constant source of worry. The boys had few playmates of their own age, and they were perhaps petted too much, if not actually spoiled. They were dressed picturesquely, and for special occasions wore belted tunics, lace collars, scarlet stockings, and slippers with straps. Although several of their parents' friends cautiously suggested that they needed the bracing effects of a boarding-school, they were kept at home for a long time because school would mean cutting their shoulder-length hair. Tennyson was often impatient with them, but he wanted to be a good father, and he tried to make up for their lack of playmates by teaching them games and the lore of the countryside. Emily poured out on them all the love that she had been denied in childhood by her mother's early death, but the boys might have profited from a more detached concern.

When writing to Patmore to thank him for congratulations on the birth of Lionel ('if the births of babes to poor men are matters of congratulation'), Tennyson said that his troubles were keeping him from writing. 'We have hardly seen a human face since we came here, except the members of our household. Happy, I certainly have not been.' Yet at the same time that he felt lonely Tennyson was increasingly worried that the Isle of Wight was being overrun and that he was in danger of being invaded by Cockneys in his hiding place at Farringford. That year a young boy who was staying with his tutor at Freshwater went to Farringford, hoping to see the author of the poems he loved. At last he was admitted to the house by Emily, then through the door he heard Tennyson ask anxiously, 'Who is it? Is it an impostor?' It was to avert such neurotic touchiness that Emily encouraged their friends to come to Farringford. The journey was not easy, and guests had to be prepared, after crossing the Solent, to go by foot for two and a half miles to Freshwater. Emily's instructions to Lear on his first visit told him that 'if you would like to walk from Yarmouth the gardener's donkey-cart should be there for your luggage. We have not ourselves yet attained to the dignity even of a garden chair.'[10] All the same the friends and admirers swarmed to Farringford; most of them at the time were bachelors, because the journey was thought too much to ask of a woman. Among the early visitors were Lear, Patmore, Clough, Millais, Richard Doyle, the Lushingtons, and Tom Taylor.

Even FitzGerald came for nearly a fortnight to attend Lionel's christening, where he stood as proxy godfather for Drummond Rawnsley. Fitz was constantly amusing, and he translated Persian for Tennyson, who had been trying to learn the language but had to give it up because the characters so bothered his eyes that Emily had hidden his textbooks. Fitz played endless Mozart and Handel on Emily's rickety piano, and he brought her sketches of poppies and orchids and yellow irises. One day Tennyson took the paints from Fitz and tried his own hand at a seascape of the rocks below the downs, which is now in the library of Trinity College. As a picture it amounts to little, but it reveals a good deal about Tennyson's sight. Even when due allowance is made for his lack of skill, it shows that he saw little but swirling colour and form almost without definition. There is no sense of individual waves or of anything more precise than a great undifferentiated wash of light, in colour and composition like a very inferior late Turner.

FitzGerald, who came from a far grander background than Tennyson, was put off by the mode of life at Farringford. He was often asked to come again, but he would never do so, saying that if Tennyson 'did not live on a somewhat large scale, with perpetual Visitors, I might go once more to see him'.[11] FitzGerald was unnaturally sensitive to pretension, but his intransigence about returning to Farringford indicates clearly that he thought Tennyson was too big for himself.

On 6 June, when Fitz was returning to the house with the Tennysons from Lionel's christening, they found a caller in the house, Sir John Simeon, who had driven over from his home some eight or nine miles away. Simeon and Tennyson had such friends as de Vere and Milnes in common, and they had met years before with Carlyle, but they apparently had not seen each other in the interval. That year Simeon had inherited Swainston Hall, which was to become almost a second home to Tennyson. Simeon was a highly cultivated man, a bibliophile who wrote poetry himself and loved Tennyson's works, but their friendship was in other ways unlikely. Simeon had become a Roman Catholic convert in 1851, which automatically meant that he was suspect to Emily, and he was master of the local hunt, a sport of which Tennyson disapproved. All the same, he was to be the person who came nearest to replacing Hallam in Tennyson's affections, and until his death sixteen years later they were each other's closest confidants.

The year they met, the Simeons and their guests were frequently back and forth to Farringford, and occasionally the Tennysons went to Swainston, but Emily wrote that 'we are bad guests for however gladly we welcomed our friends at home we felt that our work and our chief pleasure was there & that there we must for the most part be'. Aubrey de Vere came to the island to stay at both houses and was delighted to find that he was even more impressed with Emily's spirituality than he had been at Coniston. Emily was slightly suspicious of him at first, for he had been converted to Roman Catholicism the same year as Simeon. She felt particularly threatened when the Simeons and de Vere were joined by Baron de Schroeter, 'who was like an old mediaeval monk in his faith. . . . [We] had frequent and long conversations on Romanism. . . . Still we remained true to our Church.'[12] All her life she was afraid that the Roman Catholics she knew were secretly trying to convert her, but Alfred, though he never liked the Roman Church itself, became surprisingly tolerant of the faith of its members.

Sir John Simeon had a small part in the writing of Tennyson's next major poem, *Maud*, which Tennyson had in mind by the spring of 1854, and which he was presumably writing at the time of Lionel's birth. The poem had grown out of the fragmentary 'Oh! that 'twere possible', which he wrote in 1833 and published in 1837. It has been conjectured that he had come to a halt in his writing of the new poem, and that Simeon suggested that he continue by working backward from 'Oh! that 'twere possible' to provide it with a narrative background. In any case, Simeon provided encouragement and Tennyson ever after connected the poem's composition with his help.

Throughout 1854 the Tennysons were in the bellicose mood they had felt since 1852, with the difference that it was now the Russians rather than the French who were the enemy. Shortly before Lionel's birth Tennyson had built a hut of rushes for Emily to lie in shelter looking at the downs. 'Sitting there we heard the sound of the cannon practising for the Crimea. Their booming sounded somewhat knell-like.' In September Emily vowed that the first songs she would teach her sons would be patriotic ones, and the mood of the house may be judged by little Hallam's war games in which he would roll on the floor and say, 'This is the way the Russians fall when they are killed.'[13] On 14 November *The Times* printed an account of the gallant and bungled charge of the Light Brigade at Balaclava, in which so many brave men died as the result of incompetent leadership. The newspaper leader spoke of 'a hideous blunder', which became transformed in Tennyson's mind into 'someone had blundered', so that he believed it was what he had read; from the new phrase were generated the compulsive rhythm and theme of one of the most famous war poems in the language. Tennyson was so moved by the newspaper account that on 2 December he wrote 'The Charge of the Light Brigade' in one sitting and sent it off to John Forster at the *Examiner*, where it was printed on 9 December.[14] Tennyson was worried that the number of men riding into the valley of death had actually been 700 rather than the 600 mentioned in *The Times*, but he and Emily decided that the metre was more important than numerical accuracy. Despite his worries about the quality of the poem it was an instant success, and within a few months Tennyson was sending 1,000 copies to the soldiers at Sevastopol for their inspiration.

One place he did not send a copy of the poem was Bayons Manor, but that did not prevent his uncle from reading it and expressing his distaste. Alfred's fame was coming just at the most painful time for his uncle Charles. It had been bad enough that the Queen had honoured Alfred when she had so signally and ungratefully failed to award the Tennyson d'Eyncourts the peerage they deserved, and that Alfred's poems were popular all over the world when *Eustace* went unnoticed. Now, only the previous month, Mr Tennyson d'Eyncourt had disowned his son Edwin as a social and moral disgrace to his family; at such a time it was unfair to hear everywhere the praises of his untalented and graceless nephew: 'What a strange thing that such a writer shd be so generally admired & crowned with Laurels by the Queen. Perhaps it is our want of taste which blinds us to his merits!' He sent his thanks to his son George for forwarding the verses, 'not for *their own merit*! but on acct of the trouble you have kindly taken to procure them. Horrid rubbish indeed! What a discredit it is that British Poets & Poetry shd have such a representative before the Nations of the Earth & Posterity! for a Laureate will so appear. Posterity will, it is hoped, have a sound judgment on such matters, & if so, what an Age *this* must appear when such trash can be tolerated & not only tolerated but enthusiastically admired!! However I do not wish to have my opinion circulated as to my Nephew's talents—for it wd only appear to many that I was either without Taste or spiteful, & he hearing of it wd deem it ungracious &c.'[15]

Like the martial poems of 1852, 'The Charge of the Light Brigade' contributed background to *Maud*, on which Tennyson had been working sporadically during most of 1854. A trip to Somerset in the summer suggests that he had abandoned *Maud* temporarily with the idea of working once more on his long-delayed Arthurian epic, but on his return he kept more assiduously than usual to his study to complete the poem. By January 1855 it was sufficiently polished for Emily to note in her journal that he read it aloud, the first of hundreds of times that he did so before his death. On 25 April he copied out the poem, which was essentially complete, although he did not send it off to Moxon for another three months; it was published on 28 July.

In the mean time the Tennysons went in June for Alfred to receive the honorary degree of DCL from the university whose initial letter he had once been unable to bring himself to capitalize. The degree had initially been proposed by Frederick Temple, then Principal of the training college at Kneller Hall, a short distance from Chapel House in Twickenham, where the Vice Principal was Palgrave, who had been at Balliol with Temple. Both men were friends of a young Fellow of Balliol, Benjamin Jowett, and Palgrave had brought the others to Chapel House to meet Tennyson. Initially Tennyson was nervous about acquaintance with a don, whom he expected to be hypercritical, but eventually Jowett became a close friend of the entire family and normally spent his Christmases at Farringford. He was one of the few men of first-class intellect with whom Tennyson maintained intimacy the rest of his life. In 1855 Jowett was helpful in getting the degree through Convocation at Oxford.

'I have strangely enough accepted the Oxf. Doctorship,' Tennyson wrote to his wife. 'Friends told me that I ought to accept so I did.' It was apparently the first time since their move to Farringford that Emily had so much as left the Isle of Wight. They took their children and their nurse to the Lushingtons, and in Oxford they stayed with Robert Scott, Master of Balliol, who had been a supporter of Temple's original proposal. Both of them were terribly nervous in anticipation of the ceremony in the Sheldonian Theatre, and from the gardens of Balliol where they waited to cross Broad Street, 'the shouts from the Theatre seemed to him like the shouts of the multitudes in early Christian times when they cried "Christians to the Lions".' He was still pale as he entered the Sheldonian, and though he was dressed with more than usual care his hair hung in disorder, making him look rather bedraggled. From the gallery a voice shouted, 'Did your mother call you early, dear?' Tennyson recovered his composure when there was one shout for *In Memoriam*, one for Alma, and one for Inkerman. He sat directly under the Chancellor, Lord Derby, with the other recipients of degrees: Sir George de Lacy Evans and John Burgoyne, British commanding officers in the Crimea, and the Comte de Montalembert. With innocent pride he afterwards remembered, 'I'm afraid I got the larger share of the undergraduates' applause.'[16]

In spite of his habitually dirty clothes, Tennyson took a childish pleasure in dressing up, and when the ceremony was over he wore his scarlet robe at lunch in Balliol, then when he smoked his pipe in the college gardens, and finally when he walked down the High Street to show Emily the buildings of Magdalen, to which they returned that evening to meet Montalembert and Gladstone. The next day they looked at the Raphael sketches in the Ashmolean, the illuminated manuscripts in the Bodleian, and walked in Christ Church meadows and New College garden. 'A strange & delightful feeling of strange worlds,' wrote Emily. They picked up the children at Park House and went back to Farringford. '*Maud* was finished, which added to the delight of returning.'[17]

Not surprisingly, many of the early reviews of *Maud* were puzzled and hostile. With hindsight it is easy to see that it grew directly out of his earlier works, but it is in part so different from them that it seemed to have come from another pen entirely, for it is probably the most original and highly experimental poem that Tennyson ever wrote. Even with a lapse of more than a century it is still a startling work, which many modern critics think of as his most important poem, but it was not what his readers in 1855 were expecting. It is a fusion of what he had learned in writing *The Princess* and *In Memoriam*, although the derivation is not immediately apparent.

Like *The Princess* it is narrative in conception, but instead of being a straightforward story in which the burden of emotion is carried by intercalated lyrics, in *Maud* the story itself is told by completely detached, self-contained lyrics. As in *In Memoriam*, the lyrics imply rather than state what has happened, but in this case there is a fictional plot, complete with characters and incident, lying behind the lyrics that make up the poem.

Unlike *The Princess*, which is told from several viewpoints, *Maud* is held within the changing consciousness of one unnamed central figure, who is at once actor, narrator, commentator, and lyricist. In spite of the implied plot, the real action of the poem is the fluctuating awareness of this central figure, and the lyric intensity is embodied in many moods as he moves from hatred and self-disgust through a too intensely passionate love affair to the killing that is the mirror image of that passion, finally coming to a wider love and the self-realization that is consequent upon it.

Briefly, the story is of a highly neurotic young man, son of a father who has killed himself over the failure of a business venture, falling in love with the daughter of the man who drove his father to suicide. In their absorption with money and power, both Maud's brother and father try to push her into marriage with a rich, vapid young lord, heir to a new fortune and an even newer and rawer 'cockney' house built to celebrate that fortune. When her brother discovers Maud and the narrator in the garden at midnight, a duel ensues, and the brother is killed. Maud dies, and the protagonist goes mad, is confined to an asylum in Brittany, and at last is cured of his madness by a purified love of the dead Maud that leads him to a more generalized love of mankind, which finally manifests itself by his going to the Crimea to fight on the side of right. He has at last achieved sanity and calm but is shattered in the process. The warfare that has raged in his soul, between his father and Maud's father, between himself and her brother, is but a parallel to the war between men in a world that is outwardly peaceful but inwardly full of greed and hatred worse than actual warfare, so that even the Crimean War, horrible though it is, seems at least an honest admission of the struggle between good and evil.

The basically manic-depressive alternations of the narrator before he is finally cured are the occasions for lyrics of heightened emotion, which made Tennyson append the sub-title, *A Monodrama*, some twenty years after the first publication. The monodrama, as Professor Culler has pointed out, derives from the eighteenth-century stage, where the passions were explored in speech alternating with music, for the purpose of investigating a range of intense emotions. As Tennyson uses the form, the music is embodied in the outbursts of passion themselves, so that the result is startlingly operatic.

Tennyson's employment of an initially unbalanced protagonist allows him the opportunity to run through a range of emotions so high-pitched as to be morbid, then later to stand back and see the emotions as overcharged. Although the poem is about hysteria, the distance between the two viewpoints is what keeps the poem itself from being hysterical.

Tennyson was as vehement (and quite as misleading) about denying the autobiographical significance of *Maud* as he was when talking of *In Memoriam*, but it is easy enough to see that many of the details of the story had parallels in his own life, and that the emotions were far from unfamiliar to him. The unbalanced state of the narrator's father that leads to his suicide after the failure of the speculation has obvious affinities with George Clayton Tennyson's neuroticism over his lost inheritance and his virtual suicide through drugs and drink, as well as to Tennyson's own breakdown after the failure of the woodworking scheme. The madness of the son, inherited from his father, suffered through young manhood, and at last cured by the power of love, is only too closely related to Tennyson's view of the history of his own mental troubles. The economic pressures that separate Maud and the protagonist are clear transmutations of the pressures of poverty that were symbolized for Tennyson first by the impossibility of his even contemplating marriage with a rich young woman like Rosa Baring, then by the barriers of imagined penury that kept him from marrying Emily Sellwood. Closely akin to this was Tennyson's awareness of the financial difficulties that he thought had kept Frederick from marrying either his cousin Julia or Charlotte Bellingham, and that kept Arthur Hallam and his Emily apart until his death. Many of the subsidiary characters and situations clearly derive their existence from persons or happenings in Tennyson's life. Maud's father, the 'gray old wolf', owes something to the Old Man of the Wolds; the 'new-made lord' with his 'gewgaw castle' on the moor glances at Charles Tennyson d'Eyncourt and Bayons; and the lord's grandfather, self-made mine-owner and 'Master of half a servile shire', may be taken in part from

Mrs Russell's father-in-law, as she thought. Clearly the madhouse scenes come from Allen's asylum at High Beech and the various water cures which Tennyson had patronized. Finally, Maud herself is undoubtedly derived in part from both Rosa Baring and Emily Sellwood.

In spite of all this, Tennyson was partly right when he denied that the poem was autobiographical. We recognize many sections that correspond to his own life, but we cannot therefore read backwards and assume that everything else is of necessity a direct transcription of his own experience. The emotions attributed to the narrator are autobiographical, the action is not.

In Memoriam was the result of Tennyson's trying to come to terms with the dehumanizing of the universe following Hallam's death. In *Maud* he attempts to deal with the other sources of deepest pain in his life. By the time he came to write the poem he had begun to realize that some of that pain was self-inflicted, the result of his profound inability to see the world in any but subjective terms, which in turn blinded him to the truth.

The deep and neurotic self-absorption of the narrator of *Maud*, which may be both cause and result of his mental instability, is responsible for his inability to judge others and their actions accurately. We really know little of what the other characters are like, only how they impress the mind of a man who is constitutionally unable to perceive them except as projections of his own psyche. Maud's brother, for example, is finally revealed as the possessor of a gentleness to Maud and a generosity to the protagonist that the latter has refused to see previously. 'The fault was mine, the fault was mine', the brother says as he is killed, but the protagonist knows that it was his own guilty hand that did the murder. The effect is to bring into question all the narrator's assumptions about the nature of those whom he hates; his self-absorption has denied him understanding of others and of society as a whole, so that it is only when he is willing to commit himself to others that he begins to see clearly. Even the insubstantiality of Maud herself as a character is the result of his never seeing her directly, only in the mirror of his own egotism.

But it is more than the protagonist's judgement that is brought into question. By the use of so much personal experience, Tennyson is investigating the validity of his own perceptions during those periods of great pain. His dealings with this autobiographical matter, however, are very indirect, no more than the implicit admission that he had perhaps been mistaken in his earlier opinions. His judgements of his father, uncle, grandfather, Allen, Rosa, even of Emily, and his attributions of blame in his unhappiness may have been coloured by his own egocentricity: that much he could bring himself to admit indirectly, even if he could never have said it bluntly in his own person.

The obliquity of the narration and the ambiguity of the narrator's perceptions are admirably suited to capitalize on Tennyson's lyrical genius while minimizing his general weakness at action and his inability to create a mind unlike his own. His use of an unbalanced protagonist is part of his strategy of simultaneous revelation and concealment, for the neuroticism of the speaker allows Tennyson to make passionate denunciations of his society, then to stand back and dissociate himself from statements that would be inappropriate to the Laureate. Once a vivid statement is made, however, it cannot be erased from the consciousness of the reader, even if the speaker is discredited. The deep disillusionment with the selfish, commercial exploitation of England remains after Tennyson has formally withdrawn from it.

The matter is particularly important in the closing section of the poem, with its invocation of the 'blood-red blossom of war with a heart of fire'. At this point the protagonist, according to Tennyson, is sane but shattered, which immediately makes one suspicious of his protestations. The critical battles ever since its publication about how the section is to be read are proof enough of the difficulty of deciding the final commitment of the poem. When we remember how bellicose Tennyson's attitudes had been ever since 1852, it is tempting to feel that he must be emphasizing the justice of the Crimean War. On the other hand it is difficult to believe that the poet is allying himself with a speaker who has so often been proved wrong. But Tennyson was subtler than his critics, for in leaving the finale of the poem so open he was creating not muddle but ambiguity, the considered opinion that what is finally mysterious is the value of personal heroism, patriotism, and the meaning of the 'purpose of God, and the doom assigned'. It is not a conclusion that can be generally popular today, but it is perhaps wiser than either a glorification of war at any cost or a wholesale dismissal of courage and commitment because the principles which prompt them may be suspect.

Maud was drawn from many of the conflicts that most perplexed Tennyson in his own life, and like *In Memoriam* it bears the marks of deep perturbation. If the protagonist seems remarkably like an extension of Tennyson himself, that is why he could both enter fully into his consciousness and still find him mysterious. It was when Tennyson had to imagine himself into the skin of someone totally unlike himself, as he did in the *Idylls of the King*, that the emotional intensity which is so Tennysonian suddenly seems dilute.

✳

CHAPTER XXV

A LITERARY LION,
1855–1856

To anyone else it would have been obvious that *Maud, and Other Poems* might run into trouble with the reviewers, but Tennyson was completely taken aback by their hostile reactions. In the first place, it was natural for them to find it hard to forgive him for the success of *In Memoriam* and so to be unusually critical of his next major work. If *Maud* had been more like *In Memoriam*, he would undoubtedly have been taken to task for lack of variety; as it was, he was reproved for a change that was a sad falling-off. The unattractive subject-matter of madness was asking for trouble, and he had not made it easy for readers to distinguish between the hero's glorification of the Crimean War and the poet's own attitude towards that unpopular campaign. Surely, it was also unwise to describe himself on the title-page as 'D.C.L., Poet-laureate', since it was apparent that the degree had been inserted in haste after the Oxford ceremony. Tennyson would have been genuinely surprised that anyone could think the simple truth about his degree and position was ostentatious. As late as 1886 both were still printed in his books and his name was given as 'Alfred Lord Tennyson'. Since he had already begun instructing the publisher about the use of his name in 1827, with the *Poems of Two Brothers*, and had been exigent about its form in the 1830 *Poems*, it is safe to assume that the description in 1855 was not added by Moxon without his knowledge.

The other poems in the volume included the 'Ode on the Death of the Duke of Wellington', 'The Daisy', 'The Brook', and 'The Charge of the Light Brigade', but most of the reviewers' attention was paid to the title poem, and the hostility centred on the hero's apostrophe to the Crimean War. George Eliot, who had admired Tennyson's earlier poetry greatly, took exception in the *Westminster* to the morbid story and its 'faith in War as the unique social regenerator'. Tennyson never forgot and seldom forgave unfavourable reviews, so their later friendship makes it improbable that he knew she had written this one.

Gladstone, who waited until 1859 to put his feelings into print, called the ending of the poem mere 'sound and fury' and said drily that 'we do not recollect that 1855 was a season of serious danger from a mania for peace and its pursuits'. He also took a passing swipe at Tennyson's DCL, 'which we perceive he always wears on his title-page'.[1] In 1879 he recanted in a second article on *Maud*, but that did not, for Tennyson, take the sting out of the original review.

Goldwin Smith, writing in the first issue of the *Saturday Review*, acutely noticed what was wrong with the protagonist's commitment in the conclusion, which was precisely what Tennyson's friends had been saying of him for years, that he tended to 'rely on external sensations instead of internal efforts for a moral cure'. As Smith pointed out, 'To wage "war with a thousand battles and shaking a thousand thrones", in order to cure a hypochondriac and get rid of the chicory in coffee, is a bathos.'[2]

Patmore said in private that he would not change one of his own poems for fifty *Mauds*. His public statement in the *Edinburgh Review* is a curious example of his divided attitude towards Tennyson, since it contains a good bit of disparaging criticism under the guise of a wordy defence of the poem: 'The public are widely afflicted just now with certain odd notions of what poetry ought to be. . . . The oddest of these notions is that a poet must belong to his age; whereas our forefathers have always held that a poet ought to belong to no age. All great poets, and even small ones, do and must "reflect the character of their time", as the cant phrase runs; but how? Not by taking the bread out of the mouth of the demagogue, or by doing the work of the parliamentary committee-man; but by the possession and consequent reflection of those peculiarities which constitute the permanent contribution of the age, whether for ill or for good, to the ever-growing tradition of civilization. Such possession and reflection evidently cannot be conscious. Accordingly, no man reflects our age more truly than Mr. Tennyson does, when he is not thinking of doing so.'[3]

Matthew Arnold, whose innate priggishness was often drawn out by Tennyson's poetry, said the volume was 'a lamentable production, and like so much of our literature thoroughly and intensely *provincial*, not European'.[4]

Rather more amusingly, one reviewer suggested that *Maud* had one too many vowels in the title and that it would make sense no matter which was deleted. Another warned solemnly: 'If an author pipe of adultery, fornication, murder & suicide, set him down as the practiser of these crimes.' For once Tennyson's sense of humour triumphed, and he answered, 'Adulterer I may be, fornicator I may be, murderer I may be, suicide I am not yet.'[5]

Unfortunately, he had no sense of humour at all about an anonymous letter he received: 'Sir, I used to worship you, but now I hate you. I loathe and detest you. You beast! So you've taken to imitating Longfellow.' It was signed simply, 'Yours in aversion'. Hallam Tennyson said that his father enjoyed repeating it 'with a humourous intonation', but the truth was that Tennyson was deeply wounded and nearly drove his friends mad for a year or two by pitifully repeating it and asking whether they had ever been so abused. He made some wholly inaccurate guesses about the identity of the writer, but he never found out who it was. Thereafter, nearly annually, 'Yours in aversion' would write to him, but Emily Tennyson soon became adept at spotting the envelope and removing it from the post before her husband could see it and become upset all over again.

Tennyson had put so many of his own emotions into the poem that he was inordinately sensitive to any adverse criticism of it, and he began defensively reading it aloud at every opportunity in order to demonstrate that it was only misunderstanding of its music that kept readers from loving it. He called the poem his 'bantling abused' and explained away his reactions: 'You know mothers always make the most of a child that is abused.' Even Emily rushed defiantly if not wisely to the defence, writing archly humorous letters of explication to friends and critics whom she suspected of not appreciating the poem fully.

The ease with which Tennyson could be wounded was always painful to see, but his theatrical exhibition of hurt was fortunately not repeated after *Maud*, both because he learned a little about how to conceal his distress and because the reviewers never again were so hostile. The truth was that there were also a number of favourable reviews, particularly from those critics who had read the poem several times, but Tennyson typically did not notice those, nor was he comforted by word that in little more than two months 8,000 copies had been sold, news that would have sent any of his contemporary poets into blissful transports.

There was plenty of other evidence about his standing in the world of poetry, had he cared to consider it. Although it was not so flattering as the Oxford degree, he was being honoured in Cambridge by an exhibition of his works in the church of St. Sepulchre. In London

Moxon was going ahead with the grand edition of his works that he had been planning for the past year, to be illustrated by some of the best young artists of the day, including Millais, Holman Hunt, and Rossetti, and though Tennyson was always awkward about having his words translated into pictures, it promised to be the finest volume of poetry of the decade. Yet it all seemed paltry to Tennyson in the face of bad reviews.

When he felt that the world was against him, it was heartening to hear that Browning, who had received an early copy of *Maud*, had read it four times and solemnly declared it to be a great poem. It was enough to prove that Browning understood about dramatic monologues and monodramas, to reconcile Tennyson to his flamboyant behaviour at Hallam's christening, and almost sufficient to make him warm to Browning's poetry. Emily's response was to ask the Brownings to Farringford. They sent their regrets and instead invited the Tennysons to London, although they must have known that Emily could not go. Tennyson spent five or six days in London and went on two evenings to the Brownings in their rented house in Dorset Street, Manchester Square, where William and Dante Gabriel Rossetti were asked in after dinner. The evening of 27 September perhaps tells us more about Tennyson's relations with his fellow poets than any other evening of his life.

Dante Gabriel Rossetti, whose first extended meeting with Tennyson this was, had long had mixed feelings about his poetry, recognizing its importance without being able to acquiesce totally to its language. Some measure of his attitude is given by the partially playful list of some 60 'Immortals' that he and Holman Hunt had compiled, in which Tennyson was given one star out of a possible four, above Spenser, Byron, Wordsworth, and Milton, but below Homer, Chaucer, Keats, Shelley, Thackeray, and Browning, not to mention Jesus Christ, Shakespeare, and the author of Job. Some of Tennyson's contemporaries who were also awarded one star were Patmore, Mrs Browning, and Longfellow. Although the diction of Tennyson's poems sometimes seemed inflated, Rossetti admired them for those pictorial qualities that made them the Bible of the Pre-Raphaelites; he had already made a woodcut of a scene from 'Mariana in the South' and he hoped to illustrate 'The Palace of Art' and 'The Vision of Sin' for Moxon's new edition. Out of admiration for *In Memoriam* he went in the summer of 1855 to see Hallam's tomb in Clevedon church, accompanied by Lizzie Siddall, who had loved Tennyson's poems ever since she first encountered one of them wrapped around a pound of butter. Rossetti was uncertain about his judgement of *Maud*, part of which he thought beautiful, 'but much is surely artificial, and some very like rubbish'. The occasionally overblown quality of Tennyson's verse had an irresistible fascination for a born parodist like Rossetti, who had shown many of his friends, including Allingham, his own version of 'The Kraken'. When he met Tennyson he was ready to be pushed either way in his regard for him.

At dinner Tennyson enchanted both the Brownings and Browning's sister, speaking well of everything that was on his mind; afterwards he smoked his pipe and drank two bottles of port, which made him even more confidential. 'If I had a heart to spare,' wrote Mrs Browning, 'certainly he would have won mine. He is captivating with his frankness, confidingness, and unexampled *naïveté*.' The intimate mood was broken with the arrival of William and Dante Rossetti. Tennyson continued drinking, and as he did he began his old recital of the letter from 'Yours in aversion', repeating the same stories, said Rossetti, 'at the very least six or eight times in my hearing, besides an odd time or two as I afterwards found, that he told them over to members of the company in private'. Instead of eliciting sympathy from Rossetti, the plaintive account amused him, and he was beginning to find Tennyson's conversation a 'perpetual groan'. The others tried to look as 'sympathising as their view of the matter permits', but Browning succeeded only in looking incredulous at any poet's caring so much for the opinion of others. Tennyson kept insisting that for the period between 1830 and 1842 'no notice whatever was taken of him, and seemed rather annoyed at anyone recollecting to the contrary'.

Mrs Browning saved the evening by asking Tennyson to read to them from their volume of *Maud*. He sat on the sofa facing her, his back supported by a cushion, his left hand pulling a foot up under him as he read, his right holding the book close to his near-sighted eyes, for he was not wearing spectacles. In his deep and resonant voice ('like an organ', according to Mrs Browning) he began the poem, his rough Lincolnshire accent colouring the vowels: 'Ai hate the dreadful hollow behaind the little wood'. Knowing how sympathetic the Brownings were to his 'bantling', he would frequently stop to say ingenuously, 'There's a wonderful touch!' or 'That's very tender.' During the softer passages the tears coursed down his cheeks.

Rossetti, sardonically listening in the shadow where he could not be seen by Tennyson, sketched the Poet Laureate as he read from the slim green volume, his face working with emotion behind the straggly beginning of a new moustache and beard. The drawings (Rossetti made two copies of the original) might be termed affectionate caricatures, showing both the dignified intensity of Tennyson's reading and his earnest awkwardness (see Plate XIII).

Two or three hours and 1,400 lines later he came to the end of Maud; one wonders whether Mrs Browning had expected the entire thing. Browning was then persuaded to read 'Fra Lippo Lippi', which was mercifully not more than a quarter the length of Maud. The difference in the reading of the two poets was marked, and William Rossetti's account indicates as much about their differing conceptions of poetry as it does of their voices: Tennyson's 'grand deep voice sways onward with a long-drawn chaunt, which some hearers might deem monotonous, but which gives noble value and emphasis to the metrical structure and pauses. Browning's voice, which was at once rich and peculiar, took much less account of the poem as a rhythmical whole; his delivery had more affinity to that of an actor, laying stress on all the light and shade of the composition—its touches of character, its conversational points, its dramatic give-and-take. In those qualities of elocution in which Tennyson was strong, and aimed to be strong, Browning was contentedly weak; and vice versâ.'

The basic difference between the dramatic irony of Browning's monologues and the focused emotional intensity of Tennyson's monodrama was acutely noted by William Rossetti, remarking on a physical peculiarity of Browning, who had one eye that was short-sighted, one long-sighted. 'This discrepancy of physical vision always appeared to me a singular parallel or emblem of the duality of mental vision which is so apparent in Browning's poems.' On the other hand Tennyson's acute myopia seemed emblematic of his usual perception of persons and emotions in unity rather than duality.

Tennyson was fond of saying that he had no training in music and no real appreciation of it, whereas Browning knew a great deal about it and loved it, but that ironically Browning's poetry had no music while his own overflowed with it. Thomas Moore, that rare combination of poetical lyricism and musical gifts, put the matter another way, when he said it was those poets who have no real ear for music who attempt to give their poems musicality by chanting them. The fragmentary recordings of Tennyson's readings made at the end of his life demonstrate his emphasis on metre and the lyrical qualities of his poems at the expense of discursiveness.

After his reading Tennyson inscribed *Maud* for Mrs Browning. She had not read her own poetry, and Rossetti had not been asked to read. Was it forgetfulness on Mrs Browning's part that Rossetti was a poet too that kept her from asking him, or was it simple fatigue after the readings of the two older men, which lasted until 2.30 a.m.? Tennyson and Dante Gabriel Rossetti walked back to their respective lodgings together, and as they paced the dark streets of Bloomsbury Tennyson reverted once more to 'Yours with aversion'. When they passed the Holborn Casino, before which the cabs were still busy, Tennyson asked what the building was. 'I'd rather like to go there, but la!' and after a minute, 'there'd be some newspaper man, and he'd know me.' To his credit Rossetti recognized that Tennyson's attitudes, however naïve, were utterly without striving for effect: 'there was something most delightful in the genuineness of all this, and he is quite as glorious in his way as Browning in his, and perhaps of the two even more impressive on the whole personally'.

The walk through the London night, however, was to cement no friendship. Once Rossetti was away from the rugged integrity of Tennyson's presence he began to concentrate on those aspects of his personality that seemed ridiculous in retrospect, and as the years passed he liked Tennyson's poems less and less. By 1868 he no longer wanted even to see him, and when he did send Tennyson a copy of his new poems in 1870 he considered the letter of thanks 'rather shabby'. It was not until 1882, the year of his death, that Rossetti could come around again to an open admiration of Tennyson, saying sadly that he would rather have written 'Tears, idle tears' than the entirety of his own poems.

For his part Tennyson found Rossetti's illustrations for the Moxon edition unacceptable, since they departed from the text. As he heard more gossip about Rossetti, he was deeply shocked by his brand of Bohemianism and was finally convinced that he had corrupted Swinburne, 'the puny youth', and taught him bad practices. In Dorset Street he had been unaware that Rossetti was sketching him, so it was a rude shock to find Browning's copy of the caricature lent to an exhibition at the Burlington Fine Arts Club. After Rossetti's death he wrote tartly to William Sharp, who had asked for help on his biography of Rossetti: 'I have neither drawing nor painting by Rossetti . . . nor have I the slightest recollection of his being present when I was "reading . . . Maud".

However, all the disillusionment lay in the future when he left

Rossetti in Lincoln's Inn Fields so late on that September night. 'I dined yesterday with the Brownings and had a very pleasant evening,' he wrote home. 'The two Rossettis came in during the evening.' Perhaps significantly, there is no mention in the letter of Browning's reading. Mrs Browning wrote to Emily too, saying that Tennyson's visit had been 'an increase of joy and life' and made it 'worth while coming from Italy to England'.[6]

Tennyson also went for an ill-fated six o'clock family dinner with the Carlyles while he was in London. After the meal there was talk of what should be done if one were offered a title. Tennyson said emphatically that he would decline one for himself and that 'no title could excel the simple name of "Thomas Carlyle"'. While they sat smoking their long clay pipes at the cleared table, the other guest, David Davidson, an old friend of Mrs Carlyle, noticed that Tennyson would tactfully supply a quotation when Carlyle was unable to remember it. Tennyson talked a good bit about *Maud* to Carlyle, who had tried to read it without being able to finish it. Fresh from his evening with the Brownings, Tennyson offered to read the poem to Mrs Carlyle.

It was a thoroughly inauspicious occasion to read the poem aloud, but Tennyson was not to know that Jane Carlyle was suffering from terrible jealousy that brought out all her native sharpness, particularly to those she loved. She was brooding over her knowledge that Carlyle was fascinated, perhaps infatuated, with Lady Ashburton, and that her own intelligence and wit seemed totally outweighed by the wealth, flair, and social position of her supposed rival. Their friends noticed that Lady Ashburton was the only person who could mimic Carlyle when he was in a black mood and turn his depression to laughter, and even Tennyson remarked about the way Carlyle 'rollicked' with her. That autumn Carlyle often left his wife alone in Chelsea while he went off to Bath House for the evening with Lady Ashburton. 'Oh, good gracious!' wrote Jane Carlyle, 'when I first noticed that heavy yellow house without knowing, or caring to know, who it belonged to, how far I was from dreaming that through years and years I should carry every stone's weight of it on my heart!' It was certainly not the time for her to listen sympathetically to poetry about mad infatuation, and she was not disposed to feel much compassion for Tennyson in his worry over the reviews.

When Tennyson had finished reading, he asked how she liked the poem, and was told, 'I think it is perfect *stuff*!' Believing that only unfamiliarity could account for dislike of it, Tennyson plunged in again and read it through once more. 'It sounds better this time,' she said grudgingly when he was finished, but he was still not satisfied. A third reading finally bludgeoned her into saying that she liked it a great deal, which was certainly untrue. One need not believe every word of the story of the six-hour ordeal to see how doggedly Tennyson could pursue total surrender to his poor abused *Maud*.[7]

John Ruskin, who was in absolute agreement with the conclusion of *Maud*, wrote to Tennyson a month later to tell him how much he admired the poem, and the almost inevitable result was an invitation to Farringford; in her diary Mrs Tennyson recorded 'Another kind letter from Mr Ruskin but he does not accept As invitation to visit us only says he should like it'.[8] In spite of Ruskin's admiration for the delicate finish of the poem, he used the lines 'For her feet have touched the meadows/And left the daisies rosy' as an example of the pathetic fallacy, of describing nature as actuated by human feelings. Tennyson, who prided himself on his accuracy in matters of flora and fauna, constantly complained that he had only been referring to the delicately pink underside of the daisy petal. Once he pointed out a sheet of the flowers to his sons' tutor and said that he 'thought of enclosing one to Ruskin labelled "A pathetic fallacy"'.

It was perhaps fortunate for his relationship with Tennyson that Ruskin never got to Farringford, but there were many other successful visitors, chiefly chosen by Mrs Tennyson for their ability to keep Alfred happy. Thomas Woolner came to stay while he modelled a medallion of Tennyson, which she thought 'the best likeness that has yet been made', in spite of the hauteur of the handsome head and the deep lines around the mouth that lent arrogance to the expression (see Plate XVI). Edward Lear spent some time there in October, singing in his high untrained voice his own settings of 'Mariana', 'The Lotos-Eaters', and 'Oh! that 'twere possible', with an intensity that made his lack of technique unimportant and made even Tennyson approve of the songs, although he usually hated having his poems set to music. Lear thought briefly of settling down on the Isle of Wight and wrote to ask Tennyson: 'Do you think there is a Pharmouse or a Nin somewhere near you, where there would be a big room looking to the North?—so that I could paint in it quietly, & come & see you & Mrs Tennyson promiscuously?'[9] There is no indication that he received any encouragement in the plan, which was soon forgotten.

Frederick Pollock the eminent barrister and his wife visited 'Ffaringford' in the autumn of 1855 from their hotel in Freshwater. On the evening of the first day Tennyson began reading *Maud* but was unable to finish it before they went back to their hotel. The next day the Pollocks returned and sat in the garden while he completed the reading. At Christmas Jowett and Palgrave came for a few days and helped put up holly and evergreens through the house. On Christmas Eve several neighbours came in, and when the talk became too formal Tennyson insisted on playing blind-man's buff, which even Emily enjoyed.

Tennyson loved Farringford itself and he frequently liked its isolation, but even with a constant flow of house guests he was beginning to feel cut off from the life of London. One clear sign of his discontent with the island was that he was complaining again of his poverty, which might force him to move. Emily, who was seldom totally happy except when she was at home, tried to keep him so engaged that he had no time to long to be away, but she sometimes succeeded only in making him feel more caged. Try though she would, she worried about his unconventional ways and gently attempted to reform them. When he wrote to her of his weekend activities in London with the 'naughty infidel' Spedding, she replied: 'I must say I am puritan enough to be sorry thou shouldst have spent Sunday morning so. May be it was but a slip of the pen & yesterday meant the day before. My idea of Sunday is a day of high spiritual enjoyment thou knowest.' By autumn of that year she noted his reform in her diary: 'We go in the afternoon to church whenever able, the morning service being too long for my strength except on Communion Sundays when I go for that service only.' It was a reform that was only temporary in its effects, and the residents of Freshwater often spoke of the infrequency with which Tennyson was seen in church. Emily hid his books of Persian to save his eyes and instead played backgammon with him. At the end of 1855 she wrote in her diary, 'We make a bonfire of leaves & burn the box with all the pipes in it having just put the last bit of tobacco into his study fire, for he thinks that he will smoke no more.' Like his appearances in church, the stern resolve to stop smoking did not last long, no matter how often Emily suggested it should be renewed, and he was still smoking incessantly at the end of his life, although he had burned a good many pipes before then. On at least one other matter her opinion had even less effect: 'I wish', she told Woolner, 'the public could compel Alfred by act of Parliament to cut off his beard!' Her incessant vigilance over his life was necessary, but it was somewhat chafing.[10]

All his tender concern for her and all her thoughtfulness to make him content at home were not enough to tame the vagrant spirit that had so long driven him around the country before his marriage. The deep difference in their habits made life difficult for them, and it is a mark of their love and their determination to make their marriage happy that there was never a rift between them, painful as their differences must have been at times. At the end of 1855 there seems to have been some kind of decision, probably unspoken, that he would accept invitations by himself, while she stayed at home with the boys. Contented without him she could never be, but she was less unhappy than she was away from her home and children, worried whether her health would stand up to the strain of travelling. For some years Tennyson had been refusing invitations from Lady Ashburton to go to one of her brilliant Christmas house parties at the Grange, near Alresford, because Emily had not been able or willing to accompany him. When Jowett arrived at Farringford for Christmas in 1855 he brought an urgent invitation for Tennyson from Lady Ashburton. On the last day of the year Tennyson left Farringford, protesting but happy at the thought of the literary gathering to which he was going. With his usual solicitude, he wrote to Emily from Southampton on his way; she said that it 'makes my New Years Day happy just as I had been saying to myself "it is dreary without him"'.

With the help of the Baring fortune, the brilliant, sarcastic Lady Ashburton entertained large parties at the Grange, at which the aristocracy to which she was born rubbed shoulders with the literary circle she had joined, both for her own pleasure and for the introduction of her intelligent but retiring husband to a wider world of art than he would otherwise have known. At the end of 1855 such social lions as the Bessboroughs, Lady Sandwich, Lord Clarendon, and Sir James Parke were beginning to leave as the literary contingent (her 'printers') were arriving. Carlyle, who had been there with his wife since Christmas, wrote that 'We are a fluctuating company, come like shadows, so depart'. Lady Ashburton liked social or political or literary eminence, but even more she liked entertaining conversation at her table, and for what was to be her last and most brilliant holiday party she had invited the Brookfields, Venables (he and Carlyle were her favourites guests), the Tom Taylors, Henry Taylor, Spedding, Richard Doyle, and others. During Tennyson's stay there were at least twenty-five guests in the house.

Most of the others had been there before, but as Carlyle wrote, 'The agreeable phenomenon at present is Alfred Tennyson. He has a big moustache, carefully cultivated, and with his new wideawake looks flourishing.' Somewhere between the bonfire of old pipes and his arrival at the Grange Tennyson had been back-sliding. 'Good company to smoke with in the conservatory,' Carlyle said of him.

Although their hostess thought of herself as having a *salon*, some of her contemporaries wrote her off as a tuft-hunter, and like others of that breed she sometimes made social gaffes. On this occasion she had made two. When Tennyson arrived, he found that the author of the review of *Maud* in the *Saturday Review* was already there, and typically he got his name wrong in reporting the guests to Emily: 'among others the Mr Golding Smith who wrote that article in the S.R. but I cannot say I find his presence particularly annoying.' Despite Tennyson's unusual tolerance of him, Goldwin Smith was an odd man out throughout his stay, for he had also managed to offend his hostess's two favourites, Venables and Carlyle, and they avoided him whenever possible.

The atmosphere was made more tense by Lady Ashburton's careful kindness to Jane Carlyle, who had not wanted to come to the Grange in the first place and was prickling with readiness to be offended by the woman her husband so admired. When she had arrived Mrs Carlyle was taken aback by the magnificence of the dresses and jewels that the other women were wearing. At Christmas her hostess gave her a silk gown, at which Jane Carlyle flew into a temper and said she was being insulted. Lady Ashburton had to seek her out in her room and apologize in tears before Jane would consent to join the party again. Surface calm was restored, but there was still thunder in the air. The cause of Mrs Carlyle's temper, which might not be obvious today, was that a silk dress was the usual gift for the housekeeper of a large establishment. For Lady Ashburton to have given a friend a dress that was not made specifically for her was to seem condescending at the least, even though her snub was surely not intentional.

In the midst of the cross-currents of emotion, Tennyson was unwontedly calm, taking no offence, charming everyone, and liking them in return. 'I cannot see in [Lady Ashburton] a touch of the haughtiness which Fame attributes to her,' he wrote to Emily, 'she is most perfectly natural tho' like enough she sometimes snubs her own grade now & then, when she sees presumption or folly.' Her husband was 'very tender-mannered and amiable'. Tennyson found smoking among the oranges, lemons, and camellias less pleasant than filling his own study with guilty fumes, but he repaired to the conservatory with the other men, among them Dickie Doyle, who made a quick sketch of him tamping his pipe with a long fore-finger, looking somewhat quizzical at his own inability to quit the habit (see Frontispiece).

On the second day of his stay, after several refusals, Tennyson was persuaded to read and to the surprise of no one chose *Maud*. Mrs Brookfield, who had heard him read it in London, was delighted with his choice, but Jane Carlyle, who felt that she had already had more than enough of the poem, was furious. When the guests were all assembled and waiting for him, Carlyle announced that he could not bear being read to and that he intended to take a walk instead, not adding that he had already tried *Maud* with considerable lack of success. But he also refused to walk alone. There was an awkward moment before Brookfield volunteered to come with him, saying he had already had the pleasure of hearing Tennyson. They were fortunately joined by Goldwin Smith, which spared Tennyson the embarrassment of having to perform under the hostile eye of his critic. The tension of the little incident made Tennyson nervous, but he felt that he 'got thro' it very well on the whole'. Though he read with unusual fire and variety, he was a little depressed by the silence of the circle of listeners, who were too '*politely shy* to encourage him by any interruptions of "how beautiful" &c.', to which he was accustomed. Mrs Brookfield said that he had 'converted Lord A. to the real beauty of it though *the plot* is too ghastly for his taste'. Lady Ashburton was reported to like him immensely, and all the guests agreed that he was very handsome in his new moustache and tiny beard.

Tennyson's deep insecurity, so badly aggravated by his fears for *Maud*, led him to ask his fellow guests what they thought of it, but it was unfair of Jane Carlyle to say that he went 'about asking everybody if they like his *Maud*—and reading *Maud* aloud—and talking Maud, Maud, Maud, till I wished myself far away among people who only read and wrote prose or who neither read nor wrote at all'. But she was sulking in her room until luncheon each day, while Carlyle and Lady Ashburton were riding, and she needed someone on whom to take out her unhappiness.

Tennyson, sublimely unconscious of her bad temper, enjoyed himself thoroughly, his lack of sensitivity to the emotions of others standing him in good stead on this occasion. Once at luncheon he was caught in the cross-fire of teasing without realizing what was happening. Henry Taylor was chaffing his hostess, saying that once he had been new man at her table and sat by her side, that last year it had been Goldwin Smith, this year it was Tennyson, and next year someone else would have supplanted him. Venables came to her defence, when to his horror Tennyson turned to him and began, 'Why, you told me yourself that Lady Ashburton had been very kind to you at first, but that now—'. Venables managed to stop him, and Taylor said, 'Well, Tennyson, all I can say is that my advice to you is to rise with your winnings and be off.' Truly, as Venables told Mrs Brookfield, Alfred was an innocent *enfant terrible*.

It was probably with relief that Lady Ashburton received a summons from the Queen to come to Windsor. Tennyson, who had originally intended to stay only three or four days, had been there twice that time, and he left with most of the other guests before his hostess's departure. Something of Lady Ashburton's taste in poetry is shown by her reading Browning aloud when Tennyson was gone, with Carlyle, who had claimed he could not bear listening to readings, sitting at her elbow, praising equally the poetry and her reading of it. On her return to London Jane Carlyle wrote to William Allingham about the party, adding that Tennyson had 'seemed strangely excited about *Maud*—as sensitive to criticisms as if they were imputations on his honour'.[11]

The party was never to be repeated, for by the following Christmas Lady Ashburton was dead. It had been an important event for Tennyson because it showed that it was possible for him as a married man to take part in social life even when Emily was unable to accompany him. He had been used for years to being made much of, but this was part of his gradual move to the top of the social ladder, so that in a few years he was as accustomed to the company of dukes and duchesses as once he had been to the illiterate parishioners of Somersby. It was a change in his fortunes that his uncle Charles found hard to stomach. All his life Tennyson remained curiously classless, and though it would be grossly unfair to say that he was a snob, in time he found as much pleasure in meeting other artists and intellectuals in the great houses of the aristocracy as he had taken in a chop and a pint of indifferent port at the Cock with his Cambridge friends when he was a young man.

Emily was ecstatic at Tennyson's return to Farringford. 'A peace comes to one from the quiet here *and one feels it good to have one's home* & I hope feels thankful for the beautiful home tho' I for my part prefer one on some heathy hill on the mainland.' But they had both had enough of looking for suitable houses before they came to Farringford. The lease was soon to be finished, and they decided to make an offer to Mr Seymour. They had earlier turned down the option price of £4,350, and now, after months of negotiations, they had to pay £6,900 for the house and park, plus a piece of farmland not included in the original option. In the mean time, the lease had fallen in on Chapel House, so they had to store their furniture from there, then to move into a house in Freshwater while Seymour had a sale of his own furniture. From him they bought a mahogany sideboard, cellaret, dining table, and six dining-room chairs for £15. Dr Tennyson's pictures from Somersby had been at Park House, and the Lushingtons sent those to help furnish the house, but there were not enough to cover the stains on the wallpaper, so Emily wrote to Woolner asking him to find oil paintings of 'red and flesh colour and bright frames' from a pawnbroker, preferably 'oldest copies of oldest pictures to be sold for one farthing each barring the discount on ready money'.[12]

In early May, while the house was in confusion, with the Seymour furniture set out for the sale and their own things stacked in boxes all over the rooms, a terrified maid came to Emily in the drawing-room and whispered, 'His Royal Highness Prince Albert.' Emily asked his equerry, Colonel du Plat, to bring him into the drawing-room, then went in search of Alfred, whom she could not find for some time. When he finally arrived, he found the Prince looking out of the big window at the view of Freshwater Bay. The Prince shook his hand in a friendly fashion and said that he was in the neighbourhood and had wanted to call when he heard that Tennyson lived there. Nervously, Tennyson rummaged among the boxes and found wine to offer to the Prince, but he was so taken aback by Albert's informal friendliness and by his own tardy arrival that he totally forgot to ask him to sit down. The Prince talked to him 'very gaily' and asked one of his gentlemen to pick a bouquet of the cowslips that grew on the untended lawn. When he left, he kept repeating that it was a very pretty place and that he intended to bring the Queen to see it very soon. It seemed fitting that the first nightingale the Tennysons had heard at Farringford should choose that night to sing.

It was a signal mark of Albert's friendliness that he should call so informally, just as he had paid his respects in Esher so unexpectedly. The Laureateship had been another indication of his admiration, and it is probable that the two men would have become closer had the Prince not died young. The Queen's kindness to Tennyson after Albert's death was a reflection of his feelings, but she was not capable of Albert's informality, and though there was community of heart between Sovereign and Poet Laureate there was little of the sharing of mind that could have made her husband a friend of Tennyson's on a man-to-man basis.

Four days after the Prince's visit, the Tennysons received word that the Queen was in Yarmouth and on her way to Farringford. Hastily they spread rugs in the entrance hall between the packing-cases, dressed the boys in their best rose-coloured costumes, and waited in the damp garden all during the stormy morning, but she did not appear, nor did she during the following week, while they stayed on the tiptoe of expectation. Even when she and Tennyson knew each other better, she always summoned him to Osborne or Windsor but never came to either of his houses.

On 3 June Farringford was still in upheaval, but the children's nursery was ready. Their parents installed them, went back to their temporary house for dinner, then in the calm summer evening they returned, entering by way of the garden. They inspected the barn that was now theirs, and in the kitchen garden Alfred gathered a rose for Emily before they went in the back door. 'An evening to be remembered. A gave me a welcome to our home which will be ever dear to memory.'[13] At last Farringford was their permanent home.

The final payment on the house was made in the autumn of 1856. Moxon had offered to advance Tennyson £1,000, but it was unnecessary. That year Tennyson made £2,058 from his English publications, and from America the payments were coming in from Ticknor, who was at that time the only American publisher to pay an English poet.

The new contentment that was evident in Tennyson's life was reflected in his work by his return to the task that had been alternately beckoning and frightening him since boyhood. For nearly forty years he had been pondering the Arthurian matter and planning an epic, writing out prose histories of Arthur, reading Malory, then the *Mabinogion*, Layamon, and all the sources of the legend he could lay his hands on. The 'Morte d'Arthur', written on the death of Arthur Hallam, had been intended to inaugurate the composition of the epic, but he claimed that Sterling's review of the poem in 1842 had stifled the project; rather oddly, perhaps, if he had waited eight years to find out what others thought of it before continuing. According to his son, it 'was not until 1855 that he determined upon the final shape of the poem' and began writing the first of the new idylls. It is true that he did

XVII. Lionel and Hallam Tennyson, 1857, by Lewis Carroll.

XVIII. Tennyson, c. 1857, probably by Lewis Carroll.

begin 'Merlin' early in 1856, but it is far from certain that he knew the final shape of the poem even then, since he was to continue revising that shape almost to the end of his life. What seems much more likely is that he felt sufficiently peaceful and established to take the risk of what he called the greatest of all poetical subjects, which might occupy him for years. Perhaps even more importantly, he had found out that he need not have the total shape of the poem in the forefront of his mind when he began it. *In Memoriam* and *Maud* had both been written as fragments and later assembled into a whole. Even so large a project as the Arthurian work might be handled in the same way, and that was how he set out to write it. Certainly, he had central ideas in mind, but the ultimate form was the result of tinkering, patching, and plugging, rather than a detailed knowledge from the first of what the *Idylls of the King* were to become.

By March he had finished enough of the first idyll, which finally became 'Merlin and Vivien', for him to read parts to Emily. On 10 April she wrote in her journal that 'A finishes writing out Merlin and gives it to me to read'. He was so pleased with the result and so hopeful about the larger project that he began another idyll, and within six days had already written the first part of 'Enid', which was later divided into 'The Marriage of Geraint' and 'Geraint and Enid'.

In August and September they let Farringford and took the boys to Wales, where Alfred would leave the others in a moderately comfortable spot while he went alone to the more remote areas to fill in his Arthurian background. All the time they were gone, he was working on 'Enid' and they were both studying Welsh, with the help of dictionaries and the schoolmasters they sought out wherever they stopped. Travelling without reservations meant that they often had bad accommodation, as on their first stop in Wales in Llangollen, when they had to move out of the hotel into a cottage, where, however, 'the harper played the children Welsh airs, and all soon forgot the uncomfortable quarters'. They went from Dolgelly to Barmouth, to Harlech, finally working their way to Caerleon. Emily was constantly ill and depressed by the bad weather, but she was forbearing and brave. When they arrived at Caerphilly station, there was no vehicle to take them to town until they found an old cart and an arm-chair, on which she entered the town in triumph. At Caerleon Tennyson was entertained by the Vicar and by a local landowner, who gave him all his own books about the town, but Tennyson was neurotically afraid of revealing his identity to his hosts. 'I suppose they have found me out', he wrote to Emily, 'though they have never alluded to my status.'[14]

After their return he worked hard at the last touches on 'Enid', which was finished in November. His writing habits were not easy, as Spedding told Milnes after Tennyson had stayed with him: 'The Laureate cannot breakfast with anybody. The process of excretion (I speak spiritually) begins immediately after the last cup of tea; is accompanied with desire of solitude and tobacco; followed (when no disturbing cause interferes) with the production of some five & twenty lines of Idyll; which the slightest obstruction offered to the natural process shuts up for the day.'[15]

At Farringford the visitors continued without let. Among others there was Richard Doyle, who came to sketch Tennyson (see Plate XIV) and the view from the drawing-room window. Arthur Hugh Clough spent a good deal of time with him while staying at the Freshwater hotel and wrote of him: 'I like him personally better than I do his manner in his verses; personally he is the most unmannerly simple big child of a man that you can find.' Woolner came once more, this time to model a bust, making rather perfunctory noises about his worry over bothering Tennyson: 'I feel certain he anticipates the operation with shoulder-shrugging horror and I feel sorry to torture him, but as it is a duty I owe myself and country I nerve myself to disregard the fact'.[16] Not surprisingly, Tennyson refused to be at all helpful, sitting only at night, when Woolner had to hold a candle in one hand while he modelled with the other, which may account for the result, Woolner at his blandest, a startlingly vacuous likeness of a Poet Laureate not a man.

Once he and Emily had come to an almost certainly unspoken understanding that he was to be away from home more often, Tennyson spent increasing amounts of time in London. Rather than tell him of her loneliness when he was away, Emily wisely learned to confide the briefest of entries to her journal, as she did in June 1856 when she had seen him off for the mainland: 'How cold & blank the drawing-room felt when I returned.'[17] In London Alfred had to discuss publication and finances with Moxon; he made innumerable visits to his dentist; he showed his poems to Spedding for advice; but chiefly he needed the reassurance that came with invitations from literary London. He constantly complained that he was being dinnered to death, but he felt neglected if left to himself. General conversation had never been congenial, but now he had stumbled upon what best suited him in dealing with a large party: his own readings. As both Mrs Brookfield and Mrs Browning had noticed, when he thought there was inadequate comment on his poems he would supply it himself, with the added advantage that he knew precisely where to praise. What he felt was not simple conceit, rather a deep insecurity that could be alleviated only by constant reassurance. Even at Cambridge he had always thought of his readings as occasions for congratulation not criticism. It was a tortuous problem for him: the more famous he became the more he was in demand to read, but the more he read the more he needed to believe that he was being praised for the intrinsic worth of the poetry not for the fame of the poet. There was no solution to the convolutions of such a problem, and it is understandable why he became so demanding of the full attention of his audience and so distracted if he did not receive it.

The place to which he most often repaired in London was Little Holland House in West Kensington, the home of Thoby Prinsep and his wife. As Holland House itself had been the spiritual—or at least temporal—home of the Whig aristocracy, Little Holland House became the Temple of the Arts in the 1850s and 1860s, with Mrs Prinsep as its presiding priestess. Her husband was a distinguished former Indian civil servant, noted for his erudition and his large, expansive manners, but beside his wife and her family he receded palely into the backcloth. Mrs Prinsep (known as the Principessa) was one of seven half-French Pattle sisters who had been born in India and brought to England at their father's death. They were rich, exuberant, intelligent, eccentric, and all but one of them were beautiful, so they naturally were soon dispersed in marriage through the aristocracy and peerage, where they stood out like peacocks in the flowing eastern draperies and scarves that they affected. Collectively, they were known as Pattledom and their meetings as Pattlefields.

At this distance, accounts of life at Little Holland House make it sound like a discarded act of *Patience*. The rambling old house with thatched porch and gabled roofs had started life as a farm to the great house of the Foxes, and though under the Prinseps it still had cows and pastures, barns and haystacks, there was something a touch theatrical about the effect, more than a hint of Marie Antoinette and *rus in urbe*. To populate the stage Mrs Prinsep would assemble all the available artists of any sort that she could find, to swell the cast of her Sunday at-homes, which went on the year round. Burne-Jones, Holman Hunt, Rossetti, Doyle, Leighton, and the hostess's son young Val Prinsep represented painting and drawing; Hallé and Joachim stood for music; Woolner for sculpture; George Eliot, Thackeray, Tom Hughes, the Brownings, Bulwer-Lytton, Patmore, and Henry Taylor were some of the most frequent literary guests; and there were others like Gladstone, Spedding, and Jowett who were not quite artists except by courtesy title. Besides all these, the chorus, there were two indubitable stars recognized by Mrs Prinsep. G. F. Watts had come on a visit, extended his stay, had a studio built, and finally was a guest in the house for twenty-one years; in his hostess's mind there was no doubt that he was England's Michelangelo. And there was Tennyson.

Chivvying them all around were the seven members of Pattledom, who included one of the most beautiful women in England, the Countess Somers, and her sister Julia Margaret Cameron, surely one of the plainest. Of all the sisters it was Mrs Cameron who was quickest-witted and whose gorgeous, slightly tawdry robes dragged the grounds of the Pattlefield most, so that one's impression of her was inevitably compounded of quirky intelligence and several layers of dust. Tennyson had met her shortly after his marriage, with the Henry Taylors in Mortlake, and the friendship was blossoming in Little Holland House, to come to full ripeness some years later in Freshwater.

On summer days Mrs Prinsep would have the furniture dragged out of the house on to the lawn and the tea urn put on a table under a tree. One of the visitors, the young George du Maurier, thought the Prinseps were 'conventional ... *par excellence*, cultural snobs', and uncharacteristically he worried about the atmosphere of loose morals that seemed to him to hang over the 'nest of prae-raphaelites'. After being at Little Holland House for a Sunday he wrote to his mother that the great artists 'receive dinners and incense, and cups of tea handed to them by these women almost kneeling'.[18]

It was a heady atmosphere, but Tennyson was no fool whatever his need of praise, and he would sometimes rebel against the adulation and affectation, like a great woolly Newfoundland that suddenly decides it has been patted sufficiently. Once when Mrs Prinsep brought a journalist to him, she effected the introduction by saying, 'Mr Tennyson is delighted to make your acquaintance.' Mildly he turned to her without acknowledging the other man and asked, 'What made you say that? I didn't say that I was delighted to make his acquaintance.'[19]

Usually, however, he was content to be made much of in the way that seems epitomized in Watts's famous 'moonlight' portrait of him, painted for Lady Somers at Little Holland House and telling more of what was believed about him than of what he was. All his roughness is smoothed away into an almost feminine beauty, his truculence softened to a Christ-like spirituality, as if he were an idealized relative to Pattledom (see Plate XIX). As was so often true in Tennyson's life, Little Holland House represented what he badly needed, but it also stood for much that was harmful to him. Only Mrs Cameron provided a bracing and welcome touch of scepticism; perhaps it was because she always thought Henry Taylor the better poet that she never hesitated to tell Tennyson when she thought he was selfish or foolish or badly behaved. And it is to his credit that he also welcomed this treatment, the nettle that was antidote to the dock of Little Holland House.

CHAPTER XXVI

❀

THE EROSION OF FRIENDSHIPS,
1857–1859

'I do badly to stay in a house', wrote Emily Tennyson on her return to Farringford from a visit to London, 'and should always like my private house like a snail to moor alongside of that of a friend.' She wanted to believe that Farringford floated in luminous isolation, so that she and Alfred were divorced from the dictates of the world that was symbolized by London. Early in 1857 she wrote in her journal: 'We begin our half-past six o'clock dinner. Hitherto we have dined at five or half past five & our friends say have kept our clocks half an hour too fast. Very likely. There is no very exact record of time here.'[1]

But on the same day that their dinner hour was changed, the Tennysons got their first carriage, a gift from Archibald Peel and implicit recognition that they could not remain cut off from the world. And more than Greenwich mean time intruded on their fastness, for the world was increasingly curious to know the details of Tennyson's home life and personality. When Holman Hunt was staying at Farringford, he and Tennyson were coming back from their morning walk and saw a group of apparently inoffensive people standing near the gate. Quickly Tennyson led him the long way around to the house, escaping their observation. He told Hunt that often, working in the garden, he would hear voices saying, 'There he is—look', and half a dozen Cockney heads would appear in a row over the wall, staring intently. Once an intruder had got into the garden, and as they were sitting at luncheon he flattened his nose against the window, crying, 'You can see him well from here.'[2] Tennyson exaggerated the extent to which he was spied upon, but the annoyance was surely considerable. As always, he was divided in his reactions: furious if stared at, worried if he were paid no attention.

Almost as annoying as the intrusion of the trippers were the little houses being built in Freshwater, spoiling the view from Farringford. A great mound of earth was thrown up at the edge of the park and planted with trees to preserve the sense of isolation. Then Tennyson set about enclosing the house itself in a deep blanket of trees, succeeding so well that in a few years Alexander Macmillan had to admit that he would like to stretch the un-treed part of the lawn some twenty or thirty yards, to leave a free space for air and sun. In 1860 they bought 'The Terrace', a small house in Freshwater, the first of several that they bought in order to preserve their views, and in which members of their families lived from time to time.

Rather more welcome than either new houses or the intruders climbing in were the Americans who were beginning to make the island a regular stop in their tours of literary England. One of the earliest of these was a young writer Bayard Taylor, who first stayed at Farringford in the summer of 1857. He was introduced by Thackeray, stayed but two days, and behaved so well that Tennyson was nearly convinced that an American could be a gentleman. In turn Taylor found Tennyson 'a noble fellow every inch of him . . . with a head . . . of a dilapidated Jove, long black hair, splendid dark eyes, and a full mustache and beard'. With such visitors Tennyson put himself out to be charming and open, slightly larger than life. He would show them his two-gallon tobacco jug and tell them that he drank his tea in a bowl because a 'teacup is such a niggardly allowance'. As he decanted the port for the ante-room, he would add a glass of water, saying that 'it makes it wholesomer and gives me one glass more'.[3] With an enthusiastic response like Taylor's to warm him, Tennyson gradually unfolded. But a few occasions on which his confidences were revealed in American papers, usually because of an innocent slip on the part of his visitors, convinced him that 'Yankees' existed only to exploit his private life and disclose his secrets, so that they joined Cockneys as the declared enemies of his peace in Farringford.

More and more he escaped to London, often staying with either the Prinseps or the Camerons. He found the 'wild beaming benevolence' of Mrs Cameron and the courtly manners of her elderly husband very attractive, and it was not long before they began to speak of moving to the Isle of Wight to be near him. As Jowett said of Mrs Cameron, 'perhaps she has a tendency to make the house shake the moment that she enters, but in this dull world that is a very excusable fault'.[4]

Although he could be unpredictable in his behaviour, Tennyson was a great social catch for London hostesses, even those of the first rank like the Duchess of Argyll, whose husband Tennyson had come to like and admire. Both the Argylls were charmed by Tennyson's naïve frankness but apprehensive about what friends would think of his manners. The Duchess often asked him to Argyll Lodge, where he read to her and her guests; he enjoyed reading and she liked listening, but there is something unpleasantly reminiscent of a professional entertainment about the accounts of his performances there and in some other London drawing-rooms. He used to tell how once he had called on the Duchess's mother, the Duchess of Sutherland, in Stafford House, where he found with her the Duchess and another daughter, Lady Grosvenor, later Duchess of Westminster. He walked in the garden with the trio, then read them part of *Maud*. As he was leaving, one of the servants discreetly pointed to his throat and Tennyson found that he had totally forgotten to wear a necktie. 'There I was', he said, 'spouting my lines to the three graces, as *décolleté* as a strutting turkey cock.'[5] Both his innocent vanity over the rank of his friends and his engaging amusement at his own gaucherie are implicit in the story.

Since his death the legend has grown of how Tennyson shambled through Victorian society as naturally as a great animal, awkward in manner and appearance but totally oblivious of rank and degree. The reality was somewhat different. With an obstinacy that still seems winning, he indeed kept his clothes and manners unchanged, but he was far from unconscious of social station. Understandably, he was probably too impressed at first by the grandeur into which he had been pitched; one letter to Emily in 1858 might stand as an example, when he wrote to her of how, at the Queen's Ball, the Duchess of Sutherland had twice come up to Mrs Prinsep '& asked after me, you & the children & said all manner of gracious & kind things, how the Argylls valued us, grand simplicity of character &c wh. was the more remarkable says Mrs P. because the Duchess never notices her in general—'.[6] It takes superhuman strength of character not to love a duchess, and Tennyson had no more than his fair share. Had his reactions continued unchanged, the pity would have been not that he overvalued social standing but that he accepted the diminished valuation of himself by his social superiors.

When the novelty of such a world began to wear off, Tennyson's own rugged arrogance asserted itself, and the accounts written by new acquaintances comment increasingly on how seriously he took himself and how little he put himself out to be agreeable to those around him. He was unable to give up the pleasures of life among the aristocracy, but he had constantly to flaunt his independence by gruffly behaving as if it were they who were to be congratulated on his acquaintance. In accepting invitations he would specify how many guests he was prepared to meet, and stipulate that he be allowed to smoke his pipe, and agree to come to dinner only if it were at an early hour. Once there, he might refuse to talk if he found the company uninteresting. Graceless it was, probably even more so than his earlier obsequiousness, but it was the healthier reaction, since at least it allowed him to feel that he was his own man, to be taken as he was found.

It would be wrong to suggest that all his noble acquaintances thought of him as a social curiosity, and some, like the Argylls, became close friends. Another who did so was among the audience at one of his readings in the garden of Argyll Lodge, a reticent young Irishman, Lord Dufferin, who sought out Tennyson's acquaintance afterwards, telling him shamefacedly that he had never been able to like or understand poetry until he came across a volume of Tennyson's: 'Naturally enough I could not help feeling very grateful to the Orpheus whose music had made the gate of poet-land fly open.' It was an excuse for friendship that might have made some poets wary, but not Tennyson. After that Dufferin would shyly ask permission to call in at Farringford from his yacht, which he took for that purpose to the Isle of Wight, or invite the Tennysons to dine in London, always treating Tennyson with a delightful deference, unlike some of Tennyson's noble friends.

On his forays into London Tennyson liked to read his new poems aloud, gaining confidence from the comments before publishing them. Somewhat naïvely, he was surprised and hurt when his audience failed to keep total secrecy about what they had heard. Once he read 'Guinevere' aloud at Little Holland House before publication, then passed out copies of it to his audience. Among those present was Lady Somers, who spent most of the night making her own surreptitious copy of the poem. In a heavily facetious letter that barely concealed his anger, Tennyson asked Mrs Prinsep to make 'the Goddess of Eastnor Castle' burn what she had copied. Loyally, and far more bluntly, Emily Tennyson called Lady Somers 'an atrocious thief'.

Not everyone easily forgave Tennyson his duchesses and Dufferins. FitzGerald, for one, ran into him in the London Library in the spring of 1857, '*bearded*, & seeming very well but staying in a great House in Kensington with which I won't meddle'. Few people would have described Little Holland House in that fashion, but Fitz was preternaturally sensitive to anything resembling social climbing. 'He talks, however, of going to *Spedding*, for some days, and then we are to meet if I be yet heareabout.' It was on this trip to London that seven newspapers grandly announced Tennyson's arrival 'from his seat, Farringford, Freshwater, I.W.'.[7] He liked to tell others of his 'disgust' at the announcement, but there seemed considerable disingenuousness in his remembering it and repeating it so often. Fitz's continual sniffing at Tennyson's motives explains in large part the breach that was gradually growing between the old friends, although Tennyson was not guiltless in his negligence about answering letters, which Fitz took as a snub.

In any case this was the low point of FitzGerald's life, and he was desperately in need of love from his old friends. His misjudged marriage to the middle-aged daughter of his old friend Bernard Barton, undertaken in charity and grown into contempt, was nearing its miserable end, and his normally thin skin was now nearly abraded out of existence. 'I sometimes wonder if People used to be so indifferent about seeing one another as all of us, so old Friends, seem to be!' he lamented in one letter to Farringford.[8] He seldom knew when to leave a matter alone, and he would repeat over and over how much he preferred Tennyson's early poetry, how much he hated Browning's poetry, how disappointed he was at not getting answers to his letters to Tennyson. It was hard for him to accept that 'old Alfred' was internationally famous, and in his turn Tennyson could not face the inevitable attrition of Fitz's former unclouded adoration.

Tennyson was disappointed too by the failure of the *Illustrated Edition* of 1857. He had never been sanguine about it because he disliked having artists distort his words, but he had agreed to let Moxon publish it because he was told he would make at least £2,000. Tennyson had been less than co-operative with Rossetti, Millais, Arthur Hughes, Holman Hunt, and the other artists who contributed to the volume, taking them sternly to task if any of their illustrations contained a single detail that could not be plainly justified by the words of the poems. When he first met Hunt, he demanded to know why the Lady of Shalott in the illustration had 'her hair wildly tossed about as if by a tornado'. Hunt mildly explained that he wanted to convey the idea of the catastrophe that had overtaken her, but Tennyson insisted, 'I didn't say her hair was blown about like that.' Step by step he went through the illustrations, objecting to the web winding around the Lady: 'But I did not say it floated round and round her.' He took exception to the flight of steps up which Cophetua leads the beggar maid, since steps had not been specifically mentioned. To each of Hunt's explanations of the needs of the artist he would say, 'Yes, but I think the illustrator should always adhere to the words of the poet!' Reasonably, Hunt suggested that he had but half a page to do what it took Tennyson fifteen to express. At last he said playfully, 'I am afraid I was not a suitable designer for the book.' Realizing that he had gone too far, Tennyson apologized for his frank criticism and Hunt assured him that he was honoured by his candour.[9]

But niggling of this kind had not made the task of the artists easy, and Rossetti said that Tennyson loathed his designs. When the handsome edition failed to sell well, Tennyson naturally blamed the illustrations. Moxon had printed 10,000 copies, but hardly more than 2,000 of these were sold. Generously, the publisher paid Tennyson £2,000, even though the sales had by no means justified his doing so; it was an act of generosity that was to cause later trouble. The blocks and the remaindered copies were sold to Routledge, who managed to dispose of another 5,000, but when he wanted to publish a further run of the book Tennyson's demands for what seemed excessive royalties stopped the plans. Such a setback, combined with the adverse criticism of *Maud*, worried Tennyson into thinking that his reign as England's premier poet might be approaching an end.

Instead of going abroad in the summer of 1857, the Tennyson's took a holiday that was longer than usual, three months in Scotland and the north of England. On their way they stopped for a fortnight with the Turners at Grasby. The time seemed ripe for a reconciliation with the Tennyson d'Eyncourts, and one afternoon Charles drove them to Bayons. Rather disappointingly, their uncle was away, but his wife showed them all through the now nearly completed house and seemed very friendly. In the more than twenty years that it had been building, Bayons had not ceased to be a source of mockery for Lincolnshire. Only a few months before their visit Colonel Cracroft had recorded in his diary his return visit to the house: 'Whoever would think for all the pomp and circumstance and pretended ancestry of Bayons Manor that its owner was the son of my grandfather's attorney at Market Rasen? Beautifully done in every respect as is Bayons its the ridicule of the County. . . . I was walking about it . . . its sham keep and drawbridge and moat, and thought what an exquisite piece of tomfoolery it is—but still an enchanting pretty situation.'[10] Old Mr Tennyson d'Eyncourt was still trying to make himself out a great man, but he had given up on county society and turned to charity, building a fine new Gothick village schoolhouse, for which he had been sole architect. It was a calm but sad end to a life that had been alive with throbbing ambition, and Alfred Tennyson no longer found it worthwhile to be contemptuous of the man who had once represented all that he disliked. They were never to meet again, and four years later Tennyson d'Eyncourt was dead.

The Tennysons had been invited by the Marshalls to stay once more in Tent Lodge, where they had spent their honeymoon, and on their way from Grasby to the Lakes they went for an overnight stop in Manchester, to hear Dickens read *The Christmas Carol* and to make a flying visit to the Great Exhibition, which had been opened by the Queen and Prince Consort and which was intended to show the succession of painting from the time of Giotto to that of the Pre-Raphaelites. Woolner met them and accompanied them around the exhibition rooms. One of the other visitors was the American consul from Liverpool, Nathaniel Hawthorne, who had come in the hope of changing his rooted dislike of pictures: 'Doubtless, I shall be able to pass for a man of taste, by the time I return to America. It is an acquired taste, like that for wines; and I question whether a man is really any truer, wiser, or better, for possessing it.' But he persisted.

There were two living figures in the gallery that Hawthorne thought far more interesting than those by Ruysdael, Murillo, Velázquez, Titian, Van Dyck, Hogarth, Turner, or even the vulgar Etty, whose undue interest in women's buttocks he found deplorable and fascinating. Moving swiftly through the rooms with a queer shuffling gait, 'as if he were walking in slippers too loose for him', was Tennyson, accompanied by Woolner, 'a small, smug man, in a blue frock and brown pantaloons'. Tennyson wore his black wideawake as he walked the galleries, and beneath its irregular brim his hair hung tangled, almost meeting his pointed beard. With his black eyes and black frock coat, there was 'nothing white about him except the collar of his shirt, which methought might have been clean the day before'.*

Tennyson carried his spectacles in his hand, putting them on for a better look at the most interesting paintings. He was perfectly polite to those who spoke to him but gave the impression of wanting to get away as quickly as possible. Hawthorne did not make himself known as he stalked Tennyson and Woolner around the galleries; he drew the line at following them out into the neighbouring Botanical Gardens,

---

* AT was still worrying about the matter in 1891, when he told Sir Henry Craik what Hawthorne had written. 'I asked my wife, if she could have let me wear a dirty shirt at the exhibition, & she said "No certainly not." ' (Sir Henry Craik, MS memoir, National Library of Scotland.)

where they went to smoke. In walking Tennyson seemed to turn his feet inward slightly, as if he were an American Indian. 'He might well enough pass for a madman at any time, there being a wildness in his aspect, which doubtless might readily pass from quietude to frenzy.' All in all, Hawthorne found him quite the most picturesque figure he had ever seen.

While Hawthorne was dogging Tennyson through the saloons, his wife kept watch on Emily and the boys. In contrast to Alfred's careless good looks, she thought Emily had 'a slightly peasant air'. He rejoined the family in the gallery of engravings and listened to the orchestra, then he took them along to see a few of the paintings and pointed to his own likeness, one of the entries in the photography section. Wherever they went, the Hawthornes followed, the epitome of Yankeedom that Tennyson most disliked. As they were leaving the hall, Mrs Hawthorne said she impetuously grabbed one of the boys 'and kissed him to my heart's content; and he smiled and seemed well pleased. And I was well pleased to have had in my arms Tennyson's child. After my raid I went on.'[11] One understands something of Tennyson's dread of appearing in public.

The entire Tennyson family spent more than two months at Tent Lodge in August and September, and during that time many of their old friends came to stay with the Marshalls. There were picnics and excursions to the fells, and Tennyson even took to riding, a pastime to which he was not addicted. Emily hardly liked to join the excursions, since 'Our poor little boys cry very much when we leave them. Small pleasure to me to go anywhere without them.'[12] On 26 September she wrote in her diary: 'Mr Dodgson comes to photograph.' At that time Dodgson's only distinctions were that he was a competent photographer and that he was a lecturer in mathematics at Christ Church; 'Lewis Carroll' still lay in the future. He sent in his card to Tent Lodge, and though Tennyson was away he was received by Emily Tennyson and met Hallam and Lionel, whom he solemnly pronounced the most beautiful boys he had ever seen. All thought of crying over their father's absence disappeared at once, and by the time he was ready to leave, the two boys proposed that they come with him. During the next week he was often at Tent Lodge, photographing the boys and even Tennyson, who hinted that he would like to learn the art of photography (see Plates XVII, XVIII). Dodgson walked with Tennyson, listened to his explanations of *Maud*, and left Coniston with an invitation to come to Farringford when he could.

From Tent Lodge the Tennysons went to Inverary to stay in the castle with the Argylls, but something had gone wrong with the exchange of letters, so that the Duke was at Balmoral when they arrived, and the Duchess at Dunrobin. Alfred and Emily walked in the grounds, feeling rather disconsolate, but they preferred to stay in a local inn while waiting for the Argylls, even though the young Marquis of Lorne invited them to the castle. The Duchess hurried home by specially chartered 'steam Vessel' and took them from the inn to the castle; the Duke came back from Balmoral. For a week Alfred and Emily lived in splendour, with pipers walking up and down beneath their windows in the morning, playing to waken them. Tennyson went on the lake with the Duke's fishermen and read them poetry. By the time they went back to Farringford, by way of Carstairs, their friendship with the Argylls was firmly cemented.

It was to be Emily Tennyson's last long trip for several years. Almost immediately after their return to Farringford she fell ill with the mysterious weakness that plagued her the rest of her life. In 1858 she was forty-five years old, and the probability is that her illness was connected with the menopause, complicated by her long-standing trouble with her spine. At the end of the year Sir John Simeon gave her an invalid chair, which became her chief means of locomotion. Her helplessness brought out all Tennyson's innate tenderness, and he would drag her in the chair to the top of the downs, wrapped in his cloak so that only her face was exposed to the wind. Behind them came the boys laden with cushions and rugs. With his own hands Tennyson built a summer-house in which she could sit on sunny days, even in winter, and he painted the windows himself with writhing dragons and serpents in brilliant colours. When there was an unusually heavy snowfall he built a snowman for her and the boys, crowning it with his own black sombrero.

Tennyson probably felt that Emily was more conscious of her physical infirmities than she need be, for he encouraged her to be more active. When she resumed her playing and singing at his suggestion, she concluded that she was 'too weak and out of practice to sing decently'. He even got her once to play briefly at battledore and shuttlecock with him. Her weakness frequently kept Tennyson at home at Farringford with her, and there may be some unconscious psychological significance in one entry in her journal: 'Rather a wild night & day of pain but it is almost worth while to have the pain to be so tenderly nursed as I am by A.'[13] The boys, who had once played at horses with their mother, now had to tiptoe around her and to reserve their high spirits for their father. Jowett's visits were special occasions for romping, and with Tennyson he would toss both boys in his shawl.

Whatever her suffering, Emily continued to run the house with a firm hand, to manage their financial affairs with considerable shrewdness, and to carry on most of her husband's correspondence. She seems to have made many of the decisions about money before Tennyson wrote the letters conveying them. He constantly complained at the number of books of poetry sent to him, saying that he had calculated by the number of verses which the books contained that he got a verse for every three minutes of his life. But it was Emily Tennyson who actually wrote the answers. When she was busy she sometimes made mistakes, and once she wrote a too-hurried note of thanks to a Lincolnshire clergyman. Without quite saying so, she gave the impression that Tennyson had read his book; unfortunately, she had not even looked at the title-page and the name of the author, J. W. King, instead taking his name from his huddled signature. She received a brisk reply from the nettled Mr King, pointing out that his name was not 'J. Whing', that she had the title of the book wrong, and had totally mixed up another name to which she referred.

Tennyson's deep aversion to commenting to other poets on their works was responsible for his curious reaction to the twenty-year-old Swinburne, who came to Farringford with a college friend early in 1858. Tennyson was busy when they arrived but invited them to come back for dinner, after which he read them *Maud* and part of 'Guinevere'. 'I thought him a very modest and intelligent young fellow', he wrote of Swinburne, '. . . but what I particularly admired in him was that he did not press upon me any verses of his own.'

Another younger poet about whom he was always edgy was Arnold; his feelings are surely reflected in a letter from the faithful Woolner, who would not have dared so much sarcasm had he not been certain of Tennyson's agreement. Woolner had met Arnold with Patmore at John Parker's: 'He was a regular swell in brilliant white kid gloves, glittering boots and costume cut in most perfect fashion. He had a long talk with Patmore: whose countenance the whole time beamed radiant joy with the satisfaction of holding intercourse with such a high Oxford don of critical propensities.' Since he was so deliberately untidy in his own dress, Tennyson was particularly hard on poets who were dandies, from Bulwer through Arnold to Browning, to whom the harshest words he ever spoke were, 'You'll die in a white tie!'[14]

While Tennyson was finding more new acquaintances at Little Holland House and Argyll Lodge, he seemed to move further and further away from his old friends, as Fitz had feared. In 1857 Milnes had been disparaging about the trial volume of *Enid and Nimuë*, and a year later Tennyson was still waiting for an expression of contrition, which he was not apt to get. Tennyson's irritation was sharpened by his belief that Milnes was too absorbed with his own position as town wit and successor to Samuel Rogers as the busiest host in literary London. Tennyson used to repeat with pleasure Carlyle's remark that if Jesus Christ and the Devil were both in London, Milnes would ask them to dinner together. Milnes said that Tennyson liked his flattery unmixed and took some pleasure in the irritation that he could so easily produce in him. Once at dinner they were chatting amicably when Milnes said calmly, 'Tennyson, I have got a number of your earliest unpublished poems in your own handwriting, and as soon as you are dead, I shall print them.' Tennyson looked grimly at him until the whole table was silent, then said distinctly, 'You beast!' He spoke half humorously, but his anger was apparent. In many ways Milnes had totally changed from the undergraduate whose face was so good-natured that Tennyson asked to meet him. Now he was a gross-looking middle-aged man, who showed only too clearly the effects of a lifetime of self-indulgence and dissipation. He often drank too much in company, and his penchant for obscene drawings and photographs was common knowledge. A few years later Arthur Munby found 'nothing noble' in his face, which was 'sly, sensuous, and potentially wicked'.[15] His delight in showing his collection of pornography was not apt to appeal to Tennyson, who was somewhat puritanical in such matters. The two men were never totally alienated, and when Tennyson was introduced to the House of Lords he asked Milnes to attend him, but the old intimacy had long been dead.

Like many over-sensitive men, Tennyson looked for insult when none was intended. In 1857 Charles Kingsley published his novel *Two Years Ago*, in which one of the main characters is a Spasmodic poet who dies of too much opium. In spite of Kingsley's patent admiration of him, Tennyson took it into his head the following year that the character was a caricature of himself and that Kingsley was covertly accusing him of drug-taking. F. D. Maurice, who was a friend of both men, intervened with Kingsley on Tennyson's behalf: 'I believe Tennyson's life to be a perfectly simple & innocent one, & the charge about opium which I suppose Kingsley accepts to be utterly false. I know no reason to think there was any foundation for it in past years—he declares solemnly that there was not—I feel as convinced as I can be that he is entirely free from the sin now.'[16] By 1860 Kingsley and his wife had been invited to Farringford, which seems adequate proof that Tennyson was satisfied of the innocence of Kingsley's intentions.

The accusation of opium addiction was one that dogged Tennyson from the time of his honeymoon until the end of his life. At the time of his misunderstanding with Kingsley, Tennyson's brother Charles had relapsed briefly into taking too much opium again, which would have increased Alfred's sensitivity on the subject. Tennyson himself suffered great pain from neuralgia in 1858 and had to have a 'lowlying tooth & another old stump' pulled out. At the time he may have taken opium, the standard pain-killer of the period, but there is nothing to indicate that he was ever addicted to it. Fact, however, spreads less readily than rumour, and there must have been many Victorians who took it for granted that Tennyson was an addict. Even Gladstone's niece, Lady Frederick Cavendish, reported going to Downing Street and meeting 'Tennyson, a dirty man with opium-glazed eyes and rat-taily hair hanging down his back'.[17] It was the kind of remark that his unconventional appearance naturally attracted, but it was no less wounding for that. The canard still surfaces occasionally, and will probably continue to do so, but there is absolutely no evidence for it.

Early in 1859 Henry Hallam died, after suffering a stroke that left him paralysed in his right leg and arm and partially so in his speech. On hearing of his last illness Tennyson read some of *In Memoriam* aloud to Emily, which indicated how much the loss of his last tie with Arthur Hallam meant to him. 'Generally when he was asked to read the poem, he refused, saying, "It breaks me down . . . I cannot." '[18] In his will Mr Hallam left £500 to Tennyson and twice that amount to Emily Jesse.

Tennyson suffered another sort of loss with the death of Edward Moxon. For some years they had been less intimate than formerly, but it would have been difficult to better their relationship as publisher and author. Moxon's early faith in Tennyson's poetry had been amply repaid by the profits on it, and now his works were the mainstay of the firm. After Moxon's death the new management, which included his brother William, were disturbed to see how much money had been lost on the *Illustrated Edition* and asserted that it had all been undertaken at the request of Tennyson himself, who should therefore be responsible for the loss. Emily Tennyson secured the services of her brother-in-law, Charles Weld, a lawyer of literary bent, to deal with the Moxons and even offered to go to London herself to help straighten out matters. Fortunately, she kept records and correspondence assiduously, so that she was able to produce the letters in which Edward Moxon had urged the edition on Tennyson. The rupture was apparently healed, but it had taken up the emotional energies of both Alfred and Emily during most of the autumn of 1858, and thereafter he never felt the same about the firm.

There was no question, however, of Tennyson's leaving them before 1859 when he published the first volume that bore the title of *Idylls of the King*. In spite of its name, this group of four idylls is only part of the final poem, which consists of twelve separate idylls. There were to be many later verbal and structural changes in these first idylls, but essentially half of the final version was now written, since 'Enid' was later separated into two idylls ('The Marriage of Geraint' and 'Geraint and Enid'), and 'The Passing of Arthur', which was not included in 1859, was already nearly complete as 'Morte d'Arthur'. What was most important was that Tennyson had finally begun publication of the long poem he had been talking about for more than a quarter of a century.

After such a long gestation, it was a hard birth. Tennyson's first impulse had been to publish 'Enid' and 'Vivien' (under its original title of 'Nimuë') as a simple pair of alternatives set in contrast. In 1857 he had six copies struck off of *Enid and Nimuë; The True and the False*, then he quickly withdrew them when he 'heard of "a blustering mouth"' . . . a man, a friend it was said, to whom I read or showed The Nimuë, who in lieu of giving his opinion honestly at the moment, appears to have gone brawling about town, saying that such a poem would corrupt the young, that no ladies could buy it or read it &c &c such chatter is as unhandsome, as the criticism is false. Nevertheless why should I expose myself to the folly of fools . . . ? I should indeed have thought that the truth & purity of the wife in the first poem might well have served as antidote to the untruth of the woman in the second. Perhaps I shall wait till I get a larger volume together & then bring out these with others.'[19]

Idylls of the King is perhaps the best example in Tennyson's career of his having writer's block; he had been talking about the project for so long that it had become almost impossible to carry out. The 'unhandsome' chatter he heard in 1857 served as sufficient excuse to disguise the deep reluctance to publish that had been building up for so many years, and he dropped plans for publication. As he often did in the face of criticism of his work, he began adding rather than revising, and within a month or two he had written 'Guinevere'; he wrote 'Elaine' in 1858.

By 1859, however, his confidence had been bolstered again by the praise he received from his constant readings of the poems. 'I so thoroughly nauseate publishing', he wrote to the Duchess of Argyll, 'that I could be well content to be silent for ever; however the Poems, there are four of them (your Grace heard two) are finished &, for want of a better name, to be called "The King's Idylls".'[20]

The Moxons had no reason to be sorry for having made peace with him. There were 40,000 copies printed, and in the first weeks after publication in June 1859 more than 10,000 copies had been sold. The reviews, too, were generally favourable, and there was little abuse of 'Vivien' for immorality, as Tennyson had feared. Gladstone was so enthusiastic that he carried the poems around in his pocket, and the Duke of Argyll warned Tennyson that he might be responsible for a spoilt Budget.

Not all his fellow poets were delighted, however, and their reservations cannot be ascribed entirely to envy. Elizabeth Browning, that most constant of Tennyson's admirers, confessed to Allingham that she was disappointed, in part from having expected the poems for too long. 'Perhaps the breathing, throbbing life around us in this Italy, where a nation is being new-born, may throw King Arthur too far off and flat. . . . The colour, the temperature, the very music, left me cold. Here are exquisite things, but the whole did not affect me as a whole from Tennyson's hands. I would rather have written *Maud*, for instance, than half a dozen volumes of such *Idylls*.' Matthew Arnold, regretting that the poems lacked the magical charm of the Middle Ages, which he felt himself capable of dealing with even though Tennyson was not, said that the 'real truth is that Tennyson, with all his temperament and artistic skill, is deficient in intellectual power'.[21]

Arthur's long speech of condemnation of Guinevere, delivered as she grovels on the floor in contrition, with her arms around her husband's feet, was wildly popular with most of Tennyson's readers. A good bit of its appeal is lost today, when it may seem merely priggish, and even some of Tennyson's contemporaries found it unpalatable. George Meredith, who knew something of unfaithful wives from personal experience, thought Arthur sounded like a 'crowned curate', and said that his answer to Guinevere's pleading should have been, 'Get up!'[22]

The year following the publication of the *Idylls*, when royalties from their sales began coming in, Tennyson was paid £4,542 by Moxons, triumphant repudiation of any fear that his popularity was slipping. As soon as it became clear how successful sales were, the editor of *Once a Week* offered him £100 for 'The Grandmother', while allowing him to keep the copyright, and after some days of discussion Alexander Macmillan gave £300 for the rights to 'Sea Dreams' for *Macmillan's Magazine*. Thackeray had been asking for a contribution to the newly-founded *Cornhill*, so he sent him 'Tithonus', written a quarter-century before, for which he received £50. Shortly thereafter, the publisher of *Cornhill*, George Smith of Smith and Elder, offered him 5,000 guineas for the publication rights for a period of three years of a new set of *Idylls* of the length of those that had just been published. He wanted to print them first in the magazine, then in book form. It was the largest offer ever made for a book of poetry. Without answering Smith, Tennyson waited until Emily came into the room, then said, 'My dear! We are much richer than we thought we were. Mr. Smith has just offered me five thousand guineas for a book the size of the "Idylls". And, if Mr. Smith offers five thousand, of course the book is worth ten.'[23] However unworldly he might be in other matters, Tennyson was certainly not in his demands for royalties.

If he needed further proof of his popularity, he might have found it in the purchase of his bust by Woolner for the library of Trinity College, said to be the first time that a living poet had been so honoured.

There was a worm in the bud, however, and it was connected with the narrative of 'The Grandmother'. The germ of that poem had been suggested to Tennyson by Benjamin Jowett in response to Emily Tennyson's request that he give the poet subjects on which he could write. Among the many others that Jowett fluently suggested were the 'Dogma of Immortality', St. Francis of Assisi, the statuary of Phidias, the coronation of Charlemagne, and an *In Memoriam* for the dead of the Indian Mutiny complete with 'the fatal missive suddenly announcing their death'. Truly, as Jowett said, 'Subjects like blackberries seem to me capable of being gathered off every hedge.' And those he suggested were often worth about as much as blackberries. What is at issue is not that Jowett had little idea of what might be the nugget of a good poem, but the fact that Tennyson so often accepted and attempted to use what was offered to him. Woolner, too, had been pressed into service to think up subjects for Tennyson, and he told Emily that he wished he could persuade Tennyson 'to do the tale of the Sailor which I told him of years ago . . . for I think it capable in his hands of growing into one of the greatest of poems, altho told of persons not princes, philosophers, or chiefs'.[24] For two more years he continued to urge 'The Fisherman' upon Tennyson until he finally took it and made it into 'Enoch Arden'. Not many lovers of Tennyson can find it in themselves to be thankful for Woolner's pertinacity.

As a young man Tennyson had often plunged into black despair when he was not immediately inspired, but he had accepted that it might be so and that he might be better for having lain fallow for a time. Now, however, he was the most popular poet in the world, and it might look as if he were in decline if he were to stop writing for any length of time. He was fifty years old and aware that his youth was gone: 'A poet's work should be finished by the time he is sixty. Anything I write must be in the next ten years!' Publishers were constantly asking for more copy; friends urged causes, philosophical positions, religious doctrines, and more grandiose statements of morality on him with the injunction that it was his duty to write about each; most demanding of all was Tennyson's own dark fear that the sacred stream might be drying up at the source. 'Ally cannot find a subject & this troubles him,' Emily wrote to Lear early in 1860. 'He is never so happy when not at work.' More ominously, Tennyson told Henry Taylor that he needed 'a story to treat, being full of poetry, with nothing to put it in'.[25]

Emily Tennyson's whipping-up of suggestions of subjects was undertaken in the loving hope of keeping Alfred from the depression of having nothing to write, but it was also the result of a profound ignorance on her part that poetry was anything more than the mechanical union of a moral subject and the decoration of rhyme. Since Tennyson's poetry so often sprang from a nucleus of language or imagery, it was easy for her to believe that the overt subject was finally unimportant so long as it was unobjectionable, if only it were draped with 'poetry'. Yet, curiously, she seems to have believed that ultimately the actual sound of the poetry was a kind of distraction from what was important. When first she read 'Elaine', she did not want to hear it spoken aloud: 'It is well to read things to oneself without the glamour of his reading, which may beguile one.'[26] It is an acute but somewhat surprising, perception of how Tennyson's own readings sacrificed meaning to the demands of auditory pleasure.

As always, Tennyson's deepest need was for uncritical praise, which she supplied in generous measure, for without it she thought he would be rendered incapable of creation. 'It is a mistake in general for him to listen to the suggestions of others about his poems,' she said, but she did not include herself among those who were dangerous. Mrs Browning put the matter another way when she said that 'Tennyson is too much indulged. His wife is too much his second self; she does not criticise enough.'[27] Like most of the world, Tennyson was easily persuaded that anyone who warmly approved his work was a good judge of such matters, so that he was increasingly inclined to take Emily's advice.

But no serious artist is totally reliant upon others, and if her ideas had not fallen in with his own inclinations they would have been ineffective. His complaint to Henry Taylor suggests that he had begun thinking dangerously of himself as a poetic machine producing fretwork for decoration, much as Allen's 'Pyroglyphs' had done in the 1840s. It was hard for him to accept suggestions from others initially, as Woolner found, but when a subject had been introduced often enough and had had sufficient time to roll around in his head it began to seem as if it had originally come from his own thinking, so that eventually he used even some of Jowett's blackberries. Once when Fitz was suggesting an old Lincolnshire story to Tennyson, he acknowledged that 'there is no use in my finding and sending it now, because it doesn't do (with Paltry Poets) to try and drag them to the water'.[28]

It was partially in this spirit that Tennyson had originally come to the Arthurian legend, as the sculptural armature upon which he could mould his poetry. It had taken years for some parts of it to become assimilated into his own thinking, and it was to take many years before it had assumed final shape as a model of his own views of the world. The reception of the first four *Idylls* was so encouraging that he set to work at once on another, which became 'Pelleas and Ettarre'.

His own dependence upon Emily was never easy for Tennyson to accept, and it occasionally made him seem irritable and unappreciative of her efforts. Immediately before the publication of the *Idylls*, while Tennyson was worrying about how they would be received, Edward Lear went for a stay of several days at Farringford, and for the first time he was vaguely apprehensive about the atmosphere. Everything should have been splendid, for Farringford was at its prettiest and Lear fell even further under Emily's kindly spell. To his friend Chichester Fortescue he sent his famous calculation: 'I should think computing moderately, that 15 angels, several hundreds of ordinary women, many philosophers, a heap of truly wise and kind mothers, 3 or 4 minor prophets, and a lot of doctors and schoolmistresses, might all be boiled down, and yet their combined essence fall short of what Emily Tennyson really is.'[29] Under her benign influence he was at the piano constantly, and on one enchanted night as he sang his settings of Tennyson's poems, the drawing-room candles guttered unnoticed until the room was dark. Sir John Simeon at last got up, went to the window, and threw the curtains open to the calm moonlight and the distant prospect of the cliffs.

But there were ripples of discontent beneath the idyllic surface. On the day he arrived Lear had been put out slightly by being asked to move from his usual room into an attic since other guests were expected. The house was less comfortable than usual because of alterations to Alfred's study. Tennyson looked well, but all her duties had made Emily look 'very pale & worn & sad'. The next day Lear and Alfred walked on the cliffs, while Tennyson recited 'Elaine', which Lear found 'most wonderfully beautiful & affecting—so that I cried like beano'. It was unnerving, however, to see how little such a sensitive poet should notice his wife's state. 'E.T. is assuredly a most complete angel—& no mistake—but—poor dear—she is ill & weary. "Please God, if I live one, or 2 years more" she said once today. But what labour for him!—& how little he seems to regard it!' Tennyson's constant hypochondria annoyed Lear, who felt himself 'less able now than before to combine with him at times—he is so odd'. To Holman Hunt he wrote that Farringford's whole atmosphere had a sadness that he could not help feeling, and that he found it impossible to make his hours suit those of Tennyson. 'I cannot but be sad. Mrs Tennyson's looks compel me to be so—she is so worn—& so weary often. And whether Alfred sees this I cannot tell.'[30]

It was a situation that was more and more noticed by visitors. Tennyson was undoubtedly slightly insensitive to the sufferings of others, but he also liked to keep a decent reserve about his troubles, so that he seemed less understanding than he actually was. Emily suffered from real pain, but with sympathetic observers she was not always inclined to minimize her sacrifices for Alfred. It was a complicated situation and capable of both the interpretation of Lear and that of

FitzGerald, who thought that Emily was too deviously managing. Neither was wholly true, but it all made Farringford full of vibrations and strains, usually hidden beneath the well-rehearsed pattern of hospitality.

Within a fortnight of Lear's stay the Argylls were in Freshwater to be near the Tennysons, and their visit was totally different, for all went so pleasantly with walks and geologizing for Tennyson, Argyll, and the young Lord Lorne that the Argylls returned annually for several years. Even in such company Tennyson remained somewhat suspicious. Argyll used to tell how he said during the course of a walk that his unpublished poems were always being copied unscrupulously; then he took the Duke to the middle of a large stubble field and repeated 'Boädicea' in a conspiratorial tone so that he might not be overheard. As they walked Tennyson showed the Duke his recently purchased farm, which brought the total of his acres to about 150, then asked, 'How many acres have you in Argyllshire?' Rather shamefacedly, Argyll had to admit that he did not know, for 'in Scotland, we generally measure in square miles'. On one of their visits, when the Argylls arrived for dinner, Tennyson apologized charmingly for not having changed: 'I can't dress for you, for I never dress for any one, and if I made an exception and dressed for a duke, my butler would set me down as a snob.'[31] The Duke was somewhat disconcerted by being addressed as 'Your Grace' by Tennyson, but they got on well, particularly over their common love of bird-life.

✳

CHAPTER XXVII

TWO AND THIRTY YEARS AGO,
1860–1864

IN 1860 the Isle of Wight was invaded by a benevolent force of nature more overpowering than Cockneys, Yankees, and new houses combined. In that year Julia Margaret Cameron came to Freshwater, bringing her elderly husband (with whom she was as engagingly besotted as a young girl with her first lover), and settled down to rule the place as a charitable despot. She bought two cottages, joined them by a central tower, converted a conservatory into a fowl-house, and named the congeries Dimbola from her Indian past. At this time she was forty-five; she had not yet found the outlet for her wayward genius that was to ensure her a place in the history of photography, for she did not even own a camera until three years later, when she received one as a gift.

Like all the best eccentrics, Julia Cameron was original, intelligent, and totally unaware of behaving oddly. Dressed in crimson and purple robes, with gorgeous Indian shawls draped around her frequently unwashed neck, she would trail unannounced into Farringford at any hour of the day or night, her visits so frequent that at last a special gate was made into the park for her. Usually as she came in she was brandishing an inappropriate gift: a picture she had found in a shop full of rubbish, a pair of yew trees for Alfred to plant, rolls of ugly blue wallpaper with a border taken from the Elgin marbles, two legs of Welsh mutton from her sister's estates at Eastnor, a violet poncho for Emily's father, old catalogues for Hallam and Lionel to read, or anything else that caught her eye. Her relentless generosity nearly always produced gifts that were totally unwelcome to the recipient. Carlyle once unwrapped a Christmas parcel and found a prayer-book, at which he exclaimed, 'Either the Devil or Julia Cameron must have sent me this!' In vain Emily Tennyson would protest feebly, but the flood continued; it was equally useless to give presents to Mrs Cameron. When Emily sent her a jacket, she wrote in return that she was 'a grandmother with every vestige of grace gone, not preserving as you do, a youthful figure; and truly I am not worthy of the lovely jacket and *therefore I shall bring it back*'.[1]

She had an admirable facility for remaining totally oblivious to differences in age, so that she organized dances and entertainments for guests whose ages were as much as seventy years different, never imagining that any of them might lack her own catholic interest in everyone she met. She filled Dimbola with guests whose names she often forgot. Her warm chaotic hospitality and her artistic efforts, which amounted in her photography to great artistry, always had something slapdash and amateur about them. When one of the plays she produced for her friends resulted in laughter, she rang down the curtain, clapped her hands, and climbed on a chair to explain to the audience that it was a tragedy and that they were not to laugh but cry.

But she had native intelligence that belied her flamboyant, rather foolish exterior; her real love was for genius, and to it she offered nothing so commonplace as idolatry. Her reason for coming to Freshwater was to be near Tennyson, and as she tried to keep him firmly in line with what she thought he should be doing, it never occurred to her to toady to him. Shortly after her arrival a lovely night lured her out on to the beach after her guests were all in bed; she stood looking at the sea with a shawl wrapped around her head, then decided it was wasted on only one person, so she woke Tennyson, took him back to the edge of the luminous water, and left him there to ponder the sight for the good of his soul and poetry. Her managing ways seldom disturbed him, since he knew they concealed real love, and he was touched by her hesitant, tiptoe devotion to Emily. Most of all he was taken with her magnificent unselfconsciousness of a kind he could never achieve. Almost at once she called him by his Christian name.

'You exaggerate the horrors of Mrs. Cameron', Browning wrote shrewdly to a friend, '. . . after all, what harm does she do Alfred? If he considered her while he made his verses, *then* indeed! . . . Depend upon it, nobody has done him the least harm at any time: nobody has more fully found out at the beginning what he was born to do—nor done it more perfectly.'[2]

Inconveniently, Mrs Cameron regarded Dimbola and Farringford as provinces of one domain, and she was inclined to take over the Tennysons' guests. Usually it worked, but with Lear it only contributed to his lack of ease at Farringford. On his first visit after she had come to Freshwater, there was a sound of footsteps on the gravel path coming from Dimbola, which Emily attributed to Americans on a pilgrimage of devotion to Alfred. Instead it was eight men carrying Mrs Cameron's excellent grand piano, which she thought would be more pleasant for Lear to play than Emily's tinkly instrument.

Lear, who could not have been more unlike Mrs Cameron, was grateful for the piano, but when after a pleasant, quiet evening with the Tennysons, 'Mrs. C. & her train' came in, 'an odious incense palaver & fuss succeeded to quiet home moments'. More and more he found her overpowering, almost a reason not to come to Farringford.

There were other reasons for Lear's disenchantment, and most of them were connected with Tennyson himself. On this same visit Lear and Frank Lushington went for a walk with him, 'but AT was most disagreeably querulous & irritating & would return, chiefly because he saw people approaching'. Lushington wanted to take a back path to the sea, but Tennyson was 'snubby & cross' and insisted on avoiding the villagers coming from church by leading his guests home along a path that oozed mud over their shoes. At dinner he repeated himself incessantly. 'So I came to bed,' wrote Lear: '& believe that this is my last visit to Farringford:—nor can I wish it otherwise all things considered.'[3] It was not, in fact, to be his last visit, although it might as well have been for all the contentment he was to find thereafter at Farringford. He returned the next year, immediately after his sister's death, but Farringford was full so that he had to stay at a hotel in Freshwater, and the Tennysons seemed too preoccupied to pay much attention to his bereavement. Emily talked consolingly with him, and Alfred walked with him, but he felt as if he were intruding. The combination of grief and his feeling of exclusion aggravated his epileptic attacks, and finally he slipped away without saying good-bye. It seemed a long time since he had wanted to settle down in a 'Pharmouse or a Nin' in the neighbourhood.

In 1860, because of his worries over his poetry, Tennyson was in a particularly difficult frame of mind during his summer trip to the West Country. For the past two years travelling had been disappointing to him, even though the trips had both involved longer sea voyages than he had ever before undertaken. In 1858 he had gone to Norway alone when Emily was unable to take the trip they had planned to the Styrian Alps. There was a grand storm in the North Sea that broke the mast of the ship with a tremendous wave, and he looked at innumerable Norwegian waterfalls, but generally he kept away from the mountains because of the reputation of the inns. He sought out English society at the Consul's house in Christiania, and found it even less interesting than that in London. All in all, he said he could find little difference between Norway and Scotland. In 1859 he went with Palgrave to Portugal in search of the tropics he longed to see, hoping to go on to Seville, Cadiz, Gibraltar, and Tenerife. Lisbon was disappointing, and Cintra, of which he knew from Byron and Beckford, turned out to be a parched version of Richmond populated by expatriates and lionizing foreigners who followed him around the streets, bowing, introducing themselves, and trying to shake his hand. The mosquitoes were so bad that he slept inside a complicated net he had brought with him, but he had to give that up in order to smoke in bed, wishing only that he had a tiny baby beside him as a whiter and more appetizing morsel for the insects. Finally the fleas, flies, and overpowering sun drove him to cancel the rest of the trip, still unaware that he was ill-adapted for tropical landscapes. However, he did remember the atmosphere and much of the fauna, later using them as background for 'Enoch Arden'.

In 1860 he hoped to travel with Spedding, perhaps to the Levant, but that trip fell through, and eventually he was reduced to the ever-acquiescent Palgrave, who suggested Brittany but capitulated when Tennyson held out for Devon and Cornwall, where he wanted to get more background for the *Idylls*. On several earlier occasions Palgrave had proved himself invaluable for making arrangements and taking the burdens of travelling off Tennyson's shoulders, but he was literal-minded to the point of fatuity. Not that Tennyson was an easy companion. In the wrong mood he would turn quickly on the younger men who served him as acolytes. Once when walking with Allingham he had been increasingly chafed by the slowness of his speech until at last he snapped, 'Have a care, have a care, Allingham; you are rapidly developing the faculty of becoming a bore.' A kind of imperiousness was growing on him, making him feel that it was unnecessary to hide his feelings. Jowett, who was frequently ill at ease and awkward when alone with him, humbly confessed, 'I know that I must bore him sometimes, but I hope he will forgive this.' Woolner was generally an easier companion, for he was shrewd enough to confine his exuberance to Emily and to be quiet with Alfred. One evening Tennyson called on him and they sat smoking silently together until 11 p.m. without exchanging a word. As Tennyson left, he told Woolner, 'I've had the happiest evening I remember.' The story is also told of Carlyle, but it seems less credible, since it is harder to believe in his total silence for an entire evening than in Woolner's.[4]

Woolner was unable to devote his entire holiday to Tennyson in 1860, so he had to be content with Palgrave as companion. Emily, who worried about Tennyson's climbing on the rocks of the coast without being able to see well, took the precaution of asking Palgrave to keep an eye on him. When Tennyson arrived in Oxford in August to begin the trip, he was already in a bad mood, which was worsened when Palgrave announced that he would be delayed in his departure because he intended to spend a week with his brother Gifford before he returned to the Middle East. Tennyson found Gifford interesting and was fascinated with his story of his escape from a convent in the Syrian desert, 'but Frank P. kept up such a shouting with Woolner that I could not very well hear what the brother said'. At Oxford he read a new poem to Jowett, who had the temerity to say, 'I think I wouldn't publish that, if I were you, Tennyson.' 'If it comes to that, Master,' answered Tennyson coldly, 'the sherry you gave us at luncheon was beastly.'[5]

When Woolner heard of Tennyson's perturbation at having to go on alone, he good-naturedly changed his plans and agreed to stay with him until Palgrave arrived. The first week they travelled quietly and companionably to Bideford, Clovelly, Bude, and Tintagel, walking at least ten miles a day and bathing frequently when they were at the sea, although it was 'so roary and rough that none but a good swimmer could enter with impunity'.

At Tintagel Palgrave joined them and Woolner intended to leave, but so vehement was Tennyson's urging that he consented to stay another week in spite of 'prudence, desire to get to work, hatred of continuous wet'.[6] Tennyson could scarcely hide his reluctance to be left alone with Palgrave, although he continued to make good-natured jokes with both of the younger men. With Palgrave's advent what had been a simple swim was swollen into a vignette; what was, after all, only a naked, middle-aged poet creeping on tender feet over jagged rocks became in Palgrave's eyes a Renaissance landscape as Tennyson 'bathed from the scattered rocks in that peacock sea of green and azure. And as the nobly modelled figure, the point of warm colour in the view, as Titian or Veronese would have treated it, moved cautiously over the fragments to find a spot for a "header", the contrast between the rude cruel rocks and soft, "many-jointed man", as some Greek philosopher named him, (if I may quote a remark with which Tennyson agreed), impressed me forcibly.'[7] Tennyson's reactions to Palgrave are understandable on stylistic grounds alone, even had he not followed him over each rock, bawling disconsolately, 'Tennyson, Tennyson!' whenever he disappeared from view. He was only carrying out what he considered to be Emily's instructions, but it was infuriating to Tennyson.

At Helston they were joined by Holman Hunt and Val Prinsep shortly after Woolner had left them. Hunt and Prinsep were busy painting all day, and Tennyson was thrown entirely on Palgrave's company. When he wanted to be by himself to compose poetry, he was conscious of the silent Palgrave crouching behind a nearby rock in an attempt to be inconspicuous as he kept Tennyson in sight. If he moved, the rocks would resound with his name in the plaintive voice of Palgrave, who had discovered that Tennyson's fear of being found out was the best blackmail he had to make him call out where he was.

In the evenings after finishing painting Hunt and Prinsep joined them for dinner in the inns where they stayed as they moved along the Cornish coast. Tennyson had hurt his feet on the rocks in a manner unbecoming the subject of Titian, and now he had to go in a dog-cart. At table Palgrave would insist on referring loudly to Tennyson by name, in order to call attention to themselves. At last Tennyson suggested mildly that the younger man might call him 'the other gentleman' and help preserve his anonymity. In spite of this slight ruffle in its surface, the talk was so good and so fast that they had to agree to raise their hands before speaking if anyone was to be heard.

One night at dinner, Palgrave fussily told the waiter to be particularly careful of the port because 'the old gentleman' was fastidious about his wine. When the waiter was gone, Tennyson asked, 'Do you mean *me* by the old gentleman?' At fifty-one he was sensitive about his age, but he only repeated his request that Palgrave call him 'the other gentleman'. Palgrave, with his usual tactlessness, could not understand what he had done wrong, and he continued to use the phrase, insisting that it was perfectly accurate.

After several nights of repetition of 'the old gentleman' and Tennyson's subsequent expostulation, Palgrave accused him of always losing his temper. With dignity Tennyson said that he was sorry the trip had gone badly and that he intended to go by himself to Falmouth the following morning and get a train home, hoping that his departure would restore placidity to the others. To Hunt and Prinsep he apologized for having spoiled their holiday by becoming upset at the sound of Palgrave's insistent voice, 'like a bee in a bottle'.

The next morning Palgrave tried to countermand the dog-cart that

Tennyson had ordered, and when he failed at that, he asked Tennyson at least to wait a moment before leaving. He went back into the inn and returned after some time with his own luggage, which he threw into the cart, jumped in beside the startled Tennyson, and drove off with him, his protestations of fidelity to Emily Tennyson's instructions floating back on the wind to Hunt and Prinsep as the cart disappeared. When they went back into the inn they discovered that Palgrave, worried that no one had heard Tennyson's name and that his own association with him might perish from memory, had spent his last few minutes drawing a cartouche on the wall of the dining-room, with all four names inscribed in it.[8]

Even Palgrave realized that his own tact left something to be desired, and he confessed to Emily Tennyson that he had not altogether succeeded as a companion and 'was cross and nasty more than once', asking for absolution.[9]

A more enduring moment to the trip than his contrition, which was soon forgotten, was Palgrave's edition of *The Golden Treasury of Songs and Lyrics*, for many years the most popular English anthology. The first conception of the book had been broached by Palgrave to Tennyson on the trip in Cornwall, and Tennyson was largely responsible for the choice of lyrics in it. Since he refused to let his own poetry be included, there was none by living authors in the final selection. It remains a good guide to Tennyson's own favourite works, although subsequent editions included a far wider range. It must have been undertaken by Tennyson originally through a combination of generosity to Palgrave and a thoroughly understandable willingness to fall in with anything that would keep him quiet.

There now seemed to be few limits to his fame and following. The Prince Consort, for example, was so impressed by the *Idylls of the King* that he wrote to 'My dear Mr Tennyson' to ask for his autograph in his own copy of the poem, which he had been reading aloud to his family. In the spring of 1861 Tennyson was invited to accept an honorary degree from Cambridge with the assurance that 'the Undergraduates, from the Prince of Wales downwards', would be disappointed if he did not do so.[10] Tennyson agreed tentatively, then had to give up the trip altogether when he was half-way to Cambridge, because he was suffering from heart palpitations. Rather mysteriously, he converted the return journey to Farringford into a fortnight of visits in London and the country around Winchester, which suggests that his decision not to take the degree must have sprung from something besides his health, perhaps a recurrence of the shyness that had made him ask Venables to read his prize poem when he was still an undergraduate.

The heart palpitations were real enough, however, to make him resolve once more to give up smoking. He had one final puff, then broke his pipes and scattered his tobacco into the wind. His new life lasted at least twelve days, until his return to Farringford, when he told Emily 'of the glowing feelings of health he has had in the mornings since he left smoking & of his having been so hungry'.[11] It was, however, the last that was heard of that particular resolution, of the feelings of health, or indeed of the heart palpitations. Gloomily, FitzGerald recalled Dr Gully's prognostication that Tennyson would be paralysed by the time he was fifty-five, and earlier if he did not stop smoking.

Fame was not enough for Tennyson. Once he had been reassured on one cause of worry, his family 'black blood' was adept at finding a new one. That same year he told the envious Henry Taylor that he was making about £2,000 annually, 'But alas, Longfellow, he says, receives three thousand, and he has no doubt that Martin Tupper receives five thousand.'[12] Tennyson sometimes had the saving ability to laugh at his own determination to see only the dark side of a matter, but he was unable to summon it up on this occasion.

During the spring of 1861 Tennyson spent a good bit of time with two new additions to his train of younger friends. One of these was the first of a series of tutors who taught the boys. Emily Tennyson hated to give over her tuition, but she realized that she was unable to cope with either Latin or mathematics, so she asked help of Granville Bradley, headmaster of Marlborough, in finding a tutor, offering £100 annually. Bradley suggested Graham Dakyns, a twenty-two-year-old Rugbeian just down from Cambridge. From the first he was popular with the entire family and particularly so with Lionel, who probably resented his mother's favouritism with Hallam. He was a good classicist, and though he was small he was athletic and taught games to the boys, who had few friends of their own age. Tennyson so enjoyed talking classical prosody with him that he soon began taking Dakyns away from his pupils to accompany him on his walks.

It has been suggested that Farringford was a particularly happy place for a young tutor. Actually Dakyns, who stayed just over a year, was probably the only one who was totally satisfactory to the Tennysons and who remained friendly with them after his departure. During

XIX. Tennyson, 1859, oil by G. F. Watts.

XX. Hallam, Alfred, Emily, and Lionel Tennyson,
1863, by Rejlander.

the next three years, until 1865 when the boys were at last sent to school, some half-dozen recent graduates came to Farringford, each brought there with great expectation, each found wanting eventually. They were hired by the year, but most of them left before their time. No one could have suited the Tennysons as teacher to their sons, and though they tried to be kind to the young men they were not wholly satisfactory employers. Curiously enough, Emily was even forgetful about paying salaries, so that the tutors were sometimes reduced to having to ask for money. Letters written to Dakyns by his successors indicate that the boys were rebellious about tuition, and that their over-protective parents refused to support any plans for firmer discipline. Hallam, though abnormally acquiescent to his parents' wishes, was almost churlish with the tutors who followed Dakyns. Lionel was easier to deal with because he had a quicksilver interest in anything beautiful and could be charmed into studying. He lacked Hallam's firmness of purpose, but he had more imagination, a magical touch with animals, and a love of the countryside like his father's.

In March 1861 Arthur Hugh Clough and his wife came for six weeks to Freshwater, in part to be near Farringford. Clough was seeking respite from the disease that killed him later that year, and Mrs Clough was pregnant, so that they could not take full part in Freshwater activities. Like Dakyns, Clough was fond of Hallam and Lionel, and though he was not well enough at first to leave the hotel in the evenings, he none the less romped with the boys and taught them chess. When he was able, he climbed with Tennyson to see the view from the platform at the top of the house from which Tennyson watched the stars. The two poets discussed at length the problems of translating Homeric verse into English, a problem with which they were both wrestling. Tennyson liked Clough, but, apparently because he did not realize how much his illness affected his spirits, he thought the younger man rather wanting in a sense of humour. The judgement is disproved by Clough's remark to his wife after Tennyson had treated them to one of his notorious hours-long readings of *Maud*: 'That was rather a debauch, wasn't it!'[13] Shortly after this Clough left Freshwater, but he was to spend time with Tennyson a few months later in France.

Although she was still in bad health, Emily Tennyson had recovered sufficiently by 1861 to agree bravely to go with Alfred on his annual summer trip, this time to the Dordogne, the Auvergne, and the Pyrenees. After his experience the previous summer, Tennyson was not inclined to go with Palgrave, and he hated travelling alone. As Clough said of him, 'A.T. is but helpless by himself and thinks himself even more so than he is.' They took Dakyns with them to deal with trains and inns, besides taking care of the boys, who had been ill with whooping-cough. There was a personal maid to help Mrs Tennyson and to cook for the family when they were not in hotels. They expected their progress to be slow, so that the entire family could rest frequently. At the back of Tennyson's mind was the intention of going once more to Cauteretz, the lovely valley in which he had spent the happiest holiday of his life with Arthur Hallam in 1830.

They left at the end of June and returned in mid-September. The first part of the trip through Bourges and Clermont was pleasant, although they were surprised to find that there was garlic in French cooking, that the drains were not impeccable, and that 'the difficulty of getting rooms carriages or even donkeys in those days & the impossibility of finding proper food for children took away most of the pleasure'. At least the insects were not so bad as they had been in Italy and Portugal. Tennyson, who continually dreaded having his identity made public, found that the French instead of fawning on him were overtly hostile and cared little who he was. He firmly believed that the boys in the street were singing 'songs against him'. After he and Dakyns had climbed the Puy-de-Dôme they all moved to Mont-Dore.

The boys were still ill, Emily was weaker than ever, and Alfred had stomach trouble. It was a lift to drooping spirits after they had been in France three weeks to find Clough walking across the square in Mont-Dore. He stayed with them a few days, then arranged to meet them again in the Pyrenees.

From Bordeaux the Tennysons went through Tarbes and so to the Pyrenees, where they stayed in Bigorre and Luchon, which Clough thought was like a mountainous Brighton, full of Parisians in city clothes. The Tennysons were too ill to be worried by the suburban air of the place and settled down for three weeks in a pretty little house in the midst of maize fields near the river. Emily and the boys were confined to the house, but Tennyson and Dakyns walked and climbed daily.

At the end of August the family had recovered sufficiently to join Clough in Luz, only a few miles from Cauteretz. When he was near the place where he had been so happy in 1830, Tennyson talked constantly of that long-ago summer. 'Tennyson was here with Arthur Hallam 31 years ago and really finds great pleasure in the place,' Clough wrote to his wife. 'They staid here and at Cauterets—Oenone, he said, was written on the inspiration of the Pyrenees—which stood for Ida.' When he was able, Clough on a mule accompanied Tennyson and Dakyns on their walks, and he watched them swim although he could no longer do so himself.

As the time to go to Cauteretz came near, Clough noticed that Tennyson had done a complete volte-face and now seemed increasingly remote, buried in the past, so that Dakyns and Clough were almost intruders on his thoughts. When the three men went to the Cirque de Gavarnie, where Tennyson had composed the line 'slow dropping veils of thinnest lawn' in 1830, he fell silent contemplating its beauty. Without the company of Hallam even the central cataract, though 'still the finest thing in the Pyrenees', was diminished from his memory of it.

On 6 September the entire party moved to Cauteretz. Clough drove with Emily, the boys, and the maid in the carriage, while Tennyson with Dakyns as his 'walking-stick' went by foot through the mountain pass. When they came to the green declivity of the valley of Cauteretz, Dakyns recognized from Tennyson's manner that it was a 'sacred place', and instinctively dropped behind so that Tennyson could walk alone.

Emily Tennyson wrote happily that the scenery at Cauteretz pleased them more than any they had seen. 'Before our windows we have the stream rushing in its rocky bed from far away among the mountains & falling in a cataract with dark pines for a setting.' From their room they could hear 'the deepening of the Voice in the night'. But to Tennyson the charming village he remembered had become an 'odious watering-place'. With Clough he walked to 'a sort of island between two waterfalls with pines on it, of which he retained a recollection from his visit of 31 years ago—and which, moreover, furnished a simile to the Princess'. Now, however, the magical island seemed as overgrown as the village, the lone pine become a thicket. None the less, as Clough said in colossal meiosis, 'He is very of fond of this place evidently.'

Two days after he had arrived in Cauteretz Tennyson took a sheet of flimsy pink paper and jotted down the first version of the poem that had been forming in his head as he walked silently ahead of Dakyns, 'In the Valley of Cauteretz':

Brook that runnest madly, brook that flashest white
Deepening thy voice with the deepening of the night
All along the valley where thy mad waters go
I walked with Arthur Hallam two & thirty years ago.

All along the valley thou ravest down thy bed
Thy living voice to me is as the voice of the dead
All along the valley by rock & cave & tree
The voice of the dead is a living voice to me.

All the immediacy of his feelings is there in the two unpolished little stanzas, not least in the banality of the fourth line. The revisions to which it then became subject show both how instinctively Tennyson retreated from nakedly revealing his personal emotions and how conscientious a craftsman he was, rubbing and honing until the roughness was gone. The final version he believed to be the finest lyric he ever wrote:

All along the valley, stream that flashest white,
Deepening thy voice with the deepening of the night,
All along the valley, where thy waters flow,
I walked with one I loved two and thirty years ago.
All along the valley, while I walked today,
The two and thirty years were a mist that rolls away;
For all along the valley, down thy rocky bed,
Thy living voice to me was as the voice of the dead,
And all along the valley, by rock and cave and tree,
The voice of the dead was a living voice to me.

From his unconscious he drew upon other poetry with deep meaning about energized, moralized landscapes: Wordsworth's 'A slumber did my spirit seal', Meredith's 'Love in the Valley', his own 'Check every outflash, every ruder sally', and a poem by Hallam himself, 'The Soul's Eye'. The resonance created by the references to the other works only indicates the depth of Tennyson's feelings.

What is curious about the poem, of course, is that Tennyson wrote 'two & thirty years ago', when he had twice told Clough that he had been there thirty-one years earlier. Whether consciously or not, he had altered the number to achieve a more melodious line, which became particularly important after the revisions, when the true number would have been an awkward repetition of 'one I loved'. Years later he said, 'A brute of a —— has discovered that it was thirty-one years and not thirty-two', and according to his son he was still considering changing it in the year of his death. But it was not true. Clough's letters prove that Tennyson had known all along how many years it had been since his first visit; he could bring himself neither to spoil a good line nor to admit that he was consciously manipulating the facts. More than almost any other poem, it shows clearly how literal accuracy and artistic truth might be at odds for Tennyson when they involved both the depth of his emotional life and his artistic integrity.

Clough had noticed when staying at Freshwater that Tennyson was still without a subject for a new poem. It seems significant that the best new poem of the period derived from his experiences of three decades earlier, and that the other finest poem published at the time was 'Tithonus', which had chiefly been written in 1833 after Hallam's death. The two poems shine out from the other works of the early 1860s, when Tennyson's poetry too often seemed derivative, hesitant, or lacking in immediate feeling.

The return journey to England was undertaken in haste because Tennyson fell ill with the 'Pyrenaean complaint' as a result of a chill caught in Cauteretz, and he could think of little but getting home. The standard treatment of stomach upsets was rice, and at their Paris hotel Emily was incensed at 'having to pay *nine francs* for a rice pudding'. They stopped at Amiens on their way to the Channel, and as they were getting on the Boulogne train a middle-aged man with a boy put his head out of the window and saw them getting into another carriage. It was Robert Browning with his son, going to join his father and sister. At Boulogne he met Tennyson in a doorway, looking strange in the beard that he had grown since their last meeting. Browning was just trying to begin life anew after his wife's death three months earlier, and talking with the happy-looking Tennyson family was too much for him: he pulled his hat over his face and passed by the myopic Tennyson without speaking.[14]

It is improbable that the Tennysons had yet heard of the death of Mrs Browning. There were more deaths to come that year. During their absence Tennyson's uncle Charles had died, putting an end to the long history of bitter feelings between the Bayons and the Somersby branches of the family, so that Tennyson began seeing his Tennyson d'Eyncourt cousins when he was in London. Charles Tennyson d'Eyncourt died a disappointed man, who had never reached the pinnacles of political and social position to which he aspired. Only a few days after his return to Farringford Tennyson heard of the death of Clough in Florence. Before the end of the year came the news of the death of

Tennyson's royal patron, Prince Albert, to whom he owed so much, although they had met twice at most.

Emily Tennyson was 'in a perfect ecstasy' at being back in Farringford after the rigours of the Continent, sure of having 'seen no place in our wanderings where I should so well like to live'. But the world was becoming a colder place for her husband, who knew acutely the pain of his 'passion of the past'.[15]

Within a fortnight of Albert's death Tennyson had completed the 'Dedication' to his memory for the new edition of the *Idylls of the King* that was already in press. Emily Tennyson's role in its composition is not certain. At the time she was both asking for suggestions of poetic subjects from his friends and making her own, in some cases writing out prose summaries of what she thought he ought to write. A decade later she was directly responsible for the writing of the companion-piece to the dedication, 'To the Queen', which concludes the *Idylls*. It is probable that she had a large part in conceiving the dedication as a proper public expression of Alfred's deep admiration for the dead Prince and his gratitude for all that Albert had done for him, and it was her idea to forward it to Princess Alice, for transmission to her mother. Within a week came the Princess's friendly letter of thanks for the Queen, saying that his lines had calmed 'her aching, bleeding heart'. It was, wrote Emily, 'A day to be remembered by us. A letter of thanks to A from Princess Alice telling us that his lines have soothed our Queen. Thank God!'[16] Whatever her part in its composition, her own deep emotional involvement in the reception of the poem is indicated by the unconscious sliding from 'letter of thanks to A' into 'telling us'.

Emily Tennyson had few ambitions for herself, but there were no limits to what she thought her husband deserved, and she surely had an inkling that the poem might lead to his closer acquaintance with the Queen if she were to look to the Laureate for consolation.

The Queen had only a superficial interest in poetry for itself, and she usually relied upon her private secretary's advice as to what she should read. Tennyson's works, however, in particular *In Memoriam*, already had the best of recommendations, the approval of Albert, and for that reason she turned to them after his death.

All readers of poetry require that it have in some measure a relation to their own lives, but she demanded more, for her judgement of a poem frequently depended upon how closely its subject-matter and details tallied literally with her own experience. For example, one of the most telling touches in *In Memoriam* for her was that both Arthur

Hallam and Prince Albert had blue eyes. In her copy of the poem she substituted 'widow' for 'widower' in section XIII, beginning 'Tears of the widower', and changed 'her' to 'his'. Henry Ponsonby noticed that when she inaugurated amateur theatricals at Balmoral and Osborne, one of her chief interests was in ruthlessly altering the script of the plays to her own liking. It is probable that both literature and persons were important to her primarily in so far as they could be turned to reflect her own emotions faithfully.

In March 1862 Argyll wrote to Tennyson to say that the Queen would like to have him call at Osborne when next she was there, a plan suggested to her by Argyll and his mother-in-law, the Duchess of Sutherland. There was never any pretence that this was the Queen's tribute to poetry; rather, it was an occasion for one of her Household to comfort her. At this time, four months after Albert's death, her sorrow was real enough, but there were already signs that it was hardening into her 'over-indulgence in what may be called the luxury of woe'. And mixed with her grief was indignation that death had dared strike so close to the Throne. As one who knew her well wrote, 'one almost expects to find some directions in her best style of political indignation instructing her Private Secretary to address some remonstrance to the Almighty'.[17]

Tennyson had a deep veneration for the institution of royalty and great personal fealty to the Queen, and was moved by the pathos of her widowed condition. Without question he was willing to help comfort her, although, as he wrote to Argyll, 'I am a shy beast and like to keep in my burrow.' He was nervous about details of his visit: how to enter and leave the room where he saw her, how to address her, what to talk about. Argyll responded with delightful letters of detailed instruction, making the point that he should not be afraid to say anything that came naturally in the course of the conversation. 'Talk to her as you would to a Poor woman in affliction—that is what she likes best.'[18]

The meeting of two such egocentric persons should have been catastrophic, but it was saved by simplicity of heart. Each recognized the shyness, the imperfectly mastered sentiments, and the crippling sensitivity that lay behind the apparent arrogance of the other. It was the beginning of an understanding between two very difficult persons. Since the Queen could never have forgotten the difference in their stations, there was no chance that it could ever become a close friendship, such as Tennyson might have enjoyed with the Prince, but it was none the less firmly grounded in mutual affection.

This first meeting was an emotional one for each of them, although for different reasons. Tennyson, who was standing by the fire when she entered the room, was unable to see her clearly, because of both his near-blindness and the tears that sprang to his eyes, but he made out that she was much prettier than he had expected. Her voice was quiet and sad; in the turmoil of his feelings he could remember little of what she had said except that she once remarked, 'I am like your Mariana now.' Later, when Edmund Venables asked him about her conversation, Tennyson could only say, 'I can't remember, I lost my head. I only remember what I said to the Queen—big fool that I was.' 'What was that?' asked Venables. 'Why, what an excellent King Prince Albert would have made. As soon as it was out of my mouth I felt what a blunder I had made. But, happily, it proved to be the very right thing to have said. The Queen replied that that had been the constant sorrow of her life—that she was called to govern, while he who was so worthy of the first place was obliged to take a secondary position.' The interview was a long one, and Tennyson found it difficult to stand still during its length. 'The Queen is accustomed to it, and does it well', he said; 'I did it awkwardly.' When he left she asked him to come again, and he requested that she might one day shake his sons by the hand.[19]

A month after Tennyson's visit to Osborne Argyll wrote to him: 'I repeated your "Rocky Valley" to the Queen—in her own Rocky Valley, where she walks under the weight of a fresher grief than "two & thirty years ago"—and She was delighted with it.' At Christmas the Queen sent her picture to Tennyson with a copy of the speeches of Albert, inscribed 'from the beloved Prince's broken-hearted widow Victoria Rg.'.[20] He was invited to the wedding of the Prince of Wales, for which he had written 'A Welcome to Alexandra', but the invitation arrived too late for him to attend. Instead there was a supper and dance at Farringford, with fires on the downs above the house.

In May 1863 the Queen remembered her invitation to Tennyson and asked him to bring his whole family to Osborne. On his second reception by the Queen Tennyson was almost at ease, but Emily was overcome: 'She gave me her hand & I found myself on my knees kissing it but I dont exactly know how I got there. . . . Ally talked very eloquently with the Queen & we all laughed & talked. . . . We talked of everything in heaven & earth almost Jowett Huxley the stars the Millennium. I never felt it so easy to talk with any stranger before.'[21]

In spite of such honours as the day at Osborne, Tennyson soon longed as usual to get away from the island, where Emily said he felt 'rather moss-grown. . . . Men want change.' With only a trace of self-pity she added, 'A book is change enough for me I think.' During the summer of 1863 Tennyson had no plans for a trip, and he suffered from hay-fever, which was aggravated when he was bored or unable to write. With Mrs Cameron he went to London, 'hardly sneezing at all. . . . We got a coupé to ourselves she being in the immoral habit of bribing the guard.' But it was probably Mrs Cameron who had been responsible a month earlier for the disaster that spoiled the rest of his summer. Emily and the boys had planned on being vaccinated, but at the last moment Tennyson balked. When Mrs Cameron heard of his refusal, she came at once to Farringford and began to harangue him. He fled to his study at the top of the house and locked himself in, but she followed and hammered at the door, calling out repeatedly, 'Alfred, you are a coward.' When he could be heard, he shouted back, 'Woman, go away, I will be vaccinated to-morrow.' He kept his word, but he thought that the vaccine came 'from a gouty baby', infecting him with eczema.[22] Whatever the medical probability of such infection, the fact is that he fell ill with a badly inflamed leg and high fever, so that he was bedridden for more than a month. The previous year he and Palgrave had patched up their differences for a moderately successful trip to the Peak District. Now, when Tennyson was ill, Palgrave and his new wife took him in and nursed him.

Many of his old friends came to his bedside at Palgrave's. Browning was there several times, and even Carlyle, 'with a certain ungainly kindness', came from Chelsea to York Gate 'for a very few hurried minutes to see him'. One medical man told Tennyson he had varicose veins, and he bought the first of the elastic stockings that he wore for the rest of his life. It was like a repetition of the bad old days as he went from doctor to doctor, settling at last on James (later Sir James) Paget, who decided that he had a 'goutish affection' of the sort that he had often seen in families where gout was hereditary. It was an echo of Dr Gully's words, and though gout no longer concealed the threat of epilepsy, some measure of how seriously Tennyson took the diagnosis is his decision to change his drinking habits: 'It will be better I think to exchange the greatest part of the port, tho' I must say I hate claret.'[23] But, as with his snipe-like darts at temperance during the 1840s, this resolution was as short-lived as his attempts to stop smoking.

It was impossible for him to go to a hydropathic establishment, for that would have been tacit admission that he was in as bad shape as he had been before his marriage, but Tennyson still believed in the beneficial effects of water. When he was able to move from Palgrave's he went off for five lonely weeks at Harrogate, to drink the mineral waters of the spa. On his return to the south he bought himself a vapour bath for Farringford, and in London he again patronized the old Hummums, where he had so often gone to bathe when he was a bachelor. By the end of the year he was in fair shape again.

The period of his illness had only served to dry up further the creativity with which he had been so prodigal for years, when he had negligently forgotten to write down his poems, thrown them away, or used them as spills for his pipe, sure that there were always more where they came from. In 1863 he had finished giving flesh to Woolner's tale of the fisherman, now complete as 'Enoch Arden', and he finished another narrative poem, 'Aylmer's Field', the story of which had also been supplied by Woolner. Reverting to the habits of his youth when studying with his father, he experimented with the classical metres of which he had talked with Clough and Dakyns. He had always been a thoroughly experimental poet, but his successes were seldom written as demonstrations of theory, and so it was now. Most of all, the experiments seemed excuses to keep from writing the kind of poetry at which he had once excelled.

At Christmas the Bradleys, the Montagu Butlers, Palgrave, and Allingham were at Farringford, and the talk was almost entirely on the subject of classical prosody, to which, said Allingham, 'I naturally have little to contribute, nor can I see that the discussion throws much if any light on English metrical effects'. In such a group, conversation was relentless, and Mrs Bradley, who was feeling ennui for the first time at Farringford, decided that the 'tendency to discuss meanings of Gk. words makes conversation duller when Mr. Butler is there'. Perhaps her remark should be judged in the light of being said about the headmaster of Harrow by the wife of the headmaster of Marlborough. But even Emily finally made practically the only bored comment recorded in her long life: 'Mrs. T. confessed herself tired of hearing about "Classic Metres".'[24]

At the end of 1863 Tennyson's old friend Thackeray died, and his two lonely daughters came to Freshwater to stay in a cottage belonging to Mrs Cameron. Annie Thackeray used to tell how they arrived late on a bitterly cold afternoon, when a heavy snow lay on the grounds. As the two sisters walked aimlessly up and down before the fire, wondering what the future held, they slowly became aware of a tall figure immobile in the snow outside the window, muffled in a heavy cloak, his features hidden by a broad-brimmed hat. It was Tennyson, come down from Farringford to show them his silent sympathy without intruding on their grief.

Once the Thackeray girls' deepest mourning was over, the Camerons and Tennysons embarked on a positive orgy of entertaining to divert them. Before long they were all joined by Watts and the Prinseps, who were considering removing to the Isle of Wight and to that end had bought a field as a possible building site. With them was Watt's beautiful seventeen-year-old bride, Ellen Terry, twenty years his junior. And each of the families attracted a brilliant group of friends until Freshwater seemed an outpost of Little Holland House. No wonder that one of Annie Thackeray's guests said in perplexity, 'Everybody is either a genius, or a poet, or a painter or peculiar in some way; is there nobody commonplace?'[25] Jowett was encouraged to bring presentable Oxford undergraduates on reading parties to act as partners for the young ladies in the evening.

There were balls at Dimbola, with the dancers moving out into the fields and downs to drift in the moonlight. At the more sedate Farringford dances, the white-gloved Tennyson loved to lead off with a stately old-fashioned waltz or an elephantine polka with one of the young girls.

Busily recording it all was Mrs Cameron, who would drag them off in turns to the conservatory-turned-fowl-house, which now she had made into a studio where, with her new camera, she compulsively photographed anyone who caught her eye: Tennyson, a guest, a passing woman with a child, the postman, her own maids, and occasionally her patient old husband. It was a lengthy business, for the sitter had to sit perfectly still for fifteen minutes or more as Mrs Cameron tried by exhortation and threat to produce the expression she was looking for.

Annie Thackeray, who loved Tennyson as a second father, soon became one of the family, finding at Farringford the security she had not known at home because of her mother's illness. She was as good a walker as Tennyson himself, and she accompanied him on his daily course along the downs, while he talked about poetry, his voice rising above the scream of the gulls. He was only beginning to learn that women could be companions in laughter and fun, as well as helpmates or objects of distant respect. From then until the end of his life there was a succession of girls or young women to whom he was devoted, walking with them, lecturing them benignly on poetry, flirting ponderously, sometimes demanding attention in a way that approached bullying, but always giving them a sense of paternal affection. It was as if he had become the enchanter of the island, shuffling along with the great staff he carried on walks, speaking of his rough magic in the tones of Prospero instructing a series of Mirandas.

As reward for his companionship Tennyson frequently asked an innocent kiss from the young women, a habit that started up yet another rumour about him, that his interest in them was far from avuncular. It is not difficult to see that they supplied him with the kind of feminine companionship that Emily Tennyson could not provide on her invalid's sofa, and if in the relationship there was an unconscious, sublimated touch of sexual attraction on his part, it is not to be wondered at. But there is no evidence of anything more than that in his feelings for his young female friends.

When Annie first began trying her hand as a writer, she showed her efforts to Tennyson, not guessing then that his scrupulosity about language would be as applicable to prose as to poetry. Even after she had become an established author, she always tried to show him her proofs: 'He read, he said flummery flummery, he corrected a word here & there. I was not Dante but he most assuredly was Virgil & it was joy to have such a convincing lesson in style, simply given & indisputably felt by me.'[26]

Ellen Terry, too, flew to Tennyson during the summer of the one year of her disastrous marriage to Watts. Mrs Prinsep was constantly correcting her, telling her how to behave, generally trying to make her worthy of Watts, whom Mrs Prinsep believed (accurately but for the wrong reasons) she should not have married. 'I was 17 in years then, but scarcely 7, in wisdom I fear', she wrote after Tennyson's death.[27] In her unhappiness she would creep away to Farringford in her childish clothes, to play at Red Indians or a paper chase with Lionel and Hallam, with whom she felt more at home than with her husband. Tennyson took her for walks, pointing out birds and flowers, patiently teaching her their names, which she as a city child had never known. She always remembered his kindness, and it was a particular satisfaction to her years later to take the leads in his plays.

One sixteen-year-old with whom he had no success was Janet Duff Gordon, who walked with him while she was staying with her parents in Freshwater. As she used to tell the story, his shoe-string came untied, and he pointed imperiously to his foot, saying, '"Janet, tie my shoe." . . . I answered; "No, tie your own shoe. Papa says men should wait on women, not women on men." . . . He afterwards told my father that I was a clever girl, but extremely badly brought up.'[28] Improbable as the details sound, the spirit of the story was perhaps accurate. Janet was so incensed that she never liked him again, and she was almost certainly the source of many of the malicious stories that her friend Meredith used to tell of Tennyson.

Of all the festivities of that spring of 1864 the outstanding one was the reception at Farringford of Garibaldi, who spent a cold April afternoon there. The Italian hero was the hero of England that spring, and was fresh from receiving the freedom of the City of London. The Duchess of Sutherland had tried unsuccessfully to bring Tennyson and Garibaldi together at her home, but Tennyson preferred to see him at Freshwater. It was all rather rushed, but by the time their guest drove through the crowds surrounding the gates and alighted at the portico, Alfred, Emily, and the boys were waiting under the flags that they had hurriedly hung out. Inside the house the rooms were full of primroses gathered from the garden. It must have been a splendid picture as Tennyson and Garibaldi walked together up the stairs to his study: Tennyson in his habitual frock-coat spotted with food, Garibaldi in a red shirt under a red-lined poncho.

As reported by Tennyson, the conversation in the study was somewhat inconclusive. Both men spoke English but failed almost totally to understand each other. After they had talked for some time at cross purposes, things went better when they quoted Italian poetry to each other: Tennyson recited from Manzoni, and when his turn came Garibaldi quoted Ugo Foscolo. Like Gladstone, Tennyson was shocked to find that Garibaldi had little appreciation of Dante; as the Duke of Argyll explained, 'his horror of the Romish Priesthood, and his ignorance of religion in any better form, has divorced him from all definite belief: and in this way as well as in others, some of the best parts of Dante are a sealed book to him'.[29]

When Garibaldi had finished his cigar, Tennyson took him back downstairs so that he might plant a commemorative tree in front of the house. Mrs Cameron, her hands blackened with photographic chemicals, rushed up and knelt before them, imploring Garibaldi to come to the fowl-house at Dimbola and have his picture taken. For a moment there was a misunderstanding as Garibaldi took her for an overdressed beggar woman asking for charity. Mrs Cameron, realizing what was passing through his mind, waved her hands in front of his face and explained, 'This is not dirt but art!'[30] Even so he was not persuaded.

He planted the little wellingtonia, shook hands with the Tennysons, and drove off, presumably wondering what the purpose of the visit had been. Hallam ran behind the carriage as far as he could go. Meanwhile Tennyson, who claimed to have been taken by his noble simplicity, said musingly that he had the 'divine stupidity of a hero'. As a meeting of heroes, it left something to be desired. That night many of the branches of the little tree were stripped away by souvenir-hunters, so that today, when full-grown, it is still deformed.

※

CHAPTER XXVIII

NEW FRIENDS,
1864–1868

THE volume containing 'Enoch Arden' nearly had another title on publication in the summer of 1864. The story of the quiet tug-of-war preceding the final choice illustrates Tennyson's care for titles, as well as the tenacity with which Emily could oppose him when acting in what she conceived to be his own best interests. It is a picture quite unlike the usual one of her as a retiring, silvery spirit emitting faint exhortations from the sofa, as she was so often painted in contemporary reminiscences.

At the end of June, only a short time before publication, Tennyson was in London seeing the Moxons about the new volume. Before he left Farringford, Emily had decided upon *Enoch Arden and Other Poems* as a title. There is surprise and a ghost of peremptory irritation in her letter a few days after he had gone: 'Ally dearest I see in the Reader the title is to be Idylls of the Hearth. Surely not. Will not "Enoch Arden & Other Poems" be more in thy usual simple style? I dont like this Idylls of the Hearth. Wilt thou not change it?'

In reply Tennyson suggested an alternative, *Idylls, Chiefly of Seventy Years Ago*, but that met with equal disfavour at Farringford: 'I am anxious about the title dearest, will this do?' She reminded him that she had chosen the titles of *In Memoriam* and *Idylls of the King*, and that they had proved successful, 'so perhaps I may be right in this too. . . . Perhaps it would be giving it undue pre-eminence to call the book Enoch Arden & Other Poems, if not perhaps this is the best, not Idylls of the Hearth. This was not thy name I am sure. Macmillan's probably, but I may wrong him.'

When she received no reply, she wrote in apparent resignation: 'Thou hast not answered about the title so I fear it is true.' As a last alternative she offered another suggestion that seems almost designed by its ineptness to bring Alfred back to her first choice: ' "Idylls of the People" let it be.'

Unfortunately, her letter crossed one from Alfred making a last-ditch effort to name his own poems, telling her that time had run out for changes: 'I have to decide upon a title today. "Home Idylls" seems to me the best.' Deadline or no, Emily replied swiftly, and two days later Tennyson wrote in his letter diary as if the idea had just struck him, 'I now think of "Enoch Arden etc." as a title.' And so it was.[1]

Tennyson had hoped to earn £2,000 for the volume; as it turned out, he made £8,000 that year alone. More than 40,000 copies were sold within a short time of publication, and they continued to sell well until his death, making it easily his most popular volume.

As has been mentioned earlier, the two most accomplished poems in the book were 'In the Valley of Cauteretz' and that beautiful example of the burst of elegiac classicism in 1833, 'Tithonus'. There is surely significance in the fact that both are concerned with the past, with removal from contemporary society, yet they are in a volume with which Tennyson intended to mark his own direct involvement with his contemporaries by making an appeal to the common man.

It is Tennyson's very attempt to invoke everyday, elemental emotions that has made this probably the least well-regarded of his volumes in our own day. The truth is that when he deserted the landscape of his own mind in order to portray the feelings of others unlike himself he sometimes failed to distinguish sentiment from the sentimental, the moral from the maudlin. At his best there was no one who could write so well of the interchange between one's own emotions and the external world, but understanding of others had never been strong in him, so that he was inherently limited at dramatic and narrative poetry.

The point is made in the first fifteen lines of 'Enoch Arden'. It opens with a sure-footed description of the little port, in which every image is concrete, while at the same time it hints at themes to be developed later in the poem. Each detail seems directly observed, recorded in simple language pared of superfluity and hence charged with intensity. It is a style so personal to Tennyson that it would be hard to mistake it for the work of another:

> Long lines of cliff breaking have left a chasm;
> And in this chasm are foam and yellow sands;
> Beyond, red roofs about a narrow wharf
> In cluster; then a mouldered church; and higher
> A long street climbs to one tall-towered mill;
> And high in heaven behind it a gray down

With Danish barrows; and a hazelwood,
By autumn nutters haunted, flourishes
Green in a cuplike hollow of the down.

Here on this beach a hundred years ago,
Three children of three houses, Annie Lee,
The prettiest little damsel in the port,
And Philip Ray the miller's only son,
And Enoch Arden, a rough sailor's lad
Made orphan by a winter shipwreck . . .

When Tennyson shifts from landscape to children, he no longer seems to be keeping his eye on the ball. In the last six slack lines there is little that is unique to him. The language seems more second-hand than Woolner's plot, the well-worn one of the mariner, shipwrecked for ten years, who comes home to find his wife married to his best friend, then lives near the pair unrecognized until his death.

Tennyson himself knew at least subliminally that he was playing on ready-made emotions not valid ones, a fact indicated by his instructions to the audience at a reading of 'Enoch Arden': 'He begged us not to go into hysterics.' Henry Taylor recorded in his *Autobiography* that on another occasion one of Tennyson's audience when he was reading the poem actually did have hysterics.[2] Tennyson's remark was not dictated by easy cynicism about his audience but by a belief in the automatic nature of the reactions he could invoke in a manner unpleasantly reminiscent of a pop star playing upon the mass emotions of a crowd of teenagers.

Popular Victorian sentiments were no more mawkish than our own, but because we no longer share them their inertness is obvious to us, and in such poems as 'Enoch Arden' it is hard not to believe that Tennyson was writing about what he thought his readers wanted rather than anything that had ever touched him nearly.

The same problem is at the core of the failure of the other long poem of the volume, 'Aylmer's Field'. Once more the plot came from Woolner at Emily's instigation, and it relies upon easy, sentimental responses. It is only a slight variation upon Tennyson's familiar theme of the doomed love of a well-born, impoverished young man for a girl with rich, proud parents. The defeat of love by financial and social ambition provides the occasion for more diatribes against wealth and Mammonism. Again part of the trouble is the inadequate characterization of the parents and the girl (in this case her name is Edith, but she is indistinguishable from Maud or the heroines of the other poems with the same theme). Clearly, the fact that the parents are wealthy is enough for Tennyson to explain their behaviour; their roots in his own experience were nourished with everything he knew of his uncle and grandfather, in part perhaps with what he had known of the Edens, but little of that gets into the poem.

Significantly, the most moving passage is not concerned with human beings but with the unchanging earth that outlives snobbery, pride, avarice, cruelty, and the lives of all those in the poem:

> Then the great Hall was wholly broken down,
> And the broad woodland parcelled into farms;
> And where the two contrived their daughter's good,
> Lies the hawk's cast, the mole has made his run,
> The hedgehog underneath the plantain bores,
> The rabbit fondles his own harmless face,
> The slow-worm creeps, and the thin weasel there
> Follows the mouse, and all is open field.

When he could write like that of a symbolic nature, it is hard to see how Tennyson could ever have mistaken where his genius lay.

In the volume he also included a number of the experiments he had been making in translation and in adapting classical metres to English. In the light of the other poems, these too seem an attempt to graft his own style on to something already formed, as if he were incapable at the moment of a wholly original work.

His own expressed worries about the poems in the volume indicate that he was concerned about the turn his poetry had taken, but the reviews were all he could possibly have hoped for. To some of his admirers who wanted him to be a public mouthpiece for the more unexceptionable ideas of the era, the success of *Enoch Arden etc.* opened up limitless avenues. As Woolner wrote to Emily Tennyson, congratulating her on the success of their joint effort to ginger up Alfred's production: 'I only hope it will inspire him to write heaps more poems; for now he has only to think out a good subject and write it straight off; as his command over language is quite absolute now, and the verses must fashion themselves so perfectly in his mind at once as scarcely to require correction.' Like Jowett, Woolner thought the Indian Mutiny a subject tailor-made for Tennyson, for if he would 'spend 4 or 5 years hard healthy work upon it . . . he might make the greatest, most English, and sublime poem that has been done since

Paradise Lost'.[3] Any proposal for poetry that includes both 'healthy' and 'sublime' should be automatically rejected.

Matthew Arnold, who thought that the function of poetry was something more than merely rhyming *Hansard* or *The Times*, was inconstant in his reaction to Tennyson's works except for a rooted disapproval of them, and he blew hot and cold, at one time reportedly saying that 'Tithonus' was among the finest poems in the language, at another preferring 'Enoch Arden'. All in all, however, he did not think Tennyson 'a great and powerful spirit in any line—as Goethe was in the line of modern thought, Wordsworth in that of contemplation, Byron even in that of passion'.[4]

For years FitzGerald had been lamenting the decline of his old friend's poetic powers, and now he thought he perceived more clearly some of the complicated reasons for his capitulation to a vulgar taste. Tennyson should never have left 'his old County, and gone up to be suffocated by London Adulation. He has lost that which caused the long roll of the Lincolnshire Wave to reverberate in the measure of Locksley Hall. Don't believe that I rejoice like a Dastard in what I believe to be the Decay of *A Great Man*: my sorrow has been so much about it that (for one reason) I have the less cared to meet him of late years, having nothing to say in sincere praise. Nor do I mean that his Decay is all owing to London, &c. He is growing old: and I don't believe much in the *Fine Arts* thriving on an old Tree'.

To Fitz much of Tennyson's loss of powers could be laid at the door of Emily Tennyson. 'She is a graceful Lady, but I think that she & other aesthetic and hysterical Ladies have hurt A.T., who, *quoad* Artist, wd have done better to remain single in Lincolnshire, or married a jolly Woman who would have laughed & cried without any reason why.' Only a few years later he was to describe her as 'a Lady of a Shakespearian type, as I think AT. once said of her: that is, of the Imogen sort, far more agreeable to me than the sharp-witted Beatrices, Rosalinds, &c. I do not think she has been (on this very account perhaps) so good a helpmate to AT.'s Poetry as to himself.'[5]

Lear's view of Alfred's marriage was quite different: 'I believe no other woman in all this world could live with him for a month.' In the autumn after the publication of *Enoch Arden*, Lear went for several days to Farringford, but it seemed crowded. Mrs Cameron was in and out, and he decided that he disliked her in addition to finding her a bore; there were so many other guests that he complained, 'One always seems to live in public here.' Tennyson's 'ravings about England "going down hill"—"best thing God can do is to squash this planet flat!"—&c &c are wearying & distressing'. When they walked, Tennyson paid little attention to the scenery and talked of nothing but the intrusion of the railway upon their part of the island. Driven to distraction, the mild Lear at last gave him an 'outspoken opinion about his morbid absurdity & unphilosophical bothers'. Because of his love of Emily, Lear found that 'it always wrings me to leave Farringford—yet I doubt—as once before—if I can go again. I suppose it is the anomaly of high souled & philosophic writings combined with slovenliness, selfishness, & morbid folly that prevents my being happy there:—perhaps also vexation at myself for not being more so.' But Lear had his own ways of being annoying, and when he did return he found Tennyson excited about 'another farmer', which he had just written as companion-piece to the 'Northern Farmer, Old Style'. Lear suggested that 'if he wrote many he might publish them all as a Farmercopia—wh. disgusted him'.[6]

In the summer of 1864 the entire family travelled to France for a two-month trip through the Arthurian country in Brittany and Normandy. In part they wanted to escape the continual uninvited visitors to Farringford. Emily was particularly bothered by the people 'who stand in the drive staring at us & one gentleman actually in the Portico'. Some of the windows in the summer-house that Tennyson had built were smashed by 'Cockneys', and the ship's figurehead over its door was stolen. By the time they returned from France she had convinced Alfred that they needed a summer retreat, and she had decided on Surrey: 'I liked the country so much when living with my Father at Hale that I think A will like it too for a second home.'[7] They went briefly to stay near Haslemere while looking at a plot of land, and though they decided not to buy it, by now they felt committed to having at least a summer cottage.

Part of Emily's wish to have a second home was connected with her fear of the loneliness of Farringford when the boys went to school. She had tried to hold on to them as long as possible, first by teaching them herself, then by a series of tutors. But Hallam was now pubescent, and their family friends were united in suggesting that the boys needed wider horizons. Even Gladstone and Jowett said that they needed firmer discipline. In particular Lionel was stammering badly, and it was thought this might be cured in another environment. Tennyson was concerned that Lionel was reading the unexpurgated *Don Quixote* from his library; 'there are some wanton tales in it very unfit for such young boys if I recollect right'.[8] With some justice he was worried; Lionel's 'propensities' were to get him into several scrapes, both before and after his marriage. In 1864 Emily held on as long as she could, saying that it would be dangerous to cut the boys' shoulder-length hair in cold weather, thus winning a reprieve until the following Easter, when they were sent to a preparatory school in Dorset run by Charles Kegan Paul, a former chaplain at Eton, who was later to become Tennyson's publisher.

On his expeditions to London, which it was now understood should take place several times a year, Tennyson was the occasion of dinners nearly every night, often with Trollope, Milnes, Tom Taylor, Spedding, Thomas Hughes, or Lord Stanley among the guests. Usually the dinners were entirely male, since Emily had remained behind in Farringford. One face that had formerly been familiar at these dinners was not often there, that of John Forster. He and Tennyson had always been prickly with each other, and they had fallen out when Forster invited Tennyson to dinner and was told it was against his principles to dine out. Forster, who could see only too easily that this was not true, was naturally offended and said, '"All your principles are eccentric," and this seemed to stick in the poet's gizzard.'[9] Tennyson was not a liar, nor was he simple-minded, so it seems probable that he had meant that it was impossible to dine at a particular time, but Forster chose to ignore that interpretation of his words, and thereafter their already fragile relationship was on the wane.

There were, however, two men who could usually be found at table with Tennyson at least once during each of his London stays: Browning and Gladstone. As a widower Browning was embarked upon the strenuous social life that surprised his friends who had known him during his marriage; as a poet he was only beginning to be regarded as the 'other' great Victorian besides Tennyson. Recognizing that they were not apt to agree, they seldom discussed poetry, but they kept their regard, particularly on the part of Browning, who said that he liked even the smell of Tennyson's tobacco, adding, 'I never see enough of Tennyson, nor yet to talk with him about subjects we either of us value at three straws.'[10] He may have wanted to be with Tennyson more, but Emily was still unable to get him to Farringford, since he always pleaded vaguely that his engagements prevented his coming.

Tennyson had met Gladstone a few years after Hallam's death, but they had never been much together until in 1862 they were both guests of the Duchess of Sutherland at Cliveden. 'Gladstone spent all the time with him I think there from Friday to Monday', Emily told Dakyns, '& dined with him once in Town besides so they have seen a good deal of each other.' Tennyson found Gladstone 'a very agreeable, and intellectual and most gentlemanly man. I read the "Fisherman" with which he seemed to be greatly struck.'[11] Thereafter they often sought each other out when Tennyson was in town. The only difficulty was that Gladstone, who had been writing about Homer and translating him, insisted on speaking of subjects of which Tennyson regarded himself as master: 'very interesting he was, even when he discoursed on Homer, where most people think him a little hobby-horsical'.

A typical occasion when Browning, Gladstone, and Tennyson were all present was the dinner given in 1864 by the Palgraves, where Tennyson took the lead in conversation in a way that he had not always done. One of the guests, Thomas Richmond, afterwards recorded his impressions of the stars of the party: 'I shall never forget the evening. The grand head and shoulders, the tender yet powerful eyes of Tennyson. The sharpness and coxcombery of little Browning. The bad manners of Woolner and his horrid laugh. The grace of Giffy Palgrave. The tender power of Gladstone, and the odd, funny expression of Sir Francis Doyle!'[12]

On another evening later that year, when they were walking home together from a dinner, Tennyson invited Gladstone to Farringford: 'he said with great earnestness "I will take the very earliest opportunity". . . . He is a very noble fellow & perfectly unaffected.'[13] It was another seven years, however, before Gladstone found the opportunity.

Actually the curious, unstated rivalry that had sprung up years before when Tennyson displaced Gladstone in Hallam's regard still simmered beneath the friendly surface of shared evenings. It first bubbled over into the open at a dinner given by Woolner in December 1865 for guests that included Gladstone, Tennyson, Holman Hunt, and the Bristol physician Dr Symonds. A lively impression of the party was written by the young John Addington Symonds, who went in later for the evening.

When young Symonds entered, the others were still in the dining-room over their port, talking about the recent uprising in Jamaica, where Governor Eyre had savagely put down a riot in which some twenty Europeans were killed. By the time Eyre was finished, more than 600 natives had been killed or executed. Tennyson, who must have seemed to Gladstone a long way from the young liberal who had gone to France with Hallam in 1830, kept defending Eyre, saying that anyone might be panicked into cruelty in the face of danger. While Gladstone was deploring the slaughter in the 'rich, flexible' tones with which he dominated the House of Commons, Tennyson kept interrupting, not with logical rebuttal but with an irritating repetition *sotto voce*, 'We are too tender to savages, we are more tender to a black than ourselves.' Over and over he said it, varying it occasionally with an *obbligato* of 'Niggers are tigers, niggers are tigers.' His annoying assertion of his 'prejudices & convictions' was in turn interrupted by the arrival of Palgrave, 'a little man in morning dress, with short beard & moustache, well cut features & a slight cast in his eye, and impatient dissatisfied look & some self assertion in his manner'. Symonds likened the ensuing conversation to an unorthodox string quintet, with Gladstone as violin, Tennyson cello, Woolner bass viol, Palgrave viola, '& perhaps Hunt a second but very subordinate viola'.

At the table Tennyson kept moving 'his great gaunt body about', all the while 'drinking glasses of port, & glowering round the room through his spectacles. His moustache hides the play of his mouth, but as far as I cd see that feature is as grim as the rest.' Repeatedly the two great men differed, each speaking his convictions in a strong provincial accent, 'Tennyson with his deep drawl rising into an impatient falsetto when put out. Gladstone arguing, Tennyson putting in a prejudice . . . Gladstone full of facts, Tennyson relying on impressions.' According to Symonds, Gladstone's delicate repartee was that of a man of the world, and he treated Tennyson like a child, answering him with 'a tinkling laugh' when he spoke against the Reform Bill. Gladstone's condescension must have been as hard to put up with as Tennyson's dogmatic, irrational assertions.

When they moved to the drawing-room, Woolner handed Gladstone a manuscript book of Tennyson's unpublished translations from the *Iliad*, which Gladstone looked at silently. Woolner asked Tennyson to read aloud from the book. '"No, I shant" said Tennyson . . . with a pettish voice & jerking his arms & body from the hips.' Then he realized for the first time that Gladstone had been reading the manuscript. 'This isn't fair—no, this isn't fair', he said, taking it out of Gladstone's hands, '& nothing would pacify him.'

As Tennyson occasionally did when he was ill at ease in company, he began dominating the conversation totally, perhaps urged on by the port. He spoke of his own poems, of his ideas of infinity, the universe, and space, finally about the puzzling nature of matter and how it was harder to understand a brick than to understand God. 'In all this metaphysical vagueness about Matter, Morals, the existence of Evil, & the evidences of God there was something almost childish,' said Symonds, who thought Tennyson's metaphysics commonplace. 'Such points pass with most men for settled as insoluble.'

Gladstone held his fire all during the long monologue. At last Tennyson agreed to go back to the dining-room to read his translations of the *Iliad* to Gladstone and the elder Symonds, while the others stayed with the ladies. Young Symonds slipped in unperceived by Tennyson. 'He began by reading in a deep bass growl the passage of Achilles shouting in the trench.' Gladstone, who had put up for too long with interruptions about his own field of competence, now began revenging himself, and 'interrupted him with small points about words'. Tennyson could not deny that Gladstone knew what he was talking about, but it totally ruined his reading. From parliamentary experience Gladstone knew exactly how to break in most tellingly. 'He has a combative House of Commons mannerism, wh gives him the appearance of thinking too much about himself. It was always to air some theory of his own that he broke Tennyson's recital; & he seemed listening only in order to catch something up.' As Symonds noticed, 'Tennyson invited criticism' by his obvious irritation. The reading was a fiasco.

And so the long evening wore on. 'It seemed as if Gladstone were a champion in the medieval schools, throwing down theses & defending them for pure argument sake, not for any real love of truth.' It was not a pretty display by either man as their deep antagonism revealed itself over and over. One sympathizes with Mrs Woolner in the drawing-room, hearing the explosions from the dining-room, wondering when her guests would leave. Gladstone was the first of the party to go, at 1 a.m., with the honours fairly even.[14] Surprisingly, Tennyson afterwards said that he had never seen Gladstone so much at his ease and so delightful. It is one of the few ironic remarks attributed to him. Gladstone made no comment about the evening in his diary.

Bound together both by their old friendship for Hallam and by their position as the two most famous men of their generation, Tennyson and Gladstone were like brothers, very different from each other, who feel reluctant affection without ever ceasing to wonder how their lots should have been cast together. It is to their credit that they constantly smothered the antipathy that otherwise could have flashed out dangerously, and after the evening at Woolner's there were few examples of their behaving badly when together, although they continued to comment adversely on each other all their lives.

It was during the same visit to London in December 1865 that the end came to any possibility of intimacy between Tennyson and Swinburne, although it is improbable that it would have flourished in any case. For once the fault was not Tennyson's. Some time earlier he had written to compliment Swinburne on *Atalanta in Calydon* and he said of him, 'That young fellow has caught the true spirit of the old Greek poets. He thinks their thoughts, speaks their language, and sings with their own music'.[15] The omens were good for the meeting between them that had been arranged by Milnes (who had recently become Lord Houghton). Swinburne was in such awkward high spirits that Houghton thought he was drunk when they met, although Swinburne denied that he was. When Houghton took him up to Tennyson, Swinburne apparently said a few words, turned his back on him, and spent the remainder of the evening talking about Romantic art to Palgrave and George Lewes. Tennyson was understandably upset by what he took to be deliberate rudeness, and his admiration for Swinburne quickly turned to dislike.

The tarnishing of some of his acquaintances was compensated for in part by the tokens of admiration that were constantly coming to Tennyson. In March 1865 he was invited to become a member of 'The Club', which had been founded a century before by Samuel Johnson and Reynolds; it had about thirty members, chosen from the most eminent men of all interests, with 'some flavour of literature about them'. Tennyson, who was apparently proposed by Houghton and the Duke of Argyll, hesitated for some time before agreeing to be considered for election, since he was worried about the cost. On his first journey to London to be introduced to the members, he got cold feet and returned to the country, pleading that he had a swollen mouth from the dust on the express train by which he had travelled to town, and hence could not attend. The fact was, as Henry Reeve told Hallam Tennyson when speaking of the Club, that 'Houghton had a passion for society & social gossip, which your father was quite without. Never were two men more unlike. It seemed to cost your Father as much to dine in a mixed company, as it cost Houghton to dine without it. But when he came he talked well.'[16] The Club's records indicate that he attended but once in the year of his election and twice thereafter. It was a pattern he repeated all his life, from the Apostles onward, with the Sterling Club, the Cosmopolitan, the Club, later the Metaphysical

Society and the Athenaeum; he joined each in hope, then dropped out or seldom attended because of his shyness in unfamiliar company.

Although not a scientist, he had been invited in 1864 to become a Fellow of the Royal Society, but he declined. The invitation was repeated the following year, he accepted, and was introduced to the Society the day before his awkward dinner with Gladstone. It is some indication of how Tennyson appealed to men of all interests that he should have been so popular with Victorian scientists, even though their reasons for liking his poetry seem wrong-headed today. Among his scientific friends were Sir John Herschel, Charles Pritchard, Norman Lockyer, John Tyndall, James Paget, and Huxley, who told Edmund Lushington of his 'unbounded admiration' of Tennyson's poems and said, 'We scientific men claim him as having quite the mind of a man of science', which was Huxley's greatest accolade.[17]

Tennyson liked to hear men of science talk, and he had a decided penchant for factual accuracy in his poetry, but there is little evidence that his mind was strongly speculative about science or that his knowledge of any branch of it but astronomy was more than that of an intelligent amateur. Typical of the scientists' regard for his poetry is Norman Lockyer's curious study, *Tennyson as a Student and Poet of Nature*, in which he quite properly suggests that it was to Tennyson's credit that he made the study of science a subject for poetry; after that the book becomes a splendid example of how readers try to wrench poetry into something in which they feel secure. Patiently, Lockyer goes through Tennyson's nature images, explaining their accuracy, happily conferring poetic validity upon them by careful scientific identification. When Tennyson refers to the 'gilded summer-fly', Lockyer gives its entomological classification, and proceeds from identification to the assumption that accuracy proves the greatness of Tennyson's poetry. It is probably a harmless process, but it does indicate how Tennyson could be admired for odd, not to say wrong, reasons. The point of view was carried to fatuity by the mathematician Charles Babbage, who wrote to Tennyson after reading 'The Vision of Sin' to say that he was bothered by two lines:

> Every minute dies a man
> Every minute one is born.

'I would therefore take the liberty', wrote Babbage, 'of suggesting that in the next edition of your excellent poem the erroneous calculation to which I refer should be corrected as follows: "Every minute dies a man/And one and a sixteenth is born." "[18] In the next edition 'minute' was changed to 'moment'. Perhaps because he was less at home in the Royal Society than he had hoped, Tennyson rarely attended after his introduction.

In 1866 he was invited to be a candidate for the chair of Professor of Poetry at Oxford, but he declined at once. He never liked speaking in public, and he could scarcely have stood up to the strain of lecturing, since he was so shy that he hated to enter a room with strangers in it, and so self-conscious that when he passed a smiling stranger in the street he automatically assumed that he was being laughed at. One wonders, too, what his reaction would have been to being Matthew Arnold's successor at Oxford.

Almost inevitably, Tennyson's visits to the Queen gave rise to rumours that he was about to receive a title, and when he was sounded out early in 1865 about accepting a baronetcy the *Spectator* carried an article on the subject, which Alfred and Emily found embarrassing, since they were afraid the Queen would think they had talked to others about it. After some deliberation on whether a refusal would offend Victoria, Tennyson turned down the approach.

Although Queen Victoria had never come to Farringford, as her husband had promised, another queen came there in the autumn of 1865, Emma, young black queen of the Sandwich Islands, who was in England raising money for an Anglican cathedral in her homeland. While she was in London, Queen Emma stayed in Gore Lodge with Lady Franklin, the widow of Emily Tennyson's uncle, Sir John. She was pretty and good-natured, but she was an awkward guest, since her taste in food was expensive (although she claimed that her favourite food was poi and fish), she was so indolent that she would sometimes get up in the middle of dinner to go and rest on a sofa, and she apparently expected to be provided with a personal maid. Her tiny suite was difficult too, particularly the Revd Mr Hoapili, her aide-de-camp, whose womanizing was a constant embarrassment, as was his wish to fling off his clothes and bathe in the Serpentine. His wife, the Queen's lady-in-waiting, was six feet tall with a black moustache, stupid, and even more torpid than her mistress. It was with some relief that Lady Franklin received the Tennysons' invitation to bring the Queen to Farringford.

Although Emily Tennyson said she was not up to entertaining royalty, she organized Emma's visit with her customary thoroughness. An arch was erected over the front door, with red dahlias spelling out

'Aloho' on a background of ivy. The boys were brought home from school and put up in the lodge, since all the beds in the house were occupied. For four days the Queen was at Farringford. Between naps there were drives in the carriage to show her the island, including the exterior of Osborne, where she had unsuccessfully hinted to Victoria that she would like to be invited, endless guests for tea, state attendance at banquets organized to raise money for the cathedral, and a memorable morning when she walked up to the downs with Hallam and threw off her lethargy as they laughed and chased one another. Unfortunately, the sea wind gave her a bad cold, which rather spoiled the last day of her visit. Sitting on the throne that had been built from the trunk of a huge ilex in the park, she told Tennyson of her late husband's translation of the Prayer Book into their native language, and he gallantly talked about poetry to her, apparently never remembering that 'Niggers are tigers'. It is doubtful that she understood much of his talk, but she was delighted to find that the great Poet Laureate was not frightening. When she left with Lady Franklin, carrying two belated magnolia blossoms Tennyson had picked, the boys accompanied her to the boat, and as they turned to go, she called after them. Lionel did not hear, but Hallam came back to be kissed, which she did so thoroughly that the boat had pulled away from the shore before she released him. Back in London she sent the Tennysons a recent photograph of herself, a copy of her husband's translation of the Prayer Book, and after two months a thank-you note on the writing-paper she had carefully removed from her room in Farringford.

All Tennyson's activity only served to underline the fact that the poetic stream had become a trickle ever since the publication of the volume containing 'Enoch Arden'. Its popular success was gratifying, but Tennyson was clearly afraid that he was becoming nothing but the 'People's Poet' that he had been triumphantly proclaimed. Popularity, no matter how difficult to gain, was not quite enough. His poetic output was impeded, too, by a series of family troubles. In less than two years came the deaths of his mother, his brother Septimus, and Emily's father, Henry Sellwood. Tennyson had been an infrequent visitor to the house in Hampstead that he and his brothers and sisters had rented for his mother, but the fact of her death was hard to accept. He arrived in town too late for her last hours and then refused to look at her body. 'We all of us hate the pompous funeral we have to join in,' he wrote to Emily, 'black plumes, black coaches & nonsense. We should like to go in white and gold rather—but convention is against us.' The funeral at Highgate cemetery was confused, with hearses ahead of them and behind, so that Tennyson longed for the quiet of a country churchyard. Afterwards, to help begin life over again, Mrs Tennyson's children had a jolly, noisy luncheon, not realizing that in another year they would be called together again for the funeral of Septimus. 'No, Ally has not been writing,' Emily told Lear. 'These losses have been so sad a break in his life. He is not yet as he was before.'[19]

After Mrs Tennyson's death Alfred's sister Matilda came to make Farringford her home during most of the year; she was kind and affectionate, but her eccentricity made her difficult to live with, and it was some years before she learned that Alfred and Emily occasionally wanted to be together without her company. The fall into a coal-scuttle in infancy to which the family attributed her oddness had made her oblivious to conventional behaviour, and it could be embarrassing to Emily when she hoisted an umbrella in church to keep the draughts from the back of her neck. Perhaps because he was too overcome by the thought that his younger brother was now dead, his great promise totally unfulfilled, Tennyson did not go to Cheltenham to the funeral of Septimus.

The boys were giving difficulty too. Kegan Paul's school was unsatisfactory, and Lionel suffered from bullying, so that after a year they were withdrawn. Hallam then went to Marlborough, where he led an exemplary life, with the only interruption to his predictable progress being a bad attack of pneumonia 'with low symptoms', which frightened the Tennysons into thinking they would lose him.

Lionel's stammer was increasingly bad, and when Hallam went to Marlborough it was presumably at the recommendation of Charles Kingsley that Lionel was sent to have lessons with Dr James Hunt, a speech therapist at Hastings who had helped alleviate Kingsley's own stammer. Hunt was secretive about his methods, which worried Lionel's parents, and Emily was afraid that a combination of cold baths and beer at lunch was keeping him from recovering quickly. In 1868 Lionel entered Eton, on the theory that he was not strong enough for Marlborough. Lear thought that he was beginning to manifest the 'morbid Tennysonian turn'.

The boys' general lack of physical strength disturbed FitzGerald when he heard of their ill-health; he asked Pollock, 'Is it to be with A.T., as is said to be the Fate of your great Men: to leave no Posterity?'

Tennyson's own worry about the boys made him irritable, and his love of them often came out as bad temper. Lear 'loathed the brutal and snubbing way in which he treated' them,[20] but he was so abnormally sensitive to unkindness in Tennyson that it is probable he suffered a good deal more from it than the boys themselves did. At least Hallam adored Tennyson and devoted his life to him; Lionel's feelings for his father were less overt and probably more critical.

With reason Tennyson was becoming somewhat neurotic about his privacy, particularly when the invaders on Farringford were becoming more brazen; on one occasion he had to double up his fist in a most uncharacteristic gesture of threat before the tourists would go. Another time he found a Cockney up a tree with his gardener standing beneath it holding a shotgun with which he threatened the unwelcome visitor. Mrs Cameron once sent a party of Americans to Farringford with a note of introduction. When they returned to her disappointed because they had not been admitted, she took them back to Farringford, searched out Tennyson, and said, 'Alfred, these good people have come 3000 miles to see a lion and they have found a bear.'[21] This time Tennyson was too amused to refuse them admittance any longer.

'It is a sad pity but this place seems to have a very depressing influence on him now,' Emily wrote to her sister Anne from Farringford.[22] At the beginning of 1867 she went with Alfred to London for their first long stay together, renting Gore Lodge, Lady Franklin's house in Kensington. Immediately, in spite of her health, she set about entertaining even more freely than she was used to doing in Farringford. The lists of their guests and their engagements during that spring remind us how much the Victorians liked to entertain, and how often they saw one another within the circle in which they moved. To look at Emily Tennyson's journal is to suspect that there was hardly an evening when Alfred read to her or when she played the piano to him. Reading the names that jostle each other in the accounts of their activities is like looking at one of those great occasional paintings by Frith in which familiar and half-familiar faces leap out of the multitude and then are lost again in the swirl of bodies. One day, for example, they saw Dean Stanley and his wife Lady Augusta, Lord Boyne, the Simeons, Marshalls, Carlyles, Prinseps, Forster, the Argylls, the Maurices, Gardens, Lushingtons, Mrs Clough, Gladstone, Houghton, Lord John Russell, and assorted d'Eyncourt cousins. Most of their friends came for dinner that spring, and Spedding, Venables, and Browning were in and out of the house. At a large reception given by Lady Stanley of Alderley, the other guests noticed a remarkable group of literary men talking together: Tennyson, Browning, Houghton, and Carlyle. For the first time Emily Tennyson was beginning to understand why her husband often felt that Farringford was restricting. Alfred could walk into the centre of London in his rusty cloak, and Lionel used Kensington High Street as an exercise ground, racing his pony up and down that thoroughfare as if he were at home on the Isle of Wight.

Tennyson was subjected to a good deal of mindless adulation, simply because he was famous. Mrs Bradley, wife of the headmaster of Marlborough, put away the cup and saucer from which he had taken his tea, never to let them be used thereafter by ordinary mortals. People introduced themselves on the street or bowed reverently in his direction. Oscar Browning, that most egregious of Victorian snobs, went to Freshwater in 1865 to seek him out; according to the well-known story he went up to Tennyson, shook him by the hand, and introduced himself: 'I am Browning.' Tennyson, who knew but one Browning, looked at him coolly before turning on his heel as he said, 'No, you're not.'[23] Tennyson's name was so well-known that when he stayed in a hotel he had to wait until leaving to sign the register, for fear of being mobbed, and he was surely the only poet in history whose name was frequently used without permission in advertisements in the sure knowledge that it would sell goods. He found a grim amusement in telling how Cockles' Pills printed an entirely fictitious letter reading:

Dear Sir, Like most literary men I am subject to violent constipation, & your pills I find of the greatest possible comfort. Yrs A Tennyson.[24]

Annoying as it all was, it was still flattering and hard to resist, but it is not surprising that Tennyson's shyness was beginning to change its manifestation from simple diffidence to an apparently arrogant wish to avoid his fellow men. Nor can one blame him much after the treatment he so often received from the public.

Far more gratifying was the second offer in 1868 of the honorary degree of LL.D from Cambridge, which Tennyson turned down because of his dislike of taking part in public ceremonies. The invitation was renewed the next year and Tennyson refused once more, although he did happily accept Trinity's offer of an honorary fellowship in spite of Thompson's jocular warning that without the degree he would still be *in statu pupillari* and could be convened for not attending lectures. In 1868 he was also invited to stand for election as Lord

Rector of the University of Edinburgh, in succession to Gladstone and Carlyle; his refusal to accept the nomination was inevitable, since he would have hated equally the public appearances and the possibility of being defeated in the election.

One pleasant result of the adulation was that he actually had more self-confidence than ever he had before, and it came out rather surprisingly in his next visit to the Queen, just after he and Emily had returned to Farringford from Gore Lodge. Emily was too tired and ill from her exertions in London to accept the invitation, but Tennyson found that he was totally at ease with the Queen. They talked of Queen Emma, of hexameters, and Tennyson told her about the Cockneys at Farringford. She said that she had not been much troubled with them at Osborne, and then broke into laughter when Tennyson said, 'Perhaps I should not be either if I could stick a sentry at my gates.' She asked him what was new in poetry, and he told her of Browning and Swinburne, adding, 'but verse writing is the common accomplishment in the world now, every one can write verses. I dare say Y.M. can.' To which the Queen said, 'No—that I cannot. I never could make two lines meet in my life.' When they returned to more general topics, one suspects they were both less at ease: 'The Queen asked Ally why he did not do some great work. He said it was such an age and they talked about the age.'[25]

In February 1867 Bayard Taylor, who had been at Farringford a decade earlier, returned, bringing with him his wife. On his earlier visit Taylor had behaved so well that Tennyson nearly forgot his distrust of Americans, and now he welcomed him with open arms, going so far as to broach a magnum of thirty-year-old sherry that had been sent to him by a 'poetical wine-dealer'. Tennyson said it was worthy of being drunk by Cleopatra or Catherine of Russia. After dinner they drank a bottle of Waterloo port from 1815, which further cemented their friendship. Over the bottle Tennyson was moved to read 'Guinevere', boasting that he, unlike Taylor, could read it without weeping. But in the event Arthur's forgiveness of his errant wife was too much for him, and he joined Taylor, Mrs Taylor, and Emily, who were all raining tears. When he had finished, Taylor asked, 'How can you say . . . that you have no surety of permanent fame? This poem will only die with the language in which it is written.' From where she had been lying on her couch wiping her eyes, Emily started up. 'It is true!' she exclaimed. 'I have told Alfred the same thing.'[26]

The waves of shared loyalty and alcoholic *bonhomie* concluded the visit in a positive wash of pro-Americanism on Tennyson's part. The following year he entertained Longfellow, who 'arrived with a party of ten'. Emily was so impressed that she gave Longfellow her highest compliment: 'Very English he is, we thought.' Some forty or fifty neighbours were invited for tea in the Farringford orchard, with the ladies sitting on shawls and rugs. Emily took their guest gently by the arm and led him under the trees, introducing him to their friends: 'she could not possibly have done it to an Englishman but to an American it would not be objectionable'. The two poets talked of spiritualism, in which both were interested, and of poetry; Tennyson was careful not to compliment Longfellow: 'told him I didn't like his hexameters: he rather defended them'. Then Tennyson took his guest off to Mrs Cameron for the photograph that she demanded, saying as he left, 'Longfellow, you will have to do whatever she tells you. I'll come back soon and see what is left of you.'[27] The result was a beautiful photograph in which even Longfellow's untroubled features took on that faintly harried look characteristic of Mrs Cameron's sitters.

Unfortunately, after hands had been clasped so firmly across the sea, Bayard Taylor innocently described his visit to Farringford in a private letter to a friend, which was somehow acquired by an American newspaper and printed. Tennyson never forgave what he thought was total treachery to hospitality, saying that Taylor 'saw in me, not a man but a paragraph, and even out of that made a parody'. After that it was rare for Tennyson to be even decently polite to Americans. In 1870 the unlucky George Henry Boker, another minor American poet, who was a friend of Taylor, was taken to meet Tennyson: 'He is as reserved and cold with strangers as if it paid like diamonds. The Great American Three Minute Ice Cream Freezer would be a red hot stove beside him. And yet he *did* try to be civil, and let fall six large *hailstones* in the words "I heard you were in London." '[28]

It was not only Americans whom Tennyson suspected of betraying his friendship. Palgrave had been somewhat insecurely restored to favour after the West Country trip, but he fell from grace again in 1868 when Tennyson had to scold him for showing others the unpublished poems that he had been given to read. Tennyson forgave him but asked that 'please, hereafter, if I give you any little unpublished piece, keep it to yourself'.[29] Within a few months Tennyson discovered that Palgrave once more had been unable to restrain his self-importance and had been showing another of his poems. Gently Tennyson reproached him for 'not considering it a sacred deposit', and asked Palgrave to show his poems to no one, 'or if you can't depend upon yourself, forward them to me'. For all his unwonted mildness Tennyson was seriously annoyed.

As always, there was an understudy ready in the wings when one of Tennyson's attendants had to be let go. In this case it was William Allingham, who had moved in 1863 to Lymington, only a few minutes from Yarmouth by ferry. Since their meeting in Twickenham Tennyson had been almost a god to Allingham, and he was eager to serve him, to talk of poetry, to meet the famous people who passed through Farringford. His detailed diary, which he kept scrupulously for years, is one of the best records of Tennyson in his informal state, giving us a wonderful idea of what conversation on walks with Tennyson was like, or those long evenings in the smoke-filled study as he read aloud his poems, or the nocturnal climbs to the leads to watch the heavens on Tennyson's platform built for that purpose. The after-dinner port made the climb hazardous, and once Tennyson slipped and fell ten feet while gazing at a falling star. Allingham was forever uncertain of his own importance and wondering what he had to offer to Tennyson, a doubt that the latter shared, so that he could be somewhat brutal to the younger man. Once he had gone on for some time about his own intuitions about immortality, when Allingham said blandly that he had felt something of the same sort. 'I don't believe you have,' said Tennyson with a growl. 'You say it out of rivalry.' On another occasion the two men were walking on the cliffs when Allingham asked as he followed Tennyson, 'Suppose I were to slip and catch hold of you, and we both rolled down together?' Tennyson stopped, turned around, and said briefly, 'You'd better go on first.'[30]

Most of all Tennyson snubbed Allingham's over-elaborate language and Irish pronunciation. The first time he showed Allingham around Farringford, the younger man, overcome with high-flown emotions, tentatively said of a huge tangled fig-tree in blossom, 'It's like a breaking wave.' 'Not in the least,' replied Tennyson brusquely. 'Such contradictions, *from him*, are noway disagreeable,' wrote Allingham meekly. It is to be hoped that Tennyson felt a moment of shame five years after this when he was showing a later visitor 'a fig-tree of curious form; it grows along the ground throwing its branches forward till it looks "like a wave" as the poet said. "All the artists like that" he added.' Three years after Allingham's death and only a few months before his own, Tennyson went to the bottom of the garden to look at the fig-tree '"like a breaking wave", as he said'. Had Allingham known, he would have been happy to have provided Tennyson with a repetitively useful metaphor.[31]

Allingham's self-doubts were almost an invitation for imposition by Tennyson. Nothing could have been less true of another young man who made Tennyson's acquaintance in the 1860s, James Knowles, who was then practising as an architect although he was considering changing his career for one connected with literature. At his death he had fulfilled his ambition so completely that he had been editor of two major periodicals and had been knighted for his services to literature. It is hard not to smell calculation in his initial cultivation of Tennyson, as if he were hoping to make use of him. But he certainly did not hoodwink Tennyson, who recognized his ambition and diverted it to his own purposes, quite aware of how much Knowles would put up with so long as he thought it would advance his interests. Curiously enough, the suspicion with which the two men regarded each other brought about a kind of mutual respect that Tennyson shared with few of his other followers. Many of Tennyson's friends knew what lay behind the relationship and were not charmed. Carlyle thoroughly disliked Knowles and called him Tennyson's bricklayer; until Knowles had become a force in the literary world, Tennyson often had to keep him away from his other friends.

In 1861 Knowles had asked Tennyson, then unknown to him personally, for permission to dedicate to him his own retelling of the Arthurian legend, *The Story of King Arthur and His Knights*. In 1866 he came to Freshwater to see his old tutor and called at Farringford. He was invited up to Tennyson's study, where he requested, 'would he read to me one of his Poems, as I desired earnestly to hear from his own lips what I already knew and loved?' Tennyson complied with his wish and, when he left, invited him to claim acquaintance if ever they met elsewhere, since his short sight would prevent him from recognizing Knowles. It was not until the following year that Knowles met him on the platform of Haslemere station and made himself known. Tennyson said that he was in the vicinity looking for a place to build a second home. 'You are an architect, why should you not make the plans of it for me?' he asked. Knowles accepted happily, specifying that he would take no fee, since Tennyson's works had long paid him twice over in delight. 'He protested, but in the end accepted my terms.'[32] It was a proposition to their mutual advantage, a fitting start to a friendship that lasted a quarter of a century and made Knowles's career.

✽

CHAPTER XXIX

ALDWORTH AND LONDON,
1867–1872

SINCE their first journey to the neighbourhood of Haslemere in 1864
to look at land for a second house, the Tennysons had felt committed
to the area. At the end of 1866 they took Greyshott Farm for two
years, with an option to extend the let, and they lived there in the
spring of 1867 as they continued their search. Their intention was to
build a cottage of some four rooms, to which they could retreat when
the influx of summer visitors and Tennyson's hay fever coincided.
Knowles changed all that, but he could not have done so had the
Tennysons not agreed.

On 5 June 1867 they visited Greenhill, 900 feet up the southern face
of Blackdown, just over the Surrey border into Sussex. To reach it
from the rough track that led to Haslemere two miles away, they had
to put Lionel on a donkey and Emily in a small cart that could be lifted
over the deep ruts of the ground. The property included thirty-six
acres with an old farmhouse and three fields at the foot of the hill, and
a high, flat natural ledge scooped out of the side of the down, on which
potatoes were growing when they first saw it. The ledge was protected
by the hill above and surrounded by stretches of heather, mixed that
day with foxglove in early bloom. Best of all was the glorious view,
covering, as they estimated, hundreds of square miles of the Weald to a
glimpse of the sea. 'It wants nothing', said Tennyson, 'but a great river
looping along through the midst of it.'[1] There and then they determined to buy the land and build on the ledge, which was totally
secluded except for the view of it from miles away. By the end of the
month they had paid £1,400 and the land was theirs. On 23 April
1868, Shakespeare's birthday, there was a ceremonial laying of the
corner-stone, with Sir John Simeon speaking briefly, followed by a
picnic lunch.

Simple though it was, the ceremony sounds grand for a summer
cottage, and it was. Gradually the plans had expanded until the
cottage became a medium-sized country house, larger than Farring-

ford. It was built of pale grey stone in what was usually known as French Gothic style, although it seems an arbitrary description of an eclectic building with bits of whatever suited their fancy or Knowles's. Because of the narrowness of the ledge on which it was built, it was curiously huddled by the hillside, crowded in spite of the large garden surrounding it. And it would be difficult to imagine an architectural style less suited to the simple heath and expansive view than the hard-edged, elaborate carving of the crockets, pinnacles, and arches of the house that Knowles designed. The interior was sensibly planned to take advantage, by large windows and uncluttered rooms, of the landscape receding into obscurity, but there was a patent discrepancy between the interior and the pretentious exterior, which clashed with its surroundings and could be seen like a monstrous grey growth from far away on the plain beneath the hill.

Seeing the house from a distance, anyone who knows Tennyson's poetry inevitably thinks of the lines in *Maud* that describe the new lordling's recent house:

> Seeing his gewgaw castle shine,
> New as his title, built last year,
> There amid perky larches and pine
> And over the sullen-purple moor
> (Look at it) pricking a cockney ear.

If 'cockney' here means the imposition of urban values upon the country, Aldworth (as the house was finally called, in honour of the village from which Emily Tennyson's ancestors had come) seems almost a definition of the word. The lines from *Maud* are oddly premonitory of Aldworth, and it seems no accident that they derived from Tennyson's idea of Bayons Manor. But the amateur architect, Charles Tennyson d'Eyncourt, was far more sensitive than the professional, Knowles. Bayons had been designed to harmonize with its landscape and become part of it, changing it only by making apparent the order already implicit there. Aldworth exerted an alien tyranny over the countryside, insensitively imposing suburban qualities upon the land.

So much of Tennyson's boyhood and early manhood had been dominated by reaction to everything represented by his uncle Charles that it is not surprising that much had soaked into his assumptions; opposition is as effective as emulation at keeping values alive. With the death of his uncle in 1861 Tennyson had lost the cause for his resistance to Bayons, and now it was as if he had become the spiritual heir to old Mr Tennyson d'Eyncourt in a succession as irregular as his uncle's had been in 1835. Aldworth is like a reduced and less successful version of Bayons and as much an emblem of its owner as the home of Charles Tennyson d'Eyncourt. There were emblazoned shields on the windows, a motto cut into the stone of the cornice under the roof, corbels, arcades, parapets, heraldic beasts and birds, and—final testimony to Bayons—the arms of the Tennyson d'Eyncourts on the chimney-pieces. It was as if Tennyson were trying to demonstrate how a country house should be built, as his uncle had once attempted to show Alfred how an elegy was written. As one guide to Sussex has it, 'Choice of architect and style do not add much to one's opinion of the poet; the result is a fussy small hotel half-way between the French and English C16 style'[2] (see Plate XXI).

It took more than two years after the corner-stone was laid before the family could occupy Aldworth, and even then the extensive gardens were not complete. In time a stone balustrade was built at the edge of the fall of the garden, with two cypresses to frame the view, and crimson flowers set along the terrace to 'burn like lamps against the purple distance'.

One of the features of the house that most attracted Tennyson was the bathroom with running hot water, which they never had at Farringford. At first he took four or five baths a day, saying that his idea of luxury was 'to sit in a hot bath and read about little birds'.[3] When he was finished, he would throw the water out of the window to help the growth of the new-laid turf, brought all the way from Farringford.

Even better was that London was within reach of a day's return, so that he could go to town without difficulty from Haslemere station, and friends could be invited for luncheon without having to be put up overnight. There was hope that Gladstone, the Carlyles, Spedding, Browning, FitzGerald, and the others who had been evasive about making the trip to the Isle of Wight might be lured to Aldworth. This was nearly sufficient compensation for Emily, who discovered immediately that the house she had wanted for so long was no substitute for Farringford, and that the winds of Blackdown were far less kind to her than the soft air of Freshwater. For the rest of Tennyson's life they normally spent half of the year at each of their houses. Emily loved Farringford best, but Alfred fretted at its unvarying routine: 'Sunday touches Sunday,'[4] he used to say of life there, and he would be impatient to return to Aldworth. Since he lived there for forty years, Farringford has naturally always been associated with Tennyson, but there is some justice in thinking of Aldworth as his true home for the last quarter-century of his life. It may not look like a poet's home, but it could not be a more suitable seat for a Poet Laureate.

The grandeur of Aldworth was impressive, but it was not apparent to all their friends why the Tennysons needed two houses in the country, even though it was now abundantly evident that they could easily afford them. After his first visit, Lord Houghton wrote that 'the bard . . . has built himself a very handsome and commodious home in a most inaccessible site, with every comfort he can require, and every discomfort to all who approach him. What can be more poetical?' Walter White caught the spirit of Aldworth exactly when he called it 'a palatial-looking house on a small scale'.[5]

In at least one way Aldworth was to be the success that Bayons never was. Charles Tennyson d'Eyncourt had built his splendid seat with the idea that it was to be the emblem of his ennobled family once he had received his peerage. But the title never came to him, and family tradition had it that on one occasion near the end of his life, as his carriage bowled through the wooded park of Bayons, down the long winding drive to the lodge gates, he put his uncoroneted head out of the window, looked back at the drawbridge, the moat, the embattled towers, and as he stared at the forest of stone he had erected, sank back into his seat and muttered, 'I must have been mad.'[6] Tennyson was to grasp what had always eluded his uncle, who never imagined that his untidy nephew might one day outstrip him.

In World War II Bayons was turned over to the military, who paid little heed to its care. When their damaging tenancy was finished, it was sold out of the family that had occupied it for a century. At last even the solidity of its construction yielded to nature as it declined into picturesque decay with trees poking out of the ruined walls. A few years later the entire house was blown up in a morning and the rubble taken away to build roads. Today Charles Tennyson d'Eyncourt's school surveys the valley, near the church and its splendid row of monuments to the family; a small lodge stands at the end of the long drive up the hill to the site of the vanished house; for a few years after its demolition the spears and lances bought from the Eglinton Tournament to grace its corridors were used to prop up lines of washing in the village. But Bayons and all that it represented are gone from Tealby. Aldworth, too, has passed out of the hands of its first owner's descendants, but it still gleams on the face of Blackdown, as solid and as alien as it was when first built.

As his grandson has written, the purchase of land for Aldworth in 1867 'brought to an end a period of stagnation and uncertainty' in Tennyson's creative life. In the early months of 1868 he published five separate poems in *Good Words*, *Once a Week*, and *Macmillan's*. Although he had published in periodicals before, the appearance of so many poems within a short time surprised his contemporaries, many of whom thought that his dignity was compromised by association with magazines: 'cannot you, as a friend of Mr. Tennyson prevent his making such a hideous exhibition of himself as he has been doing for the last three months?' wrote Swinburne to Houghton. 'I thought there was a law against "indecent exposure"?'[7] Emily Tennyson tried ineffectually to convince Alfred that early publication of poems would spoil their impact when they appeared in a volume, but he had his own reasons for wanting to get them into print as soon as possible. In the first place, now that he had committed himself to a new house, he was reverting to his old obsessive fear that he would soon be penniless. For one poem of fewer than eighty lines, 'The Victim', *Good Words* paid him £700 and allowed him to retain the copyright; it was more money than he had had for an entire year not long before. Besides this, he was genuinely worried about the dry season of his creativity, which sometimes made it seem possible there would never be another volume of poetry. It was common gossip at the time that Tennyson's day would soon be over, and the publication of these poems was an answer to the rumours, asserting that the old master had lost neither his inspiration nor his cunning.

Perhaps what weighed even more heavily on him was the worry over his relations with Edward Moxon's heirs. The new manager of the firm, Bertrand Payne, was less interested in the quality of the work he published than in making money by any form of publicity he could manage. In addition, it became apparent that Payne was demanding exorbitant sums for republication of Tennyson's poems, then pocketing the fees himself. Aside from the trouble it caused Tennyson, Payne's behaviour seemed to indicate that the publishing house was in precarious circumstances. In 1867 Tennyson demanded a financial statement, saying that he heard persistent rumours that the firm could not last more than two or three months. 'Seeing that I have stuck to the house of Moxon from the beginning through evil report and good report, and really have been and am the main pillar of it, it seems to me

... that I should be fully informed of the state of affairs.'[8] The answer he got from Payne was unsatisfactory. To sell his poems to periodicals was to ensure their publication without having to deal with Payne.

Of the many publishers eager to get Tennyson on their lists when they heard that he wanted to leave Moxons', he chose Alexander Strahan, who settled with him to pay £5,000 p.a. for five years for the right to republish what had already appeared in print, and to publish new volumes for 10 per cent of the profits, the rest to go to Tennyson. So great was Tennyson's reputation that Strahan at first offered not even to take the 10 per cent, relying instead on the boost to his own list that his name would give, but Tennyson insisted that such an arrangement would be unfair to Strahan. Once the new contract was signed, probably the most generous ever made with a poet, he no longer felt the need to publish in periodicals, and he could once more forget temporarily the imminence of starvation.

Payne's reaction to Tennyson's leaving substantiated everything that had been suspected; it was well known that he ran 'him down even as a poet: he regards him as selfish, narrow in money-matters, not of lively affections'. According to Frederick Locker, Payne had attacked Tennyson in the *Queen's Messenger* and had even fastened a pair of ass's ears to the portrait of Tennyson hanging in the Moxon premises.[9] Tennyson saw a letter from Payne to Mortimer Collins, asking him to write a whole 'slashing' volume about Tennyson's works, making 'him out a third-rate poet', and Tennyson said he supposed that Payne would have paid him out of the money he had dishonestly withheld in the past. Collins declined the suggestion and, according to Tennyson, Payne then persuaded young Alfred Austin to write anonymously to the same effect in the May 1869 issue of *Temple Bar*.[10] Austin obligingly placed Tennyson among the lesser third-rate poets, since he had totally failed to deal with the great sweep of the Arthuriad. It was an article Austin later regretted, for Payne's fees lasted a shorter time than Tennyson's influence. In spite of Payne's behaviour, Tennyson remained constant in his friendship to Edward Moxon's widow, anonymously giving her an annual allowance, first £300, later £100, as a token of his affectionate memory of her husband.

The best indication of the end of Tennyson's period of dark stagnation was his resumption of work on the *Idylls of the King*, that gigantic incubus that hung over him for a half a century. He could neither bring himself to work at it steadily nor allow himself to desert it. One of his greatest obstacles had been the necessity of treating the Holy Grail itself; in 1859, after the publication of the first four idylls, he had told the Duke of Argyll that he doubted 'whether such a subject could be handled in these days, without incurring a charge of irreverence. It would be too much like playing with sacred things. The old writers *believed* in the Sangreal. Many years ago I did write "Lancelot's Quest of the Grail" in as good verses as I ever wrote, no, I did not write, I made it in my head, and it has now altogether slipt out of memory.' When he resumed working on the subject in 1868, the writing was completed in little more than a week, suggesting that he was recovering it from memory as much as composing freshly. No doubt he had forgotten details and changed many, but he had been able in 1830 to reconstruct an entire book of poems when he lost the manuscript one dark night near Spilsby, and it is hard to believe that he was speaking literally when he said now that he had altogether forgotten the earlier version of 'The Holy Grail'. More probably, his ideas about the objective reality of the Grail had changed over the years, as is indicated by his remark that the 'old writers *believed* in the Sangreal'. For in 1868 what he believed was that it was the product of man's imagination, not an actual vessel and that the pursuit of it was ultimately destructive for most of mankind; such a treatment obviously might incur 'a charge of irreverence'.

There can be little doubt that much of the impetus for 'The Holy Grail' came from others, mostly from Emily, who wrote that she doubted whether the poem would have been written 'but for my endeavour, and the Queen's wish, and that of the Crown Princess'. But Tennyson was happy to be pushed into this work, and his contentment is evident in a tranquil passage from Emily's journal during the week in which the first draft was made: 'A.T. took me thro' our fields, and walked again to the beacon at (night) nine o'clock and lay on his back up there to look at the stars.'[11] Since their publication there has been a good deal of debate about the intrinsic quality of the *Idylls of the King*, but there can be no doubt about the contentment it brought to Tennyson to be working on them again. For the first time he had a comprehensive idea of the eventual structure of the long poem; within a few months he had written the introductory idyll, 'The Coming of Arthur', then 'Pelleas and Ettarre', and then the revamped 'Morte d'Arthur', which he used to close the series under the title of 'The Passing of Arthur'.

The four new idylls were all in the volume published at the end of

1869 (it was dated 1870) as *The Holy Grail and Other Poems*. The increasingly speculative tone of his poetry is indicated by 'Lucretius', a dramatic monologue about the suicide of the philosopher, who is destroyed by the intrusion into his rationalistic world of overwhelming sexual passion, against the force of which there is inadequate provision by a religion that denies the soul and the existence of an afterlife. Some critics have felt that it is a too-decorous treatment of an indecorous subject, but of all his poems this most openly treats erotic excitement; his language makes it clear that Tennyson was deliberately using sexual symbolism of the sort that came to be known as Freudian. It was not the first time he had done so, but it seems particularly apparent here. Tennyson was proud of his inoffensive frankness and is reported by Oscar Browning as saying, 'What a mess little Swinburne would have made of this.'[12] Emily had passed the section on 'budded bosom-peaks', so that it is certainly inoffensive, but not all readers feel that it is frank, or even very effective, as a description of breasts. The whole poem is almost a mirror-image of 'The Holy Grail', dealing with the destructive potentiality of too much reason, as the idyll treats the perils of an abstracted ideal.

Besides the poems that had been printed in periodicals, the volume contained 'Flower in the Crannied Wall' and, as comic relief, 'Northern Farmer, New Style'. This last marks a great divide in Tennyson's readers, between those who think it rollicking evidence of his all-encompassing sense of humour and those who find it heavy-footed and schoolboyish. Tennyson himself, as his contemporaries were forever noting, had a fine spirit of fun when he was in good temper, and such friends as Frederick Locker asked, 'Did anybody ever make one laugh more heartily than Alfred Tennyson? He tells a story excellently, and has . . . an entirely natural and a very kindly laugh.' It was, however, the laughter of good spirits, which his friends found difficult to reproduce in writing, since it was not primarily verbal, and for all its humour of the moment it was not witty. Droll looks, funny tones of voice, irresistible grimaces, imitative postures: they all figure in descriptions of his humour but mean little once the moment is past. He had half-a-dozen favourite stories that he told over and over, and some of them were dependent upon verbal felicity, but there is little of the delicacy of wit in those of his own remarks that have been preserved. Almost never is there a sense of the constant assessment of language that comes through the best examples of the wit of men like Sydney Smith or Oscar Wilde. Nowadays we undoubtedly have a mistaken idea of his solemnity in daily life, perhaps because his poetry is seldom really funny; nor are most of his frequent puns that have come down to us. A not totally fair example was passed on by Emily Tennyson to Hallam: 'Oh I must tell thee a pun made by Papa. Cousin Kate was saying how tiresome the Te Deum was sung to one single chant, to which Papa replied, "The Te Deum becomes tedium."'[13] Many of Tennyson's comic poems are in Lincolnshire dialect, but once the joke of phonetic spelling is past, there is little of the inventive grasp of language that is characteristic of the best of his other work. As Fitz had said years before, 'Alfred, whatever he may think, cannot trifle.' His best qualities are to be found in his serious poetry.

Tennyson need not have worried yet about his popularity, for of the 40,000 volumes of the first edition, 26,000 copies were bespoke before publication. That year he made more than £10,000, his largest income so far. The reviews were enthusiastic on the whole, but there was some grumbling about the sameness in the works of the Laureate and some feeling that they were too didactic. The actual content of Alfred Austin's essay in *Temple Bar* can be ignored as an independent judgement, since it was written to order for Payne, but its tenor coincided with a subterranean reaction against Tennyson for the next few years; a recent critic has said that 'it is with "The Holy Grail" that adverse criticism begins to be noticeable'.[14] Emily Tennyson recognized what was happening and kept the least favourable reviews from his notice.

Criticism of another sort, that Tennyson was not at his best in dealing with the human psyche, came from the friendliest of observers, Robert Browning, who charitably put it down to a difference in the aims of Tennyson and himself. Of 'Pelleas and Ettarre' he wrote: 'We look at the object of art in poetry so differently! Here is an Idyll about a knight being untrue to his friend and yielding to the temptation of that friend's mistress after having engaged to assist him in his suit. I should judge the conflict in the knight's soul the proper subject to describe: Tennyson thinks he should describe the castle, and the effect of the moon on its towers, and anything *but* the soul.'[15] Beyond the difference in method of the two poets, however, Browning's comment does indicate a fundamental weakness in Tennyson's narrative poetry, his inability or refusal to come to terms with the psychology of his characters.

It happened that Tennyson had the bulk of his longest poem in print in 1869, the year in which Browning published his longest and greatest poem, *The Ring and the Book*. Before he began its composition Browning had offered the raw material of his Roman murder case to Trollope as the basis of a novel, and when Trollope refused it, he suggested it to Tennyson as a subject for a narrative poem, almost as if he subconsciously realized that he must write it himself and had therefore offered it to the poet least apt to find use for it. We can only be thankful that Tennyson did not undertake it, but it is probably equally fortunate that Browning had not been attracted to the Arthurian legend. Tennyson read *The Ring and the Book* as it appeared and expressed cautious enthusiasm for it, but he doubted that it could ever be popular.

Despite their guarded statements about each other's poetry, Tennyson and Browning remained on the best of terms, and in 1872 a volume of selections from Browning's poetry was 'Dedicated to Alfred Tennyson. In Poetry—illustrious and consummate: In Friendship—noble and sincere.' In London they saw each other frequently, but even with a house so near to town as Aldworth, Emily Tennyson was never able to lure Browning into staying with them. With a trace of the subacid she said, 'We should like to see him oftener, he is delightful company, but we cannot get him to come here; we are too quiet for him!'[16]

In the period between 1868 and 1872 Tennyson was preternaturally concerned with the dangers of sexual licence, a problem that comes through acutely in 'Lucretius' and in his remark about what Swinburne would have made of that poem. He had always been conservative, even prudish, in his attitudes to sex (although his language in male company could certainly be uninhibited), but now he seemed to smell it out everywhere. Two years after writing 'Lucretius' he was still talking 'despondingly of Swinburne's last book and of the tone of literature as he did now from time to time, he said that it was monstrous that Swinburne should have written a sonnet in praise of *Mdlle. de Maupin*. He foreboded the fiercest battle the world had ever known between good and evil, faith and unfaith.' When Knowles took him to a ballet, he was so shocked at the entry of scantily-clad dancers that he 'rushed at once out of the box, walked up and down in an agony over the degradation of the nineteenth century, and nothing would induce him to go in again'. Another time he nearly worried himself sick: 'He hears such bad things of the state of morals in London that this helps to depress him.'[17]

There is no evidence of anything specific in his life or that of his family to account for this morbid concern. At Eton Lionel was involved in a minor sexual scandal, apparently innocently, but that would have hardly caused such a reaction. Tennyson was sixty years old, and perhaps the very passing of the urgency of sexual appetite (if indeed it had ever been very strong) made him unduly aware of its sway over most men and of its potential danger. Whatever the reason, the whole problem was intimately connected with his growing preoccupation with religion and the old duality of spirit and matter that had perplexed him for so long; now lust became the most dramatic manifestation of materialism. As 'Lucretius' indicates, it was essential for him to believe in an afterlife in order to believe in morality in this world. Repeatedly he told his friends that if there were no afterlife he would jump into the Seine or the Thames, put his head in the oven, take poison, or fire a pistol at his own temple. *In Memoriam* had been written about the necessity of belief in immortality, but that belief was based on faith. Now he needed more exact proof, and the lack of it was anguishing. 'What I want', he told Allingham, 'is an assurance of immortality.'[18]

Frederick Tennyson, Mary Ker, and Emily Jesse were all convinced spiritualists, and Tennyson himself had been interested in the subject since boyhood, when he used to tell ghost stories to his family; at Cambridge his one abortive effort to read a paper to the Apostles had been on the subject of ghosts. It was no novelty, then, when he turned in 1869 to spirits for reassurance, but it was probably the first time he had ever attended a seance when he and Emily entertained Dr and Mrs James Acworth at Aldworth in October. Emily Tennyson was deeply disapproving of the whole proceedings and of Mrs Acworth, who was a medium, but she wrote that Alfred and his sister Matilda were 'much amazed by raps on the table in the middle room. In A's study a table heaves like the sea.'[19] Apparently Tennyson made no more experiments with seances for some years, but a very concrete result of his interest in the whole subject was the foundation of the Metaph ical Society.

In November 1868 at Knowles's house in Clapham, Tennyson spent an evening discussing the future state with his host and the astronomer Charles Pritchard, and Knowles suggested the formation of a society to consider such questions, if Pritchard and Tennyson would agree to join. As always, Knowles's motivation was a bit suspect, for it seems from later events that he was primarily interested in becoming intimate with the famous men whom the other two would attract. At first the group was intended to include only those who were worried about the decline of religious faith, drawn from practically every complexion of Christianity; then it was broadened to take in agnostics with some of the same interests. According to the historian of the Society, there were five former Apostles among the original twenty-six members and others soon joined; from the first the Cambridge society had been the model for its constitution. The original members were a distinguished group, including Huxley, Froude, Bagehot, Gladstone, Archbishop Manning, Henry Sidgwick, and the Dean of Canterbury. Within a year or two they were joined by Ruskin, the Duke of Argyll, Maurice, and the Archbishop of York. As Knowles had foreseen, Tennyson's name was useful in assembling such a group. Diversity of membership by no means ensured unanimity of opinion, nor was it meant to do so. After one meeting Sir John Simeon met Lord Arthur Russell as he was leaving and asked, 'Well, is there a GOD?' 'Oh, yes,' replied Russell, 'we had a very good majority.'[20]

Sir Frederick Pollock said that 'Knowles invented the Metaphysical Society for the purpose of convincing Tennyson of the immortality of the soul. . . . Knowles was in bond of the vulgar opinion that eternal life is an indefinitely continued existence in Greenwich time under improved conditions.' Tennyson attended the preliminary meeting, then missed the first regular meeting of the Society, but at Knowles's earnest request he sent a poem, 'The Higher Pantheism', for Knowles to read aloud. It is one of Tennyson's less successful efforts at metaphysical speculation, and when the meeting was over, John Tyndall said wryly, 'I suppose *this* is not offered as a subject for discussion.'[21]

During the decade of his membership Tennyson attended eleven meetings in all. Just as he had done when he was an Apostle, he would sit listening to the discussion without offering an opinion of his own, suffering from his usual inability to participate in the give-and-take of discussion in a large group unless he had set the subject himself. Grant Duff thought that his silent presence 'added dignity to a dignified assemblage', but Frederic Harrison less charitably remembered only his 'superior' aloofness and said, 'I am not sure that he always followed the arguments of opponents with understanding.' On one disastrous occasion he innocently asked Huxley if sap rising in a plant did not dispose of the argument that the law of gravity was of universal force. Huxley was so baffled by the question that he could only assume that it was a joke. To Harrison it seemed that the problem of life beyond the grave haunted Tennyson's 'mind until it became a kind of cerebral nightmare. When I first met him at the table of the Society he expressed this with the bluntness that incessant adulation had led him to assume as his privilege.'[22] After intermittent attendance for four years Tennyson went to only one more meeting before he resigned in 1879. A few months later the whole Society collapsed because, as Tennyson complained, in 'ten years of strenuous effort no one had succeeded in even defining the term "Metaphysics"'. From the discussions he had learned to respect the integrity of the agnostics without in any way changing his own convictions about the irrationality of pure materialism. And he had come to a greater toleration of Roman Catholics. Of the proofs of eternal life he knew little more than he had at the founding of the Society.

When he was in London, Tennyson often stayed at The Hollies on Clapham Common, where Knowles was only too pleased to invite Tennyson's famous friends. The constant dinners there were an easy way for the indolent Tennyson to seem a quasi-host returning some of his invitations, and they were an opportunity for Knowles to meet possible contributors to the *Contemporary Review*, of which he became editor in 1870. Having been Knowles's guests in Clapham, Tennyson's friends found it difficult not to include him at their own tables, but many of them disliked having him constantly riding on Tennyson's coat-tails. Palgrave, probably jealous of Knowles's intimacy with Tennyson, of the sort he had once known, referred to him contemptuously as Tennyson's keeper. There was a growing suspicion, too, that Knowles intended to use Tennyson as a subject after his death, and even Spedding ironically called him 'AT's new Bozzy'. Tennyson himself knew that Knowles was manipulating him, but he was willing to put up with it for the convenience of the relationship, and he seems to have had a real affection for the younger man without having illusions about him. After his death Hallam and Emily fell out with Knowles for publishing what they described as inaccurate accounts of private conversations he had had with Tennyson, and they were convinced that he retained possession of papers that he should have returned to them.

Another new intimate, rather more popular with most of Tennyson's friends than Knowles, was Frederick Locker, whose wife, Lady Charlotte, was the sister of Lady Augusta Stanley, wife of the Dean of Westminster and lady-in-waiting to the Queen. In 1878 Locker became even more closely connected with Tennyson by the marriage of his daughter to Lionel. At the end of 1868 Locker and Tennyson went to Paris for a brief holiday, and together they took a longer trip to Switzerland the following summer. Tennyson made no attempt to use Locker as an unpaid companion, as he had done with so many others, but habit occasionally asserted itself, and during their Swiss trip he expected Locker to put his effects into his portmanteau for him, complaining when Locker had packed something he wanted but encouraging him by sitting near, smoking his pipe, 'looking on with a sort of curious admiration, and drawling out "Why Locker you seem to have quite a *ge-e-nius* for packing!"' He loved to talk about literature to Locker, who duly recorded his pronouncements and contributed them to Hallam Tennyson's biography of his father. In 1870 it was in part the desire to be near the Lockers that made Tennyson take a small *pied-à-terre* in Albert Mansions, Victoria Street, which he kept for several years. Lady Charlotte did all the work of furnishing and stocking it for him.

Tennyson's dependence upon others increased with his age, and some acquaintances like Browning's sister, who thought him well worth cosseting, felt that 'he rather affected "the old man"', overdoing his shortsightedness and wanting help on every occasion. Miss Browning put it down to 'the habit of having every least thing done for him, about his person even' by Emily or Hallam. It was 'as if he wanted 15 or 20 people to gather his strawberries for him, and then 5 or 6 more to put them into his mouth'. But there was a childlike innocence about his selfishness that put off criticism, as did his unawareness of how much adulation he took for granted. 'No flatterer is a friend of mine,' he once declared to Jowett with some complacence. He looked to Jowett for assent, but there was no answer. 'Don't you agree with me?' he persisted. At last Jowett replied: 'Well, Tennyson while you have been talking I have been reflecting that in this house and in this room I have seen a good deal of incense offered.' With a mischievous smile he added, 'And it was not unacceptable.' But as Jowett reflected afterwards, the good humour with which Tennyson took the comment proved that he had utterly failed to realize its applicability to himself.[23]

Tennyson's close friendships sometimes seemed to be on a delicately poised balance, so that when one was added, another had to be taken away, and *vice versa*. With the rise of Knowles and Locker came the break with Lear that had been threatening for a long time. Just before Tennyson's trip to Paris with Locker, he had complained to Lear of being 'so melancholy' at Farringford in the company of his brother

Horatio, whose wife had just died; 'as if Emily were not!' wrote Lear indignantly. 'How queer is the smallness & egotism of such a man! He is going to Paris "for a run".' When Lear told him of the death of a child from infected teeth, he observed that Tennyson thought only of himself: "'*I* nearly died of teeth: I was given over, & lay for dead a long time–&c&c&c.'" From Tennyson's talk, Lear concluded bitterly, 'one would fancy him a mere child & a foolish one too', except for his sharpness in financial dealings. 'Verily o Poet! you are a wonder.'

On Tennyson's return from Switzerland Emily said that he was 'depressed & nervous of late suffering a good deal from that internal trembling which is so hard to bear', and she put it down to the 'disagreeable hits continually recurring in different newspapers.' The brunt of his depression fell on Lear when he came for his first visit to Aldworth, bringing a few of his own pictures at the request of Emily, who was still furnishing her new house. Lear found it insulting that Tennyson should be surrounded by the obvious evidence of wealth while he complained about the modest price of ten guineas for the water colours. He also fretted about the cost of framing them and debated whether the money could not be better used, as if, said Lear, 'it were carpets I was selling'. Then he grumpily announced that it was Emily who wanted the pictures not he, which provoked Lear into reaction at last: 'I said he was given to worry & everyone knew it—& he said I was irritable & what not, & so we all exploded.' Lear went to pack his bags, but when he came down Emily handed him a cheque for a picture and convinced him he should stay. Lear took a walk alone and recovered his temper. At dinner Tennyson seemed to have forgotten the whole incident of the afternoon, so that Lear, on going to bed, apologized for having spoken angrily. Tennyson said that he had not minded anything except that the statement that his tendency to worry was well-known; 'how characteristic!' thought Lear to himself.[24] Not long after, Lear went abroad to live, and they were not together again for nearly a decade; by then theirs was a meeting of near-strangers.

A far more acrimonious break, albeit with a less intimate friend, was with 'Lewis Carroll', who had been at Farringford several times and had been particularly kind to the Tennyson boys, with whom he played and to whom he sent presents and at least one enchanting letter. Some time thereafter, probably in 1868, he wrote to Tennyson about a manuscript copy of 'The Lover's Tale' that his cousin had shown him. Tennyson replied, asking that he destroy the copy, which he reluctantly did. In 1870 Carroll wrote again to say that he was in possession of a privately printed copy of 'The Window, or, The Song of the Wrens', a song-cycle that Tennyson had written for Sullivan to set to music, and which he later so disliked, with good reason, that he had tried to prevent its publication. Carroll asked for permission to keep the poem and, since so many copies of it were already in circulation, to show it to friends, although he promised that no more copies would be made. It was a thoroughly courteous letter, which did not deserve the brief and icy reply to 'Dear Sir' by Emily Tennyson, who said that it was 'useless troubling Mr Tennyson with a request' that would only revive his annoyance, and 'that a gentleman should understand that when an author does not give his works to the public he has his own reasons for it'.

Carroll replied moderately, objecting to the implication that he was no gentleman. Either Tennyson or Emily answered with a letter that has now disappeared, apparently offering no apology or regret but grudgingly admitting that Carroll was innocent of any malice in his misdoings. Carroll's formal reply this time was less conciliatory: 'it seems to me, that you first do a man an injury, and then forgive him—that you first tread on his toes, & then beg him not to cry out'. To this there was, of course, no response.

Two years later Carroll wrote to tell Tennyson of a doctor in Sheffield who treated stammering and might be useful to Lionel. Tennyson's terse reply indicated merely that since Lionel's speech impediment was better '& will probably pass or nearly pass away with advancing life, I scarce think it worth while to send him to Sheffield'.[25] That was all. It seems scarcely coincidental that part of 'The Garden of Live Flowers' in *Through the Looking-Glass*, which was published in the following year, is an obvious parody of parts of *Maud*.

In 1870 the death of two friends touched him far more intimately than did the slow attrition of amity with the living. In June came the news of the death abroad of Sir John Simeon, with whom he had been more confidential than with any person since Arthur Hallam. Simeon's body was brought back to Swainston for burial, and Tennyson felt that he had to attend the service, although he hated all the panoply of funerals. The family were behaving with the extravagance of grief that seemed a permitted exception to the decorum of Victorian behaviour. The body 'lay in state with lights burning . . . & a Roman Catholic priest in the room', the 'shrieks and sobs were terrible', and Lady Simeon threw herself on the coffin to embrace it. It was too much for Tennyson to bear, and before the procession left the house he asked the eldest son if he might borrow a pipe of Sir John's and an old hat and cloak. 'Come for me yourself', he asked, 'when it is time to start, and do not send a servant.' In a gesture of identity with his dead friend, he put on the hat and cloak, lit the pipe, and walked into the gardens, then perhaps the most beautiful on the island. Roses were climbing the medieval walls of the private chapel in the June sunshine, lilacs were in blossom, and from a wood came the song of nightingales; the contrast between the serenity of the natural beauty and the horror of death overcame him, and he tenderly remembered the two other men to whom he always said he had felt closest, Arthur Hallam and Henry Lushington, feeling beneath his sorrow for his friends the inevitable sense of his own mortality. When young Simeon came to fetch him, he found Tennyson lying full length in Sir John's clothes beneath one of the cedars he had written about in *Maud*, smoking the pipe, tears flowing from his eyes as he wept for his friends and for himself, in his hand the first rough draft of the little elegy he had written for Simeon, 'In the Garden at Swainston':[26]

> Nightingales warbled without,
> Within was weeping for thee:
> Shadows of three dead men
> Walked in the walks with me,
> Shadows of three dead men and thou wast one of the three.
>
> Nightingales sang in his woods:
> The Master was far away:
> Nightingales warbled and sang
> Of a passion that lasts but a day;
> Still in the house in his coffin the Prince of courtesy lay.
>
> Two dead men have I known
> In courtesy like to thee:
> Two dead men have I loved
> With a love that ever will be:
> Three dead men have I loved and thou art last of the three.

Curiously enough, in spite of so many of his best poems having been inspired by the death of friends, Tennyson never wrote an elegy for Lushington, of whom only the scantiest records have survived.

Less than a fortnight later Tennyson sat within the sanctuary rails of the Abbey at the funeral of Dickens, where it seemed that the congregation was more interested in seeing him than in attending to the service. Dickens had been three years younger than Tennyson, and the passing of the greatest English novelist brought the cold smell of death close to the Poet Laureate. After the service he stood waiting to leave, but the congregation surged towards the altar to stare at him, as if looking at a survivor, 'Ladies climbing on the benches & parents holding up their children that they might see too'. Tennyson had to be led out of a private door before the congregation could be persuaded to leave. Although he had never been intimate with Dickens, Tennyson had always been aware of an almost symbiotic relationship with him that extended even to their appearance, particularly since he had grown a beard, which, as FitzGerald observed, made 'rather a Dickens' of him. Dickens's death was a reminder of his own to Tennyson, and when he saw the beautiful pencil sketch that Millais made of the dead Dickens (see Plate XXII), he said musingly, 'This is the most extraordinary drawing. It is exactly like myself.'[27] It is hardly surprising that he was so preoccupied with death and an afterlife.

So far as it was possible, Simeon's place in Tennyson's life was filled by W. G. Ward, who came to live near Farringford after Sir John's death and most improbably became a devoted friend to Tennyson. The two men had met several times before without much admiration on either side, and their friendship did not flourish until Ward built a large house at Weston a mile from Farringford. Like Simeon he was a Roman Catholic convert, but there the resemblance ended, for he had, as the saying was, become more Catholic than the Pope, taking up an extreme conservative position in thorough opposition to the Protestantism from which he had sprung. All his talent at controversy and a good bit of his considerable wealth were put at the disposal of what he proudly admitted were extremely narrow religious views, and as editor of the *Dublin Review* he supported orthodoxy of a virulent rigidity. He had considered Simeon dangerously liberal, and he was far to the right of Father Peter Haythornthwaite, his own private chaplain at Weston. He was totally unlike Simeon, too, in his dislike of the countryside in which he lived, professing to be unable to distinguish wheat from barley and once horrifying Tennyson by calmly saying that he offered a bounty of a guinea for every nightingale killed near Weston, which they made hideous with their noise. Yet behind the belligerent intelligence and the pose of barbarian was a gentle, simple, loving man who quickly responded to Tennyson. Before long his huge, ungainly frame was to be seen most days walking the Freshwater lanes beside Tennyson, the air they shared filled with prejudice and affection.

The same year that Ward appeared at Farringford, Aldworth was made more pleasant by Tennyson's new acquaintance with the novelist who came into his life after the death of Dickens. Living nearby were George Henry Lewes and George Eliot, who was given the courtesy title of Mrs Lewes. Once more the friendship was an unlikely one, particularly as Emily Tennyson might have been expected to disapprove of an unmarried union, but she surprisingly called on George Eliot both with and without her husband. George Eliot and Lewes had both on occasion written scathing reviews of Tennyson's poetry, but he probably never knew that, for he went twice to read aloud to them, among other poems 'Tears idle tears' and the whole of 'Guinevere', to which George Eliot added her own tears. But it must have taken some control for her not to smile when for two or three hours Tennyson read out in its entirety what was still his favourite poem, *Maud*, unaware that his hostess had written a long attack on its morbidity in the *Westminster*. They were in total agreement, however, that English literature was greater than French, and that it was a namby-pamby age that feared tragedy. When Tennyson rode off on his hobby-horse about materialism, George Eliot defended it in part; as he left, Tennyson said, 'Well, good luck to you and your molecules', but it was all in good nature, as 'sweet as summer'. By the end of the summer of 1871 George Eliot was calling him 'mi caro Poeta', and he 'thought her a humble woman despite a dogmatic manner of assertion that had come upon her latterly in her writings'.[28]

Farringford seemed particularly confining to Tennyson after the availability of London, and to Emily's chagrin he would sometimes insist on going to Aldworth even without her. Her relief at his return lights up one of her journal entries when he had been away for only four days: 'A day never to be forgotten. Surely love as one grows older has the tenderness of the eve of a parting—the long parting. A never seemed to me so beautiful & touching & I never had moments of the same sort of happiness.'[29] For all of Tennyson's love of Emily, it was of a different quality from hers, and he could not long share her unclouded happiness in the solitude of Farringford, since he felt discontented without other company. The difference in their attitudes often threw a shadow between them.

Soon visitors such as Palgrave and Leslie Stephen noticed that even at Aldworth Tennyson was fretting for companionship, reminding Stephen of the Soul in the Palace of Art, although Tennyson continued to say he was thankful 'that none of the damned Cockneys' could get near him. The great plain before the house, which had been one of the attractions of the site, now weighed heavily on his spirits, and he would be off to his rooms in Albert Mansions. All during 1870 and 1871 he suffered from a recurrence of the eczema on his leg, and when buttermilk diets and sea bathing did little to help, he would go to London, saying that he had to see the doctors but really preferring the discomforts of his little flat, so long as he had plenty of visitors, to the loneliness of Farringford or Aldworth.

As always, Emily tried vainly to keep him happy at home by a succession of guests. In 1871 Jenny Lind came to Farringford and sang 'some of Handel's Milton verses finely & one piece from Elijah', as well as the Scottish and Swedish folk-songs Tennyson asked for. Shortly afterwards Turgenev came to stay and pleased Tennyson's most conservative instincts by telling him of the inability of the liberated Russian serfs to understand what freedom meant. Even Gladstone and his wife came at last to Aldworth in the summer of 1871. Tennyson and Hallam walked to the end of Blackdown with the Gladstones, who played in the heather as if they were children. A few days later Houghton brought Fanny Kemble and Mrs Sabine Greville to Aldworth, complaining bitterly that the last part of the drive to the house was as steep as Parnassus. After luncheon Fanny Kemble read Shakespeare with the tears streaming down her cheeks. Mrs Greville was a huge woman and Fanny Kemble was not small, but as they drove back up the difficult bit of drive, the Tennysons could hear Fanny Kemble in her most tragic tones commanding Houghton, 'Get down, my lord, from off the top, for you are no inconsiderable weight.'[30] Since the two ladies insisted on remaining inside the carriage, in a few miles the post-horses broke down completely; the trio was saved from a moonlight walk only by encountering a London cab returning from Goodwood.

Apart from the actual entertaining which tapped her strength, Emily Tennyson had to plan carefully to manage relations between Alfred and their less welcome guests. In the autumn of 1871 she told Hallam that Mary Ker was coming to Aldworth with Emily and Captain Richard Jesse: 'I must try to stop Papa's return or send him on to Farringford. The Captains chatter would drive him wild.'[31] All the juggling of arrangements was beginning to be too much for her, although she bravely continued to try everything in her power to keep Alfred happy. At Farringford she supervised the addition of a large first-floor study for Tennyson, directly over a new ballroom in which the boys could entertain at dances and where Tennyson could walk in bad weather; at Aldworth she busied herself with overseeing the widespread repairs necessitated by the bad work of the builders who had put up the house. It is difficult to guess whether Tennyson saw how much her health was deteriorating; her courage in complaining to him so little over either her health or her own loneliness probably misled him into thinking that she felt neither.

Her constant care had precisely the effect that she hoped for: Tennyson was freed for writing and publishing. In September 1871 he received a letter from the editor of the New York *Ledger*, offering £1,000 for any poem, 'even if not more than twelve lines in length'. In reply Tennyson sent 'England and America in 1782', which he had written forty years earlier. In spite of giving good measure (the poem had twenty lines), he was somewhat shamefaced at the generosity of the offer, but the editor, Robert Bonner, said, 'as it was quite satisfactory to me, I do not see why you should deem it extravagant'.[32]

Far more satisfying, if less profitable, was his publication in Knowles's *Contemporary Review* of the new idyll, 'The Last Tournament', in December 1871, for which he received £150. Immediately he then turned to finishing 'Gareth and Lynette', which he had begun some years before. The two new idylls were published together at the end of 1872 as *Gareth and Lynette, etc*. To most readers this seemed a natural conclusion to the series, but when one suggested as much to Tennyson, 'with a grim smile' he said, 'I must have two more Idylls at the least to make *Vivien* come later into the Poem, as it comes in far too soon as it stands.'[33] One of the additional idylls was created by splitting 'Enid' into two, and in 1872–4 he wrote 'Balin and Balan', last of the idylls, which was not published until 1885. With that exception the *Idylls of the King* were in print by the end of 1872, their design and intention clear enough without the completing idyll.

⁂

CHAPTER XXX

IDYLLS OF THE KING, 1872–1874

THERE is good reason to feel that Tennyson's most ambitious poem is his most disillusioned and bitter, since it is concerned with the decay of a whole world, not merely a family or a section of society. *Maud* had treated the cancer of England, but it ended with a vision of a rejuvenated national consciousness. The *Idylls of the King* conclude with a wan hope of a new order fulfilling itself in new ways, but it is not an order for this time, for this world. The last battle of the poem has nothing of the sense of renewal that the problematical conclusion to *Maud* manages to impart even to the Crimean War; what is left after Arthur's going is an exhausted, questioning world from which leadership, inspiration, magic have all departed. (It is appropriate that T. S. Eliot should have drawn on the last idyll for so many images in *The Waste Land*.) Part of the effect of decay and dissolution comes from the fact that Tennyson shows the court of Arthur in the ascendant in the first idyll only. The next, 'Gareth and Lynette', takes place well after the rot has set in, and in spite of Gareth's bright young idealism, 'the whole point of the idyll is that he is almost alone in exemplifying this spirit'.[1] The tone of the idylls is darkened by Tennyson's disgust at the sin of lust which lies behind the fall of Camelot. All his morbid worry about sex in the 1860s and early 1870s reinforces the shattering effect of the guilty love of Lancelot and Guinevere.

When we remember that Tennyson worked on the *Idylls* for some four decades, the whole poem at first seems surprisingly unified. The formal opening and closing act as a frame to the other ten idylls, which he referred to as 'The Round Table'. Tennyson's insistence in 1873 that he needed two more idylls to complete the poem indicates that his vision of it as a whole had come to him by then, but it was not a vision that had been before his eyes all during the long conception of the work, and what unity it has was imposed upon it, rather than growing organically from its matter. It is ultimately no critical judgement to say that it was composed piecemeal, but that may help to explain the curious contrast between the formal balancing of many of the idylls and the effect of discontinuity in both narrative and style.

Tennyson certainly recognized the danger of disunity that his method of writing risked, and he deliberately paired sections that referred to each other both by likeness and by contrast. 'Gareth and Lynette', for example, has the same initial situation as 'Pelleas and Ettarre', with a young and untried knight acting as champion for a beautiful maiden; 'Gareth', however, shows how Lynette finally learns to respect constancy, service, and bravery, while Ettarre reflects the moral decadence of the court in her deceit, trickery, and sexual betrayal of Pelleas. In the 'Enid' idylls the situation is reversed, and the wife is the patient, uncomplaining servant of an unreasonable husband, her steadfastness standing in contrast to the behaviour of Isolt and Guinevere. The same point is made by the constancy of Elaine in her idyll. The death of Balin and Balan as a result of Guinevere's adultery is an only too clear parallel to her coming between Arthur and Lancelot, while the restoration in death of the fraternity of Balin and Balan is meant as a contrast to the final sundering of the king and his favourite knight.

The connection between idylls is also reinforced by verbal parallels. The opening and closing idylls, for example, are both written in language more archaic than the ten central ones: 'The Passing of Arthur' because it was an enlargement of the already archaic 'Morte d'Arthur', and 'The Coming of Arthur' because it needed to match the other. Although he was writing the initial idyll at a later date, Tennyson tried hard to make verbal anticipations in the opening that would be echoed in the conclusion.

Tennyson himself indicated another way in which the idylls are unified, pointing out that Arthur's coming is on the night of the New Year, he is wedded in the spring, the vision of the Holy Grail comes on a summer night, the Last Tournament takes place in early autumn, Guinevere's flight in full autumn, and Arthur's death at midnight in mid-winter. Since then there have been many conscientious—and ingenious—attempts to show the essential unity of the idylls through theme, narrative structure, and allegorical intent.

Tennyson thought of the vast poem as an allegory, saying that there was 'an allegorical or perhaps rather a parabolic drift in the poem', but he naturally refused to make a flat statement of its relationships, aside from the suggestion that it was concerned with 'Sense at war with Soul'. 'I hate to be tied down to say, "*This* means *that*," because the thought within the image is much more than any one interpretation.' But he was equally at pains to point out that the narrative was rooted in a literal reality and that everything that might be taken as magical or supernatural could be adequately accounted for by naturalistic explanation. 'Ideal manhood closed in real man', he wrote of the King in the 'Epilogue'. The effect of his statements is to equate the importance of the allegorical and that of the literal.

The problem that arises is that the careful structural unity he imposed upon the poem may be valid on the allegorical level so long as it remains theoretical, but it is hardly to be substantiated by the experience of reading the poem. In short, the further one stays away from the poem itself, the more plausible the unity seems. Too often the allegorical values of the poem remain unexceptionable theories that are unsupported by adequate intensity in the characters and events meant to embody them. Thus, in a scheme of the poem Arthur is totally acceptable as its moral centre so long as one judges him as 'ideal manhood', but when he is looked at as 'real man', in his relations with Lancelot and Guinevere, he seems a mere absence of vice rather than a powerful moral force; the allegorical and the literal simply do not enforce each other.*

Part of the difficulty is that, as he had demonstrated so often before, Tennyson had little sense of the causal qualities of human personality and hence little sense of narrative, those qualities as they are seen in action. The problem is reflected in the language of the idylls, where a kind of inertness stems directly from a failure to recognize logical and verbal connections between events. Tennyson no doubt initially intended his story to be told in a primitive form in which the narrator simply puts one event after another on a temporal string, rather than allowing character to dictate action. It is presumably for that reason

* It may be that the inadequate characterization of Arthur stems from Tennyson's having known the model too well to give life to Arthur, that the original from which he was drawn existed so vividly in Tennyson's mind's eye that he was unaware that he had failed to transfer that vision to the page. Although not intended as a literal portrait, the blue-eyed Arthur of Camelot owed a great deal to the blue-eyed Arthur of Cambridge, even to the likeness of the names of the places with which they associated. The *Idylls* were developed out of the 'Morte d'Arthur', which was written in grief at Hallam's death; throughout the *Idylls* King Arthur's character seems made to fit that of the dying king in the final idyll, who of course recalls Hallam. It is more than poetic coincidence that Tennyson called Sir John Simeon 'the Prince of courtesy' in the elegy that brackets him with Henry Lushington and Hallam as the poet's dearest friends; in 'Balin and Balan' Arthur is described as 'the king of courtesy', as if to establish Hallam's primacy in the trinity of Tennyson's affections.

that he chose to stress the pictorial qualities of the individual episodes not their narrative aspects; he called them 'idylls' rather than 'epyllia', as Edmund Lushington thought he ought to do. Certainly they lose the name of action by too little interest in cause and effect; the point is made by Tennyson's actual diction and his over-use of the simple conjunction 'and'. Undoubtedly, he used it deliberately to underline the antiquity of his method of storytelling, but the flaccidity into which it fell only too easily is demonstrated at the beginning of 'The Coming of Arthur':

> And thus the land of Cameliard was waste,
> Thick with wet woods, and many a beast therein,
> And none or few to scare or chase the beast;
> So that wild dog, and wolf and boar and bear
> Came night and day, and rooted in the fields,
> And wallowed in the gardens of the King.
> And ever and anon the wolf would steal
> The children and devour, but now and then,
> Her own brood lost or dead, lent her fierce teat
> To human sucklings; and the children, housed
> In her foul den, there at their meat would growl . . . (lines 20–30)

It is a pattern that Tennyson was to repeat hundreds of times in the course of the entire poem; at a rough guess, 'and' occurs at least once a line. The difficulty is not only one of poetic immediacy; the slackened language also robs the characters of any appearance of 'real man' because there is no feeling of behaviour resulting from antecedents, and hence it destroys the first term of the relationship between the literal and the ideal. The result is that the literal is less believable than the allegorical, totally reversing Tennyson's intention.

The problem of the use of obsolete language was one that Tennyson never solved satisfactorily. He attempted to make the diction lofty and grave, but the result is sometimes another kind of gravity than he intended, that of heaviness. Kay's outburst at Gareth's quest, for example, shows how carefully Tennyson had swotted up his archaisms, and perhaps how much Browning he had read, but it hardly reflects spoken speech, either in the court of Arthur or in that of Victoria:

> 'Bound upon a quest
> With horse and arms—the King hath past his time—
> My scullion knave! Thralls to your work again,
> For an your fire be low ye kindle mine!

Will there be dawn in West and eve in East?
Begone!—my knave!—belike and like enow
Some old head-blow not heeded in his youth
So shook his wits they wander in his prime—
Crazed!'   (lines 692–700)

The entire poem seems infected with a flabbiness of diction quite uncharacteristic of Tennyson. The deadly repetition of 'and', and the jaw-breaking attempts at Kay's speech are paralleled by redundancies that would be hard to duplicate anywhere else in his poetry, so that the reader occasionally feels that Tennyson is merely filling out the metre. For example, in 'The Marriage of Geraint' the description of Geraint's waning reputation is robbed of its intended effect by the superfluity:

And by and by the people, when they met
In twos and threes, or fuller companies,
Began to scoff and jeer and babble of him
As of a prince whose manhood was all gone,
And molten down in mere uxoriousness.   (lines 56–60)

In the first line 'by and by' is as nearly meaningless as a cliché can be. The second line adds precisely nothing to the specification of number: can 'people' meet in any other groups than 'two and threes, or fuller companies'? 'Scoff', 'jeer', and 'babble' seem insufficiently distinguished from each other to merit the inclusion of all. The phrase 'whose manhood was all gone' is surely stated more graphically in the following line. Of these five lines, half seems pure stuffing of the blank verse.

What is most interesting is that Tennyson's verbosity and lack of precision nearly always occur in his attempts to deal with human nature rather than the natural world. Were there no more than this, the *Idylls of the King* would have to be counted a failure. What come close to redeeming the whole poem (or poems? the uncertainty of critics whether to refer to the whole as 'it' or 'them' seems indicative of a dangerous lack of unity) are the descriptions and metaphors, almost all drawn from natural imagery, which linger in the mind after the main concerns of the work are forgotten. Some of the most miraculous lines Tennyson ever wrote are scattered with a lordly prodigality throughout the poem, so complete in their rhythm and language that they are unforgettable even when they are not closely related to the main concerns of the poem.

> Then, because his wound was deep,
> The bold Sir Bedivere uplifted him,
> And bore him to a chapel nigh the field,
> A broken chancel with a broken cross,
> That stood on a dark strait of barren land:
> On one side lay the Ocean, and on one
> Lay a great water, and the moon was full.
>   ('The Passing of Arthur', lines 174–89)

With great rhythmical tact Tennyson slows down the long series of consonantal 'b' sounds to accommodate the variations on the 'o' and 'u' sounds, which have barely been hinted at before; the heavy caesura in the last line ensures adequate length given to the peace of the final word. All the hurry and transience of man is set in contrast to the slow-moving tranquillity of unheeding nature. The image may not say much that is immediately relevant to Sense and Soul, but it brings the reader to a momentary resolution.

From the same idyll comes the evocation of a loneliness in man that can be communicated only in natural phenomena:

>   and from them rose
> A cry that shivered to the tingling stars,
> And, as it were one voice, an agony
> Of lamentation, like a wind that shrills
> All night in a waste land, where no one comes,
> Or hath come, since the making of the world. (lines 366–71)

Once more, the clicking into place of the conclusion of the simile is a short-lived resolution, momentarily giving the reader a feeling of concord.

In 'Merlin and Vivien', the idyll most explicitly concerned with sensuality, the most arresting simile seems slightly off the main theme of the poem as it describes Merlin's premonition of disaster, in an image made many years before in the caves of Ballybunion:

>   he was mute:
> So dark a forethought rolled about his brain,
> As on a dull day in an Ocean cave
> The blind wave feeling round his long sea-hall
> In silence ...   (lines 227–31)

The words that Tennyson puts into the mouth of Arthur when he speaks of his search for God might, with an appropriate change of

pronoun, apply equally well to his own search for meaning in nature
and in man:

> 'I found Him in the shining of the stars,
> I marked Him in the flowering of His fields,
> But in His ways with men I find Him not.'
> ('The Passing of Arthur', lines 9–11)

The *Idylls of the King* are indeed hard to resist, but one wonders
whether many impartial readers ever responded to the whole, as it is so
easy to do to parts. With his usual gift for reducing theory to practi-
cality, even vulgarity, Carlyle summarized the matter for Emerson:
'We read, at first, Tennyson's *Idyls*, with profound recognitn. of
the finely elaborated executn., and also of the inward perfectn. of
vacancy,—and, to say truth, with considerable impatience at being
treated so very like infants, tho the lollipops were so superlative.'[2]

Carlyle's remark is relevant, but it slightly misses the point of what
Tennyson was up to. In the war of Sense with Soul, he might be
described as a tactician rather than a strategist, for the energy of the
poetry goes not into over-all planning but into smaller engagements
and local skirmishes. As the total of the minor climaxes and resolutions mounts, so does the sense of resolution of the whole poem; the
cumulative effect is nearly satisfactory, but the answers that are given
are not in response to the questions that the over-all design of the poem
leads one to expect. It is almost as if Tennyson were saying that the
large questions are ultimately impossible to answer and that man finds
a sense of meaning by ignoring them and looking to particulars for
satisfaction. It is a poetical process that is spendthrift with language,
and only a poet with inexhaustible gifts of metaphor like Tennyson
could afford to work in this way. Great as the achievement of the *Idylls*
is, it seems almost perverse, the awkward imposition of lyricism upon
a narrative form that is singularly hostile to it.

Idylls of the King sold extraordinarily well and soon took a place
among Tennyson's most popular publications, but it was apparent
that few of his poetic and literary contemporaries were enthusiastic.
Much of the criticism centred on his unconvincing re-creation of the
life of an earlier age, in which the props for play-acting are more
believable than the actors, so that we are apt to visualize Arthur's
palace as remarkably like real-life houses such as Bayons or Aldworth.
Alfred Lyall was not alone in 'confessing to an occasional feeling of
something abstract, shadowy, and spectacular in the company of these

knights and dames'. Swinburne pretended to be shocked 'that our Laureate should find in the ideal cuckold his type of the ideal man'. Even Emily Tennyson admitted reluctantly that his scenes of violence 'always ring just a little false'. She was, however, more than pleased with the new epilogue, 'To the Queen', which had been composed at her suggestion; so urgent had she been that she wrote for Alfred a long prose summary of what thought he should say, beginning:

> Victoria the beloved with your name let
> me end my Task as with His it is begun.
> Some there are who say, wherefore
> these idle tales of a day gone by?

Luckily, Tennyson seems not to have used any of what she proposed, but even so the combination of the epilogue with the dedication to Prince Albert caused a good deal of sardonic laughter at what sounded like time-serving. Swinburne called the poem 'the Morte d'Albert, or Idylls of the Prince Consort', and FitzGerald, who had not really liked any of Tennyson's poetry since 1842, found the idylls and their epilogue too much for him; with misogynic insight he saw shrewdly but uncharitably what at least part of the trouble was: 'he has sunk in Coterie-worship, and (I tremble to say it) in the sympathy of his most Ladylike, gentle Wife. An old Housekeeper like Molière's would have been far better for him, *I* think.'[3]

But an old housekeeper would not have thought of getting Tennyson to write the epilogue, nor would she have seen to it that a copy was dispatched to the Queen. It had been six years since Tennyson's last meeting with his Sovereign, and though she had written to thank him for the books intermittently sent to her in the mean time, there had been no invitation to Osborne. On 26 February 1873 she sent her thanks for the epilogue in a letter in her own hand, concluding: 'She also hopes that Mr Tennyson will not find Osborne too far a drive from Freshwater.'[4] This was immediately followed by an invitation to Windsor, so that she might show him Albert's mausoleum at Frogmore. Tennyson's admiration of the tomb was all that she could have desired, and he was able to reiterate his own feelings about his mother's funeral and his wish that such services could be light and cheerful.

It is hard to believe that the Tennysons were unable to foresee the next move, which was a telegram from Dean Stanley four days after Tennyson had been with the Queen, asking whether he would con-

XXI. a. Aldworth.

b. Bayons Manor.

XXII. a. Dickens after death, by Sir John Millais.

"GLAD, MY LORD, YOU HAVE BEEN TEMPTED TO CHANGE YOUR HAT!"

b. From *Punch*, 22 December 1883.

sider accepting a Royal honour. His cautious reply was 'that if it were hereditary it would be prized by him for his boys'.[5] Obviously the family expected a peerage, but at the end of March Gladstone wrote to offer a baronetcy. According to his son, Tennyson refused it after considering the matter a day or two; however, in the British Library is a letter from Tennyson to Gladstone, dated 28 March 1873, accepting the baronetcy in recognition of the Royal feeling that had prompted the letter. It is not certain what happened to this letter or why it is among Gladstone's papers, since it was apparently never sent. Instead, on 30 March, Tennyson declined the honour, saying that he and Emily preferred to 'remain plain Mr and Mrs', although they would like it if the title could be given instead to Hallam at whatever age seemed suitable. When he broached the matter to Hallam, he said he would not want the title during his father's lifetime, and the matter was dropped; in any case it had never been clear that the baronetcy could be given to him under those conditions. Gladstone wrote a note for the next Prime Minister, stating that the Queen was willing to confer the title on Hallam after Tennyson's death.

The following year Disraeli, who succeeded Gladstone, renewed the offer of a baronetcy at the same time that he offered one to Carlyle. His letter seemed condescending to Tennyson, who declined in a curt note saying that he had already refused the honour from Gladstone and implying that he was not apt to accept it from Disraeli's hands, but he did hedge his bets by repeating his hope that it would be offered to Hallam after his own death. His opinion of Disraeli's tone was vindicated by the Prime Minister's letter to Carlyle, in which he described Tennyson as 'if not a great poet, a real one'. Surprisingly, Carlyle was more touched than Tennyson by the offer of a title, even though he had always despised Disraeli, but it was not long after he declined it that he was once more speaking of him as a 'cursed old Jew, not worth his weight in cold bacon'.[6]

In the summer of 1872 the entire Tennyson family went to France and Switzerland; Alfred and Lionel spent an uncomfortable night at the Grande Chartreuse, where Tennyson remained only a few minutes at the mass he had asked to hear, afterwards saying the entire monastery was bare and uninteresting. The following year they all returned to Switzerland and northern Italy in the summer before the boys went off to Cambridge, where Hallam was beginning his second year at Trinity and Lionel his first. When Alfred and Emily returned to Farringford, they seemed bleakly cut off from Cambridge before taking Lady Franklin's house for two months of frenetic social activity. Tennyson went once to Cambridge, and the sons were able to join them at least once in London, then to accompany them back to Farringford for Christmas. Hallam seems to have been homesick in Cambridge, and he tried to persuade his parents that they should let Aldworth for ten years and take a town house, so that they would be nearer him and Lionel. To Tennyson it would probably have been a welcome move, for Allingham believed that 'if he had not two big houses tied to his legs, like cannon balls, he would come and live near London'.[7]

Three residences and their expenses were frightening to Tennyson, and he set about consolidating his income. At the urging of Knowles he insisted on regularizing his relations with James Fields, his American publisher, and settled for an annual payment of £500 for advance copies of his poems before they were published in England. In London he found that Strahan felt that his payment of £5,000 p.a. was putting his firm into financial difficulties, so that he was unable to continue his contract with Tennyson after 1873. Tennyson had no trouble in negotiating another contract with Henry King, who guaranteed him £25,000 for the following five years: 'Let us hope', wrote Emily, '. . . that he has found a steadfast publisher in Mr King, with whom he may stay to the end. That he is most liberal there can be no doubt.'

When they were in London Browning came to the house nearly every Sunday, while the literary and the near-literary society of the city jostled each other to entertain them until Tennyson was afraid that he would die of hospitality. Forster asked him to dine, with only Spedding and Carlyle as the other guests. It was probably the company of old friends that made him remember old grievances from the days when he was beginning to make his name as a poet: 'Tennyson was distinctly rather wearisome,' wrote Carlyle; 'nothing coming from him that did not smack of utter indolence, what one might almost call torpid sleepiness and stupor; all still enlivened, however, by the tone of boylike naïveté and total want of malice except against his *Quarterly* and other unfavourable Reviewers.'[8]

On their return to Farringford Emily was more than usually worn out. 'No doubt it is good for one to be a little in London, but how glad & thankful I am to be in our peaceful home!' she wrote in her journal. 'I of course am very busy with bills & letters but I am more happy than I can say & more thankful to be at home alone with my three.'[9] Her exhaustion stubbornly persisted, and by April she had given up even writing in her journal, saving her strength for the correspondence she still felt she must carry on for Alfred.

By mid-summer 1874 she was feeling well enough to go to France with Alfred and their sons. Tennyson and Hallam left Emily and Lionel in Tours when they went to Cauteretz for Tennyson's last visit there. He arrived at the village on 6 September, thirteen years to the day since he had walked into it with Dakyns and just over forty-four years since he had left it on his first visit. He and Hallam scrambled among the rocks above the valley and went to Pont d'Espagne, where in 1830 he and another Hallam had met the Spanish revolutionaries and turned over their money and coded messages. He pointed out again the 'stately pine' that he had mentioned in *The Princess* and said that ever since 1830 he had remembered 'the exquisite shadows on the mountains, cast by the morning light in this valley'. At the end of a long day that had begun with sunrise they returned to Cauteretz after walking nineteen miles; Tennyson felt a renewal of his youth when in the spot he loved so well, and he said that 'he really wondered at his walking powers when once he had not to go on the English dusty, leg-wearying high-road'.[10] In all his trips to Cauteretz Tennyson seems never to have been touched by its historical associations with Charlemagne, Roland, or even his own hero, Wellington; it brought back memories of Arthur Hallam and no one else.

This last visit to Cauteretz was farewell to more than forty years of his life. When they returned to Farringford Emily suffered a total collapse, which the doctor put down to overwork. In the references to her illness there is nothing to indicate its cause or exact nature. Certainly, her arm was so painful that she was unable to write, and her back troubled her so much that she was often unable to move from her couch without the help of Alfred or Hallam, but the vagueness of the accounts seems to point to a psychological basis. It is noticeable that thereafter she was seldom alone with the servants; when Alfred had to go to London, Hallam took care of her. When Hallam accompanied his father, Lionel would stay at home. Her journal entries had always indicated something of the loneliness she suffered when Alfred was away, although she felt she had to repress it and never mention it to him. Previously, she had always taken care of someone: when her mother died, she took her place with Mr Sellwood; after her marriage she had tended Alfred like a child; when it became clear that he needed to escape occasionally, she still had her sons to look after; now they too were grown and on the verge of leaving her. In the absence of other evidence, her sudden collapse seems like a mute call for help, a stifled cry from a woman who had for a quarter of a century choked the expression of her own emotions in order to preserve a calm atmosphere for a husband always on the edge of nervous disaster.

Most of his life Tennyson had been cared for by others: first by his family, then his friends, then Emily, and now suddenly his security was inexplicably gone. 'My wife I am sorry to say from overwork and over-letterwriting is still obliged to lie flat & must not exert herself in any one thing (the doctor says) if she be to recover', he wrote to Palgrave, '& so a good deal of the work falls on me, who you know abhor letter writing.'[11] It was too late for him to learn to handle his own business affairs, let alone run the houses, take care of a correspondence that sometimes brought as many as forty letters in the morning post, or even look after his own clothes, a task that Emily had taken on from the servants because he was so impossibly untidy. To have coped with everything that Emily had handled capably for years would have meant that he had no time in which to compose poetry; apart from his own satisfaction and his feelings of duty to his poetry, a cessation of writing would have meant the severe curtailment of their income. Although he could easily have afforded to do so, his shyness and intense hatred of letting outsiders know anything of his private life made it impossible for him to hire a secretary to manage his affairs and keep up his correspondence. At first glance it may seem selfishness, but it was considerably more than self-pity that caused his panic over Emily's breakdown. It was an almost impossible situation in which one can feel nothing but sympathy for both Emily and Alfred, even in their subsequent desperate step, which was to call Hallam home from Cambridge to take over Emily's work.

Tennyson's feelings of guilt at Emily's breakdown are evident enough in his protestations that it had come about because of her own over-zealousness: '*She has overwrought herself with the multifarious correspondence of many years, and is now suffering for it,*' he told Knowles; '*. . . it will never again do for her to insist upon answering every idle fellow who writes to me. I always prayed her not to do so, but she did not like the unanswered . . . to feel wroth and unsatisfied with me.*' Sadly he had to recognize that it would be a long time before she would 'be able to write letters for five hours a -day', as he told the Duchess of Argyll, 'not that I ever shall let her do it again'.[12]

After a few months of total rest and treatment with phosphorus by the local practitioner, Dr Dabbs, she began to recover her strength and within a year or two she was able to run the house from her couch, but she never again carried on a voluminous correspondence, and she never resumed writing regularly in her journal, which she had kept almost obsessively since her marriage. Like so many others of Tennyson's intimates, she had once thought of writing about his conversation: 'I feel that perhaps I have been wrong in not having fulfilled my half formed purpose of making a book of the great thoughts & sayings of Tennyson. Perhaps not for great thoughts & sayings lose much of their life when riven from their natural place.'[13] Even in its present state, chopped and ruthlessly edited as it was after his death, the journal remains a useful record of the day-to-day life of Farringford and Aldworth, of Tennyson's comings and goings, and of his troubles in writing poetry, but it seldom demonstrates wit or more than ordinary understanding in its author. Easily the most arresting single entry is the only gnomic sentence Emily Tennyson ever wrote. Behind the three dis-ordered words we can easily discern the hysterical frustration that goes far to explain her breakdown. On 1 February 1867 in isolation on the page occurs the stark entry: 'Words is enigmas.' It tells more than any-thing else she ever wrote what it must have been like for a literal-minded women of moderate imagination living with a husband whose exis-tence was essentially verbal.

Tennyson often spoke of his sorrow at taking Hallam away from Cambridge, but he knew he could never let him return. 'We are grieved that our absolute need of Hallam at home has prevented him from accomplishing his University career,' he wrote to Thompson at Trin-ity; 'but you at least will not think the worse of him for this.'[14] Clearly visible through the words of the last part of the sentence is the hope that Thompson will not think ill of Hallam's father either. Without protest Hallam accepted the end of his plans for a career of his own, but something of his quiet desperation colours his account of the monotonous routine he had dutifully assumed. 'I did not return to Cambridge after the long vacation of this year but remained at home as my Father's secretary. Otherwise our life did not undergo much change. We stayed at Farringford as of late till the end of June or the beginning of July and then went to Aldworth, which having entirely removed my Father's tendency to Hay fever he could now thoroughly enjoy his walks and drives in the beautiful country around. To make fresh plantings & to watch the growth of trees & shrubs already planted continued sources of unfailing pleasure to him. His hours of work were somewhat changed, Sir Andrew Clark having insisted on his walking before luncheon & resting afterwards. The time after this rest he generally spent in one of the lawns where he would read the Daily Papers or some book, or receive friends from the neighbourhood or talk to those who were guests in the house. By degrees we got to lunch later & to dine later partly because of the earlier walk and partly perhaps because of the trains which often brought us friends from London.' It is hard to realize that is the description by a young man of his life at twenty-two. After his father's death, when he was beginning his biography, he condensed it to this passage: 'I was summoned home from Cambridge & became my father's secretary, & hardly left home again for a single night until his Death.' Then, as if aware of how much he had inadvertently revealed, he dutifully crossed out the entire part of the sentence after the comma.[15]

Hallam's self-effacing resignation was in distinct contrast to the wayward, graceful manners of Lionel, whom, according to his son, it would have been useless to ask to give up his own career. He was not particularly scholarly, but he did remain at Trinity until he had taken an undistinguished degree. Shooting, music, theatre, the light poetry for which he had a marked talent, and young women were his chief interests, but in spite of his gaiety and charm he was the heir of the Tennysons' black blood, and he was probably far less stable emotionally than his brother. When he was only seventeen his mother had noticed a significant difference between her sons: 'Hallam comes into a room like a spirit as A does, Lionel with a grand step like an old Baron in his armour.' Hallam was 'so cheerful & so devoted in his attentions' to his father, but Emily could only hope that Lionel would outgrow his shyness with Tennyson, so that he would be 'more able to shew himself to his Father'. One indication of how Lionel felt that his father stood in his light was that he used to get so tired of being asked if he were the poet's son that he would say, 'As a matter of fact, he's *my* father.'[16]

A natural delight in meeting people and a real interest in literature combined to bring Lionel into contact with many of the writers of the day whom his father knew but slightly if at all, and his letters home describing them are usually fresh and observant. At Oxford he met Swinburne: 'I can't say I was very much fascinated with him; he has a peculiar habit of bobbing up & down on his chair: he was however very civil to me. . . . He went out to an evening party, he took too much. He made a beast of himself, he said it was the lobster sauce.' Lionel's long oval face and curly hair made him slightly resemble

Oscar Wilde, who was his own age; in 1877 he said he had 'made the acquaintance of my double, Oscar Wilde; he is not so absurd as people have represented & is a decidedly capable young man. . . . [Woolner] talked a long time to Oscar Wilde at Oxford under the impression he was me. N.B. I hope I don't look like that.'[17] He apparently did not share his father's slight distrust of Matthew Arnold, whom he saw not infrequently at London parties. He also made a special effort to meet 'H. James Junr. the American' long before James was famous. Beside Lionel's gregariousness Hallam's self-conscious propriety seemed slightly stuffy.

Once Tennyson's guilt over Hallam had worn off or returned only sporadically, he realized that his son was even better at managing his life than Emily had been. He wrote all his father's letters, and, unlike Emily, he knew how to snub unwanted correspondents, he was better than she at managing money, he could accompany Tennyson on his walks once or twice a day, he acted as audience for his readings when there was no other company in the house, and he went with him on his London jaunts and summer walking holidays. All this meant that for the first time Tennyson did not have to rely upon the adulation of other young men, and he began divesting himself of their company.

James Knowles in particular resented being displaced by Hallam, and his irritation increased when it became apparent that Tennyson had decided on Hallam as his biographer after his own death, a position for which Knowles had been preparing himself. For some time Hallam had tried to get Tennyson to confide less in Knowles: 'My Father in his simplicity told too much to Knowles which he has misrepresented,' he wrote in 1893. 'My Father gave answers to Knowles' pumping at Knowles' own table, but he was aware that he had done so, and was sorry that he had said so much afterwards. "He is the cleverest fellow I know but he is sure to make a good thing of me. Can't I see it?"' Hallam insisted that after he became his father's companion 'K's examinations came to an end'.[18] Knowles liked Hallam about as much as Hallam liked him, and in the manuscript notes for his article about his friendship with Tennyson he wrote about how he and Tennyson used to laugh together at Hallam's jealousy. Probably he invented the malicious story for the purpose of wounding Hallam, but fortunately he seems not to have published it.

It was not only Emily Tennyson who was quickly ageing. Even that apparently inexhaustible source of energy, Mrs Cameron, had begun to slow down and for the first time to seem in need of sympathy. By 1873 the Camerons' investments had turned out badly, and she was apparently nearly penniless except for gifts from her sisters and friends. In addition, her health had suddenly deteriorated, and her doctor told her that one of her lungs was badly affected by disease. She had always adored Emily Tennyson, and now she climbed the path to Farringford for mutual consolation whenever Alfred was away. 'When your Father is *with* her I do not often go up,' she told Hallam. 'They are so complete in their lives I always feel as if the presence of a third took something from & added nothing thereto, but when she is alone I go to *fill* my Soul with light & love.' To Alfred she confessed, 'although I bully you I have a corner for you in my heart'.[19]

Bully him she did. Even in her illness she persuaded one of the Simeons to plait a wreath of red and white flowers, which she then made Tennyson carry to the water's edge and throw into Freshwater Bay to celebrate the marriage of the land and sea, as if he were Doge of Freshwater. Nor were others safe from her still powerful gusts of energy. One of her last photographic projects was to illustrate the *Idylls of the King*; it was undertaken at Tennyson's own request, which suggests an act of deliberate kindness since he hated illustrations of his poems, even when he supervised them. Forgetting her illness, she threw herself into the work, waylaying passers-by with suitable faces to act as models. At Yarmouth she spotted a porter who looked to her like King Arthur, and before he knew what was happening he was dressed in borrowed robes with a bemused summer visitor grovelling on the floor as the penitent Guinevere, her arms locked around his feet. Mild old Mr Cameron was shepherded to Farringford and pushed into the trunk of a hollow tree to impersonate the imprisoned Merlin. One Sunday as she walked with Tennyson into the Wards' house, still talking about the illustrations, they found the family assembled after mass with their guest, Bishop Herbert Vaughan, the future cardinal. Mrs Cameron took one look at his handsome face and impulsively exclaimed, 'Oh Alfred, I have at last found a Sir Lancelot.' 'Where is he?' demanded Tennyson, peering myopically around the room. 'There,' cried Mrs Cameron, pointing at the embarrassed bishop. 'No,' said Tennyson equally loudly, 'he won't do, his face is too goodlooking. For Lancelot you must have a man with a face seamed and scarred by human passions.'[20]

Age might make her customary pace fail, but it could not wither Mrs Cameron. In 1875 she saw the fifty-one-year-old William Allingham on the platform of Haslemere station, and in a loud aside said to a friend, 'What white beards our younger poets are getting.' The same year the Camerons finally sold Dimbola and moved to Ceylon, where they hoped to recoup their finances. Their going left a lonely hole in Freshwater that was not filled by the advent of the Prinseps and Watts to the Briary near Farringford. Four years later Mrs Cameron died in Ceylon, looking out of the window at a glorious evening. Her last word was typical: 'Beautiful.'[21]

In part Mrs Cameron's place in Tennyson's life was taken by another eccentric and even more flamboyant friend, Mrs Sabine Greville, a well-connected and wealthy follower of the arts with an undiscriminating passion for literature, celebrities, and the theatre. Henry James called her 'the queerest creature living, but a mixture of the ridiculous and the amiable in which the amiable predominates. She is crazy, stage-struck, scatter-brained, what the French call *extravagante*; but I can't praise her better than by saying that though she is on the whole the greatest fool I have ever known, I like her very much and get on with her most easily.'[22] She was a massive woman, draped in clothing as spectacular as Mrs Cameron's, although a good bit cleaner and more expensive, and, like her, she had a deep devotion to Tennyson. Her exuberant notes were on brilliantly coloured writing-paper with a facsimile of her own sprawling signature engraved on it, addressed to Tennyson as 'Dear Heart, Our Master'. After a series of disconnected one-sentence paragraphs, one letter was dated 'the dawn of Wednesday' and left unsigned, although a signature was hardly necessary.

Mrs Cameron's admiration of Tennyson had been well seasoned with tart comment on what she disapproved of in him, for she loved him too well to tolerate bad manners, but Mrs Greville followed him unquestioningly and, like Palgrave and Allingham, willingly put up with rudeness and condescension for the pleasure of claiming his acquaintance. She gave public witness of her worship by kissing his hand in greeting. Once she had a special dish made for him when he was at her house and asked him to tell her how he liked it. Henry Irving heard that he had replied, 'If you really wish to know, I thought it was like an old shoe.' When Irving asked if it were true, Tennyson negligently denied the story: 'I said it was like an old boot.'[23] After one particularly unpleasant demonstration of deliberate incivility to her, August Hare decided that for 'the poet's bearish manners the Tennyson family are to blame in making him think himself a demigod', but that he none the less gave a 'favourable impression. He could scarcely be less egotistic with all the flattery he has.'[24]

As a genuine eccentric, Mrs Cameron had been unaware that she was out of the ordinary, which was not true of Mrs Greville, whose behaviour seemed modelled on the melodrama she loved, so that she was always on-stage. After Brookfield's death in 1874 Tennyson wrote a charming little farewell to 'Brooks, for they called you so that knew you best', full of nostalgia for Cambridge, Hallam, and long-gone youth. Before the poem was published in a volume of Brookfield's sermons the following year, he went to present a copy to Brookfield's widow, accompanied by Mrs Greville in too-tight violet velvet with a long train. After greeting his hostess he handed the poem to Mrs Greville, saying, 'Here, you'd better read this.' To Jane Brookfield's wicked delight, Mrs Greville 'took the scroll in both hands, partially unrolled it, advanced to the centre of the room, read a few lines to herself in a stagewhisper, with much facial expression, as though she had never seen the script before, then, suddenly falling upon both knees, exclaimed in tragedy tones, "Oh! this is too divine to be read in any other attitude!" and forthwith proceeded to declaim it by heart'.[25] If Tennyson felt any embarrassment at the display, Mrs Brookfield left no record of it.

Browning had said astutely that Mrs Cameron's eccentricity did not matter, since she had no influence on Tennyson's poetry. Mrs Greville's foolishness was innocent enough in itself, but her excessive adoration was precisely what was worst for Tennyson, particularly as he so enjoyed it. Her constant and unbridled flattery may even have had a part in encouraging Tennyson to turn in 1874 to what was certainly the least satisfactory part of his poetic career.

CHAPTER XXXI

✤

TENNYSON AND THE THEATRE,
1874–1882

EVER since he had first seen Fanny Kemble perform during the
Christmas vacation of 1829, when he was still an undergraduate,
Tennyson had loved the theatre, but he was hardly the serious student
of the drama that his son's biography suggests. Shakespeare he knew
well, although he had little chance to see most of the plays performed
until after the middle of the century; his love of them was chiefly for
their poetry rather than their dramatic quality. Until the 1870s there
was a clear distinction between the drama that he saw and that which
he read: most of the former consisted of farce and melodrama that he
attended as a bachelor with friends like Spedding when he was in
London, but that must be put down in part to the fact that so little
serious drama held the London stage until after his marriage. He read
many of the classical dramatists and most of the Elizabethans, but as if
they had written poems not plays.

By the 1870s, however, he had behind him twenty years of increasing experiment with the creation of character in his own poems, and if
it was not totally successful, that fact had not been pressed home to
him by his family and close friends. As the foremost poet of day he was
inevitably compared to Shakespeare, and it was natural for him to
begin equating the talents of the greatest Elizabethan dramatist with
his own and to consider the possibility of his being Shakespeare's
successor in what was generally regarded as a new Elizabethan age.

During the 1870s and early 1880s the Tennysons took a London
house for a month or two each year, which gave Alfred more opportunity to attend the theatre, often in the flattering company of Mrs
Greville. The improvement of stage machinery and lighting in the
middle of the century inevitably led to more spectacular productions,
which in turn demanded larger theatres and stages. To fill these vast
spaces there grew up a world of oversize drama, ringing set speeches,
heroic (or at least broad) acting, and voices and gestures to suit. Chief
among the new generation of actors and managers was the young

Henry Irving, who was acting at the Lyceum theatre, then leased by the American impresario Hezekiah Bateman and his wife. Apparently Tennyson did not see Irving's first success in *The Bells*, but he did see him in Bulwer Lytton's *Richelieu* in 1873. A few months later, in March 1874, he attended a performance of Irving's triumphant Hamlet. After the curtain had fallen, Irving and some of the other actors crowded into the box where Tennyson sat with his sons and Annie Thackeray. Tennyson took it upon himself to explain how he thought the parts should be played. 'You are a good actor lost,' said Irving.

What seemed more apparent to Tennyson was that he was a good playwright lost to the world, and by the spring of 1874 he was casting around for a subject, preferably connected with the English Reformation, to be a kind of continuation of Shakespeare's historical plays. Knowles suggested the Armada, and Emily talked of his choosing either Lady Jane Grey or William the Silent as a subject. By mid-April he had written a few scenes of a play about Mary Tudor; he had read considerable historical background but his chief source was Froude's *History of England*, itself as dramatic as anything on the stage. A year later *Queen Mary. A Drama* was published, the second part of its title signalling the change of direction by the Poet Laureate. It is an inordinately long work, with twenty-three scenes and forty-four characters, betraying little dramatic sense, either in construction or in characterization. Probably the most acute brief criticism of it came from a visitor to England with ambitions of his own for the stage, Henry James: 'It is simply a dramatised chronicle, without an internal structure, taking its material in pieces as history hands them over, and working each one into an independent scene—usually with rich ability. It has no shape; it is cast in no mould; it has neither beginning, middle, nor end, save the chronological ones.'[1] Another writer who had already proved his lack of skill in the theatre, Robert Browning, delicately skirted the matter of Tennyson's achievement by thanking him 'for "Queen Mary", the gift, and even more for "Queen Mary", the poem'. Of *Queen Mary* the play he tactfully said nothing. According to Domett, Browning had deserted a projected drama of his own when he heard that Tennyson was writing for the theatre.

Some of the newspapers, in particular *The Times* and the *Spectator*, were rather unrealistic in their claims for Tennyson's new work, and Swinburne wrote to Watts to ask, 'But isn't the press fun—above all the incomparable Spectator, which sets it high above the ordinary work of Shakespeare and only a little lower than his highest. And yet I am not very much alarmed at the advent of this conquering rival.'[2]

Actually, it is a surprisingly good try for a man writing his first play (unless *The Devil and the Lady* be counted) at the age of sixty-five, but it is far from first-rate theatre. Irving recognized that its central theme of the birth of modern England out of the defeat of Roman Catholicism might appeal to audiences concerned about the new threat from Rome in the shape of Papal Infallibility, which had been promulgated only five years before and which seemed to make national loyalty impossible for English Roman Catholics: 'you will have hit Manning & Co. a more fatal blow than a thousand pamphleteers & controversialists,' Froude wrote to Tennyson.[3] In addition there was sure to be a good deal of curiosity about the first drama by the Poet Laureate. Irving suggested that Tennyson shorten the play for presentation at the Lyceum.

Rather amateurishly, Tennyson cut it to half its length, sacrificing many of the central characters and turning it into what has been called 'an attenuated psychological study' of Mary Tudor and her husband Philip.[4] Then, as a friend described the process to Frederick Tennyson, the 'Yankee manageress Mrs. Bateman . . . slashed at it with her bowie knife—& has reduced it to 2 scenes an act, & all the dramatis personae to 7 or 8! . . . Yr. brother said they wanted him to go up to rehearsals, but it would make him sick—& he should probably never see it on the stage, unless he cd. smuggle himself into the house unsuspected—I said if they found he was there they would be sure to yell for him to come forward—"They may yell and be d——d," quoth he, mildly.'[5]

Tennyson had asked that the music for the play be entrusted to the young composer Charles Villiers Stanford, a friend of Hallam's. His first suggestion to Stanford was that he rearrange some of Beethoven's music to accompany the drama, and Stanford tactfully pointed out that it would no more do to excerpt Beethoven than it would for Tennyson to put one of Lady Macbeth's speeches in Queen Mary's mouth. Bateman, who disliked Stanford's music, cut out most of it and wanted to put Stanford and a tiny band under the stage. When Tennyson heard of this, he immediately offered to pay for the sixty seats in the stalls that Bateman claimed would have to be removed to provide a sufficient orchestra pit. Bateman then backed down, the seats remained, and Tennyson did not have to pay.

The opening on 18 April 1876 was to an enthusiastic audience chiefly made up of Tennyson's friends, including Browning, George Eliot and Lewes, Millais, Tom Taylor, Locker, and Frederic Leighton. Knowles thought that the Batemans' daughter, Mrs Kate Crowe, who played the title role, suffered from the 'main & fearful drawback of the outrageous and decadent *quack* which America has put into her instead of a voice',[6] but most of the audience complained only of her want of power. There was nothing but praise for Irving in the comparatively small role of Philip. Tennyson did not go to a performance until a fortnight after the opening and said then he was pleased with the acting. The audiences quickly fell off, however, and the play was withdrawn after twenty-three performances, for each of which Tennyson had received £10. It was not a successful run, but it was not disastrous enough to frighten Tennyson away from the theatre, and he had already begun another play.

Harold, which was published at the end of 1876, is half the length of *Queen Mary* and far less sprawling, but his first play had scared producers off Tennyson and *Harold* did not reach the stage until half a century after publication. It deals with many of the same events that Bulwer Lytton had used in *Harold, Last of the Saxon Kings*, but rather than present it as a challenge to his old enemy's work, as he had done with the *Idylls of the King*, Tennyson dedicated the play to his son, the second Lord Lytton: 'Your father dedicated his "Harold" to my father's brother; allow me to dedicate my "Harold" to yourself.' It was a conciliatory gesture, but it put Lytton in a difficult position, since he had said the previous year of *Queen Mary*, 'I cannot fancy the possibility of a really *dramatic* conception having issued from the brain of that blameless monarch of the milder muses.'[7] The sight of the dedication made Swinburne's 'blood run cold at the unutterable idea'[8] that he too might one day be reconciled to his enemies. Even the lukewarm reception of the printed version and his failure to get the play performed did not put off Tennyson, and he now embarked on a play about Thomas Becket.

In the summer of 1875 Emily Tennyson was able to go on a gentle trip to the Continent with her husband and sons. As travelling companion she invited Eleanor Locker, who was at a loose end following her mother's death. At Pau Tennyson and Hallam left the others while they went on a walking trip in the Pyrenees. Because of Emily's weakness Lionel and Eleanor were thrown on each other's company, and by the end of the summer they were engaged.

It seemed a thoroughly suitable match for Lionel in many ways:

Eleanor was extremely pretty, and she came of a wealthy family that was well connected through her grandfather, the Earl of Elgin. The speed with which Lionel became engaged at the age of twenty-one was a gesture of independence making it clear that he was going to lead his own life and that he had no intention of remaining unmarried to take care of his parents, as Hallam seemed set to do. Behind Hallam's descripion of his parents' reaction lies a reservation about the engagement, which 'was as welcome as so anxious an event can be to those whose life has been with and for their children'. The half-hearted language also seems to reflect Hallam's sense of his own self-sacrifice. In any case there was little prospect of Lionel's marrying immediately, since he had first to finish the University and then begin a career.

The following year Tennyson took Hallam to visit two old friends, the first time that he had stayed at the home of either. In September 1876 he and Hallam were in East Anglia and dropped in without warning on FitzGerald in Woodbridge. Fitz was now even blinder than Tennyson, wearing blue spectacles to protect his eyes, which had been burned when a paraffin lamp blazed up in his face, and he had become an old man since last he had seen Tennyson, but all the affection that he had suppressed over the years when he had received no letters from Alfred now came to life again in a joyous burst. In the two days the old friends spent together, Fitz said, it was as if they had been separated twenty days, not as many years. They went down the river Orwell and back by steamer, sat on the bank telling 'some of the old Stories', and gossiped in Fitz's garden where the pigeons wheeled down to sit comfortably on his shoulder. They reminisced about Cambridge and Mirehouse and Windermere, and Tennyson confessed that he was still hurt by the review in the *Quarterly* forty-three years before, but he took it surprisingly well when Fitz urged him to stop writing, telling him to 'ship his Oars now'. All the poems that were being sent to Alfred for reading he thought should be thrown 'into his neighbour's cucumber frames'.[9]

'I suppose I may never see him again,' wrote Fitz to Fanny Kemble after Tennyson was gone: 'and so I suppose we both thought as the Rail carried him off: and each returned to his ways as if scarcely diverted from them.' Fitz decided that the time had come to give his Laurence portrait of 'old Alfred' to Emily Tennyson, even though it was one of his dearest possessions. His correspondence after the visit rings with joy at having recovered an old friend, then the slow realization that nothing had changed after all. His letters were answered by

Hallam not Alfred, and the following year he told Frederick Tennyson that he had 'let the whole thing drop, only being ready to answer at once, & at full, if any of them ever writes to me'. But the letters did not come, and it is probable that Tennyson never wrote to him again before his death. Reluctantly Fitz had to accept the judgement he had made a quarter of a century earlier, hoping it would be disproved: 'Alfred himself never writes, nor indeed cares a halfpenny about one, though he is very well satisfied to see one when one falls in his way.'[10] Fitz had never learned that affection might remain alive behind apparent neglect, and Tennyson had never learned that friendship had to be cultivated, or that others needed occasional gestures of affection as much as he did.

The month after visiting Woodbridge Tennyson was invited with Hallam to stay with the Gladstones at Hawarden. His letter of acceptance reads in full: 'On Monday then—if all be well. As you are good enough to say that you will manage anything rather than lose my visit—will you manage that I may have my pipe in my own room whenever I like?'[11] Apparently it never occurred to him that it might lack anything in courtesy; as Hare had noticed, his family had put up with his ways for so long that they seemed perfectly normal to him.

Unfortunately, no picture seems to have survived of Gladstone and Tennyson as they walked at Hawarden. Tennyson wore his usual untidy dark cloak and sombrero, and at home Gladstone was in the habit of wearing an ancient slouch hat with brim turned down, off which the rain dripped on to a thick tweed cloak reaching his knees, equally old trousers frayed at the bottom, and a pair of thick boots on his large flat feet. Tennyson carried a long stick like a shepherd's crook and Gladstone had a heavy rustic stick, crudely made. Since neither of them would have considered that they were strangely dressed, it would not have occurred to them to preserve for future generations the outlandish appearance of England's greatest statesman and her first poet. Their conversation was wide-ranging but, if Hallam Tennyson's decorous description is accurate, surprisingly impersonal. The morning after his arrival Tennyson read the entirety of *Harold* aloud to the Gladstones. He had not warned them that it would take two and a half hours; Gladstone struggled to keep awake, his son Willy had a fit of suppressed giggles, and his daughters worried that their father would fall fast asleep. The reading began at midday, and the hour for luncheon had long passed by the time it was finished. The fact that he read aloud for so long was probably an indication of nervousness, for Tennyson seldom did so during the day.

As usual, it was noticeable that he was not on his best behaviour with Gladstone, but it was not radically different from that on other occasions, for he was developing a formidable reputation for bearish eccentricity that was difficult to distinguish from deliberate rudeness. Lord Houghton noted with amusement that he would accept dinner invitations only on condition that he could dine at seven and have old port to drink; once Houghton had to bring from Fryston some bottles of a vintage that his father had nicknamed 'The Alderman'. Stopford Brooke invited Tennyson for dinner and got an acceptance only when he promised to reserve a bottle of good port for him rather than the usual claret. When Tennyson arrived, he was in a morning jacket and apologized for his 'working clothes'. During the course of the evening he read aloud an unpublished poem, then as he left he took the hands of one of the lady guests and said, 'You must promise not to tell anybody what you have heard. Come! you must promise—you are a woman, remember.'[12] Another evening Edmund Gosse noticed with surprise that Tennyson, after an adequate amount of sherry and champagne, proceeded to drink a bottle and a half of old port, meanwhile smoking six pipes. At the end of the evening he was telling bawdy stories.

Not that Tennyson always treated the old wine he demanded with the respect its age deserved. At Trinity, Cambridge, he was once honoured by being given some of the college's famous '34 port; to the horror of his hosts he poured a tumbler of hot water into it. When he realized that they were shocked, he said imperturbably, 'Horace mixed water with his Falernian.'[13]

Even to the Argylls, of whom he had once stood in awe, he would submit conditions about the hour, the number of guests, and the entertainment before accepting invitations. Once arrived, he would often refuse to answer even direct questions if he was not in the mood for conversation. Lady Warwick said that at Lord Rosslyn's house he remained 'in a throne-like chair . . . receiving the homage of men and women, and only condescending to reward it occasionally with a monosyllable'.[14] When all allowances are made for the pleasure the contemporaries of great men take in recording their least engaging aspects, Tennyson must still have been a sore trial for hostesses.

His reading, which often covered embarrassment, as it presumably did at Hawarden, could also seem remarkably like a weapon. One listener said after Tennyson had read *Maud* to him, 'I think he always did so to persons he never wanted as guests again.' The luckless Charles Jerningham stayed in the 1870s at Weston with the Wards when Tennyson and both his sons were of the party. Wishing to be civil, Jerningham on the first night told Lionel and Hallam that he particularly admired *Maud*, although the truth was that he had only skimmed a bit of it. 'At night, when we had all gone to bed; and I was half-undressed in my bedroom, there was a knock at my door and in came Tennyson. He told me that his sons had repeated to him what I had said, and he thanked me so much for having paid him the compliment of liking his poetry; and to me, in my half-clothed, shivering state, he proceeded to spout the whole of "Maud" from beginning to end!'[15]

Tennyson's reputation for bad manners was only partially deserved. He was indeed careless of the feelings of others, but his rudeness more often sprang from a deep uncertainty and awkwardness than from intentional cruelty or even from deep egotism. Self-centred he certainly was but not wholly selfish. Sometimes his brusquerie seemed almost deliberately assumed because he knew he could never attempt the graceful manners that came naturally to his well-born friends. But what was probably behind the snarling at strangers was his awareness that in meeting him, many of them were primarily concerned to fulfil their own preconceptions not to see the man as he was. In appearance they expected the young Shelley or perhaps the ethereal Watts 'moonlight' portrait of himself, not a shambling, partially bald man of seventy, whose teeth fitted poorly. In conversation they were not really interested in how he composed a poem, writing, rewriting, endlessly changing and correcting, for they wanted to be told of fits of tempestuous inspiration in which he was in the grip of a power that dictated his poetry. They were curious to see a famous poet but their interest in poetry was slight. It was probably naïve of him to expect strangers to be more interested in Alfred Tennyson than in the Poet Laureate, but the knowledge that he was an object of idle curiosity made him lash out in barely concealed anger: 'his instinctive desire was to hide as much of himself as possible from observation until he found his companion sympathetic'. Three decades earlier in the late 1840s, when he first met Frederick Robertson in Cheltenham, he had taken refuge behind a screen of irrelevance: 'I felt', he said, 'as if he had come to pluck out the heart of my mystery—so I talked to him about nothing but beer.'[16]

In the echo of this last sentence lies the explanation of his talk on the well-known occasion when he first met Henry James in March 1877 at a dinner given by Houghton for the archaeologist Schliemann, with James, Tennyson, and Gladstone among the guests. With more enthusiasm than rhetorical nicety James had looked forward to a revelation of the poetic personality: 'Fine, fine, fine could he only be'. The actuality of the poet he had 'earliest known and best loved' was a shock to his 'fond prefigurements of youthful piety'. (In cold fact, his piety was approaching middle age, since he was thirty-four years old.) He sat two places away from the poet, straining his ears for every word he spoke, apparently ignoring the luckless man who separated them, as well as his unnamed neighbour on the other side. Although he missed Tennyson's conversation with Schliemann about the site of Troy, he 'heard most of his talk, which was all about port wine and tobacco: he seems to know much about them, and can drink a whole bottle of port at a sitting with no incommodity. He is very swarthy and scraggy, and strikes one at first as much less handsome than his photos: but gradually you see that it's a face of genius.' But all that talk of port and tobacco! Slowly it was borne in upon James that he was facing 'the full, the monstrous demonstration that Tennyson was not Tennysonian'. Probably Tennyson was not interested in the young-middle-aged American eavesdropping over his neighbour, but he must have been aware of his disconcerting attention. James was seeing a good example of Tennyson's instinctive camouflage before inquisitive strangers. Thirty years before his talk had been of beer and now it was of port and tobacco, but the method was the same as that he had used on Robertson.

What saves James's description and makes it unlike the other disillusioned accounts of meeting Tennyson for the first time is his flickering irony about the ingenuousness of his own expectations, but, like the others, he was interested only in his own reactions and did not try to understand what might be going through Tennyson's mind.

In November 1878, more than a year after Houghton's dinner, James was staying in the country with Mrs Greville, 'friend of the super-eminent', who took him to call on George Eliot and to have luncheon with the Tennysons. As he made his hesitant entrance into the long corridor at Aldworth, James heard behind him in the porch the effusions of Mrs Greville, then a deep growl as Tennyson said to her, 'Oh yes, you may do what you like—so long as you don't kiss me before the cabman!' Tennyson seems fortunately not to have remembered meeting James, and it is most unlikely that he knew of his criticism of *Queen Mary*, for he gradually warmed to his guest despite his being both a stranger and an American. It was a dark and blustery day, and the talk inevitably turned to that most English of conversation-evaders, the weather. Perhaps the dining-room seemed gloomy, for James complained of the badly lit rooms in England, putting their obscurity down to everyone's being used to fog; in America, he said, where they were more used to strong sunlight, they lit rooms brilliantly. After luncheon Tennyson took James upstairs to the better-lit study, with the 'windows that hung over space', where James had to force his attention, pinching himself while Tennyson read 'Locksley Hall', 'not at all to keep from swooning, but much rather to set up some rush of sensibility'. Instead of heaving and flushing, he could only repeat to himself, 'Oh dear, oh dear', at the low pitch of Tennyson's reading. James found himself at last 'reconciled to learning what a Bard consisted of; for that came as soon as I had swallowed my own mistake—the mistake of having supposed Tennyson something subtly other than one'.

A year or two later James had luncheon in London with the Tennysons, and this time, with his sights set lower, he actually looked at Tennyson the man, afterwards remembering chiefly that the other guest was his fellow-American, James Russell Lowell, and that Tennyson, who came into the dining-room late, launched into conversation by peering across the table at the dimly perceived guest with an American accent and asking, 'Do you know anything about *Lowell*?' only to have Emily say anxiously, 'Why, my dear, this *is* Mr. Lowell!'[17] But few other persons took the trouble to follow such a tortuous path to the realization that poets were as other men, and Tennyson's reputation for bad manners grew as he became older.

More amusing and easier to deal with were the patently mad or illiterate admirers like the farmer of Market Harborough who asked politely whether Tennyson would say 'if Isolt in your beautiful Idyll of Guinevere is a female character. I am founding a family of highly bred short horns descended from a . . . cow called Guinivere & I propose to call her female produce Isolt 1st, 2nd, 3rd &c but I cannot quite satisfy myself from the context as to the sex of Isolt.'[18]

During the season in 1877 and 1878 the Tennysons took houses in Upper Wimpole Street and Eaton Square; they still had large parties, and the regulars among the guests were still Browning and Gladstone. With the passage of years the reserve between the two poets had constantly lessened, and occasionally Tennyson 'would rally Browning playfully on his harshness of rhythm, the obscurity and length of his poems', although there is no record of his allowing Browning to tease him in return. Once when Browning heard it asserted that Tennyson was guilty of plagiarism, he said indignantly, 'You might as well accuse the Rothschilds of picking pockets.'[19] Browning used to hold private exhibitions of his son's indifferent paintings, and he invariably invited Tennyson, receiving him at the door with a low bow and the straight-faced greeting, 'Magister meus.' It was noticeable that Tennyson seldom looked at the paintings, which may have ensured the continuance of their friendship. At one of these exhibitions a young girl, Elspeth Thompson (who later married Kenneth Grahame), was looking at the pictures when she felt a touch on her arm and, as she turned, saw a pair of bright eyes and heard a deep voice saying, 'Child, look at that group & don't forget that it was pointed out to you by Fanny Kemble.' There stood Ruskin, Browning, and Tennyson in earnest conversation.

Elspeth Thompson had become acquainted with Tennyson while she was still at school and used to accompany him on walks when he was in London. She always wore her carefully subdued schoolgirl clothes, 'as quietly attired as a grey mouse', while Tennyson strode beside her in his flowing cloak and wide-brimmed hat. One day when his distinctive, well-known face and outlandish dress had attracted an unusual number of curious glances and turned heads from the crowds through which they passed, he said reprovingly, 'Child, your mother should dress you less conspicuously—people are staring at us.'[20]

On another occasion when he and Emily were staying in London, Mrs Greville arranged a meeting at her house in Chester Square between him and the Princess of Wales, for whom he had written 'A Welcome to Alexandra' on the occasion of her wedding in 1863. The Princess had asked him to read, and he began with the poem addressed to her. As he finished, they looked at each other and suddenly the fact of his reading it aloud to her struck them as so ludicrous that the book fell from his hands to the floor and they both burst into shouts of uncontrollable laughter.

At the end of the 1870s Tennyson made a determined effort to overcome his neglect of Carlyle, which had been increasing for some years. Both men were difficult and, as Spedding said, Carlyle always needed the kind of indulgence that most of us need in a fit of violent toothache, which Tennyson had not always been willing to give. Now that he had more leisure in London, Tennyson would drop in at Cheyne Row, and Carlyle was grateful for the attention. When Tennyson read 'The Revenge' to him in 1877, Carlyle said, 'Eh! Alfred, you have got the grip of it.' For the two old men the thought of death was something with which they lived daily, and in that common knowledge they forgot the irritations they occasionally produced in each other.

A new friend was Joseph Joachim, probably the greatest violinist then playing. Tennyson had little sense of music, and when Joachim would perform for him the best he could manage was to say that he liked the poetry of the bowing, and that it produced within his head the sensation of a rushing torrent and flashes of light. In the Tennyson's evenings at home Joachim would often play sonatas with Emily Ritchie as Tennyson stood in the corner listening earnestly and Emily Tennyson lay on the sofa from which she presided on such occasions.

Eleanor Locker and Lionel were married early in 1878 in Westminster Abbey, where her uncle was Dean. It was a large and fashionable wedding, with thirty policemen to control the crowds outside the Abbey, inside which were gathered most of the literary world and a good peppering of the peerage. The most impressive figure there was Tennyson, looking 'around the Abbey as if he felt the Immortals were his compeers',[21] although guests who had not seen him for some time noticed how old he looked, and the representative of an American newspaper mistook his stumble over some steps for a sign of his advanced infirmity. No doubt the splendour of the wedding was the choice of the bride and her father, but Emily Tennyson seems to have helped with suggestions. At Farringford there was a celebration in the ballroom for the servants and local residents, with dancing beneath a great display piece reading, 'Long life and happiness to L & E Tennyson.' To old friends of the family it all seemed too ostentatious. According to FitzGerald, Frederick Tennyson put it 'down to the account of *Mrs.* Alfred's ambition. He does not like her on that account. *I* never saw any sign of it in her; but Fred is positive.' As William Rossetti told a friend, Emily Tennyson 'attaches to position & appearance a certain value beyond what you do'.[22]

It was not to be a happy marriage. Both Emily and Alfred were difficult and demanding parents-in-law for Eleanor, whose letters indicate that she never felt comfortable with them and could not even find a suitable way to address them. Lionel continued to be interested in all conditions of men, not only the eminent with whom his mother felt it would be prudent to ingratiate himself; when he failed to take her advice, she mistakenly blamed it on Eleanor. He was almost certainly unfaithful during the eight years of their marriage, and probably in reaction Eleanor, who felt that she had never understood him, became known in London society as a great flirt. One of their friends said that 'she did exactly what she pleased, and he went his own way'.[23] Their marriage was not made easier by one of their three sons having inherited the mental instability of Somersby and Tealby. Lionel and Eleanor were both charming, but they never should have married.

By 1879 Tennyson had finished the long writing of *Becket* and had it run off in trial sheets, to be submitted first to Irving, who now held the lease of the Lyceum. Tennyson had been unable to scant any of the material he had assembled, so that the play is nearly as long as the original *Queen Mary* and considerably longer than an uncut *Hamlet*. Apparently Irving genuinely admired it, but he calculated that even if it were well cut it would still be financially impossible to produce, since it could not take more than £150 a night and the expenses of each performance would be at least £135, with no fee for Tennyson: 'with an outlay of two thousand pounds upon the production you may calculate the position of the manager at the end of a run of one hundred nights'. Rather ambiguously he added that 'a less remarkable work . . . would have a greater chance of success'.[24] Probably remembering how cross Mrs Bateman had been that *Queen Mary* was published before the performance, Tennyson decided to shelve *Becket* for the time being, and it was not published until 1884. Just before Tennyson's death Irving said he thought the times were ready for the play, and he produced it in 1893; it became one of his greatest successes with Ellen Terry as Rosamund and himself as Becket.

Wilfred Ward, who thought Irving something of an opportunist, went by train to Haslemere with him at the time of his dealings with Tennyson over *Becket*. As they drove together to Aldworth Irving told Ward, 'Tennyson is a great poet, but he cannot write plays; what a pity he tries, they are the greatest rubbish!' On entering the drawing-room at Aldworth, however, Irving made a series of obeisances to his host like 'a horse that had got the staggers', saying, 'You don't disdain . . . to be ranked with Shakespeare?' Tennyson, who was by now somewhat deaf, could not understand Irving's peculiar accent, so that Ward had to repeat the remark to him at full voice twice before he understood, then he said shortly, 'I think he must be chaffing me.'[25]

After dinner Tennyson's butler filled Irving's glass with port, then put the bottle down by Tennyson. He was talking and absently filling his own glass as he did so, not noticing that Irving's was empty. When the decanter was finished, he suggested another bottle, and once more Irving was given one glass by the butler while Tennyson finished the decanter. Next morning Irving found Tennyson standing solicitously by his bed, asking how he felt. 'Ah, but pray, Mr Irving, do you always drink two bottles of port after dinner?'[26]

Irving was quite alive to the value of a connection with a poet as famous as Tennyson, even if he believed the plays were indifferent. He was so impressed with him as a man that he copied his voice and intonation for his Shylock, a fact Tennyson apparently did not know; he disliked the characterization, thinking Irving 'made you pity Shylock too much'.[27]

Even before his disappointment over *Becket* Tennyson had begun another play, *The Falcon*, based on an incident in Boccaccio. This time the play was extremely short (*Queen Mary* was some seventeen times as long in the first version), with only four characters, so that it was too small to fill an entire evening. For such a slight play there was, for a change, almost too much plot: it turns upon a woman asking a poverty-stricken count to let her have his last precious possession, his falcon, to give to her little son, who is ill. The Count then tells her that the bird that had been served for her meal was the falcon, since there was no other food in the house. Tennyson realized that this was not material for Irving, and he gave the play instead to the Kendals at the St. James's Theatre, where it was produced in December 1879. Tennyson was concerned about the staging and attended a rehearsal, sitting in the stalls with a screen around him, a rug over his knees, and a hot-water bottle at his feet. *The Falcon* lasted for sixty-seven performances in spite of lukewarm notices and unenthusiastic audiences. It was unfortunately a play that aroused unintended hilarity, particularly because of the bird of the title, which was originally played by a fierce falcon that terrified the actors until it strangled itself with its chain on-stage. After that its role was taken by a stuffed understudy. Fanny Kemble told Tennyson that the play was 'an exquisite little poem in action', but her real opinion seems to have been much that of FitzGerald, who wrote to her making fun of 'two People reconciled to Love over a roasted Hawk; about as unsavoury a Bird to eat as an Owl, I believe. No doubt there was a chicken substitute at St. James'.' The story, he said, 'had been dramatised before: I wonder why'.[28]

But once more Tennyson had already begun another play, *The Cup*, which Irving took for the Lyceum in 1881. He and Ellen Terry played the leads, Synorix and Camma. Synorix contrives the death of Camma's husband in order to marry her; she tries to evade the marriage, then accedes. At the wedding she and Synorix pledge their love by drinking to each other, but the cup has been poisoned by Camma, and she dies with the name of her husband on her lips. Like *The Falcon*, it was a very short play, and it had to be coupled with a revival of the popular drama *The Corsican Brothers*. The somewhat earnest affirmation of the power of marital love caught the public fancy, and Tennyson had what might be called his first success, a run twice as long as that of *The Falcon*. There was a huge cast, with elaborate costumes and magnificent settings made historically accurate with the help of experts from the British Museum. Fanny Kemble loved the setting and thought there were 'some fine lines' in the text, but she said that 'Irving . . . walks as if he was drunk, & his pronunciation of common English words is really ludicrous. . . . Miss Terry looked *tumbled*.'[29]

Tennyson attended two performances of the play. On his first visit, a month or two after the play had opened, he was so nervous and irritable at dinner beforehand that he terrified the young Albert Baillie, a cousin of Eleanor's who was still at Eton and had been invited by Hallam to go with him and Tennyson. In his fluster he forgot his spectacles, so that he could hardly see the actors from his box near the stage. 'He drew the curtains of the box about him, fussing about not wanting to be seen, and then behaved in a way to draw the utmost attention to the box. He thundered applause when there was silence, and was silent when there was applause.' Half a century later Baillie remembered his schoolboy embarrassment: 'It was an awful evening.'[30]

After *The Cup* Tennyson wrote two other plays. The first of these, *The Foresters*, was a dramatization of the Robin Hood story, undertaken at the suggestion of Irving, who then declined to produce it; it did not reach the stage until the year of Tennyson's death, when it appeared in New York before coming to London. His last play, *The Promise of May*, his only prose work, was a melodramatic story of seduction, concealed identity, and remorse, played out in rural Lincolnshire and complete with pages of carefully phonetic dialect. He had difficulty in placing it with a manager, since neither Irving nor the Kendals would take it. Today it is almost unreadable, and it was a total failure on the stage at the Globe theatre, where it opened in November 1882. Tennyson for some time tried to defend the play, but he was bitterly disappointed, for it was at last clear that his theatrical career was finished without having reached either artistic or financial success. It had been a singularly brave attempt to storm a whole new area of writing when he was more than sixty-five, but to a modern reader only *Queen Mary* and *Becket* show intermittent flashes of his genius, and none of the plays has much sense of theatre. Many years before, he had written to an aspiring playwright who sent him a copy of his work: 'I cannot be considered as a good judge of how a play might tell in being acted.'[31] The disclaimer applied only too well to his own plays; more than seven years hard work had been largely wasted.

* * *

Tennyson's favourite brother, Charles Turner, had been ill more than a year before his death in April 1879; he went slowly downhill from general debility to seizures and paralysis in the last month or two of his life. During his illness his wife Louisa, Emily Tennyson's sister, whose hold on reality had been tenuous for years, fell into deep religious mania about her sinfulness, which she was convinced was the cause of her beloved Charles's decline. At last she was so deranged that she had to be confined on the Isle of Wight while Charles was treated in Cheltenham, where he died. Less than a month after his death, when all her reason for living was gone, Louisa Turner died and was buried in the same grave with her Charles.

It was, of course, a cruel blow to Tennyson. He suggested that his son Hallam and James Spedding should co-operate on an edition of Charles's sonnets, and to the volume he contributed an introductory poem of his own, one of two beautiful elegies he wrote for Charles:

I

Midnight—in no midsummer tune
The breakers lash the shores:
The cuckoo of a joyless June
Is calling out of doors:

And thou has vanished from thine own
To that which looks like rest,
True brother, only to be known
By those who love thee best.

II

Midnight—and joyless June gone by,
And from the deluged park
The cuckoo of a worse July
Is calling through the dark:

But thou art silent underground,
And o'er thee streams the rain,
True poet, surely to be found
When Truth is found again.

III

And, now to these unsummered skies
The summer bird is still,
Far off a phantom cuckoo cries
From out a phantom hill;

And through this midnight breaks the sun
Of sixty years away,
The light of days when life begun,
The days that seem today,

When all my griefs were shared with thee,
As all my hopes were thine—
As all thou wert was one with me,
May all thou art be mine!

For some time Tennyson had been almost abnormally interested in the spirit world that he half-believed lay around him, so that his conduct seemed distinctly peculiar to those who were unused to his obsession. He often played Dummy Whist by himself, and one young house-guest fled to her room in confusion when she realized that he was talking to Dummy as if to a real person. Whether he actually attended seances at this time is not certain, but he made enquiries to his friends about reliable mediums. After the death of his brother Charles he became very unwell and began to hear ghostly voices whispering in his ear.

It is not surprising that in the year of Charles's death, which was also that of Tennyson's own seventieth birthday, he should have been so occupied with spirits and thoughts of mortality. Emily had aged so much that Mountstuart Grant Duff found that she had 'turned into quite an old lady', and by now Tennyson had attained an age where he could expect his intimates to be falling away. That year Mrs Cameron died, as did G. H. Lewes, of whom Tennyson had seen a great deal with George Eliot. The following year, 1880, Tom Taylor and George Eliot died, and in 1881 and 1882 the deaths of Spedding, Carlyle, Dean Stanley, and W. G. Ward made it seem as if a whole generation of Tennyson's England was being wiped out. Not that he always felt his age: 'I am seventy,' he told Bram Stoker, 'and yet I don't feel old—I wonder how it is!' He liked to tell how he had remarked to an old friend, 'I don't feel the weight of age on my shoulders. I can run up-hill; I can waltz—but when I said this to Fanny Kemble she replied in a ghastly voice, "I hope I shall never see you do it!" '[32]

At seventy a man's thoughts may turn to the grave, but it is also an age beyond which he can expect to have outlived most hostile criticism, and so it was with Tennyson. The plays, to be sure, did not succeed in the next two or three years, and occasionally there was unfriendly carping at his having outgrown his simple origins, but in general his fame aroused much less envy and bitterness, and he was undergoing a process of beatification if not sanctification. What had once been chiefly admiration for his poetry and curiosity about his personality was now transmuted into the sort of love that most people feel for the aged, of which at least part is wonder at their having survived so long. Even his eccentricity had become a matter for indulgent amusement.

The young as well as the middle-aged and elderly felt affectionate admiration for him. In 1880 the undergraduates of Glasgow University asked permission to nominate him for the Lord Rectorship. Tennyson had by now conquered some of the reticence that had kept him from accepting a similar offer in 1868 from Edinburgh, and at first he consented, since he believed that the invitation had come from the entire undergraduate body; when he discovered that he was expected to stand as a Conservative candidate he declined the offer, unwilling to be involved in party matters and refusing to run the risk of defeat in the election.

Gladstone became Prime Minister again in 1880 and offered once more during what he called 'my last and I hope shortest tenure of office' to present Tennyson's name for a baronetcy. Once more Tennyson declined, saying that he still hoped the title might be offered to Hallam before his own death. In the light of subsequent events, there is good reason to think that Tennyson's refusal for himself stemmed from his belief, or possibly that of Emily, that anything short of a peerage would be insulting to poetry and inadequate recognition of his own achievement. Gladstone certainly considered offering a peerage, but he had heard from Tennyson for so long of his poverty that it was hard to believe that he could afford the additional expenditure a peerage would entail. The result was that the matter was dropped again.

The feeling by 1880 that the time for carping at Tennyson was past surely helped the reviews of *Ballads and Other Poems*, his first major book of non-dramatic poetry for eight years. In part, too, there was relief that the old poet was still capable of writing something besides the plays, even though the war songs and ballads of the new volume were very unlike the lyrics on which his fame had been grounded. 'The Revenge' and 'The Defence of Lucknow' were predestined to popularity by their celebration of stout English hearts, and such ballads as 'Rizpah', in praise of maternal love, showed Tennyson still trying to live up to the title of 'The People's Poet'. Largely they proved the durability of a technique that had been practised for decades, rather than demonstrating perennially youthful fire in an old poet.

His own awareness of the flagging of his inspiration is probably indicated by his reaction to 'A New Study of Tennyson', by John Churton Collins in the January 1880 issue of the *Cornhill*. Collins tried to show in the article that Tennyson's imagery was often an echo of his great predecessors, particularly the classical poets. In tracing some of the influences upon Tennyson's poems the article inadvertently places him firmly in the mainstream of world poetry, but Tennyson naturally took it as an attack on his originality. In his own copy of the article he wrote his furious comments, often noting 'nonsense' against Collins's frequently foolish remarks. At the end of the article Tennyson wrote with a pen that fairly spluttered: 'I will answer for it that no modern poet can write a single line but among the innumerable authors of this world you will find somewhere a striking parallelism. It is the unimaginative man who thinks everything borrowed.'[33] Such anger leaping out in naked pain at criticism was like that of Tennyson's youth; by 1880 he was almost out of practice. His fury lies behind the often-told story that at the end of his life he called Collins 'a Louse on the Locks of Literature'. The anecdote is probably apocryphal, but the tenor of it is accurate enough.

The difficulty with his liver and the constant voices in his head that he had been suffering from since Charles Turner's death were so bad by the spring of 1880 that his physician, Sir Andrew Clark, advised him to stop drinking port and to take a trip to rid himself of the voices.

With Hallam he set out for Venice, through Germany and Austria. When he heard of their departure, FitzGerald wrote enviously to Frederick Tennyson: 'he is apparently not so superannuated as you and I. But then he has a Son who acts as Courier for him.' Tennyson, however, was less fit than Fitz thought, for on the train he had to travel in a 'coupé lit' because of the 'little "commodité" at one end of the seat: it is revealed on raising a small cushion'.[34]

After a short stay in Munich they went to Tegernsee for two days with Lord Acton and his family. The damp of the mountains and the unfamiliar food made Tennyson unwell, so that he was a difficult guest. Acton, who disliked his 'want of reality, his habit of walking on clouds . . . the indefiniteness of his knowledge . . . the looseness of his political reasonings', found his ways 'a shell to crack' when Tennyson was pontificating to his host's family. 'I could not stay among the lofty entities that surround Tennyson even when he butters toast,' Acton confessed. But when the two men were alone, his dignity and his readiness to hear a joke, coupled with his generosity about Browning and Swinburne (but not Henry Taylor), at last won Acton over.[35]

For so many years Tennyson had looked forward to Venice that it was almost inevitable that he should be disappointed. Like other travellers, he found the side canals of the city noisome, and he complained that the pictures in the churches were so badly lit that he could not see them, which was not surprising for a man who boasted of being the second most short-sighted man in England.

From Venice they went through Verona to Sirmio, the little peninsula jutting into Lake Garda, and there, remembering two of Catullus's poems that he loved, he wrote of the tender sorrow that came to him in the midst of beauty as he thought of the death of Charles. Deliberately, almost as if flouting Collins, he echoed Catullus throughout. As it so often did, the elegiac mood drew from Tennyson one of his freshest poems, a farewell that only in its autumnal mood suggests that he was in this eighth decade:

> Row us out from Desenzano, to your Sirmione row!
> So they rowed, and there we landed—'O venusta Sirmio!'
> There to me through all the groves of olive in the summer glow,
> There beneath the Roman ruin where the purple flowers grow,
> Came that 'Ave atque Vale' of the Poet's hopeless woe,
> Tenderest of Roman poets nineteen-hundred years ago,
> 'Frater Ave atque Vale'—as we wandered to and fro

Gazing at the Lydian laughter of the Garda Lake below
Sweet Catullus's all-but-island, olive-silvery Sirmio!

('Frater Ave atque Vale')

When he returned to England the voices had been exorcized by the enchanted day at Sirmio and the composition of his farewell to Charles.

⁂

CHAPTER XXXII

DEATH OF OLD FRIENDS,
1880–1884

ONE of the most jarring anomalies of Tennyson's personality was the disjunction between his treatment of friendship in poetry and his actual relations with persons. The list of those whom he celebrated in verse is long, and the majority of the poems in which he did so are among his unqualified successes: Hallam of course, but also Spedding, Maurice, Simeon, FitzGerald, Brookfield, his brother Charles, Palgrave's brother Gifford, Kemble, Lear, his son Lionel, the Marquis of Dufferin and Ava, Jowett, and others. A poet who had written only the epistles or elegies inspired by these men would have an assured place in the history of English poetry on that basis alone. What is disheartening is to realize with how many of them Tennyson had misunderstandings or quarrels and with how many his intimacy lapsed. There can be few poets in the language who more consistently and successfully wrote about friendship, and there were probably equally few with whom it was more difficult to maintain untroubled relations over a long period. As a friend he was a born sprinter rather than a long-distance runner. It was not always easy, as we have seen, for those who met him for the first time to break through the crust of his shy truculence, but when they did there was often a honeymoon period of intimacy, usually falling into disrepair as the years passed.

One graceful tribute was written in thanks to Sir Edward Hamley, who came to Aldworth and helped Tennyson with the facts for 'The Charge of the Heavy Brigade at Balaclava'. The 'Prologue to General Hamley' is more memorable than the poem to which it forms a preface, although both bear witness to Tennyson's admiration of military heroism. It consists of one long sentence (a favourite device of Tennyson's in his epistolary poems) of thirty-two lines, adroitly mingling compliments to Hamley with the memory of the autumn day they spent together at Aldworth:

> Our birches yellowing and from each
> The light leaf falling fast,

XXIII. Tennyson, 1888, by Barraud.

XXIV. Tennyson, 1890, red chalk sketch by G. F. Watts.

While squirrels from our fiery beech
  Were bearing off the mast,
You came, and looked and loved the view
  Long-known and loved by me,
Green Sussex fading into blue
  With one gray glimpse of sea;
And, gazing from this height alone,
  We spoke of what had been
Most marvellous in the wars your own
  Crimean eyes had seen;
And now—like old-world inns that take
  Some warrior for a sign
That therewithin a guest may make
  True cheer with honest wine—
Because you heard the lines I read
  Nor uttered word of blame,
I dare without your leave to head
  These rhymings with your name,
Who know you but as one of those
  I fain would meet again . . .

It is perhaps not irrelevant that in spite of the nicely judged tone of the poem, Hamley was not an intimate nor did he ever become so.

Part of Tennyson's increasing difficulty as a friend was consequent upon the bad health from which he suffered during the last dozen years of his life. He had never had robust health, but his physical and mental resistance to disease was sapped by the advance of old age. Gout constantly racked him, and he was forever giving up port on the advice of his doctors in the hope of defeating the pain, but the numbers of times over the years that guests mentioned his most recent resolves to supplant it with whisky or brandy suggest that he was no more successful in this than he had been at stopping smoking. For years it had been evident that his ease of manner was in direct ratio to the amount of port he had consumed, and when he was denied its comfort he could be even more brusque and tetchy than usual, frequently ignoring the little gestures upon which friendship survives. The end of his life was a sad parade of friendships ended as often by his negligence over small details as by death.

Froude, for example, was distressed to hear that Tennyson, after reading his biography of Carlyle, had said that he had sold his master for thirty pieces of silver. He wrote an aggrieved letter to Hallam

Tennyson explaining that Carlyle had left to him the decision about what to publish and asking that Hallam tell his father the facts of the case. Rather than receiving an apology or explanation from Tennyson, as he clearly expected, Froude got a letter from Hallam by return of post: 'My father *never* said such a thing about you . . . nor could he have dreamt of it. . . . your informant must have been unaware of the very high regard in which he holds you.'[1] Froude could not have complained of the denial, but he had reasonably anticipated something more personal from the man to who he had given so much help over *Queen Mary* and 'The Revenge', and there was a subsequent cooling in their relations.

It had been nearly twenty years since Patmore and Tennyson had stopped seeing each other; they were both difficult and morbidly sensitive, but the difference was that Patmore was wounded by the lapse in their friendship, while Tennyson apparently thought little of it. In 1881 Patmore wrote at last, saying that he had heard that Tennyson believed that he had for a long time 'ceased to desire the continuance of our former friendly intercourse'. He explained that in 1862, when his first wife was dying, he had received a well-meant letter from Emily Tennyson saying that Alfred had presented a memorial to the Committee of the Literary Fund in support of a request for a grant of money for Patmore. Although he realized that it had been done in kindness, Patmore was insulted, since he had no need of the money, but he had finally swallowed his unreasonable pride and written to the Tennysons, thanking them and inviting Tennyson for an evening at his cottage. As he explained in 1881, he had never received an answer to his invitation, nor had Tennyson written in sympathy when his wife died, and therefore he had reluctantly decided to stop seeing him. Two decades later he realized that he had been stiff-necked and indicated that he would like to resume the intimacy. It took a great deal of unwonted humility for Patmore to write the letter explaining what had happened, but all that he got was a brief reply:

My dear Patmore,

As I am perfectly certain that I never received any such letter as you allude to, I can only regret that this long estrangement has taken place—and pray you to believe that I am

Always yours,
A. Tennyson.

In spite of the coolness of the letter, Patmore made one more gesture the following month, when he sent a copy of his poems to Tennyson and received in return:

My dear Patmore,
Many thanks for your 'Unknown Eros', which reached me this morning.
Yours very truly,
A. Tennyson.

It is not surprising that Patmore made no more overtures and never saw Tennyson again.[2]

Matthew Arnold was another poet who was at least as prickly as Patmore and even more adept at sniffing out a patronizing tone. Although he and Tennyson met occasionally at the dinner tables of their common friends, they never liked each other, and on one occasion Tennyson, when asked if he wanted Arnold as a fellow-guest, said he 'didn't much like dining with Gods!' The feeling was mutual, as is indicated in Arnold's negligent reply to an invitation from the Tennysons to come in after dinner: 'We are dining far away in South Kensington on the 16th, and your hours are rather early: but we shall try to reach you before the fatal hour strikes.' When Arnold and Hallam Tennyson found themselves together at table another time, Arnold was as self-important as Tennyson at his worst, leaning over to say pompously, 'I have come to the conclusion that your Father's fame is established.' After Arnold had turned to writing criticism he called at Aldworth, and when he was gone, Tennyson said to Hallam, 'Tell Matt not to write any more of those prose things but to give us something like his Forsaken Mermaid & Gipsy Scholar.' Maliciously amused at both Tennyson's condescension and his mistake over the titles of the poems, Arnold 'told it gleefully in London'. In his biography of his father, Hallam Tennyson carefully corrected the titles of both poems and said that Arnold told the story 'about himself'.[3] The explanation seems disingenuous.

In March 1881 Tennyson lost one of his oldest friends, James Spedding, who died some days after being run over by a cab. There had never been a rupture in their friendship, but they had seen little of each other since 1864, when Spedding gave up his rooms in Lincoln's Inn Fields and went to Westbourne Terrace, characteristically making the move in order to provide a home for his nieces. Tennyson, who had been an almost-too-constant guest in Spedding's other quarters for years, never went so far afield as Westbourne Terrace to seek out his old friend. In 1870, thanking Spedding for his comments on *The Holy Grail and Other Poems*, he asked, 'Where is Westbourne Terrace? If I had ever clearly made out I should assuredly have called.' He added that he had often passed the old rooms 'with a groan, thinking of you as no longer the comeatable, runuptoable, smokeablewith J.S. of old, but as a family man, far in the west, sitting cigarless among many nieces, clean and forlorn'. They met occasionally at dinner parties, and Spedding was several times invited to Farringford, but Tennyson was too indolent to look him up in London. During those years Spedding had kept all his affection for Tennyson. He lay in the hospital for several days before his death, clear-headed in spite of his pain, typically spending 'more strength in exculpating the poor driver than on any personal matter'. At the time Tennyson was living in London and called once at St. George's Hospital, which was only a short distance from their house in Belgravia, but he was not allowed to see Spedding on that occasion, and he never tried again to see him before his death, although Hallam did go to see him. When Spedding heard that another visitor had been turned away, he caught the doctor's arm and asked anxiously, 'Was it Mr. Tennyson?'[4] Nor, apparently, did Tennyson go to Spedding's funeral, although that would have been difficult, since it was held in the little church across the fields from Mirehouse. Probably more than the distance, however, lay behind his failure to attend, for he hated funerals and seldom went to those of his friends, or even to those of the three brothers and two sisters who died before he did.

Some feeling that Tennyson was no longer much interested in those who had known him longest, perhaps that he had not done enough for Spedding, caused FitzGerald's reaction the following year when he came to London during the period that the Tennysons were living once more in Belgravia: 'Tennyson was in London, I heard: but in some grand Locality of Eaton Square; so I did not venture down to him. But a day scarcely passes without my thinking of him, in one way or other.'[5]

Fitz's last letter to Tennyson was written in April 1883, and like the others of the previous few years it was directed to Hallam, since he knew that Tennyson would never answer. Emily, of course, was too feeble to write, but a reply from her would in any case have been a mere matter of duty, undertaken in spite of her dislike of him, for she knew that all during her marriage Fitz had thought old Alfred would have done better with someone more critical and less ambitious. After his death she looked at an article about FitzGerald and told Hallam:

'Pleasant enough but somehow I have not much taste for such reading as you know. Fitz-Gerald is Fitz-Gerald to me after all.'[6]

Fitz's affection for Alfred had to be expressed jokingly and tentatively, but it shines forth transparently in his last letter: 'You see that bronchitis, ever flourishing his dart over me, fails to make me graver, that is at least while referring to my dear old comrade, whom I should call "master", and with whom (in spite, perhaps *because*, of his being rather a "gloomy" soul sometimes, as Carlyle wrote to Emerson) I always did talk more nonsense than to anyone, I believe.' But there was to be no more nonsense: two months later FitzGerald was dead.

What he could not have known was that Tennyson, for all his apparent neglect, had always kept a corner of his heart for him. At the very time that Fitz was writing the letter, certain that his old friend seldom thought of him, Tennyson had dug out 'Tiresias', one of his 'dead dogs', written at the time of Hallam's death with all 'the old champagne flavour' that Fitz loved, and was rewriting it for publication with a prologue 'To E. FitzGerald'. The two poems, so contradictory in style because of the half-century intervening between them, are worthy of that most faithful but most contradictory of Tennyson's friends. Christopher Ricks has written of the dedicatory poem that it 'comprises a single sentence (fifty-six lines) of such unhurried calm, such imaginative yet unostentatious transitions, such dignity, such affectionate tact, as takes the reader's breath away, while leaving the poet amusedly unflustered. His poem breathes friendship.'[7] The first section concludes with birthday wishes to 'My Fitz', and the accompanying gift of 'Tiresias',

> welcome, as I know
> Less for its own than for the sake
> Of one recalling gracious times,
> When, in our younger London days,
> You found some merit in my rhymes,
> And I more pleasure in your praise.

The sting in the tail was intentional, and Anne Thackeray Ritchie said that Tennyson had kept the poem back, 'knowing how critical EFG was, & afraid he might not like the end'.[8] When the news came of Fitz's death, he added an epilogue, praying that

> My close of earth's experience
> May prove as peaceful as his own.

As Palgrave wrote, 'The central poem is in his finest early style; the two other poems seemed to me to be also perfect masterpieces.'[9]

Yet, for all the devotion that went into this splendid tribute, Tennyson seems never to have understood that he might have hurt his old friend, or that Fitz might have any reason to feel neglected. After his death Tennyson told Herbert Warren that Fitz 'never really read any of my poems after he had ceased to see me'.[10] It is one of the most puzzling aspects of Tennyson that he could have been so sensitive about his affection for others and so crashingly insensitive to their feelings and needs.

Intimacy may not be the exact term to describe Tennyson's relationship to the Queen, but friendship of a kind grew up between them, a wholly successful one that never faltered, as so many others had done, because its limits had been set from the beginning. Since 1873, when he had walked around Frogmore with her, he had loyally if not brilliantly fulfilled his duties as Poet Laureate, writing among others a poem of welcome to the Russian Duchess of Edinburgh, another to the memory of Princess Alice, and a greeting to the Princess Frederica on her marriage; they scarcely swell his poetic reputation, but they were just what the Queen wanted: respectful, sentimental, and not too taxing to the intellect.

In March 1883 Tennyson wrote two letters of sympathy, on the occasion of a bad fall when the Queen hurt herself and on the death of her beloved and bad-tempered servant John Brown. The Queen was touched by the expressions of concern, and in May Lady Horatia Stopford wrote to ask whether there was a chance of persuading him to come to Osborne before the end of the month, when the Court was leaving for Balmoral, so that he might 'see the Queen quite quietly, and alone. . . . The Queen says he should not have *any* thing to do with the *Court*, which H.M. knows is his own great objection to coming here, and that he might be allowed to drop all formalities &c.'[11] Tennyson, however, was too unwell to risk a long drive to Osborne in the teeth of the east wind, and the visit had to be postponed until summer, when the invitation was renewed.

On 7 August the Queen saw 'the great Poet *Tennyson* in dearest Albert's room for nearly an hour;—and most interesting it was. He is grown very old—his eyesight much impaired *and he is very shaky on his legs.*' She put him at ease at once by asking him to sit beside her: 'You and I, Mr. Tennyson, are old people, and like to sit down.' Curiously, the role of comforter seems to have been hers on this occasion. When he talked despairingly of the irreligion and socialism pervading modern life, she said in response:

> Oh yet we trust that somehow good
> Will be the final goal of ill . . .

'I thought that very pretty', said Tennyson, 'to quote my own words in answer to me.' When they spoke of a future state and wondered whether they would recognize their old friends when they met there, Tennyson told her in one of his engagingly simple parallels that he had once been bathing and had taken his dog with him, and that when he came naked from the water his dog did not know him; this suggested to him that recognition might be difficult if not impossible in heaven. Once more she flattered him by quoting from *In Memoriam*:

> Eternal form shall still divide
> The eternal soul from all beside;
> And I shall know him when we meet.

They parted with inchoate feelings of deep gratitude to each other, and over the next month they exchanged a flurry of letters, the Queen for the first time writing in the first person. At her request Tennyson composed a couplet of suitably complimentary aspiration to be inscribed on the base of the bronze statue of Brown that she had commissioned.[12]

There is not the slightest written evidence to suggest that the Queen mentioned any honour to be bestowed on Tennyson himself, but the warmth they felt must have brought the matter to her mind and perhaps to his. Certainly, she could scarcely have been better disposed to him, a fact they both recognized.

On 8 September 1883 Tennyson and Hallam joined Gladstone, Mrs Gladstone, their daughter Mary, and their son Herbert at Chester, where they took the train to Barrow to board the *Pembroke Castle* on a fortnight's cruise. As the tug pulled out for the yacht thousands of people lining the shore cheered for the Prime Minister and the Poet Laureate.

The magnificently appointed new ship of 4,000 tons was the property of Sir Donald Currie, an immensely rich shipping magnate and MP for Perthshire, who had invited a party for the trial cruise of the ship up the west coast of Scotland and then to Norway; it was essentially a gathering of Liberals that included Algernon West, Sir Arthur Gordon, Governor of New Zealand, and Sir William Harcourt, who came with them to Tobermory, where his place was taken by Tennyson's physician, Sir Andrew Clark, with his wife and daughter. One morning after breakfast Harcourt met Tennyson on deck having a smoke and asked, 'The earliest pipe of half-awakened bards?' Tennyson was not amused and for some years insisted that 'Harcourt has spoilt a beautiful line by making a burlesque of it'.[13]

At Kirkwall Gladstone and Tennyson were given the freedom of the borough. Since Tennyson refused to speak, Gladstone accepted for them both in a graceful speech paying tribute to the immortality of poetry as opposed to the fleeting fame of public life. During the voyage, while the younger guests walked the decks, Gladstone and Tennyson sat and talked, touching on the noble intellect of Arthur Hallam and how great a loss he had been to Dante studies, on Scott's novels, even on the translation of Homer, a dangerous topic for two men who had already fallen out over the subject. But by now they had learned to avoid too much disputation, and 'they took good care to keep off the quagmire of politics'.

After putting in at Christiansand, they extended the cruise to Denmark, at the suggestion of Tennyson, who wanted to see Elsinore and Copenhagen. Its position in low land made Elsinore a disappointment, but they spent two days in the capital, walking through the picturesque city. The party on the ship was invited to a dinner for eighty at the King's country palace; the Gladstones, Gordon, Currie, and Hallam Tennyson accepted but Tennyson did not go. Staying in the palace were the Princess of Wales, the Tsar and Tsarina, the King and Queen of Greece, assorted grand dukes and duchesses, princes and princesses, and countless counts.

The following day the entire flock of royalties and nobility came aboard the *Pembroke Castle* for luncheon served at three large tables at which Gladstone, Currie, and Tennyson presided. On Tennyson's right was the Queen of Greece, on his left the Princess Mary of Hanover. Gladstone at the centre table proposed the health of the King of Denmark, the Tsar proposed Queen Victoria's, the King of Denmark proposed the Gladstones', and the Queen of Denmark toasted Tennyson. It was a heady occasion, and it is not surprising that after all the toasts Tennyson stumbled into a breach of etiquette. The Princess of Wales asked him to read aloud after luncheon in a small smoking-room, where he sat wedged between her and the Tsarina. In the excitement of the occasion he mistook the Tsarina for a maid of honour, and as he read 'The Bugle Song' and 'The Grandmother' he absent-mindedly beat time on her. When he was finished, she complimented him on his performance of the poems, and unable to distinguish her features through the reading-spectacles he was still wearing, he patted her on the back and said, 'My dear girl, that's very kind of you, very kind.' She was amused, but the Tsar was taken aback. The court fool, holder of a post that Tennyson had said he was surprised to find still existed in Denmark, looked in the window of the cabin and said, 'That man ought to be taught Court manners.'[14] When the royal party had gone, the *Pembroke Castle* steamed off for England amidst cheers and the boom of cannons.

One morning when Gladstone had left the saloon after breakfast, Tennyson sat with Sir Arthur Gordon and worked the conversation around to the four times that he had declined a baronetcy, adding that he now thought he had made a mistake and that if Gladstone were to renew his offer, he would gladly accept. Naturally, Gordon acted on the broad hint, and Gladstone said he would happily offer the title again. According to Gordon, 'I then asked him whether he did not think he might go a step further and offer Mr. Tennyson a peerage. His first answer was characteristic: "Ah! Could I be an accessory to introducing *that hat* into the House of Lords?" He thought the matter over, and the following day told me that he had made up his mind to make the offer, subject to certain information which he required.'[*15]

Gladstone, who said that the idea of a peerage had been in his mind from the beginning, then cornered Hallam on deck: '"Preparatory to making this offer I must ask you two questions, one, whether you think that your father would occasionally vote, if an urgent question of state-policy required it." I answered that he was an old man but that I felt sure that he would vote whenever he felt it to be his duty. The second question Mr Gladstone put was "How much income has your father a year, & how much are you likely to have?" . . . He was particularly anxious to know whether Lionel was settled in life. He then said that he thought that the income was large enough to warrant the offer of a peerage.'[16] It was naturally hard for Gladstone to realize that a man still receiving a Civil List pension could afford to hold a title.

* Characteristically, Lord Houghton told Browning that he had first suggested Tennyson's peerage to Gladstone, who replied, 'What! a man so independent that he refuses to dine with you at half-past seven, because he usually dines at seven—*he* accept a peerage!' (Domett, p. 305.) The story may be taken with a grain of salt, since Houghton liked to boast of his beneficent exertions on behalf of his friends and since veracity stood low in the calendar of his virtues.

For two or three days Tennyson refused to allow Gladstone to prepare the recommendation, taking so long, apparently, to make up his mind that even Hallam did not realize that the whole question of a title had been reopened at his father's wishes. After endless mulling Tennyson at last agreed, saying that he was accepting for the greater honour of literature: 'By Gladstone's advice I have consented to take the peerage, but for my own part I shall regret my simple name all my life.' It was a further instance of the repetitive denials of any pleasure for himself in accepting honours: whether it was the Civil List pension, the Laureateship, an honorary degree, or the peerage, he felt compelled to say that he was accepting it only on the urging of others, against his own wishes. The evidence does not support his assertions.

On 20 September Gladstone forwarded his advice to the Queen to offer a barony to Tennyson, reminding her that twenty years before a peerage had been offered to the historian Grote (who had refused it), so that there was adequate precedent for a literary peerage. He also reminded her of the offers of a baronetcy to Tennyson: 'Mr. Gladstone has reason to believe that Mr. Tennyson's fortune has since that time improved.' Two days later Gladstone received a blast from the Queen, who was furious that her Prime Minister had gone ashore in a foreign country without her permission; she was doubly angered, no doubt, because the guilty Prime Minister was Gladstone. In a pusillanimous answer that is understandable, in view of her temper, Gladstone tried to avert the storm by pointing out that the idea of the Danish visit had been Tennyson's in the first place. Since no matters of state had been discussed in Denmark, she ultimately forgave Gladstone and did not hold the Prime Minister's indiscretions against Tennyson. The Duke of Argyll was amused at the whole imbroglio and teased Tennyson about being 'the *culprit* who brought on a great European Complication'.[17]

The pattern of years was hard to break, and Gladstone had been quite right in worrying about the financial aspects of the title, for immediately after Tennyson had told him to go ahead with the letter to the Queen, he began worrying about how much it would all cost him. 'My sisters say I shall have to pay more for my wine,' he said. Finally he refused to proceed unless Gladstone arranged to have the fees involved in the assumption of the peerage all remitted. 'I am sorry, especially considering *our* time of life, that there should be any delay,' wrote Gladstone reprovingly, for he was beginning to weary of the subject, but he promised that the 'Peerage will be accompanied with that remission of Fees' customary for military peerages and 'in a few civil instances'.[18] It was a good example of how Tennyson became so obsessive about approaching penury that others finally agreed to pay his share.

Because Gladstone was afraid that the press would sniff out jobbery if the announcement of the peerage came immediately after he and Tennyson had returned from a cruise together, he asked that it be kept secret for three months. Inevitably there were leaks, the whole matter was public knowledge within a few weeks (see Plate XXII), and the Tennysons were hard put to avoid confirming the rumours without actually lying. In the mean time there was the problem of what title Tennyson should take. His first choice, made within a few days, shows how little he had forgotten all the injuries of his youth, for he wanted to take the title that had eluded his uncle, by becoming Lord d'Eyncourt. To Sir Arthur Gordon it seemed 'an incredible folly. Who would talk of Lord D'Eyncourt's poems?' Tennyson's next choice was an even more direct assault on his uncle's ambitions: Baron Tennyson d'Eyncourt. 'The younger branch of my father's family, who succeeded to the . . . fortune . . . say they are descended from the old branch of the D'Eyncourts who came in with William & from the later creation of the same name in tempore Charles II—if they, then I.'[19] What had once appeared to Tennyson unbelievable *folie de grandeur* in his uncle now seemed a reasonable view for himself. More than ever he seemed the spiritual heir of Charles Tennyson d'Eyncourt. There is no record of what title Emily preferred, but it seems safe to assume that she was also in favour of Tennyson d'Eyncourt, since both Lionel and Hallam also thought it the best choice.

Gladstone, who recognized how closely revenge and emulation were associated in Tennyson's motivation, tried to discourage him: 'however reprehensible the act of disinheriting may have been, I suspect you will have difficulty in taking the name appropriated (if so it be) by the younger branch'. But Tennyson was determined, and he wrote to Admiral Tennyson d'Eyncourt, his senior cousin, to ask if there would be any objection to his using the name as a title. His cousin sent 'a handsome letter' of permission and the matter was turned over to the College of Arms, but there it was decided that 'The Poet Laureate is descended from Alice Deincourt who married William Lord Lovell, but he is not the representative or co-representative nor is he entitled to quarter the Arms of Deincourt'.[20] Rouge Dragon told Lionel that neither his father nor any of his mother's family was entitled to arms. There was no further appeal, and reluctantly Tennyson gave up his wish to accomplish what his uncle had achingly striven for all those years. By the end of 1883 he had decided on Baron Tennyson of Aldworth and Freshwater. Since the title might be said to be a manifestation of the 'Aldworth' side of his life, the order of places was fitting.

When the announcement of the peerage was made official, Tennyson was subjected to a renewal of hostile criticism from one section of the press, who thought that there was something inherently wrong about 'The People's Poet' taking a title. There were a few ill-natured parodies of his poetry, particularly when several journals solemnly published the elaborate and somewhat fanciful pedigree that had been made up years before at the request of Charles Tennyson d'Eyncourt, but the hostility soon died down in the face of Tennyson's innate dignity about the title and his manifest belief that he was taking it as much for literature and for the good of the arts as for himself. He had never been a democrat at heart, and without striving for false modesty he said that 'he deemed the House of Lords a much finer set of men than the Commons:—the Lords were distinguished men, or the sons of such, and "good old blood" . . . he believed in heredity'.[21] It was a statement that would have not have been incongruous in the mouth of his uncle, but it was redeemed by his sincerity. As Hallam had indicated to Gladstone, he was too old to take an active part in the debates of the House of Lords, but he was willing to do what he could.

At seventy-five his skin was still thin, however, and he felt the barbs acutely. His awareness of how easily others believed the worst of successful men was obvious some years later when T. W. Reid was interviewing him for a biography of Milnes. He told Tennyson the story of the day that Milnes took his title and met a friend in Piccadilly, who asked him how it felt to be a lord. With twinkling eyes the newly-created Houghton said, 'I never knew until to-day how immeasurable is the gulf which divides the humblest member of the peerage from the most exalted commoner in England.' Still sore with the memory of how he had been accused of snobbery at the time of his own new title, Tennyson said anxiously to Reid, 'If you tell that story, every fool will think that Milnes meant it.'[22]

Among poets there was almost no jealousy, for however much they might jib at Tennyson they recognized his supremacy. Lewis Morris, a second-rate poet who on this occasion engagingly admitted his limitations, wrote to Tennyson congratulating him in words that generally represented the feelings of his fellows: 'in the opinion of a subaltern in the army of which you are Commander in Chief, the Queen has done the most graceful thing in offering you a Peerage and you an eminently sensible and graceful thing in accepting it'.[23]

Most of Tennyson's friends were genuinely delighted, and only Jowett, who had often felt that Tennyson was too anxious for praise and recognition, tactlessly included in his congratulations a detailed list of all those who would be displeased with the news. 'O criky Jamkins!!!!!' wrote Lear to Hallam, 'your Father is going to be made a Peer . . . I for one am delighted; the Author of In Memoriam might be made 10 Peers at once so far as merit quâ Poet goes.' Less reverently but with equal delight he told Chichester Fortescue, who had recently become Lord Carlingford, that he looked forward to Tennyson's being a peer so that he could find out 'whether Sovereigns, Princes, Dukes and even Peers generally—cut their own toe-nails'. Frederick Pollock suggested that in his new arms Tennyson should have as supporters 'two Muses, all proper, for he has certainly never written a line he could have wished to blot for its impropriety'.[24]

The only serious reservation about Tennyson's elevation came from his brother Frederick, who wrote uncharitably to his own son: 'As to the Peerage which is the crowning honour—at least so considered—of a literary life, I do not believe that the desire to obtain it originated in your uncle's mind. Mrs—now Baroness T. of Aldworth & Freshwater—has not been laid upon her back most of her life without nursing ambitious dreams, now realised. She, of course, will plead the advantages accruing to her children, & theirs. Many years ago the Queen—whose heart he had gained by the poetical incense offered to the late Prince Consort—would have done the same—but he did not then seem to regard it in any other light than as an empty adjunct to an already honoured & illustrious name. But doubtless he has been drawn into the wake of his wife's worldliness.'[25] Frederick's dislike of his sister-in-law had become almost rancour, and no doubt it was fanned by a feeling that history was repeating itself as the younger son took precedence over the elder, but all the same it is hard to deny a grain of truth in his overstatement of the case. In reality, Emily Tennyson had few aspirations for herself. It is not surprising that the frustrations of her younger years should have been resolved into ambition, but any wishes for personal achievement had long since been sublimated into the advancement of her husband and sons.

On 11 March 1884 Tennyson took his seat in the House of Lords, introduced by Argyll and Lord Kenmare, who was standing in for Houghton, then absent in Greece. Gladstone need not have worried about his appearance, for years of wearing his shabby old cloak had given Tennyson an unusual assurance in moving when encumbered by yards of heavy cloth, and he presented a grandly poised figure in the robes that he had borrowed from Lord Coleridge for the occasion. He took his seat on the cross benches, explaining that 'he could not pledge himself to party thinking', wanting to be 'free to vote for that which to himself seemed best for the Empire'.[26]

After the presentation there was a luncheon party in the Deanery at Westminster, and the Bradleys' butler was so overcome by the presence of peers and poets that he inadvertently called Browning 'my lord'. Good-naturedly, Browning replied, 'Don't "my lord" *me*, my good man, I pray.'[27] On his return to Farringford, Tennyson went to call on his old friend Mary Brotherton, who was just finishing tea. He put the tea-cosy on his head in place of a cocked hat and re-enacted the entire ceremony for her.

It was natural to expect that Gladstone's part in conferring the peerage would reconcile Tennyson totally to him, but it was not to be so. His refusal to take a party seat in the House was his notice that he was not to be taken for Gladstone's man, and to make his independence perfectly clear he told a large number of different persons that he loved Gladstone but hated his politics. It was a statement that seemed to indicate a clearly defined distinction in his thinking, but in reality it was often blurred.

Tennyson was too old to undertake any real political activity in the House of Lords, even if he had been so inclined. He attended only a few times and never spoke. Reluctantly he voted for Gladstone's bill for the extension of the franchise in July 1884, after exacting from him a solemn pledge that it would not become law before redistribution took place. Later that year, when he thought that Gladstone was heading into open conflict with Salisbury and the Conservatives, he sent him the admonitory lines called 'Compromise':

> Steersman, be not precipitate in thine act
>   Of steering, for the river here, my friend,
>   Parts in two channels, moving to one end—
> This goes straight forward to the cataract:
>   That streams about the bend;
> But though the cataract seem the nearer way,

Whate'er the crowd on either bank may say,
Take thou the 'bend', 'twill save thee many a day.

When Lord Acton read the poem he wrote to Gladstone's daughter: 'Tennyson's really profound animosity against the P.M. has long been known to people in his confidence, and has come out at last. It was one reason, but not the only one, of my dislike to his peerage.'[28] If he could say this so openly to Mary Gladstone, Acton was probably aware that the whole of her family knew of Tennyson's feelings and reciprocated them.

During 1884 and 1885 Tennyson wrote two other pieces of rhymed advice to Gladstone, and an exhortation to maintain the strength of the Navy, but this brief gust of political verse was his last real attempt to get involved with the government of the country. With unfailing politeness Gladstone would acknowledge his advice and thank him, but there is no indication that he was in any way influenced in his decisions. It is worth pondering what Tennyson would have said if Gladstone had presumed to give him equally explicit directions about his poetry. The blandness of Gladstone's replies indicates that he no longer took Tennyson seriously except as a poet, and this was probably a further irritation to Tennyson.

The difference in their thinking had been made clear only a month after the two men returned on the *Pembroke Castle*, and not surprisingly it was connected with Arthur Hallam. In 1883 Charles Milnes Gaskell printed privately the letters of his father, which included letters from Hallam to the elder Gaskell. Tennyson was so sensitive on the subject of Hallam that his family thought they had to conceal Gaskell's book from him when it arrived. He complained to Gladstone that he had not received a copy, and Gladstone assured him that no offence had been meant, not knowing that Emily and Hallam Tennyson believed that the letters would disturb the 'public ideal' of Arthur Hallam: 'For the same reason but on infinitely stronger grounds, we have withheld the book from my Ally,' wrote Emily. 'One has to be specially careful with so very sensitive a nature, as you know.'[29]

In November 1883 Gladstone wrote to Tennyson to say that he still possessed the letters Hallam had written to him, and he mentioned the possibility of their publication by Knowles in the *Nineteenth Century*, to supplement what Milnes Gaskell had published. Over the years Tennyson had gradually come to assume that the author of *In Memoriam* was the true guardian of the memory of Hallam, and that permission to publish Hallam's letters belonged to himself, not to Hallam's sister or to Gladstone, no matter to whom the letters had been written. 'Don't let Knowles print A.H.H. Letters—at least let them be first submitted to me,' he told Gladstone. 'I think that I of all living men should be allowed a voice in this matter. K. is a very clever man & a kindly, but he is . . . Knowles of the 19th Century & would set the fame of his Review above the fame of your old friend & mine, at least I fear so.'[30] His wish was simply to protect Hallam's memory, but the bland assumption that any decision in the matter should be made by himself was breathtaking; it is a tribute to Gladstone's equanimity that he did not allow himself to lose his temper.

In 1885 Tennyson became innocently involved in what must have seemed to Gladstone an intolerably impudent plan to get him to retire from politics. On this occasion the difficulty originated with the Queen, who disliked Gladstone and hoped that he would leave public life after his government's defeat in June 1885. The evidence of what happened is slight, but it is clear that the Queen thought Tennyson could persuade Gladstone to retire, and on 12 July 1885 she wrote to him with the suggestion that he approach Gladstone: 'Ever since he took office in 80 he said he wished soon to retire and quite lately repeated & now the contrary.' Unusually, Tennyson took more than a week to answer the Queen, then told her that 'Mr Gladstone differs in so many of his political views from myself that whatever I might say on these subjects would have I fear little or no weight with him'. It was an exceedingly uncomfortable position for Tennyson, with the option either of refusing his Sovereign's request or of making a thoroughly presumptuous suggestion to Gladstone. Understandably, he delayed nearly three weeks until he was reminded by a peremptory postscript from the Queen: 'Have you heard from Mr Gladstone?' There was no help for it now, and he had to beard Gladstone to ask him either to retire or at least to cause the Queen no more trouble. On 9 August 1885 he reported back to the Queen: 'Mr Gladstone goes no further than to say he will not if he can help it.'[31] Apparently no record remains of the interview between Tennyson and Gladstone, but it can hardly have been pleasant or even apt to improve their always awkward relations. Subsequent events prove that Gladstone generously tried not to hold the affair against Tennyson, but it would have taken the patience of a saint not to feel some resentment against the Queen and against her Poet Laureate who had acted as her emissary.

In a way that once would have been unimportant to him, Tennyson's new title was useful, for it was good advertising for his poetry. His unsuccessful experiments with drama and his lessening output of non-dramatic poetry meant that sales had been falling off for some time. His shrewd, perhaps hard, business terms had made both Strahan and King lose money on publishing his works, and when Charles Kegan Paul, his sons' old teacher, took over the firm of Henry S. King, he renegotiated Tennyson's contract, dropping the guaranteed annual payment from £5,000 to £2,500. At the end of 1883 it was time for a new contract, and Kegan Paul's dry comment on the negotiations suggests that his offer was low: Tennyson, he said, was 'a thorough man of business, and our final parting at the end of one of our periods of agreement was that we, as publishers, and he, as author, took a different view of his pecuniary value'.[32] There was, however, one publisher who had been diffidently waiting for years to secure Tennyson: Alexander Macmillan. On 15 January 1884 Tennyson signed a ten-year contract with him that was to outlast his life; it gave him a third of the advertised price of all books sold, with a minimum guarantee of £1,500 annually, which was to be 'absolute payment in case the royalty any year did not reach that amount'.[33] Tennyson's relations with Macmillan remained excellent until his death; the publisher lost no money and, though his income dropped considerably for several years, Tennyson was content to have a publisher he could trust and also respect intellectually.

The falling off of the sheer quantity of his poetry was natural for a man in his seventies, and it is reflected in the conversations that his friends recorded during the last decade of his life. Tennyson talked about the novels he incessantly read, and for the first time he spoke a great deal more about the poetry of other men than he did of his own. The diaries of William Allingham and Alfred Domett, for example, are full of the illuminating asides he made on Milton, Keats, Wordsworth, Byron, Browning, Catullus, and Dante, glancing remarks that add up to a history of his poetic taste since boyhood. Tennyson's was not a primarily critical intelligence, but he brought to the reading of other men's poetry the intimate knowledge of what was involved in its composition, as well as a robust common sense that he did not always apply to other topics of his conversation. But his attention to the poetry of others was sufficient indication that he was thinking less about his own because he was composing less. Once, as he admitted, the praise he needed so badly had slid off him unnoticed while adverse criticism remained to fester; now, for the first time, he seemed able to express gratitude for admiration of his works. It was sad that only the diminution of his powers caused the change.

Hovering loyally in the background to support him was his son Hallam, listening patiently to his complaints, walking with him, writing his letters, acting as courier and companion. Guiltily both Alfred and Emily had recognized that they were absorbing all his energies and that each year he remained at home made it more difficult for him to settle into a career of his own. Emily made a half-hearted attempt in 1881 to get him placed as secretary to Gladstone, but nothing came of it. According to Edward Lear, the deep dislike of Gladstone's politics by both Emily and Alfred made it impossible for Hallam to go into the house, 'as he could not vote against G if by Gs interest he got into any borough'.[34] Now his father's peerage meant that he no longer needed to think of a career, since he would in time simply inherit the title and an adequate income from the capital that Tennyson had been accumulating.

The longer that Hallam remained unmarried the higher his somewhat snobbish standards in such matters seemed to go, so that Richard Jebb predicted he would marry no one below the rank of the daughter of an earl. However, in 1883 his engagement was announced to a beautiful but penniless Irish girl, Audrey Boyle, whom he had met when she was staying with relatives in Freshwater, and in June 1884 they were married in the Henry VII chapel of the Abbey. Like Lionel's, it was a grand wedding, with such literary guests as Browning, Arnold, and Houghton nodding benignly in the stalls. Emily was believed to be too ill to come, but at the last moment she arrived and was brought into the chapel in a bath-chair, although she was unable to go into the Jerusalem Chamber for the signing of the register.

It was very painful for Emily Tennyson to lose her favourite son, 'Hallamee', and two days after the marriage she became so ill that she was unable to travel to Farringford from Aldworth. Hallam and Audrey had to come home from their honeymoon and settle down as companions to the elder Tennysons until Emily's death in 1896. It was tacitly accepted that Hallam would leave Audrey behind with Emily when he was needed to accompany his father, and when he was at home he and Audrey occupied a bedroom near his parents, so that they might be easily available at night. On 8 July 1889, more than five years after their marriage, Audrey noted that she and Hallam had their first dinner alone since their honeymoon. It was an arrangement that seemed perfectly natural to Hallam, for his parents always had first place in his consideration, but his wife was often unhappy, feeling left out of the close triangular intimacy of Alfred, Emily, and Hallam. As Sir Charles Tennyson tactfully observed, 'Perhaps her task was made harder by the feeling that the intellectual level of the house was rather too high for her.'[35] The guileless records she kept on the occasions when she was allowed to accompany her husband and father-in-law indicate that Tennyson was irritated by her chatter and often did not conceal the fact. Audrey's negligible role in the household is clearly shown in a letter Emily wrote about the place of woman in marriage: 'we three are strongly impressed by St. Paul's words. The head of the woman is the man and therefore we object to competition between the two though we would have both developed to the utmost. . . . Woman should be the complement of man not his rival, his helpmate. I don't know what Audrey thinks but the same I am sure.'[36] It must have been a great relief to Audrey when she had her own children with whom to occupy herself. Alfred and Emily surely had moments of self-reproach over their monopoly of the marriage of their son, but they could scarcely afford to admit it, and there is no indication that the matter was mentioned before Tennyson spoke of it on his death-bed.

During the first five years of their marriage Hallam and Audrey were childless, then became the parents of three sons between 1889 and 1896. The eldest, Lionel, became a celebrated cricketer and eventually inherited the title. The two younger sons both died during the First World War.

The decline in his sales was not an accurate reflection of Tennyson's poetic reputation in the 1880s, for he remained without question the first poet of the day, the one name that seemed synonymous with English poetry. The honours continued to come in, and in 1884 he was given an honorary degree by Edinburgh University, in company with Browning. In 1885, after the death of Houghton, who had been President of the London Library, Tennyson was asked to succeed him in the office. He was proposed by Leslie Stephen and assured that the presidency involved no responsibility save taking the chair at the annual general meetings when he was able. He accepted, but according to the minutes of the Library he never presided during the seven years before his death.

More concrete proof of his fame was an invitation from J. B. Pond, a New York lecture agent, offering a tour of fifty lectures in the United States with a guaranteed fee of $1,000 for each lecture, which was equal to the highest fees ever paid in America. Even had he been willing to undertake such a tour, Tennyson was by now far too infirm to do so.

A problem springing from his fame was occupying the entire Tennyson family, that of his posthumous reputation. With the sure knowledge that he could not live many more years, Tennyson began facing up to the inescapable fact that his biography would be written after his death. Froude's life of Carlyle had been particularly offensive to him; that had only confirmed what he already feared, that all the years he had spent concealing his private life from public gaze would have been in vain unless he had a peculiarly reticent biographer. In particular, he was worried that the history of his grandfather, his father, and his uncle would become public, and that the family tendency to melancholia, epilepsy, madness, drink, and drugs would no longer be secret. He had concealed the sad tale from even his sons, and of the friends he made in maturity only Benjamin Jowett seems to have known most of it.

As early as 1860 he had told Mrs Cameron that 'he believed that every crime and every vice in the world were connected with the passion for autographs and anecdotes and records,—that the desiring anecdotes and acquaintance with the lives of great men was treating them like pigs to be ripped open for the public; that he knew he himself should be ripped open like a pig; that he thanked God Almighty with his whole heart and soul that he knew nothing, and that the world knew nothing, of Shakespeare but his writings; and that he thanked God Almighty that he knew nothing of Jane Austen, and that there were no letters preserved either of Shakespeare's or of Jane Austen's, that they had not been ripped open like pigs'.[37]

In 1883 he wrote to Gladstone, retelling the story of Mrs Procter, the widow of 'Barry Cornwall': 'I heard of an old lady the other day, to whom all the great men of her time had written. When Froude's Carlyle came out, she ran up to her room & to an old chest there wherein she kept their letters, & she flung them into the fire. "They were written to *me*" she said "not to the public." & she set her chimney on fire, & her children & grandchildren ran in—"the chimney's on fire" "never mind" she said & went on burning. I should like to raise an altar to that old lady & burn incense upon it.'[38]

Both statements, extreme as they sound, are accurate representations of Tennyson's fear of biography, and they go far to explain why he was so careful to choose his son as his biographer and then to tell him precisely what he wanted included in the account of his own life. For nearly a decade he talked to him daily on the subject. But it should not be assumed that the evasions of Hallam's biography of his father were all due to Tennyson himself; many of them came from Hallam and from his mother, who carefully tried to remove all traces of the rough Lincolnshire poet with his black blood, his inability to keep friendships cultivated, his reluctance to marry, his occasional obscenity and bad language, his terrible fits of depression, his obsessive fear of poverty, and his slowness to assume the responsibilities of maturity. Until his death there was constant scrubbing of his history going on in Farringford and Aldworth. It is emblematic of the process that in the same years Emily Tennyson was looking for someone to repaint the Samuel Laurence portrait of her husband that Edward FitzGerald had given to her. In 1884 Watts refused to touch it, saying that the work of another hand would be out of key with the original. It was not until two months after Tennyson's death, when the picture was needed as an illustration for his biography, that Burne-Jones consented to repaint it, changing the background and the tone of the shirt and coat. It is not certain whether he also changed the face, but it seems probable, since the portrait today is much softer in expression than engravings made of it in the mid-nineteenth century, its prettiness far more in the style of Burne-Jones than of Laurence. The portrait, like the life of Tennyson, was changed and rearranged, in order to present a more suitable romanticized likeness of the poet to the world. When the picture had been altered to the taste of Hallam and Emily Tennyson, it hung for many years in Aldworth and Farringford, and then it was given to the National Portrait Gallery as the official likeness of Queen Victoria's Poet Laureate.

CHAPTER XXXIII

DECLINING YEARS,
1885–1890

IN November 1885 Macmillan published *Tiresias, and Other Poems*, Tennyson's first new volume of lyric and narrative poems since 1880, and only the second since 1872. During those years he had been publishing his shorter poems individually in periodicals, and in 1884, realizing that its production on the stage was not apt to take place, he had finally published *Becket*, as well as a volume containing *The Cup* and *The Falcon*. Many of the poems in *Tiresias, and Other Poems* had appeared elsewhere, but a new volume from the seventy-six-year-old poet was treated as a major event, and the reviews were all that he could have wished. It was dedicated 'To My Good Friend/Robert Browning,/Whose Genius and Geniality/Will Best Appreciate What May Be Best,/And Make Most Allowance For What May Be Worst'. When Browning heard of the dedication, he said, '"Sir, my good friend—I'll change that name with you": I loved him always, and have venerated his genius fifty years long.' He told Tennyson that he had recently been burning old letters, but one that he could not bear to destroy was Tennyson's friendly offer of the house at Twickenham for the use of himself and Mrs Browning.[1]

Besides the title-poem, the 1885 volume contained, among others, 'Frater Ave atque Vale', 'The Charge of the Heavy Brigade', 'To Virgil', a comic Lincolnshire dialect poem called 'The Spinster's Sweet-Arts', 'The Ancient Sage', and 'Balin and Balan'. Of the last Jowett said, 'I trust that we have really heard the last of the Arthur legend. It was his first love, and he seems to find it difficult to shake off.'[2]

But Jowett did greatly admire 'The Ancient Sage', in which Tennyson reaffirmed his faith in the divinity of the world and the immortality of the human spirit. It is told as a dialogue between the settled confidence of the older seer (surely representing an optimistic picture of Tennyson's own opinions), who has learned that faith is not dependent upon rational proof, and the gloomy scepticism of a younger man. The radiant description of the old man's ability in former years to escape from self into the Nameless is a clear transmutation of the trances into which Tennyson had fallen as a young man, but the description of 'what has been' is veiled by a light sorrow that it will come to no more. For Tennyson the escape into trance, however frightening, had always been connected with the surge of his poetic imagination, and 'The Ancient Sage' suggests that both his total confidence in mysticism and his poetic vision seem at best beautiful memories. The suspicion that nostalgia is at the heart of the overtly cheerful poem is strengthened by Emily's statement that 'toward the end of his life' Tennyson lost his ability to enter into visionary trances.

Tennyson's recurrent feelings of terror lest faith should be mistaken cut through any complacency; on the occasion when he and Hallam climbed over Westminster Abbey, listening to the organ and choir, he suddenly said in anguish: 'It is beautiful, but what empty and awful mockery if there were no God!' When the phenomenal world, with its sciences and its philosophies, seemed emptiest, like nothing 'but a murmur of gnats in the gloom', his most frequent refuge was in the consciousness of love that transcended death. In 'Vastness', written at the time he was publishing the 1885 volume, he turned once more to the memory of Arthur Hallam, which had sustained him for more than half a century:

> Peace, let it be! for I loved him and love him for ever:
> the dead are not dead but alive.

For many years Tennyson's health had never been better than mediocre, and his friends were so used to his complaints and illnesses that they could see little alteration. In the summer of 1885 Allingham found him 'unchanged in mind and not much changed in body by these last ten years. He walks two or three hours every day, and goes on writing.'[3] In spite of recurrent bad health, Tennyson had always been so proud of his body that it was hard for him to admit that it was deteriorating, and when there were visitors he would walk further than usual and occasionally break into a shambling run to demonstrate his fitness. But the truth was that he was going downhill generally, and his eyesight had become so bad that he complained he could no longer write cheques without help. Emily, who had always been fragile physically, now seemed little more than spirit, lying on her couch most of the day, swathed in shawls, happy to see visitors but so feeble that it was a major effort to make the move from Farringford to

Aldworth and back, even with chartered private trains and boats for the journey. After 1883 they no longer took a house for the London season. For some years she had accepted no invitations while staying in town, but she had entertained frequently; now even that was too much for her.

During 1885 one of the few guests who came to stay was Margot Tennant (later Asquith), who had asked Lionel to take her to Aldworth for a weekend as a present for her twenty-first birthday. She found Tennyson a 'magnificent creature to look at. He had everything: height, figure, carriage, features and expression. . . . he asked me if I wanted him to dress for dinner, adding, "Your sister said of me that I was both untidy and dirty. . . . Do you think I'm dirty?"' Diplomatically she answered, 'You are very handsome.' To her delight he replied, 'I can see by that remark that you think I am. Very well then, I will dress for dinner.' Later he read *Maud* to her, then pulled her on to his knee, as he frequently did with attractive young women, and said, 'Many may have written as well as that, but nothing that ever sounded so well.' He also took her for a two-hour walk over rough ground, making her wish that she had not accepted out of gratification at the invitation.

In spite of holding her on his knee, Tennyson disapproved of Margot Tennant, thinking her too racy; shortly afterwards he told Wilfrid Ward's wife an improper story, watching her face carefully before saying, 'Ah, you blush. I told that story to Margot Tennant and she didn't blush.' When Margot Tennant asked him to write out a poem for her, he refused, although he rarely ignored direct requests.[4] Part of his disapproval probably stemmed from his awareness that, as Sir Charles Tennyson once indicated, she was an indiscreet chapter in Lionel Tennyson's married life. There is no record of what she and Emily Tennyson thought of each other.

In October 1885 the Tennysons made their farewells to Lionel and Eleanor, who were going to India at the invitation of Lord Dufferin, the Governor-General, in the belief that a better knowledge of the country would be useful to Lionel in a career at the India Office. Their two elder boys, Alfred and Charles, were left in Scotland with Eleanor's aunt, Lady Frances Baillie, for what was expected to be a long visit. Early in February 1886 Dufferin wrote to Tennyson to say that Lionel was 'at Government House laid up with a slight attack of fever. He seems to have caught a chill, but . . . the Doctor tells me that it will not be a matter of more than a few days. . . . we regard attacks of the kind pretty much in the same light as we do colds in England, so you need not be uneasy.'[5] The illness became worse, and some weeks later the doctors found that Lionel's lungs and heart were affected. He was operated on, without effect on the fever, and at the beginning of April he was put on a ship with Eleanor, under the care of an English doctor returning to England. The sea breezes were expected to bring back his health after the heavy air of India.

In spite of bad abscesses from the operation, he was calm on the ship, and everyone noticed his thoughtfulness of others even when he became delirious. With his big head and flowing beard, he looked the picture of his father as he lay in his bed on deck, unaware of how ill he was, while the ship went through the Red Sea. In the Tennyson Research Centre may still be seen the series of telegrams that Eleanor sent to the Tennysons, culminating on 25 April: 'He passed away very peacefully on April twentieth all possible done hope reach London via Marseilles about May fourth communicate with my Father.' Lionel died in mid-afternoon, and six hours later his body was committed to the sea, 'under a great silver moon.'

Tennyson had seemed old before, but now he was broken, so that his agitation easily spilled over into the unbidden tears of one who could no longer fully control his emotions. To Hallam he could say only, 'The thought of Lionel tears me to pieces—he was so full of promise & so young.' As Lionel's son wrote many years later, 'Though much more akin to his father in temperament than Hallam—perhaps because of this—he had never been so close to the poet as his elder brother.' With the obscure feeling that he had failed Lionel, Tennyson tried to make amends to his memory. When Laura Gurney went to stay with the Tennysons, the house had a deep stillness, and even the servants crept about silently. Tennyson came to fetch her to accompany him on a walk, bringing with him a huge Russian wolfhound that jumped on her, nearly knocking her down. All that Tennyson said was 'Lionel's dog.' For Laura Gurney it was enough. 'I understood the reference to his dead son. Lionel's dog might do anything, and not a word must be said.'[6]

Lionel's death brought to a head all Tennyson's interest in spiritualism; through it he tried to regain the faith in the continued existence of the dead that he had sought so painfully in the years after Arthur Hallam's death. Like many recently bereaved, he felt constantly aware of an unseen world of spirit that he once described as 'a great ocean pressing round us on every side, and only leaking in by a few chinks'.

At his request Laura Gurney took him to a seance, where the moving table indicated that a control or spirit wanted to speak to him. In a broken voice he cried out, 'Are you my boy Lionel?' It was too much for the others, and the seance broke up.[7] Once more Emily demonstrated that she was the stronger of the two emotionally, and she helped Tennyson through the worst of the crisis by her rock-firm faith.

Two years later Tennyson had sufficiently recovered his poise to shape his emotions into poetry with the haunting elegy dedicated 'To the Marquis of Dufferin and Ava'. Dufferin had felt guilty over having invited Lionel to the place where he contracted his fatal illness, and the poem is in part extending to him the consolation that had been so hard-won for Tennyson himself. It concludes not with the recrimination of a bereaved father but the shared love found in sorrow:

> But ere he left your fatal shore,
>   And lay on that funereal boat,
>   Dying, 'Unspeakable' he wrote
> 'Their kindness', and he wrote no more;
>
> And sacred is the latest word;
>   And now the Was, the Might-have-been,
>   And those lone rites I have not seen,
> And one drear sound I have not heard,
>
> Are dreams that scarce will let me be,
>   Not there to bid my boy farewell,
>   When That within the coffin fell,
> Fell—and flashed into the Red Sea,
>
> Beneath a hard Arabian moon
>   And alien stars. To question, why
>   The sons before the father die,
> Not mine! and I may meet him soon;
>
> But while my life's late eve endures,
>   Nor settles into hueless gray,
>   My memories of his briefer day
> Will mix with love for you and yours.

The poem is remarkable in linking Tennyson's grief over Lionel with his sorrow so many years before at the death of Arthur Hallam. His feelings on the two occasions, separated by half a century, are brought together by the ironic recollection of the coffin falling into the sea as the Tennysons wait at home for news of their son; it seems a repetition of the premonitory passage in *In Memoriam*, written when Tennyson was trying to come to terms with the death of Hallam:

> O mother, praying God will save
>   Thy sailor,—while thy head is bowed,
>   His heavy-shotted hammock-shroud
> Drops in his vast and wandering grave. (VI)

The connection between the shocking deaths of the two young men he loved must have been in Tennyson's mind from the first, for he used the same stanza form in Lionel's elegy that he had first used in *In Memoriam*.

Tennyson's sorrow infects 'Locksley Hall Sixty Years After', the long poem he wrote during the months after Lionel's death, and it even provided the name and circumstances of the death of the narrator's son, 'our sailor son thy father, Leonard early lost at sea'. More centrally, it contributes to the deep feeling of estrangement between the narrator and the world in which he lives. As an old man he can recognize how wrong his anger and his pain had been over the events of the first 'Locksley Hall', when he was a young man. He no longer resents the plighting of shallow-hearted Amy to her 'honest, rustic Squire', he no longer hates 'the tyrant of my youth' (which glances at Tennyson's own grandfather), and he has long since recognized the beneficence of the love of his wife of forty years. But, in spite of the air of personal reconciliation that breathes over the poem, the narrator at eighty has little but scorn for the whole idea of progress as embodied in Victorian England. There is almost no facet of his society that has not undergone disintegration. Tennyson insisted that *'There is not one touch of biography in it from beginning to end'*, but the assertion is surely disingenuous, for the emotions are biographically his even if the events of the poem are not. There can be little doubt how closely he identified with the narrator's pitying self-description:

> Poor old voice of eighty crying after voices that have fled!
> All I loved are vanished voices, all my steps are on the dead.
>
> All the world is ghost to me, and as the phantom disappears,
> Forward far and far from here is all the hope of eighty years.

Unfortunately, in the enumeration of the forces of disorder in nearly 300 long lines, the narrator (or more precisely, Tennyson's voice speaking through him) becomes increasingly hysterical, so that the force of the argument is gradually dissipated until it touches banality. In this poem the narrator, unlike that of *Maud*, is meant to be well balanced mentally, so that the poet's hysteria shows through. The effect is not helped by the repetitive quality of the trochaic metre, which is used far more mechanically here than in the earlier poem.* 'Locksley Hall Sixty Years After' is not one of Tennyson's successes, but it demonstrates both his growing recognition of the need for personal reconciliation at the end of his life, and his old man's anger at a world with which he could no longer cope.

The general tenor of the poem, poking awkwardly through the pretence of dramatic monologue, was uncomfortably like that of Tennyson's increasingly bitter remarks about the way that Gladstone had been running the country, and in the *Nineteenth Century* of January 1887, only a month after the publication of the poem, Gladstone answered it with an article rebutting its central tenets by listing the achievements of the age. Somewhat disingenuously he points out that many of his contemporaries do not take Tennyson seriously intellectually, and then he immediately denies the validity of their attitude, but the general tone of the article makes it seem that Tennyson's intellectual qualifications are set up for the sole purpose of being demolished. Gladstone makes a token nod to the fact that the poem is a dramatic monologue and hence cannot be identified as the direct feelings of Tennyson, but his criticism seems slightly off-centre in such a case, since it treats the poem as political or social theory rather than poetry. Almost certainly Gladstone felt that the poem as an attack upon the age was in part an attack upon himself, and the article becomes an externalization of the usually unspoken antagonism that the two men felt. The irreconcilable differences in their ideological positions were reinforced by the personal opposition that they had fought for so long to stifle; it is to their joint credit that a public disagreement remained so ostensibly impersonal. The article concludes with what was perilously near an accusation of disloyalty to the

---

* There are moments when the thump of the metre sounds almost like a parody. Any reader who knows the old music-hall song 'She was poor, but she was honest' can hardly help being reminded of it by lines 219–20:

There among the glooming alleys Progress halts on palsied feet,
Crime and hunger cast our maidens by the thousand on the street.

Is it possible that the song itself is a parody of Tennyson's poem?

Crown by the Poet Laureate: 'Justice does not require, nay rather she forbids, that the Jubilee of the Queen be marred by tragic notes.' Probably a defensible point of view for a recent Prime Minister, but it is hard not to feel that it was also a long-delayed rebuke to Tennyson for meddling with public affairs, a rebuke that Gladstone had smothered for years. Most appropriately, it was administered as an admonishment about political affairs, but it was concerned with poetry, a subject on which Gladstone was more authoritative than Tennyson was on the conduct of the country. Both men were far too decent to be deliberately offensive in their remarks, but Tennyson's criticism of Gladstone's politics and Gladstone's strictures on Tennyson's poetry were blows aimed directly at the most important beliefs of the other man. The terms sounded impersonal, but the feelings were something else. The position into which they had been put by their common admiration of Hallam had meant that they could never ignore one another, but they were constitutionally incapable of thorough mutual liking.

On the occasion of great anniversaries and honours, old men in the public eye are showered with good wishes, as Tennyson had been, but in between them there is occasionally a feeling that they have been around too long. As Gladstone had once had to listen to Tennyson bringing the Queen's proposal for his retirement from public life, now Tennyson in his turn had to put up with the younger poets who felt that he had long since written his best and that there was little more to expect of him. Lewis Morris, who had wanted to speak for the other poets of England in congratulating Tennyson on his peerage, now said that it was the duty of the 'Commander in Chief' to step down in favour of the 'subaltern', as Morris had his eye on the post of Laureate, regarding himself as Tennyson's natural heir even if no one else did so. When Morris spread rumours that Tennyson was on the verge of retirement, Hallam wrote to Theodore Watts to assure him that his father had 'not really the slightest intention of resigning until he feels that he can no longer do the work. It was by the personal wish of the Prince Consort & the Queen that he accepted the Laureateship: & he has had too much kindness from HM, to think of resigning except into her own hands & with her full concurrence.' As a snub to Morris's hopes he added that it was probable that the Laureateship would be abolished on the death of Tennyson.[8]

Tennyson's poetic energies were naturally flagging, but he was still writing regularly, and Morris's hope that he would retire must have seemed particularly galling when he had just completed 'Demeter and Persephone', a lovely retelling of the classical legend as a harbinger of Christianity. All the serenity of mind that seems so desperately lacking from 'Locksley Hall Sixty Years After' is reflected in the dignified blank verse and noble imagery. It is clearly the work of an old man, but there is only maturity and no senility in its conception.

He still thought as much as ever of poetical theory, sometimes as justification for his own practice, increasingly as it applied to all poetry. In particular he was exercised over what he considered a mean and pinchbeck view of originality. When he was accused of lifting the thoughts of others, he 'hotly maintained that every good poet has the right, has the duty, to steal anything that strikes him in a bad poet and improve it'. After all, as he told Edmund Gosse, it is only the dunces who 'fancy it is the thought that makes poetry live; it isn't, it's the expression, the form, but we mustn't tell them so, they wouldn't know what we meant'.[9] Plagiarism chiefly meant to him unacknowledged use of the language or the metre of another poet, not the discursive content of the poetry. It was this belief that lay behind his willingness to embroider the incidents and anecdotes that Hallam and Emily encouraged his friends to write out for him. Quite unselfconsciously he would acknowledge his indebtedness in such matters, confident that it was his treatment of them that made them worth considering; he was no more embarrassed at incorporating into a poem an American tale told him by Lowell (Henry James also used it, as the subject of a short story) than he was at reworking the legend of Demeter and Persephone; both were part of the legacy of educated men.

In the summer of 1887 he chartered Sir Allen Young's yacht, the *Stella*, for a cruise off Wales and the West Country, then to the Channel Islands, accompanied by Hallam and his wife. At Solva they took a dog-cart for a rough drive along a riverbed to St. David's. According to Audrey's ingenuous account, 'When we came to the cathedral we found the Dean waiting outside who took us in & showed it to us but being much snubbed by my father in law, said at last he saw he was in the way & that he preferred looking at it alone so he would leave us to our selves after asking us to go & have some tea in his house which H refused.' Embarrassingly, after snubbing him they discovered that the Dean was the brother of Tennyson's old Cambridge friend, John Allen. On the return drive to Solva the horses took fright at the noise of the water and ran away in the starlight, with Tennyson sitting 'perfectly still perfectly silent awaiting [his] doom'.[10]

In the Channel Islands they put in at St. Helier to visit Frederick Tennyson, and the two brothers gossiped lovingly a whole day, finding when Frederick was free of Emily's presence that their concord was as complete as it had been in Somersby. The older he got, the more convinced Frederick became of the spirit world and of the ghosts in whom he believed with the credulous innocence of the great boy that he had always remained. For years Alfred had been considering the same ideas, but now he reacted against his brother's deep convictions, as he often did in the face of confident assertion, even of those things in which he believed himself. 'I grant you that spiritualism must not be judged by its quacks,' he said: 'but I am convinced that God and the ghosts of men would choose something other than mere table-legs through which to speak to the heart of man.' But it was all in good temper, and as Alfred left, Frederick told him that 'not for twenty years had he spent such a happy day'.

Tennyson was in better health than he had a right to expect at his age. When Sir Andrew Clark examined him carefully in the autumn of 1887, he sent a wire to Emily reporting that there was 'nothing whatever to cause the slightest anxiety'. One of his eyes was so blind that it was of no use to him, but he could still read with the other through his heavy-lensed spectacles. He had to have a nap every day after lunch, and another after an early dinner, but he still rose at 7.30 each morning to walk before breakfast half an hour later. In bad weather he took his outings in a carriage, but when the day was fine and he felt unusually well he could still walk several miles without a stick, his shambling gait slower but hardly more remarkable than it had ever been. Strangely piratical in appearance, with flapping sombrero and rusty black broadcloth coat under his old blue cloak, he claimed the lanes around his houses as his own, impatiently waving away strangers with the book that he carried under his arm so that he might read when he rested.

He was becoming much easier for those near him. Mrs Bradley was struck in 1888 'by his great unselfishness & thoughtfulness for others—and thinks him less self-absorbed than he used to be—he certainly is most genial in company now'; his mind, she thought, took bothers and worries far more calmly. Not everyone agreed about his lack of self-absorption, but it was at least far easier to take than it had once been. Thomas Hughes said that he felt 'as fond of the dear old man as anyone in spite of his vanity, which is so open and superficial as to be quite inoffensive'. On a visit to Aldworth in 1888 Lord Carnarvon, who knew him but slightly, found that in conversation 'one is struck by the power and force of what he says, though it is the speech of a man who has lived in books; or in a very small world of his own and who sees things through a narrow vista—the constant contrast of broad and fine ideas with very narrow ideas is unusual—and from the same cause I suppose he brings everything back to himself. His own writings are the central point of all his thoughts. It is not unnatural and it would be unpleasant if it were not so entirely unconscious.' He told Carnarvon of his hatred of modern radicalism, his total loss of admiration for Gladstone, 'and if he expresses an occasional belief in human or social progress it is a very frigid and doubtful expression of faith'.[11]

What would once have seemed unpleasant vanity now became recognizable as simple truth when he compared himself to the immortals of English poetry. 'I have been reading in the Spectator that Wordsworth, Keats & myself were the three masters of blank verse who are also great in rhyme,' he told a companion on a walk. 'Keats was not a master of blank verse. It might be true of Wordsworth *at his best*. He ought only to have published a sixth of what he did, either in blank verse or rhyme.'[12] At his age it would have been false modesty for him to add parallel strictures on his own work.

His opinion of his poetry was amply supported by the dozens of letters that nearly every post brought from all over the world, praising him, asking his advice, more often for his autograph. There had never been a serious poet with such wide esteem: a greeting-card manufacturer offered him a thousand guineas for twelve lines of verse to be put on a Christmas card. Drily he once said at a local fête that 'if the organizers could ever get hold of the parings of his toe nails, they would sell them at one of the stalls!' There were, of course, frequent pleas for money, most of which he ignored. One of the most winning was that from an English artist living in Canada, who said that his speciality was drawing cows, 'but that he must have a cow of his own to live with and make proper studies of, would therefore Alfred Tennyson give him a cow?'[13]

For all his increased ease with others, on one subject Tennyson remained nearly paranoiac: intrusion on his privacy. Several memoirs of the period record how he would drive away innocent guests approaching Farringford or Aldworth, in his fury at what he took to be intrusion refusing to hear their explanations that they had appointments, until they had finally to retire in defeat. Then he would be full of recrimination at their rudeness in missing their appointments. He remained convinced that everyone on a lane or road within miles of either of his houses had no reason to be there except to spy on him, but when he was unnoticed he would fall into despondency about how quickly his public had forgotten him. Usually it was merely funny but seldom so for the unfortunate victims of his suspicion.

In particular he remained hostile to Americans, all of whom he thought crossed the ocean with no purpose save to intrude on him. He liked to say that the United States must be the worst place in the world, but he could be won over briefly by exceptional modesty or good manners in an American or, still better, by admiration for his own poetry. Once when he was entertaining the American actress Mary Anderson and an old American friend of hers aged eighty-five, they were discussing charm of manner, and Miss Anderson gave the palm to Longfellow. Tennyson's reply was 'perhaps—if an American *could* be a gentleman'. One of his few approving remarks about Arnold was made to A. D. Coleridge: 'I am glad Matthew Arnold has shewn up American vulgarity.'[14]

In the 1880s young John Jay Chapman, recently graduated from Harvard, came to call at Aldworth, bringing a letter from Annie Ritchie. His own nervousness communicated itself to Tennyson, who could find little to say before luncheon or at table, except to boast that Emily's iron garden-chair had cost £80, then relapsing into silence. After luncheon Lewis Morris came in and talked with Tennyson about insects. Chapman found no opening into the conversation until the talk turned to polecats, about which he felt that he knew as much as the others, since he had considerable familiarity with the American skunk. In his excitement at breaking his awkward silence, he fished out a quotation from *Hamlet*, 'He smote the sledded polecats on the ice', forgetting that it was all part of an undergraduate joke in which Harvard men substituted 'polecats' for 'Polacks'. Neither Tennyson nor Morris laughed, and Chapman was too overcome by embarrassment to explain. Shortly thereafter he slunk away. In the entrance-hall he said good-bye to Audrey, who had been so unstrung by the tension of the luncheon table that she could scarcely speak and could think of no response to Chapman except nervously to tear off the last sheet of a newspaper lying on a table and silently hand it to him as a memento of the visit.

On another occasion Annie Ritchie gave a letter of introduction to Georgina Schuyler, a New York friend, thinking that Tennyson would enjoy meeting a woman of such charm and distinction. He had, however, decided unreasonably that Miss Schuyler was thrusting herself upon him, and throughout her call he was even more boorish then he had been to Chapman, scarcely bothering to answer her polite attempts to keep the conversation going. At last, uneasily aware of his own bad behaviour, he tried to force out a civil word as she was making her farewells, but it was too late. Fed to the teeth with his manners, Miss Schuyler merely looked him in the eye and said coolly that 'She was always glad to meet any friend of Mrs. Ritchie's'.[15] It was the kind of treatment that Tennyson deserved more often than he received; had it occurred more frequently he would perhaps not have come to the end of his life with so little imagination about the needs of others.

So suspicious of outsiders was Tennyson that when his daughter-in-law Eleanor became engaged two years after Lionel's death, his first question to her fiancé, Augustine Birrell, was 'Why do you want to force an entrance into my family?' Throughout her unhappy marriage to Lionel, Eleanor had felt an outsider in his family, and the intervening time since his death had made her feel even more remote from her parents-in-law. In spite of this, both Tennyson and Emily thought she ought not to remarry, for they disapproved of second marriages. Birrell was a respectable thirty-eight-year-old widower, a barrister who later became famous as a man of letters and politician, but his humble background and his radical politics did not recommend him to the Tennysons. It was apparently a relief to Eleanor when she was finally free of her connection with them; there is no indication of a break or quarrel, but immediately she remarried, her letters to the Tennysons dropped any pretence of intimacy and became chiefly communications about her three sons by Lionel. Emily particularly resented the marriage and Eleanor's withdrawal. 'I had hoped to have seen Eleanor often & to have become acquainted with Mr Birrell,' she wrote to her sister Anne. 'We have had perpetual nurses & sickness almost ever since their marriage.' To Hallam she complained that 'Poor Eleanor has deeply wronged us & it is, no doubt, difficult to be just to her'.[16]

For all their disappointment, the Tennysons remained devoted grandparents to the children of Eleanor's first marriage, who normally spent a large part of their vacations in Aldworth, where Tennyson took them around the countryside to teach them the names of birds and plants. The boys grew up loving their grandparents dearly, although it must occasionally have been difficult for them to restrain their spirits in an elderly, strictly-run household where they were expected to be quiet because of Emily's delicate health and Alfred's need of concentration. The second son, Charles, has told how they used to kiss Tennyson's great brown-spotted hand in greeting each morning as he came down the stairs, but the old-fashioned courtesy was undertaken in affection not fear. For Eleanor her second marriage was everything that her first had not been. She was deeply in love with Birrell, and she felt an intimate understanding with him that she had not known with Lionel. Five years after marrying Birrell she said she 'felt a sort of excitement still at having his society for a whole afternoon to herself'.[17] For Lionel's children as well as his own, Birrell proved a wholly successful father.

At the beginning of September 1888 Tennyson complained of a swollen, painful knee when walking at Aldworth. According to his son he had sat on the terrace too soon after a rain, so that the damp brought on a severe attack of arthritic gout which was the beginning of the most serious illness he had yet suffered. For more than two months he was so ill he could not be moved from his bed by the south windows of the first floor of the house, where he lay with his hand in Emily's, peering out at the landscape spread beneath Blackdown, feeling that he was looking into eternity. In his illness he again had the flashes of illumination, half-way between trance and dream, of the kind that had once troubled him as the probable onset of epilepsy. As always, his visions were full of brilliant colour, once of a succession of beautiful pagodas piled up to heaven, again of evergreen forests, cliffs, and temples, like the wonderful amalgam of Cauteretz and Ida in which he had once imagined Œnone living. But now he could speak of what he dreamed, as he had been unable to do when a young man, for the latent terror behind the visions was gone. He dreamed of John Bright and once that he was Pope, with the burden of the whole world on his shoulders.

By November he was well enough to be moved by special train to Lymington and thence to an invalid chair across the Solent by boat. As he was towed along in the chair, he amused himself by looking at the legs of the people at Yarmouth Quay, trying to guess their characters from their legs without seeing their faces, but the small pleasures of the journey were ruined when he heard that the special train had killed a dog. At Farringford he had a serious relapse after the journey, and he became preoccupied with his own approaching death. 'The face of the clock seemed to him to expand & fill up the whole end of the room.

The clock pointed to a quarter past six & he said superstitious people would say that he would die then.'[18] When he tried to read 'De Profundis' and 'The Human Cry' to Wilfrid Ward, he broke down and sobbed aloud at the concluding lines:

> We know we are nothing—but Thou wilt help us to be.
> Hallowed be Thy name—Halleluiah!

His weight had fallen to nine and a half stone before Christmas, but by January he was able to walk a little. He was still pathetically weak and sometimes seemed like a child, totally dependent upon others for direction. One visitor told of seeing him just before dinner, when he became confused at not finding Hallam, who had gone to dress. At last he held his hands out to the visitor and asked if they were clean enough for the table. When told hesitatingly that they were not, he obediently went away to wash them. It was not long, however, before he was on the mend and reassuringly complaining in his normal fashion. When he was tucked in bed, he said fretfully that he was wrapped so warmly he felt like a goose tied by the fire to enlarge its liver.

As spring came on, he and Emily were carried into the garden and put side by side in their chairs to see the flowers. His hands were still bandaged against the pain of the gout. When the great old fig tree came into leaf, he remarked casually that it was 'like a breaking wave',[19] totally forgetting that a quarter of a century before he had reproved Allingham for the same figure, saying sharply, 'Not in the least.'

By mid-May he was well enough to take a cruise of a fortnight on the *Sunbeam*, the luxurious three-masted schooner that Lord Brassey lent to him. He was accompanied by Hallam and Nurse Durham, who had cared for him in his illness. The weather was too bad to go to Ireland, as they had planned, and they spent the two weeks investigating the coast and rivers of Devon and Cornwall once more. The unexpected cold depressed Tennyson, but he lay in his deck-chair telling all the old stories that he had most enjoyed since his youth, recalling friends now gone, sometimes forgetting that they were no longer alive. 'Thackeray', he said solemnly, 'is the greater artist, but Dickens is more affluent.'[20] He talked of Lear, who had died the previous year in the Villa Tennyson in San Remo, and of Venables, who had died during his own illness. When he read 'Guinevere' aloud he said that Gladstone had once called it the high-water mark of English poetry, and he was so affected by his own poem that his voice kept breaking as the tears washed down his face. When they returned to Freshwater he had gained strength, but no one could predict that he would long outlive his old friends.

By July he had so far recovered his health that he felt there was no longer any need for Nurse Durham, although he knew that he would sadly miss her affectionate bullying and the spirit with which she had put up with his growling. But she had become too independent to take his directions, even over her dismissal, and she refused to go, telling him that he would be better employed in writing a hymn of thanksgiving for his recovery than in dismissing a faithful helper.

The following month, on his eightieth birthday, he seemed as well as he had been before his illness, and not long after that Cecil Spring-Rice was surprised to look out of his bedroom window at Farringford and see the old man running like a boy in the early sunlight. His birthday was the occasion for hundreds of letters and telegrams of congratulations; the Queen and nearly every poet in the kingdom wrote to him, and at least for the time there was no more mention of a successor as Laureate. 'I don't know what I have done to make people feel like that towards me,' he said, 'except that I have always kept my faith in Immortality.'

Of all the attempts made to sum up Tennyson on his eightieth birthday, perhaps the best was the simple statement of Edmund Gosse: 'He is wise and full of intelligence; but in mere intellectual capacity or attainment it is probable that there are many who excel him. This, then, is not the direction in which his greatness asserts itself. He has not headed a single moral reform nor inaugurated a single revolution of opinion; he has never pointed the way to undiscovered regions of thought; he has never stood on tip-toe to describe new worlds that his fellows were not tall enough to discover ahead. In all these directions he has been prompt to follow, quick to apprehend, but never himself a pioneer. Where then has his greatness lain? It has lain in the various perfections of his writing. He has written, on the whole, with more constant, unwearied, and unwearying excellence than any of his contemporaries. ... He has expended the treasures of his native talent on broadening and deepening his own hold upon the English language, until that has become an instrument upon which he is able to play a greater variety of melodies to perfection than any other man.' As Jowett asked, 'Was there ever an octogenarian poet before?'[21]

Best of all, his recovered health meant that he was once more writing poetry, some of it as good as that of his younger years. In August, almost as if giving himself a birthday present, he composed that riddling poem 'Merlin and the Gleam', which was his own attempt at a poetical autobiography, one so puzzling, however, that no one but its creator has ever been certain of its meaning, except that it is clearly a celebration of a lifelong worship of the creative imagination.

In October 1889 the Tennysons made their annual return to Farringford from Aldworth, and the crossing from Lymington to Yarmouth inevitably brought back to Tennyson the memory of the same trip the previous year in an invalid chair, when no one could believe that he would long survive. Having once stared death down, he was now far more at ease with his own mortality, and he could accept, for the time at least, that he might never again make the short trip across the Solent. In a fit of instantaneous inspiration, the sixteen lines of 'Crossing the Bar' sprang into his mind in almost their final form. Less than twenty minutes later, when the boat pulled into Yarmouth, it was written down on a piece of used paper.

That evening Nurse Durham came into his study to light the candles and found him sitting alone in the dark. 'Will this do for you, old woman?' he asked gruffly and recited the poem. Forgetting that she had asked him for a hymn of thanksgiving, she thought that he had been overtired by the journey and had composed his own death song; in her agitation she fled without replying, leaving him in the dark room. Later that night he read the poem to Hallam, who said with justice, 'That is one of the most beautiful poems ever written.'*[22] On his death-bed Tennyson told him, 'Mind you put "Crossing the Bar" at the end of all editions of my poems', an injunction that has usually been followed since then. In its grave, simple beauty, it is a fitting encapsulation of the childlike faith he felt in his most serene hours at the end of his life.

His renewed activity made it imperative to publish another volume of his poetry, and by the beginning of November he was preparing copy for the press. Warmly dressed against the unseasonable cold in 'two Jaeger vests, his cashmere shirt & his thick coat', he sat with Nurse Durham before the fire, handing her old copies of the poems 'to tack in . . . with needle & thread, so as to spare [him] writing'. In their

---

* Hallam, who apparently thought his own spontaneous remark insufficiently solemn, later changed the printed version to 'That is the crown of your life's work', a more debatable judgement.

well-meant efforts to remove excessive burdens from his shoulders, Emily and Hallam were occasionally insensitive to a marked degree when they took their own decisions about the poems without consulting him. Emily insisted that he remove the notes he wanted to append to some of the poems, and when she had handed the final copy over to Hallam to be taken to Macmillan, she warned him: 'Papa says that you are on *no* account to alter anything; that all the corrections are well considered.'[23]

On its publication on 12 December 1889 *Demeter and Other Poems* was deservedly welcomed by the critics, and 20,000 copies were sold in the first week. Many of the poems it contained would be remarkable works at any age, let alone at eighty. Besides the title-poem and others already mentioned, the volume included 'Roses on the Terrace', 'Far—Far—Away', 'To Ulysses' (addressed to W. G. Palgrave), 'To the Marquis of Dufferin and Ava', and other poems that proved his lyric gift was still very much alive, even if the inspiration for the poems often lay in the past.

Among the kindest and most generous letters of congratulations that Tennyson had received for his birthday was that from Browning. By a sad coincidence, the date of publication of *Demeter* was the same as that of *Asolando*, Browning's final volume of poetry, and was also the last day of the life of its author, who died that night in Venice. In the three weeks that intervened between Browning's death and his burial on the last day of the year, Tennyson was active in persuading the Dean of the Abbey to have Browning's body interred there, and later he was the head of the committee of literary men who wrote to thank the Dean. He was of course invited to be a pallbearer, but he was too feeble to attend the ceremony and Hallam stood in for him. Years before, when he had been in the habit of walking around London with the schoolgirl Elspeth Thompson, Tennyson used to take her to the Abbey and tell her that one day he would lie there. Now he knew that it would not be long before he joined Browning.

Less than a month before Browning's death had come the news of the death of William Allingham, who was fifteen years Tennyson's junior. With so many of his friends gone, it was a comfort to Tennyson to remember Allingham's last words, which he often repeated for his own consolation: 'I am seeing things that you know nothing of.'[24]

It was at about this time that Tennyson wrote three lines in his prayer-book that might have applied to many friends who had recently died; it seems reasonable, however, to agree with Professor Ricks that they refer to the death in 1833 of Arthur Hallam:

> Oh but alas for the smile of smiles that never but one face wore,
> Oh for the voice that has flown away like a bird to an unseen shore,
> Oh for the face the flower of flowers that blossoms on earth no more.

❊

CHAPTER XXXIV

SILENT VOICES,
1890–1892

IN February 1890 Tennyson fell ill again, this time with a combination of bronchitis and influenza. In the confusion caused by fever he constantly returned to the past; in the initial stages he 'talked about his firstborn, & broke down describing the fists clenched as if in a struggle for life'. During his recovery he told stories of his grandparents, of his own childhood and schooldays, and of his first visit to the cataracts of the valley of Cauteretz.[1] The national newspapers carried grossly exaggerated accounts that were more alarming than the illness itself, and it was some time before Hallam discovered that a beggar from Haslemere, who came to the door for scraps of food each day, was being paid by newsmen to bring them kitchen gossip. Tennyson's recovery was slower than it would have been a few years earlier, but it was still amazingly fast. By the end of April he was entertaining large tea-parties nearly every day in the ballroom at Farringford, from which a few privileged guests were allowed into the drawing-room to talk to Emily on her sofa. He was able to get up twenty times in succession from a low chair without using his hands, and he took to waltzing again. When Mrs Brookfield came to Farringford, he suddenly turned to her and said, 'Jane, let us dance.' On her refusal to join him, protesting that they were both too old for such nonsense, he 'proceeded with deliberation and stateliness, to pirouette by himself all down the room'.[2] He regularly walked a mile or two, accompanied by his nurse and the dogs, usually up the steep hill to the Beacon on the cliffs, and he could still climb a difficult gate or run down the hill on the way home.

Thomas Edison's representatives came to Farringford in May to record Tennyson's readings of his own poetry, and for several days he shouted into a tube: 'Blow, bugle, blow', 'The Charge of the Light Brigade', 'Come into the garden, Maud', 'Ask me no more', and other extracts and short poems. For many years the original wax cylinders leaned against a radiator in Farringford, their continued existence proving, as his grandson said, something of the efficiency of the heating in the house. In recent years they have been transferred to discs. The fidelity of the recording was primitive, so that only a ghost of his powerful voice emerges from the mechanical scratching, but it is still possible to fall under the hypnotic quality of his reading. Either because of the quality of the recording and the conditions under which the cylinders were kept or because of his advanced age, his voice is curiously high, almost contralto in quality (he said it sounded like the squeak of a dying mouse), but it does not obscure the magnificent control of breathing and the length of his phrasing. It is old-fashioned recitation, with heavy stress on the rhythm in poetry that already seems to have sufficient of that, and with what sounds like deliberate neglect of the prose meaning. When Edmund Gosse heard him read 'Boädicea', he said that 'He hangs sleepily over the syllables, in a rough monotonous murmur, sacrificing everything to quantity. Had I not known the poem well beforehand it would have been entirely unintelligible.' It is difficult, however, to understand Gosse's judgement that 'His reading is worse than anyone's I ever heard',[3] for it conveys a startlingly vivid impression of how Tennyson wanted his works read aloud. Today the record gives the listener a *frisson* to be in such intimate contact with the greatest Victorian poet, a man born in 1809.

Before leaving Farringford for the summer Tennyson sat for two portraits by Watts, rather under protest, although he seemed perfectly happy once the sittings had begun (see Plate XXIV). During the winter he had been amusing himself by painting in water-colours; 'Add a daub every day', Watts told him, and he 'would then soon have a picture'.

In late June he went to London to be examined by Sir Andrew Clark, who said his general condition was better than it had been for years, although it was obvious to his friends that his ill-used, once magnificent body was running down. He was told that his eyes and ears were in surprisingly good shape for his age, but since he always brushed aside any qualifications in statements about his health, he then claimed that he was going totally blind but that his hearing was perfect. Visitors had noticed, however, that Emily carefully arranged the seating so that he could be near enough to his guests to hear what they said.

While Tennyson and Hallam were in London they stayed with Knowles. Shortly before their arrival Knowles had met Gladstone in the street, and Gladstone had said he would like to see Tennyson when next he was in town. Since his review of 'Locksley Hall Sixty Years After' he and Tennyson had exchanged several letters that were sufficiently affectionate in tone, but the memory of his rap over the knuckles still rankled with Tennyson. He also violently disapproved of Gladstone's campaign for the Home Rule Bill, and when he heard that his old acquaintance was coming for dinner he was so annoyed that he refused to sit down at the table with him, saying that he would instead have his meal in his room, quite unrepentant that one of the busiest men in the kingdom was making time to come to see him.

When the Gladstones and the other guests arrived, Knowles invented an imaginary illness to explain Tennyson's absence during the meal. After the ladies had left the dining-room, Knowles turned to Gladstone and said, 'Lord Tennyson may be much better now; don't you think you could go up and persuade him to come down?' He accompanied Gladstone to the door of Tennyson's room, then left him. Ten minutes later the two old men came shuffling down the stairs, arm in arm. They sat together on a sofa, so that they could hear each other well, discussing Homer, Browning, and finally even Home Rule. They were both aware of their advanced age and of the fact that they were bound together by memories that were more important than the differences that separated them. As Gladstone wrote after Tennyson's death, 'He and I had both lived with great loneliness after beginning in the midst of large bands of friends.' Gladstone was at his most charming and Tennyson seemed gradually to forget his disapproval. Their unspoken reconciliation was appropriate, for it was apparently the last time they ever saw one another. When the guests were gone, Tennyson turned to Knowles and his wife as he took his candle to go to bed and said with embarrassment, 'I'm sorry I said all those hard things of that old man.' Even more grudgingly he admitted of Home Rule: 'He has quite converted me. I see it all; it is the best thing if one looks at it from all sides.'

At breakfast the next morning Tennyson was gloomy as he talked over the previous evening: 'It is all right; he spellbound me for the time and I could not help agreeing with him, it was the extraordinary way in which he put it all; his logic is immense, but I have gone back to my own views. It is all wrong, this Home Rule, and I am going to write and tell him so.' He thought it over, then with a clatter he threw down his knife and fork: 'I never said anything half bad enough of that damned old rascal.'[4]

Some time after this when he was reading the 'Ode on the Death of the Duke of Wellington' to the Duke of Argyll at Farringford, he suddenly stopped at the words:

> Who never sold the truth to serve the hour,
> Nor paltered with Eternal God for power . . .

'As I am afraid Gladstone is doing now,' he added.[5]

During his London visit in 1890 Tennyson also had his last glimpse of the Queen, who bowed to him when driving in Hyde Park; although she invited him to come to see her again, he was never able to do so.

The Royal Family had by no means forgotten the old man. Princess Mary, Duchess of Teck, asked to see him, but he claimed to be too afraid of newspaper reporters to be seen going to her; instead, she good-naturedly came to Knowles's house, where he read parts of *Maud* to her. When he was back in Aldworth, the Duchess of Albany came to luncheon with him on his birthday, and he read to her, as he had done two years earlier for Princess Beatrice and Prince Henry of Battenberg when they called. Other visitors noticed his alternation between gaiety and the lethargy of old age. Occasionally his old sense of fun would flash out as it did when a guest said of the tangles of wild roses, 'What beautiful hips!' to which Tennyson demurely replied, 'I'm so glad you admire 'em, ma'am.'[6]

His good health and spirits continued into 1891. In February, when Princess Louise visited him at Farringford, he walked with her to the top of the down and raced her to the Beacon. He still liked having the house full of guests, although their presence soon tired him. In the summer he went by yacht to Devon, where he and Hallam went up the river Exe by rail. As he had always done on such trips, he asked to be left alone to smoke at the places where the scenery made poetry spring to his mind.

In June he wrote for Emily, in honour of their forty-first wedding anniversary, the gentle little poem called 'June Heather and Bracken' that stood as the dedicatory poem for his last volume of poetry:

> There on the top of the down,
> The wild heather round me and over me June's high blue,
> When I looked at the bracken so bright and the heather so brown,
> I thought to myself I would offer this book to you,
> This, and my love together,
> To you that are seventy-seven,
> With a faith as clear as the heights of the June-blue heaven,
> And a fancy as summer-new
> As the green of the bracken amid the gloom of the heather.

It is a poem that more adequately states the quality of his love for her than any other that he ever wrote.

When the composer Hubert Parry stayed at Farringford in January 1892 he found Tennyson much exercised about eternal punishment, which, as other visitors had noticed, seemed to frighten him. Tennyson told Parry that he had been discussing the subject with a bishop (probably Boyd Carpenter of Ripon) and had asserted that he simply did not believe in hell, 'whereon the Bishop replied in a whisper that he didn't either'. But his feelings of the imminence of death had not made Tennyson conventional, for he told racy anecdotes, said he preferred 'bloody' to 'awfully', drank from two bottles of brandy placed before him at dinner, read 'The Lotos-Eaters' aloud while holding a candle by his nose, repeated his wonder at the lack of music in Browning's poetry, and kept Parry up late listening to his conversation.[7] On such occasions the old man of eighty-two could rouse himself to behave as if he were fifty.

In spite of his age he was still interested in the work of younger poets and wrote to congratulate Kipling on his 'English Flag'. Kipling replied in suitably military language: 'When the commander in chief notices a private of the line the man does not say "thank you", but he never forgets the honour and it makes him fight better.'[8]

A natural reluctance to leave familiar surroundings was overtaking Tennyson, and he seemed more than ever disinclined to quit Farringford that spring, as if knowing that he would not return. It was unusually sunny, and he sat in the summer-house talking to friends, pointing out the fruit blossoms, or walking with them to the kitchen garden to see the fig tree, which he still contentedly described as 'like a breaking wave'. There had always been something otherworldly about the seclusion of Farringford, and now it had become almost ghostly, with the remote stillness of its gardens, the outmoded furniture and faded wallpaper of its rooms, and the dim candle lamps in the passages that made Parry think it 'the most old-fashioned house I ever saw'.[9]

In part the strange tranquillity of the house was due to the increased gentleness of its owner, who was remarked by his guests to have lost much of the awkwardness and truculence that had so often marked his behaviour in the past. He was simpler, more like a boy, tender in his consideration of others. There were, however, still outbursts of the old Tennyson, as is indicated by a letter written on the eve of the general election to an unknown correspondent. It reads in its entirety:

Sir,

I love Mr Gladstone but hate his present Irish policy.
I am yours faithfully,
Tennyson.

In June Tennyson and Hallam went by borrowed yacht to the Channel Islands, where Tennyson climbed like a young man on the rocks of Sark. In Jersey he visited his brother Frederick for the last time, renewing all the old ties of love in the knowledge that they would never see one another again, and trying unsuccessfully to get Frederick to come back on the yacht with them to Farringford.

On his last day at Farringford Tennyson took solemn farewell of it by having the Rector of Freshwater, Dr Merriman, come to administer Holy Communion to the family in his study. Tennyson, who had never been a regular church-goer, was determined that there would be no High-Church practices in his house, and before taking the sacrament he stoutly quoted Cranmer's Protestant assertion in *Queen Mary*:

> It is but a communion, not a mass,
> No sacrifice, but a life-giving feast.

On the first day of June the annual removal to Aldworth was made, and Tennyson went from there for his final visit to London, where he was characteristically occupied with two of his strongest interests: science and money. Sir William Flower, director of the Natural History Museum, escorted him around the new building, where he was most interested by the ichthyosaurus and the display of birds' nests. At Macmillans' he spent some time with G. L. Craik, arranging for a new volume of poetry and discussing arrangements for payment; as it turned out, the volume was not published until some three weeks after Tennyson's death. Craik was able to tell him that he had earned more than £10,000 that year, which was one of the most successful financially of his entire career. (After a lifetime of worry about money, he left an estate of more than £57,000 at his death.) In London Tennyson also heard that after its success on the New York stage, *The Foresters* had been published, and that Irving was once more making plans to produce *Becket*. Other indications of his popularity, if he had needed them, were the honorary degrees offered to him by Cambridge, for the fourth time, and by Trinity College, Dublin. He declined both.

At Aldworth he was happy to receive visitors, but he could seldom take his usual long walks with them. Instead, he would sit in the shelter of the hedges on the lawn or in his large study overlooking it, his head protected from draughts by a velvet skull-cap like that worn by one of Rembrandt's models. When he was talking to friends, he would sometimes seem to absent himself from the conversation, and without the stimulation of direct response to others, his watery old eyes would recede beneath the heavy bony brow, and his face, framed by straggly hair and unkempt beard, would settle into the elongated wrinkles of old age.

At the end of July, just before his eighty-third birthday, Tennyson came down with 'a slight cold which has affected the right side of his face & throat', as Hallam informed Sir Andrew Clark. He had 'a good deal of neuralgic pain', which was ascribed to a 'horrible & perpetual North Easter', and he could eat but little.[10] The neuralgia soon resolved itself into Tennyson's old enemy, gout, and though he had periods of relative freedom from pain, he was never well again. Tennyson realized that the end could not be far off, but he was chiefly concerned to keep the news of his condition from being made public, knowing that the last days of famous men are often made more terrible by the curiosity engendered in others, and that there may be a scarcely concealed anticipation of their death. With the onset of his final illness began the well-meant persecution by his friends, of whom even the closest seem to have been divided in motive between genuine sympathy and the wish to be among the last to have seen him alive. For a fortnight they streamed to Aldworth, then Hallam, who was making a brief trip to Somersby to see the old Rectory before it was sold, put a strict ban on visitors during his absence. When he returned, the visitors began again, and they could not be turned away for fear of alarming Tennyson unduly about his own condition. During the late summer Dakyns was there, bringing with him John Addington Symonds, accompanied by his Venetian gondolier, who hid in the bushes outside the house. Bram Stoker came to discuss Irving's plans for *Becket*; Craik brought proofs of the new volume with him; Jowett came to suggest loyally but unrealistically that Tennyson should continue writing daily. Tennyson's weakness is shown by his unwillingness to continue his years-old debate with Jowett; he begged him 'not to consult with him or argue with him, as was his wont, on points of philosophy and religious doubt'. The fragility of his religious position flickers through 'The Silent Voices', presumably composed in the last two or three months of his life:

When the dumb Hour, clothed in black,
Brings the Dreams about my bed,
Call me not so often back,
Silent Voices of the dead,
Toward the lowland ways behind me,
And the sunlight that is gone!
Call me rather, silent voices,
Forward to the starry track
Glimmering up the heights beyond me
On, and always on!

As his remark to Jowett suggests, there were moments of utter desolation when eternity seemed as uncertain as it ever had; once he told Wilfrid Ward that when he tried to pray in his illness, he felt as if God did not hear him. When Allingham's widow came to see him and said rather tentatively that she trusted he would soon be in better health, he said with a flash of his old irritability, 'Aren't we both being rather hypocritical?'[11]

On 29 September Tennyson took his last drive in the carriage. After eating, he was so nauseated that Hallam summoned the doctor from Petworth, then sent for both Sir Andrew Clark and Dr Dabbs of Freshwater, who had tended the family for years. Tennyson lay dying for a week in a ritualized hush that seems more like an elaborate death-bed scene from a Victorian novel than the end of an actual man's life. According to the doctors he was suffering from a combination of influenza and gout. No visitors were allowed, Hallam's children were sent away, and Tennyson had the constant attendance of the three physicians, several nurses, and the faithful Hallam, who scarcely slept for a week. Emily Tennyson was too feeble to help with her husband, but she was brought into his bedroom and put on a couch at his feet. Apparently Audrey was not thought to have much ability as a nurse, but she was detailed to keep a record in a notebook of every symptom, every conversation, in preparation, it seems, for Hallam's account of the death-bed in his biography of his father.

Part of Hallam Tennyson's deep love of his father was his total adoration of everything that Tennyson represented for his countrymen, so it is perhaps churlish to feel that he occasionally lost sight of a worn-out old man dying in a draughty bedroom on a Sussex hillside and saw instead the apotheosis of Victorian poetry. More of the sense of the end of Alfred Tennyson comes from Audrey's patient, factual record of his physical functions than from the elaborate hagiography of her husband, which was only the obverse of the morbid interest that Tennyson feared from the press.

At 8 a.m. on 3 October Tennyson asked for the volume of the Steevens edition of Shakespeare that contained *Cymbeline*, but when he had it in his hands he could read only a word or two before putting it down on the bed and saying to Dr Dabbs that now he was convinced of his approaching death. That night at midnight he woke, found Hallam at his bedside, and asked with concern why he was not asleep. 'I make a slave of you,' he said in remorse for the life that his son had given to him.

The following morning he called out fretfully, 'Where's my Shakespeare, I must have my Shakespeare', but his reaction to the book the day before had frightened the family, and he was told he must not read. He was at first pleased to hear that the Queen had sent a telegram of concern, then he muttered, 'O, that Press will get hold of me now!' Early in the evening he awoke from a vivid dream and asked, 'Have I not been walking with Gladstone in the garden this morning and shewing him my trees?' That night he was once more disturbed until he had the Shakespeare beside him on the bed.

The next day, 5 October, he found that the volume had again been removed, and when it was returned at his insistence he fumbled with it, then put it face down with his hand laid heavily on it, cracking the spine, so that today it still falls open to the speech of Posthumus to Imogen: 'Hang there like fruit, my soul,/Till the tree die', a passage that had always moved him to tears. He tried again that afternoon to read but could not, although he handled the book and said something that sounded like '. . . opened it'. As Hallam told the Duke of Argyll, Tennyson then spoke his last words, calling out, 'Hallam, Hallam', and whispering indistinctly to Emily, 'God bless you, my joy.' Audrey's more unimpassioned version was that 'it was almost impossible to make out more than a word here and there of what he said owing greatly I think to his having no teeth in'. When he had spoken to the family, he lapsed into unconsciousness from which he never recovered.

The family sat waiting for the end, with only the glow of the fire in the unlit room, like a group in a Victorian narrative painting. The account by Dr Dabbs shows the visual terms in which they comprehended Tennyson's death: 'On the bed a figure of breathing marble, flooded and bathed in the light of the full moon streaming through the oriel window; his hand clasping the Shakespeare which he had asked for but recently, and which he kept by him to the end; the moonlight, the majestic figure as he lay there, "drawing thicker breath," irresistibly brought to our minds his own "Passing of Arthur".' At 1.35 a.m., 6 October, after a few spasms that Dr Dabbs had calmed with chloroform, he died peacefully.[12]

The coffin in which he lay remained open until 10 October. On his head was a wreath of laurel from Virgil's tomb, gathered specifically for the purpose eleven years before by Alfred Austin, who hoped to succeed him as Poet Laureate. On his chest lay a bunch of roses from Emily, and in one hand was a copy of *Cymbeline*: it was not, however, that which had been in his hands during his illness but a volume taken from Audrey's edition of Shakespeare.

Emily Tennyson sent a wire to the Dean of Westminster after her husband's death: 'Decide as you think best. If it is thought better, let him have the flag of England on his coffin, and rest in the churchyard of the dear place where his happiest days have been passed. Only, let the flag represent the feeling of the beloved Queen, and the nation, and the empire he loved so dearly.' But there was no real question in her mind of where he should be buried, and Dean Bradley of course chose the Abbey. Emily Tennyson was too weak to attend the service on 12 October.

The Abbey was filled for the funeral, the nave was lined by men of the Balaclava Light Brigade, the London Rifle Volunteers, and boys of the Gordon Boys' Home, and there were huge crowds standing outside, but the service turned out to be disappointingly impersonal and conventional. The procession was long, swollen by what Edmund Gosse called a stream of nonentities. Among the twelve pallbearers were one duke, two marquises, two earls, a baron, and the American minister, but there was not a poet among them, not a Lincolnshire man, not an Apostle, and of the twelve Jowett was probably the only one who had ever called Tennyson by his Christian name. There was no lyricism, no beauty, no passion, no spontaneity: it was hardly to be distinguished from the funeral of any eminent public servant or military hero. Nearly every poet in the country who could lay claim to a modest reputation was there, and all of those who were hoping to succeed to the Laureate's bays, but Swinburne, who was acknowledged as the greatest poet after Tennyson, refused to attend. The Queen sent two wreaths, but there was no member of the Royal Family present. As Gladstone explained, he had 'been kindly invited to be a pall-bearer at the funeral: but unhappily his occupations of the moment are so heavy, that he could not spare the two days it would have required'.[13] Nor, apparently, could he spare the two hours it would have required to attend the funeral.

Henry James, who had once worried that the Laureate was not sufficiently Tennysonian, wrote that it was 'a lovely day, the Abbey looked beautiful, everyone was there, but something—I don't know what—of real impressiveness—was wanting'. There seemed to be 'too many masters of Balliol, too many Deans and Alfred Austins'.[14]

But it was Burne-Jones who best expressed both his own disappointment and a sense of how Tennyson should have been remembered: 'O but yesterday was so flat and flattening. I'll never forgive the Queen for not coming up to it, and I wish Gladstone had. And there should have been street music, some soldiers and some trumpets, and bells muffled all over London, and rumbling drums. I did hate it so heartily, but as he sleeps by Chaucer I daresay they woke and had nice talks in the night, and I have spent much of the early dark morning making up talks for them; I suppose he'll be hurrying off to Virgil soon. I wish I hadn't gone.'[15]

Within a fortnight Hallam Tennyson was hard at work on his biography, soliciting the return of letters that Tennyson had written, asking for contributions from all of his respectable friends. Palgrave and Henry Sidgwick helped him to read and sort out some 40,000 letters, then to destroy three-quarters of them, including practically all of Tennyson's letters to Emily before their marriage and those he had received from Arthur Hallam, as well as anything else that Hallam and Emily Tennyson had decided was unworthy of the tame, saintly character whose image they wanted to perpetuate. The process of making Tennyson's memory respectable was well in hand, and it was so successful that it took another half-century before the world began to suspect that behind the bland features of the Watts portraits and Hallam Tennyson's biography was the complicated mind and awkward personality of one of England's greatest poets.

In spite of the bad health from which she had suffered for sixty years, Emily Tennyson survived her husband by four years, and he continued to occupy her thoughts until the end. When Hallam assumed his inherited title, she asked not to be addressed as the Dowager Lady Tennyson but as Emily Lady Tennyson: 'A small matter but there seems to be in it a feeling that one is still his wife as one feels that one is.'[16] Suitably, she died shortly after the completion of *Alfred Lord Tennyson: A Memoir*, on which she had given her son so much help. The great task of her life was complete.

FAMILY TREE OF THE TENNYSONS

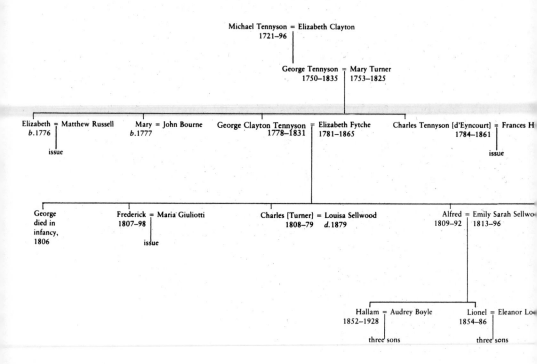

Michael Tennyson = Elizabeth Clayton
1721–96

George Tennyson = Mary Turner
1750–1835 · 1753–1825

Elizabeth = Matthew Russell Mary = John Bourne George Clayton Tennyson = Elizabeth Fytche Charles Tennyson [d'Eyncourt] = Frances H
b.1776 b.1777 1778–1831 · 1781–1865 1784–1861

issue issue

George Frederick = Maria Giuliotti Charles [Turner] = Louisa Sellwood Alfred = Emily Sarah Sellwo
died in 1807–98 1808–79 · d.1879 1809–92 · 1813–96
infancy,
1806 issue

Hallam = Audrey Boyle Lionel = Eleanor Lo
1852–1928 1854–86

three sons three sons

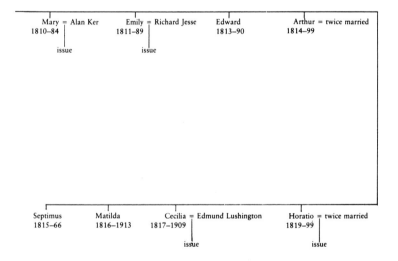

Mary = Alan Ker
1810–84

      issue

Emily = Richard Jesse
1811–89

      issue

Edward
1813–90

Arthur = twice married
1814–99

Septimus
1815–66

Matilda
1816–1913

Cecilia = Edmund Lushington
1817–1909

      issue

Horatio = twice married
1819–99

      issue

ACKNOWLEDGEMENTS

I am grateful to the present Lord Tennyson and the Tennyson Trustees for their kind permission to publish Tennyson material still in copyright; to Major Alfred Tennyson d'Eyncourt for permission (extended through Mr Michael Lloyd) to publish family material in the Lincolnshire Archives Office; to Sir Stephen Lennard, Bt., for permission to publish letters of A. H. Hallam and his family; to Professor J. E. Kerrich for permission (extended through Mrs A. McK. Terhune) to publish letters of Edward FitzGerald.

The following persons also have kindly allowed me to examine unpublished material in their possession and/or have given permission to use material in copyright: the Duke of Argyll, Miss Barham Johnson, the Viscount Boyne, Mr William Collins, Miss Janine Dakyns, Lady Elton, Mr J. H. Fryer-Spedding, Sir William Gladstone, Bt., the Hon. David Lytton Cobbold, Mrs Edward Norman-Butler, Mr R. H. Taylor, and Lady Delia Venables-Llewelyn (permission extended through the National Library of Wales). Mr Jeremy Maas, Professor Richard Purdy, Professor Gordon N. Ray, and Mr John Whale have generously supplied me with copies of material in their possession.

I hope that any copyright owner whom I have failed to trace, or from whom I have inadvertently not sought permission when I should have done so, will accept my apologies.

Extracts from the holdings of the following institutions are published with their kind permission: Bodleian Library; Trustees of the British Library; Cambridge University Library; Governing Body of Christ Church, Oxford; William R. Perkins Library, Duke University; Houghton Library, Harvard University; Hertfordshire Records Office; Huntington Library, San Marino; Lilly Library, Indiana University; University of Iowa Libraries; Brotherton Collection, University of Leeds; Lincolnshire Archives Office; Pierpont Morgan Library; Department of Rare Books and Manuscripts, Princeton University Library; National Library of Scotland; George Arendts Research Library for Special Collections, Syracuse University; Tennyson Research

Centre; Master and Fellows of Trinity College, Cambridge; National Library of Wales; Wellesley College Library; Beinecke Rare Book and Manuscript Library, Yale University.

Professor Cecil Y. Lang and Professor Edgar F. Shannon, Jr., have most kindly allowed me to read and quote from their forthcoming edition of the letters of Alfred Tennyson. Other scholars to whom I am pleasantly indebted, for permission to read and quote from unpublished editions and writings, are Professor Jack Kolb, Mrs A. McK. Terhune, Sir Francis Hill, Dr Susan Shatto and Dr Marian Shaw, Professor Philip L. Elliott, Professor Peter Allen, and Miss Mary Barham Johnson. Mr Bernard Aspinwall and Dr Priscilla Metcalf have also been kind enough to let me see copies of unpublished work.

For advice, help, and generosity too various to specify, I am indebted to: Mr Derek Auger, Mr Wilfrid Blunt, Professor Philip Collins, Professor T. J. Collins, Mr Aidan Day, Mrs Hope Dyson, Mr Laurence Elvin, Miss S. J. Flower, Professor James O. Hoge, Mrs W. F. Kochan, Mr Terence R. Leach, Professor R. M. Ludwig, Lady Maitland, Lady Mander, Miss Dorothy Milnes, Mrs Michael Noakes, Professor Ralph W. Rader, Professor C. R. Sanders, Mrs Arthur Sherwood and the Princeton University Press, Mr Hallam Tennyson, Professor Kathleen Tillotson, Dr J. M. Walker, Dr R. S. Woof, Mrs J. D. Wrisdale, Mrs G. F. Yates, University Research Committee of Princeton University, National Endowment for the Humanities, American Council of Learned Societies, Rockefeller Foundation, American Philosophical Society.

I regret that it is impossible to acknowledge all the excellent works of Tennyson criticism and research that have appeared in recent years and that have been of such help to me, but their authors and other scholars will recognize my debt. It would be real ingratitude, however, not to mention two works that have deeply influenced my thinking: *Tennyson, the Growth of a Poet*, by J. H. Buckley, and *Tennyson*, by Christopher Ricks.

Finally, with affection, I must acknowledge help that went far beyond any recognizable category, that of the poet's grandson, the late Sir Charles Tennyson, most generous of scholars and most patient of friends.

ABBREVIATIONS USED IN THE NOTES

❊

Persons

AHH	Arthur Henry Hallam
AT	Alfred Tennyson
CTDE	Charles Tennyson d'Eyncourt, born Tennyson, uncle of AT
CTT	Charles Turner, born Tennyson, brother of AT
EFG	Edward FitzGerald
EFT	Elizabeth Tennyson, born Fytche, wife of GCT, mother of AT
EST	Emily Tennyson, born Sellwood, wife of AT
ETJ	Emily Jesse, born Tennyson, sister of AT
ETR	Elizabeth Russell, born Tennyson, aunt of AT
FHTDE	Frances Tennyson d'Eyncourt, born Hutton, wife of CTDE
FT	Frederick Tennyson, brother of AT
GCT	George Clayton Tennyson, father of AT
GHTDE	George Hildeyard Tennyson d'Eyncourt, son of CTDE
GT	George Tennyson, grandfather of AT
HT	Hallam Tennyson, son of AT
JS	James Spedding
RMM	Richard Monckton Milnes, later Lord Houghton
WEG	William Ewart Gladstone

Books

Alfred Tennyson	Charles Tennyson, *Alfred Tennyson*, 1949.
Background	Charles Tennyson and Hope Dyson, *The Tennysons: Background to Genius*, 1974.
DHL	Hope Dyson and Charles Tennyson, ed., *Dear and Honoured Lady: the Correspondence Between Queen Victoria and Alfred Tennyson*, 1969.
EFG	*Letters and Literary Remains of Edward FitzGerald*, ed. W. A. Wright, 7 vols., 1902–3.
Friends	*Tennyson and His Friends*, ed. Hallam Tennyson, 1911.
Letters, AHH	*The Letters of Arthur Henry Hallam*, ed. Jack Kolb, forthcoming. The inclusion of the cue-title in parentheses in the notes indicates that the text was taken from another source but is also included in this edition.

Letters, A ?	*The Letters of Alfred Lord Tennyson*, ed. Cecil Y. Lang and Edgar F. Shannon, Jr., vol. i, forthcoming. The inclusion of the cue-title in parentheses in the notes indicates that the text was taken from another source but is included in this edition.
Letters, EFG	*The Letters of Edward FitzGerald*, ed. A. McK. and Annabelle T. Terhune, forthcoming.
Letters, EST	*The Letters of Emily Lady Tennyson*, ed. James O. Hoge, 1974.
Mem.	[Hallam Tennyson], *Alfred Lord Tennyson: a Memoir*, 2 vols., 1897.
Poems	*The Poems of Tennyson*, ed. Christopher Ricks, 1969.

Unpublished Material in the Tennyson Research Centre

'Annales Tennysoniani'	scrapbooks assembled by Tennyson's nephew, Eustace Jesse.
'CT Notebooks'	MS notebooks used by Sir Charles Tennyson in preparing *Alfred Tennyson*.
'Journal, EST'	kept by Emily Tennyson, 1850–74, after which there are a few entries by Emily Tennyson and her son Hallam.
'Marlborough'	notebook in which Hallam Tennyson as a schoolboy at Marlborough recorded his father's conversation.
Materials	'Materials for a Life of A.T. Collected for My Children', 4 vols., 1894–5, largely printed from *MS. Mats.*
MS. Mats.	'MS. Materials', 10 vols., 1894, largely in MS, earliest surviving version of Hallam Tennyson's *Alfred Lord Tennyson: a Memoir.*
T. and Friends	'Tennyson and His Friends', 2 vols., 1896, second printed stage of *Mem.*
'Talks and Walks'	notebook in which Audrey Tennyson recorded her father-in-law's conversation.

Locations of MS Material

Barham Johnson	family letters owned by Miss Mary Barham Johnson; also her study of the Apostles in preparation, provisionally known as *Cambridge 'Apostolic' Episodes, 1827–1837.*
BL	British Library.
Boyne	Russell family letters, in possession of the Viscount Boyne.
Brotherton	Brotherton Collection, Brotherton Library, University of Leeds.
Cambridge	University Library, Cambridge.
Christ Church	Hallam family papers, Christ Church Library, Oxford.
Dakyns	family letters in possession of Miss Janine Dakyns.
Duke	Tennyson Collection, Duke University Library.
Elton	family papers in possession of Lady Elton.
Harvard	Houghton Library, Harvard University.
Huntington	Henry E. Huntington Library and Art Gallery.
Iowa	University of Iowa Library.

LAO	Tennyson and Tennyson d'Eyncourt papers in the Lincolnshire Archives Office.
Lilly	Lilly Library, Indiana University.
Lytton	Lytton family papers, Hertfordshire Records Office.
Morgan	Pierpont Morgan Library.
Princeton	Department of Rare Books and Manuscripts, Princeton University Library.
Spedding	family papers in possession of Mr J. H. Fryer-Spedding.
Syracuse	George Arendts Research Library, Syracuse University.
TRC	Tennyson Research Centre, Lincoln.
Trinity	Trinity College Library, Cambridge.
Wellesley	Wellesley College Library.
Yale	Beinecke Library, Yale University.

NOTES

The primary printed source for Tennyson's biography is *Alfred Lord Tennyson: a Memoir* by his son Hallam, who had complete access to the voluminous family papers before he destroyed some three-quarters of them. In order to avoid printing even more notes than are here, quotations from the *Memoir* are documented only when they are of special interest, since the work is so well known and so easily available. For the convenience of that rare reader who wants to know still more about the sources of this biography, I have deposited copies of the working typescript in the Tennyson Research Centre and in the Department of Rare Books and Manuscripts, Princeton University Library. That typescript contains references to the quotations from the *Memoir*, as well as the hundreds of other sources that it would be supererogatory to mention here.

Chapter I. The Foundation of a Family

1. Carpenter, p. 268.
2. A full and lively account of the family and its fortunes is given by Sir Charles Tennyson and Mrs Hope Dyson in *The Tennysons: Background to Genius*.
3. *MS. Mats.* ix. 9.
4. FHTDE to Mrs Hutton, 7.11.13, 4H.6/44, LAO.
5. 'Marlborough.'
6. *Background*, p. 34.
7. Quoted by William Collier to Sir Charles Tennyson, 22.10.1971, TRC.
8. *Alfred Tennyson*, p. 6; the statement was changed in the reissue of 1968.
9. To Mr Robinson, 30.6.1793, TRC.
10. 13.5.1799, TRC.
11. 11.7.1799, TRC.
12. 1.3.1800, TRC.
13. 1.6.01, H.149/3, LAO.
14. McCabe, p. 734.
15. 6.8.05, TRC.
16. 20.6.07, H.144/36, LAO.
17. Nicoll and Wise, ii. 423.

Chapter II. Childhood and Schooling, 1809–1820

1. GCT to CTDE, 24.4.19, H.84/11, LAO.
2. Fragment in the hand of AT, TRC.
3. One-volume *Mem.*, 1906, p. 546.

4. Graves, *Grove*, pp. 197–8.
5. *Mem*. i. 11; in the preliminary drafts of 'Aspects of Tennyson' Knowles recorded Tennyson's words as 'I hear a voice that whispers in the wind', TRC.
6. *MS. Mats*. i. 2.
7. *Background*, p. 56.
8. Mrs GT to GT, 21.2.09, H.67/6, LAO.
9. HT's 1876 notebook, TRC.
10. GT to CTDE, 5.3.15, H.73/26, LAO.
11. Mrs GT to CTDE, 31.3.[16], 4H.11/-, LAO.
12. AT to B.P. Blood, 7.5.74, Harvard.
13. TRC.
14. Blathwayt, p. 40; *MS. Mats*. i. 21.
15. *MS. Mats*. ix. 6.
16. 'Marlborough.'

Chapter III. Dr Tennyson's Breakdown, 1820–1827

1. 24.4.20, 'CT Notebooks', i.
2. To GT, 16.1.22, H.88/31, LAO.
3. CTDE to GT, 14.7.18, H.79/20; GT to CTDE, 16.7.18, H.77/5; CTDE to GT, 18.7.18, H.79/25, LAO.
4. FHTDE to CTDE, 19.10.[19?], H.151/4, LAO.
5. H.144/142, LAO.
6. Copy, H.144/144, LAO.
7. Ridding, p. 76.
8. GCT to Mrs GT, 15.4.22, H.144/149; FT to GT, 28.4.22, 4H.48/-, LAO.
9. E. S. Turner, pp. 115–16.
10. 9.11.22, 4H.24/-, LAO.
11. GT to CTDE, 23.11.22, 4H.24/-, LAO.
12. Mary Bourne to CTDE, 2.3.24, H.91/41, LAO.
13. 'Marlborough'; Maisie Ward, pp. 167–8; [Peter Haythornthwaite], 'Tennyson: A Reminiscence by a Catholic Priest', MS, TRC.
14. GCT to GT, 21.1.24, H.144/159, LAO.
15. 1.2.24, H.144/160, LAO.
16. To CTDE, 5.3.25, 4H.33/-; 9.3.25, H.144/165, LAO.
17. 17.3.25, H.144/167, LAO.
18. J. H. Vane, 14.5.25, H.144/168, LAO.
19. GT to CTDE, 22.7.25, H.144/170, LAO.
20. H.147/4, LAO (*Letters, AT*).
21. AT to GT, 9.10.[25], H.147/5, LAO (*Letters, AT*).
22. GCT to GT, 23.1.26, H.97/26; GCT to GT, 1.2.26, H.97/27, LAO.
23. [July 1826?], H.97/33, LAO (*Letters, AT*).
24. 24.8.24, H.91/59, LAO.
25. Robert Gooch to CTDE, 1.10.25, 4H.33/-, LAO.
26. To GT, 23.2.21, H.86/46, LAO.
27. To CTDE, 12.9.25, H.94/15, LAO.
28. 28.7.25, H.144/182, LAO.

29. Ritchie, *Records*, p. 6.
30. 29.12.12, H.66/24, LAO.
31. W. F. Rawnsley, p. 6.
32. *Tennyson in Egypt, passim.*
33. GCT to GT, 27.10.26, H.144/173, LAO.
34. 22–24.1.27, H.148/1a, LAO.
35. 4.6.27, 2H.16/10, LAO.
36. 10.10.27, 4H.39/-, LAO.
37. W. B. Bousfield to CTDE, 17.10.27, 4H.39/-, LAO.
38. To ?, 23.10.27, 4H.39/-, LAO.
39. 24.10.27, 4H.39/-, LAO.
40. 23.11.27, H.148/12, LAO.

Chapter IV. Early Days at Cambridge, 1827–1829

1. AT to GT, 5.12.[27], H.147/6, LAO (*Letters, AT*).
2. [Leslie Stephen], p. 1.
3. *EFG* iv. 100.
4. Teichman, p. 1.
5. Thackeray: *The Uses of Adversity*, p. 128.
6. 5.12.[27], H.147/6, LAO (*Letters, AT*).
7. For GT's arrangements: GT to CTDE, 12.12.27, H.101/18; GT to CTDE, 31.12.27, H.101/16, 17; J. Fytche to GT, 15.1.28, 2H.85/4; CTDE to GT, 14.1.28, 2H.85/3, LAO.
8. 26.11.27, H.148/13, LAO (*Letters, AT*).
9. Copy, GT to CTT, 29.11.27, H.148/16, LAO.
10. CTDE to GT, 21.1.28, H.104/5; 27.2.28, 2H.85/9, LAO.
11. [23.9.28], 2H.85/18, LAO.
12. 18.4.[28], Boyne (*Letters, AT*).
13. Merivale: pp. 99–100.
14. GHTDE to CTDE, 5.12.28, 2H.85/25, LAO.
15. 5.10.28, 2H.23/31, LAO.
16. 20.1.29, 2H.23/34, LAO.
17. GHTDE to CTDE, 25.10.28, 2H.85/22, LAO.
18. 20.3.29, 2H.86/30, LAO.
19. CTDE to GHTDE, 7.11.28, 2H.23/31a, LAO.
20. 24.1.29, 2H.23/35, LAO.
21. G. A. Browne, 16.12.28, 2H.85/27, LAO.
22. To [H.P.] Brougham, 6.6.[29], 2H.86/53, LAO.
23. 26.1.29, 2H.86/3, LAO.
24. GCT to GT, 4.2.29, 2H.86/10, LAO.
25. EFT to GT, 27.2.29, 2H.86/19, LAO.
26. 24.2.29, 4H.58/-, LAO.
27. EFT to GT, 27.2.29, 2H.86/19; GCT to CTDE, 23.3.29, H.107/14, LAO.
28. 27.2.29, H.1/135, LAO.
29. 12.3.29, 2H.86/22, LAO.
30. To CTDE, 7.5.29, H.107/19, LAO.

Chapter V. Arthur Hallam at Cambridge, 1829

1. *MS. Mats.* i. 62.
2. Gaskell: p. 164.
3. Fox: p. 153.
4. *Friends*, p. 447.
5. Gaskell: p. 139.
6. Miller, p. 136.
7. *Friends*, p. 450.
8. To Ellen Hallam, [3.12.]28, Christ Church (*Letters, AHH*); Gaskell: p. 130; Gaskell to WEG, 5.1.30, BL.
9. 28.2.29, *Letters, AHH*.
10. Ritchie, *Records*, p. 19.
11. Frances Brookfield, *Apostles*, pp. 229, 127; 10.11.31, Spedding.
12. Alford: pp. 94, 65.
13. Rader, p. 12; 7.9.[31], Spedding.
14. *Friends*, p. 451.
15. Thackeray: *The Age of Wisdom*, p. 84; Jebb, p. 273.
16. 15.8.[29], Trinity (*Letters, AHH*).
17. *Friends*, p. 451.
18. Gaskell: p. 164.
19. 7.6.29, 2H.86/49; 11.6.29, 2H.86/50, LAO.
20. *Friends*, p. 263; [12.7.29], H.147/2, LAO (*Letters, AT*).
21. 'Annales Tennysoniani.'

Chapter VI. The Apostles, 1829

1. Copy, GT to EFT, 15.8.29, 2H.86/74, LAO.
2. 24.5.29, H.147/12; 27.6.29, 2H.86/55; 6.7.29, 2H.86/61, LAO.
3. To GT, 31.7.29, 2H.86/71, LAO.
4. To GT, 12.8.29, 2H.86/73, LAO.
5. 24.6.29, 2H.86/52, LAO.
6. 7.6.29, 2H.86/48, LAO.
7. H. D. Rawnsley, *Memories*, p. 68.
8. Ibid.
9. To ETJ, 8.5.85, 'Annales Tennysoniani'; *Materials*, iv. 196.
10. 'Talks and Walks.'
11. Culler, pp. 2–4.
12. Adamson, p. 73.
13. Trench: i. 51.
14. de Vere:p. 34; Milnes: Pope-Hennessy, *Years of Promise*, p. 15.
15. Nicolson, *Tennyson*, p. 77; *MS. Mats*. i. 230; Frances Brookfield, *Apostles*, p. 12.
16. Quoted, Frances Brookfield, *Apostles*, p. 8.
17. EFG to W. H. Thompson, 18.21.41, *Letters, EFG*.
18. Knowles, p. 187.
19. Frances Brookfield, *Apostles*, p. 262.
20. Ibid., p. 362.

21. John Allen: A. O. Allen, p. 36; Peter Allen, p. 136; *Friends*, p. 115.
22. Peter Allen, pp. 215, 49; Hudson, *Munby*, p. 220; AHH to RMM, [31.7.31], Trinity (*Letters, AHH*).

Chapter VII. Hallam at Somersby and *Poems, Chiefly Lyrical*, 1829–1830

1. EFG's copy of AT's 1842 *Poems*, MS note, i. 44, Trinity.
2. Clark, p. 167.
3. 14.2.30, Spedding.
4. Kolb, 'Arthur Hallam and Emily Tennyson', p. 36.
5. In 'Arthur Hallam and Emily Tennyson' Jack Kolb suggests April 1830 as the date of their first meeting, in a skilfully argued and admirably documented article to which I am much indebted, but for reasons that appear subsequently I accept the date first given by HT.
6. McCabe, p. 731; A. C. Benson, p. 345; Kemble, 'An Old Woman's Gossip', p. 711.
7. AHH to ETJ, 12.12.[32], TRC (*Letters, AHH*); 'Journal, EST', 29.11.69.
8. 23.10.[32], TRC (*Letters, AHH*).
9. *MS. Mats.* i. 93.
10. Trench: i. 59.
11. [6.2.]33, TRC (*Letters, AHH*); cf. *Mem.* i. 92, where HT changes the quotation and identifies the £11 as 'the sum my father received for the 1830 volume'.
12. Frances Brookfield, *Apostles*, p. 135.
13. [30.10.32], Wellesley (*Letters, AHH*).
14. For the meeting of AT and EST see Hoge, 'Emily Tennyson's Narrative for Her Sons', pp. 96–7; alternative MS version of this last in TRC; *Mem.* i. 148.
15. JS to Edward Spedding, 27.12.30 and 6.5.30, Spedding.
16. AHH to EFT, [June 1830], TRC (*Letters, AHH*).
17. [31.5.30], *Letters, AHH*.
18. To JS, 16.8.31, Spedding.
19. 23.6.30, 14.6.31, Barham Johnson, 'Episodes'.
20. Trench: i. 111.
21. 10.2.31, Trinity.
22. 15.11.30, Trinity.

Chapter VIII. The Valley of Cauteretz, 1830

1. GCT to CTDE, 23.3.30, 2H.88/1, LAO.
2. GT to CTDE, 16.1.30, 2H.87/10, LAO.
3. 17.7.30, 2H.88/48, LAO.
4. To John Frere, 27.7.30, Yale.
5. 5.7.30, 2H.88/36, LAO.
6. [June 1830], TRC (*Letters, AHH*).
7. Stuart, p. 213.
8. CTT to John Frere, 27.7.30, Yale.
9. H. D. Rawnsley, *Literary Associations of the English Lakes*, ii, 103–5.
10. Trench: i. 109.

11. Ibid. i. 84.
12. *MS. Mats.* i. 77.
13. *Letters, AT*, where it is conjecturally dated mid-March 1832.
14. *Letters, AHH*.
15. 15.11.[30], Trinity.
16. EFG's copy of AT's *1830 Poems, Chiefly Lyrical*, MS note, Trinity.
17. JS to Edward Spedding, 5.12.30, Spedding.
18. Wordsworth: *Letters, William and Dorothy*, i. 539; JS to his mother, 16.12.30, Spedding; 10.2.31, Trinity.
19. JS to his mother, 16.12.30, Spedding.
20. *MS. Mats.* i. 180; *Materials*, i. 148.

Chapter IX. Death of Dr Tennyson, 1831

1. *Friends*, p. 219.
2. Donne: p. 5.
3. Frances Brookfield, *Apostles*, p. 310.
4. Merivale: p. 113.
5. To Milnes, 10.2.31, Trinity.
6. Henry Hallam to T. H. Rawnsley, 22.8.32, H.110/15, LAO
7. 9.3.31, Spedding.
8. [March 1831], TRC (*Letters, AHH*).
9. 28.2.31, 2H.91/2; to CTDE, 3.3.31, 2H.91/5, LAO.
10. 5.3.31, 2H.91/9, LAO.
11. H.147/3, LAO (*Letters, AT*).
12. 23.3.31, Duke; 28.3.31, 2H.91/52, LAO.
13. [March 1831], TRC (*Letters, AHH*); Allingham: *Diary*, p. 330.
14. *MS. Mats.* i. 104; *Mem.* i. 74; 'Annales Tennysoniani'.
15. 29.3.31, 2H.91/54; 22.3.31, 2H.90/8, LAO.
16. To GHTDE, 21.3.31, 2H.90/7, LAO.
17. Copy, 20.3.31, 2H.90/6, LAO.
18. 26.3.31, 2H.91/51, LAO.
19 T. H. Rawnsley to GT, 4.4.31, 2H.91/58, LAO.
20. 10.9.31, 2H.91/83, LAO.
21. 14.9.31, 2H.91/84, LAO.
22. 22.5.31, Spedding.
23. 18.5.31, 2H.91/63, LAO.
24. To CTDE, 18.6.31, 2H.91/66, LAO.
25. To CTDE, 1.10.31, 2H.91/85, LAO.
26. [Mid-March 1832], *Letters, AT*.
27. 8.7.[31], Harvard (*Letters, AHH*).
28. 13.1.[31], Iowa (*Letters, AHH*).
29. To Brookfield, 3.8.[31], Harvard (*Letters, AT*); copy 15.7.31, TRC (*Letters, AHH*).
30. Copy, [14.8.31], TRC (*Letters, AHH*).
31. Copy, AHH to FT, [5–9.10.31], TRC (*Letters, AHH*).
32. Donne: pp. 8–9 (*Letters, AHH*).

33. 15.6.31, 2H.26/8, LAO.
34. CTDE to GT, 21.6.31, 2H.92/22, LAO.

Chapter X. Journey to the Rhine, 1832

1. 18.4.32, Duke; 13.11.[32], Iowa (*Letters, AHH*).
2. [4.2.32], Morgan (*Letters, AHH*).
3. Trench to Donne, 20.4.32, Barham Johnson, 'Episodes'; Trench: i. 113; A. M. Brookfield, p. 173 (*Letters, AHH*).
4. To Brookfield, 4.3.[32], Morgan (*Letters, AHH*).
5. Copy, 4.4.32, TRC; to RMM, 8.5.[32], Trinity (*Letters, AHH*).
6. JS to Edward Spedding, [February 1832], Spedding.
7. Copy, AHH to AT, 10.4.32, TRC (*Letters, AHH*).
8. 'Talks and Walks'; Mrs Lloyd of Elmleigh, Louth, to HT, n.d., TRC.
9. To John Frere, 18.4.32, Duke.
10. Howitt, p. 702.
11. Donne: pp. 10, 14.
12. 22.6.[32], Bodleian (*Letters, AHH*).
13. AHH to ETJ, 23.6.32, Wellesley (*Letters, AHH*); Kemble, *Records*, pp. 519–20.
14. AHH to ETJ, 19.5.[32], Shorter, n.p. (*Letters, AHH*).
15. AHH to Kemble, [5–7.7.32], BL (*Letters, AHH*); 10.3.[33], Boyne (*Letters, AT*).
16. 12–14.8.32, Morgan (*Letters, AHH*).
17. [16–20.7.32], from letter in possession of Prof. Richard Purdy (*Letters, AHH*).
18. 10.3.[33], Boyne (*Letters, AT*).
19. JS to Edward Spedding, 10.8.32, Spedding.
20. To Brookfield, 20.4.[32], Harvard.
21. GT to CTDE, 27.7.32, 'CT Notebooks' iii; AHH to ETJ, 30.10.32, Wellesley (*Letters, AHH*).
22. T. H. Rawnsley to CTDE, 25.8.32, H.110/16a, LAO.
23. 22.8.32, H.110/15, LAO.
24. 23.8.32, H.111/71, LAO; [10.9.32], *Letters, AHH*.
25. Gaskell: pp. 213–14 (*Letters, AHH*).
26. Copy, 24.9.32, TRC (*Letters, AHH*).
27. 20.11.32, *Letters, AHH*.
28. 5.12.[32], TRC (*Letters, AHH*).

Chapter XI. Crushing Reviews: Bulwer, Croker, Wilson, 1833

1. Culler, p. 36.
2. Quoted, *Poems*, p. 181.
3. T. H. Rawnsley to CTDE, [26.]3.31, 2H.91/51, LAO. Since Paden (p. 120, n. 46) the date of the coming of the Edens to the neighbourhood has been given erroneously as 1825.
4. See Kolb, 'When Did Tennyson Meet Rosa Baring?'.
5. *Random Recollections*, pp. 331–2.
6. Brightfield, p. 350.
7. Kemble, 'An Old Woman's Gossip', p. 711.

8. To GHTDE, 28.11.33, H.113/62, LAO.

9. Coleridge: p. 232. AT apparently thought that Coleridge's remark referred to the *Poems* of 1830 (*Mem.* i. 50). In 1883 he was still so annoyed he wrote, 'Coleridge—spite of his great name—spoke like an ass. I had written thousands of lines in the regular Pope-metre before I knew there was a Coleridge extant.' (Jennings, p. 43, TRC copy). His irritation may have lain behind his refusal to meet Coleridge (Allingham: *Diary*, p. 337).

10. Copy, [May 1833], TRC (*Letters, AHH*).

Chapter XII. Death of Arthur Hallam, 1833

1. GT to CTDE, [March 1833], H.113/13, LAO.

2. Julia Tennyson to CTDE, 29.12.33, H.113/79, LAO.

3. 30.7.33, H.113/30; FHTDE to CTDE, 9.8.33, H.113/33, LAO.

4. For the change of the family name, see H.3, H.112, H.113, H.114, 2H.64, *passim*, LAO.

5. 10.3.[33], Boyne (*Letters, AT*).

6. Trench: i. 136; Peter Allen, p. 152.

7. To RMM, 24.9.[33], Trinity.

8. *MS. Mats.* i. 122; Peter Allen, p. 152.

9. Elliott, p. 24; Peter Allen, p. 152.

10. 26.8.33, H.113/36, LAO.

11. 27.4.34, H.116/22, LAO.

12. To J. Frere, 10.2.34, copy in *MS. Mats.* i. 204; it has been badly mutilated, presumably to get rid of other references to CTT's opium habit. The original, at Duke University, has this section deleted by heavy inking.

13. Stephen Spring-Rice to J. W. Blakesly, quoted *Letters, AHH*, 25.5.33, n.2.

14. *Mem.* i. 102–3. My dating is conjectural, since it would have been difficult for AT in Scotland to receive a letter from Somersby or London on Wednesday, 31 July, and to return to London before AHH's departure, as the *Memoir* indicates. HT and his wife, who copied out many letters for the *Memoir*, were both thoroughly inaccurate and frequently assigned dates to letters that were wrong by as much as a whole year; either the dating of the letter or the account of the visit to London must be in error. It seems probable that it is the date that is mistaken here.

15. Molloy, ii. 366.

16. Copy, to AT and ETJ, 6.9.33, TRC (*Letters, AHH*).

17. Accounts of AHH's death differ in detail; see Francis Doyle to WEG, 3.10.33, and J. M. Gaskell to WEG, 19.10.33, BL; Henry Elton to AT, 1.10.33, TRC; Napier, p. 129; *Materials*, i. 124; *T. and Friends*, i. 105; *Mem.* i. 105.

18. 'Journal, EST', 29.11.69.

19. Gladstone: *Diaries*, i. 263.

20. Butler to HT, 15.11.86, TRC.

21. 'An Old Woman's Gossip', p. 711.

22. 18.12.33, H.113/67, LAO.

23. [10.10.33], TRC.

24. *EFG* i. 26.

25. To GHTDE, 18.12.33, H.113/67, LAO.
26. Rashdall's diary is in the Bodleian Library; it was first used by R. W. Rader.
27. Copy, TRC.
28. *MS. Mats.* i. 230.

Chapter XIII. Mirehouse, and Death of Tennyson's Grandfather, 1835

1. To Princess Alice, TRC.
2. To J. Frere, 10.2.34, Duke.
3. *MS. Mats.* i. 3.
4. J. T. Fields, p. 28.
5. *MS. Mats.* i. 207; FitzGerald: Terhune, p. 121.
6. 29.3.35, H.117/64, LAO.
7. To J. Frere, 10.2.34, Duke.
8. *MS. Mats.* i. 214.
9. Elton.
10. 6.2.34, TRC; AT to GT, [July 1834], H.147/10, LAO (*Letters, AT*).
11. Details of ETJ's visit to the Hallams from Ellen Hallam's diary, Elton.
12. [14.4.35], Trinity.
13. ETJ to Ellen Hallam, [4.3.35], Trinity.
14. To CTDE, 14.3.35, H.117/54, LAO.
15. [Spring 1835], Huntington (*Letters, AT*).
16. To CTDE, 6.4.35, H.118/26, LAO.
17. *Friends*, p. 106.
18. Frances Brookfield, *Apostles*, p. 267.
19. To Ellen Hallam, 11.[5.35], Trinity.
20. Frances Brookfield, *Apostles*, p. 267.
21. W. F. Pollock, i. 129.
22. EFG's 1842 *Poems*, ii. 3–4, 63, Trinity.
23. *EFG* i. 38–9.
24. *EFG* iv. 221; Phyllis Spedding to Mrs John Spedding, 9.5.[35], Spedding.
25. To EFG, [June 1835], TRC (*Letters, AT*); *EFG* i. 35.
26. EFG's 1842 *Poems*, ii. 8, Trinity.
27. *Friends*, pp. 445, 145.
28. *Mem.* i. 155; *EFG* iv. 201.
29. In the opinion of Dr Robert Woof, who generously pointed out the entry.
30. 'Marlborough'; Frances Brookfield, *Apostles*, p. 268.
31. Frances Brookfield, *Apostles*, p. 268.
32. Norton: i. 465; Carlyle: Wilson, *1837–48*, p. 271.
33. 7.6.35, H.25/2; FHTDE to GHTDE, [30.7.35], H.116A, LAO.
34. [10.1.37], Trinity (*Letters, AT*).
35. To GHTDE, 1.8.35, H.116A/31, LAO.
36. According to Sir Francis Hill in his article on the Tennysons and the Tennyson d'Eyncourts, to be published by the Tennyson Society. Many of the figures in this chapter come from this source.
37. 29.8.35, H.116A/33, LAO.

38. To GHTDE, 1.9.35, H.116A/34; Edwin TDE, 3.9.35, H.118/54; FT to GHTDE, 25.10.35, 4H.46/-, LAO.
39. To GHTDE, 1.8.35, H.116A/31, LAO.
40. To CTDE, 29.8.35, H.118/46; to CTDE, 2.10.35, H.118/59, LAO.

Chapter XIV. Rosa Baring and Emily Sellwood, 1835–1837

1. Louis TDE to GHTDE, 29.8.35, H.116A/33, LAO.
2. FHTDE to GHTDE, 3.30.38, H.122/68; to GHTDE, 24.1.40, H.124/4, LAO.
3. Francis Hill, 'Squire and Parson', p. 343.
4. 27.5.35, H.116A/26, LAO.
5. Domett: p. 273.
6. [June 1835], TRC (*Letters, AT*).
7. The course of his acquaintance or intimacy with Rosa Baring has been fully explored by Professor Rader, in his original and scrupulously argued study of the background of *Maud*. My own partial disagreement with his conclusions arises from a belief that Tennyson's poetry indeed reflects his personal preoccupations without necessarily being a literal transcription of autobiographical experience.
8. *Alfred Tennyson*, p. 143.
9. Bodleian.
10. 17.5.36, H.119/49, H.119/50, LAO.
11. Rader, p. 59.
12. Henderson, p. 110.
13. FitzGerald: Thomas Wright, i. 114. The date is conjectural; Wright uses 1833, which is clearly wrong, since AT and EFG did not know each other then.
14. 4.4.37, Trinity.
15. To GT, 28.11.27, H.148/15, LAO.
16. Typed copy of Catherine Franklin's account, TRC; H. D. Rawnsley, *Memories*, pp. 68–70.
17. 29.12.36, H.119/111, LAO.
18. *Mem.* i. 158–60, amplified by original, 10.1.37, Trinity (*Letters, AT*).
19. Abbott, p. 202.

Chapter XV. Matthew Allen and Thomas Carlyle, 1837–1838

1. AT to EFG, [12.4.37], EFG's 1842 *Poems*, ii. 68–9, Trinity.
2. Ibid. ii. 194–5.
3. [13.7.37], BL (*Letters, AT*).
4. 23.[3].37, Spedding.
5. Allingham: *Diary*, p. 327.
6. Domett: p. 163.
7. 19.5.40, Spedding.
8. *Materials*, iv. 343.
9. 'Marlborough.'
10. To GHTDE, 1.12.37, H.121/81, LAO.
11. To Susan Haddelsey, [Summer 1837], TRC.
12. H. D. Rawnsley, *Memories*, p. 128 (*Letters, AT*).
13. To Susan Haddelsey, 23.3.[39], TRC.

14. *MS. Mats.* ii. 39.
15. To GHTDE, 1.12.37, H.121/81; FHTDE to GHTDE, 30.3.38, H.122/68, LAO.
16. 11.4.[38], TRC.
17. 2.5.37, H.120/42, LAO.
18. 31.8.37, H.121/61, LAO.
19. Milnes: Reid, i. 221.
20. *EFG* i. 53–4.
21. FitzGerald: *New Letters*, pp. 11–12, 25, 45.
22. *EFG* iv. 218.
23. [Jane Brookfield], 'Early Recollections', p. 205.
24. To the Duchess of Argyll, 26.12.63, TRC; 'Marlborough'; Thackeray: *Letters*, ii. 26.
25. Brownings: Miller, p. 44.
26. *Friends*, p. 131.
27. Carlyles: Sanders, p. 82.
28. Carlyles: *Emerson and Carlyle*, ii. 363; Tollemache, p. 265.
29. McCabe, p. 730.
30. Carlyles: Sanders, p. 85.

Chapter XVI. Break with Emily Sellwood, 1838–1842

1. To GHTDE, 20.2.[39], 4H.52/-, LAO.
2. Milnes: Reid, i. 220; Catharine Donne to B. Barton, 11.5.38, Barham Johnson; FitzGerald: *New Letters*, pp. 12–13.
3. [1841], TRC (*Letters, AT*).
4. Part of the letter is in *Letters, EST*, p. 43, where it is inexplicably dated 1844.
5. TRC (*Letters, AT*, where Glenthorne is identified as a house on the Devon coast near Lynmouth, where EST was staying. AT may have visited there on his way to Wales.)
6. TRC (*Letters, AT*, where July or August is suggested as the date).
7. Warre Cornish, January 1922, p. 267.
8. A. J. Symington to HT, 11.1.94, TRC.
9. TRC.
10. *Letters, EST*, p. 174, n. 2.
11. FitzGerald: *New Letters*, p. 19.
12. Cecilia Tennyson to Susan Haddelsey, n.d., TRC.
13. To Julia Hallam, May [1840], Christ Church.
14. *MS. Mats.* ii. 42, 149 (*Letters, AT*).
15. John Allen: Grier, p. 95; de Polnay, p. 216.
16. Elspeth Grahame, 'Some Memories of Alfred Tennyson', typescript, TRC.
17. 17.8.40, TRC.
18. To RMM, 7.11.41, Trinity.
19. Mary Anne Fytche to Susan Haddelsey, [1841], TRC.
20. 5.11.41, H.126/24, LAO.
21. [1842], Cambridge; [c.15.9.41], *Letters, EFG*.
22. 10.8.41, Lilly.

23. Crabb Robinson: *Books and Their Writers*, ii. 591; typescript of Catherine Franklin's account of meeting AT, TRC.
24. C. and F. Brookfield, *Circle*, pp. 102–6.
25. Brownings: Landis, p. 99.
26. Kolb, 'Arthur Hallam and Emily Tennyson', p. 48.
27. Typed copy, 17.3.[n.y.], TRC; Domett: p. 273.

Chapter XVII. Financial Disaster, 1842–1843

1. Allingham: *Diary*, p. 37.
2. Carlyles: *Collected Letters*, vii. 271.
3. FitzGerald: *New Letters*, p. 55.
4. Ibid., p. 57; EFG's 1842 *Poems*, ii. 147, Trinity.
5. *EFG* iii. 310.
6. [July 1842], TRC (*Letters, AT*).
7. Culler, p. 127.
8. Tuell, p. 149.
9. Allingham: *Diary*, p.150.
10. Brownings: Miller, pp. 118, 152; Landis, pp. 88, 92.
11. Brownings: Kenyon, *Browning and Domett*, p. 40; Kemble to W. B. Donne, 5.5.42, Barham Johnson.
12. Sterling to AT, 26.10.43, TRC.
13. *EFG* i. 137.
14. Eidson, p. 43.
15. 8.9.[42], *Letters, AT*.
16. MS. *Mats*. ii. 126 (*Letters, AT*).
17. Copy, July 1842, Yale.
18. 15.10.[42], TRC (*Letters, AT*).
19. Frederick Tennyson: p. 57.
20. Williams-Wynn: p. 25; H. D. Rawnsley, *Memories*, pp. 88–9.
21. BL.
22. 2.2.44, TRC (*Letters, AT*).
23. *Friends*, p. 113.
24. Henry Taylor: *Autobiography*, ii. 193.
25. 29.9.42, H.127/2, LAO.
26. [July 1842], TRC (*Letters, AT*); MS. *Mats*. iii. 3; to EFG, 2.2.44, TRC (*Letters, AT*).
27. 10.12.43, 'CT Notebooks' vi.
28. Brownings: Kenyon, *Letters*, i. 161.

Chapter XVIII. Emotional Breakdown, 1844–1845

1. Parry-Jones, p. 262.
2. Hallam Tennyson wrote that because of the failure of the woodworking scheme AT became ill '& again went off to Dr Gully's watercure near Malvern' (*MS. Mats*. ii. 138). One of the difficulties in accepting this is that it appears to postulate not one but two unrecorded visits to Malvern prior to the time that AT went to

Prestbury. Since HT subsequently deleted the statement, he presumably recognized that it was mistaken.

3. To CTDE, [6.8.44], H.129/12, LAO.
4. Carlyles: Froude, *Letters and Memorials of Jane Welsh Carlyle*, ii. 150.
5. To EFG, 2.2.44, TRC (*Letters, AT*); [6.8.44], H.129/12, LAO.
6. pp. 26, 25.
7. Pritchett, p. 231; AT to B. P. Blood, 4.5.74, Harvard; Jennings, pp. 105–6, TRC copy.
8. 2.2.44, TRC (*Letters, AT*).
9. Boyne (*Letters, AT*).
10. To RMM, 19.9.[44], Trinity.
11. *EFG* i. 210n.; Carlyles: *Emerson and Carlyle*, p. 363.
12. FitzGerald: *New Letters*, p. 97.
13. Ibid.; to FT, 6.2.43, Cambridge.
14. Carlyles: Sanders, p. 85; to Lady Peel, 27.12.44, BL.
15. WEG to Peel, 24.2.45; Hallam to Peel, 22.2.45, BL.
16. For Mrs Norton, see Moxon: p. 53; Crabb Robinson: *Books and Their Writers*, ii. 650–1, *Diary*, ii. 263–4; de Vere: p. 99; *Materials*, ii. 293.
17. Carlyles: Sanders, p. 86.
18. Carlyles: Sanders, pp. 86, 97.
19. Carlyles: *New Letters and Memorials of Jane Welsh Carlyle*, i. 180.
20. de Vere: p. 87.
21. Troubridge, p. 30.
22. Brownings: Miller, p. 245.
23. C. and F. Brookfield, *Circle*, pp. 148–50; de Vere: pp. 71–4.
24. de Vere: p. 76.

Chapter XIX. Civil List Pension and 'The New Timon', 1845–1846

1. For Wordsworth, see *Mem.* i. 208–10; de Vere: pp. 72–4; Una Taylor, p. 165.
2. H. D. Rawnsley, *Memories*, p. 136.
3. Wordsworth: *Letters of the Wordsworth Family*, iii. 319.
4. Jennings, pp. 105–6, TRC copy.
5. *MS Mats.* iv. 27.
6. [October 1845], Harvard (*Letters, AT*).
7. Carlyles: *New Letters of Thomas Carlyle*, ii. 6; 12.11.[46], TRC (*Letters, AT*).
8. Francis Hill, 'Squire and Parson', p. 343.
9. Jennings, p. 107, TRC copy.
10. Garnett, p. 284.
11. Notebook kept by HT, beginning September 1876, TRC; 'Marlborough'.
12. [January 1846], Lytton MSS.
13. Macready: *Journal*, p. 233.
14. Quoted, Shannon, *Tennyson and the Reviewers*, p. 85.
15. 15.3.46, Lytton MSS.
16. Frederick Tennyson: p. 80.
17. Bulwer: ii. 430–1.

Chapter XX. *The Princess*, 1846–1847

1. Brownings: Kintner, i. 427; *EFG* i. 237.
2. Brownings: Kintner, i. 427.
3. Ibid. ii. 701.
4. Brownings: Sharp, p. 110.
5. Brownings: Kintner, ii. 667.
6. 'Marlborough.'
7. Ossoli: iii. 98.
8. Jennings, p. 120, TRC copy; FitzGerald: *New Letters*, pp. 123–4; *Mem.* i. 279.
9. 'Talks and Walks.'
10. Champneys, i. 165.
11. Harvard.
12. Buckley, p. 88.
13. To EFG, 12.11.[46], TRC (*Letters, AT*).
14. Dickens: *Letters*, iv. 610.
15. C. and F. Brookfield, *Circle*, p. 200.
16. *MS. Mats.* ii. 166.
17. C. and F. Brookfield, *Circle*, p. 213.
18. *EFG* i. 286.
19. Frederick Tennyson: p. 81.
20. EFG to Thompson, 15.7.61, Trinity.

Chapter XXI. Financial Security and Marriage, 1848–1850

1. EFG to Cowell, 13.1.48, Trinity; Espinasse, p. 214; 31.12.47, 2H.44/1, LAO.
2. Carlyles: Wilson, *1848–53*, p. 11.
3. Emerson: *Journals*, x. 565.
4. de Vere: p. 146.
5. Allingham: *Diary*, p. 301.
6. Emerson: *Journals*, x. 537–9.
7. de Vere: p. 253.
8. Byles, pp. 190–4.
9. *Mem.* i. 276–9; *MS. Mats.* iii. 13.
10. 'Journal, EST', i. 12.
11. *MS. Mats.* iii. 3.
12. FitzGerald: *New Letters*, p. 165; *EFG* i. 275–6.
13. A. J. Symington to HT, 11.1.94, TRC.
14. Champneys, i. 179.
15. Allingham: *Diary*, p. 55.
16. Champneys, i. 181.
17. *Præraphaelite Diaries*, p. 267.
18. *Friends*, p. 143.
19. Francis Hill, 'Cracroft Diary', pp. 27–8.
20. *Alfred Tennyson*, p. 239.
21. Charles Tennyson, *Aldworth*, p. 5.

22. *Præraphaelite Diaries*, pp. 237–8.
23. [10.12.49], Harvard (*Letters, AT*).
24. TRC. The date is entered by a later hand from the postmark on the envelope. *Letters, AT* suggests reasonably that the proper day may be May 1850, but with Tennyson's fits and starts taken into account, his intention to marry within the month was probably only an interim decision.
25. Walter White: p. 142.
26. In the collection of R. H. Taylor, Princeton.
27. *EFG* i. 290–2, 305.
28. *Letters, EST*, p. 44.
29. *T. and Friends*, i. 350.
30. A. J. Symington to HT, 11.1.94, TRC.
31. W. F. Rawnsley, pp. 20–1.
32. To Ludovic Colquhoun, [10.7.50], TRC (*Letters, AT*).
33. Duke.
34. Written on flyleaf of vol. i, *Materials*.

Chapter XXII. The Golden Year: *In Memoriam* and the Laureateship, 1850

1. 21.6.50, TRC; AT to Monteith, 10.7.[50], *Letters, AT*.
2. 13.6.50, National Library of Wales.
3. Quoted by Edmund Peel to Catherine Bradshaw, 21.6.50, R. H. Taylor collection, Princeton.
4. W. F. Rawnsley, p. 21.
5. 13.6.50 and 20.6.50, TRC.
6. Carlyles: *Thomas Carlyle: Letters to His Wife*, p. 271.
7. Champneys, ii. 115.
8. de Vere: p. 158.
9. To John Carlyle, 29.4.50, National Library of Scotland; 'Journal, EST', i. 14; Carlyles: *Thomas Carlyle: Letters to His Wife*, pp. 271–2.
10. A. D. Coleridge, 'Notes of Conversations with Lord Tennyson', 1888–92, MS, TRC.
11. Shannon, *Tennyson and the Reviewers*, pp. 173–4.
12. Eliot, p. 291.
13. Knowles, p. 182.
14. Paul Turner, pp. 116–30.
15. Eliot, p. 294.
16. Walter White: p. 145.
17. [April 1850], Berg Collection, New York Public Library.
18. Rogers: Clayden, ii. 352–3.
19. Knowles, p. 167.
20. Helps: p. 215.
21. 25.11.[50], TRC; Champneys, i. 198.
22. Henry Taylor: *Autobiography*, i. 314; de Vere: p. 259 n.
23. Grant Duff, *1892–1895*, ii. 283.
24. 6.6.[50], 2H.51A/24, LAO.
25. Domett: p. 272.

Chapter XXIII. Literary London, 1851–1852

1. 'Journal, EST', i. 15.
2. Ibid. i. 26.
3. Allingham: *Letters*, p. 279.
4. Frances Brookfield, *Apostles*, p. 325; AT to EST, 6.3.51, Yale.
5. Macready: Trewin, *Mr Macready*, p. 238.
6. 'Journal, EST', 25.3.51.
7. *MS. Mats.* ix. 6.
8. For the Brownings and Tennysons, see Brownings: Heydon and Kelley, pp. 46–7; Brownings: Huxley, p. 136; 'Journal, EST', i. 29; *Mem.* ii. 16; Mitford: p. 191.
9. W. M. Rossetti: *Præraphaelite Diaries*, pp. 304, 233.
10. *Letters, EST*, p. 54; EST to Henry Sellwood, 18.8.51, TRC.
11. EST to Henry Sellwood, 27.8.51, TRC.
12. For Meredith and Tennyson, see Graves, *Parry*, i. 302; le Gallienne, p. 30; John Pollock, pp. 102–3; Stevenson, pp. 39–40.
13. Allingham: *Diary*, pp. 60–3.
14. Champneys, i. 71.
15. FMTDE to GTDE, 2.8.51, H.136/60, LAO; AT to EST, 23.1.52, TRC.
16. *MS. Mats.* iv. 27.
17. D. G. Rossetti: *Letters*, i. 106.
18. Brownings: Lubbock, p. 299.
19. Wemyss, i. 116; 'Journal, EST', i. 34; Allingham: *Diary*, p. 65.
20. C. and F. Brookfield, *Circle*, pp. 358–9.
21. RMM to AT, 19.9.[52], TRC; 16.11.52, Boyne.
22. Walter White: p. 147.

Chapter XXIV. Farringford and *Maud*. 1852–1855

1. Hudson, *Munby*, p. 24; Laughton, i. 299.
2. Mattheisen, p. 344.
3. *Materials*, ii. 84–91.
4. 'Journal, EST', i. 35.
5. Ibid.
6. *Friends*, p. 218.
7. AT to ETR, *c*.25.3.54, Boyne.
8. 'Journal, EST', i. 36; AT to C. Ellis, 6.11.87, Brotherton.
9. AT to ?, fragment, Harvard; C. Kegan Paul to EST, 29.5.[65], TRC.
10. Champneys, ii. 304; Haweis, p. 56; EST to Lear, 12.12.[54], TRC.
11. FitzGerald: Terhune, p. 185.
12. 'Journal, EST', i. 47, 41–2.
13. 'Journal, EST', i. 36, 44.
14. *Mem.* i. 381; EST, however, told Forster that it was written on 5.12.54 (6.12.54, TRC).
15. 5.2.55, H.141/10; 11.2.55, H.141/13, LAO.
16. AT to EST, 6.6.55, TRC; 'Journal, EST', i. 49; Young, ii. 283; A. D. Coleridge, 'Notes of Conversations', MS, TRC.
17. 'Journal, EST', i. 49.

Chapter XXV. A Literary Lion, 1855–1856

1 *Westminster Review*, October 1855, viii. 596–615; *Quarterly Review*, October 1859, cvi. 454–85. Like the reviews by Smith and Patmore, these were anonymous.

2. *Saturday Review*, 3 November 1855, i. 14–15.

3. *Edinburgh Review*, October 1855, cii. 498–519.

4. Arnold: *Letters to Clough*, p. 147.

5. MS. *Mats*. iv. 69. HT's treatment of the story is an amusing example of his overly prim editing. The original version is in his handwriting, and it is copied almost exactly in *Materials*. In *T. and Friends* the accusation has been toned down to: 'If an author pipe of all the crimes under the sun including suicide, set him down as the practiser of these crimes', and AT's response has become: 'Criminal I may be, suicide I am not yet.' But even HT could see that the emasculated story had lost its point, and thereafter it disappeared.

6. For the Brownings, Rossettis, and Tennyson, see W. M. Rossetti: *The P.R.B. Journal*, pp. 106–7; D. G. Rossetti: *Letters*, i. 266–7, 281–2, ii. 664, 863; Brownings: Lubbock, p. 331; Brownings: Rossetti, i. 182, ii. 248; Elizabeth A. Sharp, p. 66; *Mem.* i. 390.

7. For the Carlyles and Tennyson, see Davidson, p. 300; Carlyles: *Letters and Memorials of Jane Welsh Carlyle*, ii. 258; Carlyles: Sanders, pp. 91–2. As an old man Tennyson denied that the reading ever took place (Jennings, p. 155, TRC copy), but his memory was unreliable on such matters.

8. 'Journal, EST', i. 64.

9. Lear: Noakes, p. 127.

10. W. G. Clark to AT, 29.4.[61], TRC.

11. For the Grange party, see 'Journal, EST', i. 66; Espinasse, p. 94; AT to EST, 2.1.56, TRC; Origo, p. 179; *MS. Mats.* iv. 85; Jane Brookfield to EST, 3.1.[56], TRC; Carlyles: Sanders, pp. 91–2; Henry Taylor: *Correspondence*, pp. 210–13; Carlyles: Wilson, *1853–1865*, p. 207; Allingham: *Letters*, p. 144.

12. 'Journal, EST', i. 68; EST to Woolner, 27.5.56, TRC.

13. 'Journal, EST', i. 82.

14. *Materials*, ii. 167; MS *Mats*. iv. 96.

15. [1856], Trinity.

16. Clough: *Correspondence*, ii. 521; Woolner, p. 109.

17. 'Journal, EST', i. 82.

18. du Maurier: Ormond, p. 103; *The Young du Maurier*, pp. 112–13.

19. *Alfred Tennyson*, p. 295.

Chapter XXVI. The Erosion of Friendships, 1857–1859

1. Woolner, p. 138; 'Journal, EST', i. 102.

2. Hunt, ii. 174.

3. Bayard Taylor, i. 334; W. F. Rawnsley, p. 45.

4. Jowett: *Letters*, p. 177.

5. Coke, p. 246.

6. AT to EST, 14.6.58, TRC.

7. EFG to E. B. Cowell, 7.5.57, Cambridge; *Materials*, ii. 182.

8. EFG to EST, 19.3.58, TRC.

9. Hunt, ii. 123–5.

10. Francis Hill, 'Cracroft Diary', p. 29.

11. Hawthorne: pp. 553–6; Lathrop, pp. 331–3.

12. 'Journal, EST', i. 122.

13. Ibid. i. 135, 163.

14. Woolner, p. 145; Williamson, p. 35.

15. Smalley, p. 76; Hudson, *Munby*, p. 220.

16. Martin, p. 163.

17. AT to EST, 14.6.58, TRC; Cavendish: ii. 101.

18. 'Journal, EST', i. 158.

19. AT to the Duchess of Argyll, [May or June 1857], TRC.

20. 8.3.59, TRC.

21. Allingham: *Letters*, p. 104; Arnold: *Letters*, i. 127.

22. Cruse, p. 199.

23. Huxley, p. 98.

24. Woolner, p. 184.

25. H. D. Rawnsley, *Memories*, p. 135; EST to Lear, 23.1.60, TRC; Henry Taylor: *Autobiography*, ii. 192.

26. 'Journal, EST', 8.2.59.

27. Annie Fields, pp. 352–3.

28. *Friends*, p. 119.

29. Lear: *Letters*, p. 138.

30. Lear, diary, 2–9.6.59, Harvard; Lear to Hunt, 8.6.59, Huntington.

31. Nicoll and Wise, ii. 438; McCabe, p. 736.

Chapter XXVII. Two and Thirty Years Ago, 1860–1864

1. Brian Hill, pp. 83–4; Ritchie, *From Friend to Friend*, p. 10.

2. Brownings: Curle, p. 75.

3. Lear, diary, 16–17.6.60, Harvard.

4. du Maurier: Millar, p. 175; Jowett to EST, n.d., TRC; Ionides, p. 65.

5. AT to EST, 18.8.60, TRC; Rose, p. 48.

6. Woolner, p. 199.

7. *Materials*, ii. 310–11.

8. Hunt, ii. 203–14.

9. To EST, 2.10.60, TRC.

10. W. G. Clark to AT, 29.4.[61], TRC.

11. 'Journal, EST', i. 218.

12. Una Taylor, p. 220.

13. Scott, p. 11.

14. For the Pyrenees trip, see Clough: *Correspondence*, ii. 602–3; 'Journal, EST', i. 219–23; *Friends*, p. 211; EST to Dakyns, 3.10.61, Dakyns; James, *Wetmore*, ii. 100. The original version of the poem is at Harvard.

15. EST to Dakyns, 3.10.61, Dakyns.

16. 'Journal, EST', i. 228.

17. Ponsonby, pp. 79–80.

18. Argyll to AT, 27.3.62, TRC.
19. Edmund Venables.
20. *MS. Mats.* v. 37; *Letters, EST*, p. 169.
21. EST to EFT, 11.5.63, TRC.
22. Liddell, p. 313.
23. *Materials*, iv. 295; *MS. Mats.* v. 62.
24. Allingham: *Diary*, pp. 93, 95; Marian Bradley, diary, 23.12.63, BL.
25. Ritchie: *Thackeray's Daughter*, p. 114.
26. Anne Ritchie, diary, 15.3.83, Mrs Edward Norman-Butler.
27. To HT, 21.3.93, TRC.
28. Ross, p. 56.
29. Argyll to AT, 15.5.64, TRC.
30. Wilfrid Ward, p. 267.

Chapter XXVIII. New Friends, 1864–1868

1. EST to AT, 25, 26, 28.6.64; AT to EST, 28.6.64, TRC; *MS. Mats.* v. 81.
2. Marian Bradley, diary, 4.1.64, BL; Henry Taylor: *Autobiography*, ii. 196.
3. Woolner, p. 255; Woolner to EST, 5.2.65, TRC.
4. Arnold: *Letters*, i. 239.
5. EFG to E. B. Cowell, 5.8.63; EFG to W. F. Pollock, December 1864; EFG to Pollock, 7.12.[69], Trinity.
6. Lear, diary, 14–17.10.64, 11.7.65, Harvard.
7. 'Journal, EST', 13.6.64, 5.11.64.
8. *Materials*, ii. 408.
9. Stirling, *Richmond Papers*, p. 176.
10. Woolner, p. 244.
11. EST to Dakyns, 8.5.62, Dakyns; *MS. Mats.* v. 36.
12. Stirling, *Richmond Papers*, p. 177.
13. AT to EST, 23.11.64, TRC.
14. Symonds: i. 591–7.
15. Edmund Venables.
16. *MS. Mats.* vi. 26.
17. Edmund Lushington to EST, 6.4.66, TRC.
18. Kenner, p. 106.
19. AT to EST, [February 1865], TRC; EST to Lear, 19.4.65, TRC.
20. *EFG* ii. 239; Lear: Noakes, p. 218.
21. *Friends*, p. 314.
22. EST to Anne Weld and Henry Sellwood, 13.4.67, TRC.
23. E. F. Benson, p. 115; there are many versions of the story.
24. 'Marlborough.'
25. *DHL*, pp. 84–5.
26. Bayard Taylor: ii. 471–2.
27. Sait, p. 187; Allingham: *Diary*, p. 183; O'Connor, 'Mrs. Cameron', p. 4.
28. J. C. Fields to Bayard Taylor, 23.2.69, Huntington; Bradley, p. 264.
29. *MS. Mats.* vi. 86.
30. Allingham: *Diary*, pp. 137, 150.

31. Ibid., p. 89; T. H. Thomas, 'A Visit to Tennyson at Farringford Oct 1868', MS, TRC; *Mem*. ii. 407.
32. *Friends*, pp. 246–7.

Chapter XXIX. Aldworth and London, 1867–1872

1. *Friends*, p. 248.
2. Nairn and Pevsner, p. 106.
3. *Friends*, pp. 248, 251.
4. Allingham: *Diary*, p. 128.
5. Milnes: Reid, ii. 176; Walter White: pp. 166–7.
6. *Background*, p. 91.
7. *Alfred Tennyson*, p. 371; Swinburne: i. 293.
8. *MS. Mats*. vi. 74.
9. W. M. Rossetti: *Rossetti Papers*, pp. 333, 411, 505.
10. AT to 'my dear Sir', [1869], Lilly.
11. *Materials*, iii. 89.
12. Oscar Browning, p. 117.
13. EST to HT, 17.2.74, TRC.
14. Armstrong, p. 52.
15. Brownings: McAleer, *Dearest Isa*, p. 328.
16. Annie Fields, p. 354.
17. *Materials*, iii. 164; Hare, iv. 478; EST to HT, 21.10.70, TRC.
18. Allingham: *Diary*, p. 185.
19. 'Journal, EST', 19.10.69.
20. Grant Duff, *1851–1872*, ii. 185.
21. Frederick Pollock, p. 94; Sidgwick: p. 220.
22. Harrison, ii. 86–7, 103.
23. Domett: p. 187; Wilfrid Ward, p. 257.
24. EST to Simeon, 4.6.69, Syracuse; Lear, diary, 27.9.69, Harvard.
25. Hudson, *Lewis Carroll*, pp. 107–11.
26. EST to Lionel Tennyson, 1.6.70, TRC; Wilfrid Ward, p. 262.
27. EST to HT, 19.7.70, TRC; Carr, p. 194.
28. A. D. Coleridge, 'Notes of Conversations', MS, TRC; 'Journal, EST', 12.11.71.
29. 'Journal, EST', 31.3.71.
30. Ibid., 28.7.71.
31. EST to HT, 19.9.71, TRC.
32. Robert Bonner to AT, 16.9.71; AT to Bonner, 22.12.71, TRC.
33. Domett: p. 79.

Chapter XXX. *Idylls of the King*, 1872–1874

1. Culler, p. 220; for a consideration of the time-span of the *Idylls*, see pp. 219 ff.
2. Carlyles: *Emerson and Carlyle*, pp. 552–3.
3. For reactions to the *Idylls*, see *Friends*, p. 364; Swinburne: ii. 335; *Letters, EST*, p. 306; EST's proposed 'Epilogue', TRC; Ricks, p. 272; EFG to RMM, 12.4.[72], Trinity.

4. *DHL*, p. 91.

5. 'Journal, EST', 10.3.73.

6. Moneypenny and Buckle, ii. 697–8.

7. Bobbitt, p. 90.

8. Carlyles: *New Letters of Thomas Carlyle*, ii. 301.

9. 'Journal, EST', 28.12.73; 5.1.74.

10. *MS. Mats.* vi. 223; HT to EST, 6.9.74, TRC.

11. *MS. Mats.* vi. 226.

12. Knowles, p. 188; AT to Duchess of Argyll, 12.7.[74], TRC.

13. 'Journal, EST', ii. 90.

14. *MS. Mats.* vii. 15.

15. 'Journal, EST', ii. 252; *MS. Mats.* i. 8.

16. 'Journal, EST', 11.8.71; EST to Edward Lear, 22.2.71, TRC; Maude V. White, p. 292.

17. Lionel Tennyson to his parents, 20.10[72]; 7.7.77, TRC.

18. HT to [Henry Sidgwick], 23.[5].93, TRC.

19. Mrs Cameron to HT, n.d., TRC; Gernsheim, p. 28.

20. [Peter Haythornthwaite], 'Tennyson', MS, TRC.

21. Gosse, *Books on the Table*, p. 294; Ritchie: *Thackeray's Daughter*, p. 117.

22. James: *Letters*, i. 71.

23. Stoker, i. 198–9.

24. Hare, v. 40.

25. Frances Brookfield, *Apostles*, p. 328.

Chapter XXXI. Tennyson and the Theatre, 1874–1882

1. Quoted, Grosskurth, p. 44.

2. Swinburne: iii. 43.

3. 7.5.75, copy, TRC.

4. Grosskurth, p. 52.

5. Mary Brotherton to FT, 6.2.76, Lilly.

6. Knowles to AT, 1.10.75, TRC.

7. Lytton: *Letters*, i. 328.

8. Swinburne: iii. 257.

9. FitzGerald: Terhune, p. 321.

10. *EFG* iii. 240, i. 304; EFG to FT, 20.11.79, Cambridge.

11. 25.10.76, copy, TRC.

12. Wedmore, pp. 47–50.

13. Stanford, p. 233.

14. Warwick, p. 139.

15. [Field], p. 273; Stirling, *Life's Little Day*, pp. 343–4.

16. Knowles, p. 165.

17. For James and Tennyson, see *Mem.* ii. 217–18; James: *Letters*, i. 53, 66; James, *The Middle Years*, pp. 86–107; 'Marlborough'. The pleasurable involutions of James's style mask a spotty memory and muddled chronology. In *The Middle Years* he indicates that he first met Tennyson in Eaton Place, although their meeting was at Almond's Hotel (*Mem.* ii. 217). He also suggests that their next

meeting was in Eaton Place when the American Minister, Lowell, was his fellow guest, and that it took place between March 1877 and November 1878, which is manifestly impossible, since Lowell did not become Minister until 1880.

18. T. Holford to AT, 27.8.77, TRC.
19. Magnus, p. 102.
20. Elspeth Grahame to Sir Charles Tennyson, 6.4.1939, TRC; 'Some Memories of Alfred Tennyson', typescript, TRC.
21. Laughton, ii. 258.
22. EFG to Anna Biddell, n.d., Syracuse; W. M. Rossetti: *Letters*, p. 74.
23. Bobbitt, p. 237.
24. Irving to AT, 16.12.79, TRC.
25. Maisie Ward, p. 174.
26. Smalley, pp. 78–9; Carr, p. 196.
27. Allingham: *Diary*, p. 287.
28. *EFG* iv. 109.
29. Fanny Kemble to [HT?], 12.1.81, copy, TRC.
30. [Baillie], p. 71.
31. AT to ?, 18.9.54, Huntington.
32. Grant Duff, *1873–1881*, ii. 122; Stoker, i. 201; Allingham: *Diary*, p. 302.
33. TRC.
34. *EFG* iv. 151; John Tyndall to HT, n.d., TRC.
35. Gladstone: *Acton to Mary . . . Gladstone*, pp. 20, 55.

Chapter XXXII. Death of Old Friends, 1880–1884

1. 20.3.82, TRC.
2. Champneys, i. 184–5.
3. For Arnold and Tennyson, see Allingham: *Diary*, p. 288; Arnold to HT, 7.3.81, TRC; Domett: p. 268; 'Journal, EST', ii. 274; *Mem.* ii. 225.
4. *Friends*, pp. 431, 434–5.
5. *EFG* iv. 240.
6. 1.11.89, TRC.
7. Ricks, p. 293.
8. Anne Ritchie, diary, 8.8.83, Mrs Edward Norman-Butler.
9. Palgrave, p. 178.
10. *MS. Mats.* ix. 32.
11. To Victoria Baillie, 9.5.83, TRC.
12. *DHL*, pp. 102–3; H. D. Rawnsley, *Memories*, p. 148; Domett: pp. 278–9.
13. From a newspaper [*The Times*?]clipping, Yale.
14. McCabe, p. 736; Grant Duff, *1892–1895*, ii. 246; A. D. Coleridge, 'Notes of Conversations', MS, TRC.
15. Gladstone: *Papers*, p. 81.
16. *MS. Mats.* viii. 5.
17. Gladstone: Guedalla, ii. 245–6; Argyll to EST, 18.10.83, TRC.
18. Warre Cornish, p. 273; WEG to AT, 3.10.83, TRC.
19. Gladstone: *Some Hawarden Letters*, p. 161; AT to WEG, [2.12.83], BL.

20. WEG to AT, 5.12.83, TRC; WEG to HT, 11.12.83, TRC; A. M. Wood to HT, 20.12.83, Yale.
21. [Peter Haythornthwaite], 'Tennyson', MS, TRC.
22. Carlyles: Wilson, *1853–1865*, p. 522.
23. Morris to AT, 10.12.83, TRC.
24. Lear to HT, 7.12.83, TRC; Lear: *Later Letters*, p. 293; Grant Duff, *1881–1886*, i. 243.
25. FT to his son Alfred Tennyson, 4.1.84, Lilly.
26. 'Journal, EST', ii. 277.
27. Ellison, p. 112.
28. Gladstone: *Acton to Mary . . . Gladstone*, p. 209.
29. *Letters, EST*, pp. 330–1.
30. AT to WEG, [2.12.83], BL.
31. *DHL*, pp. 120–3.
32. Mumby, p. 188.
33. Copy of agreement, 27.9.83, TRC.
34. Lear, diary, 17.8.80, Harvard.
35. Charles Tennyson, *Stars and Markets*, p. 27.
36. *Letters, EST*, p. 355.
37. Henry Taylor: *Autobiography*, ii. 193. A quarter of a century later AT denied the truth of the story; see AT to Henry Taylor, 23.3.[85], TRC.
38. AT to WEG, [2.12.83], BL.

Chapter XXXIII. Declining Years, 1885–1890

1. Brownings: Collins, p. 45.
2. Una Taylor, p. 301.
3. Allingham: *Letters*, p. 73.
4. Asquith: i. 195–9; Maisie Ward, p. 166.
5. Dufferin to AT, 3.2.86, TRC.
6. 'Journal, EST', ii, 284; *Alfred Tennyson*, p. 488; Troubridge, p. 27.
7. Allingham: *Diary*, p. 333; Troubridge, p. 29.
8. 31.7.87, Duke.
9. Gosse to his wife [1888], BL.
10. Audrey Tennyson, 'Yachting 1887', MS notebook, TRC.
11. 'Journal, EST', 1888; Mack and Armytage, p. 188; Hardinge, iii. 309–10.
12. 'Talks and Walks.'
13. Mrs Belson to Sir Charles Tennyson, 22.10.1950, TRC; *Materials*, iv. 498.
14. 'CT Notebooks', viii; A. D. Coleridge, 'Notes of Conversations', MS, TRC.
15. Howe, pp. 37–8.
16. *Alfred Tennyson*, p. 497; EST to Anne Weld, 18.5.90, TRC; EST to HT, 30.11.89, TRC.
17. Bobbitt, p. 237.
18. *MS. Mats.* viii. 113.
19. 'Journal, EST', ii. 296.
20. *MS. Mats.* viii. 129.
21. Gosse, 'Lord Tennyson's Eightieth Birthday', p. 7; Asquith: i. 122.

22. *Materials*, iv. 233.
23. EST to HT, 1, 5, 26.11.89, TRC.
24. Allingham: *Diary*, p. 388.

Chapter XXXIV. Silent Voices, 1890–1892

1. *MS. Mats.* ix. 3–7.
2. Frances Brookfield, *Apostles*, p. 318.
3. Mattheisen, viii. 341.
4. For Gladstone and Tennyson, see WEG to HT, 8.10.92, TRC; Ernle, p. 141; *Letters, EST*, p. 350; Temple, pp. 261–2.
5. Grant Duff, *1896–1901*, i. 20.
6. Stoker, i. 215.
7. Graves, *Parry*, i. 345–7.
8. 8.4.91, TRC. For a good example of the ruthlessness with which HT changed others' writing, see his version, *Mem.* ii. 392.
9. Graves, *Parry*, i. 347.
10. 28.7.92, TRC.
11. *Alfred Tennyson*, p. 531.
12. *Mem.* ii. 428–9; see also HT to the Duke of Argyll, 24.10.92, TRC; Audrey Tennyson's journal of AT's illness, TRC.
13. Gladstone: Guedalla, ii. 443.
14. James: Edel, p. 247.
15. [Burne-Jones], i. 78.
16. To Agnes Weld, 18.10.92, TRC.

SELECT BIBLIOGRAPHY

(Unless otherwise stated, place of publication of books is London.)

Abbott, Claude Colleer, *The Life and Letters of George Darley, Poet and Critic*, 1928.
Adamson, J. W., *English Education, 1780–1902*, Cambridge, 1930.
Alford: *Life, Journals, and Letters of Henry Alford D. D., Late Dean of Canterbury*, ed. [F. O. Alford], 1873.
Allen, John: Anna Otter Allen, *John Allen and His Friends*, 1922.
        R. M. Grier, *John Allen: Vicar of Prees and Archdeacon of Salop*, 1889.
Allen, Peter, *The Cambridge Apostles: the Early Years*, Cambridge, 1978.
Allingham: *William Allingham's Diary*, Fontwell, 1967.
     Letters to William Allingham, ed. H. Allingham and E. Baumer Williams, 1911.
Armstrong, Isobel, *Victorian Scrutinies: Reviews of Poetry 1830 to 1870*, 1972.
Arnold: *Letters of Matthew Arnold*, ed. G. W. E. Russell, 2 vols., 1895.
   The Letters of Matthew Arnold to Arthur Hugh Clough, ed. H. L. Lowry, 1932.
Asquith: *The Autobiography of Margot Asquith*, 2 vols., 1920–2.
[Baillie, Albert V.], *The Making of a Man*, 1934.
Benson, A. C., *Fasti Etonenses*, 1899.
Benson, E. F., *As We Were: a Victorian Peep-Show*, 1930.
Blathwayt, Raymond, *Through Life and Round the World*, 1917.
Bobbitt, M. R., *With Dearest Love to All: the Life and Letters of Lady Jebb*, 1960.
Bradley, Edward Sculley, *George Henry Boker*, 1927.
Brightfield, Myron F., *John Wilson Croker*, Berkeley, 1940.
Brookfield, Arthur M., 'Some Letters from Arthur Hallam', *Fortnightly Review*, 1903, lxxx. 170–9.
Brookfield, Charles and Frances, *Mrs. Brookfield and Her Circle*, 2 vols., 1905.
Brookfield, Frances, *The Cambridge 'Apostles'*, 1906.
[Brookfield, Jane], 'Early Recollections of Tennyson', *Temple Bar*, February 1894, pp. 203–7.
Brown, Alan Willard, *The Metaphysical Society: Victorian Minds in Crisis, 1869–1880*, New York, 1947.
Browning, Oscar, *Memories of Sixty Years*, 1910.
Brownings: *The Brownings to the Tennysons: Letters from Robert Browning and Elizabeth Barrett Browning to Alfred, Emily, and Hallam Tennyson, 1852–1889*, ed. Thomas J. Collins, Waco, Texas, 1971.
     Robert Browning and Julia Wedgwood, ed. Richard Curle, 1937.

Elizabeth Barrett Browning's Letters to Mrs. David Ogilvy, 1849–1861, ed. Peter N. Heydon and Philip Kelley, 1974.

Letters of Robert Browning, Collected by Thomas J. Wise, ed. T. L. Hood, 1933.

Browning to His American Friends, ed. G. R. Hudson, 1965.

Elizabeth Barrett Browning: Letters to Her Sister, 1846–1859, ed. Leonard Huxley, 1929.

Robert Browning and Alfred Domett, ed. F. G. Kenyon, 1906.

The Letters of Elizabeth Barrett Browning, ed. F. G. Kenyon, 2 vols., 1897.

The Letters of Robert Browning and Elizabeth Barrett Barrett, 1845–46, ed. Elvan Kintner, Cambridge, Mass., 2 vols., 1969.

Letters of the Brownings to George Barrett, ed. Paul Landis, R. E. Freeman, Urbana, Ill., 1958.

Percy Lubbock, *Elizabeth Barrett Browning in Her Letters*, 1906.

Dearest Isa: Robert Browning's Letters to Isabella Blagden, ed. E. C. McAleer, Austin, Texas, 1951.

Learned Lady: Letters from Robert Browning to Mrs. Thomas Fitz-Gerald, 1876–1889, ed. E. C. McAleer, Cambridge, Mass., 1966.

E. C. McAleer, 'New Letters from Mrs. Browning to Isa Blagden', *PMLA*, September 1951, lxvi. 594–612.

Elizabeth Barrett to Miss Mitford, ed. Betty Miller, 1954.

W. M. Rossetti, 'Portraits of Browning', *Magazine of Art*, April and May 1890.

William Sharp, *Life of Robert Browning*, 1890.

Buckley, J. H., *Tennyson, the Growth of a Poet*, 1960.

Bulwer: the Earl of Lytton, *The Life of Edward Bulwer, First Lord Lytton*, 2 vols., 1913.

[Burne-Jones, Georgiana], *Memorials of Edward Burne-Jones*, 2 vols., 1904.

Byles, C. E., *The Life and Letters of R. S. Hawker*, 1905.

Carlyles: *The Collected Letters of Thomas and Jane Welsh Carlyle*, ed. C. R. Sanders and K. J. Fielding, Durham, N.C., 1970–.

The Correspondence of Emerson and Carlyle, ed. Joseph Slater, 1964.

Jane Welsh Carlyle: Letters to Her Family, 1839–1863, ed. Leonard Huxley, 1924.

Letters and Memorials of Jane Welsh Carlyle, ed. J. A. Froude, 3 vols., 1883.

New Letters and Memorials of Jane Welsh Carlyle, ed. Alexander Carlyle, 2 vols., 1903.

The Letters of Thomas Carlyle to His Brother Alexander, ed. E. W. Marrs, Cambridge, Mass., 1968.

New Letters of Thomas Carlyle, ed. Alexander Carlyle, 2 vols., 1904.

Thomas Carlyle: Letters to His Wife, ed. Trudy Bliss, 1953.

Alexander Carlyle, 'Thomas Carlyle and Thomas Spedding', *Cornhill*, May 1921, pp. 513–37, 742–68.

Moncure D. Conway, *Thomas Carlyle*, 1881.

J. A. Froude, *Thomas Carlyle: a History of His Life in London*, 2 vols., 1890.

C. R. Sanders, 'Carlyle and Tennyson', *PMLA*, March 1961, lxxvi. 82–97.

D. A. Wilson, *Carlyle on Cromwell and Others (1837–48)*, 1925.

—— *Carlyle at His Zenith, (1848–53)*, 1927.

—— *Carlyle to Threescore-and-Ten (1853–65)*, 1929.

—— and D. W. MacArthur, Carlyle in Old Age (*1865–1881*), 1934.

Carpenter, W. Boyd, *Some Pages of My Life*, 1911.

Carr, J. Comyns, *Some Eminent Victorians*, 1908.

Cavendish: *The Diary of Lady Frederick Cavendish*, ed. John Bailey, 2 vols., 1927.

Champneys, Basil, *Memoirs and Correspondence of Coventry Patmore*, 2 vols., 1900.

Clark, J. W., *Old Friends at Cambridge and Elsewhere*, 1900.

Clough: *The Correspondence of Arthur Hugh Clough*, ed. F. L. Mulhauser, 2 vols., Oxford, 1957.

　　　Letters and Remains of Arthur Hugh Clough, 1865.

Coke, H. J., *Tracks of a Rolling Stone*, 1905.

Coleridge: *The Table Talk and Omniana of Samuel Taylor Coleridge*, 1917.

Cowell, George, *Life and Letters of Edward Byles Cowell*, 1904.

Crabb Robinson: *Diary, Reminiscences and Correspondence of Henry Crabb Robinson*, ed. Thomas Sadler, 2 vols., 1872.

　　　Henry Crabb Robinson on Books and Their Writers, ed. Edith J. Morley, 3 vols., 1938.

Cruse, Amy, *The Victorians and Their Books*, 1935.

Culler, A. D., *The Poetry of Tennyson*, 1977.

Davidson, David, *Memories of a Long Life*, 1890.

de Polnay, Peter, *Into an Old Room*, 1950.

de Vere: Wilfrid Ward, *Aubrey de Vere*, 1904.

Dickens: *The Letters of Charles Dickens, 1844–1846*, ed. Kathleen Tillotson, 1977.

Domett: *The Diary of Alfred Domett, 1872–1885*, ed. E. A. Horsman, 1953.

Donne: *William Bodham Donne and His Friends*, ed. Catharine B. Johnson, 1905.

Doyle: *Reminiscences and Opinions of Sir Francis Doyle, 1813–1885*, 1886.

du Maurier: *The Young George du Maurier: a Selection of His Letters, 1860–67*, ed. Daphne du Maurier, 1951.

　　　C. C. H. Millar, *George du Maurier and Others*, 1937.

　　　Leonée Ormond, *George du Maurier*, 1969.

Dyson, Hope, and Tennyson, Charles, ed., *Dear and Honoured Lady: the Correspondence Between Queen Victoria and Alfred Tennyson*, 1969.

Eidson, J. O., *Tennyson in America*, Athens, Ga., 1943.

Eliot, T. S., *Selected Essays*, New York, 1950.

Elliott, Philip L., *The Making of the Memoir*, Greenville, S. C., 1978.

Ellison, Edith Nicholl: *A Child's Recollections of Tennyson*, 1907.

Emerson: *The Journals and Miscellaneous Notebooks of Ralph Waldo Emerson*, vol. x, ed. M. M. Sealts, Cambridge, Mass., 1973.

Ernle, Lord, *Whippingham to Westminster*, 1938.

Espinasse, Francis, *Literary Recollections and Sketches*, 1893.

[Field, Julian O.], *More Uncensord Recollections*, 1926.

Fields, Annie, *Authors and Friends*, 1896.

Fields, J. T., *Yesterdays with Authors*, Boston, 1900.

FitzGerald: *Letters and Literary Remains of Edward FitzGerald*, ed. W. A. Wright, 7 vols., 1902–3.

    Some New Letters of Edward FitzGerald, ed. F. R. Barton, 1923.

    A FitzGerald Friendship: Being Hitherto Unpublished Letters from Edward FitzGerald to William Bodham Donne, ed. N. C. Hannay, 1932.

    A. McK. Terhune, *The Life of Edward FitzGerald, Translator of The Rubaiyat of Omar Khayyam*, 1947.

    Thomas Wright, *The Life of Edward FitzGerald*, 2 vols., 1904.

Fox: *The Journal of the Hon. Henry Edward Fox, 1818–1830*, ed. the Earl of Ilchester, 1923.

Fuller, Hester T., *Three Freshwater Friends: Tennyson, Watts, and Mrs. Cameron*, Newport, Isle of Wight, 1936.

Garnett, Richard, *The Life of W. J. Fox*, 1910.

Gaskell: *An Eton Boy: Being the Letters of James Milnes Gaskell from Eton and Oxford, 1820–1830*, ed. C. M. Gaskell, 1939.

Gernsheim, Helmut, *Julia Margaret Cameron: Her Life and Photographic Work*, 1948.

Gladstone: *The Gladstone Diaries*, ed. M. R. D. Foot, Oxford, 1968–.

    The Gladstone Papers, 1930.

    Some Hawarden Letters, 1878–1913, ed. Lisle March-Phillipps and B. Christian, 1917.

    Letters of Lord Acton to Mary . . . Gladstone, ed. Herbert Paul, 1904.

    Mary Drew, *Acton, Gladstone and Others*, 1924.

    Philip Guedalla, *The Queen and Mr. Gladstone*, 2 vols., 1933.

    Joyce Marlow, *Mr and Mrs Gladstone: an Intimate Biography*, 1977.

    John Morley, *Life of Gladstone*, 2 vols., 1908.

Gosse, Edmund, *Books on the Table*, 1921.

—— 'Lord Tennyson's Eightieth Birthday', *St James's Gazette*, 3 August 1899, p. 7.

Grant Duff, Mountstuart E., *Notes from a Diary, 1851–1872*, 2 vols., 1897.

—— *Notes from a Diary, 1873–1881*, 2 vols., 1898.

—— *Notes from a Diary, 1881–1886*, 2 vols., 1899.

—— *Notes from a Diary, 1886–1888*, 2 vols., 1900.

—— *Notes from a Diary, 1889–1891*, 2 vols., 1901.

—— *Notes from a Diary, 1892–1895*, 2 vols., 1904.

—— *Notes from a Diary, 1896–1901*, 2 vols., 1905.

Graves, C. L., *The Life and Letters of Sir George Grove*, 1903.

—— *Hubert Parry, His Life and Work*, 2 vols., 1926.

Grosskurth, Phyllis, 'Tennyson, Froude, and *Queen Mary*', *Tennyson Research Bulletin*, November 1973, ii. 44–54.

Hardinge, Arthur, *The Life of . . . Fourth Earl of Carnarvon*, 3 vols., 1925.

Hare, A. J. C., *The Story of My Life*, 6 vols., 1896–1900.

Harrison, Frederic, *Autobiographic Memoirs*, 2 vols., 1911.

Haweis, H. R., *My Musical Life*, 1884.

Hawthorne, Nathaniel: *English Notebooks*, ed. Randall Stewart, 1941.

Helps: *Correspondence of Sir Arthur Helps*, ed. E. A. Helps, 1917.

Henderson, Philip, *Tennyson, Poet and Prophet*, 1978.

Hill, Brian, *Julia Margaret Cameron: a Victorian Family Portrait*, 1973.

Hill, Francis, 'The Cracroft Diary', *Tennyson Research Bulletin*, November 1977, pp. 26–9.

—— 'Squire and Parson in Early Victorian Lincolnshire', *History*, October 1973, lviii. 337–49.

Hoge, J. O., 'Emily Tennyson's Narrative for Her Sons', *Texas Studies in Literature and Language*, Spring 1972, xiv. 93–106.

Howe, M. A. De Wolfe, *John Jay Chapman and His Letters*, Boston, 1937.

Howitt, William, *Homes and Haunts of the Most Eminent British Poets*, 1857.

Hudson, Derek, *Lewis Carroll*, 1954.

—— *Munby: Man of Two Worlds*, 1972.

Hunt, W. Holman, *Pre-Raphaelitism and the Pre-Raphaelite Brotherhood*, 2 vols., 1905.

Huxley, Leonard, *The House of Smith Elder*, 1923.

Ionides, Luke, *Memories*, Paris, 1925.

James, Henry: *The Letters of Henry James*, ed. Percy Lubbock, 2 vols., 1920.
        The Middle Years, [1917].
        William Wetmore Story and His Friends, 2 vols., 1903.
        Leon Edel, *Henry James, the Middle Years*, 1963.

Jebb, Caroline, *Life and Letters of Sir Richard Claverhouse Jebb*, Cambridge, 1907.

Jennings, H. J., *Lord Tennyson: a Biographical Sketch*, 1884. The copy in TRC is annotated by AT.

Jowett: *Letters of Benjamin Jowett*, ed. Evelyn Abbott and Lewis Campbell, 1899.

Kemble, Frances Anne, 'An Old Woman's Gossip', *Atlantic Monthly*, June 1876, xxxvii. 711–26.

—— *Records of a Girlhood*, 2nd edn., 1879.

Kenner, Hugh, *The Counterfeiters*, 1968.

Knowles, James, 'Aspects of Tennyson, II', *Nineteenth Century*, January 1893, xxxiii. 164–88.

Kolb, Jack, 'Arthur Hallam and Emily Tennyson', *Review of English Studies*, February 1977, xxviii. 32–48.

——'When Did Tennyson Meet Rosa Baring?', *Victorian Newsletter*, Fall 1975, pp. 26–8.

Lathrop, R. H., *Memories of Hawthorne*, 1897.

Laughton, J. K., *Memoirs of the Life and Correspondence of Henry Reeve*, 2 vols., 1898.

Lear: *Letters of Edward Lear to Chichester Fortescue*, ed. Lady Strachey, 1907.
        Later Letters of Edward Lear to Chichester Fortescue, ed. Lady Strachey, 1911.
        Vivien Noakes, *Edward Lear: the Life of a Wanderer*, 1968.

le Gallienne, Richard, *The Romantic '90s*, 1951.

Liddell, A. G. C., *Notes from the Life of an Ordinary Mortal*, 1911.

Lockyer, Norman and W. L., *Tennyson as a Student and Poet of Nature*, 1910.

Lytton: *Personal and Literary Letters of . . . First Earl of Lytton*, ed. Betty Balfour, 2 vols., 1906.

McCabe, W. Gordon, 'Personal Recollections of Alfred, Lord Tennyson', *Century Magazine*, March 1902, xli. 722–37.

Mack, E. C. and Armytage, W. H. G., *Thomas Hughes*, 1952.

Macready: *The Journal of William Charles Macready, 1832–1851,* ed. J. C, Trewin, 1967.

    J. C. Trewin, *Mr Macready*, 1955.

Magnus, Laurie, *Herbert Warren of Magdalen*, 1932.

Maitland, F. W., *Life and Letters of Leslie Stephen*, 1906.

Martin, Robert Bernard, *The Dust of Combat: a Life of Charles Kingsley*, 1959.

Mattheisen, P. F., 'Gosse's Candid "Snapshots" ', *Victorian Studies*, June 1965, viii. 329–54.

Merivale: *Autobiography of Dean Merivale*, ed. J. A. Merivale, 1899.

Miller, Betty, 'Camelot at Cambridge', *Twentieth Century*, February 1958, pp. 133–47.

Milnes: James Pope-Hennessy, *Monckton Milnes, the Years of Promise, 1809–1851*, 1949.

    ——*Monckton Milnes, the Flight of Youth, 1851–1885*, 1951.

    T. Wemyss Reid, *The Life, Letters and Friendships of Richard Monckton Milnes*, 2 vols., 1890.

Mitford: *Mary Russell Mitford: Correspondence with Charles Boner and John Ruskin*, ed. Elizabeth Lee, 1914.

Molloy, Fitzgerald, *Victoria Regina*, 2 vols., 1908.

Moneypenny, W. F. and Buckle, G. E., *The Life of Benjamin Disraeli*, 2 vols., 1929.

Moxon: Harold G. Merriam, *Edward Moxon, Publisher of Poets*, New York, 1939.

Mumby, F. A., *The House of Routledge, 1834–1934*, 1934.

Nairn, Ian, and Pevsner, Nikolaus, *Sussex*, 1965.

Napier, G. G., *The Homes and Haunts of Alfred Lord Tennyson*, Glasgow, 1892.

Nicoll and Wise: *Literary Anecdotes of the Nineteenth Century*, ed. W. R. Nicoll and T. J. Wise, 2 vols., 1895–6.

Nicolson, Harold, *Tennyson: Aspects of His Life, Character & Poetry*, Garden City, 1962.

    ——*Diaries and Letters, 1945–1962*, ed. Nigel Nicolson, 1968.

Norton: *Letters of Charles Eliot Norton*, ed. Sara Norton and M. A. DeW. Howe, 2 vols., 1913.

O'Connor, V. C. S., 'Mrs. Cameron, Her Friends, and Her Photographs', *Century Magazine*, November 1897, lv. 3–10.

    —— 'Tennyson and His Friends at Freshwater', *Century Magazine*, December 1897, lv. 240–68.

Origo, Iris, *Images and Shadows*, 1970.

Ossoli: *Memoirs of Margaret Fuller Ossoli*, 3 vols., 1852.

Paden, W. D., *Tennyson in Egypt: a Study of the Imagery in His Earlier Work*, Lawrence, Kansas, 1942.

    —— 'A Note on the Variants of *In Memoriam* and *Lucretius*', *Library*, 1953, viii. 259–73.

Palgrave, G. F., *Francis Turner Palgrave: His Journals and Memories of His Life*, 1899.

Parry-Jones, William Ll., *The Trade in Lunacy*, 1972.

Pitt, Valerie, *Tennyson Laureate*, 1962.

Pollock, Frederick, *For My Grandson*, 1933.

Pollock, John, *Time's Chariot*, 1950.

Pollock, [W.] Frederick, *Personal Reminiscences*, 2 vols., 1887.

Ponsonby, Arthur, *Henry Ponsonby*, 1942.

Pritchett, V. S., *Midnight Oil*, 1971.

Rader, R. W., *Tennyson's 'Maud': the Biographical Genesis*, Berkeley, 1963.

Random Recollections of the House of Commons . . . 1830 to . . . 1835, 'By One of No Party', 1836.

Rawnsley, Eleanor F., *Canon Rawnsley*, Glasgow, 1923.

Rawnsley, H. D., *Literary Associations of the English Lakes*, 2 vols., Glasgow, 1901.

—— *Memories of the Tennysons*, Glasgow, 1900.

Rawnsley, W. F., *Tennyson, 1809–1909*, Ambleside, 1909.

Ricks, Christopher, *Tennyson*, New York, 1972.

Ridding, Laura, *Sophia Matilda Palmer, Comtesse de Franqueville*, 1919.

Ritchie, Anne, *From Friend to Friend*, 1919.

—— *Records of Tennyson, Ruskin, and Browning*, 1892.

    Thackeray's Daughter, ed. H. T. Fuller and V. Hammersley, 1951.

Rogers: P. W. Clayden, *Samuel Rogers and His Contemporaries*, 2 vols., 1889.

    R. Ellis Roberts, *Samuel Rogers and His Circle*, 1910.

Rose, Kenneth, *Superior Person*, 1969.

Ross, Janet, *The Fourth Generation*, 1912.

Rossetti, D. G.: *Letters of Dante Gabriel Rossetti*, ed. Oswald Doughty and J. R. Wahl, 4 vols., Oxford, 1965–7.

    Letters of D. G. Rossetti to William Allingham, 1854–1870, ed. G. Birkbeck Hill, 1897.

    Dante Gabriel Rossetti: His Family Letters, ed. W. M. Rossetti, 2 vols., 1895.

Rossetti, W. M.: *Letters of William Michael Rossetti . . . to Anne Gilchrist*, ed. Clarence Gohdes and P. F. Baum, Durham, N.C., 1934.

    The P.R.B. Journal, ed. W. E. Fredeman, Oxford, 1975.

    Præraphaelite Diaries and Letters, ed. W. M. Rossetti, 1900.

    Rossetti Papers, 1862 to 1870, ed. W. M. Rossetti, 1905.

    Some Reminiscences of William Michael Rossetti, 2 vols., 1906.

Sait, J. E., 'Tennyson and Longfellow', *Tennyson Research Bulletin*, November 1976, pp. 184–9.

Scott, Patrick, 'The Cloughs Visit the Tennysons, 1861', *Tennyson Research Bulletin*, November 1977, pp. 10–13.

Sendry, Joseph, 'The *In Memoriam* Manuscripts', *Harvard Library Bulletin*, April 1973, xxi. 202–20.

Shannon, E. F., *Tennyson and the Reviewers*, 1952.

—— 'The Critical Reception of Tennyson's "Maud" ', *PMLA*, June 1953, lxviii. 397–417.

Sharp, Elizabeth A., *William Sharp*, 1910.

Shorter: *The Love Story of 'In Memoriam'*, ed. Clement Shorter, 1916.

Sidgwick: 'A.S.' and 'E.M.S.', *Henry Sidgwick*, 1906.

Smalley, G. W., *Studies of Man*, 1895.

Stanford, C. V., *Pages from an Unwritten Diary*, 1914.

[Stephen, Leslie], 'A Don', *Sketches from Cambridge*, 1865.

Stevenson, Lionel, *The Ordeal of George Meredith*, New York, 1953.

Stirling, A. M. W., *Life's Little Day*, 1924.

—— *The Richmond Papers*, 1926.

Stoker, Bram, *Personal Reminiscences of Henry Irving*, 2 vols., 1906.

Stuart, James, *Reminiscences*, 1911.

Swinburne: *The Swinburne Letters,* ed. C. Y. Lang, 6 vols., 1959–62.

Symonds: *The Letters of John Addington Symonds*, ed. H. M. Schueller and R. L. Peters, 3 vols., Detroit, 1967–9.

Taylor, Bayard: *Life and Letters of Bayard Taylor*, ed. M. Hansen-Taylor and H. E. Scudder, 2 vols., 1884.

Taylor, Henry: *Autobiography of Henry Taylor, 1800–1875*, 2 vols., 1885.

Correspondence of Henry Taylor, ed. Edward Dowden, 1888.

Taylor, Una, *Guests and Memories: Annals of a Seaside Villa*, 1924.

Teichman, Oskar, *The Cambridge Undergraduate 100 Years Ago*, Cambridge, 1926.

Temple, A. G., *Guildhall Memories*, 1918.

Tennyson, Alfred: *The Poems of Tennyson*, ed. Christopher Ricks, 1969.

Tennyson, Charles, *Aldworth, Summer Home of Alfred Lord Tennyson*, Lincoln, 1977.

—— *Alfred Tennyson*, 1949.

—— *Stars and Markets*, 1957.

—— and Dyson, Hope, *The Tennysons: Background to Genius*, 1974.

Tennyson, Emily: *The Letters of Emily Lady Tennyson*, ed. J. O. Hoge, 1974.

Tennyson, Frederick: *Letters to Frederick Tennyson*, ed. H. J. Schonfield, 1930.

[Tennyson, Hallam], *Alfred Lord Tennyson: a Memoir*, 2 vols., 1897.

Tennyson, Hallam, ed., *Tennyson and His Friends*, 1911.

Thackeray: *The Letters and Private Papers of William Makepeace Thackeray*, ed. Gordon N. Ray, 4 vols., 1945.

Gordon N. Ray, *Thackeray, the Uses of Adversity, 1811–1846*, 1955.

—— *Thackeray, the Age of Wisdom, 1847–1863*, 1958.

Tollemache, Lionel A., *Old and Odd Memories*, 1908.

Trench: *Richard Chenevix Trench, Archbishop: Letters and Memorials*, ed. [Maria Trench], 2 vols., 1888.

Troubridge, Laura, *Memories and Reflections*, 1925.

Tuell, A. K., *John Sterling: a Representative Victorian*, New York, 1941.

Turner, E. S., *Taking the Cure*, 1967.

Turner, Paul, *Tennyson*, 1976.

Venables, Edmund, letter to the Editor, *The Times*, 20 October 1892.

Wallace, A. R., *My Life*, 2 vols., 1905.

Ward, Maisie, *The Wilfrid Wards and the Transition*, 1934.

Ward, Wilfrid, *Men and Matters*, 1914.

Warre Cornish, [Blanche], 'Memories of Tennyson', *London Mercury*, December 1921, v. 144–55, and January 1922, v. 266–75.

Warwick, Frances, Countess of: *Afterthoughts*, 1931.

Wedmore, Frederic, *Memories*, 1912.

Weld, Agnes Grace, *Glimpses of Tennyson and Some of His Relations and Friends*, 1903.

Wemyss, Mrs Rosslyn, *Memoirs and Letters of . . . Sir Robert Morier*, 2 vols., 1911.

White, Maude V., *Friends and Memories*, 1914.

White, Walter: *The Journals of Walter White*, 1898.

Williams-Wynn: *Memorials of Charlotte Williams-Wynn*, ed. H. H. Lindesay, 1877.

Williamson, David, *Before I Forget*, [1932].

Woolner, Amy, *Thomas Woolner, R.A., Sculptor and Poet: His Life in Letters*, 1917.

Wordsworth: *Letters of the Wordsworth Family*, ed. William Knight, 3 vols., 1907.
The Letters of William and Dorothy Wordsworth: the Later Years, ed. Ernest de Selincourt, 3 vols., Oxford, 1939.

Young, Julian C., *A Memoir of Charles Mayne Young*, 2 vols., 1871.

INDEX

Acton, John, 1st Lord, 530, 547
Acworth, Dr and Mrs James, 482
Ainslie, Sir Robert, 34
Aix-la-Chapelle, 154
Albany, Duchess of, 576
Albert, Prince Consort: first meeting with AT, 309–10; admires AT's poetry, 351, 435, 442; visits Farringford, 403–4; death, 441–2; dedication of *Idylls* to his memory, 442–3; also, 351–2, 358, 416, 443–4
Aldworth: AT buys land, 472; building of, 471–6; resembles Bayons, 212, 475–6, 499; guests at, 490–1, 519–20, 532–3, 556, 563–6, 576, 578–80; also, 220, 373, 456, 482, 490–2, 502, 505–6
Alford, Henry, 74, 95, 126
Alice, Princess, 442, 538
Allen, John, 95, 150, 240, 562
Allen, Matthew, 236–7, 241, 253–6, 261, 268–70, 274, 276, 282, 386, 387
Allingham, Helen, 580
Allingham, William: meets AT, 364; diary, 364, 470, 549; AT's opinion of, 432, 470; and fig tree, 470–1, 568, 577; death, 571; also, 304, 325, 446, 508–9
Ambleside, 201–3
Anderson, Charles, 213
Anderson, Mary, 565
Apostles, the (Cambridge Conversazione Society), 56, 67–8, 85–96, 112–13, 116, 125, 128, 148, 150, 162, 191, 226, 227, 265, 461, 482, 483
Arabin, (Serjeant) William St. Julien, 233
Argyll, Elizabeth, Duchess of, 284, 411–13, 418, 423, 428, 466, 517

Argyll, George Douglas Campbell, 8th Duke of, 358, 411–12, 418, 428, 443, 444, 449, 461, 466, 483, 517, 542, 546
Arnold, Matthew: opinion of AT, 390, 423, 455, 535; AT's opinion of, 535, 565; also, 107, 270n., 339, 340, 419, 463, 507, 550
Ashburton, Alexander Baring, 1st Lord, 242
Ashburton, Harriet, Lady, 286, 396, 399–402
Ashburton, William Bingham Baring, 2nd Lord, 242, 340, 399, 401
Athenaeum, 462
Austen, Jane, 23, 552
Austin, Alfred, 477, 480, 582, 583

Babbage, Charles, 462–3
Bagehot, Walter, 483
Baillie, Albert, 525
Baillie, Lady Frances, 556
Ballybunion, 268, 498
Baring, Fanny (later Massingberd), 215
Baring, Sir Francis, 167
Baring, Georgina, 215
Baring, Lady Harriet, *see* Ashburton, Lady
Baring, Rosa (later Shafto), 167, 180, 215–21, 223, 249, 385, 386, 387
Baring, William Bingham, *see* Ashburton, Lord
Barrett, Elizabeth, *see* Browning, Elizabeth Barrett
Barton, Bernard, 294
Betavier, the, 152–3
Bateman, Mr and Mrs Hezekiah, 512, 513, 523
Bayons Manor: significance to AT, 32, 212–13, 343, 350, 373, 385, 473–6, 499; also, 8, 24, 39, 155–6, 169,

Bayons Manor—*contd*
174–5, 205, 207, 210–14, 225, 238, 294–5, 354, 415
Beatrice, Princess, 576
Belgium, 154, 306
Bellingham, Charlotte, 136, 217, 225
Benniworth, 7, 14
Bessborough, Caroline, Countess of, 399
Bessborough, John Ponsonby, 5th Earl of, 399
Birrell, Augustine, 566–7
Birrell, Eleanor: engagement and marriage to Lionel Tennyson, 484–5, 514–15, 522–3, 556–7; marriage to Birrell, 566–7
Blackwood's Edinburgh Magazine, 111–12, 148–9, 169, 172–3, 191, 225
Blakesley, J. W., 88, 91, 101–2, 103, 112–13, 125, 126, 176
Blessington, Marguerite, Countess, 285, 297
Boker, G. H., 469
Bonner, Robert, 492
Boulogne, 197
Bourne, John, 4–5, 34
Bourne, Mary, 4–5, 6, 9, 14–15, 16, 39–40, 43, 131, 133, 157, 166, 205, 206, 207, 208, 233, 235, 295, 354
Bousfield, Dr, 41, 42, 49, 130, 131–2
Boxley, 259–60, 274
Boyd, Robert, 117, 122, 124
Boyle, Audrey, *see* Tennyson, Audrey
Boyne, Gustavus Frederick Hamilton, 7th Viscount, 80, 466
Boyne, Emma, Viscountess, 4, 80, 133, 218
Brackenbury family, 82
Bradley, George Granville, 436, 446, 546, 582, 583
Bradley, Marian, 446, 467, 563
Brancepeth Castle, 4, 32, 210, 338
Brassey, Thomas, 1st Earl, 568
Breadalbane, John Campbell, 2nd Marquis of, 358
Bright, John, 567
Brodie, Sir Benjamin, 139
Brooke, Stopford, 517
Brookfield, Frances M., 95, 103
Brookfield, Jane, 252, 258, 308, 318, 367, 399–401, 407, 510, 573

Brookfield, William, 87, 99, 123–4, 126, 128, 147–8, 177, 229, 234, 240, 252, 288, 293, 316, 318, 319, 325, 367, 371, 399, 401, 510, 532
Brotherton, Mary, 546
Brown, John, 538, 539
Brown, Lancelot, 343
Browning, Elizabeth Barrett: opinion of AT, 241, 266–7, 271, 275, 287, 301, 366, 393, 396, 423, 426; meets Tennysons, 359–60; also, 258–9, 302, 337, 351, 367, 392–6, 407, 408, 441
Browning, Oscar, 467, 479
Browning, Robert: meets AT, 257; opinion of AT and his poetry, 267, 301–2, 392, 430, 457, 480–1, 512, 521, 554; AT's opinion of, 302, 360–1, 367, 392, 419–20, 481, 520–1, 554; never visits Farringford or Aldworth, 302, 375, 392, 457, 474, 481; in Paris with AT, 359–60; at HT's christening, 367, 392; compared to AT, 361, 394, 480–1; entertains AT, 392–6; offers AT plot of *Ring and the Book,* 480–1; dedicates poems to AT, 481; AT dedicates poems to him, 554; death, 571; also, 271, 272, 285, 351, 371, 402, 408, 441, 445, 458, 466–7, 468, 496, 502, 514, 530, 546, 550, 551, 575
Browning, R. W. B., 441, 521
Browning, Sarianna, 393, 485
Buckley, Jerome, 306
Buller, Arthur, 177
Bulwer-Lytton, Edward, 1st Baron Lytton, 69, 168–9, 171, 173, 213, 226, 227, 238–9, 277, 295–300, 301, 351, 353–4, 359, 408, 419, 512, 514
Burgoyne, Sir John, 383
Burne-Jones, Sir Edward, 240, 407, 553, 583
Burns, Robert, 219, 327–8
Burton, Catherine, 178–9, 217
Burton, Robert, 14, 15, 135
Butler, Henry Montagu, 183, 446
Butler, Samuel, 58
Byron, George Gordon, 6th Lord, 79, 95, 97–8, 231, 392, 549

Cambridge University: offers AT
  honorary degree, 435–6, 467, 578;
  also, 11–12, 41, 51–6, 59–63,
  66–79, 85–96, 99, 124–7, 128–30,
  136–7, 145, 147, 155, 173, 179,
  239, 266, 391, 501–2, 510, 515
Cameron, Charles Hay, 411, 429, 508
Cameron, Julia Margaret: character,
  408–9, 411, 429–31, 508–10; love
  of the Tennysons, 508; Browning's
  opinion of, 430; Lear's opinion of,
  431, 455; photography, 429, 447,
  449, 469, 508; last days, 508–9;
  also, 273, 445, 446–7, 466
Campbell, Thomas, 181, 237
Carlyle, Jane: opinion of AT and his
  poetry, 243, 284–6, 396–7, 401–2;
  at Grange, 399–402; also, 237, 281,
  287–8, 367, 466, 474
Carlyle, Thomas: meets AT, 241–3;
  impressions of AT, 242; AT's
  opinion of him, 241; opinion of
  AT's works, 242, 267, 270, 303,
  317, 361, 396, 499, 522; difficulties
  as friend, 303, 502, 521; meets EST,
  339–40; never at Farringford, 375,
  474; on title, 396, 501; infatuation
  with Lady Ashburton, 396, 401–2;
  at Grange, 399–402; death, 528;
  also, 105, 116, 199, 230, 232, 237,
  249, 254, 262, 277, 281–2, 283,
  284–5, 291–2, 294, 304, 380, 429,
  432, 445, 466, 467, 468, 471, 533–4
Carnarvon, Henry Herbert, 4th Earl of,
  563–4
Carpenter, William Boyd, 1, 577
'Carroll, Lewis', 417, 486–7
Catullus, 530, 549
Cauteretz, 119–20, 141, 307–8,
  438–41, 503, 567, 573
Cavendish, Lady Frederick, 421
Cecil, Lord Thomas, 143–4
Chapel House, Twickenham, 357, 359,
  360, 366–7, 370, 373, 403
Chaplin, William, 48–9
Chapman, J. J., 565
Cheltenham, 38, 142–3, 251, 274–5,
  280, 295–6, 305, 322, 338, 340,
  365, 373
Christian Remembrancer, 265
Civil List Pension, 283, 291–3, 296–7,
  376, 541

Clare, John, 236–7
Clarendon, G. W. F. Villiers, 4th Earl
  of, 399
Clark, Sir Andrew, 505, 529, 540,
  563, 574, 579, 580
Clevedon, 183, 187–8, 193–4, 338,
  392
Clough, Arthur Hugh, 379, 406, 437,
  438–41
Clough, Blanche, 437, 466
Club, The, 461–2
Cock Tavern, 229–30, 402
Coleridge, Hartley, 87, 203
Coleridge, John Duke, 1st Lord, 546
Coleridge, Samuel Taylor, 105, 173,
  198, 226
Collins, John Churton, 529, 530
Collins, Mortimer, 477
Colquhoun, Ludovic, 372
Contemporary Review, 484, 492
Copenhagen, 540
Cornhill Magazine, 424, 529
Cornwall, 319–20, 432–5, 568
'Cornwall, Barry', *see* Procter, B. W.
Cosmopolitan Club, 86, 371, 376, 461
Crabbe Robinson, Henry, 257, 283–4
Crabbe, George, 273
Cracroft family, 82, 214–15, 295, 328,
  415
Craik, G. L., 578, 579
Craik, Sir Henry, 416n.
Crimean War, 381, 384, 387, 389
Croker, J. W., 169–73, 178, 226, 265
Crowe, Mrs Kate, 514
Crystal Palace, 358
Culler, A. Dwight, 385
Currie, Sir Donald, 539–40

Dabbs, Dr G. R., 504, 580–2
Dakyns, Graham, 436–7, 438–9, 579
Darley, George, 228, 288
Darwin, Charles, 277
Davidson, David, 396
De la Warr, C. R. Sackville-West, 12th
  Lord, 271
Denmark, King and Queen of, 540–1
Derby, Edward Stanley, 14th Earl of,
  383
Derby, Edward Henry Stanley, 15th
  Earl of, 457
de Schroeter, Baron, 380
de Vere, Aubrey, 90, 257, 268, 286,

de Vere—*contd*
  287, 288, 289–90, 293, 318–19,
  330, 337, 339, 380
de Vere, Sir Vere Edmond (Hunt), 61
Devonshire, 432–5, 568, 576
Devonshire, W. G. S. Cavendish, 6th
  Duke of, 285
Dickens, Charles, 272–3, 277, 285,
  302–3, 305, 308, 350, 358–9, 416,
  488–9, 490, 568
Disraeli, Benjamin, Earl of
  Beaconsfield, 501
Dodgson, C. L., *see* 'Carroll, Lewis'
Domett, Alfred, 549
Donne, W. B., 95, 112, 143
D'Orsay, Alfred, Count, 285, 302
Doyle, Sir Francis, 97, 99, 183, 458
Doyle, Richard, 379, 401, 406, 407
Dublin Review, 489
Duff Gordon, Sir Alexander, 358
Duff Gordon, Janet, 448–9
Duff Gordon, Lady, 318
Dufferin and Ava, Frederick
  Blackwood, 1st Marquis of, 413,
  532, 556–9
Dulwich, 262
du Maurier, George, 408
du Plat, Colonel, 403
Durham, Nurse, 568, 569, 570

Ebrington, Hugh Fortescue, Lord (later
  3rd Earl Fortescue), 288
Eclectic Review, 298
Eden, Arthur, 167, 214, 454
Edinburgh, Duchess of, 538
Edinburgh Review, 112, 142, 265, 390
Edinburgh University, 467–8, 528, 551
Egerton, Lord Francis, 271
Eglinton Tournament, 211
'Eliot, George', 297, 389, 408, 490,
  514, 519, 528
Eliot, T. S., 107, 341, 343, 348, 493
Elmhirst, Sophy, 82, 167, 195, 216,
  223, 328, 334
Elsinore, 540
Elton, Henry, 183, 184
Elton, Jane, *see* Brookfield, Jane
Elton, Julia, 259
Emerson, R. W., 245, 319
Emma, Queen, 463–4, 468
Englishman's Magazine, 110–11,
  141–2

epilepsy, 2, 3, 10–11, 17, 26–9, 33,
  35, 39, 41–2, 62, 83–5, 114, 140,
  237–8, 273–4, 278–80, 315, 321,
  326–7
Eton, 11, 30, 37, 69, 70–1
Evans, Sir George de Lacy, 383
Eversley, 370
Examiner, 381
Eyre, E. J., 458–9

Farringford: lease of, 372–5; purchase
  of, 402–3, 404; visitors at, 379–80,
  397–8, 399, 403–4, 406, 426–8,
  430–1, 437, 446–7, 448–50, 463–4,
  468–9, 486, 491, 576, 577; also,
  305, 310, 378–9, 382–3, 410–11,
  418–19, 441–2, 444–5, 456, 466,
  501–2, 505, 567–9, 573–4, 577–8
feminism, 312, 313–14
Fields, James, 502
FitzGerald, Edward: at Mirehouse,
  197–203; character, 198–9, 323;
  feeling for AT, 198, 201, 204, 239,
  250, 274, 282, 322–3, 413–14, 436,
  515–16, 536–8; hatred of
  snobbishness, 198, 379, 413, 536;
  offers AT money, 204, 207, 247, 270,
  272, 282, 292, 377; opinion of AT's
  poetry, 261, 262–3, 267, 270, 301,
  311, 317, 323, 330, 414, 426, 455,
  500, 524; and EST, 335, 428, 455,
  500, 515–16, 522, 536–7; at
  Farringford, 375, 379–80, 474;
  marriage, 414; AT visits, 515–16;
  death, 537; also, 53, 87, 95, 98,
  164, 185–6, 190, 222, 230, 245,
  252, 256, 257, 269, 273, 288, 293,
  303, 304, 321, 363, 532
Fitzroy, Lord James, 143
Flower, Sir William, 578
Forster, John, 285, 297–9, 303, 329,
  337, 350, 351, 354, 358, 363, 381,
  457, 466, 502
Fortescue, Chichester, 1st Lord
  Carlingford, 427, 545
Fox, Henry, 69–70
France, 118–20, 189, 197, 365,
  437–41, 456, 501, 503, 514
Franklin, Catherine, *see* Rawnsley,
  Catherine
Franklin, Jane, Lady, 463, 466, 502
Franklin, Sir John, 82, 224

Frederica, Princess, 538
Frere, John, 61, 189
Freshwater, 372, 429–31, 446–9, 489, 508
Froude, James Anthony, 483, 512, 533–4, 552
Fuller, Margaret (later Ossoli), 303
Fytche, Elizabeth, *see* Tennyson, Elizabeth (AT's mother)
Fytche, John, 64, 81
Fytche, Mary Anne (AT's Aunt), 30, 34, 50, 64, 81, 255, 315
Fytche, Mrs (AT's grandmother), 30, 50, 58

Garden, Francis, 95, 147, 148, 177, 179, 265, 327, 361, 466
Garibaldi, Giuseppe, 449–50
Gaskell, Charles Milnes, 547
Gaskell, James Milnes, 71–2, 76–7, 547
Germany, 150, 153–4, 170, 171, 530
Gilbert, Sir William Schwenck, 313, 407
Gilfillan, George, 364
Gladstone, Mary (later Drew), 539, 547
Gladstone, William Ewart: opinion of AT's poetry, 98, 390, 423, 560–1, 568; meets AT, 232; jealousy between him and AT, 74, 232, 330, 458–60, 547–8, 560–1; with AT at Cliveden, 457–8; AT's opinion of him, 458, 575–6, 578; at Palgrave's, 458; at Woolner's, 458–60; at Aldworth, 491; offers baronetcy to AT, 500–1, 528–9; entertains AT, 516–17; cruise on *Pembroke Castle*, 539–41; offers AT peerage, 541–4; political differences with AT, 546–7, 548, 550, 575–6; last meeting with AT, 574–5; does not attend AT's funeral, 582–3; also, 70–3, 79, 97–9, 177, 183, 184, 283, 325, 383, 408, 456, 466, 468, 474, 483, 519, 520, 581
Glasgow University, 528
Good Words, 476
Gordon, Sir Arthur, 539, 541, 543
Gosse, Edmund, 517, 569, 574, 582
Grange, the, 399–402
Grant Duff, Sir Mountstuart, 483

Greece, King and Queen of, 540
Greville, Mrs Sabine, 491, 509–10, 511, 519, 521
Grey, Sir George, 358
Greyshott Farm, 472
Grosvenor, Lady Constance (later Duchess of Westminster), 412
Guizot, François, 118
Gully, Dr James, 279, 280, 315–16, 321, 436, 445
Gunby Hall, 328
Gurney, Laura, 286, 557

Hallam, Arthur Henry: meets AT, 69; University prize poem, 69, 77, 79; character, 69–77, 92, 100, 129, 177; family, 69–70; friendships, 70, 72–5, 94–6, 97–9; health, 70, 76, 85, 101, 152, 177, 178, 182; in Italy, 71; and Anna Wintour, 71–2, 76, 105–6, 158; at Cambridge, 72–7, 126–7, 128–9, 145, 147, 155; Apostle, 86, 88, 89, 92, 96; love of Emily Tennyson, 96, 99–101, 103, 106, 120n., 127, 129, 130, 142–3, 145–7, 156–8, 166–7, 178, 180; at Oxford, 97–9; helps AT publish, 102–3, 106, 140–2, 159–60; father forbids publication, 105–6; reviews 1830 *Poems*, 110–11, 142; ridiculed by Wilson, 111–12; Spanish adventure, 115–23; London life, 99, 147, 150–2, 157–9, 176–7, 180–1; with AT on Rhine, 152–4; trip with father, 179–82; death and funeral, 182–8; also, 148, 171, 173, 215, 217, 219, 232, 238, 244, 258, 259, 260, 282, 293, 304, 306–8, 330, 439–40, 488, 495n., 532, 547–8, 572
Hallam, Elizabeth (AHH's aunt), 252
Hallam, Ellen (AHH's sister), 158, 177, 193, 195
Hallam, Henry (AHH's father): opinion of the Tennysons, 127, 178, 185, 214, 367–8; attitude to AHH's engagement, 129, 130, 143, 146, 155, 156–8, 177–8, 179, 185; death, 421; also, 69–70, 71–2, 75–6, 85, 105–6, 181–3, 187, 193, 201, 258, 283, 288, 292, 293, 308, 338
Hallam, Henry (AHH's brother), 367

Hallam, Julia (AHH's mother), 69, 177, 187, 194–5
Hallam, Julia (AHH's sister), 69, 195, 259, 367
Hallé, Sir Charles, 408
Hamley, Sir Edward, 532–3
Harcourt, Sir William, 539–40
Harden, John, and family, 121
Hardy, Thomas, 109
Harlaxton Manor, 155
Harrington Hall, 82, 167, 214, 219, 220
Harrison, Frederic, 483–4
Haslemere, 456, 471, 472, 474, 508
Hawker, R. S., 320, 321
Hawthorne, Mr and Mrs Nathaniel, 416–17
Haythornthwaite, Peter, 489
Head, Sir Edmund, 353
Heath, Douglas, 91, 128, 150, 177, 192, 193
Heath, John, 91, 103, 150, 160, 177, 183, 192, 193, 195, 225, 235
Heath, Julia, 167
Henderson, Philip, 219
Heneage, Mr, 7, 26, 34, 82
Henry, Prince of Battenberg, 576
Herschel, Sir John, 462
High Beech, 225, 229, 232–7, 239, 241, 245–6, 251, 253, 255, 256, 279, 386
Hoapili, the Revd Mr and Mrs, 463
Hoare, Samuel, 289
Hogg, Sir James Weir, 297
Holland, 152–3, 256
Homer, 437, 446, 459–60, 540, 575
Horlins (family coachman), 16, 49
Hort, Fenton, 90
Houghton, Richard Monkton Milnes, 1st Lord, 74, 88, 90, 96, 97–9, 102, 112–13, 128, 186, 226–8, 229, 232, 242–3, 245, 257, 265, 266, 283, 291–2, 293, 294, 327, 338, 368, 371, 380, 420, 457, 461, 466, 467, 475, 491, 517, 519, 541n., 544, 546, 550, 551
Howard de Walden, C. A. Ellis, 6th Lord, 370
Howitt, Richard, 283, 294
Howitt, William, 150, 283, 294
Hughes, Arthur, 414
Hughes, Thomas, 408, 457, 563

Hunt, Dr James, 465
Hunt, Leigh, 140–1, 177, 180, 230, 350, 351, 353
Hunt, W. Holman, 371, 392, 407, 410, 414–15, 434–5, 458–9
Huskisson, William, 121
Hutchinson, Mr, 11, 12
Hutton, Frances, *see* Tennyson d'Eyncourt, Frances
Huxley, Thomas, 462, 483
hydropathy, 237, 275, 276–8, 279–82, 309, 315–16, 321, 445

Ingilby, Sir William, 143
Ireland, 268, 318–19
Irving, Sir Henry, 509, 511–12, 514, 523–4, 525, 578, 579
Italy, 147, 189, 225, 274, 305, 359–62, 501, 530

Jacksons of Louth, 44–5, 368
James, Henry, 507, 509, 512, 519–20, 562, 583
Jerningham, Charles, 518
Jerrold, Douglas, 303–4
Jesse, Arthur Henry Hallam, 258
Jesse, Emilia: and AHH, 96, 100–1, 103, 120n., 127, 129, 130, 138, 142–3, 145–6, 156–8, 166–7, 178, 180, 183–4, 259; health, 142–3, 146, 166–7, 176, 184, 192, 193, 194–5; stays with AHH's family, 194–5; marriage, 258–9; also, 23, 148, 185, 215, 217, 235, 246, 249, 255, 482, 491
Jesse, Eustace, 133
Jesse, Richard, 195, 249, 258–9, 376, 491
Joachim, Joseph, 408, 522
Johnson, Edward, 309, 372
Jowett, Benjamin: meets AT, 382; at Farringford, 398, 399, 419, 447; suggests subjects for AT, 424–5, 426; relations with AT, 432, 433, 485, 579; also, 408, 456, 532, 545, 552, 554, 569, 582, 583

Keats, John, 78, 140, 141, 155, 168, 169, 200, 301, 392, 549, 564
Keepsake, 226
Kegan Paul, Charles, 378, 457, 465, 549

Kemble, Adelaide, 151
Kemble, Fanny, 99, 100, 101, 102, 103, 151–2, 158, 164, 167, 172, 181, 183–4, 271, 491, 511, 521, 524, 525, 528
Kemble, John, 87, 91, 95, 99, 102, 112, 116, 117, 122, 128, 150, 152, 179, 186, 190, 267, 532
Kendal, Mr and Mrs W. H., 524
Kenilworth, 252
Kenmare, Valentine Browne, 4th Earl of, 546
Kenny, James, 283
Kensington, 466–7
Kenyon, John, 257
Ker, Alan, 365–6
Ker, Mary, 21, 23, 58, 82, 83, 100, 146, 148, 176–8, 179, 182–3, 186, 192, 193, 224, 225, 233, 235, 260, 269, 333, 335, 338, 365–6, 482, 491
Killarney, 253, 268, 319
King, Henry, 502, 549
King, J. W., 419
Kinglake, A. W., 232, 288
Kingsley, Charles, 331–2, 370, 420–1, 465
Kipling, Rudyard, 577
Kirkwall, 540
Kitlands, 160, 167, 193
Knowles, Sir James: meets AT, 471; and Aldworth, 471, 472–6; and Metaphysical Society, 482–3; relations with AT, 484, 507, 547–8; relations with AT's family, 484, 507; also, 94, 304, 342, 481, 485, 514, 574–5
Knowles, James Sheridan, 292, 293, 296, 351

Lamb, Charles, 141, 166
Langton, Bennet, 19
Lansdowne, H. C. K. Petty-Fitzmaurice, 5th Marquis of, 371
Laurence, Samuel, 240, 515, 553
Lear, Edward: epilepsy, 28, 326–7, 431; meets AT, 326; relations with AT and EST, 327, 375, 397, 426–7, 430–1, 455–6, 485–6; also, 339, 379, 465, 532, 545, 568
Leeds, the 121

Leighton, Frederic, Lord, 407, 514
Lewes, G. H., 461, 490, 514, 527
Lind, Jenny, 491
Literary Gazette, 166
Little Holland House, 297, 407–9, 413, 420
Liverpool, 121
Locker, Lady Charlotte, 484–5
Locker, Eleanor, *see* Birrell, Eleanor
Locker, Frederick (later Locker-Lampson), 484–5, 514
Lockhart, J. G., 169, 265
Lockyer, Sir Norman, 462
London, 48, 99, 150–2, 176–7, 185–6, 222, 229–32, 235–6, 239–43, 257, 261, 262–3, 281, 282–8, 289–91, 304–5, 310–11, 317–18, 319, 324–6, 328–9, 357–9, 363–5, 366–8, 370–1, 398, 406–9, 411–14, 457–63, 466–7, 474, 484–5, 490–1, 501–2, 511–12, 517, 519, 520–2, 574–6, 578
London and Westminster Review, 173, 226
London Library, 86, 261, 551
Longfellow, H. W., 240, 392, 436, 469, 565
Lorne, Marquis of (later 9th Duke of Argyll), 418, 428
Louise, Princess, 576
Louth, 11, 12, 14, 29–31, 50, 58
Lowell, J. R., 520, 562
Lushington, Cecilia, 23, 35, 84, 145, 192, 233–4, 235, 249, 253, 259, 260, 334, 335, 359, 466
Lushington, Edmund, 84, 91, 94, 145, 155, 229, 253, 259, 260, 270, 287, 293, 330, 334, 359, 466, 496
Lushington, Franklin, 255, 326–7, 339, 379, 431
Lushington, Henry, 95, 96, 229, 255–6, 257, 281, 283, 288, 310, 379, 488, 495n.
Lyall, Alfred, 499–500
Lytton, Edward Bulwer-Lytton, 1st Baron, *see* Bulwer-Lytton, Edward
Lytton, Edward Robert Bulwer, 1st Earl of, 514

Mablethorpe, 22–3, 45, 47, 147, 176, 179, 197, 256, 262, 274, 310
Macaulay, T. B., 69

McLuhan, H. M., 110
Macmillan, Alexander, 424, 451, 549
Macmillan's Magazine, 424, 476
Macready, W. C., 285, 297, 358–9
Maltby, Edward, 62–3
Malvern, 97, 279, 315–16, 321, 365
Manchester, 121, 416–17
Manning, Henry, 98, 483, 513
Market Rasen, 3, 7, 8, 204
Marshall, Mr and Mrs James, 338, 416, 417, 466
Marthion family, 57, 80
Mary, Princess, of Hanover, 540
Mary, Princess, of Teck, 576
Massingberd, Algernon Langton, 328
Massingberd family, 82
Maurice, F. D., 86, 90, 92, 95, 367, 420–1, 466, 483, 532
Melbourne, William Lamb, 2nd Viscount, 75, 175, 238
Meredith, George, 363–4, 423–4, 440, 449
Merivale, Charles, 60, 77, 142, 150, 288
Merriman, Dr, 578
Metaphysical Society, 86, 461–2, 482–4
Mill, John Stuart, 70, 173, 226
Millais, Sir John, 379, 392, 414, 489, 514
Milman, Mrs H. H., 172
Milnes, Richard Monckton, *see* Houghton, Lord
Milnes, Mrs (cook), 356
Milton, John, 25, 165, 173, 200, 341, 392, 549
Mirehouse, 197–202, 338, 515, 536
Mitford, Mary Russell, 241
Montalembert, Comte de, 383
Monteagle, Thomas Spring-Rice, 1st Lord, 358
Monteith, Robert, 95, 112, 147, 148, 179, 183, 229, 293, 327, 371, 374
Moore, Thomas, 231, 394
Morier, Sir Robert, 367
Morris, Lewis, 544–5, 561, 565
Morris, Miss, 158
Morton, Savile, 281
Moxon, Edward, 103, 141–2, 149, 159–60, 166, 172, 177, 180, 244–5, 266, 268, 283, 284, 288, 289, 290–1, 301, 305, 306–9, 324, 330, 341, 368, 375, 382, 389, 392, 404, 406, 414–15, 421–2
Moxon, Mrs Edward, 166, 477
Moxon, William, 421–2, 423, 424, 451
Munby, Arthur, 420
Murray, John, 169

New Monthly Magazine, 110, 168–9, 296
'New Timon, The', 295–9
New York *Ledger*, 492
Nicolson, Sir Harold, 90–1
Nightingale, Florence, 277
Nineteenth Century, 547–8, 560–1
Nonnenwerth, 154, 171, 306
'North, Christopher', *see* Wilson, John
Northampton, Spencer Compton, 2nd Marquis of, 226–7
Norton, Mrs Caroline, 283–4, 287
Norway, 431–2

Ojeda, 118–19, 124
Once a Week, 424, 476
Osborne, House, 404, 443–4, 464, 468, 538
Oxford, 86, 90, 97–9, 266, 382–3, 389, 390, 433, 463
Oxford Magazine, 190

Paden, W. D., 46
Paget, Sir James, 445, 462
Palgrave, Francis T.: meets AT, 325–6; character, 325–6, 371–2, 433–5, 459; travels with AT, 371–2, 432–5, 445; *The Golden Treasury*, 435; also, 304, 367, 382, 398, 438, 446, 461, 469, 484, 490, 509, 583
Palgrave, William Gifford, 433, 458, 532, 571
Palmerston, Henry John Temple, 3rd Viscount, 117
Paris, 57, 80, 118, 359–60, 441, 485
Park House, 253, 259–60, 268, 274, 281, 305, 309, 311, 321, 326, 340, 350, 351, 357, 363, 383
Parke, Sir James, 399
Parker, John, 368, 419
Parkinson, Dr John, 7–8
Parry, Sir Hubert, 577
Patmore, Coventry, 304–5, 319, 321, 324–5, 326, 330, 339, 361, 364,

365, 378, 390, 392, 408, 419, 534–5

Patmore, Mrs Coventry, 325, 330, 534

Payne, Bertrand, 476–7, 480

Peel, Archibald, 410

Peel, Edmund, 305, 357

Peel, Julia, Lady, 283, 294

Peel, Sir Robert, 251, 271–2, 283, 292, 294, 305

Pembroke Castle, the, 539–41

Pitt, Valerie, 279

Poe, Edgar Allan, 267, 364

Poet Laureateship, 35, 271–2, 290–1, 310, 350–3, 354, 357–8, 365, 376, 387, 389, 403–4, 518, 538, 553, 561

Pollock, Sir William Frederick, 229, 232, 327, 397–8, 483, 545

Pond, J. B., 551

Ponsonby, Sir Henry Frederick, 442–3

Pope, Alexander, 22, 229–30

Portugal, 432

Praed, W. M., 69

Pratt, Mr, 211

Prestbury, 275–81, 309

Priessnitz, Vincenz, 276, 277

Princess Ida, 313

Prinsep, Mr and Mrs Henry Thoby, 407–9, 411, 412, 447, 448, 466, 509

Prinsep, Valentine, 407, 434–5

Pritchard, Charles, 462, 482

Pritchett, Sir Victor, 279–80

Procter, B. W., 257, 271

Procter, Anne (Mrs B. W.), 257, 552

Publisher's Circular, 341

Punch, 297–8

Pyrenees, 118–20, 307–8, 437–40, 503, 514

Quarterly Review, 142, 169–73, 265–6, 502, 515

Queen's Messenger, 477

Rader, R. W., 217

Rashdall, John, 74–5, 186–7, 189, 217, 365

Rawnsley, Catherine, 224–5, 249, 257, 329, 331, 333–4, 356

Rawnsley, Drummond, 249, 329, 330–1, 356, 367, 379

Rawnsley, H. D., 322

Rawnsley, Sophy, *see* Elmhirst, Sophy

Rawnsley, Mr and Mrs T. H., 65, 82, 134, 136, 156–7, 186, 197, 214, 268–9, 328

Reform Bill riots, 125

Repton, Humphry, 343

Ricks, Christopher, 537, 572

Ritchie, Anne, Lady, 446–8, 512, 537, 565–6

Ritchie, Emily, 522

Robertson, Frederick, 518–19

Robertson, Robert (later Robertson-Glasgow), 116, 119, 121

Robinson, George, 135

Rogers, Samuel, 160, 180–1, 196, 230–2, 264, 273, 283–4, 289–91, 292, 304, 351, 357, 420

Rossetti, D. G., 327, 392–6, 407, 414–15

Rossetti, William, 325, 329, 392–4

Rossyln, Robert St. Clair-Erskine, 4th Earl of, 517

Routledge, George, 415

Royal Society, 462–3

Rundle, Elizabeth (later Charles), 320–1

Ruskin, John, 373, 397, 483, 521

Russell, Lord Arthur, 483

Russell, Elizabeth: gift of money to AT, 4, 45, 48, 51, 60, 146, 182, 189, 207, 247, 270, 272, 293, 338, 376; also, 5, 9, 32, 33, 38, 40, 43, 59–60, 80, 130, 133, 157, 176, 207, 315, 354, 386

Russell, Emma, *see* Boyne, Emma, Viscountess

Russell, Lord John, 351, 358, 466

Russell, Matthew, 4, 32–3, 38

Russia, 12–14

Russia, Tsar and Tsarina of, 540–1

St. Helens, Alleyne FitzHerbert, Lord, 13

Salvin, Anthony, 155

Sandwich, Mary Ann, Countess of, 399

Saturday Review, 390, 400

Schliemann, Heinrich, 519

Schuyler, Georgina, 565–6

Scotland, 179, 327–8, 362, 371–2, 415, 418, 539–40

Scott, Robert, 383

Scott, Sir Walter, 22, 36, 95, 252
Seaford House, 370, 373
Sellwood, Anne, *see* Weld, Anne
Sellwood, Emily, *see* Tennyson, Emily (AT's wife)
Sellwood, Henry, 82, 248, 249, 321, 332, 356, 366, 464, 503
Sellwood, Louisa, *see* Turner, Louisa
Severn, Joseph, 301
Seymour, Mr, 403, 404
Shafto, Robert, 221
Shakespeare, William: AT compared to, 511, 512–13, 523; *Hamlet,* 107, 132, 512, 565; *Measure for Measure,* 109; *Twelfth Night,* 128; *Much Ado About Nothing,* 128; sonnets, 201–2; *Romeo and Juliet,* 221; *Timon of Athens,* 299; *The Tempest,* 346, 448; *Cymbeline,* 581, 582; also, 37, 95, 252, 392
Shelley, P. B., 97, 99, 155, 162, 168, 169, 197, 301, 392, 518
Shenstone, William, 99
Siddall, Elizabeth, 392–3
Sidgwick, Henry, 483, 583
Simeon, Sir John, 242, 380–1, 418, 427, 466, 472, 483, 487–8, 489, 495n., 532
Smith, George, 424
Smith, Goldwin, 390, 400–1
Smith, Sydney, 75, 283, 367, 479
Society of Authors, 303
Somers, Virginia, Countess, 408–9, 413
Somersby, 14, 15–16, 17, 18–23, 25–9, 35–6, 39, 48–51, 56–9, 63–5, 80, 81–5, 99–101, 103–5, 114–15, 123–4, 126, 127, 134–5, 146–7, 148, 166–7, 171, 179, 181, 182–3, 184, 186–7, 189–90, 192–3, 195–6, 197, 214, 225, 230, 232–3, 373, 579
Sotheby, Charlotte, 158
Sotheby, Kitty, 158
Sotheby, William, 152
South Willingham, 7, 14
Southey, Robert, 105, 126, 141, 271, 351
Spanish adventure, 115–23
Spectator, 110, 350, 463, 512–13, 564
Spedding, Edward, 75, 111, 150, 151, 165

Spedding, James: character, 91–2, 165, 197; entertains AT at Mirehouse, 197–203, 338; opinion of AT, 199, 203–4; AT's opinion of him, 91, 201; revises AT's poems, 330–1, 406; surprise at AT's marriage, 337; relations with EST, 338, 367, 398; reluctance to go to Farringford, 375, 474, 536; death, 528, 535–6; also, 75, 87, 95, 105, 125, 126, 130, 150, 151, 155, 172, 178, 190–1, 207, 221, 222, 229, 230, 231, 241, 249, 253, 256, 257, 261, 265, 283, 289, 293, 308, 363, 371, 399, 406, 408, 432, 457, 466, 484, 502, 511, 521, 526, 532
Spedding, John (JS's father), 197–8, 199, 200
Spedding, Mrs John (JS's mother), 200–1, 230, 231
Spedding, John (JS's brother), 99
Spring-Rice, Cecil, 569
Spring-Rice, Stephen, 186, 190, 288, 338
Stanford, Sir Charles, 513
Stanley, A. P., 466, 500, 522, 528
Stanley, Lady Augusta, 466
Stanley, Lord, *see* Derby, 15th Earl of
Stanley of Alderley, Lady, 467
Stella, the, 562–3
Stephen, Leslie, 490, 551
Sterling, John, 86, 95, 116, 117, 121–2, 241, 265–6, 267, 404
Sterling Club, 86, 241, 242, 461
Stoker, Bram, 528, 579
Strahan, Alexander, 477, 502, 549
Stratford, 252
Sullivan, Sir Arthur, 487
Sunbeam, the 568–9
Sunderland, Thomas, 90, 97–8
Sutherland, Harriet, Duchess of, 412, 443, 449, 457
Sutton, 147
Swinburne, Algernon: AT's opinion of him, 419, 461, 479, 481, 530; his opinion of AT, 476, 500, 512–13, 514; also, 395, 468, 506, 582
Switzerland, 80, 81, 222, 302, 305, 306–9, 485, 501
Symonds, J. A., the elder, 458–60
Symonds, J. A., the younger, 458–60, 579

Talfourd, Sir Thomas Noon, 303
Tatler, 140–1
Taylor, Bayard, 411, 468, 469
Taylor, Sir Henry and Lady, 273, 286, 351, 353, 357, 367, 399–402, 408, 409, 436, 530
Taylor, Tom, 287, 288, 379, 399, 457, 514, 528
Tealby, 8, 14, 15, 24–5, 44, 133–4, 135, 137, 155–6, 174–5, 178–9, 191–2, 196, 204–5, 210–14
Temple, Frederick, 382
Temple Bar, 477, 480
Tennant, Margot (later Asquith), 556
Tennant, R. J., 74, 86, 91, 103, 126, 147, 148, 155, 177, 180, 187, 189, 192–3, 195, 234, 293

TENNYSON, ALFRED, 1ST BARON TENNYSON OF ALDWORTH AND FARRINGFORD
Chief Biographical Events
birth, 16; baptism, 17; begins writing poetry, 21–2; goes to school, 29–31; returns home for study, 35–6; *Poems by Two Brothers,* 44–6; deterioration of life at Somersby, 47–51; enters Cambridge, 52–6; University Prize poem, 68–9, 77; meets AHH, 69; becomes Apostle, 85–96; visits London and Somersby with AHH, 99–101; EST in love with him, 104; publishes *Poems, Chiefly Lyrical,* 105–6; 'Christopher North' review, 111–12; Spanish adventure, 116–22; Reform Bill riots, 125; fails to meet Wordsworth, 125–7; leaves Cambridge, 129–30; death of father, 129–34; plans for career, 137; Rhine trip, 152–4; publication of *Poems* (1833), 159–60, 168–73; romantic relations, 167; death of AHH, 181–8; turns to poetry, 184–5; at Mirehouse, 197–203; death of grandfather, 204–8; inheritance, 206–7; Rosa Baring, 214–21; involvement with EST, 223–5; Mill's review, 225–6; move to High Beech, 229, 232–5; separation from EST, 245–50; move to Tunbridge Wells, 251; woodcarving scheme, 254–6,

268–70; move to Boxley, 259–60; publication of *Poems,* (1842), 263, 265–7; trip to Ireland, 268; fails in attempt to become Poet Laureate, 271–2; move to Cheltenham, 274–5; breakdown and water cure at Prestbury, 275–81; death of Dr Allen and move to London, 282; wants to marry, 282, 286, 318; fails to get pension, 283; makes Wordsworth's acquaintance, 289–91; Civil List pension, 291–4; 'The New Timon', 295–9; Swiss trip, 306–9; water cure at Umberslade, 309; Queen and Prince Albert take notice of, 310; publication of *The Princess,* 311; freed of fears of epilepsy, 316; second trip to Ireland, 318–19; trip to West Country, 319–21; last water cure at Malvern, 321; renewal of engagement, 321–2, 328–9, 331–2; publication of *In Memoriam,* 324–5, 330–1, 332–3; marriage and wedding trip, 333–40; reception of *In Memoriam,* 340–1, 349–50; Laureateship, 350–5; Warninglid, 356; Chapel House, Twickenham, 357, 359; presentation to Queen, 357–8; still-born son, 359; France and Italy, 359–63; birth and christening of HT, 366–7; death of Duke of Wellington, 368–9; move to Farringford, 372–5; birth and christening of son Lionel, 377–9; acquainted with Sir John Simeon, 380–1; Russian threat and 'Charge of Light Brigade', 381–2; Oxford DCL, 382–3; publication and reception of *Maud,* 382, 383–4, 389–91; reads to Brownings and Carlyles, 392–7; at the Grange, 399–402; buys Farringford, 403–4; visit of Prince Albert, 403–4; begins *Idylls,* 404–6; frequents Little Holland House, 407–9; failure of *Illustrated Edition,* 414–15; trip to North, 415–18; EST falls ill, 418–19; trouble with Moxons, 421–2; financial success, 424; in search of subjects, 424–6; trips to Norway, Portugal, and West

Country, 431–5; Pyrenees trip,
437–41; meets Queen, 443–4;
entertains Garibaldi, 449–50;
publication of *Enoch Arden*, 451–2;
joins The Club and Royal Society,
461–3; offer of baronetcy, 463; visit
of Queen Emma, 463–4; deaths in
family, 464–5; builds Aldworth,
471–6; leaves Moxons for Strahan,
476–7; attacked by Payne, 477;
resumes *Idylls*, 477–9; Metaphysical
Society, 482–4; breaks with Lear
and Lewis Carroll, 485–7; death of
Simeon and Dickens, 487–9;
friendship with W. G. Ward and G.
Eliot, 489–90; completes *Idylls*, 492;
sends epilogue to Queen, 500;
refuses baronetcy again, 500–1;
Continental trips, 501; changes
publisher again, 502; last trip to
Cauteretz, 503; EST's breakdown,
503–5; HT becomes secretary,
504–6; *Queen Mary*, 512–14;
Harold, 514; Lionel's engagement
and marriage, 514–15, 522–3; visits
EFG and WEG, 515–17; later plays,
523–6; death of CTT and others,
526–8; refuses baronetcy fourth
time, 528–9; trip to Germany and
Italy, 529–31; end of friendships
with Patmore, Arnold, deaths of JS
and EFG, 534–8; renewed relations
with Queen, 538–9; cruise on
Pembroke Castle, 539–41; peerage,
541–6; political activity, 546–8;
changes publishers last time, 549;
HT's marriage, 550–1; worries
about biography, 552–3; religious
problems, 554–5; death of Lionel,
556–9; *Locksley Hall Sixty Years
After* and WEG, 559–61; remarriage
of Eleanor, 566–7; serious illness,
567–9; 80th birthday, 569; renews
writing, 569–70; death of Browning,
571; recordings, 573–4; last meeting
with WEG, 574–6; leaves
Farringford last time, 578; last
illness, 579–82; funeral, 582–3;
preparation of biography, 583; death
of EST, 583

*Personal Characteristics, Interests and
Attitudes*
Americans, 240, 245, 319, 340, 411,
416–17, 466, 468–9, 502, 519–20,
551–2, 565–6
appearance, 25, 53–4, 82, 83, 104,
117, 121, 148, 151, 176, 224, 240,
242, 257, 263, 283, 308–9, 320,
328, 333, 334, 357-8, 364, 370,
383, 393–4, 397, 398, 400, 401,
409, 411, 416–17, 419, 421, 428,
449, 458, 459, 516, 519, 521, 541,
546, 556, 563, 579
composition, methods of, 36–7, 45–6,
78, 92, 105, 119–20, 140, 186,
244–5, 257–8, 311, 341–2, 344,
404–5, 406, 424–6, 440–1, 446,
493–4, 518, 562
conversation, 89, 93, 285–6, 288, 321,
328, 364, 406–7, 432, 458–60, 483,
516–17, 530
correspondence and hatred of
letter-writing, 85, 141, 274, 419,
504, 515–16
creativity, periods when lacking, 244,
268, 271, 424–6, 441, 446, 464,
476, 477–8, 529, 549
criticism, sensitivity to, 79, 92, 112,
148–9, 172, 173, 191, 261, 263,
266, 268, 304, 317, 341, 364, 391,
393, 401, 407, 420–1, 422, 426,
486, 529, 544, 549–50
drinking habits, 55, 154, 221–2, 277,
282, 320, 321, 322–3, 339, 370,
393, 411, 445, 459, 468, 470, 517,
519, 524, 529, 533, 577
financial matters and fear of poverty,
45, 52, 60, 69, 134, 137, 149, 153,
159, 185, 189, 197, 204, 206–7,
221, 234, 239, 244–5, 247–8, 252,
254–6, 268–72, 282–3, 291–3,
323–4, 352, 366, 368, 375–7, 398,
403, 404, 414–15, 421–2, 424, 436,
452, 461, 471, 472, 476–7, 480,
486, 492, 502, 514, 523, 541–3,
549, 551, 564, 578
flattery, love of, 303–4, 326, 327, 408,
420, 426, 485, 509–10, 549
friendships, 54–6, 61, 68, 72–3, 85,
91–5, 128–9, 150–2, 196, 201, 241,
282, 301–5, 306, 319, 325–8, 358,
361, 363–4, 370–2, 392–8, 419–21,

431, 432, 437, 443, 457–63, 469–71, 484–90, 507–10, 515–17, 521–2, 532–9

Gothic architecture, love of, 373, 472–6

health: general, 25, 43, 115, 116, 118–19, 122, 123, 124, 132, 139–40, 146, 147, 189–90, 193, 237–8, 239, 242, 250–1, 253–4, 256–7, 261, 269, 274–5, 276–82, 292, 301, 309, 315–16, 320, 321, 323, 372, 421, 435–6, 438, 441, 445–6, 461, 486, 491, 505, 527, 529–30, 533, 538, 555, 563, 567–71, 573–4, 576, 579–82; deafness, 523, 574; epilepsy, fear of, 10–11, 17, 29, 84–5, 139–40, 150, 237–8, 248, 278–80, 292, 293, 315, 321, 326, 340, 445, 567; eyes, 25, 77, 83, 93–4, 121, 129, 139, 358, 379, 394, 398, 485, 520, 538, 555, 563, 574; gout, 83–5, 278, 279–80, 321, 445, 533, 567–8, 579; teeth, 370, 406, 421, 486, 581; trances, 28–9, 83–5, 238, 278–80, 309, 315, 347, 554–5, 567

host, acts as, 148, 235, 241, 318, 363, 364–5, 374–5, 379, 397–8, 427–8, 431, 565–6, 573, 576–7

humour and wit, 55, 88, 90, 148, 151, 222, 235, 242, 267, 288, 317–18, 390–1, 479–80, 576

indolence, 85, 92, 270, 281, 326, 485, 502

music, 29, 36, 148, 394, 513, 522

opium, reported to take, 340, 420–1

parent, 366, 377–8, 436–7, 456–7, 465–6, 504–7, 515, 550–1, 557–9, 566, 581

'passion of the past', 1, 150, 165, 203, 212, 328, 442, 452

politics, 67–8, 116, 122, 125, 164–5, 226, 365, 381, 459, 541, 544, 546–7, 548, 560–1, 574–6

privacy, worry about, 337, 378–9, 405–6, 410–11, 417, 428, 431, 438, 456, 467, 468, 472, 504, 518–19, 525, 552–3, 563, 564–6, 579, 581

readings, 35, 55, 92, 148, 151, 180, 199–200, 229, 239, 287, 324, 364, 375, 382, 391, 393–7, 398, 401, 406–7, 412, 413, 418, 419, 421,

425–6, 437, 453, 458, 460. 468, 471, 490, 516–18, 520, 540–1, 556, 568–9, 573–4, 575–6, 577

religion, 1, 18, 40, 56, 76, 154, 262–3, 322, 329, 331, 334, 339, 348–9, 380, 398, 460, 470, 482–4, 513, 539, 554–5, 557–8, 568, 570, 571, 577, 578, 579–80

reputation and fame, 77, 82, 190, 265, 266, 317, 341, 349–50, 351, 353, 355, 360, 391–2, 415, 424, 435, 467–8, 476, 480, 518, 528–9, 544–5, 551–2, 561, 564, 569

science, 19, 36, 177, 312, 344, 345–6, 358, 462–3, 578

sea, love of, 22–3, 147, 179, 319–20, 370, 372, 431

self-consciousness, 18, 52–3, 77, 89, 203, 401, 435–6, 443, 461–2, 463, 468, 483, 517–18, 528

sex, and relations with women, 33, 37, 82–3, 94–5, 150, 151–2, 164, 167, 171–2, 177, 180, 195–6, 214–21, 223–5, 243, 245–50, 263, 266–7, 279, 282, 284–8, 294, 312–14, 318, 321–2, 331–6, 447–9, 479, 481–2, 493, 517, 551, 556, 576–7

smoking, 55, 89, 150, 154, 190, 221, 230, 239, 241–2, 243, 251, 257, 275, 277, 282, 284–5, 287, 316, 318, 323, 360, 362, 371, 398, 400–1, 411, 432, 436, 445, 516, 519

social ineptitude, 18, 83, 193, 224, 240, 305, 309, 318, 328, 401–2, 406–7, 408, 411–13, 516–20, 525, 540–1, 565–6

social position, attitude to, 53, 208–9, 227, 358, 368, 377–8, 402, 411–14, 428, 543–4

spiritualism, 132, 482, 527, 529–31, 557–8, 563

style of life, ideas on, 232, 270, 272, 283, 291, 293, 350, 375–6, 379, 413–14, 536

theatre, connection with, 99, 229, 481, 511–14, 523–6

title, 208–9, 396, 463, 500–1, 528–9, 539, 541–7

unphilosophical mind, 56, 88, 89, 343–4, 456, 459–60, 483–4, 530, 564

Works

'Adeline', 109–10, 111
'Anacaona', 124–5, 159, 227
'Ancient Sage, The', 85, 554–5
'Ante-Chamber, The', 180
'Antony to Cleopatra', 46
'Armageddon', 66, 68, 77–8
'Audley Court', 244, 264
'Aylmer's Field', 446, 453–4
Ballads and Other Poems, 529
Becket, 514, 523, 526, 554, 578, 579
'Beggar Maid, The', 414
'Boädicea', 428, 574
'Break, break , break', 219, 263
'Bridesmaid, The', 223
'Britons, Guard Your Own', 365
'Brook, The', 389
'Character, A', 98
'Charge of the Heavy Brigade at Balaclava, The', 532, 554
'Charge of the Light Brigade, The', 381, 389, 573
'Check every outflash', 141, 440
'Claribel', 109–10
'Compromise', 546–7
'Crossing the Bar', 570
Cup, The, 525, 554
'Daisy, The', 362, 389
'Day-Dream, The', 200
'De Profundis', 568
'Death of Œnone, The', 120
'Defence of Lucknow, The', 529
'Demeter and Persephone', 561–2, 571
Demeter and Other Poems, 571
Devil and the Lady, The, 37, 79, 513
'Dora', 200, 216, 217, 264, 291
'Dream of Fair Women, A', 151, 162
'Dualisms', 110
'Eagle, The', 119
'Edwin Morris', 218, 244
'Eleänore', 164
'England and America', 492
'Enoch Arden', 425, 432, 446, 452–3, 454, 455, 458
Enoch Arden, etc., 451–2, 454–5, 464
'Epic, The', 266
Falcon, The, 524, 554
'Far-Far-Away', 571
'Flower in the crannied wall', 479
Foresters, The, 525, 578
'Frater Ave atque Vale', 530–1, 554
'Gardener's Daughter, The', 180, 200, 215, 264, 267
Gareth and Lynette, etc., 492
'Grandmother, The', 424, 540
'Hands All Round!', 365
Harold, 514, 516
'Hesperides, The', 162
'Higher Pantheism, The', 483
Holy Grail and Other Poems, The, 479, 480, 536
'How thought you that this thing', 216
'Human Cry, The', 568
'I lingered yet awhile', 216
Idylls of the King: 36, 178, 212, 266, 279, 299, 318, 319–20, 382, 388, 404–6, 420, 422–4, 432, 435, 442, 451, 477–9, 492–500; 'Balin and Balan', 492, 494, 495n., 554; 'Coming of Arthur, The', 478, 493, 494, 496; 'Dedication', 442; 'Gareth and Lynette', 492, 493, 494, 496–7; 'Geraint and Enid', 405, 422, 492, 494; 'Guinevere', 413, 419, 423–4, 468, 490, 520, 568; 'Holy Grail, The', 478, 479; 'Lancelot and Elaine', 423, 425–6, 427, 494; 'Last Tournament, The', 492; 'Marriage of Geraint, The', 405–6, 422, 492, 494, 497; 'Merlin and Vivien', 268, 405, 422, 423, 492, 498; 'Passing of Arthur, The', 422, 478, 494, 498–9, 582; 'Pelleas and Ettarre', 426, 478, 480, 494; 'To the Queen', 495, 500
In Memoriam, 94–5, 183–5, 186, 187, 189, 193–4, 233, 259, 268, 278, 281, 311, 323–5, 330–1, 332–3, 340–50, 351, 354, 384–7, 392, 405, 421, 442–3, 451, 482, 539, 547, 558–9
'In the Garden at Swainston', 487–8, 495n.
'In the Valley of Cauteretz', 120, 439–41, 444, 452
'June Bracken and Heather', 223, 576–7
'Kraken, The', 106, 107, 108–9, 393
'Lady Clara Vere de Vere', 216–17
'Lady Clare', 216–17
'Lady of Shalott, The', 162–3, 226, 263, 414
'Lilian', 110, 195, 216
'Lines on Cambridge of 1830', 68
'Lisette', 164

'Literary Squabbles', 298–9
'Locksley Hall', 121, 218, 264, 455, 520, 559
'Locksley Hall Sixty Years After', 213, 559–61, 562, 575
'Lord of Burleigh, The', 200, 217
'Lotos-Eaters, The', 92, 119, 162, 163–4, 263, 308, 397, 439, 577
'Lover's Tale, The', 159–60, 161, 486–7
'Lucretius', 479, 481–2
'Mablethorpe', 23
'Madeline', 110
'Margaret', 164
'Mariana', 106, 107, 109, 118, 226, 250, 397
'Mariana in the South', 118, 162, 392
'Marion', 164
Maud, 107, 218, 219, 220, 228, 237, 278, 311, 365, 377, 380–1, 382, 383–402, 405, 412, 415, 417, 419, 423, 437, 473, 490, 493, 518, 556, 560, 573, 576
Maud and Other Poems, 389–90
'May Queen, The', 168–9, 264
'Merlin and the Gleam', 570
'Miller's Daughter, The', 151, 264
'Mine be the strength of spirit', 155
'Morte d'Arthur', 186, 190, 195, 200, 201, 219, 263, 266, 267, 404, 422, 494
'My life is full of weary days', 159
'My Rosalind', 164
'New Timon, and the Poets, The', 297–8
'Northern Farmer, New Style', 456, 479
'Northern Farmer, Old Style', 456
'O Darling Room', 168, 169–73, 296
Ode on the Death of the Duke of Wellington, 368–9, 389, 575–6
'Ode to Memory', 106
'Œnone', 119, 120n., 159, 162, 263, 267, 439
'Of old sat Freedom on the heights', 289
'Oh! that 'twere possible', 186, 228, 380–1, 397
'On a Mourner', 186
'Oriana', 111
'Palace of Art, The', 147, 162, 163, 263, 392

Poems, (1833), 120, 146, 149, 158–60, 161–6, 168–73, 190–1, 225–6, 242, 245
Poems (1842), 120, 244, 256, 257–8, 261–8
Poems, by Alfred Tennyson (Illustrated Edition), 392, 395, 414–15, 421–2
Poems by Two Brothers, 44–6, 68, 79, 102, 105, 116, 368, 389
Poems, Chiefly Lyrical, 101–3, 105–13, 140–1, 142, 148–9, 389
'Poland', 164–5
'Prefatory Poem to My Brother's Sonnets', 526–7
Princess, The: 119, 120, 278, 279, 287–8, 301, 305, 307–8, 309, 310–18, 319, 322, 323, 329, 330, 340, 356, 384, 439, 503; 'Ask me no more', 573; 'Come down, O maid, from yonder mountain height', 307–8, 314; 'Now sleeps the crimson petal', 314; 'The splendour falls on castle walls', 312, 319, 540, 573; 'Sweet and low', 329, 330; 'Tears, idle tears', 194, 395, 490
'Prologue to General Hamley', 532–3
Promise of May, The, 525–6
Queen Mary, 512–14, 520, 523, 526, 534, 578
'Recollections of the Arabian Nights', 111
'Revenge, The', 522, 529, 534
'Rifle Clubs!!!', 365
'Rizpah', 529
'Roses on the Terrace, The', 220, 571
'St. Agnes' Eve', 226
'St. Simeon Stylites', 186, 199, 264
'Sea Dreams', 424
'Silent Voices, The', 579–80
'Sir Galahad', 263
'Sir Launcelot and Queen Guinevere', 263
'Sisters, The', 148
'Spinster's Sweet-Arts, The', 554
'Supposed Confessions of a Second-Rate Sensitive Mind', 107–8, 263
'Thy rosy lips are soft and sweet', 215–16
'Timbuctoo', 66, 77–9, 98, 102
'Tiresias', 186, 537–8

Tiresias, and Other Poems, 554–5
'Tithonus', 186, 219, 424, 441, 452, 455
'To Christopher North', 149, 168, 169, 191
'To E. FitzGerald', 537–8
'To J. S.', 162, 165
'To the Marquis of Dufferin and Ava', 558–9, 571
'To the Rev. W. H. Brookfield', 510
'To Ulysses', 571
'To Virgil', 554
'Two Voices, The', 76, 186, 229, 263–4
'Ulysses', 186, 190, 219, 263, 267
'Vastness', 555
'Victim, The', 476
'Vision of Sin, The', 263, 392, 462–3
'Walking to the Mail', 264
'Welcome to Alexandra, A', 444, 521
'Will Waterproof's Lyrical Monologue', 229–30
'Window, The', 487
'Written During the Convulsions in Spain', 68, 116
'You ask me, why, though ill at ease', 289

Tennyson, Alfred Browning Stanley (AT's grandson), 556, 566–7
Tennyson, Anne (AT's great-aunt), 2
Tennyson, Arthur (AT's brother), 23, 50, 57, 138, 140, 273–4, 276, 373
Tennyson, Audrey (HT's wife), 550–1, 562, 565, 580–1
Tennyson, Cecilia (AT's sister), *see* Lushington, Cecilia
Tennyson, Charles (AT's uncle), *see* Tennyson d'Eyncourt, Charles
Tennyson, Charles, (AT's brother), *see* Turner, Charles
Tennyson, Sir Charles (AT's grandson), 13, 215, 551, 556, 566–7
Tennyson, Clara, *see* Tennyson d'Eyncourt, Clara
Tennyson, Edward (AT's brother), 10n., 23, 57, 137–8, 140, 191, 206, 274, 293
Tennyson, Edwin, *see* Tennyson d'Eyncourt, Edwin
Tennyson, Eleanor, *see* Birrell, Eleanor
Tennyson, Elizabeth, (AT's great-grandmother), 2–3, 8
Tennyson, Elizabeth, (AT's mother): character, 14–15, 17–18, 19, 100; marriage, 14–15, 23, 48–50, 57, 63–4, 80, 114, 132; relations with children, 18, 45, 57, 150, 156–7, 322, 335; financial circumstances, 134–5, 206, 255, 269, 270; takes Chapel House, 373; death, 464–5; also, 115, 116–17, 129, 143, 205, 235, 248, 251, 253, 274, 315, 333, 338, 340
Tennyson, Elizabeth (AT's aunt), *see* Russell, Elizabeth
Tennyson, Ellen, *see* Tennyson d'Eyncourt, Ellen
Tennyson, Emilia (AT's sister 'Emily'), *see* Jesse, Emilia
Tennyson, Emily, Lady (AT's wife): character, 82, 215, 331, 333, 334–6, 339–40, 451–2, 490, 504–5, 547, 558; relations with AT before marriage, 82, 104, 180, 196, 223–5, 234, 244–50, 252, 282, 286, 315, 318, 321–2, 328–33, 385, 583; relations with AT's family, 82, 104, 167, 215, 223–5, 245–6, 248–9, 335, 365–6, 377, 522, 545; relations with AT's friends, 104, 327, 335, 338–40, 427–8, 431, 455–6, 500, 536–7; health, 167, 215, 234–5, 249–50, 321, 335, 337, 357, 359, 370, 377, 405, 418–19, 427, 437–9, 468, 472, 492, 502–5, 514, 527, 550, 555–6, 573, 580, 582, 583; religious attitudes, 215, 322, 331, 334, 361, 366–7, 380, 398, 482, 558; influence on AT's poetry, 330–1, 332–3, 334–5, 340, 424–6, 442, 451–2, 476, 478, 479, 500, 571; marriage, 333–6, 398–9, 418–19, 426–8, 503–5, 576–7; ambitions, 377, 442, 522–3, 528–9, 545; doting mother, 366, 378, 436, 437, 456–7, 503, 550–1; hostess, 374–5, 397–8, 463–4, 466–7, 474–5, 481, 491–2, 555–6; lonely without AT, 398, 406, 490, 492, 503; handles AT's correspondence and affairs, 335, 419, 502, 504; journal, 503, 505; work on AT's biography, 553, 583; death, 583

Tennyson, Eustace, *see* Tennyson d'Eyncourt, Eustace

Tennyson, Frederick (AT's brother): character, 21, 61, 62–4, 81, 134, 136, 140, 269–70, 563; education, 29, 30, 37, 41, 47, 50, 52, 54–5, 57, 60–1, 62–3, 68, 81, 135, 139, 145; relations with grandfather, 43, 63, 64, 81, 136, 139, 156, 192, 206; relations with father, 63–4, 81, 115, 123, 132; inheritance, 206–7; relations with EST, 335, 361, 522, 545, 563; entertains AT, 563, 578; also, 16, 17, 39, 97, 143, 146, 147, 148, 171, 175, 179, 184, 186, 189, 198, 205, 208, 217, 224, 225, 227, 235, 255, 260, 274, 305, 323, 385, 482

Tennyson, George (AT's grandfather): birth, 2; character, 2–3, 7–8, 174; relations with children and grandchildren, 5–7, 9, 11, 14, 15–16, 23, 24–5, 26, 33–5, 38–9, 41–2, 43–4, 47, 57–8, 63–4, 65–6, 77, 80, 81, 130–1, 133–4, 135–9, 155–6, 157, 174–6, 192; wealth, 7–9; health, 10, 38, 77, 84, 130–1, 133, 147, 176, 192, 204; MP, 32–3; death of wife, 44; opinion of AT, 44, 63, 77, 139, 162, 176; death and funeral, 204–6; will, 206–7; also, 1, 114, 127, 212–13, 376, 385, 387, 454

Tennyson, George (AT's brother), 16

Tennyson, George Clayton (AT's father): birth, 5; character, 5–6, 11–12, 13–14, 15, 17, 19, 376; relations with father, 5–7, 11–12, 14–16, 24, 26, 33–5, 38–9, 41–2, 43, 47, 59, 114; relations with brothers and sisters, 6–7, 9, 24, 32, 38, 40, 41, 80, 114; destined for Church, 7, 11–12, 14; benefices, 7, 14, 15–16, 26; epilepsy, 10–11, 26–9, 35, 38, 39, 40–2, 59, 65, 131, 237; education, 11–12; foreign travels, 12–14, 51, 57, 66, 80–1, 103, 114–15; finances, 14–16, 25–6, 35, 38–9, 47, 57, 135; marriage, 14–16, 23, 48–50, 57, 63–4, 80, 114, 132; relations with children, 17, 21, 25, 35–6, 40, 48–9, 51, 58,

63–4, 114–15; general health, 25, 26, 36, 38–42, 47–51, 57, 59, 80, 129–31; becomes DCL, 25–6; mental illness, 35, 40, 48–50, 59, 63–5, 80–1, 114–15, 122, 130; drinking, 35, 38, 39, 41, 42, 48–9, 65, 81, 129, 131; drug-taking, 42, 122, 130, 131, 340; cholera, 47; death and funeral, 129–34; also, 1, 45, 127, 385, 387

Tennyson, George Hildeyard (AT's cousin), *see* Tennyson, d'Eyncourt George

Tennyson, Hallam (AT's son), 2nd Lord: biography of AT, 17, 20, 132–3, 174, 178, 202, 247, 278, 321, 323n., 351, 391, 506, 507, 535, 552–3, 570n., 580–1; birth and christening, 366–7; character, 378, 437, 465, 466, 505–6, 507; education, 436–7, 456–7, 465, 501; leaves Cambridge, 504, 505; companion to AT, 503, 505–6, 514, 515–16, 530, 539–41; early attempts at career, 550; marriage and children, 550–1; also, 240, 245, 259, 370, 371, 373, 417, 418–19, 448, 449, 464, 484, 526

Tennyson, Horatio (AT's brother), 23, 50, 57, 138, 234, 246, 270, 277, 278, 373, 485–6

Tennyson, Julia *see* Tennyson d'Eyncourt, Julia

Tennyson, Lionel (AT's son): birth and christening, 377–8, 380; character, 378, 437, 456–7, 465–6, 506–7, 515, 522–3, 557; education, 436–7, 456–7, 465, 482, 501, 506; engagement and marriage, 484–5, 514–15, 522–3, 556–7, 566–7; last journey and death, 556–9; also, 417, 418–19, 448, 467, 472, 487, 532

Tennyson, Maria (FT's wife), 260, 361

Tennyson, Mary (AT's grandmother), 3, 5, 9, 44

Tennyson, Mary (AT's aunt), *see* Bourne, Mary

Tennyson, Mary (AT's sister), *see* Ker, Mary

Tennyson, Matilda (AT's sister), 23, 57, 82, 182–3, 235, 335, 366, 373, 465, 482

Tennyson, Michael (AT's
    great-grandfather), 2, 5
Tennyson, Septimus (AT's brother),
    10n., 23, 57, 138, 140, 191, 237,
    253, 269, 274, 373, 464–5
Tennyson d'Eyncourt, Charles: birth,
    4, 6; character, 6, 23–4; courtship
    and marriage, 6, 23–4, 33, 43, 218;
    becomes father's chief heir, 6–7,
    155, 174–6, 206–8, 210–14;
    epilepsy, 9–11, 24, 26–7, 33, 41,
    114, 237, 238; education, 11;
    practises law, 24; helps rebuild
    Btancepeth, 32; MP, 32–3, 143,
    174; affair with Miss Thornhill, 33,
    44; social ambition, 44, 53, 61, 155,
    175–6, 205, 210–14, 238, 295, 300,
    378, 415, 441, 475; relations with
    Somersby, 61–2, 83, 131, 132–4,
    155–6, 191–2, 205–6, 207–9, 255,
    273–4, 323; and AT, 30, 60–1, 113,
    137, 162, 169, 172, 176, 205,
    208–9, 211–12, 295, 317, 343,
    353–4, 359, 373, 377–8, 381–2,
    385, 387, 402, 454, 473–6, 543;
    change of name, 61, 155, 175–6,
    208; duel, 143–4; friend of Bulwer,
    168, 213, 238–9, 295–300, 353–4,
    359; rebuilds Bayons, 155, 210–14,
    225, 238, 343, 475–6; difficulties
    with children, 213–14, 294–5,
    299–300, 381; *Eustace,* 353–4, 381;
    death, 415–16, 441; also, 1, 8, 9,
    14, 20, 26, 49, 127, 156
Tennyson d'Eyncourt, Clara, 179
Tennyson d'Eyncourt, Edwin, 206
    208, 214, 218, 381, 543
Tennyson d'Eyncourt, Ellen, 206, 317
Tennyson d'Eyncourt, Eustace, 191–2,
    353–4
Tennyson d'Eyncourt, Frances, 23–4,
    33, 43–4, 155, 174, 207, 208, 225,
    415
Tennyson d'Eyncourt, George (AT's
    cousin), 10, 39, 60–2, 64–5, 83,
    131, 133, 157, 192, 213, 237, 299
Tennyson d'Eyncourt, Julia, 174, 179,
    218, 225, 238–9, 294–5, 300
Tent Lodge, 338, 339, 340, 416, 417
Terry, Dame Ellen, 447, 448, 523, 525
Thackeray, Anne, *see* Ritchie, Anne,
    Lady

Thackeray, W. M.: opinion of AT,
    190, 240–1, 353, 358; AT's opinion
    of, 240, 241, 568; also 54, 79, 87,
    95, 177, 222, 267, 273, 277, 288,
    297, 358–9, 367, 371, 392, 408,
    411, 424, 446–7
Thirlwall, Connop, 232
Thompson, Elspeth, 521, 571
Thompson, W. H., 53, 74, 91, 126,
    130, 183, 202, 467, 505
Thomson, William, 483
Thornhill, Mary, 33, 44
Ticknor, W. D., 245, 404
Times, The, 309–10, 351, 381, 512
Torquay, 244, 268
Torrijos, José Maria, 116, 117
Trench, Richard Chenevix, 88, 112,
    117, 122, 147, 162
Tribute, 226–8
Trinity College, Cambridge, 52–6,
    59–63, 68–9, 86–7, 125–7, 145,
    193, 331, 424, 467, 501–2, 517
Trinity College, Dublin, 578
Trollope, Anthony, 457, 481
Trollope, Frances, 361
Tunbridge Wells, 251, 255, 256
Tupper, Martin, 436
Turgeniev, Ivan, 491
Turner, Charles: opium habit, 42,
    123–4, 136, 140, 179, 190, 191,
    196, 222, 246, 274, 323, 340, 421;
    Cambridge, 50, 52, 54, 123, 129,
    130, 135, 136, 139, 145; *Sonnets
    and Fugitive Pieces,* 105, 106, 141;
    inherits money and changes name,
    196; marriage, 222–3, 246, 260,
    321, 323; brings AT and EST
    together, 332, 333; death, 526–7,
    530–1; also, 16, 17, 21, 29, 30, 48,
    58, 63, 81, 97, 99, 137, 146, 147,
    148, 155–6, 171, 181, 192, 205,
    206, 214, 217, 224, 225, 227, 233,
    234, 248–9, 251, 255, 269, 270,
    273, 324, 338, 366, 367, 415,
    532
Turner, Louisa, 82, 196, 222–3, 246,
    321, 323, 367, 415, 526
Turner, Samuel, 3, 26, 58, 136, 139,
    155, 178, 196
Tyndall, John, 462, 483

Umberslade Hall, 279, 309, 372

Usselby Manor, 174–5, 192, 204, 206, 213

Vane, Mr, 41, 65
Vaughan, Herbert, 508
Venables, Edmund, 444
Venables, G. S., 95–6, 229, 240, 256, 257, 288, 310, 324, 330, 337, 339, 352, 367, 371, 399–402, 466, 568
Victoria, Queen: probable first meeting with AT, 309–10; expected at Farringford, 404; thanks AT for dedication of *Idylls*, 442; summons AT, 443–4, 468, 500, 538–9; bestows peerage, 542; manoeuvres AT against WEG, 542, 548; AT sees for last time, 576; sends wreaths to funeral, 582; also 289, 291, 351–3, 357–8, 416, 463, 464, 569, 581
Vienna, 182
Virgil, 155

Waite, J., 29–30
Wales, 244, 245–7, 280, 405–6, 562
Wales, Alexandra, Princess of, 444, 521, 540
Wales, Edward, Prince of, 435, 444
Ward, W. G., 489, 508, 518, 528
Ward, Wilfrid, 523, 568, 580
Warninglid, 356
Warwick, 252
Warwick, Frances, Countess of, 517
Watson, Miss, 58, 217
Watts, G. F., 371, 408–9, 447, 448, 509, 518, 553, 574, 583
Weld, Anne, 82, 104–5, 189, 235, 249, 366
Weld, Charles, 366, 422
Wellington, Duke of, 231, 242–3, 368–9, 503
West, Sir Algernon, 539
Westminster Abbey, 48, 177, 489, 522, 550, 555, 571, 582–3

Westminster Review, 110, 111, 112, 265, 389, 490
Wheeler, C. S., 245
Whewell, William, 56, 283
White, James, 372
White, Walter, 475
Wight, Isle of, 305, 324, 372–5
Wilde, Oscar, 479, 506–7
Williams-Wynn, Charlotte, 271
Wilson, Effingham, 102–3
Wilson, John ('Christopher North'), 111–12, 148–9, 169, 172–3, 191, 225–6, 351
Windsor, 500
Wintour, Anna, 71–2, 76, 85, 101, 103, 106, 127, 158
wood-carving scheme, 254–6, 261, 268–70, 385
Woolner, Thomas: meets AT, 326–7; sculpts likenesses of AT, 326, 397, 406, 424; relations with EST, 327, 339, 432; at Farringford, 397, 406; suggests subjects to AT, 425, 446, 453, 454–5; also, 304, 366, 408, 416–17, 419, 433–4, 458–60, 507
Wordsworth, Charles, 79
Wordsworth, Christopher, 54, 56, 61, 69, 98, 105, 125–6
Wordsworth, Gordon, 291
Wordsworth, William: opinion of AT, 125–6, 190–1, 289–91; relations with AT, 126–7, 202–3, 289–91; AT's opinion of, 200, 202, 290–1, 549, 564; death, 341, 350; also, 61, 87, 98, 105, 141, 179, 196, 198, 266, 271, 293, 339, 352, 353, 357, 358, 392, 440
Wortley, Lady Emmeline Stuart, 226–7

Yeats, W. B., 110
Yorkshire, 366, 371, 446
Young, Sir Allen, 562